DYNAMIC PROBABILISTIC SYSTEMS

Volume II: SEMI-MARKOV AND DECISION PROCESSES

SERIES IN DECISION AND CONTROL

Ronald A. Howard, Editor

FINITE DIMENSIONAL LINEAR SPACES

by Roger W. Brockett

DYNAMIC PROBABILISTIC SYSTEMS

Volume I: MARKOV MODELS

by Ronald A. Howard

DYNAMIC PROBABILISTIC SYSTEMS

Volume II: SEMI-MARKOV AND DECISION PROCESSES

by Ronald A. Howard

OPTIMIZATION BY VECTOR SPACE METHODS

by David G. Luenberger

INTRODUCTION TO DYNAMIC PROGRAMMING

by George L. Nemhauser

OPTIMIZATION THEORY WITH APPLICATIONS

by Donald A. Pierre

DYNAMIC PROBABILISTIC SYSTEMS

Volume II: SEMI-MARKOV AND DECISION PROCESSES

RONALD A. HOWARD
Stanford University
Stanford, California

JOHN WILEY & SONS, INC.,
New York · London · Sydney · Toronto

Library of Congress Catalogue Card Number: 74-112593
ISBN 0-471-41666-5

Printed in the United States of America.

10 9 8 7 6 5 4 3 2

To Polly,
my trapping state.

Series in Decision and Control

SERIES PREFACE

Ronald A. Howard

Modern developments intensify the effects of uncertainty, complexity, and dynamics in every aspect of personal and social life. The individual and the technologist are forced to cope with problems that were not appreciated, much less formulated or solved, only a few years ago. Fortunately, striking progress is being made in the conception and implementation of rational systems. The purpose of this series is to disseminate the understanding necessary to place man in a position of decision and control in the governance of his artifacts and enterprises.

PREFACE

Uncertainty, complexity, and dynamism have been continuing challenges to man's understanding and control of his physical environment. In the development of logical structures to describe these phenomena, the model originated by A. A. Markov stands as a major accomplishment. Where previous contributors had modeled uncertainty as a sequence of independent trials, Markov saw the advantage of introducing dependence of each trial on the result of its predecessor. While it is tempting to consider even more complex dependency of the present trial on the results of past trials, such temptation usually leads to results that are both analytically and computationally intractable.

Consequently, Markov models represent the first outpost in the domain of dependent models that is powerful both in capturing the essence of many dependent systems observed in practice and in producing the analytical and computational results necessary to gain insight into their behavior. The purpose of this book is to equip the reader to formulate, analyze, and evaluate simple and advanced Markov models of systems that range from genetics to space engineering to marketing. This book should be viewed not as a collection of techniques (although many will value it as such), but rather as a consistent application of the fundamental principles of probability and linear system theory.

It is often said that good ideas are simple; the Markov process is no exception. In fact, there is no problem considered in this book that cannot be made clear to a child. The device we use to make such expositions simple is a pond covered with lily pads among which a frog may jump. Although his jumps may be random, the frog never falls into the water. Furthermore, he may occupy the same pad after successive jumps. We can use the lily pond analogy to clarify any discussion in the text.

The book is an integrated work published in two volumes. The first volume, Chapters 1–9, treats the basic Markov process and its variants; the second, Chapters 10–15, semi-Markov and decision processes. Although the reader who is already familiar with Markov process terminology will understand the design of the book from the Contents, it should be helpful to all readers to discuss each chapter using the lily pond analogy.

Chapter 1 introduces the basic Markov model. The number of pads in the lily pond is assumed to be finite. The Markov assumption states that the probability of the frog's making his next jump to any pad depends only on the pad he currently occupies and not on how he reached his present pad. The discussion then considers the question, given the starting pad and the fact that n jumps have been made without our observing the pond, what probability must we assign to the frog's occupying each pad in the pond. Graphical and transform methods are used to find these probabilities and to illustrate the typical behavior of a variety of processes.

Chapter 2 is a diversion to present the theory of linear systems and graphical methods for their analysis. Chapter 3 shows how to apply these powerful techniques to answering the problems of Chapter 1 with respect to the lily pond.

Chapter 4 considers the case where certain pads, once occupied, cannot be left and investigates the statistics for the number of jumps required before such trapping occurs. Chapter 5 treats two types of statistics: First, how many jumps will be made onto each pad in a given number of total jumps and, second, how many jumps will be required to reach one pad from another pad for the first time.

Chapter 6 finds the statistics of jumps from one set of pads to another set of pads. It allows identifying certain jumps as being of special interest and then finding the statistics of these jumps. Furthermore, it considers the implications of the information provided by these jumps for probability assignments on the frog's location.

Chapter 7 focuses on the case where we observe only one pad and where the frog's returns to that pad can be governed by an arbitrary probability distribution. We explore the statistics of these returns from several pcints of view. This chapter also discusses for the first time the possibility that the pond may have an infinite number of pads and illustrates the analytic modifications necessary to treat this situation.

Chapter 8 investigates the possibility of having several frogs jumping in the pond at the same time. It expands the discussion to the case where at certain times frogs may be added to each pad in the pond in varying numbers. Finally, it treats the case where the frogs may breed to produce new generations of jumpers.

Chapter 9 considers the case where the probability of a jump from one pad to another may be different on successive jumps. For example, the frog may be getting tired.

Chapter 10 introduces another dimension to the discussion. We explicitly consider the time between jumps as a multiple of some time unit and let this be a random variable that depends on the jump made by the frog. We can now consider the probability of the frog's occupying each pad given both the number of jumps he has made and the total time units he has been jumping. All previous questions about the frog's behavior are re-examined in this generalized form.

Chapter 11 allows the time between jumps to be a continuous random variable and extends all previous discussions to this case. Chapter 12 considers the continuous-time Markov process, the case in which the time that the frog has occupied the same pad has no bearing on the amount of time he will continue to occupy it. It also discusses the infinite-pad lily pond once again.

Chapter 13 concerns the payment of rewards on the basis of the frog's jumping. He may earn a reward for making a particular jump or from occupying a pad. We develop and illustrate expressions for the expected total reward the frog will earn in a finite and infinite time with and without discounting.

Chapter 14 presents another diversion, a discussion of the optimization procedure of dynamic programming, the natural way to formulate optimization problems for Markov processes.

Chapter 15 combines the material of the last several chapters to develop procedures for optimizing the expected reward generated by the frog. Control is effected by altering the probabilistic structure and reward structure of his jumping.

Since the level of interest in frog-jumping is relatively low, the examples throughout are drawn from a variety of fields: consumer purchasing, taxicab operation, inventory control, rabbit reproduction, coin-tossing, gambling, family-name extinction, search, car rental, machine repair, depreciation, production, action-timing, reliability, reservation policy, machine maintenance and replacement, network traversal, project scheduling, space exploration, and success in business. The applicability of the models to still other areas is also made evident.

The background suggested for the reader if he is to achieve greatest benefit from the book is a foundation in calculus, probability theory, and matrix theory. The emphasis is on the fundamental rather than the esoteric in these areas, so preparation should not be a major stumbling block. The book may be read with ease by anyone with the basic background whether his field be engineering, management, psychology, or whatever. Specialized material from any field used in examples is presented as required. Consequently, the professional reading independently to expand his knowledge of Markov models should be able to proceed rapidly and effectively.

This book developed from courses taught at M.I.T. and Stanford University over a decade. Although the advanced undergraduate can master the subject with no difficulty, the course has always been offered at the graduate level. The material is developed naturally for course presentation. To cover the whole book typically requires the entire academic year. The two volumes serve well as texts for successive one-semester courses. If a two-quarter version is desired, then Chapters 8 and 9 can be placed in the optional category.

One feature of the development that is becoming increasingly advantageous to exploit is the suitability of examples and problems for solution by computer, particularly the time-shared variety. Virtually every chapter contains material appropriate for computer demonstration, such as simulation of Markov process behavior, or solution for statistics via difference equations. While such integration with computer methods is not necessary, it does provide an opportunity for curriculum unification.

Some of the material presented here has appeared in more primitive form elsewhere. For example, Chapter 2 is a highly revised form of "System Analysis of Linear Models," *Multistage Inventory Models and Techniques*, eds., Scarf, Shelley, Guilford, 143–184, Stanford University Press, 1963; Chapter 13 is an expanded version of "Dynamic Programming," *Management Science*, Vol. 12, No. 5, 317–348, January 1966. Much of the development in the second volume is based on "System Analysis of Semi-Markov Processes," *Trans. IEEE Prof. Group on Mil. Elec.*, Vol. MIL–8, No. 2, 114–124, April 1964, and on "Semi-Markovian Decision Processes," *Proceedings of the 34th Session International Statistical Institute*, 625–652, Ottawa, Canada, August 1963.

Finally, some credit where credit is due. Much of the original work on this book was performed during a visiting year at Stanford University under the sponsorship of what has become the Department of Engineering-Economic Systems. Most of the final touches were supplied during a visiting year as Ford Research Professor at the Stanford Graduate School of Business. The book contains research results that grew from supported research. Most of the early research was sponsored by the Office of Naval Research; more recently the research was supported by the National Science Foundation. To all these organizations I express my appreciation.

The question of personal acknowledgments is a difficult one for any author. Only he knows the debt he owes to so many over a period of several years. By selecting a few for special mention, he accepts the risk that the important contributions of others will not receive sufficient notice. Accepting that risk, let me reveal how this work is the result of many contributors.

Several individuals have provided me with advice, criticism, and suggestions on the development of the manuscript. In the early versions, I benefited greatly from my contact with Edward S. Silver and Jerome D. Herniter. Richard D. Smallwood has provided a continuing stream of suggestions that have materially improved the manuscript. Herbert F. Ayres and W. Howard Cook have each made several suggestions that clarified the text. Finally, I must credit the Herculean task of my friend James E. Matheson who read through the completed manuscript in detail with no hope of reward but the promise of a feast in a fancy New York restaurant. Having fulfilled that promise, I am happy to report that he has found and corrected all mistakes in the manuscript, thus relieving me of the necessity of making that boring statement that any idiocies in the book are the full responsibility of the author.

I believe that there is no more important part of a textbook than its problems, and so I asked Richard D. Smallwood to collate and augment the problem sets we have used in courses over the years. He has done a thorough and imaginative job and has demonstrated that the challenging need not be humorless. Many of the problems were originally composed by teaching assistants; age and evolutionary change have made their authorship obscure. However, in many I discern the deft touch of Edward A. Silver who has a special knack for making a student smile and sweat at the same time.

Any book that would illustrate complex Markov models will require extensive electronic computation. I have been fortunate in having the services of individuals who have unusual flair and ability in this area, namely, Claude Dieudonné, Richard D. Smallwood, Paul Schweitzer, Leif Tronstad, and Alain Viguier. Their contribution ranged from solution of numerical examples to the development of programming systems that treated large classes of models: The reader is the beneficiary of their ingenuity.

A challenging part of the manuscript was the translation of Markov's paper. Here I needed someone who could translate classic Russian into English—I found him in George Petelin. Mr. Petelin's English translation provided the basis for the final version that appears in the book; for its accuracy I personally bear full responsibility.

Obviously a project of this magnitude is a secretarial nightmare. Fortunately, I have found myself over the years in the hands of a succession of ladies whose secretarial skills were exceeded only by their intelligence and charm. The first was Mrs. Nobuko McNeill who personally supervised the typing of over one thousand pages of Gregg shorthand directly into finished manuscript. The second was Mrs. Edna Tweet who prepared the final chapter of Volume II. The third was Mrs. Louise Goodrich who suffered through the endless revision, galley reading, and proof checking necessary to bring this project to a successful conclusion.

Therefore, let me express to all these fine people my appreciation and thanks for helping me tell my story about the Markov process and what became of it.

Palo Alto, California
January, 1971

RONALD A. HOWARD

CONTENTS

DYNAMIC PROBABILISTIC SYSTEMS

Volume II: SEMI-MARKOV AND DECISION PROCESSES

10 THE DISCRETE-TIME SEMI-MARKOV PROCESS

All of the Markov models we discussed in Volume I have the property that a transition is made at every time instant. The transition may return the process to the state it previously occupied, but a transition occurs nevertheless. Now we want to turn our attention to a more general class of processes where the time between transitions may be several of the unit time-intervals, and where this transition time can depend on the transition that is made. As we shall see, this process is no longer strictly Markovian. However, it retains enough of the Markovian properties to deserve the name of a "semi-Markov" process. In this chapter we shall define and investigate the semi-Markov process and reveal the additional flexibility it brings to the problem of modeling dynamic probabilistic systems.

10.1 THE FORMAL MODEL

We can think of the semi-Markov process as a process whose successive state occupancies are governed by the transition probabilities of a Markov process, but whose stay in any state is described by an integer-valued random variable that depends on the state presently occupied and on the state to which the next transition will be made. Thus at transition instants the semi-Markov process behaves just like a Markov process. We call this process the imbedded Markov process. However, the times at which transitions occur are governed by a different probabilistic mechanism.

To make these notions precise, let p_{ij} be the probability that a semi-Markov process that entered state i on its last transition will enter state j on its next transition. The transition probabilities p_{ij} must satisfy the same equations as the transition probabilities for a Markov process,

$$p_{ij} \geq 0 \qquad i = 1, 2, \ldots, N; j = 1, 2, \ldots, N \tag{10.1.1}$$

and

$$\sum_{j=1}^{N} p_{ij} = 1 \qquad i = 1, 2, \ldots, N, \tag{10.1.2}$$

where, as usual, N is the total number of states in the system. Whenever a process enters a state i, we imagine that it determines the next state j to which it will move according to state i's transition probabilities $p_{i1}, p_{i2}, \ldots, p_{iN}$. However, after j has been selected, but before making this transition from state i to state j, the process "holds" for a time τ_{ij} in state i. The holding times τ_{ij} are positive, integer-valued random variables each governed by a probability mass function $h_{ij}(\cdot)$ called the holding time mass function for a transition from state i to state j. Thus,

$$\mathscr{P}\{\tau_{ij} = m\} = h_{ij}(m) \qquad m = 1, 2, 3, \ldots; i = 1, 2, \ldots, N; j = 1, 2, \ldots, N. \quad (10.1.3)$$

We assume that the means $\bar{\tau}_{ij}$ of all holding time distributions are finite and that all holding times are at least one time unit in length,

$$h_{ij}(0) = 0. \quad (10.1.4)$$

We must specify N^2 holding time mass functions, in addition to the transition probabilities, to describe a discrete-time semi-Markov process completely.

After holding in state i for the holding time τ_{ij}, the process makes the transition to state j, and then immediately selects a new destination state k using the transition probabilities $p_{j1}, p_{j2}, \ldots, p_{jN}$. It next chooses a holding time τ_{jk} in state j according to the mass function $h_{jk}(\cdot)$, and makes its next transition at time τ_{jk} after entering state j. The process continues developing its trajectory in this way indefinitely.

Figure 10.1.1 shows a portion of a possible trajectory for a discrete-time semi-Markov process. The large black dots indicate the state of the process immediately after a transition. Thus the figure shows that the process entered state 2 at time 0, held in state 2 for three time units, then made a transition to state 4. It held in state 4 for one time unit and then moved to state 3 at time 4. The process remained in state 3 for two time units before making a transition to state 1. When last seen, the process had stayed at least 2 time units in state 1.

We see that we have removed the basic connection between the time scale and the time of transition. We can thus talk about the probability of 3 transitions in a

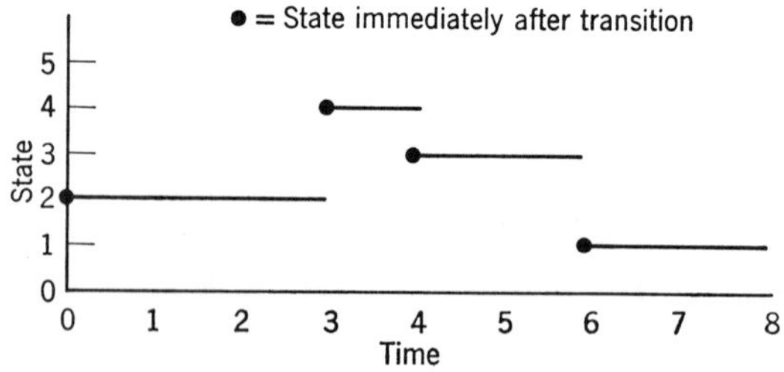

Figure 10.1.1 A possible semi-Markov process trajectory.

total time 7, etc. We also observe that we can consider the discrete-time Markov process we have been discussing in earlier chapters to be a discrete-time semi-Markov process for which

$$h_{ij}(m) = \delta(m-1) \qquad m = 0, 1, 2, \ldots; i = 1, 2, \ldots, N; j = 1, 2, \ldots, N; \quad (10.1.5)$$

that is, all holding times are exactly one time unit in length.

Real and Virtual Transitions

In Section 4.3 (Volume I) we discussed a subject that is closely related to the topic of this chapter. We made a distinction between real transitions, which required an actual change of state indices as the result of a transition, and virtual transitions, where the state indices could be the same after the transition. We saw that we could consider the discrete-time Markov process as a process that could make only real transitions and had geometric holding times, or as a process that could make virtual transitions and had all holding times equal to one unit. From either point of view, the discrete-time Markov process is a discrete-time semi-Markov process.

The distinction between real and virtual transitions is useful in the theory of the semi-Markov process itself. When modeling real systems by semi-Markov processes, we must often decide whether we want to call a movement from a state to itself a transition of the process. The decision depends on the circumstances: Some physical processes require that only real transitions be allowed, in other processes the virtual transitions are most important. The impact of the decision on the possible trajectories of the process is indicated in Figure 10.1.2. We observe that when virtual transitions are allowed, transitions can occur with no change of state. We have already noted that when the state of the process represents the last brand purchased by the customer in a marketing model, a virtual transition represents a repeat purchase of a brand, an event of frequent importance to the analyst. Since the semi-Markov process is an even more general model for marketing and other processes than is the Markov process, we must preserve our ability to speak

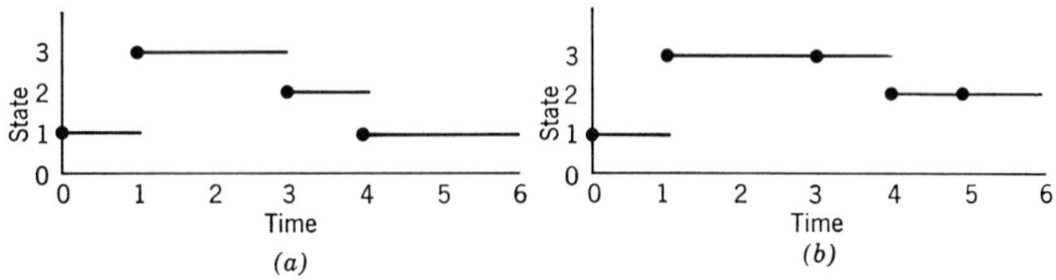

Figure 10.1.2 Real and virtual transitions. (*a*) Real transitions only. (*b*) Virtual transitions allowed.

of virtual transitions. Therefore, in our future developments we shall always allow the possibility of virtual transitions—the transition probabilities p_{ii} may or may not be zero.

Holding Times and Waiting Times

We shall find it useful to develop additional notation for the holding time behavior. We use ${}^{\leq}h_{ij}(\cdot)$ for the cumulative probability distribution of τ_{ij},

$$ {}^{\leq}h_{ij}(n) = \sum_{m=0}^{n} h_{ij}(m) = \mathscr{P}\{\tau_{ij} \leq n\} \tag{10.1.6} $$

and ${}^{>}h_{ij}(\cdot)$ for the complementary cumulative probability distribution of τ_{ij},

$$ {}^{>}h_{ij}(n) = \sum_{m=n+1}^{\infty} h_{ij}(m) = 1 - {}^{\leq}h_{ij}(n) = \mathscr{P}\{\tau_{ij} > n\}. \tag{10.1.7} $$

Suppose now that the process enters state i and chooses a successor state j, but we as observers do not know the successor chosen. The probability mass function we would assign to the time τ_i spent in i, we shall then call $w_i(\cdot)$, where

$$ w_i(m) = \sum_{j=1}^{N} p_{ij}h_{ij}(m) = \mathscr{P}\{\tau_i = m\}; \tag{10.1.8} $$

that is, the probability that the system will spend m time units in state i if we do not know its successor state is the probability that it will spend m time units in state i if its successor state is j multiplied by the probability its successor state is j and summed over all possible successor states. We shall call τ_i the waiting time in state i, and $w_i(\cdot)$ the waiting time probability mass function. Thus, a waiting time is merely a holding time that is unconditional on the destination state.

The mean waiting time $\bar{\tau}_i$ is related to the mean holding time $\bar{\tau}_{ij}$ by

$$ \bar{\tau}_i = \sum_{j=1}^{N} p_{ij}\bar{\tau}_{ij}. \tag{10.1.9} $$

We compute the second moment of the waiting time $\overline{\tau_i^2}$ from the second moments of the holding time $\overline{\tau_{ij}^2}$ using

$$ \overline{\tau_i^2} = \sum_{j=1}^{N} p_{ij}\overline{\tau_{ij}^2}; \tag{10.1.10} $$

then we can write the variance of the waiting time, $\overset{v}{\tau}_i$, as

$$\overset{v}{\tau}_i = \overline{\tau_i^2} - \bar{\tau}_i^2. \tag{10.1.11}$$

In view of Equation 10.1.7, the cumulative and complementary cumulative probability distributions for the waiting times are

$${}^{\leq}w_i(n) = \sum_{m=0}^{n} w_i(m) = \sum_{m=0}^{n} \sum_{j=1}^{N} p_{ij}h_{ij}(m) = \sum_{j=1}^{N} p_{ij}\, {}^{\leq}h_{ij}(n) = \mathscr{P}\{\tau_i \leq n\} \tag{10.1.12}$$

and

$${}^{>}w_i(n) = \sum_{m=n+1}^{\infty} w_i(m) = \sum_{m=n+1}^{\infty} \sum_{j=1}^{N} p_{ij}h_{ij}(m) = \sum_{j=1}^{N} p_{ij}\, {}^{>}h_{ij}(n) = \mathscr{P}\{\tau_i > n\}. \tag{10.1.13}$$

A Car Rental Example

Before proceeding to more theoretical developments, let us show a very simple example of a discrete-time semi-Markov process. An automobile rental agency rents cars at two locations, town 1 and town 2. Consider one car and let its state be the number of the town at which it was last rented. Thus we have a two-state system.

Transition probabilities

The experience of the company shows that when a car is rented in town 1 there is a 0.8 probability that it will be returned to town 1 and a 0.2 probability that it will be returned to town 2. When the car is rented in town 2, there is a 0.7 probability that it will be returned to town 2 and a 0.3 probability that it will be returned to town 1. We assume that there are always many customers available at both towns and that cars are always rented at the towns to which they are last returned. Then we can represent the transition probabilities of this imbedded Markov process by the transition probability matrix

$$P = \begin{bmatrix} 0.8 & 0.2 \\ 0.3 & 0.7 \end{bmatrix}. \tag{10.1.14}$$

Note that this is the same transition probability matrix we used in our two-state Markov process marketing example.

Holding times

But now we give the example a semi-Markovian flavor. Because of the nature of the trips involved, the length of time a car will be rented depends on both where it is rented and where it is returned. The holding time τ_{ij} is thus the length of time a car will be rented if it was rented at town i and returned to town j. The four possible holding time probability mass functions are found from the company's records to be:

$$h_{11}(m) = (1/3)(2/3)^{m-1} \quad m = 1, 2, 3, \ldots \quad h_{12}(m) = (1/6)(5/6)^{m-1} \quad m = 1, 2, 3, \ldots$$
$$h_{21}(m) = (1/4)(3/4)^{m-1} \quad m = 1, 2, 3, \ldots \quad h_{22}(m) = (1/12)(11/12)^{m-1} \quad m = 1, 2, 3, \ldots \tag{10.1.15}$$

Note that these holding time distributions are all geometric distributions with different parameters. However, they could have been distributions of arbitrary complexity. As we found in Section 4.1, the geometric distribution $(1 - a)a^{n-1}$, $n = 1, 2, 3$, has a mean $1/(1 - a)$, second moment $(1 + a)/(1 - a)^2$, and variance $a/(1 - a)^2$. Therefore the moments of our four holding times are:

$$\bar{\tau}_{11} = 3,\ \overline{\tau_{11}{}^2} = 15,\ \check{\tau}_{11} = 6; \qquad \bar{\tau}_{12} = 6,\ \overline{\tau_{12}{}^2} = 66,\ \check{\tau}_{12} = 30;$$
$$\bar{\tau}_{21} = 4,\ \overline{\tau_{21}{}^2} = 28,\ \check{\tau}_{21} = 12; \qquad \bar{\tau}_{22} = 12,\ \overline{\tau_{22}{}^2} = 276,\ \check{\tau}_{22} = 132. \tag{10.1.16}$$

These numbers indicate that people renting cars at town 2 and returning them to town 2 often have long rental periods; perhaps town 2 is in the center of a scenic region.

We can represent the holding time properties by a square matrix $H(\cdot)$ with elements $h_{ij}(\cdot)$. For the example,

$$H(m) = \begin{bmatrix} (1/3)(2/3)^{m-1} & (1/6)(5/6)^{m-1} \\ (1/4)(3/4)^{m-1} & (1/12)(11/12)^{m-1} \end{bmatrix} \qquad m = 1, 2, 3, \ldots. \tag{10.1.17}$$

Now that we have specified the transition probability matrix P and the holding time mass function matrix $H(\cdot)$, we have created a complete description of the semi-Markov process. Figure 10.1.3 shows how this description can be represented

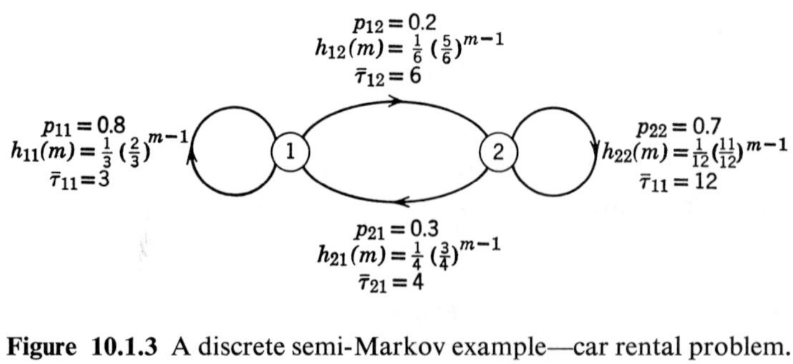

Figure 10.1.3 A discrete semi-Markov example—car rental problem.

in a transition diagram. Each branch in the diagram must be labeled not only with the transition probability that corresponds to that branch, but also with the holding time mass function for the branch.

If $h_{ij}(m)$ is the geometric distribution $(1 - a)a^{m-1}$ $m = 1, 2, 3, \ldots$, then the cumulative and complementary cumulative distributions ${}^{\leq}h_{ij}(n)$ and ${}^{>}h_{ij}(n)$ are

$$ {}^{\leq}h_{ij}(n) = \sum_{m=0}^{n} h_{ij}(m) = \sum_{m=1}^{n} (1 - a)a^{m-1} = 1 - a^n \qquad n = 0, 1, 2, \ldots \qquad (10.1.18) $$

and

$$ {}^{>}h_{ij}(n) = \sum_{m=n+1}^{\infty} h_{ij}(m) = \sum_{m=n+1}^{\infty} (1 - a)a^{m-1} = a^n \qquad n = 0, 1, 2, \ldots. \qquad (10.1.19) $$

Therefore, the matrix forms of these distributions for the example are

$$ {}^{\leq}H(n) = \begin{bmatrix} 1 - (2/3)^n & 1 - (5/6)^n \\ 1 - (3/4)^n & 1 - (11/12)^n \end{bmatrix} \qquad n = 0, 1, 2, \ldots \qquad (10.1.20) $$

and

$$ {}^{>}H(n) = \begin{bmatrix} (2/3)^n & (5/6)^n \\ (3/4)^n & (11/12)^n \end{bmatrix} \qquad n = 0, 1, 2, \ldots. \qquad (10.1.21) $$

These results show, for example, that the chance that a car rented in town 1 and returned to town 2 will be rented for n or fewer time periods is $1 - (5/6)^n$. A car rented in 2 and returned to 1 has a chance $(3/4)^n$ of being rented for more than n periods.

Waiting times

We can use Equations 10.1.8 through 10.1.13 to find the waiting time statistics for the example. We start with the means,

$$ \begin{aligned} \bar{\tau}_1 &= p_{11}\bar{\tau}_{11} + p_{12}\bar{\tau}_{12} = 0.8(3) + 0.2(6) = 3.6 \\ \bar{\tau}_2 &= p_{21}\bar{\tau}_{21} + p_{22}\bar{\tau}_{22} = 0.3(4) + 0.7(12) = 9.6. \end{aligned} \qquad (10.1.22) $$

The mean time that a car rented in town 1 will be rented, destination unknown, is 3.6 periods. If the car is rented in town 2, the mean is 9.6 periods.

We compute the second moment of the waiting time in each state i, $\overline{\tau_i^2}$, from Equation 10.1.10,

$$ \begin{aligned} \overline{\tau_1^2} &= p_{11}\overline{\tau_{11}^2} + p_{12}\overline{\tau_{12}^2} = 0.8(15) + 0.2(66) = 25.2 \\ \overline{\tau_2^2} &= p_{21}\overline{\tau_{21}^2} + p_{22}\overline{\tau_{22}^2} = 0.3(28) + 0.7(276) = 201.6, \end{aligned} \qquad (10.1.23) $$

then the variance of the waiting times from Equation 10.1.11,

$$\overset{\vee}{\tau}_1 = \overline{\tau_1^{\,2}} - \bar{\tau}_1^{\,2} = 25.2 - (3.6)^2 = 12.24$$
$$\overset{\vee}{\tau}_2 = \overline{\tau_2^{\,2}} - \bar{\tau}_2^{\,2} = 201.6 - (9.6)^2 = 109.44. \qquad (10.1.24)$$

For the distributions of waiting time we find

$$\begin{aligned} w_1(m) &= p_{11}h_{11}(m) + p_{12}h_{12}(m) \\ &= 0.8(1/3)(2/3)^{m-1} + 0.2(1/6)(5/6)^{m-1} \\ &= (4/15)(2/3)^{m-1} + (1/30)(5/6)^{m-1} \qquad m = 1, 2, 3, \ldots; \\ w_2(m) &= p_{21}h_{21}(m) + p_{22}h_{22}(m) \\ &= 0.3(1/4)(3/4)^{m-1} + 0.7(1/12)(11/12)^{m-1} \\ &= (3/40)(3/4)^{m-1} + (7/120)(11/12)^{m-1} \qquad m = 1, 2, 3, \ldots. \end{aligned} \qquad (10.1.25)$$

These expressions give the probability that a car rented in each town will be rented for m periods, destination unknown. We use Equations 10.1.12 and 10.1.13 to compute from Equations 10.1.20 and 10.1.21 the cumulative and complementary cumulative distributions of waiting time,

$$\begin{aligned} {}^{\leq}w_1(n) &= 1 - 0.8(2/3)^n - 0.2(5/6)^n \\ {}^{\leq}w_2(n) &= 1 - 0.3(3/4)^n - 0.7(11/12)^n \qquad n = 0, 1, 2, \ldots \end{aligned} \qquad (10.1.26)$$

and

$$\begin{aligned} {}^{>}w_1(n) &= 0.8(2/3)^n + 0.2(5/6)^n \\ {}^{>}w_2(n) &= 0.3(3/4)^n + 0.7(11/12)^n \qquad n = 0, 1, 2, \ldots. \end{aligned} \qquad (10.1.27)$$

The expression for ${}^{>}w_2(n)$, for example, shows the probability that a car rented in town 2 will be rented for more than n periods if its destination is unknown.

10.2 THE INTERVAL TRANSITION PROBABILITIES

The central statistics in semi-Markov processes are the interval transition probabilities, quantities that correspond to the multistep transition probabilities for the Markov process. For mnemonic reasons we shall use the same notation we used in Markov processes. We define $\phi_{ij}(n)$ as the probability that a discrete-time semi-Markov process will be in state j at time n given that it entered state i at time zero. We call this probability the interval transition probability from state i to state j in the interval $(0, n)$. Note that an essential part of the definition is that the system *entered* state i at time zero as opposed to its simply *being* in state i at time zero. We must be precise on this point because, as we shall see, the length of time a process has occupied a state can often affect the probabilities we assign to the destination of its next transition.

We now turn to the question of developing an expression for the interval transition probabilities. How can a process that started by entering state i at time zero be in state j at time n? One way this can happen is for i and j to be the same state and for the process never to have left state i throughout the period $(0, n)$. This requires that the process make its first transition after time n. Every other way to get from state i to state j in the interval $(0, n)$ requires that the process make at least one transition during that interval. For example, the process could have made its first transition from state i to some state k at a time m, $0 < m \le n$, and then by some succession of transitions have made its way to state j at time n. These considerations lead us to the equation,

$$\phi_{ij}(n) = \delta_{ij}\,{}^{>}w_i(n) + \sum_{k=1}^{N} p_{ik} \sum_{m=0}^{n} h_{ik}(m)\phi_{kj}(n-m)$$

$$i = 1, 2, \ldots, N;\ j = 1, 2, \ldots, N;\ n = 0, 1, 2, \ldots$$

$$\delta_{ij} = \begin{cases} 1 & i = j \\ 0 & i \ne j. \end{cases} \qquad (10.2.1)$$

The quantity δ_{ij} ensures that the term in which it appears occurs only when $i = j$. The complementary cumulative waiting time probability ${}^{>}w_i(n)$ is the probability that the process will leave its starting state i at a time greater than n. The second term in the equation represents the probability of the sequence of events where the process makes its first transition from the starting state i to some state k (maybe i itself) at some time m and then proceeds somehow from state k to state j in the remaining time $n - m$. This probability is summed over all states k to which the initial transition could have been made and over all times of first transition m between 1 and n. Extending the summation to include $m = 0$ is innocuous because $h_{ij}(0) = 0$.

Matrix Formulation

Let us now place Equation 10.2.1 in matrix form. In addition to the usual matrices denoted by the corresponding upper case letters, we define a set of diagonal waiting time matrices by giving their elements,

$$W(m) = \{\delta_{ij}w_i(m)\} \quad {}^{\le}W(n) = \{\delta_{ij}\,{}^{\le}w_i(n)\} \quad {}^{>}W(n) = \{\delta_{ij}\,{}^{>}w_i(n)\}. \qquad (10.2.2)$$

Then by interchanging the order of summation and by using our box notation ($\square$), we write Equation 10.2.1 as

$$\Phi(n) = {}^{>}W(n) + \sum_{m=0}^{n} [P \,\square\, H(m)]\Phi(n-m) \qquad n = 0, 1, 2, \ldots. \qquad (10.2.3)$$

We call $\Phi(n)$ the interval transition probability matrix for the semi-Markov process in the interval $(0, n)$; note that

$$\Phi(0) = I. \tag{10.2.4}$$

Equation 10.2.3 provides a convenient recursive basis for computing the interval transition probability matrix for any semi-Markov process. The quantities P and $H(m)$ come directly from the definition of the process. From Equation 10.1.13 we see that we can compute ${}^{>}w_i(n)$, the ith diagonal element of ${}^{>}W(n)$, as the sum from $m = n + 1$ to infinity of the sum of the elements in the ith row of $P \square H(m)$,

$${}^{>}w_i(n) = \sum_{m=n+1}^{\infty} \text{sum of elements in } i\text{th row of } P \square H(m). \tag{10.2.5}$$

The core matrix

We observe that computation of the interval transition probabilities rests only on the matrix $P \square H(m)$. This matrix we shall call the core matrix of the semi-Markov process, and give it the symbol $C(m)$,

$$C(m) = P \square H(m). \tag{10.2.6}$$

The ijth element of $C(m)$ is the probability of the joint event that a system that entered state i at time zero makes its next transition to state j and makes that transition at time m. If we sum the elements of $C(m)$ across the ith row, we obtain the waiting time mass function for the ith state,

$$\sum_{j=1}^{N} c_{ij}(m) = \sum_{j=1}^{N} p_{ij}h_{ij}(m) = w_i(m), \tag{10.2.7}$$

a result that leads directly to Equation 10.2.5. If we sum the ijth element of $C(m)$ for all values of m, we obtain the transition probability p_{ij},

$$\sum_{m=1}^{\infty} c_{ij}(m) = \sum_{m=1}^{\infty} p_{ij}h_{ij}(m) = p_{ij} \sum_{m=1}^{\infty} h_{ij}(m) = p_{ij}. \tag{10.2.8}$$

We shall usually write the core matrix $C(m)$ in the form $P \square H(m)$ to emphasize the relationship between semi-Markov and Markov processes.

Specialization to a Markov process

We can check Equation 10.2.3 by applying it to the discrete-time Markov process. For this process, as we observed in Equation 10.1.5, the holding time mass function matrix is

$$H(m) = U\,\delta(m - 1) \qquad m = 0, 1, 2, \ldots. \tag{10.2.9}$$

We calculate the waiting time mass functions from

$$w_i(m) = \sum_{j=1}^{N} p_{ij}h_{ij}(m) = \sum_{j=1}^{N} p_{ij}\,\delta(m-1) = \delta(m-1). \tag{10.2.10}$$

Therefore the complementary cumulative waiting time distribution for each state is

$$^{>}w_i(n) = \sum_{m=n+1}^{\infty} w_i(m) = \sum_{m=n+1}^{\infty} \delta(m-1) = \delta(n); \tag{10.2.11}$$

that is, there is probability one that the waiting time will exceed 0, and probability zero that it will exceed any number equal to or greater than one. This makes sense because the waiting time is always exactly equal to one, just like the holding time for all states. We could, of course, have made these observations without mathematical guidance. However, we have now established that the complementary cumulative waiting time matrix for a discrete-time Markov process is just the identity matrix at time zero and a zero matrix for all other times,

$$^{>}W(n) = I\,\delta(n) \qquad n = 0, 1, 2, \ldots. \tag{10.2.12}$$

We now substitute the results of Equations 10.2.9 and 10.2.12 into the recursive Equation 10.2.3 for the interval transition probabilities,

$$\begin{aligned}
\Phi(n) &= {}^{>}W(n) + \sum_{m=0}^{n} [P \,\square\, H(m)]\Phi(n-m) \\
&= I\,\delta(n) + \sum_{m=0}^{n} [P \,\square\, U\,\delta(m-1)]\Phi(n-m) \\
&= I\,\delta(n) + \sum_{m=0}^{n} P\,\delta(m-1)\Phi(n-m) \\
&= I\,\delta(n) + P\Phi(n-1) \qquad n = 0, 1, 2, \ldots.
\end{aligned} \tag{10.2.13}$$

This is, of course, just the equation we wrote in Chapter 1 for the multistep transition probability matrix for the discrete-time Markov process. We know that its solution is

$$\Phi(n) = P^n \qquad n = 0, 1, 2, \ldots. \tag{10.2.14}$$

Unfortunately, it will seldom be the case that we can solve Equation 10.2.3 in such a simple form. Generally we shall require a computing machine to assist us.

The car rental example

Let us apply this equation to the car rental example to show how the calculation proceeds and what type of results are generated. First we construct the core matrix $C(m) = P \,\square\, H(m)$ for the example from Equations 10.1.14 and 10.1.17,

$$C(m) = P \,\square\, H(m) = \begin{bmatrix} (4/15)(2/3)^{m-1} & (1/30)(5/6)^{m-1} \\ (3/40)(3/4)^{m-1} & (7/120)(11/12)^{m-1} \end{bmatrix} \qquad m = 1, 2, 3, \ldots. \tag{10.2.15}$$

The row sums of $P \,\square\, H(m)$ (or the results of Equation 10.1.25) allow us to construct the diagonal waiting time mass function matrix,

$$W(m) = \begin{bmatrix} (4/15)(2/3)^{m-1} + (1/30)(5/6)^{m-1} & 0 \\ 0 & (3/40)(3/4)^{m-1} + (7/120)(11/12)^{m-1} \end{bmatrix}$$
$$m = 1, 2, 3, \ldots. \tag{10.2.16}$$

Finally, by summing this matrix from $m = n + 1$ to infinity (or by using Equation 10.1.27), we write the complementary cumulative waiting time distribution matrix

$${}^{>}W(n) = \begin{bmatrix} 0.8(2/3)^n + 0.2(5/6)^n & 0 \\ 0 & 0.3(3/4)^n + 0.7(11/12)^n \end{bmatrix} \quad n = 0, 1, 2, \ldots. \tag{10.2.17}$$

Table 10.2.1 shows the result of substituting Equations 10.2.15 and 10.2.17 into Equation 10.2.3 for a few values of n. The interval transition probabilities $\phi_{11}(n)$

Table 10.2.1 Interval Transition Probability Matrices for Car Rental Problem

$$\Phi(0) = \begin{bmatrix} 1 & 0 \\ 0 & 1 \end{bmatrix} \quad \Phi(1) = \begin{bmatrix} 0.967 & 0.033 \\ 0.075 & 0.925 \end{bmatrix} \quad \Phi(2) = \begin{bmatrix} 0.933 & 0.068 \\ 0.133 & 0.867 \end{bmatrix}$$

$$\Phi(3) = \begin{bmatrix} 0.898 & 0.102 \\ 0.178 & 0.822 \end{bmatrix} \quad \Phi(4) = \begin{bmatrix} 0.865 & 0.135 \\ 0.213 & 0.787 \end{bmatrix} \quad \Phi(5) = \begin{bmatrix} 0.832 & 0.168 \\ 0.241 & 0.759 \end{bmatrix}$$

$$\Phi(6) = \begin{bmatrix} 0.801 & 0.199 \\ 0.262 & 0.738 \end{bmatrix} \quad \Phi(7) = \begin{bmatrix} 0.771 & 0.229 \\ 0.279 & 0.721 \end{bmatrix} \quad \Phi(8) = \begin{bmatrix} 0.743 & 0.257 \\ 0.293 & 0.707 \end{bmatrix}$$

$$\Phi(9) = \begin{bmatrix} 0.716 & 0.284 \\ 0.304 & 0.696 \end{bmatrix} \quad \Phi(10) = \begin{bmatrix} 0.691 & 0.309 \\ 0.312 & 0.688 \end{bmatrix} \quad \Phi(11) = \begin{bmatrix} 0.667 & 0.333 \\ 0.319 & 0.681 \end{bmatrix}$$

$$\Phi(12) = \begin{bmatrix} 0.645 & 0.355 \\ 0.325 & 0.675 \end{bmatrix} \quad \Phi(13) = \begin{bmatrix} 0.625 & 0.375 \\ 0.329 & 0.671 \end{bmatrix} \quad \Phi(14) = \begin{bmatrix} 0.606 & 0.394 \\ 0.333 & 0,667 \end{bmatrix}$$

$$\Phi(15) = \begin{bmatrix} 0.588 & 0.412 \\ 0.336 & 0.664 \end{bmatrix}$$

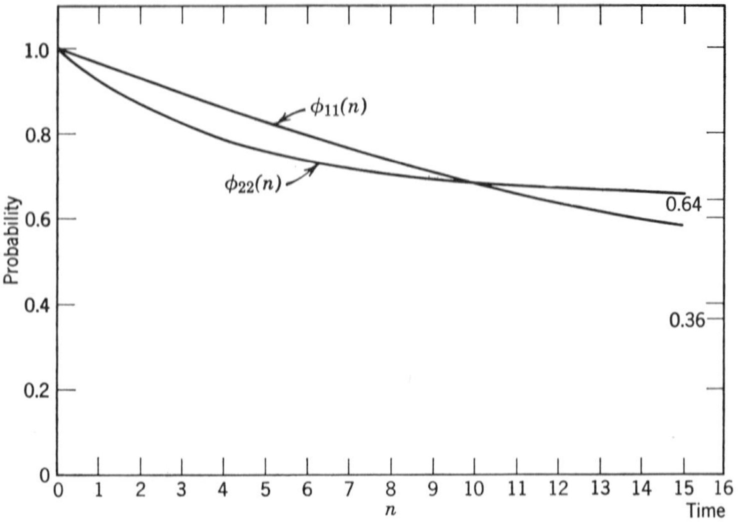

Figure 10.2.1 Plot of interval transition probabilities $\phi_{11}(n)$ and $\phi_{22}(n)$ for the car rental problem.

and $\phi_{22}(n)$ are plotted in Figure 10.2.1. We need only plot these two quantities because they jointly determine the entire $\Phi(n)$ matrix. The quantity $\phi_{11}(n)$ is the probability that a car rented in town 1 at time zero will have town 1 as its last rental point at time n. Note that both $\phi_{11}(n)$ and $\phi_{22}(n)$ appear to approach limiting values when n is large. However, the tendency is much more evident in the case of $\phi_{22}(n)$. We shall soon devote considerable attention to this limiting behavior.

10.3 TRANSFORM ANALYSIS

The recursive Equation 10.2.3 is the most practical method for finding the interval transition probabilities of discrete-time semi-Markov processes. However, for completeness and for theoretical purposes let us develop the transform analysis of such processes. We begin by writing the geometric transform of Equation 10.2.1 in our usual transform notation. Since the convolution becomes a multiplication of transforms, we write

$$\phi_{ij}^g(z) = \delta_{ij}\,{}^{>}w_i^g(z) + \sum_{k=1}^{N} p_{ik}h_{ik}^g(z)\phi_{kj}^g(z) \qquad i = 1, 2, \ldots, N;\ j = 1, 2, \ldots, N. \tag{10.3.1}$$

We obtain the transform $h_{ik}^{g}(z)$ by direct geometric transformation of the holding time mass function for the $i \to k$ transition. The transform of the ith complementary cumulative waiting time distribution is directly related to the transform of the waiting time mass function. Since ${}^{>}w_i(n) = 1 - {}^{\leq}w_i(n)$, Equation 10.1.13 and relations 3 and 25 of Table 1.5.1 (Vol. I) show that

$$ {}^{>}w_i^{g}(z) = \frac{1 - w_i^{g}(z)}{1 - z} = \frac{1 - \sum_{j=1}^{N} p_{ij} h_{ij}^{g}(z)}{1 - z} \qquad i = 1, 2, \ldots, N. \quad (10.3.2) $$

Matrix Formulation

We place Equation 10.3.1 in matrix form either directly or by transforming Equation 10.2.3,

$$ \begin{aligned} \Phi^{g}(z) &= {}^{>}W^{g}(z) + [P \,\square\, H^{g}(z)]\Phi^{g}(z) \\ &= {}^{>}W^{g}(z) + C^{g}(z)\Phi^{g}(z). \end{aligned} \quad (10.3.3) $$

Here we have used the symbol $C^{g}(z)$ for the transformed core matrix. Equation 10.3.2 becomes

$$ {}^{>}W^{g}(z) = \frac{1}{1 - z}[I - W^{g}(z)]. \quad (10.3.4) $$

We can rearrange Equation 10.3.3 to produce

$$ [I - P \,\square\, H^{g}(z)]\Phi^{g}(z) = {}^{>}W^{g}(z) \quad (10.3.5) $$

or

$$ \begin{aligned} \Phi^{g}(z) &= [I - P \,\square\, H^{g}(z)]^{-1}\, {}^{>}W^{g}(z) \\ &= [I - C^{g}(z)]^{-1}\, {}^{>}W^{g}(z). \end{aligned} \quad (10.3.6) $$

Equation 10.3.6 shows that the transform of the interval transition probability matrix for a discrete-time semi-Markov process is given by the inverse of I minus the transformed core matrix for the process postmultiplied by the transform of the complementary cumulative waiting time distribution matrix for the process. The inverse matrix will always exist for the type of process we are considering.

The inverse matrix $[I - C^{g}(z)]^{-1}$ has properties that parallel those of $[I - Pz]^{-1}$. In view of the series expansion,

$$ [I - C^{g}(z)]^{-1} = \sum_{n=0}^{\infty} [C^{g}(z)]^{n}, \quad (10.3.7) $$

we note that

$$C^{\mathscr{g}}(z)[I - C^{\mathscr{g}}(z)]^{-1} = [I - C^{\mathscr{g}}(z)]^{-1}C^{\mathscr{g}}(z). \tag{10.3.8}$$

Furthermore, for future reference,

$$[I - C^{\mathscr{g}}(z)]^{-1} = [I - C^{\mathscr{g}}(z)]^{-1}[I - C^{\mathscr{g}}(z) + C^{\mathscr{g}}(z)] = I + [I - C^{\mathscr{g}}(z)]^{-1}C^{\mathscr{g}}(z) \tag{10.3.9}$$

or, alternately,

$$[I - C^{\mathscr{g}}(z)]^{-1} = [I - C^{\mathscr{g}}(z) + C^{\mathscr{g}}(z)][I - C^{\mathscr{g}}(z)]^{-1} = I + C^{\mathscr{g}}(z)[I - C^{\mathscr{g}}(z)]^{-1}. \tag{10.3.10}$$

Equations 10.3.9 and 10.3.10 jointly show

$$[I - C^{\mathscr{g}}(z)]^{-1} - I = [I - C^{\mathscr{g}}(z)]^{-1}C^{\mathscr{g}}(z) = C^{\mathscr{g}}(z)[I - C^{\mathscr{g}}(z)]^{-1}, \tag{10.3.11}$$

a series of relationships that also follow directly from the series expansion of Equation 10.3.7.

Specialization to a Markov process

We can check the result of Equation 10.3.6 by applying it to the discrete-time Markov process. From Equation 10.2.9, we have

$$H^{\mathscr{g}}(z) = Uz. \tag{10.3.12}$$

Therefore,

$$C^{\mathscr{g}}(z) = P \,\square\, H^{\mathscr{g}}(z) = P \,\square\, Uz = Pz. \tag{10.3.13}$$

From Equation 10.2.10, we obtain

$$W^{\mathscr{g}}(z) = Iz. \tag{10.3.14}$$

By inserting Equation 10.3.14 into Equation 10.3.4 or directly from Equation 10.2.12, we find

$$^{>}W^{\mathscr{g}}(z) = I. \tag{10.3.15}$$

Now we substitute the results of Equations 10.3.13 and 10.3.15 into Equation 10.3.6 to produce

$$\begin{aligned} \Phi^{\mathscr{g}}(z) &= [I - C^{\mathscr{g}}(z)]^{-1}\,{}^{>}W^{\mathscr{g}}(z) \\ &= [I - Pz]^{-1}I \\ &= [I - Pz]^{-1}, \end{aligned} \tag{10.3.16}$$

and we have obtained our usual expression for the transform of the multistep transition probability matrix for the discrete-time Markov process.

The car rental example

The car rental example illustrates the difficulty of applying transform methods to all but the smallest problems. First we compute the transformed core matrix $C^g(z) = P \square H^g(z)$ from Equation 10.2.15,

$$C^g(z) = P \square H^g(z) = \begin{bmatrix} \dfrac{(4/15)z}{1-(2/3)z} & \dfrac{(1/30)z}{1-(5/6)z} \\ \dfrac{(3/40)z}{1-(3/4)z} & \dfrac{(7/120)z}{1-(11/12)z} \end{bmatrix}. \quad (10.3.17)$$

Then we compute the transform of the complementary cumulative waiting time matrix from Equation 10.2.17 or from Equations 10.2.16 and 10.3.4,

$$\begin{aligned} {}^{>}W^g(z) &= \begin{bmatrix} \dfrac{4/5}{1-(2/3)z} + \dfrac{1/5}{1-(5/6)z} & 0 \\ 0 & \dfrac{3/10}{1-(3/4)z} + \dfrac{7/10}{1-(11/12)z} \end{bmatrix} \\ &= \begin{bmatrix} \dfrac{1-(4/5)z}{[1-(2/3)z][1-(5/6)z]} & 0 \\ 0 & \dfrac{1-(4/5)z}{[1-(3/4)z][1-(11/12)z]} \end{bmatrix}. \end{aligned} \quad (10.3.18)$$

Mean waiting time matrix. We can develop a useful check on ${}^{>}W^g(z)$ by attempting to evaluate ${}^{>}W^g(z)$ as expressed by Equation 10.3.4 at the point $z = 1$,

$${}^{>}W^g(1) = \lim_{z\to 1} {}^{>}W^g(z) = \lim_{z\to 1} \frac{1}{1-z}[I - W^g(z)]. \quad (10.3.19)$$

Since

$$W^g(1) = \sum_{n=0}^{\infty} W(n) = I, \quad (10.3.20)$$

the limit is indeterminate. We therefore use L'Hôpital's rule,

$${}^{>}W^g(1) = \lim_{z\to 1} {}^{>}W^g(z) = \frac{d}{dz} W^g(z)\bigg|_{z=1} = \sum_{n=0}^{\infty} nW(n) = M, \quad (10.3.21)$$

where M is a diagonal matrix whose ith diagonal element is $\bar{\tau}_i$, the mean waiting time in state i. This relation recalls the general result of Equation 7.2.59 that the geometric transform of the complementary cumulative probability distribution of any random variable evaluated at $z = 1$ is equal to the mean of the variable.

For the car rental example, we obtain from Equation 10.3.18

$$ {}^{>}W^{g}(1) = M = \begin{bmatrix} 3.6 & 0 \\ 0 & 9.6 \end{bmatrix}. \tag{10.3.22} $$

The mean waiting times in the matrix M are just those found in Equation 10.1.22.

Transform representation. Returning now to the question of finding the transformed interval transition probability matrix, we compute $I - P \,\square\, H^{g}(z)$

$$ I - C^{g}(z) = I - P \,\square\, H^{g}(z) = \begin{bmatrix} \dfrac{1-(14/15)z}{1-(2/3)z} & \dfrac{-(1/30)z}{1-(5/6)z} \\ \dfrac{-(3/40)z}{1-(3/4)z} & \dfrac{1-(39/40)z}{1-(11/12)z} \end{bmatrix}. \tag{10.3.23} $$

We obtain the determinant of this matrix after some algebraic labor as

$$ |I - C^{g}(z)| = \frac{(1-z)[1-(4/5)z][1-(203/120)z+(1021/1440)z^2]}{[1-(2/3)z][1-(11/12)z][1-(3/4)z][1-(5/6)z]} $$

$$ = \frac{(1-z)[1-(4/5)z](1-0.92587z)(1-0.76579z)}{[1-(2/3)z][1-(11/12)z][1-(3/4)z][1-(5/6)z]}, \tag{10.3.24} $$

then

$$ [I - C^{g}(z)]^{-1} = \frac{[1-(2/3)z][1-(11/12)z][1-(3/4)z][1-(5/6)z]}{(1-z)[1-(4/5)z]\underbrace{(1-0.92587z)(1-0.76579z)}_{1-(203/120)z+(1021/1440)z^2}} $$

$$ \times \begin{bmatrix} \dfrac{1-(39/40)z}{1-(11/12)z} & \dfrac{(1/30)z}{1-(5/6)z} \\ \dfrac{(3/40)z}{1-(3/4)z} & \dfrac{1-(14/15)z}{1-(2/3)z} \end{bmatrix}. \tag{10.3.25} $$

Finally, we postmultiply this matrix by ${}^{>}W^{g}(z)$ from Equation 10.3.18 to produce the transformed interval transition probability matrix,

$$ \Phi^{g}(z) = [I - C^{g}(z)]^{-1}\, {}^{>}W^{g}(z) = \frac{1}{(1-z)\underbrace{(1-0.92587z)(1-0.76579z)}_{1-(203/120)z+(1021/1440)z^2}} $$

$$ \times \begin{bmatrix} [1-(3/4)z][1-(39/40)z] & (1/30)z[1-(2/3)z] \\ (3/40)z[1-(11/12)z] & [1-(5/6)z][1-(14/15)z] \end{bmatrix}. \tag{10.3.26} $$

The next step is partial fraction expansion, again a laborious process,

$$\Phi^{g}(z) = \frac{1}{1-z}\begin{bmatrix} 0.36 & 0.64 \\ 0.36 & 0.64 \end{bmatrix} + \frac{1}{1-0.92587z}\begin{bmatrix} 0.72813 & -0.72813 \\ -0.05818 & 0.05818 \end{bmatrix}$$
$$+ \frac{1}{1-0.76579z}\begin{bmatrix} -0.08813 & 0.08813 \\ -0.30182 & 0.30182 \end{bmatrix}. \qquad (10.3.27)$$

Note that the rows of $\Phi^{g}(z)$ sum to $1/(1-z)$ since the process must be in some state at time n,

$$\Phi^{g}(z)\mathbf{s} = \frac{1}{1-z}\mathbf{s}. \qquad (10.3.28)$$

Solution. Upon taking the inverse geometric transform, we obtain the interval transition probability matrix,

$$\Phi(n) = \begin{bmatrix} 0.36 & 0.64 \\ 0.36 & 0.64 \end{bmatrix} + (0.92857)^n\begin{bmatrix} 0.72813 & -0.72813 \\ -0.05818 & 0.05818 \end{bmatrix}$$
$$+ (0.76579)^n\begin{bmatrix} -0.08813 & 0.08813 \\ -0.30182 & 0.30182 \end{bmatrix} \qquad n = 0, 1, 2, \ldots. \qquad (10.3.29)$$

We check that $\Phi(0) = \mathbf{1}$, and note that when n is very large $\Phi(n)$ approaches a limiting matrix,

$$\lim_{n\to\infty} \Phi(n) = \Phi = \begin{bmatrix} 0.36 & 0.64 \\ 0.36 & 0.64 \end{bmatrix}. \qquad (10.3.30)$$

Thus the interval transition probabilities approach a limit that is independent of starting state just as did the state probabilities of a monodesmic Markov process. We shall have more to say of this limiting behavior in a moment.

We must not read too much into the form of Equation 10.3.29. Although the transient components of $\Phi(n)$ are geometrically weighted differential matrices, this property will not hold in general for all discrete-time semi-Markov processes. In the car rental example, it is a consequence of the geometric holding time distributions. Note that $\Phi(n)$ has two geometrically decaying components—in a two-state discrete-time Markov process $\Phi(n)$ would have only one component. While we appreciate the insight provided by such closed-form solutions, the problem of calculating $\Phi(n)$ by transform analysis is generally so difficult that we prefer to use the recursive method of Equation 10.2.3.

The diagonal elements of $\Phi(n)$ are

$$\phi_{11}(n) = 0.36 + 0.72813(0.92857)^n - 0.08813(0.76579)^n \qquad n = 0, 1, 2, \ldots \quad (10.3.31)$$

and

$$\phi_{22}(n) = 0.64 + 0.05818(0.92857)^n + 0.30182(0.76579)^n \qquad n = 0, 1, 2, \ldots. \quad (10.3.32)$$

These equations for $\phi_{11}(n)$ and $\phi_{22}(n)$ produce the values for these quantities already plotted in Figure 10.2.1 using the recursive method.

Limiting Behavior of Monodesmic Processes

Let us now turn to the question of finding the limiting behavior of interval transition probabilities over long intervals. We first note that the chain structure of a semi-Markov process is the same as that of its imbedded Markov process. Therefore the interval transition probabilities of a semi-Markov process can exhibit a unique limiting behavior only within the same chain of the imbedded process. We shall assume that we are dealing with a monodesmic imbedded Markov process and, therefore, with a monodesmic semi-Markov process. The extension to the polydesmic case is then straightforward.

We begin by defining a limiting interval transition probability matrix Φ for the process by

$$\Phi = \lim_{n \to \infty} \Phi(n). \tag{10.3.33}$$

From the final value theorem of geometric transforms, Φ is also given by

$$\Phi = \lim_{z \to 1} (1 - z)\Phi^g(z). \tag{10.3.34}$$

Since the limit of a product is the product of the limits if they exist, we can find Φ by taking limits in Equation 10.3.6,

$$\Phi = \lim_{z \to 1} (1 - z)\Phi^g(z) = \lim_{z \to 1} (1 - z)[I - P \,\square\, H^g(z)]^{-1} \lim_{z \to 1} {}^{>}W^g(z). \tag{10.3.35}$$

We now consider separately each limit on the right side of this equation. We have already evaluated the second limit in Equation 10.3.21 where we found that it represented a diagonal matrix M of mean waiting times. If we define $T(z)$ by

$$T(z) = (1 - z)[I - P \,\square\, H^g(z)]^{-1}, \tag{10.3.36}$$

then Equation 10.3.35 becomes

$$\Phi = \lim_{z \to 1} T(z)M. \tag{10.3.37}$$

Equation 10.3.36 can be written as

$$T(z) - T(z)[P \,\square\, H^g(z)] = (1 - z)I. \tag{10.3.38}$$

If we take the limit of this equation as z approaches 1, noting that

$$H^g(1) = \sum_{m=0}^{\infty} H(m) = U, \tag{10.3.39}$$

we obtain

$$T(1) = T(1)P. \tag{10.3.40}$$

Each row of the $T(1)$ matrix must therefore satisfy the same equation as do the limiting state probabilities for the imbedded Markov process, namely,

$$\boldsymbol{\pi} = \boldsymbol{\pi}P. \tag{10.3.41}$$

Thus the rows of the $T(1)$ matrix must each be proportional to the limiting state probability vector of the imbedded Markov process, a vector which is unique because we have assumed that the imbedded Markov process is monodesmic.

We have now reduced Equation 10.3.35 to the form,

$$\Phi = T(1)M, \tag{10.3.42}$$

where the elements of Φ must satisfy

$$\phi_{ij} = t_{ij}(1)\bar{\tau}_j = k_i\pi_j\bar{\tau}_j \qquad i = 1, 2, \ldots, N; j = 1, 2, \ldots, N. \tag{10.3.43}$$

Here k_i is an undetermined coefficient of proportionality between the ith row of $T(1)$ and $\boldsymbol{\pi}$, the limiting state probability vector for the imbedded Markov process. We use the condition that the limiting interval transition probabilities ϕ_{ij} must sum to one over all states of the process to evaluate k_i,

$$\sum_{j=1}^{N} \phi_{ij} = 1 = \sum_{j=1}^{N} k_i\pi_j\bar{\tau}_j = k_i \sum_{j=1}^{N} \pi_j\bar{\tau}_j, \tag{10.3.44}$$

and therefore,

$$k_i = \frac{1}{\sum_{j=1}^{N} \pi_j\bar{\tau}_j} \qquad i = 1, 2, \ldots, N. \tag{10.3.45}$$

The constant of proportionality k_i is therefore the same for all states. We define

$$\bar{\tau} = \sum_{j=1}^{N} \pi_j\bar{\tau}_j, \tag{10.3.46}$$

and write Equation 10.3.43 as

$$\phi_{ij} = \frac{\pi_j\bar{\tau}_j}{\sum_{j=1}^{N} \pi_j\bar{\tau}_j} = \frac{\pi_j\bar{\tau}_j}{\bar{\tau}} = \phi_j. \tag{10.3.47}$$

As we would expect, the limiting interval transition probabilities ϕ_{ij} for a monodesmic semi-Markov process do not depend on the starting state i. We shall therefore use only the second subscript j to designate these quantities. Furthermore, the limiting interval transition probability for state j, ϕ_j, is equal to the limiting state probability for that state in the imbedded Markov process, π_j, multiplied by the mean waiting time in state j, $\bar{\tau}_j$, and normalized so that the limiting interval transition probabilities sum to one over all states. The quantity ϕ_j answers the question: What is the probability of observing that the process is in state j if we observe it after it has operated for a long time? The result of Equation 10.3.47 is intuitive and important: The only statistic of the holding time distributions that affects the limiting behavior of the process is the mean.

Since all the rows of Φ are identical for a monodesmic process, we define each of them to be $\boldsymbol{\phi}$, the limiting interval transition probability vector whose components are ϕ_j. We can express this vector in terms of the limiting state probability vector for the imbedded Markov process through Equation 10.3.47,

$$\boldsymbol{\phi} = \frac{1}{\bar{\tau}}\boldsymbol{\pi}M. \tag{10.3.48}$$

The car rental example

We can apply these results to find the limiting behavior of the interval transition probabilities in the car rental example. We have on several occasions established that the limiting state probabilities for the imbedded Markov process with the transition probability matrix of Equation 10.1.14 are

$$\pi_1 = 0.6 \qquad \pi_2 = 0.4. \tag{10.3.49}$$

Equation 10.1.22 shows that the mean waiting times for each state are

$$\bar{\tau}_1 = 3.6 \qquad \bar{\tau}_2 = 9.6. \tag{10.3.50}$$

Therefore, by applying Equation 10.3.47, we find

$$\begin{aligned} \phi_1 &= \frac{\pi_1\bar{\tau}_1}{\pi_1\bar{\tau}_1 + \pi_2\bar{\tau}_2} = \frac{0.6(3.6)}{0.6(3.6) + 0.4(9.6)} = 0.36 \\ \phi_2 &= \frac{\pi_2\bar{\tau}_2}{\pi_1\bar{\tau}_1 + \pi_2\bar{\tau}_2} = \frac{0.4(9.6)}{0.6(3.6) + 0.4(9.6)} = 0.64. \end{aligned} \tag{10.3.51}$$

We observe that these values are the limiting interval transition probabilities found for the car rental example in Equation 10.3.30. Equation 10.3.47 thus provides a very simple and convenient method for finding the limiting interval transition probabilities of the semi-Markov process. We see that this calculation is but a little more difficult than computing only the limiting state probabilities of the imbedded Markov process.

Limiting Behavior of Polydesmic Processes

A word is in order here about what to do if the process is not monodesmic. If this is the case, a limiting state probability vector $\boldsymbol{\pi}$ must be associated with each starting state of the process. Then in computing ϕ_{ij} from Equation 10.3.47, we use the values of π_j that correspond to the starting state i and compute a ϕ_{ij} distribution for that starting state.

Proceeding in detail, we find for each starting state the limiting state probabilities of the imbedded process. Then we weigh each of these probabilities by the mean waiting times and normalize so that the sum of the limiting interval transition probabilities over all states is one. We shall therefore have at least as many different sets of limiting interval transition probabilities as we have chains. Transient states that can run into more than one chain will then have limiting interval transition probabilities that are linear combinations of those for the chains they can enter.

Limiting Behavior Interpretation

We must be sure that we understand the difference between the limiting state probabilities π_i and the limiting interval transition probabilities ϕ_i. The difference is best illustrated by the example. Since $\phi_1 = 0.36$, we know that if we are operating many cars in this system, at any time we expect 36% of them to have the property that they were rented at town 1. However, since $\pi_1 = 0.60$, we expect 60% of all the rental contracts to be written in town 1. In both of these interpretations we are assuming that we have no detailed information on the state of any car. We reconcile the differences between the ϕ_i's and π_i's by observing that although town 2 writes fewer rental contracts, its cars are rented for longer times on the average. Town 2 is therefore responsible for renting most of the cars on the road at any time. A moment spent pondering this contrast between the interval transition probabilities and the limiting state probabilities is well-spent. Remember that the imbedded process describes only the successive transitions and not the time behavior of the process.

10.4 AN ALTERNATE FORMULATION—CONDITIONAL TRANSITION PROBABILITIES

Although our present formal model for semi-Markov processes is valuable in its present form, we can increase its utility by considering an alternate representation of the process. In the present model, the process first selects its destination using the transition probabilities p_{ij}, and then selects its time of transition from a holding time mass function $h_{ij}(\cdot)$ that is conditional on the transition made. We can equally well reverse this procedure to allow the process to select its time of transition first and then select a destination conditional on transition time. In many physical processes this sequence of events is more natural. For example, in a marketing model where each state represents the last brand purchased, it is likely that the decision on when to buy does not depend on the brand last purchased (except possibly through its size). However, the next brand purchased may depend not only on the last brand purchased but also on the time since that purchase because of the cumulative effects of advertising during the interval between purchases.

Conditional Transition Probability Formulation

The waiting time distribution $w_i(m)$ that we have already defined in Equation 10.1.8 is the distribution of holding time unconditional on destination state. In the alternate description of the process, $w_i(m)$ would have to be specified all for states. Then we have to supply the probability of making a transition to each state given the time the process has held in its present state before making the transition. Let $p_{ij}(m)$ be the probability that a process which is now in state i and which will make a transition out of state i at time m will make that transition to state j. Thus the $p_{ij}(m)$ are transition probabilities conditional on holding time; we shall call them simply "conditional" transition probabilities.

The waiting time distributions $w_i(m)$ and the conditional transition probabilities $p_{ij}(m)$ provide a complete alternate definition of a semi-Markov process. We emphasize this by showing that each element of the core matrix $C(m)$ can be written in terms of either formulation,

$$c_{ij}(m) = p_{ij}h_{ij}(m) = w_i(m)p_{ij}(m) \qquad \begin{aligned} i &= 1, 2, \dots, N \\ j &= 1, 2, \dots, N \\ m &= 1, 2, 3, \dots . \end{aligned} \tag{10.4.1}$$

This equation simply states that the probability of the joint event of transition to state j and transition at time m can be expressed in terms of either of the conditional probabilities associated with the joint event. The joint probability is either the product of the transition probability and the holding time probability or the product of the waiting time probability and the conditional transition probability.

We can convert from one representation to the other very easily. If the process is originally described in terms of p_{ij} and $h_{ij}(m)$, we compute $w_i(m)$ from Equation 10.1.8 and then $p_{ij}(m)$ from Equation 10.4.1,

$$p_{ij}(m) = \frac{p_{ij}h_{ij}(m)}{w_i(m)} = \frac{p_{ij}h_{ij}(m)}{\sum_{j=1}^{N} p_{ij}h_{ij}(m)} \qquad \begin{aligned} i &= 1, 2, \dots, N \\ j &= 1, 2, \dots, N \\ m &= 1, 2, 3, \dots . \end{aligned} \tag{10.4.2}$$

On the other hand, if the process is originally described by $w_i(m)$ and $p_{ij}(m)$, we can convert by computing p_{ij} from Equations 10.2.8 and 10.4.1,

$$p_{ij} = \sum_{m=1}^{\infty} c_{ij}(m) = \sum_{m=1}^{\infty} w_i(m)p_{ij}(m) \qquad \begin{aligned} i &= 1, 2, \dots, N \\ j &= 1, 2, \dots, N \end{aligned} \tag{10.4.3}$$

and then using Equation 10.4.1 to produce $h_{ij}(m)$,

$$h_{ij}(m) = \frac{w_i(m)p_{ij}(m)}{p_{ij}} \qquad \begin{matrix} i = 1, 2, \ldots, N \\ j = 1, 2, \ldots, N \\ m = 1, 2, 3, \ldots . \end{matrix} \tag{10.4.4}$$

Of course, these conversions are nothing but exercises in elementary probability.

Because $W(m)$ is a diagonal matrix, we can construct a conditional transition probability matrix $P(m)$ from Equation 10.4.2 in matrix form,

$$P(m) = [W(m)]^{-1}[P \,\square\, H(m)] \qquad m = 1, 2, 3, \ldots . \tag{10.4.5}$$

The car rental example

By using the results of Equations 10.2.15 and 10.2.16 we can write the conditional transition probability matrix for the car rental example,

$$P(m) = \begin{bmatrix} \dfrac{8(2/3)^{m-1}}{8(2/3)^{m-1} + (5/6)^{m-1}} & \dfrac{(5/6)^{m-1}}{8(2/3)^{m-1} + (5/6)^{m-1}} \\ \dfrac{9(3/4)^{m-1}}{9(3/4)^{m-1} + 7(11/12)^{m-1}} & \dfrac{7(11/12)^{m-1}}{9(3/4)^{m-1} + 7(11/12)^{m-1}} \end{bmatrix} \qquad m = 1, 2, 3, \ldots . \tag{10.4.6}$$

The matrix $P(m)$ must, of course, be a stochastic matrix for any value of m.

We observe

$$P(1) = \begin{bmatrix} 8/9 & 1/9 \\ 9/16 & 7/16 \end{bmatrix}. \tag{10.4.7}$$

The odds are 8 to 1 that if the process made a transition after being in state 1 for one time unit, it made that transition once more to state 1. If the process left state 2 after one time unit, the odds are 9 to 7 that it made a transition to state 1. In terms of the car rental example, there is a 8/9 probability that a car rented in town 1 and returned after one period will be returned to town 1. There is a 7/16 probability that a car rented in town 2 and returned after one period will be returned to town 2.

If the process makes its first transition out of a state after occupying it for a very long time, the conditional transition probability matrix is

$$\lim_{m \to \infty} P(m) = P(\infty) = \begin{bmatrix} 0 & 1 \\ 0 & 1 \end{bmatrix}. \tag{10.4.8}$$

This shows that transitions made after holding in either state for a very long time are likely to be made to state 2. In car rental terminology, almost all cars rented for very long periods are returned to town 2.

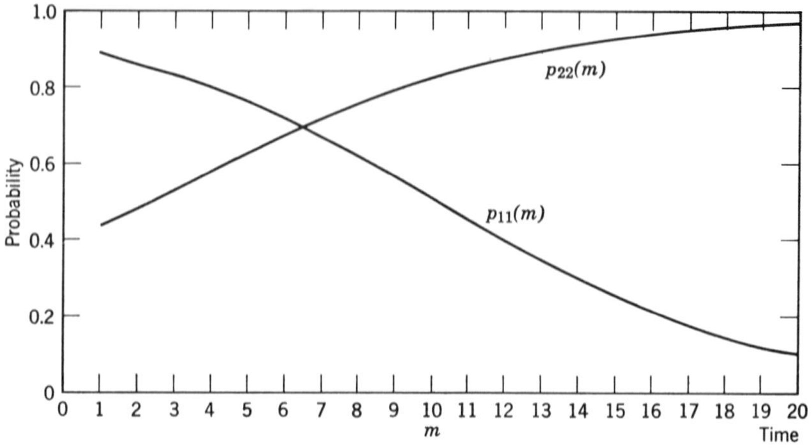

Figure 10.4.1 Conditional transition probabilities $p_{11}(m)$ and $p_{22}(m)$ for the car rental example.

Figure 10.4.1 shows $p_{11}(m)$ and $p_{22}(m)$ for the car rental example. These plots show that our feelings about the relative likelihood of transition destinations can vary quite markedly as our knowledge of the holding time changes.

Specialization to a Markov Process

Equation 10.4.2 takes an interesting form when we consider the discrete-time Markov process. We already know that the holding time and waiting time probability mass functions for this process are given by

$$h_{ij}(m) = w_i(m) = \delta(m - 1) \qquad \begin{array}{l} i = 1, 2, \ldots, N \\ j = 1, 2, \ldots, N \\ m = 1, 2, \ldots . \end{array} \tag{10.4.9}$$

Therefore Equation 10.4.2 becomes

$$p_{ij}(m) = p_{ij} \qquad \begin{array}{l} i = 1, 2, \ldots, N \\ j = 1, 2, \ldots, N \\ m = 1, 2, 3, \ldots \end{array} \tag{10.4.10}$$

or in matrix form

$$P(m) = P \qquad m = 1, 2, 3, \ldots . \tag{10.4.11}$$

The conditional transition probability matrix for a discrete-time Markov process is exactly the same as the transition probability matrix P.

Independent Semi-Markov Processes

What this means is that knowledge of when a transition occurs in such a process does not affect our assignment of probability to the possible destinations of that transition. We shall call semi-Markov processes with this probability "independent" semi-Markov processes because for them the selection of destination and the selection of transition time are independent random processes.

Since for an independent semi-Markov process Equations 10.4.10 must hold, we find from Equation 10.4.1 that for such a process

$$h_{ij}(m) = w_i(m) \qquad \begin{aligned} i &= 1, 2, \ldots, N \\ j &= 1, 2, \ldots, N \\ m &= 1, 2, 3, \ldots . \end{aligned} \tag{10.4.12}$$

This equation states that the holding times for an independent semi-Markov process are independent of destination and therefore have identical distributions for all transitions out of a given state. These distributions may, of course, be different for different states. Although a discrete-time Markov process meets this requirement, so also do other discrete-time semi-Markov processes. Equations 10.4.10 and 10.4.12 therefore provide two alternate necessary and sufficient conditions for a semi-Markov process to be an independent semi-Markov process.

In view of Equation 10.4.12, we have immediately for an independent semi-Markov process

$$P \square H(m) = W(m)P. \tag{10.4.13}$$

When we substitute this result into Equation 10.4.5, we produce Equation 10.4.11. Equation 10.4.13 allows us to write Equations 10.2.3 and 10.3.3 in specialized forms for the independent semi-Markov process:

$$\Phi(n) = {}^{>}W(n) + \sum_{m=0}^{n} W(m)P\Phi(n-m) \qquad n = 0, 1, 2, \ldots \tag{10.4.14}$$

and

$$\Phi^{g}(z) = {}^{>}W^{g}(z) + W^{g}(z)P\Phi^{g}(z) \tag{10.4.15}$$

or

$$\Phi^{g}(z) = [I - W^{g}(z)P]^{-1}\, {}^{>}W^{g}(z). \tag{10.4.16}$$

These equations emphasize that an independent semi-Markov process is completely characterized by its transition probability matrix P and its waiting time distribution matrix $W(m)$. The independent semi-Markov process is an important case of semi-Markov process theory.

10.5 FLOW GRAPH ANALYSIS

Let us now develop a flow graph analysis for discrete-time semi-Markov processes. The procedure we follow is very similar to that for discrete-time Markov processes. Equation 10.3.6 shows immediately that we can construct a matrix flow graph whose transmissions will be the geometric transforms of $\phi_{ij}(n)$; the matrix flow graph appears in Figure 10.5.1. This matrix flow graph is equivalent to the regular flow graph partially indicated in Figure 10.5.2. In this figure we have constructed an N-node flow graph and labeled its nodes from 1 to N. Then we have drawn branches with transmissions $p_{ij}h_{ij}^{g}(z)$ from each node i to each node j. Finally, we have added to each node j an output branch with transmission ${}^{>}w_j^{g}(z)$. We shall call the node at the end of this branch the output node associated with node j. The transmission of the flow graph from node i to the output node associated with node j is the transform $\phi_{ij}^{g}(z)$ of the interval transition probability $\phi_{ij}(n)$. This transmission is equal to the transmission of the flow graph from node i to node j multiplied by ${}^{>}w_j^{g}(z)$.

The flow graph thus provides a graphical and useful representation of discrete-time semi-Markov processes. The representation must, of course, specialize to the case of discrete-time Markov processes that we have studied in some detail. In particular, we note that if we introduce the results of Equations 10.3.13 and 10.3.15 developed for the discrete-time Markov process into the flow graph for the semi-Markov process in Figures 10.5.1 and 10.5.2, we obtain immediately the flow graphs for the discrete-time Markov process in Figures 3.1.1 and 3.1.2 (Volume I).

We can easily draw the flow graph for a discrete-time semi-Markov process when we know its core matrix $C(m) = P \,\square\, H(m)$. The transmission of the flow graph from node i to node j is just the geometric transform $c_{ij}^{g}(z) = p_{ij}h_{ij}^{g}(z)$ of the ijth element $c_{ij}(m)$ in the core matrix. Then we construct the transmissions ${}^{>}w_i^{g}(z)$ on the output branch associated with node i according to Equation 10.3.2. That is, we develop ${}^{>}w_i^{g}(z)$ by summing the transmissions on all branches leaving node i, subtracting the result from 1, and then dividing by $1 - z$.

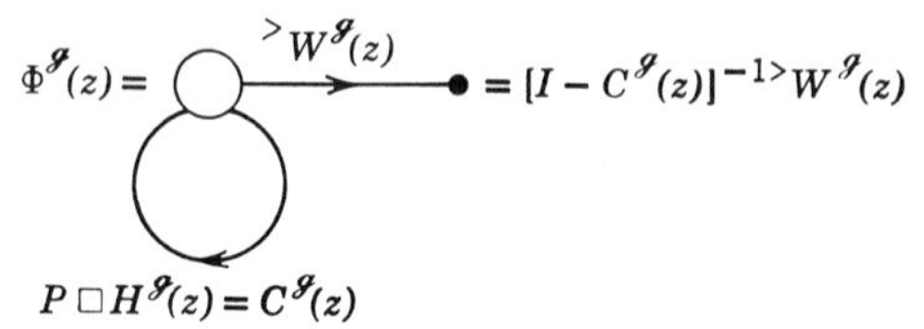

Figure 10.5.1 Matrix flow graph for the discrete-time semi-Markov process.

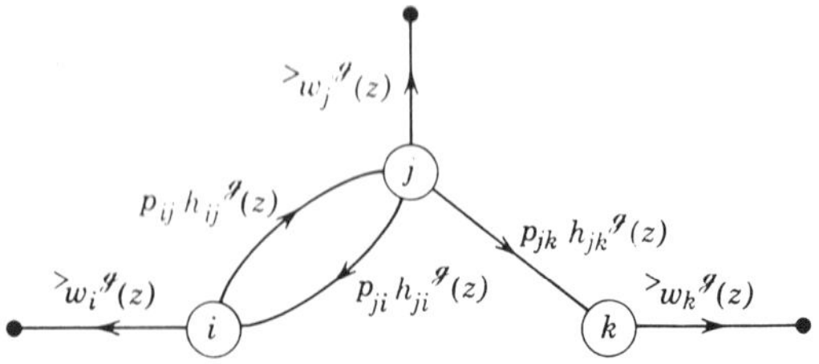

Figure 10.5.2 Partial flow graph for the discrete-time semi-Markov process.

Figure 10.5.3 is the flow graph for the car rental example constructed according to Equations 10.3.17 and 10.3.18. The transmission of this flow graph from node i to the output node associated with node j produces the transform $\phi_{ij}^{\mathscr{g}}(z)$, that is, the ijth element of $\Phi^{\mathscr{g}}(z)$ in Equation 10.3.26.

We see that the flow graph for a semi-Markov process is to be more valued as an aid to visualization than as an aid to computation. We usually draw the flow graph in setting up the problem, find the recursive equation implied by the flow graph, and then solve it for the numerical values of the interval transition probabilities.

10.6 COUNTING TRANSITIONS

Because the semi-Markov model allows a distinction between the number of time units that have passed and the number of transitions that have occurred, we have the opportunity of asking not only the probability of being in each state at time n but also the probability distribution of the number of transitions made by that time. Let $\kappa(n)$ be the number of transitions that the process has made between time zero and time n, let $s(n)$ be the index of the state that the system

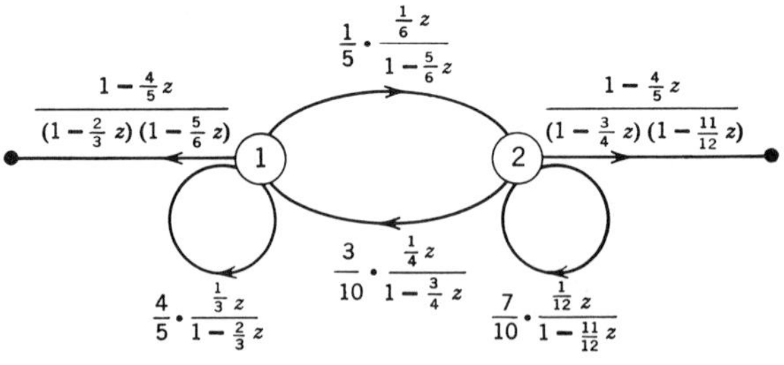

Figure 10.5.3 Flow graph for car rental example.

occupies at time n, and let $t(k)$ be the time at which the kth transition occurs. Then we can define a quantity $\phi_{ij}(k|n)$ by

$$\phi_{ij}(k|n) = \mathscr{P}\{\kappa(n) = k, s(n) = j|s(0) = i, t(0) = 0\}$$
$$i = 1, 2, \ldots, N; j = 1, 2, \ldots, N$$
$$k = 0, 1, 2, \ldots; n = 0, 1, 2, \ldots. \quad (10.6.1)$$

The quantity $\phi_{ij}(k|n)$ is the joint probability that the process is in state j and that it has made k transitions given that the time is n and that at time zero it entered state i on its zeroth transition. This probability must satisfy the recursive equation,

$$\phi_{ij}(k|n) = \delta_{ij}\, \delta(k)\, {}^{>}w_i(n) + \sum_{r=1}^{N} p_{ir} \sum_{m=0}^{n} h_{ir}(m)\phi_{rj}(k-1|n-m)$$
$$i = 1, 2, \ldots, N; j = 1, 2, \ldots, N$$
$$k = 0, 1, 2, \ldots; n = 0, 1, 2, \ldots. \quad (10.6.2)$$

By our convention that any quantity with a negative argument is zero,

$$\phi_{ij}(0|n) = \delta_{ij}\, {}^{>}w_i(n) \qquad \begin{aligned} i &= 1, 2, \ldots, N \\ j &= 1, 2, \ldots, N \\ n &= 0, 1, 2, \ldots, \end{aligned} \quad (10.6.3)$$

showing that the only way to have made no transitions within the $(0, n)$ interval is to have $i = j$ and a holding time in state i that exceeds n. The probability of achieving values of k greater than 0 is the probability of making $k - 1$ transitions after the first transition. Thus Equation 10.6.2 follows the exact reasoning that underlies Equation 10.2.1 with the addition that we are now keeping track of the number of transitions.

The relationship between $\phi_{ij}(k|n)$ and the interval transition probability $\phi_{ij}(n)$ is very simple: $\phi_{ij}(n)$ is the marginal distribution on j of the joint distribution $\phi_{ij}(k|n)$ on j and k. That is, the probability of being in state j at time n is the sum of the probabilities of achieving this event and having made various numbers of transitions,

$$\phi_{ij}(n) = \sum_{k=0}^{\infty} \phi_{ij}(k|n). \quad (10.6.4)$$

We place Equation 10.6.2 in matrix form by defining a matrix $\Phi(k|n)$ with elements $\phi_{ij}(k|n)$:

$$\Phi(k|n) = \delta(k)\, {}^{>}W(n) + \sum_{m=0}^{n} [P \,\square\, H(m)]\Phi(k-1|n-m) \qquad \begin{aligned} k &= 0, 1, 2, \ldots \\ n &= 0, 1, 2, \ldots. \end{aligned} \quad (10.6.5)$$

Equations 10.6.2 or 10.6.5 provide a convenient recursive basis for calculation.

Transform Relations

We can now write the double geometric transform of $\phi_{ij}(k|n)$ defined in our usual notation by

$$\phi_{ij}{}^{gg}(y|z) = \sum_{k=0}^{\infty} \sum_{n=0}^{\infty} y^k z^n \phi_{ij}(k|n). \tag{10.6.6}$$

Since we are already experienced in operations with this type of transform, we can immediately transform Equation 10.6.2,

$$\phi_{ij}{}^{gg}(y|z) = \delta_{ij}\, {}^{>}w_i{}^{g}(z) + y \sum_{r=1}^{N} p_{ir} h_{ir}{}^{g}(z) \phi_{rj}{}^{gg}(y|z). \tag{10.6.7}$$

By transforming Equation 10.6.5 or by writing Equation 10.6.7 in matrix form, we obtain the transformed matrix relation,

$$\begin{aligned} \Phi^{gg}(y|z) &= {}^{>}W^{g}(z) + y[P \,\square\, H^{g}(z)]\Phi^{gg}(y|z) \\ &= {}^{>}W^{g}(z) + yC^{g}(z)\Phi^{gg}(y|z) \end{aligned} \tag{10.6.8}$$

or

$$\Phi^{gg}(y|z) = [I - y(P \,\square\, H^{g}(z)]^{-1}\, {}^{>}W^{g}(z) = [I - yC^{g}(z)]^{-1}\, {}^{>}W^{g}(z). \tag{10.6.9}$$

Flow Graph Representation

This equation shows that the matrix flow graph for $\Phi^{gg}(y|z)$ in Figure 10.6.1 is the same as the matrix flow graph for $\Phi^{g}(z)$ in Figure 10.5.1 except that every transmission in the loop is multiplied by y, a very simple modification. In view of Equation 10.6.4, we relate $\Phi^{gg}(y|z)$ to the transformed interval transition probability matrix by

$$\Phi^{g}(z) = \Phi^{gg}(1|z), \tag{10.6.10}$$

a result confirmed by both Equation 10.6.9 and the corresponding flow graph.

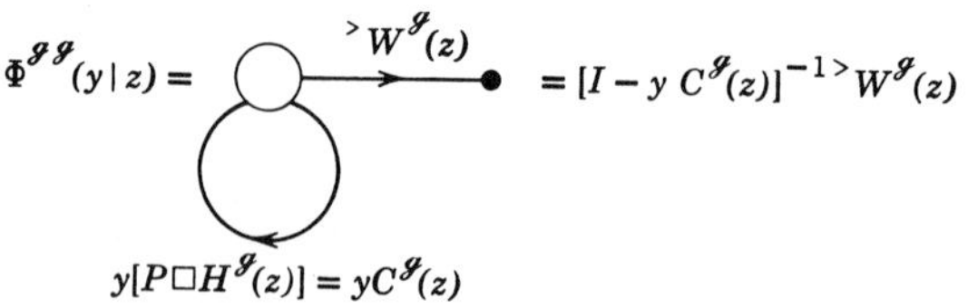

Figure 10.6.1 Matrix flow graph for counting transitions.

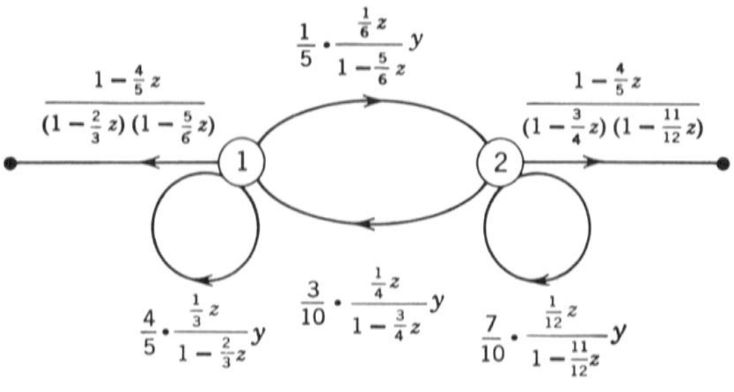

Figure 10.6.2 Flow graph for car rental example with transitions counted.

A significant interpretation of our result is that we can control what we call a transition by selecting which transmissions of the graph we multiply by y. For example, if we multiply only the diagonal elements $p_{ii}h_{ii}{}^{g}(z)$ by y, we shall count only the virtual transmissions of the process. If we multiply only the off-diagonal elements $p_{ij}h_{ij}{}^{g}(z)$, $i \neq j$, by y, then we shall count only the real transitions. Of course, we can select any subset of transitions that we wish, just as we could when we studied tagging in Chapter 6.

The flow graph we drew for the car rental example would appear as shown in Figure 10.6.2 if we intended to keep track of the total number of transitions or rentals made by the system. If we wanted to count only rentals made at town 1, then only branch transmissions leaving node 1 would be multiplied by y. If we wanted to count only rentals at town 2 that were returned to town 1, then only the transmission of the branch leading from node 2 to node 1 would be multiplied by y.

Tagging Interpretation

We see, therefore, that the development of this section is merely a variation of the tagging concept, a consideration that motivated using the same notation. We used to ask about the probability of making k special transitions in n transitions—now we ask about the probability of making k transitions in time n. The difference is a question only of interpretation. If we specialize the results of this section to the discrete-time Markov process, we find that we have produced an alternate proof of the tagging procedure.

Thus all the results of the tagging section can be applied to semi-Markov processes. We can do multiple tagging of different kinds of transitions, including placing several tagging variables on the same transition if we wish to count it in several categories. Although complete transform methods are prohibitive in solving these problems, the transforms do provide the recursive equation formulation, a very practical solution technique.

Transition Moments

Just as we used tagging to find the moments of the number of tagged transitions made by the discrete-time Markov process, so can we use the same device to obtain the moments of the number of transitions made in a semi-Markov process. We must therefore recall the necessity of making sure that all moments we calculate are computed using the proper probability for the events in the equation. Let $\overline{k_{ij}^m(n)}$ be the mth moment of the number of transitions the process makes through time n given that it started in state i and ended in state j. We can express $\overline{k_{ij}^m(n)}$ in the equation

$$\overline{k_{ij}^m(n)} = \frac{k_{ij}^m(n)}{\phi_{ij}(n)}, \tag{10.6.11}$$

where $k_{ij}^m(n)$ is a quantity whose geometric transform $k_{ij}^{m\mathscr{g}}(z)$ is obtained by successive differentiation of the tagged transmission $\phi_{ij}^{\mathscr{g}\mathscr{g}}(y|z)$ with respect to y and evaluation at the point $y = 1$. Equation 10.6.11 thus corresponds to Equations 6.1.35 and 6.1.42. The evaluation of the transform $k_{ij}^{m\mathscr{g}}(z)$ for $m = 1$ and $m = 2$ appears in Equations 6.1.33 and 6.1.40,

$$k_{ij}^{\mathscr{g}}(z) = \frac{d}{dy}\,\phi_{ij}^{\mathscr{g}\mathscr{g}}(y|z)\bigg|_{y=1} \tag{10.6.12}$$

and

$$k_{ij}^{2\mathscr{g}}(z) = \frac{d^2}{dy^2}\,\phi_{ij}^{\mathscr{g}\mathscr{g}}(y|z)\bigg|_{y=1} + k_{ij}^{\mathscr{g}}(z). \tag{10.6.13}$$

If we define a matrix $K^{m\mathscr{g}}(z)$ with elements $k_{ij}^{m\mathscr{g}}(z)$, then we write these equations in the form,

$$K^{\mathscr{g}}(z) = \frac{d}{dy}\,\Phi^{\mathscr{g}\mathscr{g}}(y|z)\bigg|_{y=1} \tag{10.6.14}$$

and

$$K^{2\mathscr{g}}(z) = \frac{d^2}{dy^2}\,\Phi^{\mathscr{g}\mathscr{g}}(y|z)\bigg|_{y=1} + K^{\mathscr{g}}(z). \tag{10.6.15}$$

First moments

Since we already know how to compute the multistep transition probability $\phi_{ij}(n)$ needed in Equation 10.6.11, we can concentrate on the problem of evaluating $k_{ij}(n)$ and $k_{ij}^2(n)$. We start by computing the derivative of Equation 10.6.9 needed in Equation 10.6.14,

$$\begin{aligned}\frac{d}{dy}\,\Phi^{\mathscr{g}\mathscr{g}}(y|z) &= \frac{d}{dy}\,[I - yC^{\mathscr{g}}(z)]^{-1}\,{}^{>}W^{\mathscr{g}}(z)\\ &= [I - yC^{\mathscr{g}}(z)]^{-1}C^{\mathscr{g}}(z)[I - yC^{\mathscr{g}}(z)]^{-1}\,{}^{>}W^{\mathscr{g}}(z),\end{aligned} \tag{10.6.16}$$

then

$$K^g(z) = \frac{d}{dy}\,\Phi^{gg}(y|z)\Big|_{y=1} = [I - C^g(z)]^{-1}C^g(z)[I - C^g(z)]^{-1}\,{}^{>}W^g(z). \tag{10.6.17}$$

Using the properties of the core matrix from Section 10.3, we can write $K^g(z)$ in the alternate forms,

$$\begin{aligned} K^g(z) &= C^g(z)[I - C^g(z)]^{-1}[I - C^g(z)]^{-1}\,{}^{>}W^g(z) \\ &= [I - C^g(z)]^{-1}[I - C^g(z)]^{-1}C^g(z)\,{}^{>}W^g(z) \\ &= [I - C^g(z)]^{-1}[(I - C^g(z))^{-1} - I]\,{}^{>}W^g(z). \end{aligned} \tag{10.6.18}$$

Note that when the semi-Markov process contains exactly one state, all these equations reduce to the result of Equation 7.2.12 that we developed for the renewal process. The identifications necessary are $P = 1$; $H^g(z) = p^g(z)$; and ${}^{>}W^g(z) = {}^{<}p^g(z)$.

Recursive equation. Equations 10.6.17 and 10.6.18 relate $K^g(z)$ directly to the core matrix and therefore provide a transform method of finding $k_{ij}(n)$ and therefore $\bar{k}_{ij}(n)$. However, to illustrate how we can use an equation like 10.6.18 to write a recursive equation for $k_{ij}(n)$, we proceed by rearranging Equation 10.6.18,

$$\begin{aligned} K^g(z) &= [I - C^g(z)]^{-1}[I - C^g(z)]^{-1}C^g(z)\,{}^{>}W^g(z) \\ [I - C^g(z)][I - C^g(z)]K^g(z) &= C^g(z)\,{}^{>}W^g(z) \\ [I - 2C^g(z) + C^g(z)C^g(z)]K^g(z) &= C^g(z)\,{}^{>}W^g(z) \\ K^g(z) - 2C^g(z)K^g(z) + C^g(z)C^g(z)K^g(z) &= C^g(z)\,{}^{>}W^g(z) \qquad (10.6.19) \\ K^g(z) &= 2C^g(z)K^g(z) - C^g(z)C^g(z)K^g(z) + C^g(z)\,{}^{>}W^g(z) \\ &= C^g(z)[2K^g(z) - C^g(z)K^g(z) + {}^{>}W^g(z)] \\ &= (P \square H^g(z))[2K^g(z) - (P \square H^g(z))K^g(z) + {}^{>}W^g(z)]. \end{aligned}$$

Equation 10.6.19 in element form is

$$k_{ij}{}^g(z) = \sum_{r=1}^{N} p_{ir}h_{ir}{}^g(z)\left[2k_{rj}{}^g(z) - \sum_{q=1}^{N} p_{rq}h_{rq}{}^g(z)k_{qj}{}^g(z) + \delta_{rj}\,{}^{>}w_j{}^g(z)\right]. \tag{10.6.20}$$

Finally, we invert the geometric transformation,

$$k_{ij}(n) = \sum_{r=1}^{N}\sum_{m=0}^{n} p_{ir}h_{ir}(m)\left[2k_{rj}(n - m) - \sum_{q=1}^{N}\sum_{u=0}^{n-m} p_{rq}h_{rq}(u)k_{qj}(n - m - u) + \delta_{rj}\,{}^{>}w_j(n - m)\right] \qquad \begin{aligned} n &= 0, 1, 2, \ldots \\ i &= 1, 2, \ldots, N \\ j &= 1, 2, \ldots, N. \end{aligned} \tag{10.6.21}$$

Thus even complicated transform equations like Equation 10.6.18 can be written in recursive form by simple algebraic operations. Although we shall seldom carry out this process in the future, we should always bear in mind that a recursive solution is possible.

Moments unconditional on final state

If we are not interested in conditioning the moments on the final state occupied, then we compute $\overline{k_{i\Sigma}{}^m}(n)$, the mth moment of the number of transitions the process makes through time n given only that it starts in state i. In this case,

$$\overline{k_{i\Sigma}{}^m} = \sum_{j=1}^{N} k_{ij}{}^m \tag{10.6.22}$$

and no denominator factor is required as in Equation 10.6.11. Thus $K^{g}(z)\mathbf{s}$ is a column vector whose ith element is $\bar{k}_{i\Sigma}{}^{g}(z)$, the transform of $\bar{k}_{i\Sigma}{}^{g}(n)$. From Equation 10.6.17,

$$\begin{aligned} K^{g}(z)\mathbf{s} &= [I - C^{g}(z)]^{-1}C^{g}(z)[I - C^{g}(z)]^{-1}\,{}^{>}W^{g}(z)\mathbf{s} \\ &= [I - C^{g}(z)]^{-1}C^{g}(z)\Phi^{g}(z)\mathbf{s} \\ &= [I - C^{g}(z)]^{-1}C^{g}(z)\left(\frac{1}{1-z}\right)\mathbf{s} \\ &= \frac{1}{1-z}[I - C^{g}(z)]^{-1}C^{g}(z)\mathbf{s}. \end{aligned} \tag{10.6.23}$$

Here we have used the fact that the rows of $\Phi^{g}(z)$ sum to $1/(1 - z)$. As in the case of the tagging in Chapter 6, we observe that computation of the moments is considerably simplified if we do not condition them on being in a certain state at time n.

Second moments

To extend all these results to the second moment we must first compute the second derivative of Equation 10.6.9 needed in Equation 10.6.15. Since we already have the first derivative in Equation 10.6.16, we easily compute the second derivative as

$$\frac{d^2}{dy^2}\Phi^{gg}(y|z) = 2[I - yC^{g}(z)]^{-1}C^{g}(z)[I - yC^{g}(z)]^{-1}C^{g}(z)[I - yC^{g}(z)]^{-1}\,{}^{>}W^{g}(z). \tag{10.6.24}$$

Then we evaluate it at $y = 1$,

$$\frac{d^2}{dy^2}\Phi^{gg}(y|z)\bigg|_{y=1} = 2[I - C^g(z)]^{-1}C^g(z)[I - C^g(z)]^{-1}C^g(z)[I - C^g(z)]^{-1}\,{}^{>}W^g(z). \tag{10.6.25}$$

Finally, we combine this result and Equation 10.6.17 to write $K^{2g}(z)$ from Equation 10.6.15,

$$\begin{aligned} K^{2g}(z) &= 2[I - C^g(z)]^{-1}C^g(z)[I - C^g(z)]^{-1}C^g(z)[I - C^g(z)]^{-1}\,{}^{>}W^g(z) \\ &\quad + [I - C^g(z)]^{-1}C^g(z)[I - C^g(z)]^{-1}\,{}^{>}W^g(z) \\ &= [I - C^g(z)]^{-1}C^g(z)\{2[I - C^g(z)]^{-1}C^g(z) + I\}[I - C^g(z)]^{-1}\,{}^{>}W^g(z) \\ &= [I - C^g(z)]^{-1}C^g(z)\{2[I - C^g(z)]^{-1} - I\}[I - C^g(z)]^{-1}\,{}^{>}W^g(z). \end{aligned} \tag{10.6.26}$$

We have thus developed a transform method for finding the quantity $k_{ij}^2(n)$ needed in Equation 10.6.11 to compute $\overline{k_{ij}^2}(n)$. We can use Equation 10.6.26 to produce a recursive equation for $k_{ij}^2(n)$ when necessary. Note that Equation 10.6.26 reduces to Equation 7.2.14 for a one-state semi-Markov process.

If we choose not to condition the second moment on the final state occupied, then we compute $\overline{k_{i\Sigma}^2}(n)$ from Equation 10.6.22. Of course, $\overline{k_{i\Sigma}^2}(n)$ is the second moment of the number of transitions the process makes through time n if it starts in state i. The quantity $K^{2g}(z)\mathbf{s}$ is then a column vector whose ith element is $\overline{k_{i\Sigma}}^{2g}(z)$, the transform of $\overline{k_{i\Sigma}^2}(n)$. From Equation 10.6.26,

$$\begin{aligned} K^{2g}(z)\mathbf{s} &= [I - C^g(z)]^{-1}C^g(z)\{2[I - C^g(z)]^{-1} - I\}[I - C^g(z)]^{-1}\,{}^{>}W^g(z)\mathbf{s} \\ &= [I - C^g(z)]^{-1}C^g(z)\{2[I - C^g(z)]^{-1} - I\}\Phi^g(z)\mathbf{s} \\ &= [I - C^g(z)]^{-1}C^g(z)\{2[I - C^g(z)]^{-1} - I\}\frac{1}{1 - z}\mathbf{s} \\ &= \frac{1}{1 - z}[I - C^g(z)]^{-1}C^g(z)\{2[I - C^g(z)]^{-1} - I\}\mathbf{s}. \end{aligned} \tag{10.6.27}$$

10.7 ENTRANCE AND DESTINATION PROBABILITIES

Entrance Probabilities – Time and Transition

We are sometimes interested not only in the probability that the process will occupy a state at some time in the future but also in the probability that the process will enter a state at some particular future time. We shall let $e_{ij}(k|n)$ be the probability that a process which enters state i at time zero and transition zero will enter state j at time n on its kth transition. That is,

$$e_{ij}(k|n) = \mathscr{P}\{\mathscr{n}(n) = k, \mathscr{n}(n-1) = k-1, s(n) = j|s(0) = i, t(0) = 0\}$$
$$i = 1, 2, \ldots, N; j = 1, 2, \ldots, N \qquad k = 0, 1, 2, \ldots; n = 0, 1, 2, \ldots. \tag{10.7.1}$$

We call this probability an entrance probability; it differs from the interval transition probability $\phi_{ij}(k|n)$ because it is concerned with the entrance of the process into a state rather than with the presence of a process in a state. Note that a virtual transition to the same state counts as an entrance.

The recursive relation for these entrance probabilities is very similar to that for the interval transition probabilities,

$$e_{ij}(k|n) = \delta_{ij}\,\delta(n)\,\delta(k) + \sum_{r=1}^{N}\sum_{m=0}^{n} p_{ir}h_{ir}(m)e_{rj}(k-1|n-m)$$
$$i = 1, 2, \ldots, N; j = 1, 2, \ldots, N \qquad k = 0, 1, 2, \ldots; n = 0, 1, 2, \ldots. \tag{10.7.2}$$

The first term follows from the requirement that

$$e_{ij}(0|n) = \delta_{ij}\,\delta(n); \tag{10.7.3}$$

if no transitions are made, the only nonzero entrance probability occurs when $n = 0$ and $i = j$. If k is greater than zero, then the process could enter state j at time n after k transitions by making its first transition at time m to some state r and then entering state j after $k - 1$ additional transitions and an additional time $n - m$. When this possibility is summed over all allowable times m and states r, we have Equation 10.7.2. This equation serves as a convenient recursive relationship for the computation of the entrance probabilities.

Transform relations

We can place Equation 10.7.2 in the transform domain by defining the double geometric transform of the entrance probability $e_{ij}(k|n)$ to be

$$e_{ij}^{gg}(y|z) = \sum_{k=0}^{\infty}\sum_{n=0}^{\infty} y^k z^n e_{ij}(k|n). \tag{10.7.4}$$

Transforming Equation 10.7.2 then produces

$$e_{ij}^{gg}(y|z) = \delta_{ij} + y\sum_{r=1}^{N} p_{ir}h_{ir}^{g}(z)e_{rj}^{gg}(y|z) \tag{10.7.5}$$

or, in matrix form,

$$E^{gg}(y|z) = I + y[P \square H^{g}(z)]E^{gg}(y|z)$$
$$= I + yC^{g}(z)E^{gg}(y|z), \tag{10.7.6}$$

where $E^{gg}(y|z)$ is the transformed entrance probability matrix. We solve explicitly for this matrix in the form

$$E^{gg}(y|z) = [I - y(P \square H^{g}(z))]^{-1} = [I - yC^{g}(z)]^{-1}. \tag{10.7.7}$$

This equation shows that the transformed entrance probability matrix is given by the matrix flow graph of Figure 10.7.1. We see immediately that this flow graph is exactly the same as that for the transformed interval transition probability matrix in Figure 10.6.1 except that the structure of associated nodes labeled with transformed complementary cumulative waiting time distributions has disappeared. Therefore, it is very reasonable to interpret the entrance probabilities as just one factor in constructing the interval transition probabilities. We see that they are related by

$$\Phi^{gg}(y|z) = E^{gg}(y|z) \,{}^{>}W^{g}(z) \tag{10.7.8}$$

or in component form by

$$\phi_{ij}{}^{gg}(y|z) = e_{ij}{}^{gg}(y|z) \,{}^{>}w_{j}{}^{g}(z). \tag{10.7.9}$$

The inverse geometric transform of this equation is

$$\phi_{ij}(k|n) = \sum_{m=0}^{n} e_{ij}(k|m) \,{}^{>}w_{j}(n-m). \tag{10.7.10}$$

Equation 10.7.10 allows us to interpret the relationship of the interval transition probabilities and entrance probabilities explicitly. The probability of being in state j after k transitions and at time n is just the probability of having entered state j at one of the mutually exclusive times $m = 0$ through $m = n$ after k transitions, and then having stayed in that state for at least the period $n - m$, summed over all values of m. Of course, all of these events are conditioned on the process's having entered state i on its zeroth transition.

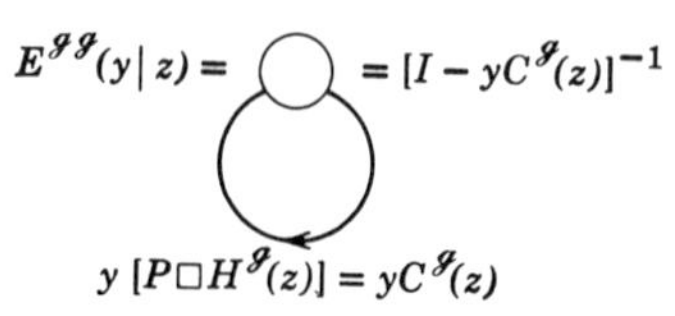

Figure 10.7.1 Matrix flow graph for entrance probabilities, counting transitions.

Thus the entrance probabilities play a key role in the analysis of semi-Markov processes. In a sense, they are even more fundamental than the interval transition probabilities. However, Equations 10.7.9 and 10.7.10 show that the relationship between them is so direct that in most of our developments we could use either with equal ease.

We obtain interesting results by evaluating the transform $E^{gg}(y|z)$ for certain values of the transform variables. We see from Equation 10.7.7, for example, that

$$\begin{aligned} E^{gg}(y|1) &= [I - y(P \,\square\, H^{g}(1))]^{-1} \\ &= [I - y(P \,\square\, U)]^{-1} \\ &= [I - yP]^{-1}. \end{aligned} \tag{10.7.11}$$

The element $e_{ij}^{gg}(y|1)$ of this matrix is the geometric transform of the probability that the process will enter state j on its kth transition given that it made its first transition into state i. Of course, this is just the transform of the multistep transition probability from state i to state j for the imbedded Markov process.

Entrance probabilities—time

If we evaluate $E^{gg}(y|z)$ at $y = 1$, we produce a matrix we shall call $E^{g}(z)$,

$$E^{g}(z) = E^{gg}(1|z) = [I - P \,\square\, H^{g}(z)]^{-1} = [I - C^{g}(z)]^{-1}. \tag{10.7.12}$$

The element $e_{ij}^{g}(z)$ of $E^{g}(z)$ is the geometric transform of $e_{ij}(n)$, the probability that a system that entered state i at time zero will enter state j at time n. Thus $e_{ij}(n)$ is an entrance probability concerned only with time and not with both time and number of transitions. The recursive equation for $e_{ij}(n)$ that corresponds to Equation 10.7.2 is

$$e_{ij}(n) = \delta_{ij}\, \delta(n) + \sum_{r=1}^{N} \sum_{m=0}^{N} p_{ir} h_{ir}(m) e_{rj}(n - m). \tag{10.7.13}$$

The quantity $e_{ij}^{g}(z)$ is also the transmission from node i to node j of the flow graph for the discrete-time semi-Markov process shown in Figure 10.5.2. You will recall that $\phi_{ij}^{g}(z)$ was the transmission of this same graph from node i to the output node associated with node j. The matrix flow graph for $E^{g}(z)$ is, of course, the graph of Figure 10.7.1 when $y = 1$, a result shown as Figure 10.7.2.

The relationship between $e_{ij}(n)$ and the interval transition probability $\phi_{ij}(n)$ is expressed by equations like 10.7.8, 10.7.9, and 10.7.10:

$$\Phi^{g}(z) = E^{g}(z) \,{}^{>}W^{g}(z), \tag{10.7.14}$$

$$\phi_{ij}^{g}(z) = e_{ij}^{g}(z) \,{}^{>}w_{j}^{g}(z), \tag{10.7.15}$$

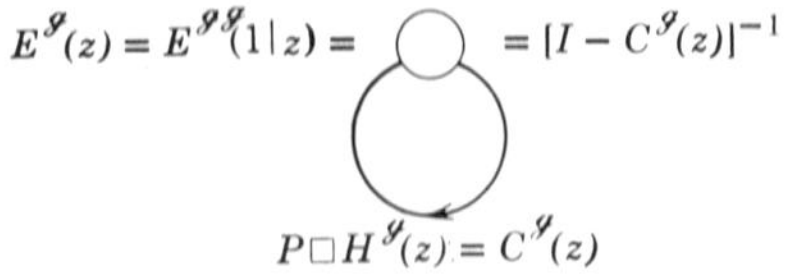

Figure 10.7.2 Matrix flow graph for entrance probabilities, not counting transitions.

and

$$\phi_{ij}(n) = \sum_{m=0}^{n} e_{ij}(m)\ {}^{>}w_j(n-m). \tag{10.7.16}$$

We shall use the term entrance probability for both $e_{ij}(n)$ and $e_{ij}(k|n)$. The context will always make clear the type of entrance probability we are using.

Limiting behavior

The entrance probabilities $e_{ij}(n)$ approach a limit for large n just as do the interval transition probabilities $\phi_{ij}(n)$. We define a matrix of limiting entrance probabilities E by

$$E = \lim_{z\to 1}(1-z)E^{g}(z) = \lim_{z\to 1}(1-z)[I - P\,\square\,H^{g}(z)]^{-1} = \lim_{z\to 1}(1-z)[I - C^{g}(z)]^{-1}. \tag{10.7.17}$$

The limiting matrix E is just the matrix $T(z)$ in Equation 10.3.36 evaluated at $z = 1$. Therefore from Equation 10.3.42,

$$\Phi = EM \tag{10.7.18}$$

or, in terms of the elements,

$$\phi_{ij} = e_{ij}\bar{\tau}_j. \tag{10.7.19}$$

Then from Equation 10.3.47 for a monodesmic process,

$$e_{ij} = e_j = \frac{1}{\bar{\tau}_j}\phi_j = \frac{\pi_j}{\sum_{j=1}^{N}\pi_j\bar{\tau}_j} = \frac{\pi_j}{\bar{\tau}}. \tag{10.7.20}$$

The rows of E are identical; the probability e_j of entering state j at any time in the steady state is independent of the starting state. Moreover, the probability e_j is just the limiting state probability π_j for the imbedded Markov process divided by

$\bar{\tau}$, the sum over all states of the mean waiting time in each state multiplied by the limiting state probability for that state.

We shall call each row of E the limiting entrance probability vector $\mathbf{e}$. We write immediately from Equation 10.7.18

$$\boldsymbol{\phi} = \mathbf{e}M \tag{10.7.21}$$

and therefore

$$\mathbf{e} = \boldsymbol{\phi}M^{-1}. \tag{10.7.22}$$

From Equation 10.7.20 we also have

$$\mathbf{e} = \frac{1}{\bar{\tau}}\boldsymbol{\pi}. \tag{10.7.23}$$

Equations 10.7.21 and 10.7.23 together imply Equation 10.3.48. Note that if all waiting times are exactly equal to one unit as they are for the basic Markov process, then the limiting entrance probability vector is just the limiting state probability vector.

The car rental example. Equation 10.3.25 provides an explicit expression for $[I - P \,\Box\, H^{g}(z)]^{-1}$ for the car rental example. Therefore we can apply Equation 10.7.17 to this result to obtain the limiting entrance probability matrix for the example,

$$E = \lim_{z \to 1} (1 - z)[I - P \,\Box\, H^{g}(z)]^{-1} = \begin{bmatrix} 3/30 & 2/30 \\ 3/30 & 2/30 \end{bmatrix}. \tag{10.7.24}$$

Since

$$\Phi = \begin{bmatrix} 0.36 & 0.64 \\ 0.36 & 0.64 \end{bmatrix} \qquad M = \begin{bmatrix} 3.6 & 0 \\ 0 & 9.6 \end{bmatrix}, \tag{10.7.25}$$

Equation 10.7.18 is confirmed in this example.

We observe from E in Equation 10.7.24 that the probability of entering state 1 at some time in the steady state is $1/10$, and for state 2 it is $1/15$. The probability of entering some state at a time in the steady state is therefore $1/10 + 1/15 = 1/6$. We conclude that in the steady state we expect $1/6$ of the time instants to be times of transition.

Since the common row $\mathbf{e}$ of E is proportional to $\boldsymbol{\pi}$, the limiting state probability vector, we might inquire further about $\bar{\tau} = \sum_{j=1}^{N} \pi_j \bar{\tau}_j$, the factor that divides $\boldsymbol{\pi}$ to produce $\mathbf{e}$. Since π_j is the probability that a transition in the steady state will be a transition to state j and since $\bar{\tau}_j$ is the average time the process will spend in state j

before making its next transition, it is clear that $\bar{\tau} = \sum_{j=1}^{N} \pi_j \bar{\tau}_j$ is the mean time between transitions of the process in the steady state. For the example, we find

$$\bar{\tau} = \sum_{j=1}^{2} \pi_j \bar{\tau}_j = \pi_1 \bar{\tau}_1 + \pi_2 \bar{\tau}_2 = 0.6(3.6) + 0.4(9.6) = 6. \qquad (10.7.26)$$

Since on the average there are 6 time units between transitions in the steady state, we have confirmed the result that on the average 1/6 of the time instants will produce transitions.

We have already interpreted ϕ_j and π_j for the car rental example. Since $e_1 = 1/10$ and $e_2 = 1/15$, the car rental company expects that 1/10 of the cars it has rented will be returned to town 1 during any period and 1/15 will be returned to town 2. Therefore, on the average, 1/6 of the cars will be returned somewhere during a period, and we expect a car to be rented for 6 periods if we have no information about where it was rented.

We must carefully distinguish the differences in the three quantities ϕ_j, e_j, and π_j. To interpret them, consider a process governed by a given transition probability matrix and a given holding time mass function matrix. Suppose it has been operating unobserved for such a long time that we have lost track of its starting state (we are in the steady state). Then we are asked various questions at some time instant. What probability do you assign to the event that the process occupies state j? We answer ϕ_j. What probability do you assign to the event that the process is just entering state j at this instant? We answer e_j. Given that the process is now making a transition, what probability do you assign to the event that the transition is to state j? We answer π_j.

Destination Probabilities

When we observe a semi-Markov process entering state i at time zero and observe it again at time n, we can ask about the probability that it is occupying state j—the probability is $\phi_{ij}(n)$, as we already know, or $\phi_{ij}(k|n)$ if we also inquire about the number of transitions it has made. However, when we observe it at time n, we could ask not only the probability that it is in state j but also the probability that it will make its next transition to state q. Even if we know that the process is in state j at time n, the probability that it will make its next transition to state q is not simply p_{jq}, because the knowledge that it is in state j gives us indirect knowledge about the holding time and therefore modifies the probability of the next transition according to the argument in Section 10.4.

Let us therefore define the quantity $\gamma_{ijq}(k|n)$ as the probability that a process which started in state i both at time 0 and transition 0 is in state j at time n, has made k transitions by that time, and will make its next transition to state q; for brevity, we call this quantity the destination probability of the process. To satisfy the conditions necessary for this event to occur, the process must enter state j on its kth transition at some time m, $m \leq n$, then determine that it will make its next transition to state q, and finally hold in state j for at least a time $n - m$. Therefore we obtain

$$\gamma_{ijq}(k|n) = \sum_{m=0}^{n} e_{ij}(k|m)p_{jq}\,{}^{>}h_{jq}(n-m) \quad \begin{array}{ll} i = 1, 2, \ldots, N & k = 0, 1, 2, \ldots \\ j = 1, 2, \ldots, N & n = 0, 1, 2, \ldots \\ q = 1, 2, \ldots, N, & \end{array} \qquad (10.7.27)$$

showing that the destination probability $\gamma_{ijq}(\cdot|\cdot)$ is the convolution of the entrance probability $e_{ij}(\cdot|\cdot)$ and the complementary cumulative holding time distribution ${}^{>}h_{jq}(\cdot)$, multiplied by the transition probability p_{jq}.

Transform relations

For the double geometric transform $\gamma_{ijq}^{gg}(y|z)$ of $\gamma_{ijq}(k|n)$, we find

$$\gamma_{ijq}^{gg}(y|z) = e_{ij}^{gg}(y|z)p_{jq}\,{}^{>}h_{jq}^{g}(z). \qquad (10.7.28)$$

If we choose to ignore the number of transitions k and deal simply with $\gamma_{ijq}(n)$, then we write its geometric transform $\gamma_{ijq}^{g}(z)$ as

$$\gamma_{ijq}^{g}(z) = \gamma_{ijq}^{gg}(1|z) = e_{ij}^{g}(z)p_{jq}\,{}^{>}h_{jq}^{g}(z). \qquad (10.7.29)$$

We can relate these results to the interval transition probabilities by noting that since the process must make its next transition to some state q, the interval transition probabilities are just the sum of the destination probabilities over all values of q. Thus from Equation 10.7.28 we write

$$\begin{aligned} \phi_{ij}^{gg}(y|z) &= \sum_{q=1}^{N} \gamma_{ijq}^{gg}(y|z) = \sum_{q=1}^{N} e_{ij}^{gg}(y|z)p_{jq}\,{}^{>}h_{jq}^{g}(z) \\ &= e_{ij}^{gg}(y|z)\sum_{q=1}^{N} p_{jq}\,{}^{>}h_{jq}^{g}(z) \\ &= e_{ij}^{gg}(y|z)\,{}^{>}w_{j}^{g}(z), \end{aligned} \qquad (10.7.30)$$

which is the result of Equation 10.7.9. Of course, summing Equation 10.7.29 over q produces $\phi_{ij}^{g}(z)$.

Limiting behavior

When n is large and the process is monodesmic, $\gamma_{ijq}(n)$ approaches a limiting destination probability γ_{jq} that is independent of i. We find it by applying the final value theorem to Equation 10.7.29, using Equation 10.7.20, and observing that ${}^{>}h_{jq}{}^{g}(1) = \bar{\tau}_{jq}$, the mean holding time for the $j \rightarrow q$ transition,

$$\begin{aligned} \gamma_{jq} &= \lim_{n\to\infty} \gamma_{ijq}(n) = \lim_{z\to 1} (1 - z)\gamma_{ijq}^{g}(z) = \lim_{z\to 1} (1 - z)e_{ij}{}^{g}(z)p_{jq}\, {}^{>}h_{jq}{}^{g}(z) \\ &= [\lim_{z\to 1} e_{ij}{}^{g}(z)]p_{jq}[\lim_{z\to 1} {}^{>}h_{jq}{}^{g}(z)] \\ &= e_j p_{jq}\bar{\tau}_{jq} \\ &= \frac{\pi_j p_{jq}\bar{\tau}_{jq}}{\bar{\tau}}. \end{aligned} \tag{10.7.31}$$

Thus the limiting destination probability γ_{jq} is equal to the product of the limiting state probability π_j, the transition probability p_{jq}, and the mean holding time $\bar{\tau}_{jq}$ divided by the mean time between transitions $\bar{\tau}$. We interpret γ_{jq} as the probability that at a time instant in the steady state the process is in state j and planning to make its next transition to state q. For the car rental example, we find

$$\begin{aligned} \gamma_{11} &= \frac{1}{\bar{\tau}}(\pi_1 p_{11}\bar{\tau}_{11}) = \frac{1}{6}(0.6)(0.8)(3) = 0.24 \\ \gamma_{12} &= \frac{1}{\bar{\tau}}(\pi_1 p_{12}\bar{\tau}_{12}) = \frac{1}{6}(0.6)(0.2)(6) = 0.12 \\ \gamma_{21} &= \frac{1}{\bar{\tau}}(\pi_2 p_{21}\bar{\tau}_{21}) = \frac{1}{6}(0.4)(0.3)(4) = 0.08 \\ \gamma_{22} &= \frac{1}{\bar{\tau}}(\pi_2 p_{22}\bar{\tau}_{22}) = \frac{1}{6}(0.4)(0.7)(12) = 0.56. \end{aligned} \tag{10.7.32}$$

Thus at a time in the steady state, we expect 24% of the rental cars to be making trips from town 1 to town 1, 56% to be making trips from town 2 to town 2, etc.

If we sum the limiting destination probabilities γ_{jq} over q, we obtain the limiting interval transition probabilities, as we would expect from Equation 10.7.30,

$$\sum_{q=1}^{N} \gamma_{jq} = \frac{\pi_j}{\bar{\tau}} \sum_{q=1}^{N} p_{jq}\bar{\tau}_{jq} = \frac{\pi_j \bar{\tau}_j}{\bar{\tau}} = \phi_j. \tag{10.7.33}$$

For the car rental example,

$$\phi_1 = \gamma_{11} + \gamma_{12} = 0.36, \qquad \phi_2 = \gamma_{21} + \gamma_{22} = 0.64, \tag{10.7.34}$$

in accordance with Equation 10.3.30.

If we let $\gamma_{\Sigma q}$ be the sum of γ_{jq} over j,

$$\gamma_{\Sigma q} = \sum_{j=1}^{N} \gamma_{jq} = \frac{\sum_{j=1}^{N} \pi_j p_{jq}\bar{\tau}_{jq}}{\bar{\tau}}, \tag{10.7.35}$$

then we can interpret $\gamma_{\Sigma q}$ as the probability that if the process is entered in the steady state it will be observed to make its next transition to state q. For the car rental example,

$$\gamma_{\Sigma 1} = \gamma_{11} + \gamma_{21} = 0.32, \qquad \gamma_{\Sigma 2} = \gamma_{12} + \gamma_{22} = 0.68. \tag{10.7.36}$$

Thus at a time in the steady state, we expect 32% of the car rental fleet to be returned to town 1 and 68% to be returned to town 2. This stands in contrast to the values of ϕ_1 and ϕ_2 in Equation 10.7.34 which show that we expect 36% of the cars to have been rented in town 1 and 64% in town 2. One might conclude from these results that since a higher fraction of cars was rented in town 1 than will be returned to town 1, town 1 will eventually run out of cars. Of course, the conclusion is erroneous; the results merely reflect the method of observation. In fact, we know from π_1 that we expect town 1 to be the source of 60% of the rental contracts. Table 10.7.1 summarizes the relationships.

Table 10.7.1 Steady-state Characteristics of Car Rental Example

		State	
	$j =$	1	2
Probability a given transition will be to each state	π_j	0.60	0.40
Probability the process occupies each state	ϕ_j	0.36	0.64
Probability the next transition will be to each state	$\gamma_{\Sigma q}$	0.32	0.68

Interpretation. The implications of these comments are more striking if we picture the same example in a marketing context. Let the state represent the last brand purchased by the customer. Then the transition probabilities in the car rental example represent brand-changing in the marketing problem, and the holding time distributions represent the times between the customer's purchases. If we use exactly the same numbers in both examples and refer to Table 10.7.1, our car rental results would lead us to expect that at any time 36% of the customers would be using brand 1, although we expect brand 1's share of purchases to be 60%. If we perform an interview experiment by asking all customers at a particular time what brand they bought last and what brand they will buy next, we expect that 36% will reply that they bought brand 1 last and that 32% will reply that they intend to buy brand 1 next. This kind of experimental result has been interpreted by some investigators as evidence that brand 1 is in the process of experiencing a decrease in its market share. We know from our results that if the customers are described by this semi-Markovian model, there is no basis for this conclusion and that brand 1's share of purchases will remain at 60%. One must not be too hasty in drawing conclusions about complex probabilistic systems.

We finish by observing that for the basic Markov process where $\bar{\tau}_{jq} = \bar{\tau} = 1$,

$$\gamma_{\Sigma q} = \sum_{j=1}^{N} \pi_j p_{jq} = \pi_q = \phi_q = e_q, \tag{10.7.37}$$

and all the various limiting probabilities are identical. The greater complexity of the semi-Markov process requires us to distinguish between a number of quantities that do not differ for the basic Markov process.

10.8 TRANSIENT PROCESSES

Just as in the basic Markov process, we are often interested in how long the process will require to leave a set of transient states, that is, a transient chain. The answer can be expressed most generally in terms of k, the number of transitions required, and n, the number of time periods required. Suppose we have a semi-Markov process with all states transient except one state, state r (for recurrent). Then we shall let $p_{ir}(k, n)$ be the probability that a process started in state i on its zeroth transition will require k transitions and n time periods to reach the trapping state r.

Flow Graph Representation

If we count all transitions in the process except virtual transitions within state r, the flow graph of the semi-Markov process in the vicinity of state r appears as shown in Figure 10.8.1. Note that because $p_{rr} = 1$, no branches connect state r with nodes representing other states of the process. The transmission of the loop around node r is just $h_{rr}{}^{\mathscr{g}}(z) = w_r{}^{\mathscr{g}}(z)$. Therefore, the effect of this loop on transmissions through node r is to multiply them by $1/[1 - w_r{}^{\mathscr{g}}(z)]$. As far as transmissions to the output node associated with node r are concerned, we can remove this loop if we change the transmission on the output branch from ${}^{>}w_r{}^{\mathscr{g}}(z)$ to

$$\frac{{}^{>}w_r{}^{\mathscr{g}}(z)}{1 - w_r{}^{\mathscr{g}}(z)} = \frac{1}{1 - z}, \tag{10.8.1}$$

in accordance with Equation 10.3.2. The new form of the flow graph also appears in Figure 10.8.1.

We know that the transmission from node i to the output node associated with node r for such a semi-Markov process is the transform of the probability $\phi_{ir}(k|n)$ that the system will be in state r at time n after k transitions if it entered state i on its zeroth transition at time zero. Since state r is the only trapping state in the process, $\phi_{ir}(k|n)$ is the probability that the system will have entered state r by time n and that it will have made k transitions external to state r for the given starting

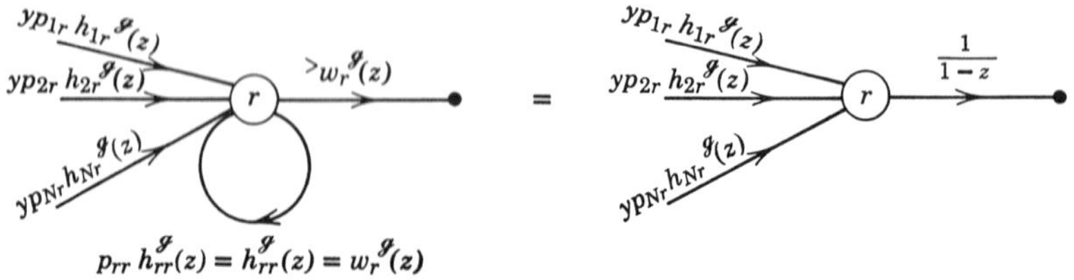

Figure 10.8.1 Portion of flow graph for a transient process.

condition. The quantity $\phi_{ir}(k|n)$ differs from $p_{ir}(k, n)$ in that $\phi_{ir}(k|n)$ is the probability that state r is entered *by* time n while $p_{ir}(k, n)$ is the probability that state r is entered *at* time n; that is, $\phi_{ir}(k|n)$ is just the cumulative of $p_{ir}(k, n)$ with respect to n,

$$\phi_{ir}(k|n) = \sum_{m=0}^{n} p_{ir}(k, m). \tag{10.8.2}$$

Therefore,

$$\phi_{ir}{}^{gg}(y|z) = \frac{1}{1-z} p_{ir}{}^{gg}(y, z), \tag{10.8.3}$$

where we have written $p_{ir}{}^{gg}(y, z)$ as the double geometric transform of $p_{ir}(k, n)$. Consequently, all we have to do to find $p_{ir}{}^{gg}(y, z)$ is to remove the output branch associated with node r in Figure 10.8.1, a branch that represents a summer, and then find the transmission of the flow graph from node i to node r. The portion of this new flow graph in the vicinity of node r appears in Figure 10.8.2.

Let us summarize. To find $p_{ir}{}^{gg}(y, z)$, the transform of the probability that k transitions and time n will be required to reach a trapping state r from a starting state i, first draw the flow graph for the process, tagging all transitions with y. Then remove the branches that leave node r—its self-loop and its associated output

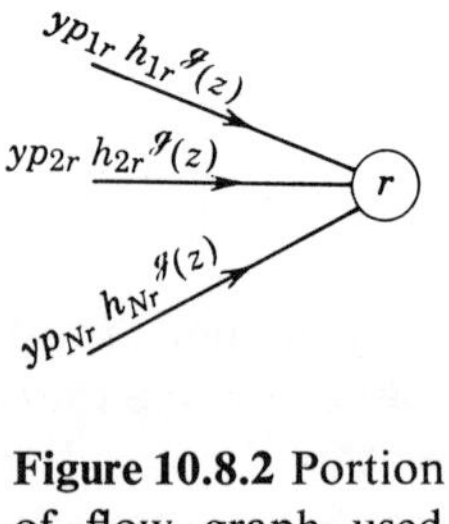

Figure 10.8.2 Portion of flow graph used to find $p_{ir}{}^{g}(y, z)$ for a transient process.

branch. The transmission of the resulting flow graph from node i to node r is the transform $p_{ir}{}^{gg}(y, z)$. An alternate interpretation of this procedure for finding $p_{ir}{}^{gg}(y, z)$ is that we have found $e_{ir}{}^{gg}(y|z)$, the transform of the entrance probability to state r, in a situation where only one entrance is permitted.

Probability distributions

Once we have the transform $p_{ir}{}^{gg}(y, z)$ we can compute $p_{ir}(k, n)$, the joint probability on transitions and time spent in the transient process. It would be wise, of course, to check first that $p^{gg}(1, 1) = 1$. We can also find the marginal probability $p_{ir}{}^{\cdot g}(k, 1)$ that k transitions will be required in the transient process and the marginal probability $p_{ir}{}^{\cdot g}(1, n)$ that time n will be spent in the transient process. We see immediately that the work on transient processes that we carried out in Chapter 4 was concerned with $p_{ir}{}^{\cdot g}(k, 1)$, the marginal probability on transitions. The present method reduces to the earlier method when $z = 1$.

Moments

We can also compute the marginal moments of the transitions and time spent in the transient process by differentiating the transform $p_{ir}{}^{gg}(y, z)$ and evaluating the derivatives when $y = 1$ and when $z = 1$. We find the mean $\bar{k}$, second moment $\overline{k^2}$, variance $\overset{v}{k}$, and standard deviation $\overset{s}{k}$ of the number of transitions in the transient process from

$$\bar{k} = \frac{d}{dy} p_{ir}{}^{gg}(y, 1)\Big|_{y=1} \qquad \overline{k^2} = \frac{d^2}{dy^2} p_{ir}{}^{gg}(y, 1)\Big|_{y=1} + \bar{k}$$

$$\overset{v}{k} = \overline{k^2} - \bar{k}^2 \qquad \overset{s}{k} = \sqrt{\overset{v}{k}}. \tag{10.8.4}$$

We find the mean $\bar{n}$, second moment $\overline{n^2}$, variance $\overset{v}{n}$, and standard deviation $\overset{s}{n}$ of the time spent in the transient process from

$$\bar{n} = \frac{d}{dz} p_{ir}{}^{gg}(1, z)\Big|_{z=1} \qquad \overline{n^2} = \frac{d^2}{dz^2} p_{ir}{}^{gg}(1, z)\Big|_{z=1} + \bar{n}$$

$$\overset{v}{n} = \overline{n^2} - \bar{n}^2 \qquad \overset{s}{n} = \sqrt{\overset{v}{n}}. \tag{10.8.5}$$

The car rental example

Let us apply these results to a simple example. Suppose we consider cars rented at town 1 in the car rental example and ask what we can say about the number of people who will rent them and the number of periods they will be rented before they are returned to town 2 for the first time. Thus state 1 in the example becomes a transient state while state 2 becomes a trapping state. We construct the flow

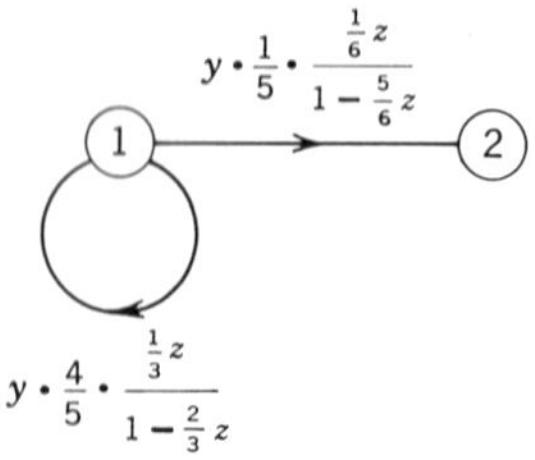

Figure 10.8.3 Flow graph for a transient process in the car rental example.

graph of Figure 10.8.3 to represent the problem by applying what we have learned in this section to the flow graph of Figure 10.6.2. Thus we eliminate all branches leaving node 2, and for convenience also remove the output branch associated with node 1 because it will not affect our computations. We find the transform $p_{12}{}^{gg}(y, z)$ as the transmission of the graph,

$$p_{12}{}^{gg}(y, z) = \vec{t}_{12} = \frac{\dfrac{(1/30)yz}{1-(5/6)z}}{1-\dfrac{(4/15)yz}{1-(2/3)z}} = \frac{(1/30)yz[1-(2/3)z]}{[1-(2/3)z-(4/15)yz][1-(5/6)z]}. \quad (10.8.6)$$

Recursive solution for joint distribution. Since the labor of inverting this double transform will seldom be justified, we prefer to find $p_{12}(k, n)$, the joint distribution of transitions and time spent in the transient process, by using the recursive equation implied by the transform. We write

$$p_{12}{}^{gg}(y, z)[1 - (3/2)z + (5/9)z^2 - (4/15)yz + (2/9)yz^2] = (1/30)yz - (1/45)yz^2 \quad (10.8.7)$$

and then

$$\begin{aligned} p_{12}(k, n) = {} & (3/2)p_{12}(k, n-1) - (5/9)p_{12}(k, n-2) + (4/15)p_{12}(k-1, n-1) \\ & - (2/9)p_{12}(k-1, n-2) + (1/30)\,\delta(k-1)\,\delta(n-1) - (1/45)\,\delta(k-1)\,\delta(n-2) \\ & k = 0, 1, 2, \ldots; n = 0, 1, 2, \ldots. \end{aligned} \quad (10.8.8)$$

This equation provides a practical method of solution for the joint probabilities of k and n; they are tabulated for values of k and n through 10 in Table 10.8.1.

Marginal distribution on transitions. In many problems we shall be content with the marginal distributions on transitions and time spent in the transient process. Thus if we are interested in the number of transitions or rentals necessary to reach town 2, we compute $p_{12}^{gg}(y, 1)$, the geometric transform of the probability distribution for k alone, and then invert the transform. We find it either from Equation 10.8.6 or from the flow graph,

$$p_{12}^{gg}(y, 1) = \frac{(1/5)y}{1 - (4/5)y}. \qquad (10.8.9)$$

Then

$$p_{12}^{\cdot g}(k, 1) = (1/5)(4/5)^{k-1} \qquad k = 1, 2, 3, \ldots. \qquad (10.8.10)$$

This marginal distribution on number of transitions in the transient process also appears in Table 10.8.1. Each marginal probability is the sum of the joint probabilities over all values of n. Since the table is truncated at $n = 10$, the marginal probabilities are greater than the row sums of the table.

From Equation 10.8.4, we compute

$$\bar{k} = 5 \qquad \overline{k^2} = 45 \qquad \overset{\vee}{k} = 20 \qquad \overset{s}{k} = 4.47. \qquad (10.8.11)$$

We see that on the average it will require 5 rentals for the car to reach town 2, with a standard deviation of 4.47.

Marginal distribution on time. If we desire to investigate only the time spent in the transient process, then we first find its transform as $p_{12}^{gg}(1, z)$,

$$p_{12}^{gg}(1, z) = \frac{(1/30)z[1 - (2/3)z]}{[1 - (14/15)z][1 - (5/6)z]}$$

$$= \frac{(4/45)z}{1 - (14/15)z} + \frac{-(1/18)z}{1 - (5/6)z}. \qquad (10.8.12)$$

After inverse geometric transformation, we obtain

$$p_{12}^{g\cdot}(1, n) = (4/45)(14/15)^{n-1} - (1/18)(5/6)^{n-1} \qquad n = 1, 2, 3, \ldots. \qquad (10.8.13)$$

The quantity $p_{12}^{g\cdot}(1, n)$ is the probability that n periods will be necessary to reach town 2; it is recorded in Table 10.8.1. This marginal probability on time spent in the transient process is the sum of the joint probabilities over all numbers of transitions k, and hence is given by the column sums of the table.

We find the moments of the number of periods required from Equation 10.8.5,

$$\bar{n} = 18 \qquad \overline{n^2} = 558 \qquad \overset{\vee}{n} = 234 \qquad \overset{s}{n} = 15.3. \qquad (10.8.14)$$

The average number of periods necessary to reach town 2 is 18, with a standard deviation of 15.3.

Table 10.8.1 Joint and Marginal Distributions of Number of Transitions and Time Spent in a Transient Process in the Car Rental Example

$p_{12}(k, n)$

k Transitions \ n Time	$p_{12}{}^{\mathcal{g}}(k, 1)$	0	1	2	3	4	5	6	7	8	9	10
$p_{12}{}^{\mathcal{g}}(1, n)$		0	0.3333	0.03667	0.03885	0.04012	0.04066	0.04063	0.04015	0.03934	0.03826	0.03701
0	0	0	0	0	0	0	0	0	0	0	0	0
1	0.20000	0	0.03333	0.02778	0.02315	0.01929	0.01608	0.01340	0.01116	0.00930	0.00775	0.00646
2	0.16000	0	0	0.00889	0.01333	0.01506	0.01519	0.01441	0.01318	0.01176	0.01032	0.00895
3	0.12800	0	0	0	0.00237	0.00514	0.00744	0.00901	0.00985	0.01008	0.00986	0.0C932
4	0.10240	0	0	0	0	0.00063	0.00179	0.00318	0.00452	0.00564	0.00645	0.00693
5	0.08192	0	0	0	0	0	0.00017	0.00059	0.00124	0.00203	0.00286	0.00363
6	0.06554	0	0	0	0	0	0	0.00004	0.00019	0.00046	0.00085	0.00133
7	0.05243	0	0	0	0	0	0	0	0.00001	0.00006	0.00016	0.00033
8	0.04194	0	0	0	0	0	0	0	0	0.00000	0.00002	0.00005
9	0.03355	0	0	0	0	0	0	0	0	0	0.00000	0.00001
10	0.02684	0	0	0	0	0	0	0	0	0	0	0.00000

Mean Time in Process

If we are interested only in the mean time spent in the transient process or even in the more detailed information represented by the mean time spent in each state of the transient process, we can use a simplified flow graph method like the one we developed in Section 4.1. We parallel the earlier argument by defining a random variable $x_{ij}(n)$ to be equal to 1 if the system is in state j at time n and 0 otherwise, given that the system entered state i at time zero. Let ν_{ij} be the total amount of time the process will spend in state j if it is started in state i. Then

$$\nu_{ij} = \sum_{n=0}^{\infty} x_{ij}(n), \tag{10.8.15}$$

and the expected time the process will spend in state j, $\bar{\nu}_{ij}$, is

$$\bar{\nu}_{ij} = \sum_{n=0}^{\infty} \overline{x_{ij}(n)}. \tag{10.8.16}$$

The probability that $x_{ij}(n)$ will equal 1 is $\phi_{ij}(n)$, the interval transition probability. The probability that $x_{ij}(n)$ will equal 0 is therefore $1 - \phi_{ij}(n)$. Consequently,

$$\overline{x_{ij}(n)} = \phi_{ij}(n), \tag{10.8.17}$$

and we can write Equation 10.8.16 as

$$\bar{\nu}_{ij} = \sum_{n=0}^{\infty} \phi_{ij}(n), \tag{10.8.18}$$

a result analogous to Equation 4.1.31 for the basic Markov process. From the definition of the geometric transform we have

$$\bar{\nu}_{ij} = \sum_{n=0}^{\infty} \phi_{ij}(n)z^n \bigg|_{z=1} = \phi_{ij}^g(1). \tag{10.8.19}$$

The expected time spent in state j of the transient process is therefore the transmission of the flow graph for the process from state i to the output node associated with state j evaluated at $z = 1$ (and, of course, with $y = 1$ since we are not counting transitions).

The augmented transition diagram

We can alternately evaluate the flow graph at $z = 1$ and then find the transmission. Since

$$h_{ij}^g(1) = 1 \qquad \text{and} \qquad \lim_{z \to 1} {}^{>}w_i^g(z) = \bar{\tau}_i, \tag{10.8.20}$$

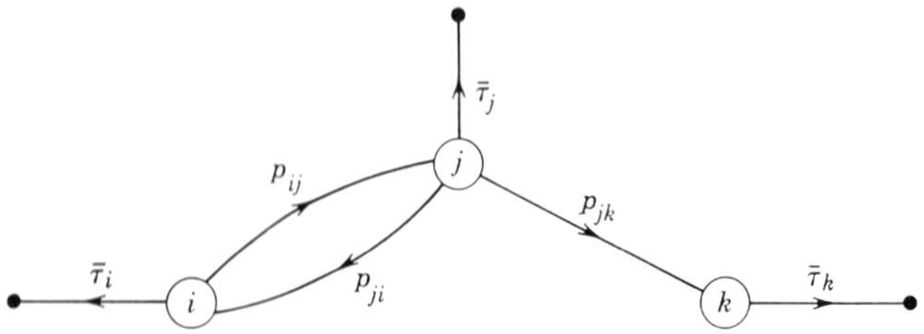

Figure 10.8.4 Augmented transition diagram for mean time spent in each state of a transient process.

we can imagine that the flow graph in Figure 10.5.2 is the flow graph of the Markov process outside the trapping state and draw it in the special form of Figure 10.8.4. This figure shows the transition diagram for the imbedded Markov process with each node connecting to an associated output node by a branch whose transmission is the mean waiting time in the corresponding state. The transmission of this augmented transition diagram from node i to the output node associated with node j is the mean time that a transient process started in state i will spend in the transient state j before it is trapped by the trapping state. Of course, the total expected time spent in the transient process is just the sum of the expected time spent in each of the transient states. We see that if we let $\overline{\mathrm{N}}$ be the matrix with elements $\bar{\nu}_{ij}$, then

$$\overline{\mathrm{N}} = [I - P]^{-1}M, \tag{10.8.21}$$

where P is now the portion of the transition probability matrix corresponding to transient states and M is a diagonal matrix of mean waiting times for these states. Equation 10.8.21 is therefore a generalization of Equation 4.1.39 developed for the basic Markov process. One way of interpreting our results is to say that we use the methods of Section 4.1 to find the expected number of times each transient state is entered before the process is trapped. Then to compute the expected time spent in each state we simply multiply this expected number of occupancies by the mean time the process will spend in that state every time it is entered.

The car rental example. Figure 10.8.5 shows the augmented transition diagram for the expected number of periods required to leave the transient process we have studied in the car rental example. This figure was constructed from Figure 10.8.3 and the knowledge that $\bar{\tau}_1 = 3.6$; it could also be drawn directly from Figure 10.5.3 with $z = 1$. The transmission of this augmented transition diagram from state 1 to the output node associated with state 1 is

$$\bar{\nu}_{11} = \frac{1}{1 - (4/5)} \times 3.6 = 18. \tag{10.8.22}$$

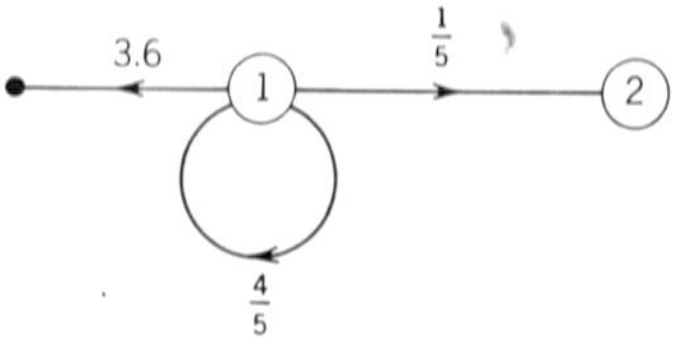

Figure 10.8.5 Augmented transition diagram for mean time in a transient process in the car rental example.

Therefore we expect the process to spend 18 periods in making its first transition to state 2. Since state 1 is the only transient state in the process, the mean number of periods spent in the transient process is also 18, a result we first observed in Equation 10.8.14.

Multiple Trapping States

The results we have developed can be applied to the case where we have several trapping states or, equivalently, we have several recurrent chains into which the transient process may run. As in Figure 10.8.2, we remove all branches that leave each trapping state (or recurrent chain). Then the transmission from a transient state i to a trapping state r is the double transform $p_{ir}^{\mathscr{g}\mathscr{g}}(y, z)$ of the joint probability that k transitions and n time periods will be required to enter state r *and that, in fact, state r will be entered.* Thus $p_{ir}^{\mathscr{g}\mathscr{g}}(1, 1)$ is not necessarily 1 but rather the probability that sooner or later the process will be trapped by state r if it is started in state i. This is, of course, just the kind of computation we performed in Section 4.1. Once we realize the nature of $p_{ir}^{\mathscr{g}\mathscr{g}}(y, z)$ in the multiple trapping state case, we can easily use this quantity to answer almost any question about the transient process. For example, we can compute the moments of the number of transitions and amount of time spent in the transient process conditional on trapping by each of the trapping states.

10.9 DURATION

We define the duration† of a state to be either the number of transitions or amount of time required after a state is entered before the first real transition is made to another state. Thus virtual transitions made to the same state all add to the

† The duration of a state is not to be confused with the duration of a process studied in Section 6.3 (Volume I).

duration. Let $d_i(k, n)$ be the probability that the duration of state i is k transitions and time n; that is,

$$d_i(k, n) = \mathcal{P}\{t(k) = n, s(n) \neq i, s(n-1) = s(n-2) = \cdots = s(1) = i | s(0) = i, t(0) = 0\} \qquad \begin{matrix} i = 1, 2, \ldots, N \\ k = 0, 1, 2, \ldots \\ n = 0, 1, 2, \ldots . \end{matrix} \qquad (10.9.1)$$

The easiest way to develop an expression for the duration of a state is to exploit the transient process model we have just analyzed. Let $d_i^{gg}(y|z)$ be the double geometric transform of $d_i(k, n)$. The transmission of the flow graph in Figure 10.9.1(a) is just $d_i^{gg}(y|z)$. The transient process starts when the system enters state i and stops when the system enters any other state. We have lumped all other states into a single composite state and have shown one branch transmission from state i to this composite state for each other state the system may enter. The possible returns to state i in virtual transitions are allowed by the loop around node i with transmission $yp_{ii}h_{ii}^g(z)$. Every branch transmission in the graph is tagged by a y so that transitions will be counted.

The flow graph of Figure 10.9.1(a) can be drawn in the simpler form of Figure 10.9.1(b). Then we note that we can write the summation in a different form as

$$\sum_{\substack{j=1 \\ j\neq 1}}^{N} p_{ij}h_{ij}^g(z) = \sum_{j=1}^{N} p_{ij}h_{ij}^g(z) - p_{ii}h_{ii}^g(z) = w_i^g(z) - p_{ii}h_{ii}^g(z), \qquad (10.9.2)$$

and draw the flow graph in the final form of Figure 10.9.1(c). We see immediately that

$$d_i^{gg}(y, z) = \frac{y[w_i^g(z) - p_{ii}h_{ii}^g(z)]}{1 - yp_{ii}h_{ii}^g(z)} . \qquad (10.9.3)$$

As a check, we observe $d_i^{gg}(1, 1) = 1$.

Equation 10.9.3 is useful for theoretical procedures, but seldom for calculation. To obtain numerical results, we prefer the recursive equation form,

$$d_i(k, n) = \sum_{m=0}^{n} p_{ii}h_{ii}(m)d_i(k-1, n-m) + \delta(k-1)[w_i(n) - p_{ii}h_{ii}(n)]$$
$$i = 1, 2, \ldots, N; k = 0, 1, 2, \ldots; n = 0, 1, 2, \ldots, \qquad (10.9.4)$$

which could, of course, have been obtained by direct reasoning.

We have already observed the calculation of a duration. The duration of state 1 in the car rental example is just the transient process we solved in Section 10.8. Thus $d_1(k, n) = p_{12}(k, n)$ and $d_1^{gg}(y, z) = p_{12}^{gg}(y, z)$ as given in Equation 10.8.6.

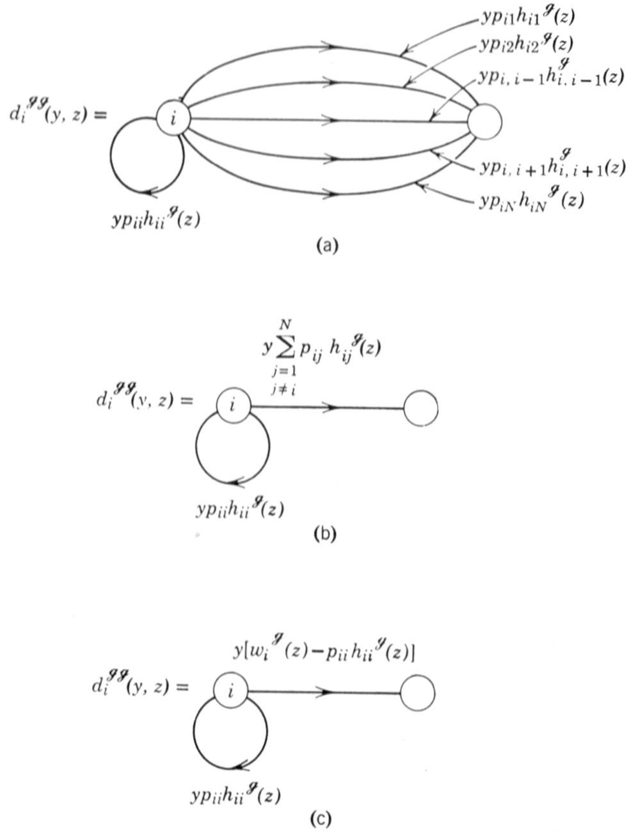

Figure 10.9.1 Flow graphs for duration calculation.

Duration in Transitions

The transform of $d_i^{gg}(y, z)$ when evaluated at $z = 1$ and then at $y = 1$ produces the transforms of the marginal distributions for duration measured in terms of transitions alone or time alone. Thus with $z = 1$, we find

$$d_i^{gg}(y, 1) = \frac{y(1 - p_{ii})}{1 - yp_{ii}} \tag{10.9.5}$$

and for the marginal distributions on duration measured in transitions,

$$d_i^{\cdot g}(k, 1) = (1 - p_{ii})p_{ii}^{k-1} \qquad k = 1, 2, 3, \ldots . \tag{10.9.6}$$

This result shows that the number of transitions required to make a real transition out of a state is geometrically distributed with parameter p_{ii}. We first observed this result in Chapter 4 for the basic Markov process. Either by differentiating the transform of Equation 10.9.5 or from the properties of the geometric distributions, we find the moments of the duration measured in transitions for state i to be

$$\bar{k}_i = \frac{1}{1 - p_{ii}} \qquad \overline{k_i^2} = \frac{1 + p_{ii}}{(1 - p_{ii})^2} \qquad \check{k}_i = \frac{p_{ii}}{(1 - p_{ii})^2}. \tag{10.9.7}$$

Duration in Time

The transform of the duration distribution measured in time is $d_i^{gg}(y, z)$ evaluated at $y = 1$,

$$d_i^{gg}(1, z) = \frac{w_i^g(z) - p_{ii}h_{ii}^g(z)}{1 - p_{ii}h_{ii}^g(z)}. \tag{10.9.8}$$

For the basic Markov process where $w_i^g(z) = h_{ii}^g(z) = z$, we have

$$d_i^{gg}(1, z) = \frac{z(1 - p_{ii})}{1 - zp_{ii}}, \tag{10.9.9}$$

which is, of course, the same transform shown in Equation 10.9.5. Therefore we have another confirmation of the result in Chapter 4 that the time spent in any state of a basic Markov process is geometrically distributed.

Time duration moments

The moments of the duration measured in time are especially interesting quantities. We obtain them by differentiating Equation 10.9.8 with respect to z and evaluating the result at $z = 1$.

Mean. For the mean duration in time for state i, $\bar{n}_i$, we write

$$\bar{n}_i = \frac{d}{dz} d_i^{gg}(1, z)\bigg|_{z=1} = \frac{\bar{\tau}_i}{1 - p_{ii}} = \bar{k}_i\bar{\tau}_i. \tag{10.9.10}$$

The mean duration in time for state i is equal to the mean duration in transitions for state i multiplied by the mean waiting time for state i, a reasonable result.

Variance. Let us now turn to the variance of the duration in time for state i, $\check{n}_i$. We compute the second moment, $\overline{n_i^2}$, from

$$\overline{n_i^2} = \frac{d^2}{dz^2} d_i^{gg}(1, z)\bigg|_{z=1} + \bar{n}_i = \frac{(\overline{\tau_i^2} - \bar{\tau}_i)(1 - p_{ii}) + 2p_{ii}\bar{\tau}_i\bar{\tau}_{ii}}{(1 - p_{ii})^2} + \bar{n}_i$$

$$= \frac{\overline{\tau_i^2}(1 - p_{ii}) + 2p_{ii}\bar{\tau}_i\bar{\tau}_{ii}}{(1 - p_{ii})^2}. \tag{10.9.11}$$

Then we write the variance as

$$\check{n}_i = \overline{n_i^2} - \bar{n}_i^2 = \frac{\overline{\tau_i^2}(1 - p_{ii}) + 2p_{ii}\bar{\tau}_i\bar{\tau}_{ii}}{(1 - p_{ii})^2} - \frac{\bar{\tau}_i^2}{(1 - p_{ii})^2}$$

$$= \frac{(1 - p_{ii})(\overline{\tau_i^2} - \bar{\tau}_i^2) + p_{ii}(2\bar{\tau}_i\bar{\tau}_{ii} - \bar{\tau}_i^2)}{(1 - p_{ii})^2}$$

$$= \frac{(1 - p_{ii})\check{\tau}_i + p_{ii}\bar{\tau}_i(2\bar{\tau}_{ii} - \bar{\tau}_i)}{(1 - p_{ii})^2}$$

$$= \bar{k}_i\check{\tau}_i + \check{k}_i\bar{\tau}_i(2\bar{\tau}_{ii} - \bar{\tau}_i). \tag{10.9.12}$$

The car rental example. The transient process of Figure 10.8.3 that represents the duration of state 1 provides a numerical check on our moment formulas. For this example, $p_{11} = 0.8$, $\bar{\tau}_{11} = 3$, $\bar{\tau}_1 = 3.6$, $\check{\tau}_1 = 12.24$. We write the moments of the duration of state 1 *measured in transitions* from Equation 10.9.7,

$$\bar{k}_1 = 5 \qquad \overline{k_1^2} = 45 \qquad \check{k}_1 = 20. \tag{10.9.13}$$

These results were found originally in Equation 10.8.11. Then we write the moments of duration of state 1 *measured in time* from Equations 10.9.10 and 10.9.12 as

$$\begin{aligned} \bar{n}_1 &= \bar{k}_1\bar{\tau}_1 = 5(3.6) = 18 \\ \check{n}_1 &= \bar{k}_1\check{\tau}_1 + \check{k}_1\bar{\tau}_1(2\bar{\tau}_{11} - \bar{\tau}_1) = 5(12.24) + 20(3.6)[2(3) - 3.6] = 234, \end{aligned} \tag{10.9.14}$$

in agreement with Equation 10.8.14.

Independent semi-Markov process. Equation 10.9.12 assumes an interesting special form for an independent semi-Markov process, the process discussed in Section 10.4 whose holding times in any state are chosen from the same distribution regardless of destination. For such a process, $\bar{\tau}_{ii} = \bar{\tau}_i$ and we can write Equation 10.9.12 as

$$\check{n}_i = \bar{k}_i\check{\tau}_i + \check{k}_i\bar{\tau}_i^2. \tag{10.9.15}$$

The duration *measured in time* for independent semi-Markov processes is an application of the theory of compound distributions. We think of the geometric process that generates returns to state i as a process that determines how many independent samples are to be taken from the waiting time distribution for state i and added together to form the duration in time. With this interpretation, Equations 10.9.10 and 10.9.15 for the mean and variance of the duration in time follow directly from the theory of compound distributions developed in Section 8.2 (Volume 1).

10.10 FIRST PASSAGE TIMES

First passage times for semi-Markov processes play the same important role that they played for the basic Markov process. However, now we can think of first passage times either in terms of transitions, or of time, or both. Let $f_{ij}(k, n)$ be the probability that k transitions and time n will be required for the first passage from state i to state j. Formally,

$$f_{ij}(k, n) = \begin{cases} \mathscr{P}\{t(k) = n, s(n) = j, s(t(k-1)) \neq j, s(t(k-2)) \neq j, \ldots, \\ \qquad s(t(1)) \neq j \mid s(0) = i, t(0) = 0\} & k = 2, 3, 4, \ldots; \\ & n = k, k+1, k+2, \ldots \\ \mathscr{P}\{t(1) = n, s(n) = j \mid s(0) = i, t(0) = 0\} & k = 1; n = 1, 2, 3, \ldots \\ 0 & k = 0 \text{ or } n < k \end{cases}$$

$$i = 1, 2, \ldots, N; j = 1, 2, \ldots, N. \qquad (10.10.1)$$

The first passage time is thus a measure of how long it takes to reach a given state from another state. The duration measured how long it took to leave a given state.

As we already know, we can solve first passage time problems using the theory of the transient process. All we must do to find $f_{ij}^{gg}(y, z)$, the double geometric transform of $f_{ij}(k, n)$, is to draw the flow graph for the semi-Markov process, make state j a trapping state, and then find the transmission of the graph from node i to node j. Thus the transient process we analyzed in Section 10.8 was the process governing the first passage time from state 1 to state 2. Therefore, $f_{12}^{gg}(y, z) = p_{12}^{gg}(y, z)$, $f_{12}(k, n) = p_{12}(k, n)$, and we have already seen a typical first passage time calculation in Equations 10.8.6, 10.8.8, etc.

However, although treating first passage time problems as a succession of transient process problems is always possible theoretically, and sometimes practically as well, first passage times are of such major importance that we find it worthwhile to develop special analyses for this computation. We begin by writing a recursive equation relating the first passage time probabilities to themselves,

$$f_{ij}(k, n) = \sum_{\substack{r=1 \\ r \neq j}}^{N} \sum_{m=0}^{n} p_{ir} h_{ir}(m) f_{rj}(k-1, n-m) + \delta(k-1) p_{ij} h_{ij}(n)$$

$$i = 1, 2, \ldots, N; k = 0, 1, 2, \ldots \qquad (10.10.2)$$
$$j = 1, 2, \ldots, N; n = 0, 1, 2, \ldots.$$

The first term in this equation accounts for the case where $k > 1$ and the process makes a transition from state i to some state r different from j at time m and then makes a first passage from state r to state j in $k - 1$ additional transitions and time $n - m$. This term is summed over all states and times that could describe this first transition. The second term accounts for the case where $k = 1$ and the process makes its first transition directly to state j at time n.

Equation 10.10.2 can be solved recursively to find the first passage time probabilities for any semi-Markov process. Moreover, since we can consider any transient process problem as a first passage time problem, Equation 10.10.2 also serves as a computational procedure for solving large transient processes.

We recognize that the first passage time distribution $f_{ij}(k, n)$ will be a proper joint probability distribution, $f_{ij}{}^{gg}(1, 1) = 1$, if and only if it is certain that state j will sooner or later be occupied. It is not necessary that state j be recurrent, only that state j be occupied at least once when the process is started in state i. For example, if i and j are members of a transient chain and the process must enter state j before leaving the chain, then the first passage time probability $f_{ij}(k, n)$ will be a proper joint probability distribution. If it is not certain that j will be occupied when the process starts in state i, then $f_{ij}{}^{gg}(1, 1)$ is the probability that a first passage from state i to state j will occur.

If we are interested only in time rather than in both time and transitions, then we define $f_{ij}(n)$ as the probability that the first passage from i to j will require time n and simplify Equation 10.10.2 to the form,

$$f_{ij}(n) = \sum_{\substack{r=1 \\ r \neq j}}^{N} \sum_{m=0}^{n} p_{ir} h_{ir}(m) f_{rj}(n-m) + p_{ij} h_{ij}(n) \qquad \begin{aligned} i &= 1, 2, \ldots, N \\ j &= 1, 2, \ldots, N \\ n &= 0, 1, 2, \ldots . \end{aligned} \tag{10.10.3}$$

The reasoning underlying this equation is the same as that used in developing Equation 10.10.2. It is the semi-Markov version of Equation 5.2.35.

Transform Relations

Returning to the general analysis, we write Equation 10.10.2 in the form,

$$f_{ij}(k, n) = \sum_{r=1}^{N} \sum_{m=0}^{n} p_{ir} h_{ir}(m) f_{rj}(k-1, n-m)$$
$$- \sum_{m=0}^{n} p_{ij} h_{ij}(m) f_{jj}(k-1, n-m) + \delta(k-1) p_{ij} h_{ij}(n), \tag{10.10.4}$$

and then transform it,

$$f_{ij}{}^{gg}(y, z) = y \sum_{r=1}^{N} p_{ir} h_{ir}{}^{g}(z) f_{rj}{}^{gg}(y, z) - y p_{ij} h_{ij}{}^{g}(z) f_{jj}{}^{gg}(y, z) + y p_{ij} h_{ij}{}^{g}(z)$$
$$= y \sum_{r=1}^{N} p_{ir} h_{ir}{}^{g}(z) f_{rj}{}^{gg}(y, z) + y p_{ij} h_{ij}{}^{g}(z)[1 - f_{jj}{}^{gg}(y, z)]. \tag{10.10.5}$$

We use $F^{gg}(y, z)$ for the matrix with elements $f_{ij}^{gg}(y, z)$ and place Equation 10.10.5 in matrix form as

$$\begin{aligned} F^{gg}(y, z) &= y[P \,\square\, H^{g}(z)]F^{gg}(y, z) + y[P \,\square\, H^{g}(z)][I - F^{gg}(y, z) \,\square\, I] \\ &= y\{C^{g}(z)F^{gg}(y, z) + C^{g}(z)[I - F^{gg}(y, z) \,\square\, I]\} \\ &= yC^{g}(z)[I + (U - I) \,\square\, F^{gg}(y, z)]. \end{aligned} \tag{10.10.6}$$

The matrix $F^{g}(z)$ whose elements $f_{ij}^{g}(z)$ are the transforms of $f_{ij}(n)$ is related to $F^{gg}(y, z)$ by

$$F^{g}(z) = F^{gg}(1, z) = C^{g}(z)[I + (U - I) \,\square\, F^{g}(z)]. \tag{10.10.7}$$

The equation in terms of the elements is

$$f_{ij}^{g}(z) = \sum_{r=1}^{N} p_{ir}h_{ir}^{g}(z)f_{rj}^{g}(z) + p_{ij}h_{ij}^{g}(z)[1 - f_{jj}^{g}(z)]. \tag{10.10.8}$$

The matrix $F^{gg}(y, 1)$ is the matrix of transformed first passage times measured in transitions,

$$F^{gg}(y, 1) = yP[I + (U - I) \,\square\, F^{gg}(y, 1)]. \tag{10.10.9}$$

We studied this kind of first passage time in Section 5.2.

Relationship to Interval Transition Probabilities

The first passage time probabilities are directly related to the interval transition probabilities by

$$\phi_{ij}(k|n) = \sum_{m=0}^{n} \sum_{u=0}^{k} f_{ij}(u, m)\phi_{jj}(k - u|n - m) + \delta_{ij}\,\delta(k)\,{}^{>}w_i(n). \tag{10.10.10}$$

This equation states that the probability of occupying state j after k transitions and time n starting from state i is composed of two terms. The first term is the probability of making a first passage to state j after u transitions and time m multiplied by the probability of occupying state j after an additional $k - u$ transitions and time $n - m$ given a start in state j. This term is summed over all numbers of transitions u and times m. The second term accounts for the only possibility of being in state j after k transitions and time n not accounted for by the first term; namely, the possibility that $k = 0$, $i = j$, and the process makes its first transition out of state i after time n.

Equation 10.10.10 is a recursive equation that can be used to produce the interval transition probabilities from the first passage time probabilities. Usually we would prefer to have a method of producing the first passage time probabilities from the interval transition probabilities. To this end, we write Equation 10.10.10 in the form,

$$\phi_{ij}(k|n) = \sum_{m=0}^{n-1} \sum_{u=0}^{k} f_{ij}(u, m)\phi_{jj}(k - u|n - m) + f_{ij}(k, n) + \delta_{ij}\, \delta(k)\, {}^{>}w_i(n), \tag{10.10.11}$$

and then rearrange it to obtain

$$f_{ij}(k, n) = \begin{cases} \phi_{ij}(k|n) - \sum_{m=0}^{n-1} \sum_{u=0}^{k} f_{ij}(u, m)\phi_{jj}(k - u|n - m) - \delta_{ij}\, \delta(k)\, {}^{>}w_i(n) & n \geq 1 \\ 0 & n = 0 \end{cases}$$

$$k = 0, 1, 2, \ldots. \tag{10.10.12}$$

This equation is a convenient recursive form for computing the first passage time probabilities from the interval transition time probabilities. If we are not interested in counting transitions, Equation 10.10.12 assumes the simpler form,

$$f_{ij}(n) = \begin{cases} \phi_{ij}(n) - \sum_{m=0}^{n-1} f_{ij}(m)\phi_{jj}(n - m) - \delta_{ij}\, {}^{>}w_i(n) & n \geq 1 \\ 0 & n = 0, \end{cases} \tag{10.10.13}$$

which is analogous to Equation 5.2.39.

Transform relations

In the transform domain, Equation 10.10.10 becomes

$$\phi_{ij}{}^{gg}(y|z) = f_{ij}{}^{gg}(y, z)\phi_{jj}{}^{gg}(y|z) + \delta_{ij}\, {}^{>}w_i{}^{g}(z), \tag{10.10.14}$$

the double convolution in the equation becoming the product of two double geometric transforms. If we solve this equation for the transform of the first passage time probabilities, we find

$$f_{ij}{}^{gg}(y, z) = \frac{\phi_{ij}{}^{gg}(y|z) - \delta_{ij}\, {}^{>}w_i{}^{g}(z)}{\phi_{jj}{}^{gg}(y|z)}. \tag{10.10.15}$$

The matrix forms for Equations 10.10.14 and 10.10.15 are

$$\Phi^{gg}(y|z) = F^{gg}(y, z)[\Phi^{gg}(y|z) \,\square\, I] + {}^{>}W^{g}(z) \tag{10.10.16}$$

and

$$F^{gg}(y, z) = [\Phi^{gg}(y|z) - {}^{>}W^{g}(z)][\Phi^{gg}(y|z) \,\square\, I]^{-1}. \tag{10.10.17}$$

Equation 10.10.17 provides an explicit method for computing $F^{\mathscr{g}\mathscr{g}}(y, z)$ from $\Phi^{\mathscr{g}\mathscr{g}}(y|z)$; however, Equation 10.10.16 does not have the converse property. To develop an equation that allows us to write $\Phi^{\mathscr{g}\mathscr{g}}(y|z)$ from $F^{\mathscr{g}\mathscr{g}}(y, z)$, we first observe the form that Equation 10.10.14 assumes when $i = j$,

$$\phi_{jj}{}^{\mathscr{g}\mathscr{g}}(y|z) = f_{jj}{}^{\mathscr{g}\mathscr{g}}(y, z)\phi_{jj}{}^{\mathscr{g}\mathscr{g}}(y|z) + {}^{>}w_j{}^{\mathscr{g}}(z) \tag{10.10.18}$$

or

$$\phi_{jj}{}^{\mathscr{g}\mathscr{g}}(y|z) = \frac{{}^{>}w_j{}^{\mathscr{g}}(z)}{1 - f_{jj}{}^{\mathscr{g}\mathscr{g}}(y, z)}. \tag{10.10.19}$$

Then for $i \neq j$ we have

$$\phi_{ij}{}^{\mathscr{g}\mathscr{g}}(y|z) = f_{ij}{}^{\mathscr{g}\mathscr{g}}(y, z)\phi_{jj}{}^{\mathscr{g}\mathscr{g}}(y|z) = \frac{f_{ij}{}^{\mathscr{g}\mathscr{g}}(y, z)\,{}^{>}w_j{}^{\mathscr{g}}(z)}{1 - f_{jj}{}^{\mathscr{g}\mathscr{g}}(y, z)} \qquad i \neq j. \tag{10.10.20}$$

Equations 10.10.19 and 10.10.20 show how to find the interval transition probability transforms from first passage time probability transforms.

Flow graph representation

These relationships imply the flow graph of Figure 10.10.1. To construct this flow graph we first make state j of the original semi-Markov process graph into a trapping state and find $f_{ij}{}^{\mathscr{g}\mathscr{g}}(y, z)$, the transmission of this graph from node i to node j. Then we return to the original graph and find the transmission around node j, that is, the transmission through the branches leaving node j through the rest of the graph and finally through the branches entering node j—this transmission is $f_{jj}{}^{\mathscr{g}\mathscr{g}}(y, z)$. Now the flow graph of Figure 10.10.1 can be constructed

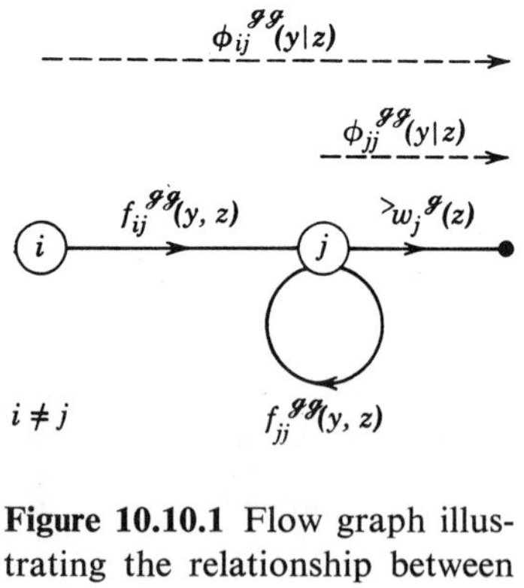

Figure 10.10.1 Flow graph illustrating the relationship between first passage times and interval transition probabilities.

and we can find $\phi_{ij}{}^{gg}(y, z)$ as its transmission. Note that if $i = j$ then only $f_{jj}{}^{gg}(y, z)$ need be computed to determine $\phi_{jj}{}^{gg}(y|z)$.

If we substitute Equation 10.10.20 into Equation 10.10.14, we obtain an expression for the interval transition probability transforms in terms of the first passage time probability transforms for all values of i and j,

$$\begin{aligned}\phi_{ij}{}^{gg}(y|z) &= f_{ij}{}^{gg}(y, z)\frac{{}^{>}w_j{}^{g}(z)}{1 - f_{jj}{}^{gg}(y, z)} + \delta_{ij}\,{}^{>}w_i{}^{g}(z)\\ &= \frac{f_{ij}{}^{gg}(y, z)\,{}^{>}w_j{}^{g}(z) + \delta_{ij}[1 - f_{jj}{}^{gg}(y, z)]\,{}^{>}w_i{}^{g}(z)}{1 - f_{jj}{}^{gg}(y, z)}\\ &= \frac{[\delta_{ij} + (1 - \delta_{ij})f_{ij}{}^{gg}(y, z)]\,{}^{>}w_j{}^{g}(z)}{1 - f_{jj}{}^{gg}(y, z)},\end{aligned} \tag{10.10.21}$$

a result in harmony with Equations 10.10.19 and 10.10.20. The matrix version of this equation is

$$\Phi^{gg}(y|z) = [I + (U - I) \,\Box\, F^{gg}(y, z)][I - F^{gg}(y, z) \,\Box\, I]^{-1}\,{}^{>}W^{g}(z). \tag{10.10.22}$$

We have thus found an explicit method for computing $\Phi^{gg}(y|z)$ from $F^{gg}(y, z)$.

Relationship to Entrance Probabilities

We could have related the first passage time probabilities to the entrance probabilities rather than to the interval transition probabilities. However, these results are easy to obtain from those we have already developed. In Equations 10.10.10 through 10.10.22, we substitute $e_{ij}(k|n)$ for $\phi_{ij}(k|n)$; $\delta(n)$ for ${}^{>}w_i(n)$; $e_{ij}(n)$ for $\phi_{ij}(n)$; and in the transform domain, $e_{ij}{}^{gg}(y|z)$ for $\phi_{ij}{}^{gg}(y|z)$; 1 for ${}^{>}w_i{}^{g}(z)$; $E^{gg}(y|z)$ for $\Phi^{gg}(y|z)$; and I for ${}^{>}W^{g}(z)$. Then we have before us the proper equations relating the entrance probabilities and first passage time probabilities. For example, in terms of entrance probabilities, Equations 10.10.19 and 10.10.20 become

$$e_{jj}{}^{gg}(y|z) = \frac{1}{1 - f_{jj}{}^{gg}(y, z)} \tag{10.10.23}$$

and

$$e_{ij}{}^{gg}(y|z) = \frac{f_{ij}{}^{gg}(y, z)}{1 - f_{jj}{}^{gg}(y, z)} \qquad i \neq j. \tag{10.10.24}$$

These equations show that $e_{ij}{}^{gg}(y|z)$ for any (i, j) pair is just the transmission from node i to node j of the flow graph of Figure 10.10.1.

From Equations 10.10.19, 10.10.20, 10.10.23, and 10.10.24 we obtain another important result,

$$\frac{\phi_{ij}^{gg}(y|z)}{\phi_{jj}^{gg}(y|z)} = \frac{e_{ij}^{gg}(y|z)}{e_{jj}^{gg}(y|z)} = f_{ij}^{gg}(y|z) \qquad i \neq j. \tag{10.10.25}$$

Of course, when $i = j$,

$$\frac{\phi_{jj}^{gg}(y|z)}{\phi_{jj}^{gg}(y|z)} = \frac{e_{jj}^{gg}(y|z)}{e_{jj}^{gg}(y|z)} = 1. \tag{10.10.26}$$

Therefore in matrix form we have

$$\begin{aligned} \Phi^{gg}(y|z)[\Phi^{gg}(y|z) \,\square\, I]^{-1} &= E^{gg}(y|z)[E^{gg}(y|z) \,\square\, I]^{-1} \\ &= I + (U - I) \,\square\, F^{gg}(y, z). \end{aligned} \tag{10.10.27}$$

The importance of this result is that by substituting it into Equation 10.10.6 we can obtain an explicit expression for the transformed first passage time probabilities in terms of the transformed core matrix of the process. We first write

$$\begin{aligned} F^{gg}(y, z) &= yC^{g}(z)[I + (U - I) \,\square\, F^{gg}(y, z)] \\ &= yC^{g}(z)E^{gg}(y|z)[E^{gg}(y|z) \,\square\, I]^{-1}, \end{aligned} \tag{10.10.28}$$

and then substitute $E^{gg}(y|z)$ from Equation 10.7.7,

$$F^{gg}(y, z) = yC^{g}(z)[I - yC^{g}(z)]^{-1}\{[I - yC^{g}(z)]^{-1} \,\square\, I\}^{-1}. \tag{10.10.29}$$

This equation thus shows how to compute $F^{gg}(y, z)$ from the basic distributions of the process; it is a matrix representation of the procedure we devised for finding each element $f_{ij}^{gg}(y, z)$ as the transmission of a transient process. As usual the transform relation implies a computable recursive equation.

Special Forms

If we are not interested in keeping track of transitions, then we use $F^{g}(z) = F^{gg}(1, z)$ and we obtain simple expressions for the first passage time probability transforms. Corresponding to Equations 10.10.16, 10.10.17, 10.10.22, and 10.10.29, we have

$$\Phi^{g}(z) = F^{g}(z)[\Phi^{g}(z) \,\square\, I] + {}^{>}W^{g}(z) \tag{10.10.30}$$

$$F^{g}(z) = [\Phi^{g}(z) - {}^{>}W^{g}(z)][\Phi^{g}(z) \,\square\, I]^{-1} \tag{10.10.31}$$

$$\Phi^{g}(z) = [I + (U - I) \,\square\, F^{g}(z)][I - F^{g}(z) \,\square\, I]^{-1}\, {}^{>}W^{g}(z) \tag{10.10.32}$$

and

$$F^{g}(z) = C^{g}(z)[I - C^{g}(z)]^{-1}\{[I - C^{g}(z)]^{-1} \,\square\, I\}^{-1}. \tag{10.10.33}$$

When we are interested only in transitions, we use $F^{gg}(y, 1)$ and obtain for the same equations,

$$\Phi^{gg}(y|1) = F^{gg}(y, 1)[\Phi^{gg}(y|1) \,\Box\, I] + I \qquad (10.10.34)$$

$$F^{gg}(y, 1) = [\Phi^{gg}(y|1) - I][\Phi^{gg}(y|1) \,\Box\, I]^{-1} \qquad (10.10.35)$$

$$\Phi^{gg}(y|1) = [I + (U - I) \,\Box\, F^{gg}(y, 1)][I - F^{gg}(y, 1) \,\Box\, I]^{-1} \qquad (10.10.36)$$

and

$$F^{gg}(y, 1) = yP[I - yP]^{-1}\{[I - yP]^{-1} \,\Box\, I\}^{-1}. \qquad (10.10.37)$$

These equations describe the type of first passage times we analyzed in Section 5.2. For example, Equation 10.10.35 was originally developed as Equation 5.2.45.

First Passage Time Moments

Let θ_{ij} be the first passage time from state i to state j measured in time. We can easily develop methods for finding the mean $\bar{\theta}_{ij}$, second moment $\overline{\theta_{ij}^2}$, and variance $\overset{v}{\theta}_{ij}$ to correspond to the results of Chapter 5 where we were interested in first passage times measured in transitions.

Mean recurrence times

First we consider the case where $i = j$; we call θ_{jj} the recurrence time of state j. Since the expected recurrence time $\bar{\theta}_{jj}$ is the mean of the distribution $f_{jj}(\cdot)$, we compute $\bar{\theta}_{jj}$ from

$$\bar{\theta}_{jj} = \sum_{n=0}^{\infty} nf_{jj}(n) = \frac{d}{dz} f_{jj}{}^{g}(z)\bigg|_{z=1} = \lim_{z\to 1} \frac{1 - f_{jj}{}^{g}(z)}{1 - z}. \qquad (10.10.38)$$

By using Equation 10.10.19 with $y = 1$, we can write

$$\bar{\theta}_{jj} = \lim_{z\to 1} \frac{{}^{>}w_j{}^{g}(z)}{(1 - z)\phi_{jj}{}^{g}(z)} = \frac{\lim\limits_{z\to 1} {}^{>}w_j{}^{g}(z)}{\lim\limits_{z\to 1} (1 - z)\phi_{jj}{}^{g}(z)} = \frac{\bar{\tau}_j}{\phi_j}. \qquad (10.10.39)$$

Then from Equation 10.7.20,

$$\bar{\theta}_{jj} = \frac{\sum\limits_{j=1}^{N} \pi_j \bar{\tau}_j}{\pi_j} = \frac{1}{e_j}. \qquad (10.10.40)$$

The mean recurrence times are the reciprocals of the limiting entrance probabilities. Note that if $\bar{\tau}_j = 1$, they are just the reciprocals of the limiting state probabilities.

Of course, Equation 10.10.39 has an interesting interpretation in its own right, especially in the form

$$\phi_j = \frac{\bar{\tau}_j}{\bar{\theta}_{jj}}. \tag{10.10.41}$$

This equation states that the limiting interval transition probability for state j is just the mean waiting time for state j divided by the mean recurrence time of state j.

Mean first passage times

To obtain a general relationship among mean first passage times, we write Equation 10.10.8

$$f_{ij}{}^g(z) = \sum_{r=1}^{N} p_{ir}h_{ir}{}^g(z)f_{rj}{}^g(z) + p_{ij}h_{ij}{}^g(z)[1 - f_{jj}{}^g(z)], \tag{10.10.42}$$

and then evaluate its derivative at the point $z = 1$,

$$\begin{aligned}\bar{\theta}_{ij} = \frac{d}{dz} f_{ij}{}^g(z)\bigg|_{z=1} &= \bar{\tau}_i + \sum_{r=1}^{N} p_{ir}\bar{\theta}_{rj} - p_{ij}\bar{\theta}_{jj} \\ &= \bar{\tau}_i + \sum_{\substack{r=1 \\ r\neq j}}^{N} p_{ir}\bar{\theta}_{rj} \qquad \begin{array}{l} i = 1, 2, \ldots, N \\ j = 1, 2, \ldots, N. \end{array}\end{aligned} \tag{10.10.43}$$

This result is intuitive in that the mean time required to go from state i to state j for the first time must be the mean time required to leave state i plus the mean time required to proceed to state j from the state which is the destination of the first transition multiplied by the probability of that destination and summed over all states except state j. When $\tau_i = 1$ we obtain the result of Equation 5.2.80.

If we multiply Equation 10.10.43 by π_i, the limiting state probability of state i, and sum over all states, we obtain

$$\begin{aligned}\sum_{i=1}^{N} \pi_i\bar{\theta}_{ij} &= \sum_{i=1}^{N} \pi_i\bar{\tau}_i + \sum_{r=1}^{N}\sum_{i=1}^{N} \pi_i p_{ir}\bar{\theta}_{rj} - \sum_{i=1}^{N} \pi_i p_{ij}\bar{\theta}_{jj} \\ &= \sum_{i=1}^{N} \pi_i\bar{\tau}_i + \sum_{r=1}^{N} \pi_r\bar{\theta}_{rj} - \pi_j\bar{\theta}_{jj}\end{aligned} \tag{10.10.44}$$

or

$$\bar{\theta}_{jj} = \frac{\sum_{i=1}^{N} \pi_i\bar{\tau}_i}{\pi_j} = \frac{1}{e_j} \tag{10.10.45}$$

in agreement with Equation 10.10.40.

First passage time second moments

We evaluate the second moment of the first passage time $\overline{\theta_{ij}^2}$ in an analogous way from another differentiation of Equation 10.10.42,

$$\overline{\theta_{ij}^2} = \frac{d^2}{dz^2} f_{ij}{}^g(z)\bigg|_{z=1} + \frac{d}{dz} f_{ij}{}^g(z)\bigg|_{z=1} = \overline{\tau_i^2} + \sum_{\substack{r=1 \\ r \neq j}}^{N} p_{ir}(2\bar{\tau}_{ir}\bar{\theta}_{rj} + \overline{\theta_{rj}^2}). \quad (10.10.46)$$

When $\bar{\tau}_i = \overline{\tau_i^2} = 1$, this equation reduces to Equation 5.2.88 for the basic Markov process. When we multiply Equation 10.10.46 by π_i, sum over all states, and solve for $\overline{\theta_{jj}^2}$, we obtain

$$\overline{\theta_{jj}^2} = \frac{1}{\pi_j}\left[\sum_{i=1}^{N} \pi_i \overline{\tau_i^2} + \sum_{\substack{r=1 \\ r \neq j}}^{N} \sum_{i=1}^{N} 2\pi_i p_{ir}\bar{\tau}_{ir}\bar{\theta}_{rj}\right]. \quad (10.10.47)$$

This equation shows that we can compute the second moment of the recurrence times very easily when we know the means of the first passage times.

The car rental example

Suppose that we wish to calculate the moments of the first passage time from state 1 to state 2 in the car rental example of Figure 10.1.3. From Equation 10.10.43,

$$\bar{\theta}_{12} = \bar{\tau}_1 + p_{11}\bar{\theta}_{12} \quad (10.10.48)$$

or

$$\bar{\theta}_{12} = \frac{\bar{\tau}_1}{1 - p_{11}} = \frac{3.6}{1 - 0.8} = 18. \quad (10.10.49)$$

From Equation 10.10.46,

$$\overline{\theta_{12}^2} = \overline{\tau_1^2} + p_{11}(2\bar{\tau}_{11}\bar{\theta}_{12} + \overline{\theta_{12}^2}) \quad (10.10.50)$$

or

$$\overline{\theta_{12}^2} = \frac{1}{1 - p_{11}}[\overline{\tau_1^2} + 2p_{11}\bar{\tau}_{11}\bar{\theta}_{12}]$$

$$= \frac{1}{1 - 0.8}[25.2 + 2(0.8)(3)(18)]$$

$$= 558. \quad (10.10.51)$$

These results for $\bar{\theta}_{12}$ and $\overline{\theta_{12}^2}$ agree with those of Equation 10.8.14 which were obtained by analyzing this first passage time problem as a transient process.

10.11 STATE OCCUPANCIES

Let $\nu_{ij}(n)$ be the number of times that a discrete-time semi-Markov process enters state j through time n given that it entered state i at time zero. When $i = j$ we shall not count the initial occupancy at time zero in computing $\nu_{ij}(n)$. We call $\nu_{ij}(n)$ the occupancy of state j through time n for a starting state i. The state occupancy $\nu_{ij}(n)$ is a random variable with mean $\bar{\nu}_{ij}(n)$, second moment $\overline{\nu_{ij}^2}(n)$, and variance $\check{\nu}_{ij}(n)$. However, let us begin by considering its probability distribution $\omega_{ij}(\cdot\,|n)$. The quantity $\omega_{ij}(k|n)$ is the probability that a process entering state i at time zero will enter state j on k occasions in the time period $(0, n)$,

$$\omega_{ij}(k|n) = \mathscr{P}\{\nu_{ij}(n) = k\}. \tag{10.11.1}$$

We can write a recursive relation for the state occupancy probability distribution in the form,

$$\begin{aligned}\omega_{ij}(k|n) &= \sum_{\substack{r=1\\ r\neq j}}^{N} \sum_{m=0}^{n} p_{ir}h_{ir}(m)\omega_{rj}(k|n-m) \\ &\quad + \sum_{m=0}^{n} p_{ij}h_{ij}(m)\omega_{jj}(k-1|n-m) + \delta(k)\,{}^{>}w_i(n) \\ &\qquad i = 1, 2, \ldots, N;\ k = 0, 1, 2, \ldots \\ &\qquad j = 1, 2, \ldots, N;\ n = 0, 1, 2, \ldots\,.\end{aligned} \tag{10.11.2}$$

This equation states that you can obtain k occupancies of state j through time n (1) by having the first transition out of state i to a state r not equal to j at time m and then having k occupancies of state j in the remaining time $n - m$, (2) by having the first transition out of state i directly to state j at time m and then having $k - 1$ occupancies of state j in the remaining time $n - m$, and (3), when $k = 0$, by having the first transition out of state i occur after time n. The probabilities of these cases are summed over appropriate destination states r and times m. Equation 10.11.2 thus is concerned basically with the nature of the first transition out of state i. This recursive relation is a very practical method for computing the state occupancy probability distributions.

Transform Relations

We define a double geometric transform $\omega_{ij}{}^{gg}(y|z)$ of $\omega_{ij}(k|n)$ and write Equation 10.11.2 in the transform domain as

$$\omega_{ij}{}^{gg}(y|z) = \sum_{\substack{r=1 \\ r \neq j}}^{N} p_{ir} h_{ir}{}^{g}(z) \omega_{rj}{}^{gg}(y|z) + y p_{ij} h_{ij}{}^{g}(z) \omega_{jj}{}^{gg}(y|z) + {}^{>}w_i{}^{g}(z)$$

$$= \sum_{r=1}^{N} p_{ir} h_{ir}{}^{g}(z) \omega_{rj}{}^{gg}(y|z) - (1 - y) p_{ij} h_{ij}{}^{g}(z) \omega_{jj}{}^{gg}(y|z) + {}^{>}w_i{}^{g}(z). \tag{10.11.3}$$

By writing $\Omega^{gg}(y|z)$ as the matrix whose elements are $\omega_{ij}{}^{gg}(y|z)$ we produce

$$\Omega^{gg}(y|z) = [P \,\square\, H^{g}(z)]\Omega^{gg}(y|z) - (1 - y)[P \,\square\, H^{g}(z)][\Omega^{gg}(y|z) \,\square\, I] + {}^{>}W^{g}(z)U$$

$$= C^{g}(z)\Omega^{gg}(y|z) - (1 - y)C^{g}(z)[\Omega^{gg}(y|z) \,\square\, I] + {}^{>}W^{g}(z)U \tag{10.11.4}$$

or

$$[I - C^{g}(z)]\Omega^{gg}(y|z) + (1 - y)C^{g}(z)[\Omega^{gg}(y|z) \,\square\, I] = {}^{>}W^{g}(z)U. \tag{10.11.5}$$

We premultiply this equation by the matrix $[I - C^{g}(z)]^{-1}$ to obtain

$$\Omega^{gg}(y|z) + (1 - y)[I - C^{g}(z)]^{-1}C^{g}(z)[\Omega^{gg}(y|z) \,\square\, I]$$

$$= [I - C^{g}(z)]^{-1}\,{}^{>}W^{g}(z)U = \Phi^{g}(z)U = \frac{1}{1 - z}U. \tag{10.11.6}$$

Here we have used the basic relation for $\Phi^{g}(z)$ and the fact that its rows sum to $1/(1 - z)$.

In the appendix we find the solution of a certain matrix equation containing the $\square$ operator. Equation 10.11.6 is in this form; therefore, we can write an explicit expression for $\Omega^{gg}(y|z)$,

$$\Omega^{gg}(y|z) = \frac{1}{1 - z}U - \frac{1 - y}{1 - z}[I - C^{g}(z)]^{-1}C^{g}(z)$$

$$\times (I + (1 - y)\{[I - C^{g}(z)]^{-1}C^{g}(z)\} \,\square\, I)^{-1}$$

$$= \frac{1}{1 - z}U - \frac{1 - y}{1 - z}[I - C^{g}(z)]^{-1}C^{g}(z)$$

$$\times (yI + (1 - y)\{I + [I - C^{g}(z)]^{-1}C^{g}(z)\} \,\square\, I)^{-1}. \tag{10.11.7}$$

We now note that from Equation 10.3.9

$$I + [I - C^{g}(z)]^{-1}C^{g}(z) = [I - C^{g}(z)]^{-1}$$

and write Equation 10.11.7 as

$$\Omega^{gg}(y|z) = \frac{1}{1-z}U - \frac{1-y}{1-z}[I - C^g(z)]^{-1}C^g(z) \times (yI + (1-y)\{[I - C^g(z)]^{-1} \square I\})^{-1}. \quad (10.11.8)$$

Equation 10.11.8 provides an explicit relationship between the transforms of the state occupancy probability distributions and the core matrix of the semi-Markov process.

Relationship to First Passage Times

The state occupancy probability distributions are directly related to the first passage time probabilities by the equation

$$\omega_{ij}(k|n) = \sum_{m=0}^{n} f_{ij}(m)\omega_{jj}(k-1|n-m) + \delta(k)\,{}^{>}f_{ij}(n) \qquad \begin{matrix} i = 1, 2, \ldots, N;\ k = 0, 1, 2, \ldots \\ j = 1, 2, \ldots, N;\ n = 0, 1, 2, \ldots . \end{matrix} \quad (10.11.9)$$

We can obtain k occupancies of state j through time n by making a first passage to state j at some time m and then having $k - 1$ occupancies of state j in the remaining time $n - m$ or, when $k = 0$, by having the first passage time from i to j exceed n. We have summed the probabilities of these events over all values of m within the interval and written ${}^{>}f_{ij}(n)$ for the probability that θ_{ij} will exceed n. Equation 10.11.9 provides a practical method for computing the state occupancy probability distributions from the first passage time probability distributions.

Transform relations

The double geometric transform of Equation 10.11.9 is

$$\omega_{ij}{}^{gg}(y|z) = yf_{ij}{}^{g}(z)\omega_{jj}{}^{gg}(y|z) + {}^{>}f_{ij}{}^{g}(z), \quad (10.11.10)$$

or in matrix form,

$$\Omega^{gg}(y|z) = yF^g(z)[\Omega^{gg}(y|z) \square I] + {}^{>}F^g(z). \quad (10.11.11)$$

However, this equation does not provide an explicit expression for $\Omega^{gg}(y|z)$ in terms of $F^g(z)$.

To obtain this explicit relationship, we write Equation 10.11.10 when $i = j$,

$$\omega_{jj}{}^{gg}(y|z) = yf_{jj}{}^{g}(z)\omega_{jj}{}^{gg}(y|z) + {}^{>}f_{jj}{}^{g}(z) \quad (10.11.12)$$

or

$$\omega_{jj}{}^{gg}(y|z) = \frac{{}^{>}f_{jj}{}^{g}(z)}{1 - yf_{jj}{}^{g}(z)}. \quad (10.11.13)$$

Renewal interpretation

Equation 10.11.13 is an especially interesting result. Referring to Equation 7.2.4, we see that we can interpret Equation 10.11.13 as the equation for the transform of the number of renewals k that will occur in a period n when the lifetime distribution is $f_{jj}(\cdot)$ and the counting of renewals begins immediately after a renewal. This recurrence time distribution for a state in a semi-Markov process plays the role of a lifetime distribution with respect to the renewals defined as occupancies of that state.

If we substitute the result of Equation 10.11.13 into Equation 10.11.10, we obtain

$$\omega_{ij}{}^{gg}(y|z) = \frac{yf_{ij}{}^{g}(z)\,{}^{>}f_{jj}{}^{g}(z)}{1 - yf_{jj}{}^{g}(z)} + {}^{>}f_{ij}{}^{g}(z) \qquad \begin{array}{l} i = 1, 2, \ldots, N \\ j = 1, 2, \ldots, N. \end{array} \tag{10.11.14}$$

This equation is analogous to Equation 7.2.33 developed for the case where the time to the first renewal is selected from a different distribution from that used to determine times between subsequent renewals. Here the occupancies of state j are the renewals; the recurrence time distribution $f_{jj}(\cdot)$ is the lifetime distribution; and $f_{ij}(\cdot)$, the first passage time distribution from state i to state j, is the distribution from which the time of the first renewal is selected. We observe once more the close relationship between Markov processes and renewal theory.

Matrix transform solution

Equation 10.11.14 provides the explicit relationship between the transforms of the state occupancy probabilities and the transforms of the first passage time probabilities that we sought. We express it in matrix form as

$$\Omega^{gg}(y|z) = yF^{g}(z)[{}^{>}F^{g}(z) \square I][I - yF^{g}(z) \square I]^{-1} + {}^{>}F^{g}(z). \tag{10.11.15}$$

However, a somewhat simpler relation can be developed by exploiting the result that

$${}^{>}f_{ij}{}^{g}(z) = \frac{1 - f_{ij}{}^{g}(z)}{1 - z} \tag{10.11.16}$$

in Equation 10.11.14,

$$\begin{aligned} \omega_{ij}{}^{gg}(y|z) &= \frac{yf_{ij}{}^{g}(z)[1 - f_{jj}{}^{g}(z)]}{[1 - yf_{jj}{}^{g}(z)](1 - z)} + \frac{1 - f_{ij}{}^{g}(z)}{1 - z} \\ &= \frac{1}{1 - z}\,\frac{yf_{ij}{}^{g}(z)[1 - f_{jj}{}^{g}(z)] + [1 - f_{ij}{}^{g}(z)][1 - yf_{jj}{}^{g}(z)]}{1 - yf_{jj}{}^{g}(z)} \\ &= \frac{1}{1 - z}\left(1 - \frac{(1 - y)f_{ij}{}^{g}(z)}{1 - yf_{jj}{}^{g}(z)}\right). \end{aligned} \tag{10.11.17}$$

Then we write this equation in matrix form as

$$\Omega^{gg}(y|z) = \frac{1}{1-z}U - \frac{1-y}{1-z}F^{g}(z)[I - yF^{g}(z) \square I]^{-1}. \qquad (10.11.18)$$

We can apply two simple checks to this result. First, the only way of having no occupancies in time n is for all first passage times to exceed n,

$$\Omega^{gg}(0|z) = \frac{1}{1-z}[U - F^{g}(z)] = {}^{>}F^{g}(z), \qquad (10.11.19)$$

which checks. Second, the chance of having some number of occupancies from 0 through infinity is 1. Therefore,

$$\Omega^{gg}(1|z) = \frac{1}{1-z}U. \qquad (10.11.20)$$

If in Equation 10.11.18 we substitute for $F^{g}(z)$ the Equation 10.10.33 giving $F^{g}(z)$ in terms of the transformed core matrix $C^{g}(z)$, then with some manipulation we obtain Equation 10.11.8 expressing $\Omega^{gg}(y|z)$ directly in terms of the transformed core matrix.

Occupancy Moments

We shall now develop expressions for the occupancy moments: $\overline{\nu_{ij}}(n)$, $\overline{\nu_{ij}^2}(n)$, and $\check{\nu}_{ij}(n)$.

Mean

We begin with the mean $\bar{\nu}_{ij}(n)$, the expected number of times that state j will be entered through time n given that the process entered state i at time zero. We obtain $\bar{\nu}_{ij}{}^{g}(z)$, the transform of $\bar{\nu}_{ij}(n)$, from

$$\bar{\nu}_{ij}{}^{g}(z) = \sum_{k=0}^{\infty} k\omega_{ij}{}^{\cdot g}(k|z) = \frac{d}{dy}\,\omega_{ij}{}^{gg}(y|z)\Big|_{y=1}. \qquad (10.11.21)$$

Since from Equation 10.11.20,

$$\omega_{ij}{}^{gg}(1|z) = \frac{1}{1-z}, \qquad (10.11.22)$$

we can make use of l'Hôpital's rule to write Equation 10.11.21 as

$$\bar{\nu}_{ij}{}^{g}(z) = \lim_{y\to 1} \frac{\dfrac{1}{1-z} - \omega_{ij}{}^{gg}(y|z)}{1-y}. \qquad (10.11.23)$$

We now define the mean occupancy matrix to be $\overline{\mathrm{N}}(n)$ with elements $\bar{\nu}_{ij}(n)$ and the transformed mean occupancy matrix to be $\overline{\mathrm{N}}^g(z)$ with elements $\bar{\nu}_{ij}{}^g(z)$. We can then write the matrix version of Equation 10.11.23 as

$$\overline{\mathrm{N}}^g(z) = \lim_{y \to 1} \frac{1}{1 - y} \left[\frac{1}{1 - z} U - \Omega^{gg}(y|z)\right]. \tag{10.11.24}$$

From Equation 10.11.8,

$$\overline{\mathrm{N}}^g(z) = \lim_{y \to 1} \frac{1}{1 - y} \Bigg[\frac{1}{1 - z} U - \frac{1}{1 - z} U + \frac{1 - y}{1 - z}$$

$$\times\ [I - C^g(z)]^{-1} C^g(z)(yI + (1 - y)\{[I - C^g(z)]^{-1} \square I\})^{-1}\Bigg]$$

$$= \frac{1}{1 - z} [I - C^g(z)]^{-1} C^g(z). \tag{10.11.25}$$

We now have a direct relationship between the transformed mean occupancy matrix and the transformed core matrix.

Recursive solution. If we rearrange Equation 10.11.25, we obtain

$$[I - C^g(z)]\overline{\mathrm{N}}^g(z) = \frac{1}{1 - z} C^g(z)$$

$$\overline{\mathrm{N}}^g(z) = C^g(z)\overline{\mathrm{N}}^g(z) + \frac{1}{1 - z} C^g(z)$$

$$= [P \square H^g(z)]\overline{\mathrm{N}}^g(z) + \frac{1}{1 - z} [P \square H^g(z)]. \tag{10.11.26}$$

In element form this equation is

$$\bar{\nu}_{ij}{}^g(z) = \sum_{r=1}^{N} p_{ir} h_{ir}{}^g(z) \bar{\nu}_{rj}{}^g(z) + \frac{1}{1 - z} p_{ij} h_{ij}{}^g(z). \tag{10.11.27}$$

After inverse geometric transformation it becomes

$$\bar{\nu}_{ij}(n) = \sum_{r=1}^{N} \sum_{m=0}^{n} p_{ir} h_{ir}(m) \bar{\nu}_{rj}(n - m) + p_{ij}\, {}^{\leq}h_{ij}(n)$$

$$= \sum_{r=1}^{N} \sum_{m=0}^{n} p_{ir} h_{ir}(m) [\bar{\nu}_{rj}(n - m) + \delta_{rj}]. \tag{10.11.28}$$

This equation provides a recursive method for computing mean occupancies. Further, it has a simple interpretation. If a process started in state i makes no transition within the interval $(0, n)$, then the contribution to the expected number of occupancies of state j is, of course, zero. But if it does make a transition to state r at time $m \leq n$ (an event with probability $p_{ir}h_{ir}(m)$), then the number of occupancies of state j will be increased by one if $r = j$, a condition represented in the equation by δ_{rj}. However, if $r \neq j$, then the expected number of occupancies of j in the remaining period $n - m$ starting in state r is $\bar{\nu}_{rj}(n - m)$. The equation shows that these contributions to the mean occupancies of state j are summed over all states r and all transition times m.

Relationship to core matrix. If we use the result of Equation 10.3.11 in Equation 10.11.25, we find

$$\overline{\mathrm{N}}^{g}(z) = \frac{1}{1 - z}([I - C^{g}(z)]^{-1} - I). \qquad (10.11.29)$$

The solution of this equation for $C^{g}(z)$ is

$$C^{g}(z) = I - [I + (1 - z)\overline{\mathrm{N}}^{g}(z)]^{-1}. \qquad (10.11.30)$$

The importance of this result is that it shows how the matrix $C^{g}(z)$ can be constructed from the matrix $\overline{\mathrm{N}}^{g}(z)$ and therefore that the transformed mean occupancy matrix $\overline{\mathrm{N}}^{g}(z)$ describes a discrete-time semi-Markov process fully as well as does the transformed core matrix $C^{g}(z)$.

Relationship to entrance probabilities. Using Equation 10.7.12 we can express $\overline{\mathrm{N}}^{g}(z)$ in terms of the entrance probabilities as

$$\overline{\mathrm{N}}^{g}(z) = \frac{1}{1 - z}([I - C^{g}(z)]^{-1} - I) = \frac{1}{1 - z}[E^{g}(z) - I]. \qquad (10.11.31)$$

This result is in full accord with Equation 5.1.19 when we realize that the present formulation does not count the original state occupancy. Equation 10.11.31 implies the recursive equation,

$$\bar{\nu}_{ij}(n) = \bar{\nu}_{ij}(n - 1) + e_{ij}(n) - \delta_{ij}\,\delta(n), \qquad (10.11.32)$$

thus showing how easy it is to construct the mean state occupancies when the entrance probabilities are known.

Second moment

An alternate and immediate method for constructing the expression for $\bar{\nu}_{ij}{}^{g}(z)$ shown in Equation 10.11.27 is to carry out the differentiation in Equation 10.11.21 using $\omega_{ij}{}^{gg}(y|z)$ as expressed in Equation 10.11.3. We shall use this method in calculating the transform of the second moment of state occupancy, $\overline{\nu_{ij}{}^{2}}{}^{g}(z)$. The relevant equation is

$$\overline{\nu_{ij}^2}{}^g(z) = \sum_{k=0}^{\infty} k^2 \omega_{ij}{}^{\cdot g}(k|z) = \frac{d^2}{dy^2}\, \omega_{ij}{}^{gg}(y|z)\Big|_{y=1} + \frac{d}{dy}\, \omega_{ij}{}^{gg}(y|z)\Big|_{y=1}$$

$$= \frac{d^2}{dy^2}\, \omega_{ij}{}^{gg}(y|z)\Big|_{y=1} + \bar{\nu}_{ij}{}^g(z). \tag{10.11.33}$$

We compute the second derivative and make use of Equation 10.11.27,

$$\frac{d^2}{dy^2}\, \omega_{ij}{}^{gg}(y|z)\Big|_{y=1} = \sum_{r=1}^{N} p_{ir}h_{ir}{}^g(z)\, \frac{d^2}{dy^2}\, \omega_{rj}{}^{gg}(y|z)\Big|_{y=1} + 2p_{ij}h_{ij}{}^g(z)\bar{\nu}_{jj}{}^g(z)$$

$$= \sum_{r=1}^{N} p_{ir}h_{ir}{}^g(z)[\overline{\nu_{rj}^2}{}^g(z) - \bar{\nu}_{rj}{}^g(z)] + 2p_{ij}h_{ij}{}^g(z)\bar{\nu}_{jj}{}^g(z)$$

$$= \sum_{r=1}^{N} p_{ir}h_{ir}{}^g(z)\overline{\nu_{rj}^2}{}^g(z) + 2p_{ij}h_{ij}{}^g(z)\bar{\nu}_{jj}{}^g(z) - \bar{\nu}_{ij}{}^g(z)$$

$$+ \frac{1}{1-z}\, p_{ij}h_{ij}{}^g(z). \tag{10.11.34}$$

Then from Equation 10.11.33,

$$\overline{\nu_{ij}^2}{}^g(z) = \sum_{r=1}^{N} p_{ir}h_{ir}{}^g(z)\overline{\nu_{rj}^2}{}^g(z) + 2p_{ij}h_{ij}{}^g(z)\bar{\nu}_{jj}{}^g(z) + \frac{1}{1-z}\, p_{ij}h_{ij}{}^g(z). \tag{10.11.35}$$

This equation can be written in recursive equation form for the purposes of calculation,

$$\overline{\nu_{ij}^2}(n) = \sum_{r=1}^{N}\sum_{m=0}^{n} p_{ir}h_{ir}(m)\overline{\nu_{rj}^2}(n-m) + 2\sum_{m=0}^{n} p_{ij}h_{ij}(m)\bar{\nu}_{jj}(n-m) + p_{ij}\,{}^{\leq}h_{ij}(n). \tag{10.11.36}$$

In calculating the second moments we make use of the means computed from Equation 10.11.28.

Matrix relations. We define $\overline{\mathrm{N}^2}{}^g(z)$ as the matrix with elements $\overline{\nu_{ij}^2}{}^g(z)$ and write Equation 10.11.35 in matrix form as

$$\overline{\mathrm{N}^2}{}^g(z) = [P \,\square\, H^g(z)]\overline{\mathrm{N}^2}{}^g(z) + 2[P \,\square\, H^g(z)][\overline{\mathrm{N}}^g(z) \,\square\, I] + \frac{1}{1-z}[P \,\square\, H^g(z)]$$

$$= C^g(z)\overline{\mathrm{N}^2}{}^g(z) + 2C^g(z)[\overline{\mathrm{N}}^g(z) \,\square\, I] + \frac{1}{1-z}\, C^g(z). \tag{10.11.37}$$

Now we solve for $\overline{N^2}{}^g(z)$,

$$\overline{N^2}{}^g(z) = [I - C^g(z)]^{-1}C^g(z)\left[2\overline{N}^g(z) \,\square\, I + \frac{1}{1-z}I\right]. \qquad (10.11.38)$$

From Equation 10.3.11,

$$N^{2g}(z) = ([I - C^g(z)]^{-1} - I)\left[2\overline{N}^g(z) \,\square\, I + \frac{1}{1-z}I\right]. \qquad (10.11.39)$$

Now we use the result of Equation 10.11.29 to obtain

$$\overline{N^2}{}^g(z) = (1 - z)\overline{N}^g(z)\left[2\overline{N}^g(z) \,\square\, I + \frac{1}{1-z}I\right]$$

$$= \overline{N}^g(z)[2(1 - z)\overline{N}^g(z) \,\square\, I + I]. \qquad (10.11.40)$$

This equation shows that the transformed matrix of second moments of state occupancies depends only on the transformed matrix of first moments. However, we proceed to another step and use Equation 10.11.31 to write Equation 10.11.40 as

$$\overline{N^2}{}^g(z) = \overline{N}^g(z)[2(E^g(z) - I) \,\square\, I + I]$$

$$= \overline{N}^g(z)[2E^g(z) \,\square\, I - I] = \overline{N}^g(z)[2[I - C^g(z)]^{-1} \,\square\, I - I]. \quad (10.11.41)$$

Equations 10.11.31 and 10.11.41 show how both $\overline{N}^g(z)$ and $\overline{N^2}{}^g(z)$ can be obtained from $E^g(z)$, the matrix of transformed entrance probabilities. Equation 10.11.41 is analogous to Equation 5.1.43 for the basic Markov process.

Occupancies and tagging

An interesting relationship exists between the mean state occupancies described by $\overline{N}^g(z)$ in Equation 10.11.25 and the matrix $K^g(z)$ in Equation 10.6.17. If we form $\overline{N}^g(z)\mathbf{s}$, we obtain the column vector

$$\overline{N}^g(z)\mathbf{s} = \frac{1}{1-z}[I - C^g(z)]^{-1}C^g(z)\mathbf{s}. \qquad (10.11.42)$$

Since we have summed over all ending states j, the ith element of this vector is just the transform of the expected number of times all states will be visited through time n if the process starts in state i at time zero. As we found in developing Equation 10.6.23, the ith element of the column vector $K^g(z)\mathbf{s}$ is the expected number of transitions the process makes through time n given only that it starts in state i at time zero. Since every state occupancy corresponds to a transition, clearly

$$\overline{N}^g(z)\mathbf{s} = K^g(z)\mathbf{s}, \qquad (10.11.43)$$

a result confirmed by comparing Equation 10.6.23 with Equation 10.11.42. Note, however, that

$$\overline{N^2}{}^g(z)\mathbf{s} \neq K^{2g}(z)\mathbf{s}, \qquad (10.11.44)$$

where $\overline{N^2}^g(z)$ and $K^{2g}(z)$s are given by Equations 10.11.41 and 10.6.27. There is, of course, no reason why the quantities in Equation 10.11.44 should be equal because the first represents the sum of the squares while the second represents the square of the sum.

Occupancies in transient chains

An important special case of our results for the occupancy moments occurs when we study the states in a transient chain. For any state in such a chain, both the mean and the second moment of the number of occupancies in an infinite number of transitions will be finite. If we define $\overline{N}$ and $\overline{N^2}$ as the matrices of means and second moments of occupancies for a set of transient states in an infinite number of transitions, then these matrices are related to those we have developed above by

$$\overline{N} = \lim_{n\to\infty} N(n) = \lim_{z\to 1} (1 - z)\overline{N}^g(z) = \lim_{z\to 1} [E^g(z) - I] = E^g(1) - I \quad (10.11.45)$$

and

$$\overline{N^2} = \lim_{n\to\infty} \overline{N^2}(n) = \lim_{z\to 1} (1 - z)\overline{N^2}^g(z) = \lim_{z\to 1} (1 - z)N^g(z)[2E^g(z) \square I - I]$$
$$= \overline{N}[2E^g(1) \square I - I]. \quad (10.11.46)$$

We must remember that these matrices are defined only for the states in some transient chain. Note, however, that $E^g(1)$ is all that we must calculate to determine $\overline{N}$ and $\overline{N^2}$. Since $e_{ij}^g(1)$ is the transmission of the transition diagram of the imbedded Markov process from state i to state j, our results are simple indeed. Formally,

$$E^g(1) = [I - P]^{-1} \quad (10.11.47)$$

where P is the transition probability matrix for this transient chain. Then

$$\overline{N} = [I - P]^{-1} - I. \quad (10.11.48)$$

Note that this equation differs from Equation 10.8.21 both because we are measuring entrances to a state rather than time spent in a state and because we are not counting the original occupancy.

The car rental example. We can illustrate these results for the transient process shown in Figure 10.8.5. We find

$$e_{11}^g(1) = \vec{t}_{11} = \frac{1}{1 - (4/5)} = 5. \quad (10.11.49)$$

Then from Equation 10.11.45,

$$\bar{\nu}_{11} = e_{11}^g(1) - 1 = 4, \quad (10.11.50)$$

showing that the mean number of times state 1 will be entered, excluding its original occupancy, is 4. From Equation 10.11.46 we compute

$$\overline{\nu_{11}^2} = \bar{\nu}_{11}(2e_{11}{}^g(1) - 1) = 4(2\cdot 5 - 1) = 36, \tag{10.11.51}$$

and then calculate the variance of the number of state occupancies of state 1,

$$\overset{\vee}{\nu}_{11} = \overline{\nu_{11}^2} - \bar{\nu}_{11}{}^2 = 36 - (4)^2 = 20. \tag{10.11.52}$$

This variance agrees with the result of Equation 10.8.11 since the variance is unaffected by whether or not we count the original state occupancy.

Relationship of Occupancy Moments to First Passage Time Moments

We can find interesting relationships between the state occupancy moments and the first passage time moments.

Mean

If we substitute the result of Equation 10.11.18 into Equation 10.11.24, we obtain

$$\begin{aligned}\overline{\mathrm{N}}^g(z) &= \lim_{y\to 1}\frac{1}{1-y}\left[\frac{1}{1-z}U - \Omega^{gg}(y|z)\right]\\ &= \lim_{y\to 1}\frac{1}{1-y}\left\{\frac{1}{1-z}U - \frac{1}{1-z}U + \frac{1-y}{1-z}F^g(z)[I - yF^g(z)\,\square\, I]^{-1}\right\}\\ &= \frac{1}{1-z}F^g(z)[I - F^g(z)\,\square\, I]^{-1}.\end{aligned} \tag{10.11.53}$$

In elemental form this equation is

$$\bar{\nu}_{ij}{}^g(z) = \frac{\dfrac{1}{1-z}f_{ij}{}^g(z)}{1 - f_{jj}{}^g(z)} \tag{10.11.54}$$

or

$$\bar{\nu}_{ij}{}^g(z) = \bar{\nu}_{ij}{}^g(z)f_{jj}{}^g(z) + \frac{1}{1-z}f_{ij}{}^g(z). \tag{10.11.55}$$

Inverse geometric transformation produces a recursive equation suitable for calculating the mean state occupancies from the first passage time probabilities,

$$\bar{\nu}_{ij}(n) = \sum_{m=0}^{n}\bar{\nu}_{ij}(m)f_{jj}(n-m) + {}^{\leq}f_{ij}(n). \tag{10.11.56}$$

This form for the recursive equation has the advantage that $\bar{\nu}_{ij}(n)$ for any pair of states (i, j) can be computed without reference to all the mean occupancies for other pairs.

Renewal interpretation. Equation 10.11.54 has an important interpretation in terms of renewal processes. Comparing it with Equation 7.2.42 (Volume I) shows that Equation 10.11.54 is just the equation that gives the transform of the number of renewals in time n for a renewal process whose lifetime distribution is $f_{jj}(\cdot)$ and whose time to the first renewal is determined by $f_{ij}(\cdot)$.

An alternate recursive equation. If we write Equation 10.11.54 for $i = j$,

$$\bar{\nu}_{jj}{}^{g}(z) = \frac{\dfrac{1}{1-z} f_{jj}{}^{g}(z)}{1 - f_{jj}{}^{g}(z)}, \tag{10.11.57}$$

then from Equations 10.11.54 and 10.11.57 we observe

$$\bar{\nu}_{ij}{}^{g}(z) f_{jj}{}^{g}(z) = f_{ij}{}^{g}(z) \bar{\nu}_{jj}{}^{g}(z), \tag{10.11.58}$$

an interesting symmetry relation between the mean occupancies and the first passage time probabilities. We can use it to write Equation 10.11.55 as

$$\bar{\nu}_{ij}{}^{g}(z) = f_{ij}{}^{g}(z) \bar{\nu}_{jj}{}^{g}(z) + \frac{1}{1-z} f_{ij}{}^{g}(z) \tag{10.11.59}$$

which leads to an alternate recursive equation for $\bar{\nu}_{ij}(n)$,

$$\bar{\nu}_{ij}(n) = \sum_{m=0}^{n} f_{ij}(m) \bar{\nu}_{jj}(n-m) + {}^{\leq}f_{ij}(n). \tag{10.11.60}$$

This equation has a direct probabilistic interpretation revealed by writing it as

$$\bar{\nu}_{ij}(n) = \sum_{m=0}^{n} f_{ij}(m)[1 + \bar{\nu}_{jj}(n-m)]. \tag{10.11.61}$$

If the first passage from state i to state j occurs at time m, the mean number of times state j will be entered through time n is 1 plus the mean number of times state j will be entered in the remaining time $n - m$. The probability of a first passage from state i to state j at time n is $f_{ij}(m)$; the product of the conditional expectation and this probability must be summed over all mutually exclusive times m at which the first passage could have occurred.

An alternate method of deriving Equation 10.11.59 is to differentiate $\omega_{ij}{}^{gg}(y|z)$ in Equation 10.11.10 with respect to y and evaluate the result at $y = 1$,

$$\begin{aligned} \bar{\nu}_{ij}{}^{g}(z) &= \frac{d}{dy} \omega_{ij}{}^{gg}(y|z)\Big|_{y=1} = \frac{d}{dy} [y f_{ij}{}^{g}(z) \omega_{jj}{}^{gg}(y|z) + {}^{>}f_{ij}{}^{g}(z)]\Big|_{y=1} \\ &= \left[y f_{ij}{}^{g}(z) \frac{d}{dy} \omega_{jj}{}^{gg}(y|z) + f_{ij}{}^{g}(z) \omega_{jj}{}^{gg}(y|z) \right]\Bigg|_{y=1} \\ &= f_{ij}{}^{g}(z) \bar{\nu}_{jj}{}^{g}(z) + \frac{1}{1-z} f_{ij}{}^{g}(z). \end{aligned} \tag{10.11.62}$$

We have used Equation 10.11.20 to evaluate $\omega_{jj}{}^{gg}(1|z)$.

Second moment

To produce the transform of the second moment of the occupancies in terms of the first passage time probabilities, we use Equation 10.11.33 but this time applied to $\omega_{ij}{}^{gg}(y|z)$ from Equation 10.11.10. We obtain

$$\overline{\nu_{ij}{}^2}{}^g(z) = f_{ij}{}^g(z)\overline{\nu_{jj}{}^2}{}^g(z) + 2\bar{\nu}_{ij}{}^g(z) - \frac{1}{1-z}f_{ij}{}^g(z). \tag{10.11.63}$$

In recursive equation form we have

$$\overline{\nu_{ij}{}^2}(n) = \sum_{m=0}^{n} f_{ij}(m)\overline{\nu_{jj}{}^2}(n-m) + 2\bar{\nu}_{ij}(n) - {}^{\leq}f_{ij}(n), \tag{10.11.64}$$

where again the calculation of means must precede the calculation of second moments.

We can use Equation 10.11.63 to develop an explicit equation for $\overline{\nu_{ij}{}^2}{}^g(z)$ by first writing the equation with $i = j$,

$$\overline{\nu_{jj}{}^2}{}^g(z) = f_{jj}{}^g(z)\overline{\nu_{jj}{}^2}{}^g(z) + 2\bar{\nu}_{jj}{}^g(z) - \frac{1}{1-z}f_{jj}{}^g(z), \tag{10.11.65}$$

and then solving for $\overline{\nu_{jj}{}^2}{}^g(z)$

$$\overline{\nu_{jj}{}^2}{}^g(z) = \frac{1}{1 - f_{jj}{}^g(z)}\left[2\bar{\nu}_{jj}{}^g(z) - \frac{1}{1-z}f_{jj}{}^g(z)\right]. \tag{10.11.66}$$

When we substitute this result into Equation 10.11.63 we find

$$\overline{\nu_{ij}{}^2}{}^g(z) = \frac{f_{ij}{}^g(z)}{1 - f_{jj}{}^g(z)}\left[2\bar{\nu}_{jj}{}^g(z) - \frac{1}{1-z}f_{jj}{}^g(z)\right] + 2\bar{\nu}_{ij}{}^g(z) - \frac{1}{1-z}f_{ij}{}^g(z). \tag{10.11.67}$$

Finally, we introduce the results of Equations 10.11.54 and 10.11.57 and simplify to produce

$$\overline{\nu_{ij}{}^2}{}^g(z) = \frac{f_{ij}{}^g(z)[1 + f_{jj}{}^g(z)]}{(1-z)[1 - f_{jj}{}^g(z)]^2}. \tag{10.11.68}$$

Renewal interpretation. Equation 10.11.68 is another equation relating state occupancies to the renewal process; it is analogous to Equation 7.2.45. We could also have derived Equation 10.11.68 by applying Equation 10.11.33 directly to Equation 10.11.14. This procedure would parallel the development in Section 7.2.

Asymptotic State Occupancy Moments

We can use the interpretation of state occupancies as renewal processes to obtain expressions for the rate of growth of the state occupancy moments. We shall consider: a renewal to be an entry into state j; the lifetime distribution to be $f_{jj}(\cdot)$, the recurrence time distribution for the state; and the time to the first renewal to be $f_{ij}(\cdot)$, the first passage time distribution from state i to state j.

Mean

From Equation 7.2.68 we have

$$\bar{\nu}_{ij}(n) = \frac{1}{\bar{\theta}_{jj}} n + \frac{1}{2\bar{\theta}_{jj}} \left[1 + \frac{\overline{\theta_{jj}^2}}{\bar{\theta}_{jj}} - 2\bar{\theta}_{ij}\right] \quad \text{for large } n. \tag{10.11.69}$$

The quantities $\bar{\theta}_{jj}$ and $\overline{\theta_{jj}^2}$ are the first and second moments of the recurrence time of state j; $\bar{\theta}_{ij}$ is the mean first passage time from state i to state j. We observe that $\bar{\nu}_{ij}(n)$ grows linearly with n when n is large at a rate,

$$\lim_{n \to \infty} \frac{1}{n} \bar{\nu}_{ij}(n) = \frac{1}{\bar{\theta}_{jj}} = e_j = \frac{\pi_j}{\sum_{j=1}^{N} \pi_j \bar{\tau}_j}, \tag{10.11.70}$$

which is equal to the limiting entrance probability for the state.

Variance

We write the variance of the occupancies of state j from Equation 7.2.77,

$$\overset{\vee}{\nu}_{ij}(n) = n \frac{\overset{\vee}{\theta}_{jj}}{\bar{\theta}_{jj}^{\,3}} + \text{constant} \quad \text{for large } n, \tag{10.11.71}$$

where $\overset{\vee}{\theta}_{jj}$ is the variance of the recurrence time for state j. Thus the variance of the state occupancies also grows linearly with n for large n at a rate

$$\lim_{n \to \infty} \frac{1}{n} \overset{\vee}{\nu}_{ij}(n) = \frac{\overset{\vee}{\theta}_{jj}}{\bar{\theta}_{jj}^{\,3}}. \tag{10.11.72}$$

Equations 10.11.70 and 10.11.72 show that the asymptotic forms for state occupancy moments found in Equations 5.2.127 and 5.2.129 also apply to the discrete-time semi-Markov process.

10.12 THE GENERAL DISCRETE-TIME SEMI-MARKOV PROCESS

Occasionally the first transition that a process makes out of any state has a different destination probability and transition time probability distribution from those of future transitions. For example, the replacement parts used in a system could have a lifetime distribution different from that for original equipment. Let ${}_fp_{ij}$ and ${}_fh_{ij}(\cdot)$ be the transition probability and holding time probability distribution for the first transition out of state i. We designate the waiting time distribution for this transition as ${}_{f}w_i(\cdot)$ by analogy with our past notation for waiting times. All transitions of the process after the first are governed by the quantities p_{ij} and $h_{ij}(\cdot)$. Thus we can define a core matrix for the first transition, ${}_{f}C^g(z)$, by

$$ {}_{f}C^g(z) = {}_{f}P \,\Box\, {}_{f}H^g(z), \tag{10.12.1} $$

and use the ordinary core matrix $C^g(z)$ for all future transitions. We shall call a semi-Markov process with an arbitrary core matrix for its first transition the general discrete-time semi-Markov process.

Let us now develop the multistep transition probabilities for the process, including the feature of counting transitions. Let ${}_{f}\phi_{ij}(k|n)$ be the probability that at time n the process is in state j and has made k transitions given that it started in state i at time zero and that it uses transition probabilities ${}_{f}p_{ij}$ and holding time probabilities ${}_{f}h_{ij}(\cdot)$ for its first transition, and corresponding quantities p_{ij} and $h_{ij}(\cdot)$ for all future transitions. By the same type of reasoning used in developing Equation 10.6.2, we can write the following recursive equation for ${}_{f}\phi(k|n)$,

$$ {}_{f}\phi_{ij}(k|n) = \delta_{ij}\,\delta(k)\,{}^{>}_{f}w_i(n) + \sum_{r=1}^{N} {}_{f}p_{ir} \sum_{m=0}^{n} {}_{f}h_{ir}(m)\phi_{rj}(k-1|n-m) $$
$$ i = 1, 2, \ldots, N;\ j = 1, 2, \ldots, N \qquad k = 0, 1, 2, \ldots;\ n = 0, 1, 2, \ldots. \tag{10.12.2} $$

Note that the quantity on the right of this Equation is $\phi(\cdot|\cdot)$ rather than ${}_{f}\phi(\cdot|\cdot)$ because this term refers to transitions made after the first and these transitions are governed by the ordinary core matrix $C^g(z)$.

Matrix Relations

We write the double geometric transform of this equation,

$$ {}_{f}\phi_{ij}{}^{gg}(y|z) = \delta_{ij}\,{}^{>}_{f}w_i{}^{g}(z) + y \sum_{r=1}^{N} {}_{f}p_{ir}\,{}_{f}h_{ir}{}^{g}(z)\phi_{rj}{}^{gg}(y|z), \tag{10.12.3} $$

and then place it in matrix form,

$$ \begin{aligned} {}_{f}\Phi^{gg}(y|z) &= {}^{>}_{f}W^g(z) + y\,[{}_{f}P \,\Box\, {}_{f}H^g(z)]\Phi^{gg}(y|z) \\ &= {}^{>}_{f}W^g(z) + y\,{}_{f}C^g(z)\Phi^{gg}(y|z). \end{aligned} \tag{10.12.4} $$

This equation relates ${}_{f}\Phi^{gg}(y|z)$ to the $\Phi^{gg}(y|z)$ from Equation 10.6.9 and to the core matrix ${}_{f}C^g(z)$ for the first transition. The matrix ${}^{>}_{f}W^g(z)$ is, of course, a diagonal matrix whose diagonal elements are the successive row sums of ${}_{f}C^g(z)$ subtracted from one and divided by $1 - z$. If we substitute the result of Equation

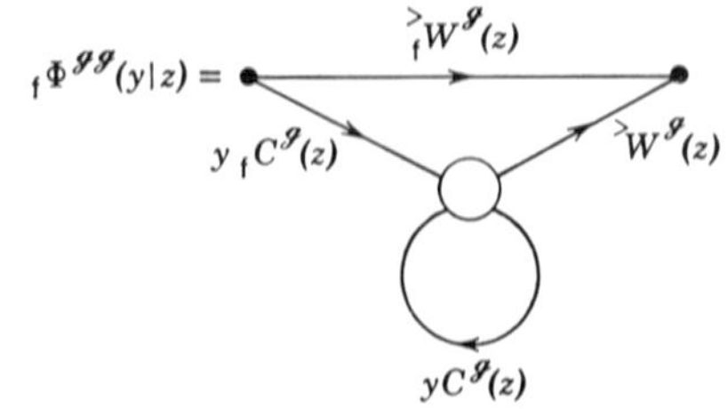

Figure 10.12.1 Matrix flow graph for interval transition probabilities of a general discrete-time semi-Markov process.

10.6.9 into Equation 10.12.4, we obtain

$$ {}_f\Phi^{gg}(y|z) = {}^>_f W^g(z) + y\,{}_f C^g(z)[I - yC^g(z)]^{-1}\,{}^> W^g(z), \qquad (10.12.5)$$

an equation which implies the matrix flow graph of Figure 10.12.1. In either form we relate ${}_f\Phi^{gg}(y|z)$ directly to the core matrices ${}_f C^g(z)$ and $C^g(z)$. If we do not wish to count transitions, then we set $y = 1$ in the flow graph and in Equation 10.12.5 to obtain

$$ {}_f\Phi^g(z) = {}_f\Phi^{gg}(1|z) = {}^>_f W^g(z) + {}_f C^g(z)[1 - C^g(z)]^{-1}\,{}^> W^g(z). \qquad (10.12.6)$$

We can confirm Equation 10.12.5 in two interesting ways. First, if ${}_f C^g(z) = C^g(z)$ so that even the first transition is governed by $C^g(z)$, then the properties of the core matrix show that Equation 10.12.5 reduces to Equation 10.6.9. Second, if there is only one state in the process and we make the identifications ${}_f C^g(z) = {}_f p^g(z)$, ${}^>_f W^g(z) = {}^>_f p^g(z)$, $C^g(z) = p^g(z)$, and ${}^> W^g(z) = {}^> p^g(z)$, then Equation 10.12.5 reduces to Equation 7.2.33 for the general renewal process as, of course, it should.

Entrance Probabilities

In some situations we might be interested in the entrance probabilities for the general discrete-time semi-Markov process. We define ${}_f e_{ij}(k|n)$ in the same way as ${}_f\phi_{ij}(k|n)$ except that it is the probability that the system enters state j at time n on its kth transition. Then by direct analogy to the procedure of Section 10.7 and what we have just done, we can write the equations

$$ {}_f e_{ij}(k|n) = \delta_{ij}\,\delta(n)\,\delta(k) + \sum_{r=1}^{N} {}_f p_{ir} \sum_{m=0}^{n} {}_f h_{ir}(m) e_{rj}(k-1|n-m)$$
$$ i = 1, 2, \ldots, N; j = 1, 2, \ldots, N \qquad k = 0, 1, 2, \ldots; n = 0, 1, 2, \ldots \qquad (10.12.7)$$

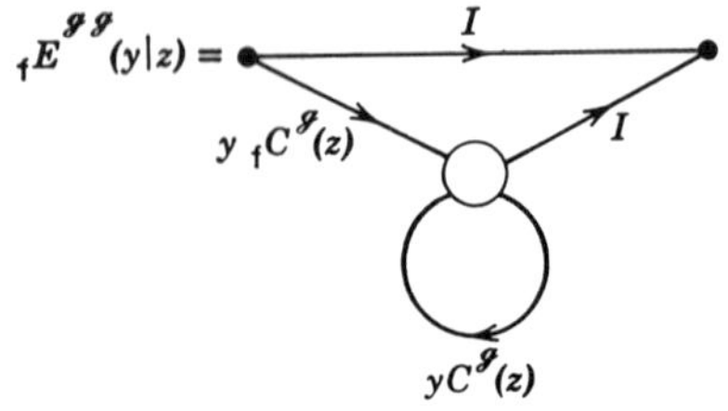

Figure 10.12.2 Matrix flow graph for entrance probabilities of a general discrete-time semi-Markov process.

$$ {}_{f}e_{ij}{}^{gg}(y|z) = \delta_{ij} + y \sum_{r=1}^{N} {}_{f}p_{ir}\; {}_{f}h_{ir}{}^{g}(z) e_{rj}{}^{gg}(y|z) \tag{10.12.8} $$

$$ {}_{f}E^{gg}(y|z) = I + y[{}_{f}P \,\square\, {}_{f}H^{g}(z)]E^{gg}(y|z) = I + y\, {}_{f}C^{g}(z)E^{gg}(y|z), \tag{10.12.9} $$

thereby relating ${}_{f}E^{gg}(y|z)$ to $E^{gg}(y|z)$ from Equation 10.7.7. The explicit form of Equation 10.12.9 in terms of the core matrix is

$$ {}_{f}E^{gg}(y|z) = I + y\, {}_{f}C^{g}(z)[I - yC^{g}(z)]^{-1}. \tag{10.12.10} $$

The corresponding flow graph appears in Figure 10.12.2. Note that in either form this result reduces to that of Equation 10.7.7 when ${}_{f}C^{g}(z) = C^{g}(z)$. By comparing Equations 10.12.5 and 10.12.10, we note that

$$ {}_{f}\Phi^{gg}(y|z) \neq {}_{f}E^{gg}(y|z) \,\square\, {}_{f}W^{g}(z), \tag{10.12.11} $$

a result that might have been tempting in view of Equation 10.7.8. If we do not count transitions, then Equation 10.12.10 becomes

$$ {}_{f}E^{g}(z) = {}_{f}E^{gg}(1|z) = I + {}_{f}C^{g}(z)[I - C^{g}(z)]^{-1}. \tag{10.12.12} $$

Moments of the General Process

We can compute the moments of the number of transitions for the general process just as we computed these moments for the basic semi-Markov process in Section 10.6. All the equations of that section apply if we add the pre-subscript f to every k and ϕ. Thus Equation 10.6.11 becomes

$$ {}_{f}\overline{k_{ij}{}^{m}}(n) = \frac{{}_{f}k_{ij}{}^{m}(n)}{{}_{f}\phi_{ij}(n)} \tag{10.12.13} $$

and shows how to compute the mth moment of the number of transitions through time n in a general semi-Markov process that begins in state i and ends in state j.

Mean

We find ${}_fK^g(z)$, the matrix of transforms of ${}_fk_{ij}(n)$ from Equation 10.6.14,

$$ {}_fK^g(z) = \frac{d}{dy}\,{}_f\Phi^{gg}(y|z)\Big|_{y=1}. \tag{10.12.14}$$

To apply this result we compute the derivative of Equation 10.12.4,

$$\frac{d}{dy}\,{}_f\Phi^{gg}(y|z) = \frac{d}{dy}\,[{}^{>}_{f}W^g(z) + y\,{}_fC^g(z)\Phi^{gg}(y|z)]$$

$$= {}_fC^g(z)\Phi^{gg}(y|z) + y\,{}_fC^g(z)\frac{d}{dy}\,\Phi^{gg}(y|z). \tag{10.12.15}$$

Then

$${}_fK^g(z) = \frac{d}{dy}\,{}_f\Phi^{gg}(y|z)\Big|_{y=1} = {}_fC^g(z)\Phi^{gg}(1|z) + {}_fC^g(z)\frac{d}{dy}\,\Phi^{gg}(y|z)\Big|_{y=1}$$

$$= {}_fC^g(z)[\Phi^g(z) + K^g(z)]. \tag{10.12.16}$$

Now we use the results of Equations 10.3.6 and 10.6.18 developed for the basic semi-Markov process to write

$${}_fK^g(z) = {}_fC^g(z)\{[I - C^g(z)]^{-1}\,{}^{>}W^g(z)$$

$$+ [I - C^g(z)]^{-1}([I - C^g(z)]^{-1} - I)\,{}^{>}W^g(z)\}$$

$$= {}_fC^g(z)[I - C^g(z)]^{-1}[I - C^g(z)]^{-1}\,{}^{>}W^g(z). \tag{10.12.17}$$

Thus we have found how to compute the matrix of transforms of ${}_fk_{ij}(n)$ necessary to evaluate ${}_f\bar{k}_{ij}(n)$, the mean number of transitions through time n for a general Markov process that starts in state i and ends in state j. We can check this result: first, when ${}_fC^g(z) = C^g(z)$, it reduces to Equation 10.6.18 for the basic semi-Markov process; second, when we consider the one-state process, the result becomes Equation 7.2.41 for the general renewal process.

Limiting behavior. We expect the matrix ${}_fK(n)$ to increase linearly with n when n is large. We find the rate by computing

$$\lim_{z\to1}(1 - z)^2\,{}_fK^g(z) = \lim_{z\to1}{}_fC^g(z)\lim_{z\to1}(1 - z)[I - C^g(z)]^{-1}$$

$$\times \lim_{z\to1}(1 - z)[I - C^g(z)]^{-1}\,{}^{>}W^g(z)$$

$$= {}_fPE\Phi, \tag{10.12.18}$$

where we have used the results of Equations 10.3.35 and 10.7.17. From the properties of E and Φ from Equations 10.3.47 and 10.7.20, we find

$${}_fPE\Phi = {}_fP\frac{1}{\bar{\tau}}\,\Phi = \frac{1}{\bar{\tau}}\,\Phi. \tag{10.12.19}$$

Therefore,

$$ {}_{\mathrm{f}}K(n) = \frac{n}{\bar{\tau}}\,\Phi + \text{constant for large } n. \tag{10.12.20} $$

Since for the general as well as the basic semi-Markov process

$$ \lim_{n\to\infty} {}_{\mathrm{f}}\Phi(n) = \Phi, \tag{10.12.21} $$

Equation 10.12.13 then shows

$$ {}_{\mathrm{f}}\bar{k}_{ij}(n) = \frac{1}{\bar{\tau}}\,n + \text{constant for large } n. \tag{10.12.22} $$

The number of transitions made through time n grows with n at an asymptotic linear rate $1/\bar{\tau}$ for a monodesmic process regardless of starting and ending state. Since $1/\bar{\tau}$ is the reciprocal of the mean time between transitions for the process, this result is hardly surprising.

Second moment

Let us now turn to the computation of the second moment of transitions in the general discrete-time semi-Markov process. We compute ${}_{\mathrm{f}}K^{2g}(z)$, the matrix of transforms of ${}_{\mathrm{f}}k_{ij}{}^{2}(n)$ from Equation 10.6.15 applied to the general process,

$$ {}_{\mathrm{f}}K^{2g}(z) = \frac{d^2}{dy^2}\,{}_{\mathrm{f}}\Phi^{gg}(y|z)\Big|_{y=1} + {}_{\mathrm{f}}K^{g}(z). \tag{10.12.23} $$

Since we have already computed the first derivative of ${}_{\mathrm{f}}\Phi^{gg}(y|z)$ with respect to y in Equation 10.12.15, we find it easy to evaluate the second derivative,

$$ \begin{aligned} \frac{d^2}{dy^2}\,{}_{\mathrm{f}}\Phi^{gg}(y|z) &= \frac{d}{dy}\,{}_{\mathrm{f}}C^{g}(z)\left[\Phi^{gg}(y|z) + y\,\frac{d}{dy}\,\Phi^{gg}(y|z)\right] \\ &= {}_{\mathrm{f}}C^{g}(z)\left[2\,\frac{d}{dy}\,\Phi^{gg}(y|z) + y\,\frac{d^2}{dy^2}\,\Phi^{gg}(y|z)\right]. \end{aligned} \tag{10.12.24} $$

At the point $y = 1$ we have

$$ \begin{aligned} \frac{d^2}{dy^2}\,{}_{\mathrm{f}}\Phi^{gg}(y|z)\Big|_{y=1} &= {}_{\mathrm{f}}C^{g}(z)\left[2\,\frac{d}{dy}\,\Phi^{gg}(y|z)\Big|_{y=1} + \frac{d^2}{dy^2}\,\Phi^{gg}(y|z)\Big|_{y=1}\right] \\ &= {}_{\mathrm{f}}C^{g}(z)[2K^{g}(z) + K^{2g}(z) - K^{g}(z)] \\ &= {}_{\mathrm{f}}C^{g}(z)[K^{2g}(z) + K^{g}(z)], \end{aligned} \tag{10.12.25} $$

where we have used Equations 10.6.14 and 10.6.15. Next we substitute the results of Equations 10.6.18 and 10.6.26,

$$ \begin{aligned} \frac{d^2}{dy^2}\,{}_{\mathrm{f}}\Phi^{gg}(y|z)\Big|_{y=1} &= {}_{\mathrm{f}}C^{g}(z)2\{[I - C^{g}(z)]^{-1}C^{g}(z)[I - C^{g}(z)]^{-1} \\ &\qquad \times [I - C^{g}(z)]^{-1}\} \,{}^{>}W^{g}(z). \end{aligned} \tag{10.12.26} $$

Equations 10.12.17 and 10.12.26 allow us to write ${}_{f}K^{2g}(z)$ from Equation 10.12.23,

$$\begin{aligned}{}_{f}K^{2g}(z) &= {}_{f}C^{g}(z)[I - C^{g}(z)]^{-1}\{2C^{g}(z)[I - C^{g}(z)]^{-1} + I\}[I - C^{g}(z)]^{-1} {}^{>}W^{g}(z) \\ &= {}_{f}C^{g}(z)[I - C^{g}(z)]^{-1}\{2[I - C^{g}(z)]^{-1} - I\}[I - C^{g}(z)]^{-1} {}^{>}W^{g}(z).\end{aligned} \tag{10.12.27}$$

We have thus obtained ${}_{f}K^{2g}(z)$ explicitly in terms of the core matrices. When ${}_{f}C^{g}(z) = C^{g}(z)$, Equation 10.12.27 becomes Equation 10.6.26. For a one-state general semi-Markov process, it reduces to Equation 7.2.44 for the general renewal process.

10.13 RANDOM STARTING

The most important case of the general discrete-time semi-Markov process arises when we enter the process at a random time. The chance that such a random entry will find the process in state i is, of course, ϕ_i, the limiting interval transition probability for state i. However, if we do find the process in state i by entering at a random time point, it will usually be very unlikely that the process has just entered state i as the result of a transition. Consequently, we have to consider the possibility that we shall begin to observe the process in, so to speak, the middle of a holding time. The probability that the process will make its next transition to each state j and the remaining holding time before that transition occurs will not be described by the quantities p_{ij} and $h_{ij}(\cdot)$, but rather by other quantities ${}_{r}p_{ij}$ and ${}_{r}h_{ij}(\cdot)$ that arise from this random manner of starting. Since all future transitions will be governed by the normal descriptors p_{ij} and $h_{ij}(\cdot)$, the analysis of this process is that of the general discrete-time semi-Markov process with ${}_{f}p_{ij} = {}_{r}p_{ij}$ and ${}_{f}h_{ij}(\cdot) = {}_{r}h_{ij}(\cdot)$.

The central problem of this section is therefore to find ${}_{r}p_{ij}$, the transition probability for the first transition, and ${}_{r}h_{ij}(\cdot)$, the holding time probability distribution for the first transition pertaining to the condition that the process was entered at a random time and observed to be in state i. When we have calculated these quantities we can find ${}_{r}w_i(\cdot)$, the waiting time probability distribution for state i under this starting condition from

$${}_{r}w_i(m) = \sum_{j=1}^{N} {}_{r}p_{ij}\, {}_{r}h_{ij}(m), \tag{10.13.1}$$

and compute its cumulative distributions in the usual way. We shall use the shortened notation that { } can represent either the probability of an event or the probability distribution of a random variable, and be similarly brief in our other definitions. Let i be the index of the present state of the system; let τ be the total

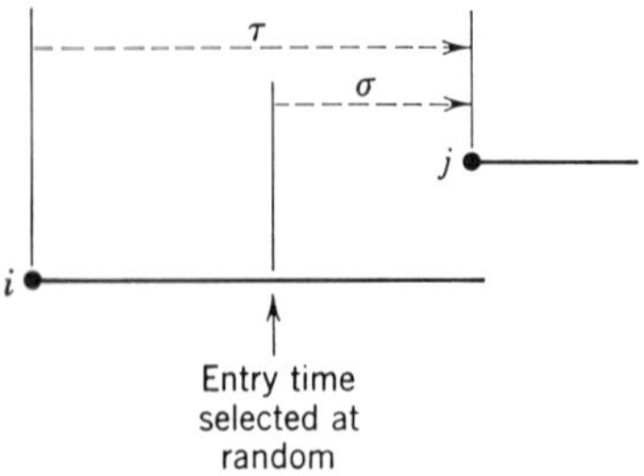

Figure 10.13.1 Diagram illustrating conditions of random entry.

length of time the system has spent and will spend in state i during its present occupancy; let σ be the portion of τ that follows the time picked at random; let R be the event that the holding time interval under examination was selected by the random entry procedure; and let j be the index of the next state to be occupied by the system. Figure 10.13.1 illustrates the relationship among these quantities. In terms of this notation we have

$$\begin{aligned} \{j|i\} &= p_{ij} & \{j|R, i\} &= {}_{r}p_{ij} \\ \{\tau|i, j\} &= h_{ij}(\tau) & \{\sigma|R, i, j\} &= {}_{r}h_{ij}(\sigma) \\ \{\tau|i\} &= w_i(\tau) & \{\sigma|R, i\} &= {}_{r}w_i(\sigma). \end{aligned} \tag{10.13.2}$$

By $\{\tau|i, j\} = h_{ij}(\tau)$, for example, we mean

$$\{\tau = m|i, j\} = \mathscr{P}\{\tau = m|i, j\} = h_{ij}(m). \tag{10.13.3}$$

We already know the quantities on the left side of Equation 10.13.2; we want to calculate those on the right.

Initial Transition Probabilities under Random Starting

We begin by using Bayes's theorem to write the joint probability of j and τ given that the process was in state i when it was entered at a random time,

$$\{j, \tau|R, i\} = \frac{\{R|\tau, i, j\}\{j, \tau|i\}}{\sum_{\tau}\sum_{j}\{R|\tau, i, j\}\{j, \tau|i\}}. \tag{10.13.4}$$

We know that $\{R|\tau, i, j\} = \alpha\tau$, where α is a constant of proportionality, because the probability that a holding time will be encountered if the process is entered at a time picked at random is proportional to its length. Then

$$\{j, \tau | R, i\} = \frac{\alpha\tau\{j, \tau|i\}}{\sum_{\tau} \alpha\tau \sum_{j} \{j, \tau|i\}} = \frac{\tau\{j, \tau|i\}}{\sum_{\tau} \tau\{\tau|i\}}$$

$$= \frac{\tau\{j, \tau|i\}}{\langle\tau|i\rangle} = \frac{\tau\{j|i\}\{\tau|i, j\}}{\langle\tau|i\rangle}, \tag{10.13.5}$$

where the symbol $\langle\ \ \rangle$ denotes the expectation of a random variable. By summing over τ, we obtain immediately

$$\{j|R, i\} = \sum_{\tau} \{j, \tau|R, i\} = \frac{\{j|i\} \sum_{\tau} \tau\{\tau|i, j\}}{\langle\tau|i\rangle}$$

$$= \{j|i\} \frac{\langle\tau|i, j\rangle}{\langle\tau|i\rangle}. \tag{10.13.6}$$

In terms of our original notation we therefore have

$${}_{\mathrm{r}}p_{ij} = p_{ij} \frac{\bar{\tau}_{ij}}{\bar{\tau}_i}, \tag{10.13.7}$$

and we have solved the problem of finding the appropriate transition probabilities for the first transition. Hence the probability that the first transition we observe from state i will be to state j is the ordinary probability of this transition multiplied by the mean holding time for the transition and divided by the mean unconditional waiting time in state i.

If we enter the process at a random time, the chance that it will be in state i is ϕ_i. If it is in state i, the chance that it will make its next transition to state j is ${}_{\mathrm{r}}p_{ij}$. Therefore if we enter the process at a random time, the probability that it will make its next transition to state j is

$$\sum_{i=1}^{N} \phi_i \, {}_{\mathrm{r}}p_{ij} = \sum_{i=1}^{N} \frac{\pi_i \bar{\tau}_i}{\bar{\tau}} \cdot p_{ij} \frac{\bar{\tau}_{ij}}{\bar{\tau}_i} = \frac{1}{\bar{\tau}} \sum_{i=1}^{N} \pi_i p_{ij} \bar{\tau}_{ij}. \tag{10.13.8}$$

This is just the limiting destination probability $\gamma_{\Sigma j}$ that we defined in Equation 10.7.35.

The car rental example

We can calculate the matrix ${}_{\mathrm{r}}P$ with elements ${}_{\mathrm{r}}p_{ij}$ very easily for the car rental example by using the results of Equations 10.1.14, 10.1.16, and 10.1.22,

$${}_{\mathrm{r}}P = \begin{bmatrix} 0.8(3/3.6) & 0.2(6/3.6) \\ 0.3(4/9.6) & 0.7(12/9.6) \end{bmatrix} = \begin{bmatrix} 2/3 & 1/3 \\ 1/8 & 7/8 \end{bmatrix}. \tag{10.13.9}$$

We already know that if we select a rented car at random, there is a probability 0.36 that it will have been rented in town 1 and a probability 0.64 that it came from town 2. Equation 10.13.9 shows that if we find that the car came from town 1, there is a probability 2/3 that it will return to town 1, and that if we find it came from town 2, there is a probability 7/8 that it will return to town 2.

Initial Holding Times under Random Starting

We now proceed to the calculation of ${}_{r}h_{ij}(\cdot)$. If we know that the process was entered at a random time, that it was in state i, and that it will make its next transition to state j, then the probability distribution of the total time the process occupies state i is designated by $\{\tau|R, i, j\}$. By the definition of conditional probability and the results of Equations 10.13.5 and 10.13.6, we find

$$\{\tau|R, i, j\} = \frac{\{j, \tau|R, i\}}{\{j|R, i\}} = \frac{\tau\{\tau|i, j\}}{\langle\tau|i, j\rangle}. \tag{10.13.10}$$

This equation shows how to calculate the probability distribution of the total time the process spends in state i. But what we want to find is $\{\sigma|R, i, j\} = {}_{r}h_{ij}(\sigma)$, the probability distribution for the remaining time the process will spend in state i given that the process will make its next transition to state j and that the entry time was selected at random. We write $\{\sigma|R, i, j\}$ in the form

$$\{\sigma|R, i, j\} = \sum_{\tau=1}^{\infty} \{\sigma|\tau, R, i, j\}\{\tau|R, i, j\}. \tag{10.13.11}$$

The quantity $\{\sigma|\tau, R, i, j\}$ is the probability that the remaining time will be equal to σ given that the total length of the holding time is τ, that the process is now in state i, and that it will make its next transition to state j. However, this last information on i and j is irrelevant. All we need to know is that the holding time was of length τ and that a time point in it was selected at random. The remaining time σ is equally likely to be any of the values $\sigma = 1$, $\sigma = 2$, through $\sigma = \tau$, or

$$\{\sigma|\tau, R, i, j\} = \frac{1}{\tau} \qquad 1 \le \sigma \le \tau. \tag{10.13.12}$$

When we substitute the results of Equations 10.13.10 and 10.13.12 into Equation 10.13.11, we obtain

$$\{\sigma|R, i, j\} = \sum_{\tau=\sigma}^{\infty} \frac{1}{\tau}\cdot\frac{\tau\{\tau|i, j\}}{\langle\tau|i, j\rangle}$$

$$= \frac{\sum_{\tau=\sigma}^{\infty} \{\tau|i, j\}}{\langle\tau|i, j\rangle}, \tag{10.13.13}$$

where the lower limit of the summation is caused by the region of definition of Equation 10.13.12. In terms of our original notation we have

$$ {}_{r}h_{ij}(\sigma) = \frac{{}^{>}h_{ij}(\sigma - 1)}{\bar{\tau}_{ij}} \tag{10.13.14} $$

or

$$ {}_{r}h_{ij}(m) = \frac{{}^{>}h_{ij}(m - 1)}{\bar{\tau}_{ij}}. \tag{10.13.15} $$

Equation 10.13.15 shows how to compute the probability distribution of the holding time to the first transition of a process entered at a random time, found to be in state i, and intending to make its next transition to state j. The probability that the holding time will equal m is the probability that the ordinary holding time for this transition will exceed $m - 1$ divided by the mean holding time of the transition. Note that if the semi-Markov process has only one state, then Equation 10.13.15 reduces to Equation 7.1.52 for the probability distribution of the time to the next renewal in a renewal process entered at a random time. We can therefore consider the present development as a more complete proof of this earlier result.

The car rental example

We compute the matrix ${}_{r}H(m)$ with elements ${}_{r}h_{ij}(m)$ for the car rental example using the results of Equations 10.1.16 and 10.1.21,

$$ {}_{r}H(m) = \begin{bmatrix} (1/3)(2/3)^{m-1} & (1/6)(5/6)^{m-1} \\ (1/4)(3/4)^{m-1} & (1/12)(11/12)^{m-1} \end{bmatrix} \qquad m = 1, 2, 3, \ldots . \tag{10.13.16} $$

By comparing this result with Equation 10.1.17 we find ${}_{r}H(m) = H(m)$, thus showing that the holding time distributions for this example are the same for the first transition as they are for all future transitions. This observation is particular rather than general; it arises from the choice of geometric holding time distributions in the original problem. If we know that a car has been rented at i and that it will be returned to j, then the probability distribution for the additional time until its return is $h_{ij}(\cdot)$ regardless of the period for which it has already been rented.

Initial Core Matrix under Random Starting

Since from Equations 10.13.7 and 10.13.15

$$ {}_{r}p_{ij}\,{}_{r}h_{ij}(m) = \frac{p_{ij}\,{}^{>}h_{ij}(m - 1)}{\bar{\tau}_{i}}, \tag{10.13.17} $$

we obtain the matrix relationship

$$ {}_{r}C(m) = {}_{r}P \,\square\, {}_{r}H(m) = M^{-1}[P \,\square\, {}^{>}H(m - 1)]. \tag{10.13.18} $$

For the car rental example we find from Equations 10.13.9 and 10.13.16,

$$ {}_{\mathrm{r}}C(m) = {}_{\mathrm{r}}P \,\square\, {}_{\mathrm{r}}H(m) = \begin{bmatrix} (2/9)(2/3)^{m-1} & (1/18)(5/6)^{m-1} \\ (1/32)(3/4)^{m-1} & (7/96)(11/12)^{m-1} \end{bmatrix} \qquad m = 1, 2, 3, \ldots . \tag{10.13.19} $$

Initial Waiting Times under Random Starting

From Equations 10.13.1 and 10.13.17 we write the unconditional waiting time probability distributions for the time to the first transition under random starting,

$$ {}_{\mathrm{r}}w_i(m) = \sum_{j=1}^{N} {}_{\mathrm{r}}p_{ij}\, {}_{\mathrm{r}}h_{ij}(m) = \frac{\sum_{j=1}^{N} p_{ij}\, {}^{>}h_{ij}(m-1)}{\bar{\tau}_i} = \frac{{}^{>}w_i(m-1)}{\bar{\tau}_i}. \tag{10.13.20} $$

Note that ${}_{\mathrm{r}}w_i(m)$ is computable for state i from the complementary cumulative waiting time distribution and mean waiting time. We place this equation in matrix form as

$$ {}_{\mathrm{r}}W(m) = M^{-1}\, {}^{>}W(m-1). \tag{10.13.21} $$

The car rental example

For the car rental example we compute ${}_{\mathrm{r}}W(m)$ by making its diagonal elements equal to the row sums of ${}_{\mathrm{r}}C(m)$ in Equation 10.13.19,

$$ {}_{\mathrm{r}}W(m) = \begin{bmatrix} (2/9)(2/3)^{m-1} + (1/18)(5/6)^{m-1} & 0 \\ 0 & (1/32)(3/4)^{m-1} + (7/96)(11/12)^{m-1} \end{bmatrix} $$

$$ m = 1, 2, 3, \ldots . \tag{10.13.22} $$

An alternative is to compute M^{-1} from Equation 10.3.22,

$$ M^{-1} = \begin{bmatrix} 1/3.6 & 0 \\ 0 & 1/9.6 \end{bmatrix} \tag{10.13.23} $$

and then combine this result with ${}^{>}W(m-1)$ from Equation 10.2.17 to produce ${}_{\mathrm{r}}W(m)$ using Equation 10.13.21.

Transform Relationships

We easily place Equations 10.13.17, 10.13.18, 10.13.20, and 10.13.21 in the transform domain as

$$ {}_{r}p_{ij}\,{}_{r}h_{ij}{}^{g}(z) = \frac{z}{\bar{\tau}_i} p_{ij}\,{}^{>}h_{ij}{}^{g}(z) = \frac{z}{\bar{\tau}_i(1-z)} p_{ij}[1 - h_{ij}{}^{g}(z)] $$

$$ = \frac{z}{\bar{\tau}_i(1-z)} [p_{ij} - p_{ij}h_{ij}{}^{g}(z)] \tag{10.13.24} $$

$$ {}_{r}C^{g}(z) = {}_{r}P \,\Box\, {}_{r}H^{g}(z) = zM^{-1}[P \,\Box\, {}^{>}H^{g}(z)] = \frac{z}{1-z} M^{-1}\{P \,\Box\, [U - H^{g}(z)]\} $$

$$ = \frac{z}{1-z} M^{-1}[P - P \,\Box\, H^{g}(z)] = \frac{z}{1-z} M^{-1}[P - C^{g}(z)] \tag{10.13.25} $$

$$ {}_{r}w_i{}^{g}(z) = \frac{z}{\bar{\tau}_i}\,{}^{>}w_i{}^{g}(z) = \frac{z}{\bar{\tau}_i(1-z)}[1 - w_i{}^{g}(z)] \tag{10.13.26} $$

and

$$ {}_{r}W^{g}(z) = zM^{-1}\,{}^{>}W^{g}(z) = \frac{z}{1-z} M^{-1}[I - W^{g}(z)]. \tag{10.13.27} $$

The transform of the matrix of complementary cumulative probability distributions for waiting time until the first transition under random starting is

$$ {}^{>}_{r}W^{g}(z) = \frac{1}{1-z}[I - {}_{r}W^{g}(z)] = \frac{1}{1-z}[I - zM^{-1}\,{}^{>}W^{g}(z)] \tag{10.13.28} $$

or

$$ {}^{>}_{r}W^{g}(z) = \frac{1}{1-z}\left\{I - \frac{z}{1-z} M^{-1}[I - W^{g}(z)]\right\}. \tag{10.13.29} $$

Note that in the case of the one-state semi-Markov process, Equations 10.13.24 and 10.13.26 reduce to Equations 7.1.53 and 7.1.54 for the renewal process entered at a random time.

Thus we have found explicit expressions for the transition probabilities and holding time distributions that govern the first transition for a process entered at a random time. Equivalently, we have found the core matrix ${}_{r}C^{g}(z)$ for this first transition. To determine further implications of random starting, all we must do is substitute these results into the equations for the general discrete-time semi-Markov process.

Interval Transition Probabilities under Random Starting

We define ${}_{r}\phi_{ij}(k|n)$ to be the probability that the process will be in state j at time n and will have made k transitions given that time zero was established by selecting a random time and that the state of the process at time zero was i. Thus ${}_{r}\phi_{ij}(k|n)$ is the interval transition probability for a process entered at a random time. The doubly transformed matrix of interval transition probabilities ${}_{r}\Phi^{gg}(y|z)$ is given by ${}_{f}\Phi^{gg}(y|z)$ for the general semi-Markov process with the transition probabilities and holding time probability distributions for the first transition given by the results for random starting that we have just developed. Thus from Equation 10.12.5 we write

$$ {}_{r}\Phi^{gg}(y|z) = {}^{>}_{r}W^{g}(z) + y\,{}_{r}C^{g}(z)[I - yC^{g}(z)]^{-1}\,{}^{>}W^{g}(z), \qquad (10.13.30) $$

which reduces to Equation 7.2.35 for the simple renewal process. Now we substitute ${}_{r}C^{g}(z)$, the core matrix for the first transition, using Equation 10.13.25,

$$ {}_{r}\Phi^{gg}(y|z) = {}^{>}_{r}W^{g}(z) + \frac{z}{1-z}M^{-1}[yP - yC^{g}(z)][I - yC^{g}(z)]^{-1}\,{}^{>}W^{g}(z). \qquad (10.13.31) $$

We can express the terms involving $C^{g}(z)$ as

$$ \begin{aligned} [yP - yC^{g}(z)][I - yC^{g}(z)]^{-1} &= [I - yC^{g}(z) - (I - yP)][I - yC^{g}(z)]^{-1} \\ &= I - (I - yP)[I - yC^{g}(z)]^{-1}. \end{aligned} \qquad (10.13.32) $$

If we use this result and Equation 10.13.28 for ${}^{>}_{r}W^{g}(z)$, we can write Equation 10.13.31 as

$$ \begin{aligned} {}_{r}\Phi^{gg}(y|z) &= \frac{1}{1-z}[I - zM^{-1}\,{}^{>}W^{g}(z)] \\ &\quad + \frac{z}{1-z}M^{-1}\{I - (I - yP)[I - yC^{g}(z)]^{-1}\}\,{}^{>}W^{g}(z) \\ &= \frac{1}{1-z}I - \frac{z}{1-z}M^{-1}(I - yP)[I - yC^{g}(z)]^{-1}\,{}^{>}W^{g}(z) \\ &= \frac{1}{1-z}I - \frac{z}{1-z}M^{-1}(I - yP)\Phi^{gg}(y|z). \end{aligned} \qquad (10.13.33) $$

This equation shows how to compute the interval transition probabilities under random starting from the ordinary interval transition probabilities.

If we do not choose to count transitions, then we compute ${}_{r}\phi_{ij}(n)$, the probability that the process will be in state j at time n given that it entered state i at time zero as the result of random starting. The transformed matrix of these quantities is

$$ {}_{r}\Phi^{g}(z) = {}_{r}\Phi^{g}(1|z) = \frac{1}{1-z}I - \frac{z}{1-z}M^{-1}(I - P)\Phi^{g}(z). \qquad (10.13.34) $$

Random starting without observation

If we are not allowed to observe the state of the process at the time-point we select as zero by the random process, we know that we should assign probability

ϕ_i to the process's being in state i. Then $\boldsymbol{\phi}$, the limiting interval transition probability row vector, shows the probabilities to assign to the entire set of states. In this situation the row vector $\boldsymbol{\phi}\,{}_{\mathrm{r}}\Phi^g(z)$ would have as its jth component the transform of the probability that the process will be in state j at time n following a time zero selected at random. From Equation 10.13.34 we compute

$$\boldsymbol{\phi}\,{}_{\mathrm{r}}\Phi^g(z) = \frac{1}{1-z}\boldsymbol{\phi} - \frac{z}{1-z}\boldsymbol{\phi}M^{-1}(I-P)\Phi^g(z). \qquad (10.13.35)$$

The two Equations 10.7.22 and 10.7.23 show that for a monodesmic process

$$\boldsymbol{\phi}M^{-1} = \mathbf{e} = \frac{1}{\bar{\tau}}\boldsymbol{\pi}. \qquad (10.13.36)$$

Therefore,

$$\boldsymbol{\phi}M^{-1}(I-P) = \frac{1}{\bar{\tau}}\boldsymbol{\pi}(I-P) = \frac{1}{\bar{\tau}}(\boldsymbol{\pi} - \boldsymbol{\pi}P) = 0, \qquad (10.13.37)$$

since $\boldsymbol{\pi}$, the limiting state probability vector of the imbedded Markov process, must satisfy $\boldsymbol{\pi} = \boldsymbol{\pi}P$. Thus we can write Equation 10.13.35 in the simple form

$$\boldsymbol{\phi}\,{}_{\mathrm{r}}\Phi^g(z) = \frac{1}{1-z}\boldsymbol{\phi}, \qquad (10.13.38)$$

with inverse transform

$$\boldsymbol{\phi}\,{}_{\mathrm{r}}\Phi(n) = \boldsymbol{\phi}, \qquad (10.13.39)$$

which shows that the probability vector $\boldsymbol{\phi}$ should be assigned as the probability of occupying each of the states for any future value of n. This result could have been anticipated, since the knowledge that we enter the process at a random time gives us absolutely no information with which to assign probabilities to each state in the future that are any different from $\boldsymbol{\phi}$.

Entrance Probabilities under Random Starting

Now let us turn to the question of entrance probabilities in a process entered at a random time. We define ${}_{\mathrm{r}}e_{ij}(k|n)$ as the probability that the process will enter state j at time n on its kth transition given that the starting point for counting both time and transitions was selected at random and that the process was in state i at that time. From Equation 10.12.10, we obtain the matrix ${}_{\mathrm{r}}E^{gg}(y|z)$ of double geometric transforms of this quantity, by substituting r for f just as we did in computing ${}_{\mathrm{r}}\Phi^{gg}(y|z)$. However, we exclude the term I because we do not want to assume that an entry occurred at the time of observation,

$${}_{\mathrm{r}}E^{gg}(y|z) = y\,{}_{\mathrm{r}}C^g(z)[I - yC^g(z)]^{-1}. \qquad (10.13.40)$$

When we substitute ${}_rC^g(z)$ from Equation 10.13.25 we find

$${}_rE^{gg}(y|z) = \frac{z}{1-z} M^{-1}[yP - yC^g(z)][I - yC^g(z)]^{-1}. \qquad (10.13.41)$$

In view of Equation 10.13.32, this equation becomes

$${}_rE^{gg}(y|z) = \frac{z}{1-z} M^{-1}\{I - (I - yP)[I - yC^g(z)]^{-1}\}$$

$$= \frac{z}{1-z} M^{-1}[I - (I - yP)E^{gg}(y|z)], \qquad (10.13.42)$$

and we have developed an expression that relates ${}_rE^{gg}(y|z)$ to $E^{gg}(y|z)$.

If we are not interested in counting transitions, we compute ${}_rE^g(z)$ from

$${}_rE^g(z) = {}_rE^{gg}(1|z) = \frac{z}{1-z} M^{-1}[I - (I - P)E^g(z)]. \qquad (10.13.43)$$

Random starting without observation

In the situation where the state entered at a random time is not disclosed to us, we may want to examine the row vector $\boldsymbol{\phi}\,{}_rE^g(z)$ whose jth component is the transform of the probability that state j will be entered at time n if time zero is selected by observing the process at a random time. We write

$$\boldsymbol{\phi}\,{}_rE^g(z) = \frac{z}{1-z}\boldsymbol{\phi}M^{-1} - \frac{z}{1-z}\boldsymbol{\phi}M^{-1}(I - P)E^g(z). \qquad (10.13.44)$$

Equations 10.13.36 and 10.13.37 then show that this equation reduces to

$$\boldsymbol{\phi}\,{}_rE^g(z) = \frac{z}{1-z}\mathbf{e}, \qquad (10.13.45)$$

with inverse transform

$$\boldsymbol{\phi}\,{}_rE(n) = \mathbf{e} \qquad n = 1, 2, 3, \ldots. \qquad (10.13.46)$$

Thus the entrance probability distribution over the states will be $\mathbf{e}$ at all future times. This result is consistent with our observation that the random method of entry provides no information about the process.

We note that as a consequence of these developments we have found a method for starting a semi-Markov process in such a way that its behavior for all future times and transitions will be indistinguishable from steady-state behavior. All we have to do is: 1) select the present state of the process according to the probability vector $\boldsymbol{\phi}$; 2) decide upon the destination state for the next transition using transition probabilities ${}_rp_{ij}$ from Equation 10.13.7; 3) obtain the time until the next transition by sampling from the holding time density functions ${}_rh_{ij}(m)$ defined by Equation

10.13.15; and 4) use the ordinary quantities p_{ij} and $h_{ij}(\cdot)$ to govern all future transitions. Knowledge of this procedure often solves the problem of getting computer simulations of semi-Markov processes off on the right foot.

Transition Moments under Random Starting

We can compute the moments of the number of transitions the process will make in a time interval after a point selected at random in time as a particular case of our results for the general discrete-time semi-Markov process. Let ${}_r\overline{k_{ij}{}^m}(n)$ be the mth moment of the number of transitions the process makes through time n given that the process was entered at a time zero picked at random, that it was in state i at time zero, and that it is in state j at time n. Following the development of Equation 10.12.13, we compute ${}_r\overline{k_{ij}{}^m}(n)$ from

$$ {}_r\overline{k_{ij}{}^m}(n) = \frac{{}_rk_{ij}{}^m(n)}{{}_r\phi_{ij}(n)}. \qquad (10.13.47)$$

We already know how to compute ${}_r\phi_{ij}(n)$ by using Equation 10.13.34. We therefore need to calculate the quantities ${}_rk_{ij}{}^m(n)$ or their matrix transforms ${}_rK^{mg}(z)$ from the results of Section 10.12.

First moments

We begin by computing ${}_rK^g(z)$ using Equation 10.12.17 with $f = r$ to show the particular type of first transition behavior implied by random starting,

$$ {}_rK^g(z) = {}_rC^g(z)[I - C^g(z)]^{-1}[I - C^g(z)]^{-1} \,{}^{>}W^g(z). \qquad (10.13.48)$$

From Equation 10.13.25 we write

$$ {}_rK^g(z) = \frac{z}{1-z} M^{-1}[P - C^g(z)][I - C^g(z)]^{-1}[I - C^g(z)]^{-1} \,{}^{>}W^g(z). \qquad (10.13.49)$$

When $y = 1$ Equation 10.13.32 shows

$$ [P - C^g(z)][I - C^g(z)]^{-1} = I - (I - P)[I - C^g(z)]^{-1}, \qquad (10.13.50)$$

therefore Equation 10.13.49 becomes

$$ \begin{aligned} {}_rK^g(z) &= \frac{z}{1-z} M^{-1}\{I - (I - P)[I - C^g(z)]^{-1}\}\{I - C^g(z)]^{-1} \,{}^{>}W^g(z) \\ &= \frac{z}{1-z} M^{-1}[I - C^g(z)]^{-1} \,{}^{>}W^g(z) \\ &\quad - \frac{z}{1-z} M^{-1}(I - P)[I - C^g(z)]^{-1}[I - C^g(z)]^{-1} \,{}^{>}W^g(z) \\ &= \frac{z}{1-z} M^{-1}\Phi^g(z) - \frac{z}{1-z} M^{-1}(I - P)E^g(z)\Phi^g(z). \end{aligned} \qquad (10.13.51)$$

We have therefore related ${}_rK^g(z)$ to quantities that have already been computed.

Random starting without observation. If we do not observe the state of the process when it is entered at a random time, then we consider the row vector $\boldsymbol{\phi}\ {}_{r}K^{mg}(z)$ whose jth component is the transform of $\sum_{i=1}^{N} \phi_i\ {}_{r}k_{ij}{}^{m}(n)$. When we divide $\sum_{i=1}^{N} \phi_i\ {}_{r}k_{ij}{}^{m}(n)$ by ϕ_j, the probability of being in state j at time n found in Equation 10.13.39 for random starting, we obtain ${}_{r}\overline{k_j{}^{m}}(n)$, the mth moment of the number of transitions made by the process through time n given that it is in state j at time n and that time zero was selected at random,

$$ {}_{r}\overline{k_j{}^{m}}(n) = \frac{\sum_{i=1}^{N} \phi_i\ {}_{r}k_{ij}{}^{m}(n)}{\phi_j}. \qquad (10.13.52) $$

We obtain the vector $\boldsymbol{\phi}\ {}_{r}K^{g}(z)$ used in computing the first moment from Equation 10.13.51 as

$$ \boldsymbol{\phi}\ {}_{r}K^{g}(z) = \frac{z}{1-z}\boldsymbol{\phi} M^{-1}\Phi^{g}(z) - \frac{z}{1-z}\boldsymbol{\phi} M^{-1}(I-P)E^{g}(z)\Phi^{g}(z). \qquad (10.13.53) $$

However, when we refer to Equations 10.13.36 and 10.13.37, we find

$$ \boldsymbol{\phi}\ {}_{r}K^{g}(z) = \frac{z}{1-z}\, \mathbf{e}\Phi^{g}(z), \qquad (10.13.54) $$

which shows that the vector $\boldsymbol{\phi}\ {}_{r}K^{g}(z)$ is computable from $\Phi^{g}(z)$.

If in addition to these considerations we do not know the state of the system at time n, then we want to calculate ${}_{r}\overline{k^{m}}(n)$, the mth moment of the number of transitions through time n if time zero is selected at random. Notice that in this computation we no longer have to condition the expectation on the occurrence of any event like the occupancy of state j at time n,

$$ {}_{r}\overline{k^{m}}(n) = \sum_{j=1}^{N}\sum_{i=1}^{N} \phi_i\ {}_{r}k_{ij}{}^{m}(n). \qquad (10.13.55) $$

The transform ${}_{r}\overline{k^{m}}{}^{g}(z)$ of ${}_{r}\overline{k^{m}}(n)$ is then

$$ {}_{r}\overline{k^{m}}{}^{g}(z) = \boldsymbol{\phi}\ {}_{r}K^{mg}(z)\mathbf{s}. \qquad (10.13.56) $$

For the mean we have

$$ {}_{r}\bar{k}^{g}(z) = \frac{z}{(1-z)^2}\,\mathbf{es}. \qquad (10.13.57) $$

From Equation 10.13.36,

$$ {}_{r}\bar{k}^{g}(z) = \frac{z}{(1-z)^2}\cdot\frac{1}{\bar{\tau}}\,\boldsymbol{\pi}\mathbf{s} = \frac{z}{(1-z)^2}\cdot\frac{1}{\bar{\tau}}\,. \qquad (10.13.58) $$

By inverse transformation we obtain

$$_r\bar{k}(n) = \frac{1}{\bar{\tau}} n \qquad n = 1, 2, 3, \ldots, \tag{10.13.59}$$

thus showing that the expected number of transitions in the n time periods following a random time entry rises linearly with n at the rate $1/\bar{\tau}$, the reciprocal of the mean time between transitions in the steady state. This result reduces to Equation 7.2.50 for the case of a one-state discrete-time semi-Markov process.

Second moments

Proceeding in an analogous way to the computation of second moments of numbers of transitions following random starting, we write $_rK^{2g}(z)$ from Equation 10.12.27,

$$_rK^{2g}(z) = {_rC^g}(z)[I - C^g(z)]^{-1}\{2[I - C^g(z)]^{-1} - I\}[I - C^g(z)]^{-1} \,{}^{>}W^g(z), \tag{10.13.60}$$

and then substitute Equation 10.13.25,

$$\begin{aligned} _rK^{2g}(z) &= \frac{z}{1 - z} M^{-1}[P - C^g(z)][I - C^g(z)]^{-1} \\ &\quad \times \{2[I - C^g(z)]^{-1} - I\}[I - C^g(z)]^{-1} \,{}^{>}W^g(z). \end{aligned} \tag{10.13.61}$$

We use Equation 10.13.50 to produce

$$\begin{aligned} _rK^{2g}(z) &= \frac{z}{1 - z} M^{-1}\{I - (I - P)[I - C^g(z)]^{-1}\} \\ &\quad \times \{2[I - C^g(z)]^{-1} - I\}[I - C^g(z)]^{-1} \,{}^{>}W^g(z) \\ &= \frac{z}{1 - z} M^{-1}\{2[I - C^g(z)]^{-1} - I\}[I - C^g(z)]^{-1} \,{}^{>}W^g(z) \\ &\quad - \frac{z}{1 - z} M^{-1}(I - P)[I - C^g(z)]^{-1}\{2[I - C^g(z)]^{-1} - I\} \\ &\quad \times [I - C^g(z)]^{-1} \,{}^{>}W^g(z) \\ &= \frac{z}{1 - z} M^{-1}[2E^g(z) - I]\Phi^g(z) \\ &\quad - \frac{z}{1 - z} M^{-1}(I - P)E^g(z)[2E^g(z) - I]\Phi^g(z). \end{aligned} \tag{10.13.62}$$

Random starting without observation. Now we compute $\phi\, {_rK^2}(z)$ for use in the determination of $_r\overline{k_j^2}(n)$ from Equation 10.13.52. We write

$$\begin{aligned} \phi\, {_rK^{2g}}(z) &= \frac{z}{1 - z} \phi M^{-1}[2E^g(z) - I]\Phi^g(z) \\ &\quad - \frac{z}{1 - z} \phi M^{-1}(I - P)E^g(z)[2E^g(z) - I]\Phi^g(z), \end{aligned} \tag{10.13.63}$$

then use Equations 10.13.36 and 10.13.37 to simplify,

$$\phi\ {}_{\mathrm{r}}K^{2g}(z) = \frac{z}{1-z}\,\mathbf{e}[2E^g(z) - I]\Phi^g(z). \qquad (10.13.64)$$

If furthermore we do not know the state of the system at time n, then we use Equation 10.13.56 to obtain ${}_{\mathrm{r}}\overline{k^{2g}}(z)$, the transform of ${}_{\mathrm{r}}\overline{k^2}(n)$. The quantity ${}_{\mathrm{r}}\overline{k^2}(n)$ is the second moment of the number of transitions in the n time periods following a random starting time. We obtain

$${}_{\mathrm{r}}\overline{k^{2g}}(z) = \phi\ {}_{\mathrm{r}}K^{2g}(z)\mathbf{s} = \frac{z}{1-z}\,\mathbf{e}[2E^g(z) - I]\Phi^g(z)\mathbf{s}$$

$$= \frac{z}{(1-z)^2}\,\mathbf{e}[2E^g(z) - I]\mathbf{s}. \qquad (10.13.65)$$

Although this result is not so simple as that for ${}_{\mathrm{r}}\overline{k^g}(z)$, it is easily computable from the entrance probabilities. If we write Equation 10.13.65 for a one-state discrete-time semi-Markov process, we find

$${}_{\mathrm{r}}\overline{k^{2g}}(z) = \frac{z}{(1-z)^2}\cdot\frac{1}{\bar{\tau}_{11}}\{2[1 - h_{11}{}^g(z)]^{-1} - 1\}, \qquad (10.13.66)$$

which is, of course, the same equation as Equation 7.2.49.

An Alternate Approach to Random Starting

The foregoing development of random starting has emphasized the idea of encountering an ongoing process without knowledge of its history. The implications of this situation for the destination and time of the next transition were derived from elementary probability theory. The reason for choosing this method of development was to demonstrate that fundamental reasoning can serve as well to produce important relationships as can the more elaborate analytical structures we have erected. However, to show that using these structures leads to the same result, let us derive by an alternate procedure the transition probabilities and holding-time probability distributions to be associated with the first transition following a time selected at random.

The viewpoint we shall take is the one used previously to derive limiting results; namely, that we have information about the process at some time in the past, but that the information has been made useless by the passage of time. We define $\zeta_{qij}(\sigma|n)$ as the probability that the process occupies state i at time n and will make its very next transition to state j at time $\sigma + n$, given that it entered state q at time 0. The event under consideration can occur only if state i is entered at some time $m \leq n$; if successor state j is selected; and if the holding time τ_{ij} in state i equals

$\sigma + n - m$. The probability of this event must be summed over all $m \leq n$. Therefore we have

$$\zeta_{qij}(\sigma|n) = \sum_{m=0}^{n} e_{qi}(m)p_{ij}h_{ij}(\sigma + n - m). \tag{10.13.67}$$

If we perform geometric transformation on n, noting, in particular, relation 8 of Table 1.5.1, we obtain

$$\begin{aligned} \zeta_{qij}^{g}(\sigma|z) &= e_{qi}^{g}(z)p_{ij}z^{-\sigma}[h_{ij}^{g}(z) - h_{ij}(0) - zh_{ij}(1) - \cdots - z^{\sigma-1}h_{ij}(\sigma - 1)] \\ &= e_{qi}^{g}(z)p_{ij}z^{-\sigma}\left[h_{ij}^{g}(z) - \sum_{m=0}^{\sigma-1} z^m h_{ij}(m)\right]. \end{aligned} \tag{10.13.68}$$

Suppose n is very large and therefore the knowledge that the process entered state q at time 0 is quite ancient. We let $\zeta_{qij}(\sigma)$ be the limiting form of $\zeta_{qij}(\sigma|n)$ corresponding to this case and determine it by applying the final value theorem for geometric transforms to Equation 10.13.68,

$$\begin{aligned} \zeta_{qij}(\sigma) &= \lim_{n\to\infty} \zeta_{qij}(\sigma|n) = \lim_{z\to 1} (1 - z)\zeta_{qij}^{g}(\sigma|z) \\ &= \lim_{z\to 1} (1 - z)e_{qi}^{g}(z)p_{ij} \lim_{z\to 1} z^{-\sigma}\left[h_{ij}^{g}(z) - \sum_{m=0}^{\sigma-1} z^m h_{ij}(m)\right] \\ &= e_{qi}p_{ij}\left[1 - \sum_{m=0}^{\sigma-1} h_{ij}(m)\right] \\ &= e_{qi}p_{ij} \, {}^{>}h_{ij}(\sigma - 1). \end{aligned} \tag{10.13.69}$$

For a monodesmic process, $e_{qi} = e_i$, regardless of q, the right-hand side becomes independent of q and we can write

$$\zeta_{ij}(\sigma) = e_i p_{ij} \, {}^{>}h_{ij}(\sigma - 1). \tag{10.13.70}$$

Here $\zeta_{ij}(\sigma)$ is the probability that if we have lost all knowledge of the process we shall observe it to be in state i and to make its next transition to state j after a time σ.

The probability we shall observe it in state i is the sum of $\zeta_{ij}(\sigma)$ over all j and σ,

$$\begin{aligned} \sum_{j=1}^{N} \sum_{\sigma=1}^{\infty} \zeta_{ij}(\sigma) &= e_i \sum_{j=1}^{N} p_{ij} \sum_{\sigma=1}^{\infty} {}^{>}h_{ij}(\sigma - 1) \\ &= e_i \sum_{j=1}^{N} p_{ij}\bar{\tau}_{ij}, \\ &= e_i\bar{\tau}_i, \end{aligned} \tag{10.13.71}$$

which, of course, is ϕ_i.

If we wish to consider the case where we have observed the process to be in state i and would like to assign the conditional probability on j and σ, we must divide the joint probability of Equation 10.13.70 by the marginal probability of Equation 10.13.71. The result is ${}_{r}c_{ij}(\sigma)$, the core transition matrix element under random starting,

$$ {}_{r}c_{ij}(\sigma) = {}_{r}p_{ij}\,{}_{r}h_{ij}(\sigma) = p_{ij}\,\frac{{}^{>}h_{ij}(\sigma - 1)}{\bar{\tau}_i}, \tag{10.13.72} $$

and we have confirmed Equation 10.13.17. Summing over σ produces the transition probability ${}_{r}p_{ij}$,

$$ \begin{aligned} {}_{r}p_{ij} &= \sum_{\sigma=1}^{\infty} {}_{r}c_{ij}(\sigma) = \frac{p_{ij}}{\bar{\tau}_i} \sum_{\sigma=1}^{\infty} {}^{>}h_{ij}(\sigma - 1) \\ &= p_{ij}\,\frac{\bar{\tau}_{ij}}{\bar{\tau}_i}, \end{aligned} \tag{10.13.73} $$

in accordance with Equation 10.13.7. Dividing Equation 10.13.72 by Equation 10.13.73 provides the holding time mass function ${}_{r}h_{ij}(\sigma)$,

$$ {}_{r}h_{ij}(\sigma) = \frac{{}^{>}h_{ij}(\sigma - 1)}{\bar{\tau}_{ij}}, \tag{10.13.74} $$

as in Equation 10.13.14. We have therefore obtained the earlier results for probabilities of destination and time of the first transition after observation begun at a random time.

10.14 BASIC MARKOVIAN EQUIVALENTS

We have now completed our investigation of the discrete-time semi-Markov process. As we have seen, the ability to assign arbitrary probability distributions for the time of each transition provides a very useful flexibility in constructing system models. We can consider all our work on the basic Markov process as a special case of the developments in this chapter.

The Car Rental Example as a Markov Process

Occasionally we encounter situations where a semi-Markov process can be represented as a basic Markov process. In fact, the car rental example we have been considering is just such a case. To represent the example as a basic Markov process we first characterize it by the flow graph of Figure 10.14.1. Note that although the semi-Markov process had 2 states, the flow graph has 6 nodes. Nodes 1 and 2 correspond to the two states of the semi-Markov process but only at the

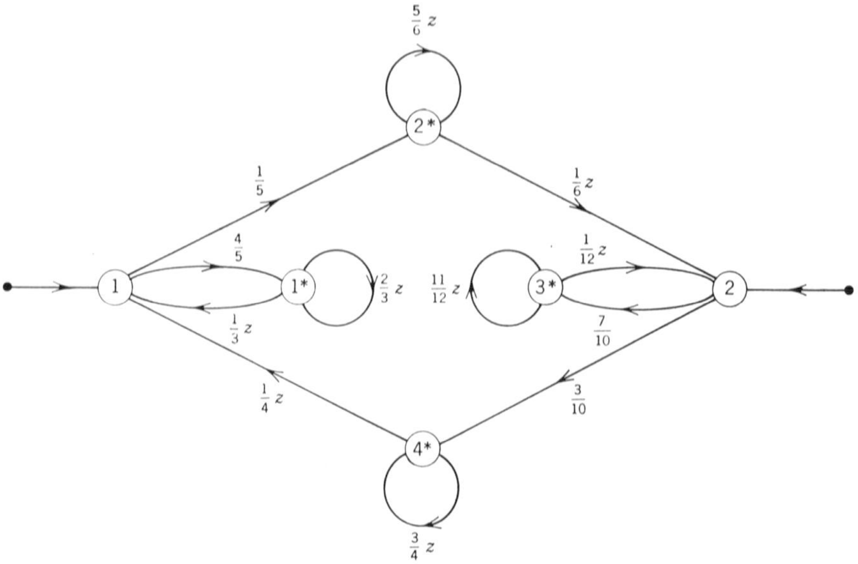

Figure 10.14.1 Another flow graph for the car rental example.

time they are first entered. Thus when state 1 is entered, we observe that the process proceeds instantly to state 1* with probability 4/5 and to state 2* with probability 1/5. The states 1* and 2* represent the holding time states for state 1 under the condition that the next transition will be, respectively, a virtual transition back to state 1 and a real transition to state 2. Thus the transmission from state 1* back to state 1 is $(1/3)z/[1 - (2/3)z]$, the transform of the holding time distribution for the virtual transition from state 1 to state 1; also, the transmission from state 2* to state 2 is $(1/6)z/[1 - (5/6)z]$, the transform of the holding time distribution for the real transition from state 1 to state 2. What we have done is to construct transient processes at nodes 1* and 2* whose transit time distributions are the appropriate holding time distributions for each transition. We see that we were able to do this only because the holding time distributions were geometric in form. Similarly, the states 3* and 4* entered from state 2 with probabilities 7/10 and 3/10 begin transient processes whose transformed transit times are $(1/12)z/[1 - (11/12)z]$ and $(1/4)z/[1 - (3/4)z]$.

Since nodes 1 and 2 in this flow graph cannot be occupied for any non-zero time, we must find the process at one of the nodes 1*, 2*, 3*, and 4*. If the process is at nodes 1* or 2*, then the process is in state 1 of the semi-Markov process; if the process is at nodes 3* or 4*, then the process is in state 2 of the semi-Markov process. Of course, to start the process in either of the semi-Markov states 1 or 2, we place it at nodes 1 or 2 and let it make the instantaneous transition to one of the other states. Thus we have for the transformed interval transition probabilities of the semi-Markov process,

$$\begin{aligned} \phi_{11}{}^{g}(z) &= \vec{t}_{11\bullet}(z) + \vec{t}_{12\bullet}(z) \qquad & \phi_{12}{}^{g}(z) &= \vec{t}_{13\bullet}(z) + \vec{t}_{14\bullet}(z) \\ \phi_{21}{}^{g}(z) &= \vec{t}_{21\bullet}(z) + \vec{t}_{22\bullet}(z) \qquad & \phi_{22}{}^{g}(z) &= \vec{t}_{23\bullet}(z) + \vec{t}_{24\bullet}(z). \end{aligned} \tag{10.14.1}$$

These equations produce the same values for the transformed interval transition probabilities that we calculated in Equation 10.3.26 and that we also obtained as the relevant transmissions of the flow graph of Figure 10.5.3.

Equivalent Markov transition probability matrix

Although the flow graph of Figure 10.14.1 is an adequate representation of the example, it is not clear whether or not it can be written as a basic Markov process because of the instantaneous transitions. Therefore we reduce it to the flow graph of Figure 10.14.2 using the residual node method of reduction described in Chapter 2. The transmissions of this graph between nodes 1 and 2 and each of the starred nodes are identical with those of the graph in Figure 10.14.1. However,

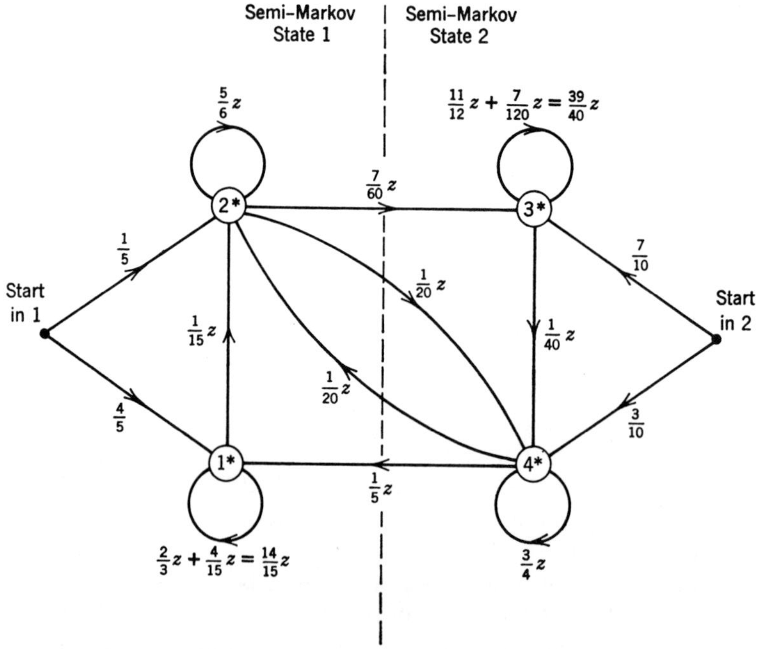

Figure 10.14.2 Flow graph for a basic Markovian equivalent of the car rental example.

now the internal structure of the graph does not contain the starting nodes 1 and 2. Furthermore, the nodes 1*, 2*, 3*, and 4* constitute a basic 4-state Markov process with transition probability matrix P^* given by

$$P^* = \begin{bmatrix} 14/15 & 1/15 & 0 & 0 \\ 0 & 5/6 & 7/60 & 1/20 \\ 0 & 0 & 39/40 & 1/40 \\ 1/5 & 1/20 & 0 & 3/4 \end{bmatrix}, \qquad (10.14.2)$$

and we have achieved our goal of representing the semi-Markov example as a Markov process. When the semi-Markov process is started in states 1 or 2, the flow graph of Figure 10.14.2 is entered at the corresponding starting nodes.

Equivalence of limiting behavior

To show the correspondence of the two representations, let us compute the limiting state probability vector $\boldsymbol{\pi}^*$ for the equivalent basic Markov process using

$$\boldsymbol{\pi}^* = \boldsymbol{\pi}^* P \qquad \text{and} \qquad \sum_{i=1}^{4} \pi_i^* = 1. \qquad (10.14.3)$$

We find

$$\boldsymbol{\pi}^* = [6/25 \quad 3/25 \quad 14/25 \quad 2/25] = [0.24 \quad 0.12 \quad 0.56 \quad 0.08] \qquad (10.14.4)$$

thus indicating, for example, that in the steady state the process will spend on the average 14/25 or 56% of its time in the process of making a virtual transition from state 2 to state 2. In fact, the entries in the vector $\boldsymbol{\pi}^*$ are just the values of the limiting destination probabilities γ_{jq} found in Equation 10.7.32. We observe that

$$\phi_1 = \pi_1^* + \pi_2^* = 9/25 = 0.36 \qquad \phi_2 = \pi_3^* + \pi_4^* = 16/25 = 0.64, \qquad (10.14.5)$$

and

$$\gamma_{\Sigma 1} = \pi_1^* + \pi_4^* = 8/25 = 0.32 \qquad \gamma_{\Sigma 2} = \pi_2^* + \pi_3^* = 17/25 = 0.68, \qquad (10.14.6)$$

thereby establishing the limiting interval transition probabilities and limiting destination probabilities we found in Equations 10.7.34 and 10.7.36.

Equivalence of first passage time

We can illustrate another interesting correspondence between the semi-Markov process and its basic Markov equivalent by considering the transient process whose flow graph appears in Figure 10.14.3. The transmission of this flow graph represents the transform of the time required for the process to reach state 2 from the moment it enters state 1, in other words, the first passage time from

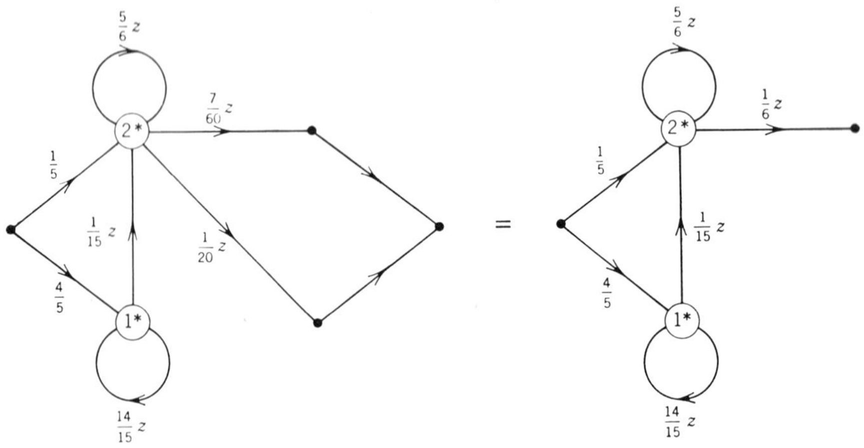

Figure 10.14.3 Flow graph for a transient process in the Markovian equivalent.

semi-Markov states 1 to 2. We find

$$\vec{t} = \frac{(1/30)z[1 - (2/3)z]}{[1 - (14/15)z][1 - (5/6)z]}, \tag{10.14.7}$$

which is, of course, just the transform found in Equation 10.8.12 when the same problem was solved as a semi-Markov rather than basic Markov transient process problem.

Tagging analysis

The basic Markov equivalent we have constructed allows us to compute process statistics measured in time. If we want to consider transitions, then we tag all branches in Figure 10.14.2 except the self-loops on nodes 1*, 2*, 3*, and 4*. Then we have a way of considering both time and number of transitions in such questions as entrance probabilities and first passage times. All of the results that we developed for the semi-Markov car rental example can therefore be verified using the basic Markov equivalent and the results of our earlier studies.

The problem of equivalent basic Markov processes is not worth pursuing further because only a rare semi-Markov process will have its holding time probability distributions expressible as basic Markov transient processes. However, since representation by an equivalent Markov process simplifies computations, we should always be alert to the possibility.

10.15 CONCLUSION

The greatest advantage of the discrete-time semi-Markov process is that the generality it provides in modeling does not cause unusual computational problems. Virtually every expression that we have developed has a simple recursive form that allows us to compute its value on a digital computer. Therefore the semi-Markov process does not exact a price in computation sufficient to outweigh its advantage of flexibility.

PROBLEMS

1. Perry Patetic is an itinerant analyst. Every time Perry enters employment on the East Coast he quits at the end of the year and obtains a new job on the West Coast. Half of Perry's West Coast jobs are of a particular type that result in Perry's obtaining new employment on the East Coast; these jobs last for only one year. The other half of Perry's West Coast jobs result in Perry's obtaining his next job also on the West Coast; 40% of these jobs last one year and 60% last two years.

a) Model Perry's travels as a two-state discrete-time semi-Markov process. Draw the flow graph for the process.

b) If Perry works on the East Coast during year zero, what is the probability that he will be working on the West Coast during year n?

c) What fraction of Perry's time will be spent on the West Coast in the long run?

d) If Perry is working on an East Coast job, what is the probability that his kth job from now will be a West Coast job?

e) If Perry is working on the East Coast in year zero, what is the probability that he will begin a new West Coast job at the beginning of year n?

f) If Perry has just started an East Coast job, what is the probability mass function for the number of years until he will begin an East Coast job again? What are the mean and variance for this first passage time?

g) What is the probability that the total duration of any one uninterrupted stay on the West Coast will be n years? What are the mean and variance of the duration of one such visit to the West Coast?

2. For the preceding problem, assume that Perry works on the East Coast during year zero.

a) What is the probability that Perry will have undertaken exactly k jobs on the West Coast by the middle of the nth year? What is the expected number of such trips?

b) What are the answers to a) if it is known that Perry is working on the West Coast during the nth year?

c) What are the answers if it is known that he is working on the East Coast during the nth year?

d) What are the answers if it is known that Perry *began* a new West Coast job at the beginning of year n?

3. Consider our traveling analyst of Problem 1. Suppose that every time Perry goes looking for a new job there is a 0.1 probability that he will give up his hectic pace and retire. If Perry starts off with an East Coast job:

a) What are the mean and variance of the number of years that Perry will stay active in his profession?

b) What are the mean and variance of the number of jobs Perry will have before he retires?

4. Use the matrix transform Equation 10.11.8 to derive an equation suitable for the recursive computation of the state occupancy probability distribution $\omega_{ij}(k|n)$ from the elements of the core matrix $c_{ij}(n)$.

5. Show that Equation 10.11.18 can be derived by writing the explicit solution for $\Omega^{gg}(y|z)$ in Equation 10.11.11 using the results for the matrix equation in the appendix.

6. Establish the recursive Equation 10.11.56 by direct argument.

7. Write the recursive equation for computing ${}_r\phi_{ij}(k|n)$ from $\phi_{ij}(k|n)$ implied by the matrix transform Equation 10.13.33.

8. Show that ${}_rp_{ij}$, the first transition probability under random starting, is related to the limiting destination probabilities γ_{ij} by the equation

$$ {}_rp_{ij} = \frac{\gamma_{ij}}{\sum_j \gamma_{ij}} . $$

9. Use Equation 10.13.42 to write a recursive equation suitable for computing the elements of ${}_rE(k|n)$ from the elements of $E(k|n)$.

10. a) Consider an arbitrary discrete-time Markov process (i.e., transitions occur at times $n = 1, 2, 3, \ldots$) with transition probability matrix P.

i) Develop the modified transition matrix P^r and the holding time matrix $H(n)$ for a semi-Markov model of this process *that allows only real transitions.*

ii) Show that the semi-Markov model gives $\Phi(n)$ values that are identical to those obtained directly from the discrete-time model.

b) Suppose the process in part a) starts in state i and we are interested in $p_i(k|n)$, the probability that the system will make k real transitions in time n. Outline a method for obtaining $p_i(k|n)$.

11. A hospital system is modeled by a four-state semi-Markov process. A patient is in state 1 when he is under intensive care and in state 2 when under intermediate care. State 3 represents the case when he is under self-care and state 4 when he is discharged (hopefully, but not necessarily, alive). The transition probability matrix P and matrix X of holding-time means and standard deviations in days in the form (mean, standard deviation) for each transition are given by:

$$ P = \begin{bmatrix} 0 & 0.8 & 0.1 & 0.1 \\ 0.2 & 0 & 0.7 & 0.1 \\ 0.1 & 0.2 & 0 & 0.7 \\ 0 & 0 & 0 & 1 \end{bmatrix} \qquad X = \begin{bmatrix} — & (5, 3) & (4, 4) & (3, 2) \\ (2, 3) & — & (6, 4) & (3, 3) \\ (3, 3) & (4, 3) & — & (10, 15) \\ — & — & — & — \end{bmatrix} $$

Find the mean and standard deviation of the number of days required to reach the discharged state from the time of entering each of the other states.

12. It is known that a certain three-state semi-Markov process has mean waiting times of $\bar{\tau}_1 = 1$, $\bar{\tau}_2 = 2$, and $\bar{\tau}_3 = 3$. If the following expected first passage times are known

$$\bar{\Theta} = \begin{bmatrix} - & 8 & 8/3 \\ 14 & - & 17/3 \\ 12 & 9 & - \end{bmatrix},$$

what are the transition probabilities of the process?

13. One possible interpretation for a semi-Markov process is the following: When the process arrives in state i, it selects its next state j according to the transition probabilities and then takes a time-interval τ_{ij} to get there, where τ_{ij} is selected from $h_{ij}(\cdot)$. If the process has been running for a long time, what fraction of its time will be spent between states i and j? Express your answer in terms of any of the basic characteristics of a semi-Markov process such as p_{ij}, $h_{ij}(\cdot)$, $\bar{\tau}_{ij}$, $\bar{\tau}_i$, π_i, etc.

14. Consider the following model of the sensory perception process of a nerve. At some time we apply a continual stimulus to the receptors (dendrites) of the nerve. The stimulated dendrites send a series of pulses along the nerve fiber (axon) to the main body of the nerve (neuron) located in the brain. The distribution of interarrival times of pulses at the neuron is given by

$$\begin{aligned} a(\ell) &= \mathscr{P}\{\text{next pulse occurs } \ell \text{ milliseconds after the last previous pulse}\} \\ &= (1/2)^{\ell} \qquad \ell = 1, 2, 3, \ldots. \end{aligned}$$

a) Show that if s milliseconds have elapsed since the last pulse, the probability that a pulse occurs ℓ seconds hence (i.e., $s + \ell$ after the previous pulse) is again given by $a(\ell)$ and is therefore independent of s.

b) Upon receipt of the first pulse, the neuron is activated to an excited state in which it remains for a period of m milliseconds with probability $r(m)$, $m = 1, 2, 3, \ldots$. While in the excited state the neuron is oblivious to incoming pulses from its dendrites. Then the neuron returns to its unexcited state. Upon receipt of the next pulse the neuron is again activated, this time for a period described by the distribution $r(m - 1)$, $m = 2, 3, 4, \ldots$; i.e., the distribution has been delayed by a millisecond and, on the average, the neuron remains activated one millisecond longer. The next time the neuron returns to its unexcited state and is reactivated by a pulse, the period of activation has the distribution $r(m - 2)$, $m > 2$. In general, the kth time the neuron is activated the period of activation has the distribution $r(m - k)$, $m > k$. If the stimulation continues long enough for the neuron to be activated K times, the neuron remains in its excited state. The stimulation is considered recognized when this Kth activation occurs.

i) If the stimulation begins at time $n = 0$ and continues indefinitely, draw the flow graph for the semi-Markov process in which there are states corresponding to *each* activation and deactivation of the neuron. Let $r^g(z)$ be the geometric transform of $r(n)$.

ii) Find the geometric transform $p^g(z)$ of the probability $p(n)$ that the stimulation is recognized for the first time by the neuron at time n.

iii) Given that the distribution $r(m)$ has mean value $\overline{m}$ and that stimulation begins at $n = 0$ and continues indefinitely, find the mean recognition time $\bar{n}$.

11 THE CONTINUOUS-TIME SEMI-MARKOV PROCESS

The discrete-time semi-Markov process we have just discussed is a convenient formulation for modeling physical systems and then computing the implications of the model. However, for certain applications and for theoretical developments we also find it worthwhile to develop the semi-Markov process model on a continuous-time basis. In the continuous-time semi-Markov process the transitions of the system can occur after any positive, not necessarily integral, time spent in a state. Or in terms of the frog pond, the jumps of the frog are not confined to any periodic time scale. The extension of our previous work to this case will be straightforward. But we shall have to increase our terminology and notation to permit discussion of this new model. In particular, we shall define and use a new transform, the exponential transform, to perform transform analysis of the continuous-time process.

11.1 THE FORMAL MODEL

The continuous-time semi-Markov process is just like the discrete-time semi-Markov process except for the domain of the holding times. The states occupied on successive transitions are still governed by the transition probabilities p_{ij} of the imbedded Markov process. However, now the time τ_{ij} that the system will hold in state i before making a transition to state j is a random variable that can take on any positive value, and not necessarily an integral value. We must now use a probability density function to describe the nature of this random variable.

The Probability Density Function

As you recall, a probability density function $f(\cdot)$ is a non-negative function with the property that its area between two arguments a and b, $b > a$, is the probability that the random variable it describes will take on a value between those arguments. Figure 11.1.1 shows a probability density function $f_x(\cdot)$ for a random variable x; the functional form of this particular density function is

$$f_x(x_0) = \lambda e^{-\lambda x_0} \qquad x_0 \geq 0. \tag{11.1.1}$$

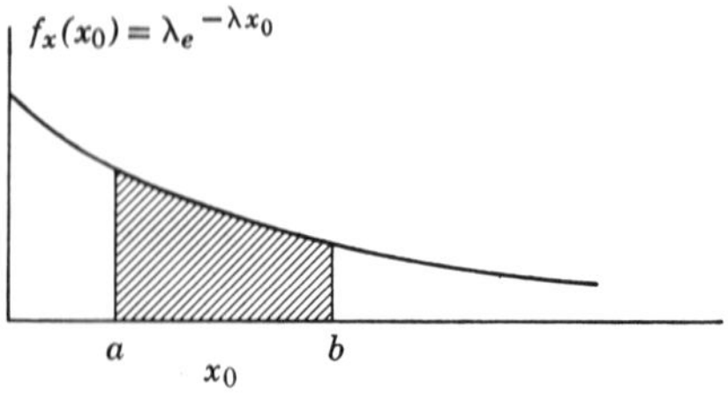

Figure 11.1.1 A density function (the exponential distribution).

We call this density function the exponential distribution. The probability that x will take on a value between a and b is the shaded area under this distribution, or

$$\mathscr{P}\{a \leq x < b\} = \int_a^b dx_0\ f_x(x_0) = \int_a^b dx_0\ \lambda e^{-\lambda x_0} = e^{-\lambda a} - e^{-\lambda b}. \quad (11.1.2)$$

The unit impulse function

We can describe the assignment of probability to any random variable including a holding time of a continuous-time semi-Markov process by constructing a probability density function. However, one situation can arise where an expansion of this concept of a density function is necessary. The situation appears when a particular value of the random variable can occur with a finite, non-zero probability. The difficulty here is that the probability density function must be infinite at such a value. We allow for this possibility by defining a unit impulse function $\delta(\cdot)$ by

$$\delta(t) = \lim_{h \to 0} \begin{Bmatrix} \dfrac{1}{h} & 0 \leq t \leq h \\ 0 & t > h \end{Bmatrix} \qquad -\infty < t < \infty. \quad (11.1.3)$$

Note that the area of the function remains one throughout the limiting process. The nature of the definition and the symbolism of the unit impulse appear graphically in Figure 11.1.2.

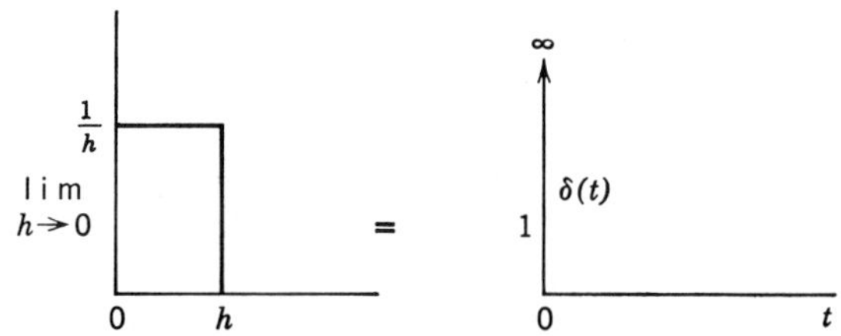

Figure 11.1.2 The definition of the unit impulse.

We shall use the same symbol $\delta(\cdot)$ for this continuous-time impulse that we used for the discrete-time impulse of Chapter 2 because the context will always make clear whether a discrete or continuous argument is to be supplied.

Suppose now that a random variable x assumes a value c with probability d. All we need do to represent this situation is to place an impulse of magnitude (area) d at the point c in the density function. The symbol for this contribution would be $d\,\delta(x_0 - c)$. Now whenever we compute the probability that the random variable x will lie in a region that includes c, we write for this probability the total area of the density function that lies over the region including, of course, the area d of the impulse.

Holding Times

Allowing probability density functions to contain impulses provides us with all the freedom we need in representing the probabilistic nature of any random variable. We can therefore allow the holding time density functions of the continuous-time semi-Markov process to contain impulses if necessary. However, there is one situation we choose to exclude: the possibility of an impulse at zero in a holding time density function. Such an impulse would mean that there was a finite, non-zero probability of a zero holding time. Since this situation leads only to difficulties in interpretation and does not add to the richness of the model, we shall assume in all our future work that there is no impulse at the origin in any holding time density function.

We shall attempt as far as possible to use the same notation for continuous-time semi-Markov processes that we used for the discrete-time version. We therefore let $h_{ij}(\cdot)$ be the holding time density function for the holding time τ_{ij}. Complete specification of the holding time behavior of the process requires an N by N matrix $H(\cdot)$ with elements $h_{ij}(\cdot)$. The kth moment $\overline{\tau_{ij}{}^k}$ of a holding time τ_{ij} is defined by

$$\overline{\tau_{ij}{}^k} = \int_0^\infty d\tau\, h_{ij}(\tau)\tau^k. \tag{11.1.4}$$

The zeroth moment is, of course, one because the area under the entire density function is one. We usually require the mean $\bar{\tau}_{ij}$, second moment $\overline{\tau_{ij}{}^2}$, and variance $\overset{\vee}{\tau}_{ij}$ defined by

$$\overset{\vee}{\tau}_{ij} = \overline{\tau_{ij}{}^2} - \bar{\tau}_{ij}{}^2. \tag{11.1.5}$$

If the holding time τ_{ij} were described by the exponential distribution of Equation 11.1.1,

$$h_{ij}(\tau) = \lambda e^{-\lambda\tau} \qquad \tau \geq 0, \tag{11.1.6}$$

then its moments would be given by

$$\bar{\tau}_{ij} = \int_0^\infty d\tau\, h_{ij}(\tau)\tau = \int_0^\infty d\tau\, (\lambda e^{-\lambda\tau})\tau = \frac{1}{\lambda} \tag{11.1.7}$$

$$\overline{\tau_{ij}^{\,2}} = \int_0^\infty d\tau\, h_{ij}(\tau)\tau^2 = \int_0^\infty d\tau\, (\lambda e^{-\lambda\tau})\tau^2 = \frac{2}{\lambda^2} \tag{11.1.8}$$

and

$$\overset{\vee}{\tau}_{ij} = \frac{2}{\lambda^2} - \left(\frac{1}{\lambda}\right)^2 = \frac{1}{\lambda^2}\cdot \tag{11.1.9}$$

We can alternately represent the probabilistic nature of a holding time by its cumulative probability distribution ${}^{\leq}h_{ij}(\cdot)$ and complementary cumulative probability distribution ${}^{>}h_{ij}(\cdot)$ defined by

$${}^{\leq}h_{ij}(t) = \mathscr{P}\{\tau_{ij} \leq t\} = \int_0^t d\tau\, h_{ij}(\tau) \tag{11.1.10}$$

and

$${}^{>}h_{ij}(t) = \mathscr{P}\{\tau_{ij} > t\} = \int_t^\infty d\tau\, h_{ij}(\tau) = 1 - {}^{\leq}h_{ij}(t). \tag{11.1.11}$$

If the holding time density function is the exponential distribution of Equation 11.1.6, then we can evaluate these two cumulative distributions by taking first $a = 0$, $b = t$, and then $a = t$, $b = \infty$ in Equation 11.1.2,

$${}^{\leq}h_{ij}(t) = 1 - e^{-\lambda t} \qquad {}^{>}h_{ij}(t) = e^{-\lambda t}. \tag{11.1.12}$$

These functions appear in Figure 11.1.3.

Note that describing the probabilistic nature of a random variable in terms of either of its cumulative distributions causes no problem when a particular value of the random variable can be assumed with a finite, non-zero probability. This situation merely requires a vertical discontinuity in both cumulative distributions at that particular value, with a magnitude equal to the probability that the value will be assumed. Thus if an impulse of area d occurs at the point c in a

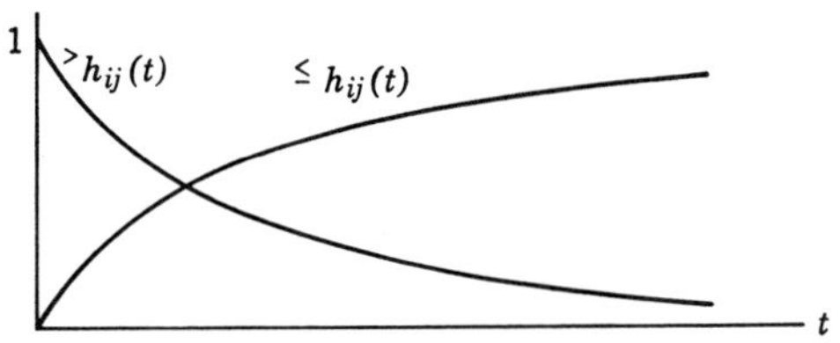

Figure 11.1.3 Cumulative distributions.

probability density function, it will require a vertical rise (fall) of d in the (complementary) cumulative probability distribution at the point c. We observe from Equations 11.1.10 and 11.1.11 that the density function is related to the cumulative probability distribution by

$$h_{ij}(t) = \frac{d}{dt}\,{}^{\leq}h_{ij}(t) = -\frac{d}{dt}\,{}^{>}h_{ij}(t), \tag{11.1.13}$$

where the dual nature of impulses in the probability density function and vertical discontinuities in the cumulative probability distributions must be remembered.

Waiting Times

We define an unconditional waiting time in state i, τ_i, just as we do for the discrete-time case. The waiting time τ_i is the time spent in state i when we do not know the successor state. Since τ_i is a continuous random variable like τ_{ij}, it must also be described by a probability density function, for which we use the symbol $w_i(\cdot)$. The waiting time density function is related to the holding time density functions by

$$w_i(\tau) = \sum_{j=1}^{N} p_{ij}h_{ij}(\tau), \tag{11.1.14}$$

where we have simply weighted the holding time density functions by the probabilities that they will occur.

The waiting time τ_i has a kth moment $\overline{\tau_i^k}$ defined by

$$\overline{\tau_i^k} = \int_0^\infty d\tau\; w_i(\tau)\tau^k. \tag{11.1.15}$$

By using Equations 11.1.4 and 11.1.14 we can express the waiting time moments in terms of the holding time moments,

$$\overline{\tau_i^k} = \int_0^\infty d\tau \sum_{j=1}^{N} p_{ij}h_{ij}(\tau)\tau^k = \sum_{j=1}^{N} p_{ij}\int_0^\infty d\tau\; h_{ij}(\tau)\tau^k = \sum_{j=1}^{N} p_{ij}\overline{\tau_{ij}^k}. \tag{11.1.16}$$

Again, we usually deal with the mean $\bar{\tau}_i$, second moment $\overline{\tau_i^2}$, and variance $\overset{v}{\tau}_i = \overline{\tau_i^2} - \bar{\tau}_i^2$ of the waiting times.

The cumulative probability distribution ${}^{\leq}w_i(\cdot)$ and the complementary cumulative probability distribution ${}^{>}w_i(\cdot)$ provide an alternate representation of the probabilistic nature of waiting times. They are given by

$${}^{\leq}w_i(t) = \mathscr{P}\{\tau_i \leq t\} = \int_0^t d\tau\; w_i(\tau) = \int_0^t d\tau \sum_{j=1}^{N} p_{ij}h_{ij}(\tau) = \sum_{j=1}^{N} p_{ij}\;{}^{\leq}h_{ij}(t) \tag{11.1.17}$$

and

$${}^{>}w_i(t) = \mathscr{P}\{\tau_i > t\} = \int_t^\infty d\tau\; w_i(\tau) = \int_t^\infty d\tau \sum_{j=1}^{N} p_{ij}h_{ij}(\tau) = \sum_{j=1}^{N} p_{ij}\;{}^{>}h_{ij}(t). \tag{11.1.18}$$

Matrix Notation

For some purposes we like to use matrices to describe all random variables in the process. In addition to $H(\cdot)$, the matrix of holding time density functions, we can define N by N matrices ${}^{\le}H(\cdot)$ and ${}^{>}H(\cdot)$ whose elements are the cumulative probabilities ${}^{\le}h_{ij}(\cdot)$ and ${}^{>}h_{ij}(\cdot)$. For convenience we define $W(\cdot)$ to be an N by N diagonal matrix whose ith diagonal element is the waiting time density function $w_i(\cdot)$. The N by N diagonal matrices ${}^{\le}W(\cdot)$ and ${}^{>}W(\cdot)$ then specify the cumulative waiting time probabilities.

11.2 THE CAR RENTAL EXAMPLE

We shall use as an example of the continuous-time semi-Markov process the two-state car rental example of Chapter 10. The only difference will be that the time for which cars are rented need no longer be an integral number of periods like days as it was before, but rather any positive length of time. We might say that the rental locations have "24-hour check-in" so that we can measure the rental duration as precisely as we like. We can consider our time unit to be 12 of the periods we used earlier for numerical convenience.

Transition Probabilities and Holding Times

The transition probability matrix is the same as before,

$$P = \begin{bmatrix} 0.8 & 0.2 \\ 0.3 & 0.7 \end{bmatrix}. \tag{11.2.1}$$

However, now we specify the holding time density functions to be the following exponential distributions:

$$\begin{aligned} h_{11}(\tau) &= 4e^{-4\tau} \quad \tau \ge 0 \qquad & h_{12}(\tau) &= 2e^{-2\tau} \quad \tau \ge 0 \\ h_{21}(\tau) &= 3e^{-3\tau} \quad \tau \ge 0 \qquad & h_{22}(\tau) &= e^{-\tau} \quad\;\; \tau \ge 0 \end{aligned} \tag{11.2.2}$$

By using the results of Equations 11.1.7, 11.1.8, and 11.1.9, we can immediately write the moments of these exponentially distributed holding times,

$$\begin{aligned} &\bar{\tau}_{11} = 1/4,\ \overline{\tau_{11}^{\,2}} = 1/8,\ \check{\tau}_{11} = 1/16 \qquad && \bar{\tau}_{12} = 1/2,\ \overline{\tau_{12}^{\,2}} = 1/2,\ \check{\tau}_{12} = 1/4 \\ &\bar{\tau}_{21} = 1/3,\ \overline{\tau_{21}^{\,2}} = 2/9,\ \check{\tau}_{21} = 1/9 \qquad && \bar{\tau}_{22} = 1,\ \overline{\tau_{22}^{\,2}} = 2,\ \check{\tau}_{22} = 1. \end{aligned} \tag{11.2.3}$$

We observe that the mean waiting times are all exactly 1/12 their corresponding values for the discrete-time case shown in Equation 10.1.16. The variances are in approximately the same relationship to each other as in the discrete-time version of the example, but they are not strictly proportional.

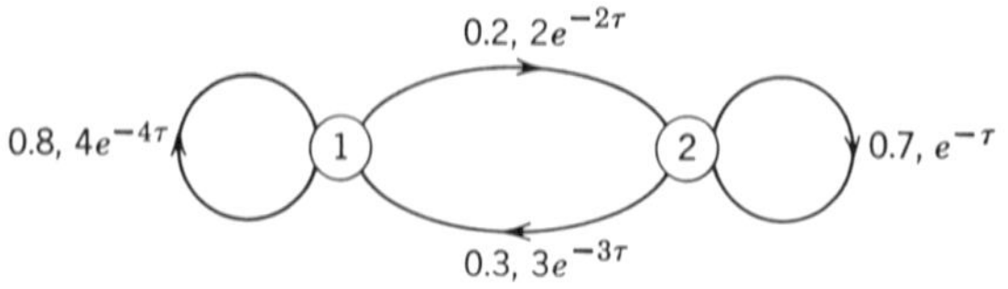

Figure 11.2.1 Transition diagram for the continuous-time car rental example: p_{ij}, $h_{ij}(\tau)$ values shown.

We can write the entire matrix of holding time density functions as

$$H(\tau) = \begin{bmatrix} 4e^{-4\tau} & 2e^{-2\tau} \\ 3e^{-3\tau} & e^{-\tau} \end{bmatrix} \qquad \tau \geq 0. \tag{11.2.4}$$

The transition probability matrix P and the holding time density function matrix $H(\tau)$ provide a complete description of the continuous-time semi-Markov process. Both of these matrices are necessary to represent the process by the transition diagram of Figure 11.2.1. Each branch in this diagram is labeled both by the transition probability and the corresponding holding time density function. As usual, the transition diagram is an important aid in visualizing the relationships of the process.

Waiting Times

We continue by using Equation 11.1.12 to construct the matrices of cumulative holding time probabilities,

$$^{\leq}H(t) = \begin{bmatrix} 1 - e^{-4t} & 1 - e^{-2t} \\ 1 - e^{-3t} & 1 - e^{-t} \end{bmatrix} \qquad ^{>}H(t) = \begin{bmatrix} e^{-4t} & e^{-2t} \\ e^{-3t} & e^{-t} \end{bmatrix}. \tag{11.2.5}$$

The waiting time density functions for the example follow from Equation 11.1.14,

$$\begin{aligned} w_1(\tau) &= p_{11}h_{11}(\tau) + p_{12}h_{12}(\tau) = 3.2e^{-4\tau} + 0.4e^{-2\tau} \\ w_2(\tau) &= p_{21}h_{21}(\tau) + p_{22}h_{22}(\tau) = 0.9e^{-3\tau} + 0.7e^{-\tau}. \end{aligned} \tag{11.2.6}$$

Equation 11.1.16 allows us to write the waiting time moments as

$$\begin{aligned} \bar{\tau}_1 &= p_{11}\bar{\tau}_{11} + p_{12}\bar{\tau}_{12} = 0.8(1/4) + 0.2(1/2) = 0.3 \\ \bar{\tau}_2 &= p_{21}\bar{\tau}_{21} + p_{22}\bar{\tau}_{22} = 0.3(1/3) + 0.7(1) = 0.8 \\ \overline{\tau_1^2} &= p_{11}\overline{\tau_{11}^2} + p_{12}\overline{\tau_{12}^2} = 0.8(1/8) + 0.2(1/2) = 0.2 \\ \overline{\tau_2^2} &= p_{21}\overline{\tau_{21}^2} + p_{22}\overline{\tau_{22}^2} = 0.3(2/9) + 0.7(2) = 1\ 7/15 = 1.467 \\ \check{\tau}_1 &= \overline{\tau_1^2} - \bar{\tau}_1^2 = 0.11 \qquad \check{\tau}_2 = \overline{\tau_2^2} - \bar{\tau}_2^2 = (62/75) = 0.827. \end{aligned} \tag{11.2.7}$$

The diagonal matrix of waiting time density functions is

$$W(\tau) = \begin{bmatrix} 3.2e^{-4\tau} + 0.4e^{-2\tau} & 0 \\ 0 & 0.9e^{-3\tau} + 0.7e^{-\tau} \end{bmatrix}. \tag{11.2.8}$$

Equations 11.1.17 and 11.1.18 then allow us to write the cumulative waiting time probability matrices as

$$\begin{aligned} {}^{\leq}W(t) &= \begin{bmatrix} 1 - 0.8e^{-4t} - 0.2e^{-2t} & 0 \\ 0 & 1 - 0.3e^{-3t} - 0.7e^{-t} \end{bmatrix} \\ {}^{>}W(t) &= \begin{bmatrix} 0.8e^{-4t} + 0.2e^{-2t} & 0 \\ 0 & 0.3e^{-3t} + 0.7e^{-t} \end{bmatrix}. \end{aligned} \tag{11.2.9}$$

We can use this example as a basis for asking all the questions in the continuous-time semi-Markov process that we asked in the discrete-time case. We shall illustrate each of them in turn.

11.3 THE INTERVAL TRANSITION PROBABILITIES

We define $\phi_{ij}(t)$ as the probability that the process will occupy state j at time t if it entered state i at time zero; we call it the interval transition probability from state i to state j in the interval $(0, t)$. By the same logic used for the discrete-time case, we have

$$\phi_{ij}(t) = \delta_{ij}\, {}^{>}w_i(t) + \sum_{k=1}^{N} p_{ik} \int_0^t d\tau\, h_{ik}(\tau)\phi_{kj}(t - \tau) \qquad \begin{matrix} i = 1, 2, \ldots, N \\ j = 1, 2, \ldots, N \\ t \geq 0 \end{matrix} \tag{11.3.1}$$

as the fundamental equation for the interval transition probabilities. In matrix form this equation becomes

$$\Phi(t) = {}^{>}W(t) + \int_0^t d\tau\, (P \,\square\, H(\tau))\Phi(t - \tau). \tag{11.3.2}$$

Once again we see the desirability of defining a core matrix $C(\tau)$ whose elements are the products of the corresponding elements in P and $H(\tau)$,

$$C(\tau) = P \,\square\, H(\tau). \tag{11.3.3}$$

The core matrix $C(\tau)$ is the basic descriptor of the continuous-time semi-Markov process. For the car rental example we write

$$C(\tau) = P \,\square\, H(\tau) = \begin{bmatrix} 3.2e^{-4\tau} & 0.4e^{-2\tau} \\ 0.9e^{-3\tau} & 0.7e^{-\tau} \end{bmatrix}. \tag{11.3.4}$$

The row sums of $C(\tau)$ are the diagonal elements of $W(\tau)$. The integral of $C(\tau)$ over all values of τ is the transition probability matrix P.

However, when we examine the form of Equation 11.3.2 we gain an appreciation for computational simplicity of the discrete-time model. Equation 11.3.2 requires us to solve an integral equation whenever we want numerical answers. Since the usual method for solving such equations is to approximate them by a discrete-time analog, we shall probably find ourselves returning to the discrete-time formulation for the computation of results in even moderately large problems.

11.4 THE EXPONENTIAL TRANSFORM

The geometric transform enabled us to represent in a scalar function vectors with a countably infinite number of components. The question we face now is how to represent a function like that shown in Figure 11.4.1 in terms of a scalar function. We can think of the continuous function in Figure 11.4.1 as a vector with a noncountably infinite number of components, one for every real number between 0 and ∞, and zero for negative arguments. The transform that will do the job of representing this vector in most cases is the exponential transform. If we transform a function $f(\cdot)$ by an exponential transformation, we denote its transform by $f^e(s)$ and define it by

$$f^e(s) = \int_0^\infty dt\, f(t)e^{-st}. \tag{11.4.1}$$

Thus exponential transformation corresponds to weighting the continuous function by an exponential function and then integrating to find the resulting area. The geometric transformation required weighting the discrete function by a geometric sequence and then summing the result. The transform variable for the exponential transform is s rather than z. Since exponential functions and geometric sequences have much in common, there is great similarity between exponential and geometric transforms.

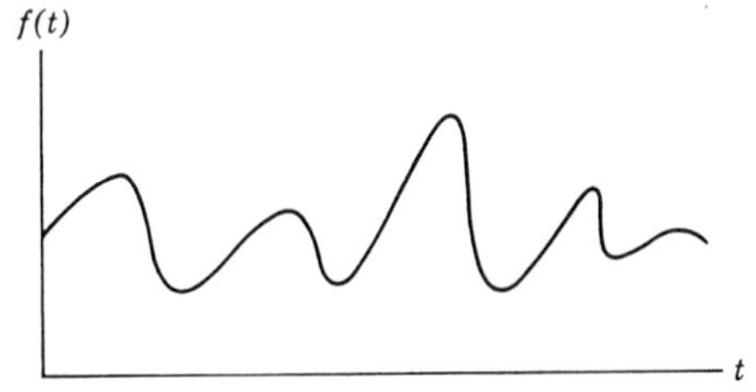

Figure 11.4.1 An unusual vector.

An Exponential Transform Table

Table 11.4.1 is a table of transform pairs for the exponential transform that is completely analogous to Table 1.5.1 for the geometric transform.

Basic relations

The first relation is the transform definition. The second relation follows directly from the definition—it states that the transform of the unit impulse is one.

Table 11.4.1 A Table of Exponential Transforms

	Continuous Function		Exponential Transform
1	$f(t)$		$f^e(s) = \int_0^\infty dt\, f(t)e^{-st}$
2	$\delta(t)$	Unit Impulse	1
3	$u(t) = 1$	Unit Step	$\frac{1}{s}$
4	$af(t)$	a is a constant	$af^e(s)$
5	$f_1(t) + f_2(t)$		$f_1^e(s) + f_2^e(s)$
6	$\int_0^t d\tau\, f_1(\tau)f_2(t - \tau)$		$f_1^e(s)f_2^e(s)$
7	$f(t - \tau)$	$(\tau > 0)$	$e^{-s}f^{e\tau}(s)$
8	$f(t + \tau)$	$(\tau < 0)$	$e^{s\tau}\left[f^e(s) - \int_0^\tau dt\, e^{-st}f(t)\right]$
9	$tf(t)$		$-\frac{d}{ds}f^e(s)$
10	$e^{-at}f(t)$		$f^e(s + a)$
11	e^{-at}		$\frac{1}{s + a}$
12	te^{-at}		$\frac{1}{(s + a)^2}$
13	t	Unit Ramp	$\frac{1}{s^2}$
14	$\frac{1}{2}t^2e^{-at}$		$\frac{1}{(s + a)^3}$

	Continuous Function		Exponential Transform
15	$\frac{1}{2}t^2$		$\frac{1}{s^3}$
16	$\frac{1}{k!}t^k e^{-at}$	k is a non-negative integer	$\frac{1}{(s+a)^{k+1}}$
17	$\frac{1}{k!}t^k$	k is a non-negative integer	$\frac{1}{s^{k+1}}$
18	$f\left(\frac{t}{a}\right)$	$a > 0$	$af^e(as)$
19	$\frac{d}{dt}f(t)$	$t \geq 0$	$sf^e(s) - f(0)$
20	$\int_0^t d\tau\, f(\tau)$		$\frac{1}{s}f^e(s)$
21	Integration Property	$\int_0^\infty d\tau\, f(\tau) = f^e(0)$	
22	Initial Value Property	$f(0) = \lim_{s\to\infty} sf^e(s)$—if it exists	
23	Final Value Property	$f(\infty) = \lim_{s\to 0} sf^e(s)$—if it exists	
24	$M(t)$ a matrix function		$M^e(s) = \int_0^\infty dt\, e^{-st}M(t)$
25	$tM(t)$		$-\frac{d}{ds}M^e(s)$
26	e^{At}		$[sI - A]^{-1}$
27	te^{At}		$[sI - A]^{-1}[sI - A]^{-1}$

Relation 3 presents the transform of the unit step $u(t)$, a function equal to one for all positive values of its argument and zero for all negative values. The transform is computed as

$$\int_0^\infty dt\, u(t)e^{-st} = \int_0^\infty dt\, e^{-st} = -\frac{1}{s}e^{-st}\Big|_0^\infty = \frac{1}{s}. \tag{11.4.2}$$

Relation 4 states that the result of multiplying a function by a constant is to multiply its transform by the same constant.

The fact that the transform of the sum of two functions is the sum of their transforms expressed in relation 5 is a direct result of the defining relation. Relation 6 states that the convolution of two continuous-time functions has an exponential transform equal to the product of the individual transforms, in direct analogy with the result for geometric transforms. To prove it we write

$$\begin{aligned}\int_0^\infty dt\, e^{-st}\int_0^t d\tau\, f_1(\tau)f_2(t-\tau) &= \int_0^\infty dt \int_0^t d\tau\, f_1(\tau)e^{-s\tau}f_2(t-\tau)e^{-s(t-\tau)}\\ &= \int_0^\infty d\tau \int_\tau^\infty dt\, f_1(\tau)e^{-s\tau}f_2(t-\tau)e^{-s(t-\tau)}\\ &= \int_0^\infty d\tau \int_0^\infty du\, f_1(\tau)e^{-s\tau}f_2(u)e^{-su} \qquad (u = t-\tau)\\ &= \int_0^\infty d\tau\, e^{-s\tau}f_1(\tau)\int_0^\infty du\, e^{-su}f_2(u)\\ &= f_1^e(s)f_2^e(s). \end{aligned} \tag{11.4.3}$$

Relation 7 shows that shifting a function to the right by an amount τ requires that its transform be multiplied by $e^{-s\tau}$:

$$\int_0^\infty dt\, e^{-st}f(t-\tau) = \int_{-\tau}^\infty du\, e^{-s(u+\tau)}f(u) = e^{-s\tau}\int_0^\infty du\, e^{-su}f(u) = e^{-s\tau}f^e(s). \tag{11.4.4}$$

Here we change the lower limit from $-\tau$ to 0 because all functions that we consider are zero for negative arguments.

Relation 8 is similar. It states that shifting a function to the left by an amount τ requires not only that its transform be multiplied by $e^{s\tau}$ but also that, before this multiplication, it be adjusted to account for any non-zero part of the function that may have been shifted across the origin:

$$\begin{aligned}\int_0^\infty dt\, e^{-st}f(t+\tau) &= \int_\tau^\infty du\, e^{-s(u-\tau)}f(u) = e^{s\tau}\left[\int_0^\infty du\, e^{-su}f(u) - \int_0^\tau du\, e^{-su}f(u)\right]\\ &= e^{s\tau}\left[f^e(s) - \int_0^\tau dt\, e^{-st}f(t)\right]. \end{aligned} \tag{11.4.5}$$

The import of relation 9 is that multiplication of a function by its argument requires that we differentiate its transform with respect to the transform variable and change its sign. We establish this result immediately by differentiating the transform definition with respect to s,

$$\frac{d}{ds}f^e(s) = \frac{d}{ds}\int_0^\infty dt\, e^{-st}f(t) = -\int_0^\infty dt\, e^{-st}tf(t). \tag{11.4.6}$$

Relation 10 states that multiplying a function by an exponential function of rate $-a$ requires that its transform variable s be replaced by $s + a$. We prove this from

$$\int_0^\infty dt\, e^{-at}f(t)e^{-st} = \int_0^\infty dt\, f(t)e^{-(s+a)t} = f^e(s+a). \tag{11.4.7}$$

Relation 11 shows the result of transforming an exponential function. It follows directly from relations 3 and 10 that the transform of $e^{-at} = e^{-at}u(t)$ is $1/(s + a)$.

We obtain relation 12 by applying relation 9 to relation 11,

$$\int_0^\infty dt\, e^{-st} t e^{-at} = -\frac{d}{ds}\left(\frac{1}{s + a}\right) = \frac{1}{(s + a)^2}. \tag{11.4.8}$$

Relation 13, which states that the transform of the unit ramp t is $1/s^2$, corresponds to the special case of relation 12 where $a = 0$.

By applying relations 4 and 9 to relation 12 we obtain relation 14,

$$\int_0^\infty dt\, e^{-st} \frac{1}{2} t^2 e^{-at} = \frac{1}{2}\left[-\frac{d}{ds}\left(\frac{1}{(s + a)^2}\right)\right] = \frac{1}{(s + a)^3}. \tag{11.4.9}$$

The parabolic ramp $(1/2)t^2$ therefore has transform $1/s^3$ as given by relation 15. We obtain relation 16 by applying relations 4 and 9 again and again to relation 11; with $a = 0$, we have relation 17.

The effect of changing the scale of a transformed function by dividing its argument by a positive constant a appears in relation 18,

$$\int_0^\infty dt\, e^{-st} f\left(\frac{t}{a}\right) = a \int_0^\infty du\, e^{-sau} f(u) = a f^e(as). \tag{11.4.10}$$

The transform variable and the transform are multiplied by a.

Relation 19 shows the effect on the transform of differentiating the function. The transform must be multiplied by s and then the value of the function at 0 must be subtracted. We establish the result by using integration by parts,

$$\int_0^\infty dt\, e^{-st} \frac{d}{dt} f(t) = e^{-st} f(t)\Big|_0^\infty + s \int_0^\infty dt\, e^{-st} f(t) = s f^e(s) - f(0). \tag{11.4.11}$$

In this development we have made the assumption that $f(t)$ grows with t when t is large at no greater than an exponential rate. This is, in fact, the general requirement for the existence of the exponential transform of a function. As in the discrete case, we shall have no concern about existence in our work.

Relation 20 illustrates the effect of integration on the transform of a function, namely, that the transform must be multiplied by $1/s$:

$$\begin{aligned}\int_0^\infty dt\, e^{-st} \int_0^t d\tau\, f(\tau) &= \int_0^\infty d\tau\, e^{-s\tau} f(\tau) \int_\tau^\infty dt\, e^{-s(t-\tau)} \\ &= \int_0^\infty d\tau\, e^{-s\tau} f(\tau) \int_0^\infty du\, e^{-su} \\ &= \frac{1}{s} f^e(s).\end{aligned} \tag{11.4.12}$$

If we take $s = 0$ in the defining relation 1, we obtain relation 21, which shows that the exponential transform with argument zero is just the integral from 0 to ∞ of the transformed function.

Relation 22 is the initial value theorem for exponential transforms rather than a transform pair. This relation shows how to obtain the value of the function at the origin by operating on the transform. The operation requires multiplying the transform by s and then letting s approach infinity. We prove the theorem by taking the limit of Equation 11.4.11 as s approaches infinity.

$$\lim_{s\to\infty} \int_0^\infty dt\, e^{-st} \frac{d}{dt} f(t) = \lim_{s\to\infty} sf^e(s) - f(0)$$

$$0 = \lim_{s\to\infty} sf^e(s) - f(0)$$

or

$$\lim_{s\to\infty} sf^e(s) = f(0). \tag{11.4.13}$$

Relation 23 is the final value theorem for exponential transforms. If the function has a limiting value $f(\infty)$ for large arguments, then we can obtain this value by multiplying its transform by s and letting s approach zero. We prove the theorem by taking the limit of Equation 11.4.11 as s approaches zero,

$$\lim_{s\to 0} \int_0^\infty dt\, e^{-st} \frac{d}{dt} f(t) = \lim_{s\to 0} sf^e(s) - f(0)$$

$$\int_0^\infty df(t) = \lim_{s\to 0} sf^e(s) - f(0)$$

$$f(\infty) - f(0) = \lim_{s\to 0} sf^e(s) - f(0)$$

or

$$f(\infty) = \lim_{s\to 0} sf^e(s). \tag{11.4.14}$$

As we shall see in our discussion of partial fraction expansion of exponential transforms, this procedure is equivalent to finding the magnitude of the step component in the function.

Matrix function transforms

To consider exponential transforms of matrix functions, we first define a matrix function $M(t)$ that specifies the elements of a matrix at any non-negative value of t. Relation 24 is the definition of the matrix transform $M^e(s)$ of this function,

$$M^e(s) = \int_0^\infty dt\, e^{-st} M(t). \tag{11.4.15}$$

We can therefore consider the ijth element $m_{ij}^e(s)$ to be the exponential transform of the ijth element $m_{ij}(t)$,

$$m_{ij}^e(s) = \int_0^\infty dt\, e^{-st} m_{ij}(t). \tag{11.4.16}$$

We can find matrix transform pairs by analogy to the procedure used for function transform pairs. For example, by differentiating Equation 11.4.15 with respect to s, we immediately obtain relation 25 for determining the effect on the transform of multiplying the matrix function by its argument,

$$\frac{d}{ds} M^e(s) = -\int_0^\infty dt\, e^{-st} t M(t). \tag{11.4.17}$$

However, to develop transforms of complicated matrix functions, it is necessary to examine functions with matrix arguments. We define a function of a matrix as the matrix we would obtain if we substituted a matrix for the variable in the power series representation of the function. Thus, for example, if a is a real number, e^{at} has the power series expansion,

$$e^{at} = 1 + at + \frac{a^2t^2}{2!} + \frac{a^3t^3}{3!} \cdots. \tag{11.4.18}$$

Therefore, if A is a square matrix, we define e^{At} by

$$e^{At} = I + At + A^2\frac{t^2}{2!} + A^3\frac{t^3}{3!} \cdots. \tag{11.4.19}$$

The definition extends, of course, to many other functions of matrices, but the representation of e^{At} is of most concern at the moment.

We can exponentially transform Equation 11.4.19 by using relation 17 of Table 11.4.1. We find

$$\begin{aligned} \int_0^\infty dt\, e^{At}e^{-st} &= I\cdot\frac{1}{s} + A\cdot\frac{1}{s^2} + A^2\cdot\frac{1}{s^3} + A^3\cdot\frac{1}{s^4} + \cdots \\ &= \frac{1}{s}\left[I + A\cdot\frac{1}{s} + A^2\cdot\frac{1}{s^2} + A^3\cdot\frac{1}{s^3} + \cdots\right] \\ &= \frac{1}{s}\left[I - \frac{1}{s}A\right]^{-1}, \end{aligned} \tag{11.4.20}$$

where the final step is justified by the series definition of the matrix function $[I-(1/s)A]^{-1}$. Of course, we can now write the exponential transform of e^{At} as

$$\int_0^\infty dt\, e^{At}e^{-st} = [sI - A]^{-1}. \tag{11.4.21}$$

The exponential transform of the matrix function e^{At} is just the inverse of the matrix formed by subtracting A from s times the identity matrix, as shown by relation 26. If A is the scalar $-a$, then relation 26 becomes relation 11.

From relations 25 and 26 we see that the transform of te^{At} should be $-\frac{d}{ds}[sI-A]^{-1}$. Since Equation 1.5.24

$$\frac{d}{dz}[F^g(z)]^{-1} = -[F^g(z)]^{-1}\left[\frac{d}{dz}F^g(z)\right][F^g(z)]^{-1}$$

applies to any matrix function and to the exponential transform in particular, we obtain relation 27 directly. If A is replaced by the scalar $-a$, then relation 27 becomes relation 12.

Relationship to Geometric Transform

We have now proved all the relations in Table 11.4.1. We could expand the table almost without limit, but the relations we have established will serve our present purposes. We note that these relations bear a close resemblance to the corresponding relations for the geometric transform. We can show the exact correspondence between the two transforms by noting that we can represent any discrete function by a string of continuous-type impulses whose areas are the values of the discrete function. Thus a discrete function $f(\cdot)$ that takes on the value $f(n)$ at the point n where n is a non-negative integer could be as well represented at the point n by a continuous-type impulse of area $f(n)$. If we used this representation at all points n, we could write the continuous function $f(t)$ as

$$f(t) = \sum_{n_0=0}^{\infty} f(n_0)\,\delta(t - n_0). \tag{11.4.22}$$

The exponential transform $f^e(s)$ of $f(t)$ would then be

$$\begin{aligned} f^e(s) &= \int_0^{\infty} dt\, e^{-st}f(t) = \int_0^{\infty} dt\, e^{-st}\sum_{n_0=0}^{\infty} f(n_0)\,\delta(t - n_0) \\ &= \sum_{n_0=0}^{\infty} f(n_0)\int_0^{\infty} dt\, e^{-st}\,\delta(t - n_0) = \sum_{n_0=0}^{\infty} f(n_0)e^{-sn_0}. \end{aligned} \tag{11.4.23}$$

If we now let $z = e^{-s}$, we can write the exponential transform as

$$f^e(s) = \sum_{n_0=0}^{\infty} f(n_0)z^n = f^g(z). \tag{11.4.24}$$

Therefore, if we have the geometric transform of a discrete function and we wish to interpret the function as a continuous-type impulse string and then write its exponential transform, we simply substitute e^{-s} for z in the geometric transform,

$$f^e(s) = f^g(e^{-s}). \tag{11.4.25}$$

Thus we can interpret all of our previous results for the geometric transform as a special case of those for the exponential transform.

Transforms of Probability Distributions

Any of the probability distributions we have discussed, whether density function or cumulative probability distribution, may be exponentially transformed. If $f_x(\cdot)$ is a probability density function for a random variable x, then its exponential transform $f_x{}^e(s)$ is defined by

$$f_x{}^e(s) = \int_0^\infty dx_0\, e^{-sx_0} f_x(x_0), \tag{11.4.26}$$

and is therefore the expectation of e^{-sx}.

Convolution

If x and y are two independent random variables with density functions $f_x(\cdot)$ and $f_y(\cdot)$, we know that their sum z will have a density function $f_z(\cdot)$ obtained as the convolution of $f_x(\cdot)$ and $f_y(\cdot)$. In view of relation 6 in Table 11.4.1 we know that the exponential transform of z is the product of the exponential transforms of x and y,

$$f_z{}^e(s) = f_x{}^e(s) f_y{}^e(s). \tag{11.4.27}$$

Therefore transforms have an important use in addition operations on independent random variables.

Moment computation

However, for our purposes a more important property of the exponential transform of the density function is that the moments of the random variable are the derivatives of the transform at $s = 0$. We see this by repeatedly differentiating Equation 11.4.26 with respect to s,

$$f_x{}^e(s) = \int_0^\infty dx_0\, e^{-sx_0} f_x(x_0)$$

$$\frac{d}{ds} f_x{}^e(s) = -\int_0^\infty dx_0\, e^{-sx_0} x_0 f_x(x_0)$$

$$\frac{d^2}{ds^2} f_x{}^e(s) = \int_0^\infty dx_0\, e^{-sx_0} x_0{}^2 f_x(x_0)$$

or, in general,

$$\frac{d^k}{ds^k} f_x^e(s) = (-1)^k \int_0^\infty dx_0\, e^{-sx_0} x_0^k f_x(x_0). \tag{11.4.28}$$

When we evaluate this result at $s = 0$ we obtain

$$\lim_{s \to 0} (-1)^k \frac{d^k}{ds^k} f_x^e(s) = \int_0^\infty dx_0\, x_0^k f_x(x_0) = \overline{x^k} \qquad k = 0, 1, 2, \ldots. \tag{11.4.29}$$

The kth moment of the random variable is therefore $(-1)^k$ times the kth derivative of its exponential transform evaluated at $s = 0$.

We observe that the zeroth moment of the random variable is just the area under the density function and therefore equals one. A useful check on the exponential transform of any probability density function is therefore that it equal 1 when $s = 0$. We are most concerned, however, with the first and second moments $\bar{x}$ and $\overline{x^2}$ given by

$$\bar{x} = -\frac{d}{ds} f_x^e(s)\bigg|_{s=0} \qquad \overline{x^2} = \frac{d^2}{ds^2} f_x^e(s)\bigg|_{s=0}. \tag{11.4.30}$$

Exponential distribution. We have already considered in Equation 11.1.1 the exponential probability density function $f_x(x_0) = \lambda e^{-\lambda x_0}$. By using relations 4 and 11 in the transform table we find that the exponential transform of this distribution is

$$f_x^e(s) = \frac{\lambda}{s + \lambda}. \tag{11.4.31}$$

We check that $f_x^e(0) = 1$, and then proceed to calculate the moments using Equation 11.4.30,

$$\begin{aligned} \bar{x} &= -\frac{d}{ds}\left(\frac{\lambda}{s + \lambda}\right)\bigg|_{s=0} = \frac{\lambda}{(s + \lambda)^2}\bigg|_{s=0} = \frac{1}{\lambda} \\ \overline{x^2} &= \frac{d^2}{ds^2}\left(\frac{\lambda}{s + \lambda}\right)\bigg|_{s=0} = \frac{2\lambda}{(s + \lambda)^3}\bigg|_{s=0} = \frac{2}{\lambda^2}. \end{aligned} \tag{11.4.32}$$

These results agree with those produced by direct integration in Equations 11.1.7 and 11.1.8.

Transforms of cumulatives

The cumulative probability distribution ${}^{\leq}f_x(x_c)$ and the complementary cumulative probability distribution ${}^{>}f_x(x_c)$ are related to the density function by

$${}^{\leq}f_x(x_c) = \mathscr{P}\{x \leq x_c\} = \int_0^{x_c} dx_0\, f_x(x_0)$$

$${}^{>}f_x(x_c) = \mathscr{P}\{x > x_c\} = \int_{x_c}^\infty dx_0\, f_x(x_0) = 1 - {}^{\leq}f_x(x_c). \tag{11.4.33}$$

In view of relations 20 and 3 of the transform table we write the exponential transforms ${}^{\leq}f_x^e(s)$ and ${}^{>}f_x^e(s)$ of these cumulatives as

$$ {}^{\leq}f_x^e(s) = \frac{1}{s} f_x^e(s) \qquad {}^{>}f_x^e(s) = \frac{1}{s} - \frac{1}{s} f_x^e(s) = \frac{1}{s}(1 - f_x^e(s)). \quad (11.4.34)$$

Thus there is a very simple relationship in the transform domain between the density functions and the cumulatives. For the exponential distribution we find

$$ {}^{\leq}f_x^e(s) = \frac{1}{s}\cdot\frac{\lambda}{(s + \lambda)} \qquad {}^{>}f_x^e(s) = \frac{1}{s}\left[1 - \frac{\lambda}{s + \lambda}\right] = \frac{1}{s + \lambda}\cdot \quad (11.4.35)$$

Moment computation from cumulative transforms

We observe an interesting and important result by taking the limit of ${}^{>}f_x^e(s)$ as s approaches zero,

$$\lim_{s\to 0} {}^{>}f_x^e(s) = \lim_{s\to 0} \frac{1 - f_x^e(s)}{s} \overset{\text{l'Hôpital}}{=} \lim_{s\to 0} -\frac{d}{ds} f_x^e(s) = \bar{x}. \quad (11.4.36)$$

The limit of the exponential transform of the complementary cumulative probability distribution as s approaches zero is the area under the complementary cumulative probability distribution and this, in turn, is the mean of the random variable. Thus for the exponential distribution,

$$\bar{x} = \lim_{s\to 0} {}^{>}f_x^e(s) = \lim_{s\to 0} \frac{1}{s + \lambda} = \frac{1}{\lambda}, \quad (11.4.37)$$

in agreement with Equation 11.4.32.

Furthermore, if we evaluate the derivative of ${}^{>}f_x^e(s)$ at $s = 0$ we find

$$\lim_{s\to 0} \frac{d}{ds} {}^{>}f_x(^e s) = \lim_{s\to 0} \frac{d}{ds} \frac{1 - f_x^e(s)}{s} = \lim_{s\to 0} \frac{-s f_x^{e\prime}(s) - (1 - f_x^e(s))}{s^2}$$

$$\overset{\text{l'Hôpital}}{=} \lim_{s\to 0} -\frac{1}{2} f_x^{e\prime\prime}(s) = -\frac{1}{2}\overline{x^2}. \quad (11.4.38)$$

The derivative of the exponential transform of the complementary cumulative probability distribution at $s = 0$ is $-(1/2)$ the second moment of the random variable. For the exponential distribution,

$$\frac{d}{ds} {}^{>}f_x^e(s)\bigg|_{s=0} = \frac{-1}{(s + \lambda)^2}\bigg|_{s=0} = \frac{-1}{\lambda^2} = -\frac{1}{2}\overline{x^2}, \quad (11.4.39)$$

in accordance with Equation 11.4.32.

Linear System Applications

The exponential transform has the same type of application in linear systems theory as does the geometric transform. We could return to Chapter 2 and develop the theory of linear systems allowing continuous-time rather than discrete-time functions throughout. However, this will not be necessary because the reader will be able to perform the conversion of our earlier results himself with very little effort. All we need are a few key steps in the translation.

First we note that the impulse response of a linear, time-variant, physically realizable system is its response to the impulse function defined in Figure 11.1.2. We then show in a manner exactly analogous to our previous work that the output of any linear system is the input convolved with the impulse response, where the form of the convolution is the integral in relation 6 of Table 11.4.1. This relation illustrates that the exponential transform of the output of such a linear system is the product of the exponential transforms of its input and its impulse response. As before, we call the exponential transform of the impulse response the transfer function of the system. The input-output relationship for continuous-time systems is therefore the same as that for discrete-time systems except that the transform involved is the exponential rather than the geometric transform. Once we make this observation we see that all the results we previously obtained in Chapter 2 have completely analogous continuous-time counterparts. In particular, all the flow graph reduction results, including the inspection method of reduction, are unchanged. The differences between the geometric and exponential transforms arise only when *entering* and when *leaving* the transform domain.

Of course, there are features in which the exponential and geometric transforms differ. For example, rather than dealing with a summer with geometric transform $1/(1 - z)$, we have used a continuous-time integrator with exponential transform $1/s$. Correspondingly, the differencer with geometric transform $1 - z$ is replaced by the differentiator with exponential transform s. However, these results are apparent from the transform table and the similarities of the two analytical models are far more significant than their differences.

An example

Let us illustrate the use of the exponential transform in systems analysis. Suppose that a system with impulse response $h(t) = e^{-bt}$ $t \geq 0$ is subjected to an input $f(t) = e^{-at}$ $t \geq 0$, $b \neq a$. What will be the output? The problem appears graphically in Figure 11.4.2. We compute first the exponential transforms of the input and the impulse response using the transform table,

$$f^e(s) = \frac{1}{s + a} \qquad h^e(s) = \frac{1}{s + b}. \tag{11.4.40}$$

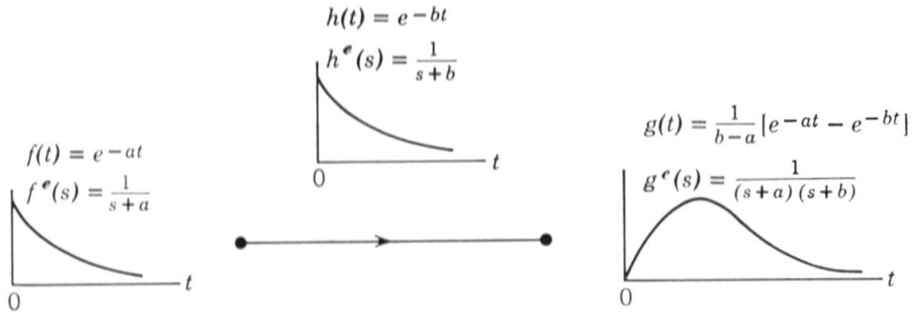

Figure 11.4.2 A continuous-time linear system problem.

The exponential transform $g^e(s)$ of the output $g(t)$ is the product of $f^e(s)$ and $h^e(s)$,

$$g^e(s) = f^e(s)h^e(s) = \frac{1}{(s + a)(s + b)} \cdot \tag{11.4.41}$$

To carry out the inverse exponential transformation we must now perform a partial fraction expansion of $g^e(s)$. One method is to use undetermined coefficients,

$$\frac{1}{(s + a)(s + b)} = \frac{A}{s + a} + \frac{B}{s + b}$$

$$1 = A(s + b) + B(s + a). \tag{11.4.42}$$

By evaluating this equation first at $s = -a$ and then at $s = -b$, we obtain

$$A = \frac{1}{b - a} \qquad B = \frac{-1}{b - a} \cdot \tag{11.4.43}$$

Note that the numerator of any term with denominator $s + s_0$ can be found by multiplying the transform by $s + s_0$ and evaluating the result at $s = -s_0$, a result in complete analogy with our findings for the geometric transform. We shall return to the case of repeated denominator factors in just a moment.

Thus

$$g^e(s) = \frac{\frac{1}{b - a}}{s + a} + \frac{\frac{-1}{b - a}}{s + b}; \tag{11.4.44}$$

and, by using the transform table,

$$g(t) = \frac{1}{b - a}[e^{-at} - e^{-bt}] \qquad t \geq 0. \tag{11.4.45}$$

The output of the linear system is the difference between two exponential terms.

Partial Fraction Expansion with Repeated Denominator Factors

Returning now to the problem of partial fraction expansion, we recall that the numerator must be a lower degree polynomial in s than is the denominator. If we desire to perform a partial fraction expansion on a transform with repeated denominator factors, then one alternative is repeated application of the principles we just developed. Thus to expand $1/[(s+a)^2(s+b)]$, we write

$$\frac{1}{(s+a)^2(s+b)} = \frac{1}{s+a}\left[\frac{1}{(s+a)(s+b)}\right] = \frac{1}{s+a}\left[\frac{\frac{1}{b-a}}{s+a} + \frac{\frac{-1}{b-a}}{s+b}\right]$$

$$= \frac{\frac{1}{b-a}}{(s+a)^2} + \frac{-\frac{1}{b-a}}{(s+a)(s+b)}$$

$$= \frac{\frac{1}{b-a}}{(s+a)^2} + \frac{-\frac{1}{(b-a)^2}}{s+a} + \frac{\frac{1}{(b-a)^2}}{s+b}. \tag{11.4.46}$$

Repeated denominator factors can also be treated using differentiation in a procedure closely analogous to that used for geometric transforms. Let $n(s)$ be the numerator function and $d(s)$ the denominator function. If the transform denominator has an mth order factor of the form,

$$\frac{n(s)}{d(s)} = \frac{n(s)}{(s+a)^m d_1(s)},$$

we expand it as

$$\frac{n(s)}{(s+a)^m d_1(s)} = \frac{A_0}{(s+a)^m} + \frac{A_1}{(s+a)^{m-1}} + \frac{A_2}{(s+a)^{m-2}} + \cdots$$

$$+ \frac{A_{m-2}}{(s+a)^2} + \frac{A_{m-1}}{s+a} + f(s). \tag{11.4.47}$$

When we multiply both sides of this equation by $(s+a)^m$, we find that the coefficients are given by

$$A_k = \left(\frac{1}{k!}\right)\frac{d^k}{ds^k}\left[(s+a)^m \frac{n(s)}{d(s)}\right]\bigg|_{s=-a} \qquad k = 0, 1, 2, \ldots, m-1. \tag{11.4.48}$$

This expression differs from that for the geometric transform type of expansion of Equation 1.5.50 only because there is no multiplication by the kth power of the negative of the value at which the expression is being evaluated.

For the example, we write

$$\frac{1}{(s+a)^2(s+b)} = \frac{A_0}{(s+a)^2} + \frac{A_1}{s+a} + \frac{B}{s+b}. \tag{11.4.49}$$

Then,

$$A_0 = \left.\frac{1}{s + b}\right|_{s=-a} = \frac{1}{b - a}$$

$$A_1 = \left.\frac{d}{ds}\frac{1}{s + b}\right|_{s=-a} = \frac{-1}{(b - a)^2}$$

$$B = \left.\frac{1}{(s + a)^2}\right|_{s=-b} = \frac{1}{(b - a)^2}, \tag{11.4.50}$$

in agreement with Equation 11.4.46.

Thus the process of partial fraction expansion is very similar for both exponential and geometric transforms. Indeed, we have found that the entire systems analysis procedure is much the same from either point of view.

11.5 TRANSFORM ANALYSIS OF THE CONTINUOUS-TIME SEMI-MARKOV PROCESS

Now that we have developed the necessary transform apparatus, we can return to the analysis of the interval transition probabilities of the continuous-time semi-Markov process. We begin by taking the exponential transform of Equation 11.3.1, using the usual notation that a superscript e means the exponential transform of the function. We obtain

$$\phi_{ij}^e(s) = \delta_{ij}\, {}^{>}w_i^e(s) + \sum_{k=1}^{N} p_{ik}h_{ik}^e(s)\phi_{kj}^e(s) \qquad i = 1, 2, \ldots, N;\ j = 1, 2, \ldots, N. \tag{11.5.1}$$

Since convolution of functions again becomes multiplication of transforms in the transform domain, this result is just the continuous equivalent of Equation 10.3.1. Here $\phi_{ij}^e(s)$ is the exponential transform of the interval transition probability; $h_{ik}^e(s)$ is the exponential transform of the holding time density function for the transition from state i to state k; and ${}^{>}w_i^e(s)$ is the exponential transform of the complementary cumulative probability distribution for waiting time in state i. In view of Equation 11.4.34, ${}^{>}w_i^e(s)$ can be expressed in terms of the transform of the waiting time density function for state i by

$${}^{>}w_i^e(s) = \frac{1}{s}(1 - w_i^e(s)). \tag{11.5.2}$$

Since we can transform Equation 11.1.14 to relate the exponential transforms of the waiting time and holding time density functions,

$$w_i^e(s) = \sum_{j=1}^{N} p_{ij}h_{ij}^e(s), \tag{11.5.3}$$

the transforms of the interval transition probabilities depend only on the transition probabilities and the transforms of the holding time density functions.

Matrix Relations

If we place Equation 11.5.1 in matrix form we obtain

$$\Phi^e(s) = {}^{>}W^e(s) + [P \,\square\, H^e(s)]\Phi^e(s) \tag{11.5.4}$$

or

$$\Phi^e(s) = {}^{>}W^e(s) + C^e(s)\Phi^e(s). \tag{11.5.5}$$

The matrix ${}^{>}W^e(s)$ is the diagonal transform matrix whose diagonal elements are defined by Equations 11.5.2 and 11.5.3. Since $C^e(s)$ is just the transformed core matrix of the continuous-time semi-Markov process, the sum of the elements in its ith row is $w_i^e(s)$, as shown in Equation 11.5.3. Therefore the transformed core matrix $C^e(s)$ allows us to construct ${}^{>}W^e(s)$ and thereby determine the transformed matrix of interval transition probabilities $\Phi^e(s)$. Solving Equation 11.5.5 for $\Phi^e(s)$ produces

$$\Phi^e(s) = [I - C^e(s)]^{-1}\,{}^{>}W^e(s) = [I - P \,\square\, H^e(s)]^{-1}\,{}^{>}W^e(s). \tag{11.5.6}$$

The matrix $\Phi^e(s)$ is therefore equal to the transformed complementary cumulative waiting time matrix ${}^{>}W^e(s)$ premultiplied by the inverse of the matrix formed by subtracting the transformed core matrix $C^e(s)$ from the identity matrix I. Once more, this inverse matrix will always exist for the type of process we are considering. Furthermore, the matrix relations given in Equations 10.3.7 through 10.3.11 for the transformed core matrix $C^g(z)$ for the discrete-time process apply as well to the transformed core matrix $C^e(s)$ for the continuous-time process.

The car rental example

Now we shall apply our results to the continuous-time version of the car rental example. We begin by exponentially transforming the core matrix of Equation 11.3.4,

$$C^e(s) = P \,\square\, H^e(s) = \begin{bmatrix} \dfrac{3.2}{s+4} & \dfrac{0.4}{s+2} \\[2ex] \dfrac{0.9}{s+3} & \dfrac{0.7}{s+1} \end{bmatrix}. \tag{11.5.7}$$

Note that $C^e(0) = P \,\square\, H^e(0) = P \,\square\, U = P$, as required. Next we exponentially transform ${}^{>}W(t)$ in Equation 11.2.9 to form ${}^{>}W^e(s)$,

$$\begin{aligned} {}^{>}W^e(s) &= \begin{bmatrix} \dfrac{0.8}{s+4} + \dfrac{0.2}{s+2} & 0 \\[2ex] 0 & \dfrac{0.3}{s+3} + \dfrac{0.7}{s+1} \end{bmatrix} \\ &= \begin{bmatrix} \dfrac{s+2.4}{(s+2)(s+4)} & 0 \\[2ex] 0 & \dfrac{s+2.4}{(s+1)(s+3)} \end{bmatrix}. \end{aligned} \tag{11.5.8}$$

We could also have developed the ith row of ${}^{>}W^e(s)$ by summing the ith row of $C^e(s)$, subtracting the sum from one, and dividing by s.

As a check on ${}^{>}W^e(s)$ and for other purposes, we should note that as a direct result of Equation 11.4.36 the matrix ${}^{>}W^e(0)$ is a diagonal matrix M whose ith diagonal element is the mean waiting time in state i, $\bar{\tau}_i$,

$$ {}^{>}W^e(0) = M. \tag{11.5.9}$$

For the example, we have

$$M = {}^{>}W^e(0) = \begin{bmatrix} 0.3 & 0 \\ 0 & 0.8 \end{bmatrix}, \tag{11.5.10}$$

a result confirmed by Equation 11.2.7.

Transform representation. To write the matrix of transformed interval transition probabilities $\Phi^e(s)$ for the example, we first compute $I - C^e(s)$ using Equation 11.5.7,

$$I - C^e(s) = \begin{bmatrix} \dfrac{s+0.8}{s+4} & \dfrac{-0.4}{s+2} \\ \dfrac{-0.9}{s+3} & \dfrac{s+0.3}{s+1} \end{bmatrix}; \tag{11.5.11}$$

then write its determinant,

$$\begin{aligned} |I - C^e(s)| &= \frac{s(s^3 + 6.1s^2 + 11.38s + 6)}{(s+1)(s+2)(s+3)(s+4)} \\ &= \frac{s(s+2.4)(s^2 + 3.7s + 2.5)}{(s+1)(s+2)(s+3)(s+4)} \\ &= \frac{s(s+0.88953)(s+2.4)(s+2.81047)}{(s+1)(s+2)(s+3)(s+4)}; \end{aligned} \tag{11.5.12}$$

and finally develop its inverse,

$$[I - C^e(s)]^{-1} = \frac{(s+1)(s+2)(s+3)(s+4)}{s(s+0.88953)(s+2.4)(s+2.81047)} \begin{bmatrix} \dfrac{s+0.3}{s+1} & \dfrac{0.4}{s+2} \\ \dfrac{0.9}{s+3} & \dfrac{s+0.8}{s+4} \end{bmatrix}. \tag{11.5.13}$$

Next we postmultiply this matrix by ${}^{>}W^e(s)$ from Equation 11.5.8 to produce $\Phi^e(s)$,

$$\begin{aligned} \Phi^e(s) &= [I - C^e(s)]^{-1}\, {}^{>}W^e(s) \\ &= \frac{1}{s(s+0.88953)(s+2.81047)} \begin{bmatrix} (s+0.3)(s+3) & 0.4(s+4) \\ 0.9(s+1) & (s+0.8)(s+2) \end{bmatrix}. \end{aligned} \tag{11.5.14}$$

To aid in writing the inverse of the exponential transforms, we now perform partial fraction expansion,

$$\Phi^e(s) = \frac{1}{s}\begin{bmatrix} 0.36 & 0.64 \\ 0.36 & 0.64 \end{bmatrix} + \frac{1}{s + 0.88953}\begin{bmatrix} 0.72813 & -0.72813 \\ -0.05818 & 0.05818 \end{bmatrix}$$

$$+ \frac{1}{s + 2.81047}\begin{bmatrix} -0.08813 & 0.08813 \\ -0.30182 & 0.30182 \end{bmatrix}. \tag{11.5.15}$$

Solution. The matrix of interval transition probabilities for the car rental example is therefore

$$\Phi(t) = \begin{bmatrix} 0.36 & 0.64 \\ 0.36 & 0.64 \end{bmatrix} + e^{-0.88953t}\begin{bmatrix} 0.72813 & -0.72813 \\ -0.05818 & 0.05818 \end{bmatrix}$$

$$+ e^{-2.81047t}\begin{bmatrix} -0.08813 & 0.08813 \\ -0.30182 & 0.30182 \end{bmatrix} \qquad t \geq 0. \tag{11.5.16}$$

We see immediately the similarity of this result to that of Equation 10.3.29. The component matrices are the same, but the coefficients are exponentials rather than geometric sequences. We note that $\Phi(0) = I$ as required and that $\Phi(t)$ approaches a limiting matrix as t becomes large. Denoting this limiting matrix by Φ, we write for the example,

$$\Phi = \lim_{t \to \infty} \Phi(t) = \lim_{s \to 0} s\Phi^e(s) = \begin{bmatrix} 0.36 & 0.64 \\ 0.36 & 0.64 \end{bmatrix}, \tag{11.5.17}$$

which is, of course, the same Φ found in Equation 10.3.30.

The rate of approach of $\Phi(t)$ to the limiting values is illustrated in Figure 11.5.1 by the plots of the diagonal elements,

$$\begin{aligned} \phi_{11}(t) &= 0.36 + 0.72813e^{-0.88953t} - 0.08813e^{-2.81047t} \\ \phi_{22}(t) &= 0.64 + 0.05818e^{-0.88953t} + 0.30182e^{-2.81047t}. \end{aligned} \tag{11.5.18}$$

Note the similarity of this graph to Figure 10.2.1. The essential differences are a change of the time scale by the factor of 12 and the use of a continuous rather than a discrete time base.

Limiting Behavior

The limiting behavior of the interval transition probabilities for the continuous-time semi-Markov process is analogous to the limiting behavior of the discrete-time process. In each case the chain structure is that of the imbedded Markov process. Only in the case of the monodesmic process are the limiting interval transition probabilities independent of the state in which the system starts. By

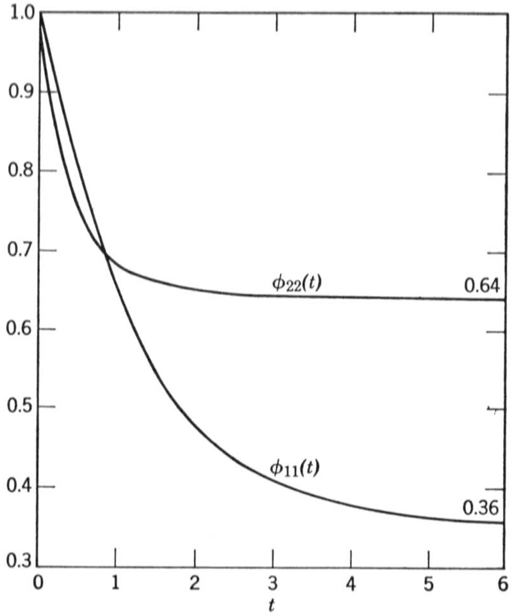

Figure 11.5.1 Two interval transition probabilities for the continuous-time car rental example.

arguments that exactly follow those in Section 10.3 except for the replacement of geometric by exponential transforms, we can show that the limiting interval transition probability ϕ_{ij} for a monodesmic process can be expressed by

$$\phi_{ij} = \frac{\pi_j \bar{\tau}_j}{\sum_{j=1}^{N} \pi_j \bar{\tau}_j} = \frac{\pi_j \bar{\tau}_j}{\bar{\tau}} = \phi_j, \tag{11.5.19}$$

the same equation as Equation 10.3.47. Here as before, π_j is the limiting state probability of state j for the imbedded process, and $\bar{\tau}_j$ is the mean waiting time for that state. The quantity $\bar{\tau} = \sum_{j=1}^{N} \pi_j \bar{\tau}_j$ is the mean time between transitions for the continuous-time process.

The car rental example

Since the continuous-time version of the car rental example has the same imbedded process as the discrete version and has mean waiting times that differ from those for the discrete version by a factor of 12, the continuous-time version of the example should have the same limiting interval transition probabilities as does the discrete-time version. We confirm this by computing first the mean time between transitions using the values $\pi_1 = 0.6$, $\pi_2 = 0.4$ for the imbedded process and $\bar{\tau}_1 = 0.3$, $\bar{\tau}_2 = 0.8$ from Equation 11.2.7,

$$\bar{\tau} = 0.6(0.3) + 0.4(0.8) = 0.5. \tag{11.5.20}$$

The mean time between transitions is therefore 0.5 units, which is 1/12 of its value for the discrete-time example. Then we write

$$\begin{aligned} \phi_1 &= \frac{\pi_1 \bar{\tau}_1}{\bar{\tau}} = \frac{0.6(0.3)}{0.5} = 0.36 \\ \phi_2 &= \frac{\pi_2 \bar{\tau}_2}{\bar{\tau}} = \frac{0.4(0.8)}{0.5} = 0.64. \end{aligned} \tag{11.5.21}$$

These are, of course, the elements in the rows of Φ in Equation 11.5.17, the same elements we obtained for the discrete-time case.

The limiting interval transition probabilities for the continuous-time example have the same interpretation as they did in the discrete-time example. If we select a rented car's number at random from the company files and ask the probability that this car was rented last in town 1, the answer is 0.36. However, if we select a completed rental contract at random from the files, there is a 0.60 chance that it was written in town 1.

11.6 ALTERNATE FORMULATIONS

Conditional Transition Probabilities

Just as we did in the case of the discrete-time process, we can construct an alternate representation of the continuous-time semi-Markov process in terms of the waiting time density functions and the conditional transition probabilities. We define the conditional transition probability $p_{ij}(\tau)$ to be the probability that the system will make its next transition to state j given that it entered state i at time zero and that it will leave state i for the first time at time τ. Then we can write the core matrix element $c_{ij}(\tau)$ in the alternate forms,

$$c_{ij}(\tau) = p_{ij}h_{ij}(\tau) = w_i(\tau)p_{ij}(\tau) \qquad \begin{aligned} i &= 1, 2, \ldots, N \\ j &= 1, 2, \ldots, N \\ \tau &> 0. \end{aligned} \tag{11.6.1}$$

All forms of this relation are the joint probability-probability density function of a transition to state j at time τ; the analogy to Equation 10.4.1 is immediate.

To compute $p_{ij}(\tau)$ from the quantities we defined earlier, we write Equation 11.6.1 in the form,

$$p_{ij}(\tau) = \frac{p_{ij}h_{ij}(\tau)}{w_i(\tau)} = \frac{p_{ij}h_{ij}(\tau)}{\sum_{j=1}^{N} p_{ij}h_{ij}(\tau)} \qquad \begin{array}{l} i = 1, 2, \ldots, N \\ j = 1, 2, \ldots, N \\ \tau > 0. \end{array} \tag{11.6.2}$$

If we let $P(\tau)$ be the N by N matrix with elements $p_{ij}(\tau)$, we can express Equation 11.6.2 in matrix form as

$$P(\tau) = [W(\tau)]^{-1}(P \,\square\, H(\tau)) \qquad \tau > 0. \tag{11.6.3}$$

The car rental example

For the car rental example this matrix is

$$P(\tau) = \begin{bmatrix} \dfrac{3.2e^{-4\tau}}{3.2e^{-4\tau} + 0.4e^{-2\tau}} & \dfrac{0.4e^{-2\tau}}{3.2e^{-4\tau} + 0.4e^{-2\tau}} \\ \dfrac{0.9e^{-3\tau}}{0.9e^{-3\tau} + 0.7e^{-\tau}} & \dfrac{0.7e^{-\tau}}{0.9e^{-3\tau} + 0.7e^{-\tau}} \end{bmatrix} \qquad \tau > 0. \tag{11.6.4}$$

Figure 11.6.1 shows a plot of the diagonal elements of $P(\tau)$,

$$\begin{aligned} p_{11}(\tau) &= \frac{3.2e^{-4\tau}}{3.2e^{-4\tau} + 0.4e^{-2\tau}} \\ p_{22}(\tau) &= \frac{0.7e^{-\tau}}{0.9e^{-3\tau} + 0.7e^{-\tau}}. \end{aligned} \tag{11.6.5}$$

We see that knowing the holding time of a transition in this example has an important effect on the probability assigned to the destination of that transition.

We observe further that $P(\tau)$ is a stochastic matrix for any value of τ. In particular, for $\tau = 0^+$,

$$P(0) = \begin{bmatrix} 8/9 & 1/9 \\ 9/16 & 7/16 \end{bmatrix}. \tag{11.6.6}$$

Thus transitions made very soon after a state is entered have $P(0)$ for their transition probability matrix. Cars rented in town 1 for very short trips have a probability 8/9 of being returned to town 1; cars rented in town 2 for very short trips have a 7/16 probability of being returned to town 2.

When τ is very large we find

$$P(\infty) = \begin{bmatrix} 0 & 1 \\ 0 & 1 \end{bmatrix}. \tag{11.6.7}$$

If a transition is made from either state after a very long waiting time, that transition is almost certainly a transition to state 2—cars rented for long times have a

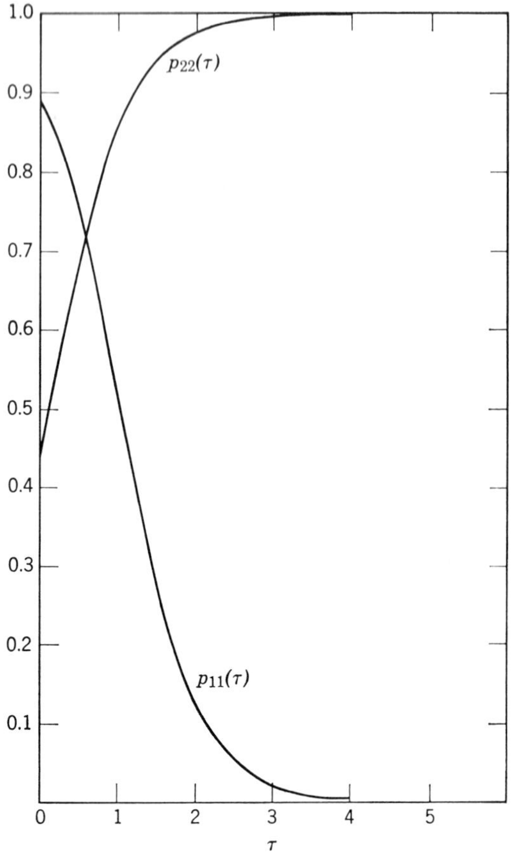

Figure 11.6.1 Two conditional transition probabilities for the continuous-time car rental example.

very high probability of being returned to town 2. These results have a direct correspondence to Equations 10.4.7 and 10.4.8.

Independent continuous-time semi-Markov processes

We can define an independent continuous-time semi-Markov process as one in which the holding times do not depend on the destination state; thus,

$$h_{ij}(\tau) = w_i(\tau) \qquad \begin{array}{l} i = 1, 2, \ldots, N \\ j = 1, 2, \ldots, N \\ \tau \geq 0, \end{array} \tag{11.6.8}$$

which implies

$$p_{ij}(\tau) = p_{ij} \qquad \begin{array}{l} i = 1, 2, \ldots, N \\ j = 1, 2, \ldots, N \\ \tau > 0. \end{array} \tag{11.6.9}$$

The conditional transition probabilities for the independent semi-Markov process are therefore the same as the transition probabilities. We write this significant property of the independent semi-Markov process in matrix form as

$$P(\tau) = P. \tag{11.6.10}$$

The Competing Process Model

Occasionally it is valuable to characterize a semi-Markov process by a model based on the concept of a race between competing processes. Thus when a process enters state i, we imagine that it selects its next state by observing N independent random variables associated with state i, one representing each possible successor state. If the random variable corresponding to successor state j is the smallest and has value τ, then the process makes its next transition to state j after holding a time τ in state i. Thus the destination state and holding time depend on the outcome of a race between the competing processes of state i. After the transition is made to some state j, the procedure is repeated using the competing processes associated with state j.

To specify the model, let $g_{ik}(\cdot)$ be the probability density function for the random variable representing successor state k when the process occupies state i. The complementary cumulative distribution ${}^{>}g_{ik}(t)$, showing the probability that the random variable will exceed t, is then defined by

$${}^{>}g_{ik}(t) = \int_t^\infty d\tau\, g_{ik}(\tau). \tag{11.6.11}$$

We require that all probability density functions $g_{ik}(\cdot)$ be finite everywhere to eliminate concern about the possibility of ties arising in determining the successor state. This requirement is the reason for discussing the competing process formulation in the context of the continuous-time rather than the discrete-time semi-Markov process.

Relationship to core matrix formulation

To relate the model to the core matrix formulation, we recall that $c_{ij}(\tau)$ is the joint probability-probability density function for the event that a process entering state i will make its next transition to state j after holding a time τ. This event will occur in the competing process model only if the random variable representing state j assumes the value τ, while those corresponding to the other $N-1$ states are all greater than τ. Thus,

$$c_{ij}(\tau) = g_{ij}(\tau) \prod_{\substack{k=1 \\ k \neq j}}^{N} {}^{>}g_{ik}(\tau) \qquad \text{all } i, j. \tag{11.6.12}$$

The transition probabilities of the process are then

$$p_{ij} = \int_0^\infty d\tau \; c_{ij}(\tau) = \int_0^\infty d\tau \; g_{ij}(\tau) \prod_{\substack{k=1 \\ k \neq j}}^{N} {}^{>}g_{ik}(\tau) \qquad \text{all } i, j, \tag{11.6.13}$$

while the holding time probability density functions are

$$h_{ij}(\tau) = \frac{c_{ij}(\tau)}{p_{ij}} = \frac{g_{ij}(\tau) \prod_{\substack{k=1 \\ k \neq j}}^{N} {}^{>}g_{ik}(\tau)}{\int_0^\infty d\tau \; g_{ij}(\tau) \prod_{\substack{k=1 \\ k \neq j}}^{N} {}^{>}g_{ik}(\tau)} \qquad \text{all } i, j. \tag{11.6.14}$$

If we wished to consider only real transitions, then the race would be between $N-1$ contestants, one for every state but i. In this case the product in the above equations would exclude $k = i$, and the diagonal elements of $C(\tau)$, P, and $H(\tau)$ would be set to zero.

While it is relatively easy to develop the usual process descriptors from the probability mass functions for the competing processes, the converse is seldom true: If $C(\cdot)$ is given, it can be very difficult to solve Equation 11.6.12 for all $g_{ij}(\cdot)$.

11.7 FLOW GRAPH ANALYSIS

Flow graph analysis of continuous-time semi-Markov processes is analogous to that for the discrete case. The major difference is that geometric transforms are replaced by exponential transforms in all the transmissions of the graph. The matrix flow graph for the continuous-time process corresponding to Equation 11.5.6 for the interval transition probabilities appears as Figure 11.7.1. This flow

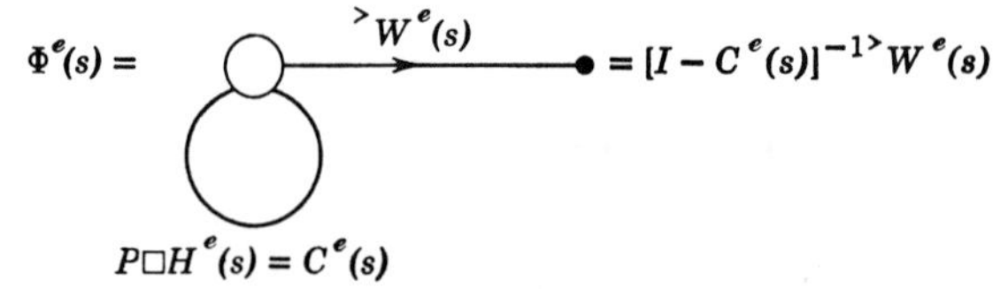

Figure 11.7.1 Matrix flow graph for the continuous-time semi-Markov process.

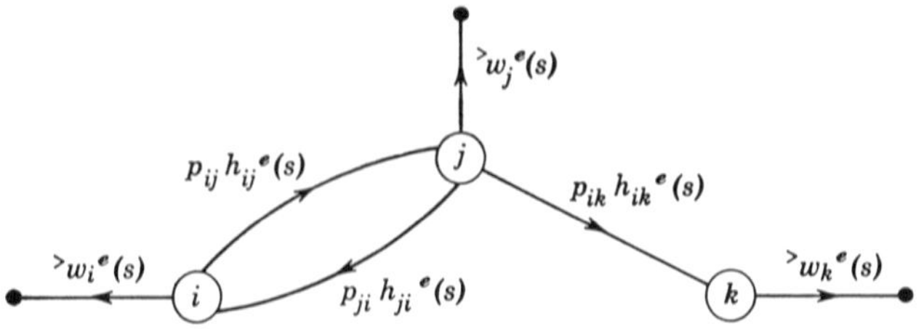

Figure 11.7.2 Partial flow graph for the continuous-time semi-Markov process.

graph is merely the continuous-time version of the flow graph in Figure 10.5.1. A portion of the ordinary flow graph that is implied by the matrix flow graph of Figure 11.7.1 is shown in Figure 11.7.2. The defining relations of the flow graph are Equations 11.5.1. This flow graph representation has its discrete-time counterpart in Figure 10.5.2. Once more we call the node at the end of the branch with transmission $^{>}w_j^e(s)$ the output node associated with node j. The transmission of the flow graph from node i to the output node associated with node j is thus $\phi_{ij}^e(s)$, the exponential transform of the interval transition probability $\phi_{ij}(t)$ for the continuous-time semi-Markov process. The flow graph analysis of such a process is therefore not changed from the analysis of the discrete-time process.

The flow graph for the car rental problem in continuous time appears as Figure 11.7.3. We can construct it directly from the transition diagram of Figure 11.2.1 and the computation of $^{>}W^e(s)$ in Equation 11.5.8. The transmission of the branch from node i to node j is just $c_{ij}^e(s) = p_{ij}h_{ij}^e(s)$, the product of the transition probability and the exponential transform of the holding time density function for that transition. We then calculate the quantity $^{>}w_i^e(s)$ by summing the transmissions on all branches leaving node i, subtracting the result from one, and dividing by s.

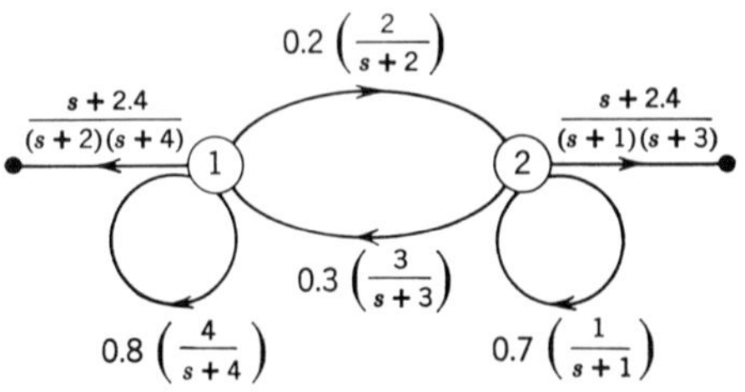

Figure 11.7.3 Flow graph for the continuous-time car rental example.

If we calculate the transmission of this flow graph from node i to the output node associated with node j, we obtain the ijth element of $\Phi^e(s)$ in Equation 11.5.14.

Although the flow graph for the discrete-time semi-Markov process had a computational advantage as a basis for developing a recursive equation, this advantage is not shared by the flow graph for the continuous-time case. Therefore the flow graph for the continuous-time semi-Markov process serves mainly as an aid to visualizing the relationships in the process.

We shall now consider the form that the results of Chapter 10 for the discrete-time process assume in the continuous-time process. Since the changes are relatively minor, we shall be brief in our treatment and concentrate only on the differences rather than the similarities. In particular, the reasoning underlying each of the basic equations is identical except for the introduction of the continuous time base. Finally, because flow graph representations of these results follow immediately from their discrete-time counterparts and the relevant equations, we shall often omit reference to these representations in this chapter.

11.8 COUNTING TRANSITIONS

To count transitions we define $\phi_{ij}(k|t)$ as the probability that the process will occupy state j at time t and that it will have made k transitions given that it made its zeroth transition into state i at time zero,

$$\phi_{ij}(k|t) = \mathscr{P}\{n(t) = k, s(t) = j|s(0) = i, t(0) = 0\}. \tag{11.8.1}$$

The integral equation for $\phi_{ij}(k|t)$ is

$$\phi_{ij}(k|t) = \delta_{ij}\,\delta(k)\,{}^{>}w_i(t) + \sum_{r=1}^{N} p_{ir}\int_0^t d\tau\, h_{ir}(\tau)\phi_{rj}(k-1|t-\tau) \qquad \begin{aligned} i &= 1, 2, \ldots, N \\ j &= 1, 2, \ldots, N \\ k &= 0, 1, 2, \ldots \\ t &\geq 0. \end{aligned} \tag{11.8.2}$$

Now we define $\phi_{ij}{}^{ge}(y|s)$ to be the result of transforming $\phi_{ij}(k|t)$ geometrically on its first variable and exponentially on its second variable,

$$\phi_{ij}{}^{ge}(y|s) = \sum_{k=0}^{\infty} y^k \int_0^\infty dt\, e^{-st}\phi_{ij}(k|t). \tag{11.8.3}$$

This notation is a direct extension of our multiple transform notation to the case where we must distinguish whether each variable is to be geometrically or exponentially transformed. Again, when any part of the multiple transform is inverted we replace the corresponding transform subscript by a hyphen.

The geometric-exponential transform of Equation 11.8.2 is then

$$\phi_{ij}^{ge}(y|s) = \delta_{ij} \, {}^{>}w_i^e(s) + y \sum_{r=1}^{N} p_{ir} h_{ir}^e(s) \phi_{rj}^{ge}(y|s), \tag{11.8.4}$$

or in matrix form,

$$\begin{aligned} \Phi^{ge}(y|s) &= {}^{>}W^e(s) + y[P \square H^e(s)]\Phi^{ge}(y|s) \\ &= {}^{>}W^e(s) + yC^e(s)\Phi^{ge}(y|s). \end{aligned} \tag{11.8.5}$$

We write the solution of this matrix equation as

$$\Phi^{ge}(y|s) = [I - yC^e(s)]^{-1} \, {}^{>}W^e(s). \tag{11.8.6}$$

Therefore, counting transitions in a continuous-time semi-Markov process requires only tagging with y the transitions in the flow graph that are to be counted. We have an exact correspondence to the discrete-time results of Equation 10.6.9.

Transition Moments

Computing the moments of the number of transitions made in any time given the starting and ending states is very similar for the discrete- and continuous-time cases; however, there are a few minor changes.

We define $\overline{k_{ij}^m(t)}$ as the mth moment of the number of transitions the process makes from time zero through time t given that it entered state i at time zero and occupied state j at time t. We can express $\overline{k_{ij}^m(t)}$ in the equation

$$\overline{k_{ij}^m(t)} = \frac{k_{ij}^m(t)}{\phi_{ij}(t)}, \tag{11.8.7}$$

where $k_{ij}^m(t)$ is a quantity whose exponential transform $k_{ij}^{m\,e}(s)$ is obtained, as before, by successive differentiation of $\phi_{ij}^{ge}(y|s)$ with respect to y. We write for $m = 1$ and $m = 2$,

$$k_{ij}^e(s) = \frac{d}{dy} \phi_{ij}^{ge}(y|s)\Big|_{y=1} \tag{11.8.8}$$

and

$$k_{ij}^{2e}(s) = \frac{d^2}{dy^2} \phi_{ij}^{ge}(y|s)\Big|_{y=1} + k_{ij}^e(s). \tag{11.8.9}$$

The matrix form of these equations is

$$K^e(s) = \frac{d}{dy} \Phi^{ge}(y|s)\Big|_{y=1} \tag{11.8.10}$$

and

$$K^{2e}(s) = \frac{d^2}{dy^2}\,\Phi^{ge}(y|s)\bigg|_{y=1} + K^e(s). \tag{11.8.11}$$

First moments

By using Equation 11.8.6 we can obtain $K^e(s)$ in the form,

$$K^e(s) = [I - C^e(s)]^{-1}C^e(s)[I - C^e(s)]^{-1} \square W^e(s), \tag{11.8.12}$$

or we can place it in any of the alternate forms,

$$\begin{aligned} K^e(s) &= C^e(s)[I - C^e(s)]^{-1}[I - C^e(s)]^{-1} \square W^e(s) \\ &= [I - C^e(s)]^{-1}[I - C^e(s)]^{-1}C^e(s) \square W^e(s) \\ &= [I - C^e(s)]^{-1}[(I - C^e(s))^{-1} - I] \square W^e(s). \end{aligned} \tag{11.8.13}$$

By using inverse exponential transformation and Equation 11.8.7, we then find $\bar{k}_{ij}(t)$, the mean number of transitions in the interval $(0, t)$ given that trajectory of the process started in state i and ended in state j.

Moments unconditional on final state

If we are not interested in the ending state, then we define $\overline{k_{i\Sigma}{}^m}(t)$, the mth moment of the number of transitions through time t given only that the system started in state i at time zero. Then,

$$\overline{k_{i\Sigma}{}^m}(t) = \sum_{j=1}^{N} k_{ij}{}^m(t), \tag{11.8.14}$$

and we no longer need the denominator factor $\phi_{ij}(t)$ used in Equation 11.8.7. Then $K^{m\,e}(s)\mathbf{s}$ is a column vector whose ith element is the exponential transform $\overline{k_{i\Sigma}{}^m}{}^e(s)$ of $\overline{k_{i\Sigma}{}^m}(t)$. From Equation 11.8.12,

$$\begin{aligned} K^e(s)\mathbf{s} &= [I - C^e(s)]^{-1}C^e(s)[I - C^e(s)]^{-1} \square W^e(s)\mathbf{s} \\ &= [I - C^e(s)]^{-1}C^e(s)\Phi^e(s)\mathbf{s}. \end{aligned} \tag{11.8.15}$$

Since the rows of $\Phi^e(s)$ each sum to $1/s$, we have

$$K^e(s)\mathbf{s} = \frac{1}{s}\,[I - C^e(s)]^{-1}C^e(s)\mathbf{s}. \tag{11.8.16}$$

Thus the summation indicated in Equation 10.6.23 by the transform operator $1/(1 - z)$ becomes an integration indicated by $1/s$ in Equation 11.8.16. Often the only changes we shall have to make in our earlier results are substitutions of integrations for summations, or of $1/s$ for $1/(1 - z)$ in the transform domain.

Second moments

Returning to the second moment of the number of transitions, we differentiate $\Phi^{ge}(y|s)$ with respect to y once more and use Equation 11.8.11 to write

$$K^{2e}(s) = [I - C^e(s)]^{-1}C^e(s)\{2[I - C^e(s)]^{-1} - I\}[I - C^e(s)]^{-1} > W^e(s). \tag{11.8.17}$$

When we are not interested in the state occupied at the end of the trajectory, we compute the vector

$$K^{2e}(s)\mathbf{s} = \frac{1}{s}[I - C^e(s)]^{-1}C^e(s)\{2[I - C^e(s)]^{-1} - I\}\mathbf{s}, \tag{11.8.18}$$

and inverse-transform its ith element to obtain $\overline{k_i^2}(t)$.

11.9 ENTRANCE AND DESTINATION PROBABILITIES

Entrance Rates

The concept of entrance probabilities is not nearly so neat for the continuous-time semi-Markov process as it is for the discrete-time semi-Markov process. We define an entrance rate $e_{ij}(k|t)$ such that $e_{ij}(k|t)\Delta$, where Δ is very small, is the probability that the process will enter state j on its kth transition and in the time interval $(t, t + \Delta)$ given that it made its zeroth transition into state i at time zero. The integral equation for this entrance rate is then

$$e_{ij}(k|t) = \delta_{ij}\,\delta(k)\,\delta(t) + \sum_{r=1}^{N} p_{ir}\int_0^t d\tau\, h_{ir}(\tau)e_{rj}(k - 1|t - \tau) \qquad \begin{aligned} i &= 1, 2, \ldots, N \\ j &= 1, 2, \ldots, N \\ k &= 0, 1, 2, \ldots \\ t &\geq 0. \end{aligned} \tag{11.9.1}$$

Transform relations

We define the geometric-exponential transform of $e_{ij}(k|t)$ as

$$e_{ij}^{ge}(y|s) = \sum_{k=0}^{\infty} y^k \int_0^{\infty} dt\, e^{-st}e_{ij}(k|t), \tag{11.9.2}$$

to permit doubly transforming Equation 11.9.1 into the form,

$$e_{ij}^{ge}(y|s) = \delta_{ij} + y\sum_{r=1}^{N} p_{ir}h_{ir}^e(s)e_{rj}^{ge}(y|s). \tag{11.9.3}$$

The corresponding matrix equation is

$$\begin{aligned} E^{ge}(y|s) &= I + y[P \,\Box\, H^e(s)]E^{ge}(y|z) \\ &= I + yC^e(s)E^{ge}(y|z), \end{aligned} \tag{11.9.4}$$

with solution

$$E^{ge}(y|s) = [I - yC^e(s)]^{-1}. \tag{11.9.5}$$

Note that $E^{ge}(y|s)$ is just the matrix of transmissions of the matrix flow graph for the continuous-time semi-Markov process with the associated output branches labeled with the ${}^{>}w_i^e(s)$'s removed. We can therefore write the transformed interval transition probabilities in terms of the transformed entrance rates as

$$\Phi^{ge}(y|s) = E^{ge}(y|s)\, {}^{>}W^e(s). \tag{11.9.6}$$

We may thus consider the entrance rates as just one component of the interval transition probabilities. Equation 11.9.6 in element form shows that the interval transition probabilities are just the entrance rates convolved with the complementary cumulative waiting time density functions,

$$\phi_{ij}(k|t) = \int_0^t d\tau\, e_{ij}(k|\tau)\, {}^{>}w_j(t-\tau). \tag{11.9.7}$$

If we choose to ignore the number of transitions made by the process, then we eliminate k from the non-transformed equations and evaluate the transformed equations at $y = 1$. Thus,

$$E^e(s) = [I - C^e(s)]^{-1} \tag{11.9.8}$$

is the matrix whose ijth element is the exponential transform of the entrance rate to state j at time t given that the process entered state i at time zero. We therefore have

$$\Phi^e(s) = E^e(s)\, {}^{>}W^e(s). \tag{11.9.9}$$

Limiting behavior

By applying the final value theorem of exponential transforms, we find

$$\begin{aligned} \lim_{s\to 0} s\Phi^e(s) &= \lim_{s\to 0} sE^e(s) \lim_{s\to 0} {}^{>}W^e(s) \\ \Phi &= EM, \end{aligned} \tag{11.9.10}$$

where E is the matrix of limiting entrance rates defined by

$$E = \lim_{s\to 0} sE^e(s) = \lim_{s\to 0} s[I - C^e(s)]^{-1}. \tag{11.9.11}$$

For a monodesmic process the elements of Equation 11.9.10 imply

$$\phi_{ij} = \phi_j = e_{ij}\bar{\tau}_j \tag{11.9.12}$$

or

$$e_{ij} = e_j = \frac{\phi_j}{\bar{\tau}_j} = \frac{\pi_j}{\bar{\tau}}. \tag{11.9.13}$$

The rows of the limiting entrance rate matrix E are therefore identical for a monodesmic process. The jth element in each row is the ratio of the limiting state probability π_j for the imbedded Markov process to the mean time between transitions $\bar{\tau}$.

The car rental example. If we apply Equation 11.9.11 to the car rental example result of Equation 11.5.13, we find

$$E = \lim_{s\to 0} s[I - C^e(s)]^{-1} = \begin{bmatrix} 1.2 & 0.8 \\ 1.2 & 0.8 \end{bmatrix}. \tag{11.9.14}$$

Since for this example

$$M = \begin{bmatrix} 0.3 & 0 \\ 0 & 0.8 \end{bmatrix}, \tag{11.9.15}$$

we obtain immediately

$$\Phi = EM = \begin{bmatrix} 0.36 & 0.64 \\ 0.36 & 0.64 \end{bmatrix}, \tag{11.9.16}$$

in agreement with our earlier results.

The numerical form of E in Equation 11.9.14 makes obvious our statement that entrance rates are not entrance probabilities. How then can we interpret the numbers 1.2 and 0.8? You recall that $1/\bar{\tau}$ is the steady-state average transition rate per unit time, equal to $1/0.5 = 2$ in the continuous-time version of the car rental example. This means that on the average there will be two rentals returned per time unit for each car in the fleet. Equation 11.9.14 shows that 1.2 of these rentals will be returned to town 1 per unit time in the steady state, while 0.8 will be returned to town 2. The probability of observing the return of a car to town 1 within a small time window of length Δ in the steady state is therefore $e_1\Delta = 1.2\Delta$.

Destination Probabilities

We do not encounter any difficulty in discussing destination probabilities for the continuous-time semi-Markov process. We define $\gamma_{ijq}(k|t)$ as the probability that the process is in state j at time t, that it has made k transitions, and that its next transition will be to state q given that it entered state i on its zeroth transition at time 0. The destination probabilities are then related to the entrance rates, transition probabilities, and complementary cumulative holding time probabilities by

$$\gamma_{ijq}(k|t) = \int_0^t d\tau\, e_{ij}(k|\tau)p_{jq}\, {}^{>}h_{jq}(t-\tau) \qquad \begin{aligned} i &= 1, 2, \ldots, N \\ j &= 1, 2, \ldots, N \\ q &= 1, 2, \ldots, N \\ k &= 0, 1, 2, \ldots \\ t &\geq 0. \end{aligned} \tag{11.9.17}$$

The geometric-exponential transform of this equation is then

$$\gamma_{ijq}^{ge}(y|s) = e_{ij}^{ge}(y|s)p_{jq}\, {}^{>}h_{jq}^{e}(s). \tag{11.9.18}$$

If we ignore the number of transitions, then the equation simplifies to

$$\gamma_{ijq}^{e}(s) = e_{ij}^{e}(s)p_{jq}\, {}^{>}h_{jq}^{e}(s). \tag{11.9.19}$$

If, on the other hand, we sum Equation 11.9.18 over the destination state q, we obtain

$$\begin{aligned} \sum_{q=1}^{N} \gamma_{ijq}^{ge}(y|s) &= e_{ij}^{ge}(y|s) \sum_{q=1}^{N} p_{jq}\, {}^{>}h_{jq}^{e}(s) \\ &= e_{ij}^{ge}(y|s)\, {}^{>}w_j^{e}(s) \\ &= \phi_{ij}^{ge}(y|s). \end{aligned} \tag{11.9.20}$$

Limiting behavior

If the imbedded process is monodesmic, $\gamma_{ijq}(t)$, the destination probability without regard to transition, approaches a limiting value γ_{jq} when t is large. We find this limiting destination probability by using the final value theorem for exponential transforms,

$$\begin{aligned} \gamma_{jq} &= \lim_{t\to\infty} \gamma_{ijq}(t) = \lim_{s\to 0} s\gamma_{ijq}^{e}(s) = \lim_{s\to 0} se_{ij}^{e}(s)p_{jq}\, {}^{>}h_{jq}^{e}(s) \\ &= \lim_{s\to 0} se_{ij}^{e}(s)p_{jq} \lim_{s\to 0} {}^{>}h_{jq}^{e}(s) \\ &= e_j p_{jq} \bar{\tau}_{iq} \\ &= \frac{\pi_j p_{jq} \bar{\tau}_{jq}}{\bar{\tau}}. \end{aligned} \tag{11.9.21}$$

The probability γ_{jq} is the probability that if we observe the process in the steady state, we shall find it in state j and planning to make its next transition to state q.

Note that the time scale of the process will not affect the limiting destination probabilities because mean times appear in both the numerator and denominator of Equation 11.9.21. As a result the limiting destination probabilities for the continuous-time car rental example are the same as those found for the discrete-time version in Equation 10.7.32.

Furthermore, if we define $\gamma_{\Sigma q} = \sum_{q=1}^{N} \gamma_{jq}$ as the probability that the next transition of the process will be to state j when it is observed in the steady state, we have obtained the same values for this quantity in the example that we obtained before. Therefore for both the continuous- and discrete-time versions of the car rental example, if we observe a car in the steady state, there is a 0.36 chance that it was rented in town 1 and a 0.32 chance that it will be returned to town 1.

Lapsed Time

Suppose that we knew that a state i had already been occupied for a time τ_ℓ that we shall designate as the lapsed time. How would this knowledge affect our probability assignments on destination state and remaining time until next transition? We would like to know how the joint probability of next transition to state j and density function for total time in state i, τ, will be affected by the knowledge that τ exceeds τ_ℓ. In the abbreviated notation of Section 10.13, this quantity is $\{j, \tau | \tau > \tau_\ell, i\}$. From elementary probability we can write this expression in the equivalent form,

$$\{j, \tau | \tau > \tau_\ell, i\} = \frac{\{\tau > \tau_\ell | j, \tau, i\}\{j, \tau | i\}}{\{\tau > \tau_\ell | i\}}. \tag{11.9.22}$$

Since $\{\tau > \tau_\ell | j, \tau, i\} = 1$ if $\tau > \tau_\ell$ and zero otherwise, we have

$$\begin{aligned} \{j, \tau | \tau > \tau_\ell, i\} &= \frac{\{j, \tau | i\}}{\{\tau > \tau_\ell | i\}} & \tau > \tau_\ell \\ &= \frac{c_{ij}(\tau)}{{}^{>}w_i(\tau_\ell)} & \tau > \tau_\ell \\ &= \frac{p_{ij} h_{ij}(\tau)}{{}^{>}w_i(\tau_\ell)} & \tau > \tau_\ell. \end{aligned} \tag{11.9.23}$$

We see that we have obtained, for $\tau > \tau_\ell$, the core matrix element $c_{ij}(\tau)$ divided by the complementary cumulative waiting time distribution for state i evaluated at τ_ℓ, which is, of course, just the integral of $c_{ij}(\tau)$ from τ_ℓ to ∞.

This joint probability allows us to compute the marginal distributions on destination state j and total time in state i, τ. The probability that the process will make its next transition to state j given that it has already spent a lapsed time τ_ℓ in state i is

$$\begin{aligned} \{j | \tau > \tau_\ell, i\} &= \int_{\tau_\ell}^{\infty} d\tau \, \{j, \tau | \tau > \tau_\ell, i\} \\ &= \frac{p_{ij}\, {}^{>}h_{ij}(\tau_\ell)}{{}^{>}w_i(\tau_\ell)}, \end{aligned} \tag{11.9.24}$$

which is just the transition probability p_{ij} multiplied by the ratio of complementary cumulative holding time distribution at τ_ℓ to complementary cumulative waiting time distribution at τ_ℓ. Note that this ratio equals one for the independent semi-Markov process.

The distribution on total time in state i, τ, given the lapsed time τ_ℓ, is just the sum of the joint distribution over all destination states j,

$$\begin{aligned}\{\tau|\tau > \tau_\ell, i\} &= \sum_j \{j, \tau|\tau > \tau_\ell, i\} \\ &= \frac{\sum_j p_{ij}h_{ij}(\tau)}{{}^>w_i(\tau_\ell)} \qquad \tau > \tau_\ell \\ &= \frac{w_i(\tau)}{{}^>w_i(\tau_\ell)} \qquad \tau > \tau_\ell,\end{aligned} \tag{11.9.25}$$

which is just the waiting time density function normalized by its complementary cumulative at τ_ℓ.

If the total time τ spent in the state is considered as the sum of the lapsed time τ_ℓ and a remaining time τ_r, $\tau = \tau_\ell + \tau_r$, then the joint probability-probability density on j and τ_r is given by Equation 11.9.23 as

$$\begin{aligned}\{j, \tau_r|i\} &= \{j, \tau = \tau_\ell + \tau_r|\tau > \tau_\ell, i\} \\ &= \frac{p_{ij}h_{ij}(\tau_\ell + \tau_r)}{{}^>w_i(\tau_\ell)} \qquad \tau_r > 0.\end{aligned} \tag{11.9.26}$$

We shall use this result in Chapter 13.

11.10 TRANSIENT PROCESSES

Consider a monodesmic continuous-time semi-Markov process with a single trapping state r. We define $p_{ir}(k, t)$ as the joint probability-probability density function that k transitions and time t will be required to reach this trapping state if the process starts in a transient state i. The geometric-exponential transform $p_{ir}{}^{ge}(y, s)$ of $p_{ir}(k, t)$ is then the transmission of the flow graph of the transient process from state i to state r. By an argument exactly analogous to that in Section 10.8, this flow graph is constructed from the transition-counting flow graph of the continuous-time semi-Markov process simply by removing all branches that leave node r. We can also consider this flow graph to be derived as a flow graph for calculating the entrance rate for a state that can be entered but once.

Transform Analysis

The transform $p_{ir}{}^{ge}(y, s)$ must satisfy the requirement that $p_{ir}{}^{ge}(1, 0) = 1$. If we invert the geometric transform and evaluate the result when $s = 0$, we obtain

$p_{ir}^{-e}(k, 0)$, the probability that k transitions will be required to reach the trapping state. If we invert the exponential transform and evaluate the result at $y = 1$, we obtain $p_{ir}^{g-}(1, t)$, the density function for the time to reach the trapping state.

We let $\bar{k}$ and $\overline{k^2}$ be the first and second moments of the number of transitions to reach the trapping state, and $\bar{t}$ and $\overline{t^2}$ be the first and second moments of the time to reach the trapping state. From our relationships for deriving the moments of distributions from their transforms, we can then write

$$\bar{k} = \frac{d}{dy} p_{ir}^{ge}(y, 0)\bigg|_{y=1} \qquad \overline{k^2} = \frac{d^2}{dy^2} p_{ir}^{ge}(y, 0)\bigg|_{y=1} + \bar{k} \tag{11.10.1}$$

and

$$\bar{t} = -\frac{d}{ds} p_{ir}^{ge}(1, s)\bigg|_{s=0} \qquad \overline{t^2} = \frac{d^2}{ds^2} p_{ir}^{ge}(1, s)\bigg|_{s=0}. \tag{11.10.2}$$

The car rental example

Suppose that in the continuous-time car rental example we consider as a transient process the number of transitions and time required to reach state 2 from state 1. We draw the flow graph of this transient process immediately as Figure 11.10.1. We find by inspection,

$$p_{12}^{ge}(y, s) = \vec{t}_{12} = \frac{\dfrac{0.4y}{s+2}}{1 - \dfrac{3.2y}{s+4}} = \frac{0.4y(s+4)}{(s+4-3.2y)(s+2)}, \tag{11.10.3}$$

a transform whose inversion is somewhat complicated.

Marginal on transitions. Turning therefore to the marginal on the number of transitions we write

$$p_{12}^{ge}(y, 0) = \frac{0.2y}{1 - 0.8y} \tag{11.10.4}$$

or

$$p_{12}^{-e}(k, 0) = 0.2(0.8)^{k-1} \qquad k = 1, 2, 3, \ldots. \tag{11.10.5}$$

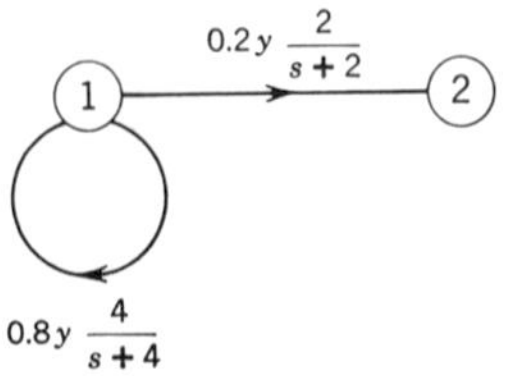

Figure 11.10.1 Flow graph for a transient process in the car rental example.

Since the transition structure of this transient process is exactly the same as it was for the discrete version whose flow graph appears in Figure 10.8.3, we are not surprised that Equation 11.10.5 is the same result found in Equation 10.8.10. The moments computed from Equation 11.10.1 including the variance $\overset{v}{k}$ and standard deviation $\overset{s}{k}$ are therefore the same as those of Equation 10.8.11,

$$\bar{k} = 5 \qquad \overline{k^2} = 45 \qquad \overset{v}{k} = 20 \qquad \overset{s}{k} = 4.47. \tag{11.10.6}$$

Marginal on time. The time until the trapping state is reached, however, has a different form in the continuous-time transient process. The density function for this time has an exponential transform,

$$\begin{aligned} p_{12}{}^{ge}(1, s) &= \frac{0.4(s + 4)}{(s + 0.8)(s + 2)} \\ &= \frac{16/15}{s + 0.8} + \frac{(-2/3)}{s + 2}, \end{aligned} \tag{11.10.7}$$

with inverse transform,

$$p_{12}{}^{g}(1, t) = \frac{16}{15}e^{-0.8t} - \frac{2}{3}e^{-2t} \qquad t \geq 0. \tag{11.10.8}$$

The density function for the time to enter the trapping state is therefore the difference between two exponential terms. Note that the area under this density function is one since $p_{12}{}^{ge}(1, 0) = 1$, and that the density function is positive for all positive values of t.

We apply Equation 11.10.2 to Equation 11.10.7 to find the moments of the time to reach the trapping state. We obtain the moments

$$\bar{t} = -\frac{d}{ds}p_{12}{}^{ge}(1, s)\bigg|_{s=0} = 1.5 \qquad \overline{t^2} = \frac{d^2}{ds^2}p_{12}{}^{ge}(1, s)\bigg|_{s=0} = 4, \tag{11.10.9}$$

and therefore the variance and standard deviation

$$\overset{v}{t} = \overline{t^2} - \bar{t}^2 = 1.75 \qquad \overset{s}{t} = \sqrt{\overset{v}{t}} = 1.32. \tag{11.10.10}$$

Thus the mean time to reach state 2 is 1.5 with a standard deviation of 1.32. If we start to measure time when a car is rented at town 1, then we expect 1.5 time units to elapse before that car will first reach town 2. The car may, of course, have been rented several times at town 1 before this even occurs. Note that the mean $\bar{t} = 1.5$ is just a factor of 12 smaller than the mean $\bar{n} = 18$ found for the discrete case in Equation 10.8.14. The standard deviation $\overset{s}{n} = 15.3$ in that equation is approximately, but not exactly, a factor of 12 larger than the standard deviation $\overset{s}{t} = 1.32$.

The augmented transition diagram

In Section 10.8 we developed a flow graph procedure for calculating $\bar{\nu}_{ij}$, the expected amount of time the process will spend in transient state j if it is started in transient state i. By defining $x_{ij}(t)$ to be equal to 1 if the process is in state j at time t and 0 otherwise given that it entered state i at time zero, we can write

$$\bar{\nu}_{ij} = \int_0^\infty dt\, \bar{x}_{ij}(t) = \int_0^\infty dt\, \phi_{ij}(t) = \phi_{ij}^e(0). \tag{11.10.11}$$

Thus $\bar{\nu}_{ij}$ is just the transmission from node i to node j of the flow graph for the continuous-time semi-Markov process evaluated at $s = 0$. Since $h_{ij}^e(0) = 1$ and ${}^>w_i^e(0) = \bar{\tau}_i$, the quantity $\bar{\nu}_{ij}$ is just the transmission from node i to the output node associated with node j of the augmented transition diagram we drew in Figure 10.8.4 for the discrete-time semi-Markov process.

To find the mean time spent in state 1 for the continuous-time car rental transient process we have been discussing, we evaluate $\bar{\nu}_{11}$ by using the augmented transition diagram of Figure 10.8.5 with $\bar{\tau}_1 = 3.6$ replaced by the value $\bar{\tau}_1 = 0.3$ appropriate to the continuous-time version. We calculate

$$\bar{\nu}_{11} = \vec{t}_{11} = \frac{1}{1 - (4/5)}(0.3) = 1.5, \tag{11.10.12}$$

which is, of course, the value for $\bar{t}$ found in Equation 11.10.9.

Duration

We can again define the duration of a state to be either the number of transitions or the amount of time required after a state is entered before a real transition is made to another state. We let $d_i(k, t)$ be the joint probability-probability density function for the number of transitions k and time t that constitute the duration of state i. The geometric-exponential transform $d_i^{ge}(y, s)$ of the duration has the flow graph representation of Figure 10.9.1 with geometric transforms replaced by exponential transforms. Thus we can write the transformed duration as

$$d_i^{ge}(y, s) = \frac{y[w_i^e(s) - p_{ii}h_{ii}^e(s)]}{1 - yp_{ii}h_{ii}^e(s)}. \tag{11.10.13}$$

Our check is that $d_i^{ge}(1, 0) = 1$.

Duration in transitions

If we measure duration in transitions alone then the geometric transform of the probability mass function for the number of transitions is

$$d_i^{ge}(y, 0) = \frac{y[1 - p_{ii}]}{1 - yp_{ii}}, \tag{11.10.14}$$

with inverse

$$d_i^{\cdot e}(k, 0) = (1 - p_{ii})p_{ii}^{k-1} \qquad k = 1, 2, 3, \ldots. \tag{11.10.15}$$

The duration measured in transitions is therefore still geometrically distributed with moments

$$\bar{k}_i = \frac{1}{1 - p_{ii}} \qquad \overline{k_i^2} = \frac{1 + p_{ii}}{(1 - p_{ii})^2} \qquad \check{k}_i = \frac{p_{ii}}{(1 - p_{ii})^2}, \tag{11.10.16}$$

just as we found in Equation 10.9.7.

Duration in time

However, if we measure duration in time alone, then the duration has a density function whose exponential transform is

$$d_i^{\mathcal{g}e}(1, s) = \frac{w_i^e(s) - p_{ii}h_{ii}^e(s)}{1 - p_{ii}h_{ii}^e(s)}. \tag{11.10.17}$$

The inverse of this transform would provide an explicit expression for the density function. To calculate $\bar{t}_i$, the mean duration of state i measured in time, we write

$$\bar{t}_i = -\frac{d}{ds} d_i^{\mathcal{g}e}(1, s)\bigg|_{s=0} = \frac{\bar{\tau}_i}{1 - p_{ii}} = \bar{k}_i\bar{\tau}_i, \tag{11.10.18}$$

which produces the same result as Equation 10.9.10, i.e., the mean duration in time is the mean duration in transitions multiplied by the mean waiting time for the state.

For the second moment of duration measured in time, $\overline{t_i^2}$, we write

$$\overline{t_i^2} = \frac{d^2}{ds^2} d_i^{\mathcal{g}e}(1, s)\bigg|_{s=0} = \frac{\overline{\tau_i^2}(1 - p_{ii}) + 2p_{ii}\bar{\tau}_i\bar{\tau}_{ii}}{(1 - p_{ii})^2}, \tag{11.10.19}$$

and therefore obtain the same result we found in Equation 10.9.11 for the discrete-time case. The variance of the duration measured in time $\check{t}_i$ is then

$$\check{t}_i = \overline{t_i^2} - \bar{t}_i^2 = \bar{k}_i\check{\tau}_i + \check{k}_i\bar{\tau}_i(2\bar{\tau}_{ii} - \bar{\tau}_i). \tag{11.10.20}$$

The car rental example

We can use these relationships to calculate the moments of duration in transitions and time for state 1 of the continuous-time version of the car rental example. Since $p_{11} = 0.8$, $\bar{\tau}_{11} = 0.25$, $\bar{\tau}_1 = 0.3$, $\check{\tau}_1 = 0.11$, Equations 11.10.16 produce the moments of duration in transitions as

$$\bar{k}_1 = 5 \qquad \overline{k_1^2} = 45 \qquad \check{k}_1 = 20; \tag{11.10.21}$$

then Equations 11.10.18 and 11.10.20 use these results to construct the moments of duration in time,

$$\begin{aligned} \bar{t}_1 &= \bar{k}_1\bar{\tau}_1 = 5(0.3) = 1.5 \\ \check{t}_1 &= \bar{k}_1\check{\tau}_1 + \check{k}_1\bar{\tau}_1(2\bar{\tau}_{11} - \bar{\tau}_1) = 5(0.11) + 20(0.3)[2(0.25) - 0.3] = 1.75. \end{aligned} \tag{11.10.22}$$

Since the transient process whose flow graph appears in Figure 11.10.1 is just the process that describes the duration of state 1, the moments in terms of transitions and time found in Equations 11.10.21 and 11.10.22 are the same results shown in Equations 11.10.6, 11.10.9, and 11.10.10.

We should finally note that for the independent continuous-time semi-Markov process the variance of the duration measured in time becomes simply

$$\check{t}_i = \bar{k}_i \check{\tau}_i + \check{k}_i \bar{\tau}_i^2, \tag{11.10.23}$$

in accordance with the theory of compound distributions.

11.11 FIRST PASSAGE TIMES

The first passage times of the continuous-time semi-Markov process can be measured in time or in terms of the number of transitions. We define $f_{ij}(k, t)$ to be the joint probability mass function-probability density function for the number of transitions k and time t required for the first passage from state i to state j given that state i was entered at time zero on the zeroth transition; we let $f_{ij}^{ge}(y, s)$ be the geometric-exponential transform of $f_{ij}(k, t)$. We already know that one method for finding first passage time transforms is to change state j of the semi-Markov process into a trapping state and then find the transmission of the flow graph for the process from state i to state j. However, this procedure follows exactly that of the discrete-time case. In fact, we have already computed $f_{12}^{ge}(y, s)$ for the car rental example in Equation 11.10.3 using this procedure.

We therefore concern ourselves with the general method for developing first passage time transforms. The integral equation for $f_{ij}(k, t)$ is

$$f_{ij}(k, t) = \sum_{\substack{r=1 \\ r \neq j}}^{N} p_{ir} \int_0^t d\tau \; h_{ir}(\tau) f_{rj}(k-1, t-\tau) + \delta(k-1) p_{ij} h_{ij}(t)$$

$$i = 1, 2, \ldots, N; \; k = 0, 1, 2, \ldots \qquad j = 1, 2, \ldots, N; \; t \geq 0 \tag{11.11.1}$$

with geometric-exponential transform

$$f_{ij}^{ge}(y, s) = y \sum_{\substack{r=1 \\ r \neq j}}^{N} p_{ir} h_{ir}^{e}(s) f_{rj}^{ge}(y, s) + y p_{ij} h_{ij}^{e}(s)$$

$$= y \sum_{r=1}^{N} p_{ir} h_{ir}^{e}(s) f_{rj}^{ge}(y, s) + y p_{ij} h_{ij}^{e}(s)[1 - f_{jj}^{ge}(y, s)] \tag{11.11.2}$$

and matrix transform

$$\begin{aligned} F^{ge}(y, s) &= y(P \,\square\, H^e(s))F^{ge}(y, s) + yP \,\square\, H^e(s)[I - F^{ge}(y, s) \,\square\, I] \\ &= yC^e(s)[I + (U - I) \,\square\, F^{ge}(y, s)]. \end{aligned} \tag{11.11.3}$$

Of course, if we are interested only in transitions, we evaluate the transforms at $s = 0$; if only in time, then at $y = 1$.

Relationship to Interval Transition Probabilities

The basic relationship between the interval transition probabilities and the first passage times is

$$\phi_{ij}(k|t) = \sum_{l=0}^{k} \int_0^t d\tau\, f_{ij}(l, \tau)\phi_{jj}(k - l|t - \tau) + \delta_{ij}\, \delta(k)\, {}^{>}w_i(t), \tag{11.11.4}$$

with geometric-exponential transform

$$\phi_{ij}^{ge}(y|s) = f_{ij}^{ge}(y, s)\phi_{jj}^{ge}(y|s) + \delta_{ij}\, {}^{>}w_i^e(s) \tag{11.11.5}$$

or

$$f_{ij}^{ge}(y, s) = \frac{\phi_{ij}^{ge}(y|s) - \delta_{ij}\, {}^{>}w_i^e(s)}{\phi_{jj}^{ge}(y|s)}. \tag{11.11.6}$$

Equation 11.11.6 leads to a matrix expression for the first passage time transforms in terms of the interval transition probability transforms,

$$F^{ge}(y, s) = [\Phi^{ge}(y|s) - {}^{>}W^e(s)][\Phi^{ge}(y|s) \,\square\, I]^{-1}, \tag{11.11.7}$$

but to write the inverse relationship we again note the two different forms that Equation 11.11.5 takes for $i = j$ and $i \neq j$,

$$\begin{aligned} \phi_{jj}^{ge}(y|s) &= \frac{{}^{>}w_j^e(s)}{1 - f_{jj}^{ge}(y, s)} \qquad i = j \\ \phi_{ij}^{ge}(y|s) &= \frac{f_{ij}^{ge}(y, s)\, {}^{>}w_j^e(s)}{1 - f_{jj}^{ge}(y, s)} \qquad i \neq j. \end{aligned} \tag{11.11.8}$$

These equations show that a flow graph like that of Figure 10.10.1 with appropriate changes of notation represents the relationship between the interval transition probability transforms and the first passage time transforms. We combine Equations 11.11.8 into the single equation

$$\phi_{ij}^{ge}(y|s) = \frac{[\delta_{ij} + (1 - \delta_{ij})f_{ij}^{ge}(y, s)]\, {}^{>}w_j^e(s)}{1 - f_{jj}^{ge}(y, s)}, \tag{11.11.9}$$

which implies the matrix relation we require,

$$\Phi^{ge}(y|s) = [I + (U - I) \,\square\, F^{ge}(y, s)][I - F^{ge}(y, s) \,\square\, I]^{-1} > W^e(s). \quad (11.11.10)$$

Finally, by noting that Equation 10.10.27 holds as well for the continuous-time case in which the second transform is an exponential transform, we can use Equation 11.11.3 to write an explicit equation for the first passage time transform matrix in terms of the transformed core matrix,

$$F^{ge}(y, s) = yC^e(s)[I - yC^e(s)]^{-1}\{[I - yC^e(s)]^{-1} \,\square\, I\}^{-1}, \quad (11.11.11)$$

a result analogous to Equation 10.10.29.

Thus the analysis of first passage times is virtually unchanged from our results for the discrete-time case.

First Passage Time Moments

If we let $\bar{\theta}_{ij}$ and $\overline{\theta_{ij}^2}$ be the first and second moments of the first passage time from state i to state j measured in time, then we find by direct evaluation that the results of Section 10.10 still apply with a change in interpretation. That is, the mean recurrence time $\bar{\theta}_{jj}$ is the reciprocal of the limiting entrance *rate* into state j, i.e., e_j,

$$\bar{\theta}_{jj} = \frac{1}{e_j}. \quad (11.11.12)$$

The mean first passage times are

$$\bar{\theta}_{ij} = -\frac{d}{ds} f_{ij}{}^e(s)\bigg|_{s=0} = -\frac{d}{ds} f_{ij}{}^{ge}(1, s)\bigg|_{s=0} = \bar{\tau}_i + \sum_{r=1}^{N} p_{ir}\bar{\theta}_{rj} - p_{ij}\bar{\theta}_{jj}$$

$$i = 1, 2, \ldots, N \qquad j = 1, 2, \ldots, N. \quad (11.11.13)$$

We compute the second moments as

$$\overline{\theta_{ij}^2} = \frac{d^2}{ds^2} f_{ij}{}^e(s)\bigg|_{s=0} = \frac{d^2}{ds^2} f_{ij}{}^{ge}(1, s)\bigg|_{s=0} = \overline{\tau_i^2} + \sum_{\substack{r=1 \\ r \neq j}}^{N} p_{ir}(2\bar{\tau}_{ir}\bar{\theta}_{rj} + \overline{\theta_{rj}^2})$$

$$i = 1, 2, \ldots, N \qquad j = 1, 2, \ldots, N. \quad (11.11.14)$$

Thus the first passage time moments have the same expressions they did in the discrete-time case.

The car rental example

We can use these equations to calculate the first passage time moments in time from state 1 to state 2 for the continuous-time form of the car rental example. We write

$$\begin{aligned}
\bar{\theta}_{12} &= \bar{\tau}_1 + p_{11}\bar{\theta}_{12} & \overline{\theta_{12}^2} &= \overline{\tau_1^2} + p_{11}(2\bar{\tau}_{11}\bar{\theta}_{12} + \overline{\theta_{12}^2}) \\
\bar{\theta}_{12} &= \frac{\bar{\tau}_1}{1 - p_{11}} & \overline{\theta_{12}^2} &= \frac{1}{1 - p_{11}}(\overline{\tau_1^2} + 2p_{11}\bar{\tau}_{11}\bar{\theta}_{12}) \\
&= \frac{0.3}{1 - 0.8} & &= \frac{1}{1 - 0.8}(0.2 + 2(0.8)(1/4)(1.5)) \\
&= 1.5 & &= 4,
\end{aligned} \tag{11.11.15}$$

and obtain results that agree with those of Equation 11.10.9 computed by analyzing the first passage time as a transient process.

11.12 STATE OCCUPANCIES

We let $\nu_{ij}(t)$ be the number of times state j is occupied in the time interval $(0, t)$ given that the process started in state i. We define $\omega_{ij}(k|t)$ to be the probability that $\nu_{ij}(t)$ is equal to k and call it the occupancy probability distribution. The integral equation for this distribution is

$$\begin{aligned}
\omega_{ij}(k|t) = \sum_{\substack{r=1 \\ r \neq j}}^{N} \int_0^t d\tau\, p_{ir}h_{ir}(\tau)\omega_{rj}(k|t - \tau) \\
+ \int_0^t d\tau\, p_{ij}h_{ij}(\tau)\omega_{jj}(k - 1|t - \tau) + \delta(k)\, {}^{>}w_i(t)
\end{aligned}$$

$$i = 1, 2, \ldots, N;\ k = 0, 1, 2, \ldots \quad j = 1, 2, \ldots, N;\ t \geq 0, \tag{11.12.1}$$

with geometric-exponential transform

$$\omega_{ij}^{ge}(y|s) = \sum_{r=1}^{N} p_{ir}h_{ir}^{e}(s)\omega_{rj}^{ge}(y|s) - (1 - y)p_{ij}h_{ij}^{e}(s)\omega_{jj}^{ge}(y|s) + {}^{>}w_i^{e}(s). \tag{11.12.2}$$

By using the methods of analysis in Section 10.11 we can express the matrix of transforms of the state occupancy probability distribution $\Omega^{ge}(y|s)$ in terms of the transformed core matrix by an equation directly analogous to Equation 10.11.8,

$$\Omega^{ge}(y|s) = \frac{1}{s}U - \frac{1}{s}(1-y)[I - C^e(s)]^{-1}C^e(s) \times (yI + (1-y)\{[I - C^e(s)]^{-1} \square I\})^{-1}. \tag{11.12.3}$$

Note that the only real change in this equation is the substitution of the integration operator $1/s$ for the summation operator $1/(1-z)$.

Relationship to First Passage Times

The integral equation that relates the state occupancy probability distribution to the first passage time probability distributions measured in time is

$$\omega_{ij}(k|t) = \int_0^t d\tau\, f_{ij}(\tau)\omega_{jj}(k-1|t-\tau) + \delta(k)\, {}^{>}f_{ij}(t) \qquad \begin{array}{l} i = 1, 2, \ldots, N;\ k = 0, 1, 2, \ldots \\ j = 1, 2, \ldots, N;\ t \geq 0, \end{array} \tag{11.12.4}$$

where ${}^{>}f_{ij}(t)$ is the probability that the first passage time from state i to state j exceeds t. The transform relationship is then

$$\omega_{ij}^{ge}(y|s) = yf_{ij}^e(s)\omega_{jj}^{ge}(y|s) + {}^{>}f_{ij}^e(s) \qquad \begin{array}{l} i = 1, 2, \ldots, N \\ j = 1, 2, \ldots, N \end{array} \tag{11.12.5}$$

or in matrix form

$$\Omega^{ge}(y|s) = yF^e(s)[\Omega^{ge}(y|s) \square I] + {}^{>}F^e(s). \tag{11.12.6}$$

However, more interesting relationships are obtained by writing Equation 11.12.5 for the case when $i = j$,

$$\omega_{jj}^{ge}(y|s) = \frac{{}^{>}f_{jj}^e(s)}{1 - yf_{jj}^e(s)}, \tag{11.12.7}$$

and then placing Equation 11.12.5 in the form,

$$\omega_{ij}^{ge}(y|s) = \frac{yf_{ij}^e(s)\, {}^{>}f_{jj}^e(s)}{1 - yf_{jj}^e(s)} + {}^{>}f_{ij}^e(s). \tag{11.12.8}$$

By noting that ${}^{>}f_{ij}^e(s) = (1/s)(1 - f_{ij}^e(s))$ we write

$$\omega_{ij}^{ge}(y|s) = \frac{1}{s}\left(1 - \frac{(1-y)f_{ij}^e(s)}{1 - yf_{jj}^e(s)}\right), \tag{11.12.9}$$

and obtain the matrix expression

$$\Omega^{ge}(y|s) = \frac{1}{s}U - \frac{1}{s}(1-y)F^e(s)[I - yF^e(s) \square I]^{-1} \tag{11.12.10}$$

as the analog of Equation 10.11.18.

Occupancy Moments

The first and second moments $\bar{\nu}_{ij}(t)$ and $\overline{\nu_{ij}^2}(t)$ can be directly evaluated from the probability distribution $\omega_{ij}(k|t)$. However, we can find the exponential transforms $\bar{\nu}_i^e(s)$ and $\overline{\nu_i^{2e}}(s)$ by differentiation of the transform $\omega_{ij}^{ge}(y|s)$ with respect to y.

First moments

Thus the transform of the mean is

$$\bar{\nu}_{ij}^e(s) = \sum_{k=0}^{\infty} k\omega_{ij}^{e}(k|s) = \frac{d}{dy}\,\omega_{ij}^{ge}(y|s)\Big|_{y=1}, \tag{11.12.11}$$

which is as well given by

$$\bar{\nu}_{ij}^e(s) = \lim_{y\to 1} \frac{\dfrac{1}{s} - \omega_{ij}^{ge}(y|s)}{1-y}\cdot \tag{11.12.12}$$

This result means that we can write $\overline{\mathrm{N}}^e(s)$, the matrix form of $\bar{\nu}_{ij}^e(s)$, from Equation 11.12.3,

$$\overline{\mathrm{N}}^e(s) = \lim_{y\to 1}\frac{1}{1-y}\left[\frac{1}{s}U - \Omega^{ge}(y|s)\right] = \frac{1}{s}[I - C^e(s)]^{-1}C^e(s)$$

$$= \frac{1}{s}\{[I - C^e(s)]^{-1} - I.\} \tag{11.12.13}$$

Since this equation implies that $C^e(s)$ can be found from $\overline{\mathrm{N}}^e(s)$,

$$C^e(s) = I - [I + s\overline{\mathrm{N}}^e(s)]^{-1}, \tag{11.12.14}$$

the matrix of mean occupancies of the process $\overline{\mathrm{N}}(t)$ is as complete a descriptor of the continuous-time semi-Markov process as is the core matrix.

We should also note from Equation 11.12.13 that the mean state occupancies are directly related to the entrance rates,

$$\overline{\mathrm{N}}^e(s) = \frac{1}{s}(E^e(s) - I). \tag{11.12.15}$$

Thus

$$\bar{\nu}_{ij}(t) = \int_0^t d\tau\, e_{ij}(\tau) - \delta_{ij}\,\delta(t) \qquad t \geq 0. \tag{11.12.16}$$

The mean number of occupancies of state j through time t for a given starting state i is just the integral of the entrance rate to state j over the $(0, t)$ interval, provided that we exclude the initial entrance if $i = j$.

Second moments

The direct method for evaluating the transform of the second moment is to differentiate $\omega_{ij}{}^{g^e}(y|s)$ twice with respect to y. We use Equation 11.12.2 and the continuous-time form of Equation 10.11.27 to write

$$\overline{\nu_{ij}{}^{2e}}(s) = \frac{d^2}{dy^2}\,\omega_{ij}{}^{g^e}(y|s)\bigg|_{y=1} + \bar{\nu}_{ij}{}^{e}(s) \tag{11.12.17}$$

$$= \sum_{r=1}^{N} p_{ir}h_{ir}{}^{e}(s)\overline{\nu_{jr}{}^{2e}}(s) + 2p_{ij}h_{ij}{}^{e}(s)\bar{\nu}_{jj}{}^{e}(s) + \frac{1}{s}\,p_{ij}h_{ij}{}^{e}(s). \tag{11.12.18}$$

If we let $\overline{\mathrm{N}^{2e}}(s)$ be the matrix form of $\overline{\nu_{ij}{}^{2e}}(s)$ we obtain

$$\overline{\mathrm{N}^{2e}}(s) = C^e(s)\overline{\mathrm{N}^{2e}}(s) + 2C^e(s)(\overline{\mathrm{N}}^e(s)\,\square\, I) + \frac{1}{s}\,C^e(s), \tag{11.12.19}$$

with solution

$$\overline{\mathrm{N}^{2e}}(s) = [I - C^e(s)]^{-1}C^e(s)\left[2\overline{\mathrm{N}}^e(s)\,\square\, I + \frac{1}{s}\,I\right]. \tag{11.12.20}$$

The results of Equations 11.12.13 and 11.12.15 allow us to place this equation in the form,

$$\overline{\mathrm{N}^{2e}}(s) = \overline{\mathrm{N}}^e(s)[2E^e(s)\,\square\, I - I]$$

$$= \overline{\mathrm{N}}^e(s)[2[I - C^e(s)]^{-1}\,\square\, I - I]. \tag{11.12.21}$$

We can therefore compute both $\overline{\mathrm{N}}^e(s)$ and $\overline{\mathrm{N}^{2e}}(s)$ from the transformed entrance rate matrix $E^e(s)$.

Relationship of Occupancy Moments to First Passage Time Moments

We can express the occupancy moments in terms of the first passage time moments by using Equation 11.12.9. We have for the first moment

$$\bar{\nu}_{ij}{}^{e}(s) = \frac{d}{dy}\,\omega_{ij}{}^{g^e}(y|s)\bigg|_{y=1} = \frac{f_{ij}{}^{e}(s)}{s[1 - f_{jj}{}^{e}(s)]} \qquad \begin{aligned} i &= 1, 2, \ldots, N \\ j &= 1, 2, \ldots, N. \end{aligned} \tag{11.12.22}$$

Note that by dividing this equation by the same equation with $i = j$ we obtain the symmetry relation,

$$\bar{\nu}_{ij}{}^{e}(s)f_{jj}{}^{e}(s) = f_{ij}{}^{e}(s)\bar{\nu}_{jj}{}^{e}(s). \tag{11.12.23}$$

For the second moment we have

$$\overline{\nu_{ij}{}^{2e}}(s) = \frac{d^2}{dy^2}\,\omega_{ij}{}^{ge}(y|s)\bigg|_{y=1} + \bar{\nu}_{ij}{}^{e}(s)$$

$$= \frac{f_{ij}{}^{e}(s)[1 + f_{jj}{}^{e}(s)]}{s[1 - f_{jj}{}^{e}(s)]^2}. \tag{11.12.24}$$

Thus the relations between state occupancy moments and the first passage time probability distributions are the direct analogs of Equations 10.11.54 and 10.11.68 for the discrete case.

11.13 THE GENERAL CONTINUOUS-TIME SEMI-MARKOV PROCESS

The general continuous-time Markov process has different transition probabilities and holding times for its first transition from the ones used for successive transitions. We consider the holding times for the first transition to be continuous random variables. We describe by a density function ${}_fh_{ij}(\cdot)$ the holding time required for the first transition from state i to state j; the transition probability for this transition is ${}_fp_{ij}$. We shall use the pre-subscript f to indicate all functions associated with the general continuous-time semi-Markov process rather than with the type we have considered up to the present point in this chapter. Thus ${}_fC^e(s)$ is the transformed core matrix for the first transition and ${}_f\Phi^{ge}(y|s)$ is the transformed matrix of interval transition probabilities when the first transition of the process is governed by such a core matrix.

We have now seen enough of the procedure of converting the discrete-time equations to the continuous-time case that we can go directly to the basic result we want. Thus the interval transition probabilities for the general process have the transform matrix

$${}_f\Phi^{ge}(y|s) = {}^{>}_{f}W^e(s) + y\,{}_fC^e(s)\Phi^{ge}(y|s)$$

$$= {}^{>}_{f}W^e(s) + y\,{}_fC^e(s)[I - yC^e(s)]^{-1}\,{}^{>}W^e(s), \tag{11.13.1}$$

while the entrance rates have the transform matrix

$${}_fE^{ge}(y|s) = I + y\,{}_fC^e(s)E^{ge}(y|s)$$

$$= I + y\,{}_fC^e(s)[I - yC^e(s)]^{-1}. \tag{11.13.2}$$

Transition Moments

We give the symbol ${}_f\overline{k_{ij}{}^m}(t)$ to the mth moment of the number of transitions made by the general continuous-time semi-Markov process during the interval

$(0, t)$ given that the trajectory started in state i and ended in state j. We know that $\overline{_f k_{ij}{}^m}$ is computed from

$$\overline{_f k_{ij}{}^m}(t) = \frac{_f k_{ij}{}^m(t)}{_f\phi_{ij}(t)} \tag{11.13.3}$$

where $_f k_{ij}{}^m(t)$ is a quantity computed by differentiating $_f\phi_{ij}{}^{ge}(y|s)$ m times with respect to y. Thus we find the matrix $_f K^{me}(s)$ of exponential transforms of $_f k_{ij}{}^m(t)$ by differentiating $_f\Phi^{ge}(y|s)$. In particular we have

$$\begin{aligned} _f K^e(s) &= \frac{d}{dy}\, _f\Phi^{ge}(y|s)\bigg|_{y=1} = {_f C^e(s)}[\Phi^e(s) + K^e(s)] \\ &= {_f C^e(s)}[I - C^e(s)]^{-1}[I - C^e(s)]^{-1} \,{}^{>}W^e(s), \end{aligned} \tag{11.13.4}$$

and

$$\begin{aligned} _f K^{2e}(s) &= \frac{d^2}{dy^2}\, _f\Phi^{ge}(y|s)\bigg|_{y=1} + {_f K^e(s)} = {_f C^e(s)}[K^{2e}(s) + K^e(s)] \\ &= {_f C^e(s)}[I - C^e(s)]^{-1}\{2[I - C^e(s)]^{-1} - I\}[I - C^e(s)]^{-1} \,{}^{>}W^e(s). \end{aligned} \tag{11.13.5}$$

11.14 RANDOM STARTING

If we begin observing a semi-Markov process at a time that has no relation to the operation of the process, we create a problem in random starting. We handle this problem by considering it as an application of the results for the general continuous-time semi-Markov process when the core matrix governing the first transition is developed for the starting condition of random entry. We shall use a presubscript r to indicate this special case of the general process.

Initial Transition Probabilities under Random Starting

If we follow the development in Section 10.13 we observe that the only change we have to make in the argument as a consequence of the continuous-time base is to convert the summations over τ to integrations. We thus obtain the same result for the initial transition probabilities under random starting,

$$_r p_{ij} = p_{ij}\frac{\bar{\tau}_{ij}}{\bar{\tau}_i}. \tag{11.14.1}$$

If we enter the process at a random time and observe it to be in state i, the probability that it will make its next transition to state j is the transition probability p_{ij} multiplied by the mean holding time $\bar{\tau}_{ij}$ and divided by the mean waiting time $\bar{\tau}_i$.

Since the ratio of $\bar{\tau}_{ij}$ to $\bar{\tau}_i$ is the same for both discrete- and continuous-time versions of the car rental example, the initial transition probability matrix under random starting is the one shown in Equation 10.13.9,

$$ {}_{\mathrm{r}}P = \begin{bmatrix} 2/3 & 1/3 \\ 1/8 & 7/8 \end{bmatrix}. \tag{11.14.2} $$

Initial Holding Times under Random Starting

As before, we let τ be the length of the holding time entered by the random observation point and let σ be the time from this point to the next transition. The density function for τ given the random method of entry and the fact that the process is planning to make a transition from state i to state j appears in Equation 10.13.10,

$$ \{\tau|R, i, j\} = \frac{\{j, \tau|R, i\}}{\{j|R, i\}} = \frac{\tau\{\tau|i,j\}}{\langle\tau|i, j\rangle}, \tag{11.14.3} $$

where $\{\tau|i, j\}$ is the holding time density function for the state i to state j transition and $\langle\tau|i, j\rangle$ is its mean. Then we can write the corresponding density function for σ in the form

$$ \{\sigma|R, i, j\} = \int_0^\infty d\tau\, \{\sigma|\tau, R, i, j\}\{\tau|R, i, j\}. \tag{11.14.4} $$

The quantity $\{\sigma|\tau, R, i, j\}$ is the density function for σ conditional on knowing τ, the random method of entering, and the transition that will be made. Since we are equally likely to enter the process at any point in the holding time τ, this conditional density function is

$$ \{\sigma|\tau, R, i, j\} = \frac{1}{\tau} \qquad 0 < \sigma \le \tau. \tag{11.14.5} $$

Equations 11.14.3 and 11.14.5 then allow us to write the density function for the time to the next transition from Equation 11.14.4 as

$$ \begin{aligned} \{\sigma|R, i, j\} &= \int_\sigma^\infty d\tau \cdot \frac{1}{\tau} \cdot \frac{\tau\{\tau|i, j\}}{\langle\tau|i, j\rangle} \\ &= \frac{\int_\sigma^\infty d\tau\, \{\tau|i, j\}}{\langle\tau|i, j\rangle} \\ &= \frac{{}^{>}h_{ij}(\sigma)}{\bar{\tau}_{ij}}. \end{aligned} \tag{11.14.6} $$

Then in terms of our usual notation, with the substitution of τ for σ,

$$ {}_{\mathrm{r}}h_{ij}(\tau) = \frac{{}^{>}h_{ij}(\tau)}{\bar{\tau}_{ij}}. \tag{11.14.7} $$

The density function for the time to the first transition given that it will be from state i to state j and that the process was entered at random is the complementary cumulative probability distribution for the holding time for this transition divided by the mean holding time for the transition.

For the car rental example we compute

$$ {}_{\mathrm{r}}H(\tau) = \begin{bmatrix} 4e^{-4\tau} & 2e^{-2\tau} \\ 3e^{-3\tau} & e^{-\tau} \end{bmatrix}, \tag{11.14.8}$$

which is the same as the matrix of holding time density functions $H(\tau)$. The equivalence of the two matrices is a direct result of the exponential distributions used for holding times.

Initial Core Matrix under Random Starting

From Equations 11.14.1 and 11.14.7 we observe

$$ {}_{\mathrm{r}}c_{ij}(\tau) = {}_{\mathrm{r}}p_{ij}\; {}_{\mathrm{r}}h_{ij}(\tau) = \frac{p_{ij}\; {}^{>}h_{ij}(\tau)}{\bar{\tau}_i} \tag{11.14.9}$$

or in matrix form

$$ {}_{\mathrm{r}}C(\tau) = {}_{\mathrm{r}}P \,\square\, {}_{\mathrm{r}}H(\tau) = M^{-1}[P \,\square\, {}^{>}H(\tau)]. \tag{11.14.10}$$

For the continuous-time car rental example,

$$ {}_{\mathrm{r}}C(\tau) = {}_{\mathrm{r}}P \,\square\, {}_{\mathrm{r}}H(\tau) = \begin{bmatrix} (8/3)e^{-4\tau} & (2/3)e^{-2\tau} \\ (3/8)e^{-3\tau} & (7/8)e^{-\tau} \end{bmatrix}. \tag{11.14.11}$$

Initial Waiting Times under Random Starting

For the waiting time distributions under random starting we obtain

$$ \begin{aligned} {}_{\mathrm{r}}w_i(\tau) &= \sum_{j=1}^{N} {}_{\mathrm{r}}p_{ij}\; {}_{\mathrm{r}}h_{ij}(\tau) = \frac{\sum_{j=1}^{N} p_{ij}\; {}^{>}h_{ij}(\tau)}{\bar{\tau}_i} \\ &= \frac{{}^{>}w_i(\tau)}{\bar{\tau}_i} \end{aligned} \tag{11.14.12}$$

or in matrix form

$$ {}_{\mathrm{r}}W(\tau) = M^{-1}\; {}^{>}W(\tau). \tag{11.14.13}$$

Transform Relations

If we place our results for random starting in the transform domain, we find

$$
\begin{aligned}
{}_{r}c_{ij}{}^{e}(s) &= {}_{r}p_{ij}\,{}_{r}h_{ij}{}^{e}(s) = \frac{1}{\bar{\tau}_i}\,p_{ij}\,{}^{>}h_{ij}{}^{e}(s) = \frac{1}{s\bar{\tau}_i}\,p_{ij}[1 - h_{ij}{}^{e}(s)] \\
&= \frac{1}{s\bar{\tau}_i}\,[p_{ij} - p_{ij}h_{ij}{}^{e}(s)],
\end{aligned}
\tag{11.14.14}
$$

$$
{}_{r}C^{e}(s) = \frac{1}{s}\,M^{-1}[P - C^{e}(s)],
\tag{11.14.15}
$$

$$
{}_{r}w_i{}^{e}(s) = \frac{1}{\bar{\tau}_i}\,{}^{>}w_i{}^{e}(s) = \frac{1}{s\bar{\tau}_i}\,[1 - w_i{}^{e}(s)],
\tag{11.14.16}
$$

$$
{}_{r}W^{e}(s) = M^{-1}\,{}^{>}W^{e}(s) = \frac{1}{s}\,M^{-1}[I - W^{e}(s)].
\tag{11.14.17}
$$

For the diagonal matrix of transformed complementary cumulative waiting time distributions for the first transition under random starting, we obtain

$$
\begin{aligned}
{}^{>}_{r}W^{e}(s) &= \frac{1}{s}\,[I - {}_{r}W^{e}(s)] = \frac{1}{s}\,[I - M^{-1}\,{}^{>}W^{e}(s)] \\
&= \frac{1}{s}\left[I - \frac{1}{s}\,M^{-1}[I - W^{e}(s)]\right].
\end{aligned}
\tag{11.14.18}
$$

Thus we have converted the basic results for random starting to the continuous-time case with only minor changes in form.

Interval and Entrance Probabilities under Random Starting

If we substitute the results for random starting into Equation 11.13.1 for the interval transition probabilities of the general process, we produce

$$
\begin{aligned}
{}_{r}\Phi^{ge}(y|s) &= {}^{>}_{r}W^{e}(s) + y\,{}_{r}C^{e}(s)[I - yC^{e}(s)]^{-1}\,{}^{>}W^{e}(s) \\
&= \frac{1}{s}\,[I - M^{-1}(I - yP)\Phi^{ge}(y|s)]
\end{aligned}
\tag{11.14.19}
$$

by following directly the reasoning of Section 10.13. Likewise, we write the transformed matrix of entrance probabilities from Equation 11.13.2 as

$$
\begin{aligned}
{}_{r}E^{ge}(y|s) &= y\,{}_{r}C^{e}(s)[I - yC^{e}(s)]^{-1} \\
&= \frac{1}{s}\,M^{-1}[I - (I - yP)E^{ge}(y|s)],
\end{aligned}
\tag{11.14.20}
$$

where we have again excluded the term I to avoid assuming that an entry occurred at the time of observation. The implications of these results for starting a semi-Markov process in the steady state are the same for both discrete- and continuous-time versions.

Moments Under Random Starting

All the moment expressions for random starting developed in the discrete-time case carry over to the continuous-time case with minor modifications such as the substitution of $1/s$ for $z/(1 - z)$ where this factor appears. We shall emphasize, however, the definition of ${}_r\overline{k^m}(t)$ as the mth moment of the number of transitions made during a time t after the process is entered at random without observation of the state. We find that the exponential transform of the first moment, ${}_r\bar{k}^e(s)$, becomes simply

$$ {}_r\bar{k}^e(s) = \frac{1}{s^2}\cdot\frac{1}{\bar{\tau}}, \tag{11.14.21} $$

implying the inverse,

$$ {}_r\bar{k}(t) = \frac{1}{\bar{\tau}}\,t. \tag{11.14.22} $$

The mean number of transitions grows linearly in time at a rate equal to the reciprocal of the mean time between transitions in the steady state.

The second moment has an exponential transform ${}_r\overline{k^{2e}}(s)$ equal to

$$ {}_r\overline{k^{2e}}(s) = \frac{1}{s^2}\,\mathbf{e}[2E^e(s) - I]\mathbf{s}, \tag{11.14.23} $$

where $\mathbf{e}$ is the row vector of limiting entrance rates, $E^e(s)$ is the exponential transform of the matrix of entrance rates measured in time, and $\mathbf{s}$ is the summing column vector. Referring to Equation 11.5.13 where $E^e(s) = [I - C^e(s)]^{-1}$ appears for the car rental example, we see that calculating the second moment of the number of transitions in time t following a random entry is not a simple task for even an elementary problem.

11.15 THE CONTINUOUS-TIME RENEWAL PROCESS

We can define a continuous-time renewal process to correspond to the discrete-time renewal process of Section 7.1. We simply let the lifetime or time between renewals be a continuous random variable described by a probability density function rather than a discrete random variable described by a probability mass function. We still use the symbol $p(\cdot)$ for the lifetime distribution of the renewal process even though it is now a density function. The renewal process generates a sequence of renewals in time—the time between any two successive renewals is an independent sample from the lifetime distribution.

The Double Exponential Lifetime Example

We shall use as an example of a renewal process the process whose lifetime distribution is the density function

$$p(\tau) = \frac{\lambda\mu}{\lambda - \mu}\,[e^{-\mu\tau} - e^{-\lambda\tau}] \qquad \tau \geq 0 \tag{11.15.1}$$

as illustrated in Figure 11.15.1.

We shall call this distribution the double exponential distribution; note that it is the system output of Equation 11.4.45 scaled to have area one so that it can serve as a probability density function.

Exponential transform

Every lifetime density function will have an exponential transform $p^e(s)$. Thus for the double exponential distribution,

$$\begin{aligned} p^e(s) &= \frac{\lambda\mu}{\lambda - \mu}\left[\frac{1}{s + \mu} - \frac{1}{s + \lambda}\right] \\ &= \frac{\lambda\mu}{(s + \lambda)(s + \mu)}. \end{aligned} \tag{11.15.2}$$

Such a transform must always satisfy the requirement that $p^e(0) = 1$.

Complementary cumulative lifetime distribution

The complementary cumulative lifetime distribution ${}^{>}p(\cdot)$ is defined by

$${}^{>}p(t) = \int_t^\infty d\tau\; p(\tau). \tag{11.15.3}$$

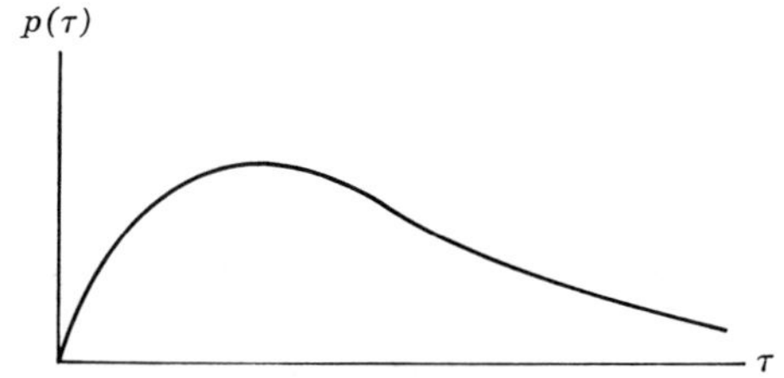

Figure 11.15.1 The double-exponential lifetime distribution.

Thus ${}^{>}p(t)$ represents the probability that the lifetime will exceed t. We know from Equation 11.4.34 that the exponential transform ${}^{>}p^e(s)$ of the complementary cumulative lifetime distribution is related to the exponential transform of the lifetime distribution by

$$ {}^{>}p^e(s) = \frac{1}{s}[1 - p^e(s)] \tag{11.15.4} $$

or, for the double exponential example,

$$ \begin{aligned} {}^{>}p^e(s) &= \frac{1}{s}\left[1 - \frac{\lambda\mu}{(s+\lambda)(s+\mu)}\right] \\ &= \frac{s+\lambda+\mu}{(s+\lambda)(s+\mu)} \cdot \end{aligned} \tag{11.15.5} $$

We find an explicit expression for ${}^{>}p(t)$ by performing a partial fraction expansion,

$$ {}^{>}p^e(s) = \frac{\dfrac{\mu}{\mu-\lambda}}{s+\lambda} + \frac{\dfrac{\lambda}{\lambda-\mu}}{s+\mu}, \tag{11.15.6} $$

and then inverting the transform,

$$ {}^{>}p^e(t) = \frac{1}{\lambda-\mu}[\lambda e^{-\mu t} - \mu e^{-\lambda t}] \qquad t \geq 0. \tag{11.15.7} $$

Note that ${}^{>}p(0) = 1$ as required if an ultimate renewal is certain. The plot of ${}^{>}p(t)$ appears in Figure 11.15.2.

We can define $p_R = p^e(0) = {}^{>}p(0)$ as the probability of eventual renewal. If p_R is less than 1, we see that the continuous-time renewal process is transient and we can analyze the consequences by the methods of Section 7.1. If p_R is equal to one, then we call the renewal process recurrent. We shall consider only recurrent renewal processes in the remainder of this section.

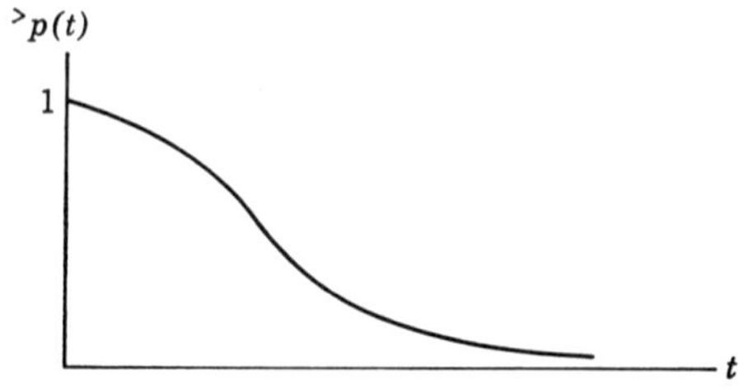

Figure 11.15.2 Complementary cumulative of the double exponential lifetime distribution.

Lifetime moments

Since a recurrent renewal process has a proper probability density function for its lifetime distribution, we can speak of the moments of the lifetime, in particular, the mean $\bar{l}$, second moment $\overline{l^2}$, and variance $\check{l} = \overline{l^2} - \bar{l}^2$. As we already know, these moments may be obtained by differentiating the exponential transform of the lifetime distribution:

$$\bar{l} = \int_0^\infty d\tau \cdot \tau \cdot p(\tau) = -\frac{d}{ds} p^e(s)\bigg|_{s=0}$$
$$\overline{l^2} = \int_0^\infty d\tau \cdot \tau^2 p(\tau) = \frac{d^2}{ds^2} p^e(s)\bigg|_{s=0} \qquad (11.15.8)$$

Thus for the double exponential example,

$$\bar{l} = -\frac{d}{ds}\left[\frac{\lambda\mu}{(s+\lambda)(s+\mu)}\right]\bigg|_{s=0} \qquad \overline{l^2} = \frac{d^2}{ds^2}\left[\frac{\lambda\mu}{(s+\lambda)(s+\mu)}\right]\bigg|_{s=0}$$
$$= \frac{\lambda+\mu}{\lambda\mu} \qquad\qquad = \frac{2(\lambda^2+\lambda\mu+\mu^2)}{\lambda^2\mu^2}$$
$$= \frac{1}{\lambda} + \frac{1}{\mu} \qquad\qquad = \frac{2}{\mu^2} + \frac{2}{\lambda\mu} + \frac{2}{\lambda^2}$$

$$\check{l} = \overline{l^2} - \bar{l}^2 = \frac{1}{\lambda^2} + \frac{1}{\mu^2}. \qquad (11.15.9)$$

Of course, we could have obtained these moments by direct integration of the lifetime distribution itself. We should also note that as a result of Equation 11.4.36, the mean lifetime is equal to the exponential transform of the complementary cumulative lifetime distribution evaluated at $s = 0$,

$$\bar{l} = {}^{>}p^e(0), \qquad (11.15.10)$$

a result confirmed by Equation 11.15.5.

Continuous-Time Semi-Markov Interpretation

The previous results of this chapter become directly applicable to the continuous-time renewal process when we realize that the renewal process is simply a one-state continuous-time semi-Markov process. Since the transition probability of this one-state system is $p_{11} = 1$, the process is completely described by its one holding time density function $h_{11}(\cdot)$, which is, of course, just the lifetime density function. Thus

$$p(\cdot) = h_{11}(\cdot) = w(\cdot) = c(\cdot), \qquad (11.15.11)$$

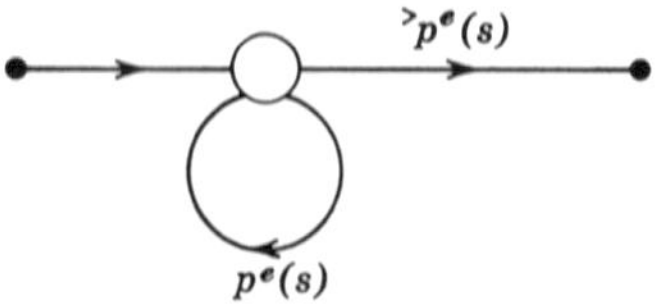

Figure 11.15.3 Flow graph for the continuous-time renewal process.

and we have a special case indeed. In the transform domain

$$p^e(s) = h_{11}{}^e(s) = w^e(s) = c^e(s) \tag{11.15.12}$$

and, of course, the matrix quantities reduce to scalar functions,

$$p^e(s) = H^e(s) = W^e(s) = C^e(s) \tag{11.15.13}$$

and

$$ {}^{>}p^e(s) = {}^{>}H^e(s) = {}^{>}W^e(s). \tag{11.15.14}$$

Flow graph

The flow graph for the continuous-time renewal process therefore assumes the form shown in Figure 11.15.3, a specialization of Figure 11.7.1. Since we consider the process as occupying a state until the expiration of the holding time and then making an instantaneous transition, it is clear that the one state in Figure 11.15.3 will be occupied at all times except for the transition instants. Therefore $\phi(t)$, the probability that this state is occupied at time t, must be equal to one for all values of t. Since $\phi^e(s)$, the exponential transform of $\phi(t)$, is just the transmission of the flow graph of Figure 11.15.3, we immediately obtain

$$\phi^e(s) = \vec{t} = \frac{{}^{>}p^e(s)}{1 - p^e(s)}. \tag{11.15.15}$$

In view of Equation 11.15.4, we write the transform as

$$\phi^e(s) = \frac{1}{s}, \tag{11.15.16}$$

with inverse

$$\phi(t) = 1 \qquad t \geq 0, \tag{11.15.17}$$

thereby confirming our conclusion.

Renewal Rates

Thus we see that although we could identify a renewal in the discrete-time renewal process as the occupancy of a particular state, this identification is no longer appropriate in the continuous-time case. Instead we choose to identify renewals with entrances to the single state and use our knowledge of entrance rates for the continuous-time semi-Markov process in order to solve certain renewal process problems. Thus we let $e(t)$ be the renewal rate of the renewal process at time t. We interpret $e(t)\Delta$, where Δ is a small number, as the probability of a renewal between t and $t + \Delta$. We know that $e^e(s)$, the exponential transform of $e^e(t)$ is the transmission of the flow graph of Figure 11.15.3 from the input to the central node. From this observation, or from Equation 11.9.8, we write $e^e(s)$ for the renewal process as

$$e^e(s) = \frac{1}{1 - p^e(s)}. \tag{11.15.18}$$

The exponential transform of the renewal rate is therefore the reciprocal of one minus the exponential transform of the lifetime distribution.

The double exponential example

The exponential transform of the renewal rate for the double exponential example is

$$\begin{aligned} e^e(s) &= \frac{1}{1 - p^e(s)} = 1 + \frac{p^e(s)}{1 - p^e(s)} \\ &= 1 + \frac{\dfrac{\lambda\mu}{(s + \lambda)(s + \mu)}}{1 - \dfrac{\lambda\mu}{(s + \lambda)(s + \mu)}} \\ &= 1 + \frac{\lambda\mu}{s(s + \lambda + \mu)} \\ &= 1 + \frac{\dfrac{\lambda\mu}{\lambda + \mu}}{s} + \frac{\dfrac{-\lambda\mu}{\lambda + \mu}}{s + \lambda + \mu}. \end{aligned} \tag{11.15.19}$$

By inversion we produce the renewal rate for the process as

$$e(t) = \delta(t) + \frac{\lambda\mu}{\lambda + \mu}[1 - e^{-(\lambda + \mu)t}] \qquad t \geq 0, \tag{11.15.20}$$

a function plotted in Figure 11.15.4. Note that the renewal rate has an impulse at $t = 0$ as a result of the initial renewal that is assumed to occur at $t = 0$. The renewal rate then starts again at zero at $t = 0+$ and gradually increases asymptotically to the value $\lambda\mu/(\lambda + \mu)$.

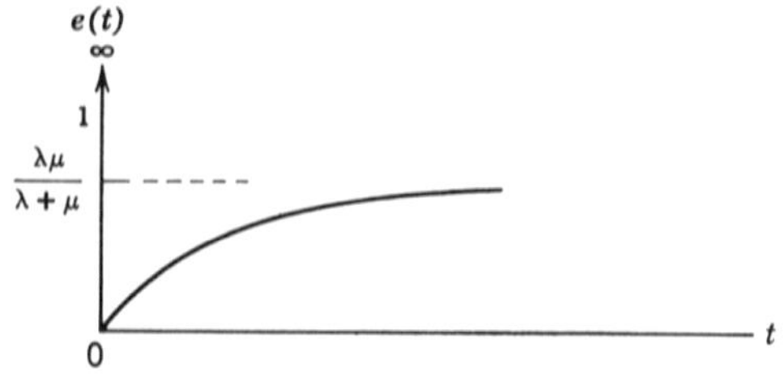

Figure 11.15.4 Renewal rate for the double exponential lifetime problem.

Steady-state renewal rate

We call $e(\infty)$ the steady-state renewal rate and give it the symbol e; for the example,

$$e = \lim_{t \to \infty} e(t) = \frac{\lambda\mu}{\lambda + \mu}. \tag{11.15.21}$$

From Equation 11.9.13 or by application of the final value theorem for exponential transforms to Equation 11.15.18, we observe that the steady-state renewal rate is the reciprocal of the mean lifetime $\bar{l}$,

$$e = \lim_{t \to \infty} e(t) = \lim_{s \to 0} se^e(s) = \lim_{s \to 0} \frac{s}{1 - p^e(s)} = \frac{1}{-\frac{d}{ds} p^e(s)\Big|_{s=0}} = \frac{1}{\bar{l}}. \tag{11.15.22}$$

Since the mean lifetime for the double exponential example was found in Equation 11.15.9 to be $(\lambda + \mu)/\lambda\mu$, the steady-state renewal rate e for the example must be

$$e = \frac{\lambda\mu}{\lambda + \mu}, \tag{11.15.23}$$

in agreement with Equation 11.15.21.

Counting Renewals

The results developed for counting transitions in the continuous-time semi-Markov process can be applied immediately to the problem of counting transitions in the continuous-time renewal process. We simply tag renewal with a y in the flow graph of Figure 11.15.3 to produce the flow graph of Figure 11.15.5. The discrete form of this flow graph appeared as Figure 7.2.1. The transmission of the flow graph in Figure 11.15.5 is $\phi^{ge}(y|s)$, the exponential transform of the probability $\phi(k|t)$ that we shall observe k renewals in the interval $(0, t)$ if a renewal is known

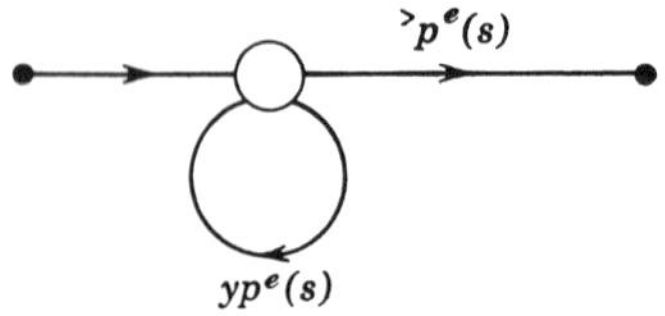

Figure 11.15.5 Flow graph for counting renewals.

to have occurred at time zero. Therefore by computing this transmission or directly from Equation 11.8.6 we have

$$\phi^{ge}(y|s) = \frac{{}^{>}p^e(s)}{1 - yp^e(s)}, \tag{11.15.24}$$

a result which provides a continuous-time analog to Equation 7.2.4.

If we find the transmission from the input to the central node of the flow graph in Figure 11.15.5 we obtain the geometric-exponential transform $e^{ge}(y|s)$ of the entrance rate counting renewals,

$$e^{ge}(y|s) = \frac{1}{1 - yp^e(s)}. \tag{11.15.25}$$

This equation is also a direct consequence of Equation 11.9.5. The inverse $e(k|t)$ we interpret as the renewal rate for the kth renewal alone. Naturally, if we sum this rate over all values of k from 0 on up, we obtain the total renewal rate $e(t)$ already discussed. The summation in the transform domain produces the simple relation,

$$e^{ge}(1|s) = e^e(s). \tag{11.15.26}$$

Renewal moments

The derivatives of $\phi^{ge}(y|s)$ with respect to y evaluated at $y = 1$ provide the moments of the number of renewals $k(t)$ in the interval $(0, t)$ given that a renewal occurred at $t = 0$. We define $\overline{k^m}(t)$ as the mth moment of this number of renewals and let $\overline{k^{m}}^e(s)$ be its exponential transform. Then by operating on Equation 11.15.24 or directly from Equation 11.8.16 we find the exponential transform of the mean number of renewals $\bar{k}(t)$ as

$$\bar{k}^e(s) = \frac{d}{dy}\phi^{ge}(y|s)\Big|_{y=1} = \frac{d}{dy}\frac{{}^{>}p^e(s)}{1 - yp^e(s)}\Big|_{y=1}$$

$$= \frac{{}^{>}p^e(s)p^e(s)}{[1 - p^e(s)]^2} = \frac{p^e(s)}{s[1 - p^e(s)]}, \tag{11.15.27}$$

a continuous-time version of Equations 7.2.12 and 7.2.13. By another differentiation or by using Equation 11.8.18, we obtain the transform of the second moment of the number of renewals as

$$\overline{k^{2e}}(s) = \frac{d^2}{dy^2}\phi^{ge}(y|s)\Big|_{y=1} + \bar{k}^e(s)$$

$$= \frac{p^e(s)}{s[1 - p^e(s)]}\left[2\frac{1}{1 - p^e(s)} - 1\right]$$

$$= \frac{p^e(s)[1 + p^e(s)]}{s[1 - p^e(s)]^2}, \qquad (11.15.28)$$

the analog of Equation 7.2.15.

Renewals as state occupancies

We can produce the relations we have developed for the exponential transforms of the renewal moments in other ways. For example, Equation 11.12.15 expresses the exponential transform of the mean state occupancy matrix in terms of the exponential transform of the entrance rate matrix. Since state occupancies for the single-state renewal process are just renewals, we can use this expression directly to produce $\bar{k}^e(s)$,

$$\overline{\mathrm{N}}^e(s) = \bar{k}^e(s) = \frac{1}{s}[E^e(s) - I] = \frac{1}{s}[e^e(s) - 1] \qquad (11.15.29)$$

or

$$\bar{k}^e(s) = \frac{1}{s}\left[\frac{1}{1 - p^e(s)} - 1\right] = \frac{p^e(s)}{s[1 - p^e(s)]}. \qquad (11.15.30)$$

The same reasoning applies to the expression for the matrix of exponential transforms of the second moments of state occupancies in Equation 11.12.21,

$$\overline{\mathrm{N}^{2e}}(s) = \overline{k^{2e}}(s) = \overline{\mathrm{N}}^e(s)[2[I - C^e(s)]^{-1} \square I - I]$$

or

$$\overline{k^{2e}}(s) = \bar{k}^e(s)\left[\frac{2}{1 - p^e(s)} - 1\right] = \bar{k}^e(s)\left[\frac{1 + p^e(s)}{1 - p^e(s)}\right]$$

$$= \frac{p^e(s)[1 + p^e(s)]}{s[1 - p^e(s)]^2}. \qquad (11.15.31)$$

Renewals as first passages

Still another route to the exponential transforms of the renewal moments is through the first passage time moments of Equations 11.12.22 and 11.12.24. Since in the renewal process every renewal constitutes a first passage from the single state to itself with a first passage time density function $p(\cdot)$, the exponential transform $f_{11}{}^e(s)$ of the first passage time distribution is just $p^e(s)$. Therefore from

Equation 11.12.22 we write the transform of the first moment of the number of renewals as

$$\bar{\nu}_{11}{}^e(s) = \bar{k}^e(s) = \frac{f_{11}{}^e(s)}{s[1 - f_{11}{}^e(s)]} = \frac{p^e(s)}{s[1 - p^e(s)]}, \tag{11.15.32}$$

and from Equation 11.12.24 the exponential transform of the second moment as

$$\overline{\nu_{11}{}^2}^e(s) = \overline{k^2}^e(s) = \frac{f_{11}{}^e(s)[1 + f_{11}{}^e(s)]}{s[1 - f_{11}{}^e(s)]^2} = \frac{p^e(s)[1 + p^e(s)]}{s[1 - p^e(s)]^2}. \tag{11.15.33}$$

These alternate developments of the same result provide additional insight into the meaning of our general continuous-time semi-Markov analyses.

The double exponential example

Mean. We find the expected number of renewals in time t following a renewal for the double exponential lifetime process by substituting $p^e(s)$ for this process from Equation 11.15.2 into Equation 11.15.27,

$$\bar{k}^e(s) = \frac{p^e(s)}{s[1 - p^e(s)]} = \frac{\lambda\mu}{s^2(s + \lambda + \mu)}$$

$$= \frac{\dfrac{\lambda\mu}{\lambda + \mu}}{s^2} + \frac{\dfrac{-\lambda\mu}{(\lambda + \mu)^2}}{s} + \frac{\dfrac{\lambda\mu}{(\lambda + \mu)^2}}{s + \lambda + \mu}, \tag{11.15.34}$$

and then find the inverse transform,

$$\bar{k}(t) = \frac{\lambda\mu}{\lambda + \mu}t - \frac{\lambda\mu}{(\lambda + \mu)^2}[1 - e^{-(\lambda + \mu)t}]. \tag{11.15.35}$$

The plot of $\bar{k}(t)$ in Figure 11.15.6 shows that the expected number of renewals in time t grows linearly with t at the rate $\lambda\mu/(\lambda + \mu)$ after an initial transient that ultimately subtracts an amount $\lambda\mu/[(\lambda + \mu)^2]$ from the linear growth term. As we shall see, we can interpret the quantity $\lambda\mu/[(\lambda + \mu)^2]$ as the expected reduction in the long-run number of renewals caused by starting to observe the system after a renewal rather than at a random time. As Equation 11.15.29 shows, the expected number of renewals through time t is equal to the integral through time t of the renewal rate, provided that we exclude the initial impulse in the renewal rate. The graph of Figure 11.15.6 is therefore the integral of the graph in Figure 11.15.4 from $t = 0+$ onward.

Second moment. We write the second moment of the number of renewals for the double exponential lifetime process from Equation 11.15.28,

$$\overline{k^2}^e(s) = \frac{p^e(s)[1 + p^e(s)]}{s[1 - p^e(s)]^2} = \frac{\lambda\mu[s^2 + (\lambda + \mu)s + 2\lambda\mu]}{s^3(s + \lambda + \mu)^2}. \tag{11.15.36}$$

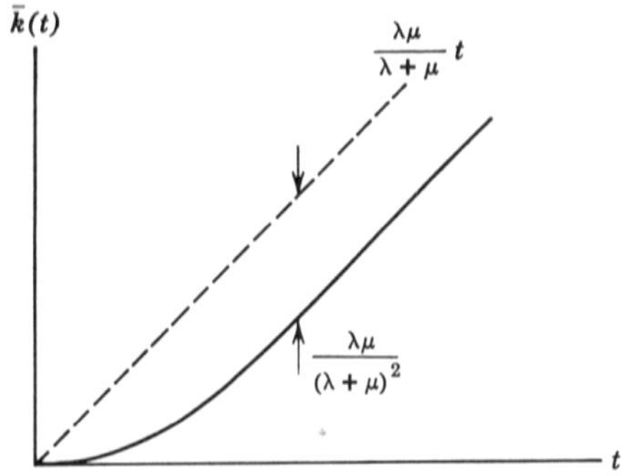

Figure 11.15.6 Expected number of renewals in time t following a renewal for the double exponential lifetime problem.

Rather than perform a complete partial fraction expansion we shall concentrate on the terms with denominators s^3 and s^2,

$$\overline{k^{2e}}(s) = \frac{\dfrac{2\lambda^2\mu^2}{(\lambda+\mu)^2}}{s^3} + \frac{\dfrac{\lambda\mu(\lambda-\mu)^2}{(\lambda+\mu)^3}}{s^2} + \frac{f(s)}{s(s+\lambda+\mu)^2}, \tag{11.15.37}$$

and write the inverse in the form,

$$\overline{k^2}(t) = \frac{\lambda^2\mu^2}{(\lambda+\mu)^2}t^2 + \frac{\lambda\mu(\lambda-\mu)^2}{(\lambda+\mu)^3}t + \text{constant} \quad \text{for large } n. \tag{11.15.38}$$

The second moment thus contains terms that grow as t^2 and as t, as well as other terms that remain bounded for large t.

Variance. By using the results of Equations 11.15.35 and 11.15.38, we can produce the variance $\check{k}(t)$ of the number of renewals in time t following a renewal in the form,

$$\check{k}(t) = \overline{k^2}(t) - (\bar{k}(t))^2 = \left[\frac{\lambda\mu(\lambda-\mu)^2}{(\lambda+\mu)^3} + \frac{2\lambda^2\mu^2}{(\lambda+\mu)^3}\right]t + \text{constant}$$

$$= \frac{\lambda\mu(\lambda^2+\mu^2)}{(\lambda+\mu)^3}t + \text{constant} \quad \text{for large } n. \tag{11.15.39}$$

The terms involving the square of t thus vanish and we find that the variance of the number of renewals grows linearly with t.

The General Continuous-Time Renewal Process

If the time to the first renewal has a lifetime density function ${}_fp(\cdot)$ different from the lifetime density function $p(\cdot)$ governing the time between successive renewals, we perform our analysis using the results for the general continuous-time semi-Markov process from Section 11.13. We begin by drawing the flow graph of the general continuous-time renewal process shown in Figure 11.15.7. We obtain this flow graph by drawing the matrix flow graph of Figure 10.12.1 for the continuous-time case with $y = 1$ and then specializing the results to the one-state renewal process. The transmission of this graph is ${}_f\phi^e(s)$, the exponential transform of ${}_f\phi(t)$, the probability that the state is occupied at time t given that the time to the first renewal was selected from ${}_fp(\cdot)$. Of course, this probability must be one, as we readily confirm by writing

$$ {}_f\phi^e(s) = \vec{t} = {}^{>}_{f}p^e(s) + \frac{{}_fp^e(s)\,{}^{>}p^e(s)}{1 - p^e(s)} = \frac{1}{s}[1 - {}_fp^e(s)] + \frac{1}{s}\,{}_fp^e(s) = \frac{1}{s}; \qquad (11.15.40) $$

therefore,

$$ {}_f\phi(t) = 1. \qquad (11.15.41) $$

As Figure 10.12.2 shows, we obtain the flow graph for ${}_fe^e(s)$, the transform of the renewal rate ${}_fe(t)$ for the general process, by substituting ${}^{>}_{f}p^e(s) = {}^{>}p^e(s) = 1$ in the flow graph of Figure 11.15.7. Then we easily find

$$ {}_fe^e(s) = 1 + \frac{{}_fp^e(s)}{1 - p^e(s)}. \qquad (11.15.42) $$

The more interesting case is where we count renewals and use the tagged flow graph of Figure 11.15.8 rather than that of Figure 11.15.7. The discrete-time version of this flow graph appeared as Figure 7.2.4. The transmission of the flow graph of Figure 11.15.8 is ${}_f\phi^{ge}(y|s)$, the geometric-exponential transform of the probability

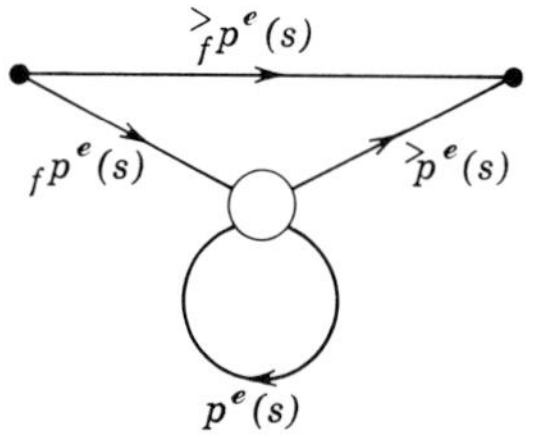

Figure 11.15.7 Flow graph for the general continuous-time renewal process.

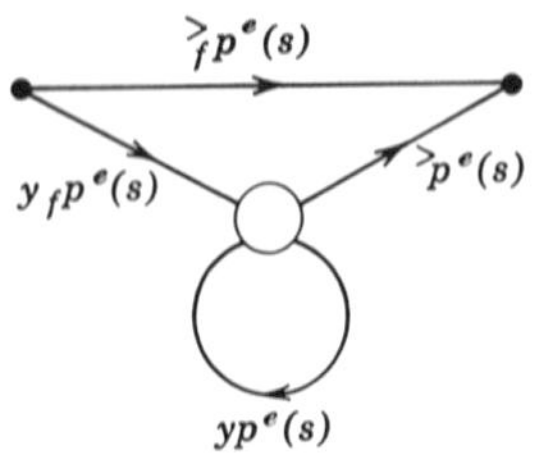

Figure 11.15.8 Flow graph for counting renewals in the general continuous-time renewal process.

${}_{f}\phi(k|t)$ that k renewals will occur in time t if the time to the first renewal is selected from ${}_{f}p(\cdot)$. We obtain

$$ {}_{f}\phi^{ge}(y|s) = \vec{t} = {}^{>}_{f}p^{e}(s) + \frac{y\,{}_{f}p^{e}(s)\,{}^{>}p^{e}(s)}{1 - yp^{e}(s)}, \tag{11.15.43} $$

which is also the result of applying Equation 11.13.1 to the one-state process.

If again we substitute ${}^{>}_{f}p^{e}(s) = {}^{>}p^{e}(s) = 1$, we can write ${}_{f}e^{ge}(y|s)$, the geometric-exponential transform of the renewal rate ${}_{f}e(k|t)$ for the kth renewal in the general process, as

$$ {}_{f}e^{ge}(y|s) = 1 + \frac{y\,{}_{f}p^{e}(s)}{1 - yp^{e}(s)}. \tag{11.15.44} $$

Equation 11.13.2 for the one-state renewal process produces this equation directly.

Renewal moments

Proceeding to the moments of the general process, we let ${}_{f}\overline{k^{m}}(t)$ and ${}_{f}\overline{k^{me}}(s)$ be the mth moment and the exponential transform of the mth moment of the number of renewals in time t if the time to the first renewal is selected from ${}_{f}p(\cdot)$. Since the analysis of the one-state process does not require the denominator division by ${}_{f}\phi_{ij}(t)$ (indicated in Equation 11.13.3), Equations 11.13.4 and 11.13.5 immediately provide expressions for the transforms of the first and second renewal moments,

$$ {}_{f}\bar{k}^{e}(s) = \frac{{}_{f}p^{e}(s)\,{}^{>}p^{e}(s)}{[1 - p^{e}(s)]^{2}} = \frac{{}_{f}p^{e}(s)}{s[1 - p^{e}(s)]} \tag{11.15.45} $$

and

$$ {}_{f}\overline{k^{2e}}(s) = \frac{{}_{f}p^{e}(s)[1 + p^{e}(s)]\,{}^{>}p^{e}(s)}{[1 - p^{e}(s)]^{3}} = \frac{{}_{f}p^{e}(s)[1 + p^{e}(s)]}{s[1 - p^{e}(s)]^{2}}. \tag{11.15.46} $$

The discrete-time version of these results appeared as Equations 7.2.41, 7.2.42, 7.2.44, and 7.2.45.

Random Starting

As usual, an especially interesting case of the general continuous-time renewal process is that of random starting. By random starting we mean beginning to observe the process at a time point that is in no way related to the operation of the process. The time to the first renewal we observe will then have some density function ${}_{\mathrm{r}}p(\cdot)$, while the time between all successive renewals will be selected from $p(\cdot)$. Therefore the results for random starting are just the results of the general continuous-time renewal process with ${}_{\mathrm{f}}p(\cdot) = {}_{\mathrm{r}}p(\cdot)$ and with all the rest of the f subscripts replaced by r subscripts to indicate the method of starting.

Initial lifetime distribution under random starting

We begin by finding ${}_{\mathrm{r}}p(\cdot)$, the density function for the time to the first renewal if we start to observe the process at a random time. Equations 11.14.7 or 11.14.12 show that the density function ${}_{\mathrm{r}}p(\cdot)$ must be given by

$$ {}_{\mathrm{r}}p(t) = \frac{1}{\bar{l}}\,{}^{>}p(t), \qquad (11.15.47) $$

that is, the complementary cumulative lifetime distribution divided by the mean lifetime. The discrete-time form of this result appeared as Equation 7.1.52.

For the double exponential lifetime example we find

$$ {}_{\mathrm{r}}p(t) = \frac{1}{\bar{l}}\,{}^{>}p(t) = \frac{1}{\dfrac{\lambda + \mu}{\lambda\mu}} \cdot \frac{1}{\lambda - \mu}\,[\lambda e^{-\mu t} - \mu e^{-\lambda t}] \qquad t \geq 0 \qquad (11.15.48) $$

$$ = \frac{\lambda\mu}{\lambda^2 - \mu^2}\,[\lambda e^{-\mu t} - \mu e^{-\lambda t}] \qquad t \geq 0. \qquad (11.15.49) $$

This density function looks just like Figure 11.15.2 after the ordinate of that graph is divided by $\bar{l} = (\lambda + \mu)/\lambda\mu$. Note that even though ${}_{\mathrm{r}}p(t)$ and $p(t)$ are similar in that both are the difference between two exponentials, the two density functions are quite disparate in graphical representation.

The exponential transform ${}_{\mathrm{r}}p^e(s)$ of the density function for the time to the first renewal under random starting is

$$ {}_{\mathrm{r}}p^e(s) = \frac{1}{\bar{l}}\,{}^{>}p^e(s) = \frac{1}{\bar{l}s}\,[1 - p^e(s)], \qquad (11.15.50) $$

a result we compare with Equations 7.1.53 and 7.1.54. For the double exponential lifetime we have

$$ {}_{\mathrm{r}}p^e(s) = \frac{1}{\bar{l}}\,{}^{>}p^e(s) = \frac{\lambda\mu}{\lambda + \mu} \cdot \frac{s + \lambda + \mu}{(s + \lambda)(s + \mu)}, \qquad (11.15.51) $$

with the inverse transform shown in Equation 11.15.49.

Initial lifetime complementary cumulative under random starting

We write the exponential transform of the complementary cumulative distribution of time to the first renewal after a random start as

$$ {}^{>}_{\mathrm{r}}p^e(s) = \frac{1}{s}\,[1 - {}_{\mathrm{r}}p^e(s)] = \frac{1}{s}\left[1 - \frac{1}{\bar{l}}\,{}^{>}p^e(s)\right] = \frac{1}{s}\left[1 - \frac{1}{\bar{l}s}\,(1 - p^e(s))\right]. \quad (11.15.52) $$

We use Equation 11.15.51 to produce ${}^{>}_{\mathrm{r}}p^e(s)$ for the double exponential lifetime process,

$$ {}^{>}_{\mathrm{r}}p^e(s) = \frac{1}{s}\left[1 - \frac{\lambda\mu}{\lambda + \mu}\,\frac{s + \lambda + \mu}{(s + \lambda)(s + \mu)}\right] $$

$$ = \frac{s + \dfrac{\lambda^2 + \mu\lambda + \mu^2}{\lambda + \mu}}{(s + \lambda)(s + \mu)} $$

$$ = \frac{\dfrac{\mu^2}{\mu^2 - \lambda^2}}{s + \lambda} + \frac{\dfrac{\lambda^2}{\lambda^2 - \mu^2}}{s + \mu}. \quad (11.15.53) $$

The complementary cumulative distribution for time to the first renewal is then

$$ {}^{>}_{\mathrm{r}}p(t) = \frac{1}{\lambda^2 - \mu^2}\,[\lambda^2 e^{-\mu t} - \mu^2 e^{-\lambda t}] \qquad t \geq 0, \quad (11.15.54) $$

which properly is one at $t = 0$. This function has the same general form as the ${}^{>}p(t)$ distribution of Figure 11.15.2, but they are not identical.

Initial lifetime mean under random starting

The mean time to the first renewal following a random time point is ${}_{\mathrm{r}}\bar{l}$, the mean of the ${}_{\mathrm{r}}p(\cdot)$ density function. We know that this mean is just the exponential transform of the complementary cumulative ${}^{>}_{\mathrm{r}}p(\cdot)$ evaluated at $s = 0$,

$$ {}_{\mathrm{r}}\bar{l} = \lim_{s \to 0} {}^{>}_{\mathrm{r}}p^e(s) = {}^{>}_{\mathrm{r}}p^e(0). \quad (11.15.55) $$

For the double exponential lifetime example,

$$ {}_{\mathrm{r}}\bar{l} = \frac{\lambda^2 + \mu\lambda + \mu^2}{\lambda\mu(\lambda + \mu)} = \frac{(\lambda + \mu)^2 - \lambda\mu}{\lambda\mu(\lambda + \mu)} $$

$$ = \frac{\lambda + \mu}{\lambda\mu} - \frac{1}{\lambda + \mu} $$

$$ = \bar{l} - \frac{1}{\lambda + \mu}. \quad (11.15.56) $$

The mean time to the first renewal after a random time point is therefore less than the mean time between renewals.

We can develop an explicit expression for ${}_{\mathrm{r}}\bar{l}$ in terms of the moments of the lifetime density function $p(\cdot)$ by writing

$$ {}_{\mathrm{r}}\bar{l} = -\frac{d}{ds}\,{}_{\mathrm{r}}p^e(s)\bigg|_{s=0} = -\frac{d}{ds}\frac{1}{\bar{l}}\,{}^{>}p^e(s)\bigg|_{s=0} = -\frac{1}{\bar{l}}\frac{d}{ds}\,{}^{>}p^e(s)\bigg|_{s=0}. \qquad (11.15.57)$$

Equation 11.4.38 shows that the derivative of the exponential transform of the complementary cumulative probability distribution is minus 1/2 the value of the second moment of the random variable. Therefore we immediately have

$$ {}_{\mathrm{r}}\bar{l} = \frac{\overline{l^2}}{2\bar{l}}; \qquad (11.15.58)$$

the mean time to the first renewal after a random time point is 1/2 the ratio of the second to first moments of the lifetime distribution. We encountered the discrete-time version of this result in Equation 7.2.70, where the extra additive factor of 1/2 is a direct consequence of being able to observe the renewal process of Section 7.2 only at discrete instants. The moments $\bar{l}$ and $\overline{l^2}$ recorded for the double exponential lifetime process in Equation 11.15.9 show that Equation 11.15.58 immediately produces the value of ${}_{\mathrm{r}}\bar{l}$ found in Equation 11.15.56.

Counting renewals with random starting

We can obtain the geometric-exponential transform of the probability of the number of renewals in time t following a random time point by substituting the values of ${}_{\mathrm{r}}p^e(s)$ and ${}^{>}_{\mathrm{r}}p^e(s)$ from Equations 11.15.50 and 11.15.52 into Equation 11.15.43 for the general process, or by specializing Equation 11.14.19 directly,

$$ {}_{\mathrm{r}}\phi^{ge}(y|s) = \frac{1}{s}\left[1 - \frac{1-y}{\bar{l}}\cdot\frac{{}^{>}p^e(s)}{1-yp^e(s)}\right]. \qquad (11.15.59)$$

For example, ${}_{\mathrm{r}}\phi(0, t)$, the probability of observing no renewals in time t following a random point, is necessarily ${}^{>}_{\mathrm{r}}p(t)$ since

$$ {}_{\mathrm{r}}\phi^{\cdot e}(0|s) = {}_{\mathrm{r}}\phi^{ge}(0|s) = \frac{1}{s}\left[1 - \frac{{}^{>}p^e(s)}{\bar{l}}\right] = \frac{1}{s}[1 - {}_{\mathrm{r}}p^e(s)] = {}^{>}_{\mathrm{r}}p^e(s). \qquad (11.15.60)$$

We obtain the exponential transform ${}_{\mathrm{r}}e^e(s)$ of the renewal rate for the random starting case from Equation 11.14.20 with $y = 1$,

$$ {}_{\mathrm{r}}e^e(s) = \frac{1}{\bar{l}s}, \qquad (11.15.61)$$

and the renewal rate itself as

$$ {}_{\mathrm{r}}e(t) = \frac{1}{\bar{l}}. \qquad (11.15.62)$$

The renewal rate is a constant equal to the reciprocal of the mean lifetime. We obtained the discrete-time form of this result in Equation 7.1.58. Note that Equation 11.15.62 is the basis for our saying in the interpretation of Equation 11.15.35 that $\lambda\mu/[(\lambda + \mu)^2]$ is the saving in expected renewals observed over a long time period caused by beginning to watch the system after a renewal rather than at a random time.

Renewal moments under random starting. We find the exponential transforms of the moments of the number of renewals in time t after a random start either from Section 11.14 or from earlier results in this section. For the transform of the mean we use either Equation 11.14.21 or Equation 11.15.45 to produce

$$ {}_{\mathrm{r}}\bar{k}^e(s) = \frac{1}{s^2}\cdot\frac{1}{\bar{l}} \tag{11.15.63}$$

or

$$ {}_{\mathrm{r}}\bar{k}(t) = \frac{1}{\bar{l}}\,t, \tag{11.15.64}$$

thus showing that the expected number of renewals following a random point of observation grows linearly with time at a rate equal to the mean lifetime. Either Equation 11.14.23 or Equation 11.15.46 shows that the transform of the second moment is

$$ {}_{\mathrm{r}}\overline{k^2}^e(s) = \frac{1 + p^e(s)}{\bar{l}s^2(1 - p^e(s))}\,. \tag{11.15.65}$$

The discrete-time versions of Equations 11.15.63 and 11.15.64 were Equations 7.2.48 and 7.2.50.

Asymptotic Moments

By paralleling the methods used in Section 7.2, we can easily develop expressions for the asymptotic renewal moments of the general continuous-time renewal process. Of course, these same results apply to the case of random starting.

First moment

For the first moment we write

$$ {}_{\mathrm{f}}\bar{k}^e(s) = \frac{{}_{\mathrm{f}}p^e(s)}{s[1 - p^e(s)]} = \frac{{}_{\mathrm{f}}p^e(s)}{s^2\ {}^{>}p^e(s)} = \frac{a_1}{s^2} + \frac{a_2}{s}$$

$$+ \text{ transform of terms that vanish for large } t, \tag{11.15.66}$$

where

$$a_1 = \lim_{s \to 0} \frac{{}_{f}p^e(s)}{{}^{>}p^e(s)} = \frac{1}{\bar{l}}, \tag{11.15.67}$$

$$a_2 = \lim_{s \to 0} \frac{d}{ds} \frac{{}_{f}p^e(s)}{{}^{>}p^e(s)} = \lim_{s \to 0} \frac{{}^{>}p^e(s)\,{}_{f}p^{e'}(s) - {}_{f}p^e(s)\,{}^{>}p^{e'}(s)}{[{}^{>}p^e(s)]^2} = \frac{-\bar{l}\,{}_{f}\bar{l} + (1/2)\overline{l^2}}{\bar{l}^2}. \tag{11.15.68}$$

Therefore,

$$_{f}\bar{k}(t) = \frac{1}{\bar{l}}\,t + \frac{1}{\bar{l}}\left(\frac{\overline{l^2}}{2\bar{l}} - {}_{f}\bar{l}\right) \quad \text{for large } t. \tag{11.15.69}$$

The interesting term in this expression is the constant term. Equation 11.15.58 shows that this term vanishes if we begin observing the process at a random time, thereby placing Equation 11.15.69 in agreement with Equation 11.15.64. If we begin observation of the process just after a renewal then ${}_{f}\bar{l} = \bar{l}$ and the constant term is

$$\frac{1}{\bar{l}}\left(\frac{\overline{\ell^2}}{2\bar{l}} - \bar{l}\right). \tag{11.15.70}$$

For the double exponential lifetime process this becomes

$$\frac{\lambda\mu}{\lambda + \mu}\left(\frac{\lambda^2 + \lambda\mu + \mu^2}{\lambda\mu(\lambda + \mu)} - \frac{\lambda + \mu}{\lambda\mu}\right) = -\frac{\lambda\mu}{(\lambda + \mu)^2}, \tag{11.15.71}$$

the lag in renewals we observed in Figure 11.15.6.

Second moment

For the second moment we write

$$\begin{aligned} {}_{f}\overline{k^{2}}^{e}(s) &= \frac{{}_{f}p^e(s)[1 + p^e(s)]}{s[1 - p^e(s)]^2} = \frac{{}_{f}p^e(s)[1 + p^e(s)]}{s^3[{}^{>}p^e(s)]^2} \\ &= \frac{b_1}{s^3} + \frac{b_2}{s^2} + \text{transform of terms that remain bounded for large } t, \end{aligned} \tag{11.15.72}$$

where

$$b_1 = \lim_{s \to 0} \frac{{}_{f}p^e(s)[1 + p^e(s)]}{[{}^{>}p^e(s)]^2} = \frac{2}{\bar{l}^2}, \tag{11.15.73}$$

$$b_2 = \lim_{s \to 0} \frac{d}{ds} \frac{{}_{f}p^e(s)[1 + p^e(s)]}{[{}^{>}p^e(s)]^2} = \frac{2\overline{l^2} - 2\bar{l}\,{}_{f}\bar{l} - \bar{l}^2}{\bar{l}^3}. \tag{11.15.74}$$

Therefore,

$$_{f}\overline{k^2}(t) = \frac{1}{\bar{l}^2}\,t^2 + \left[\frac{2\overline{l^2} - 2\bar{l}\,{}_{f}\bar{l} - \bar{l}^2}{\bar{l}^3}\right]t + \text{constant} \quad \text{for large } t. \tag{11.15.75}$$

Variance

The asymptotic variance is thus

$$ {}_t\overset{\vee}{k}(t) = {}_t\overline{k^2}(t) - [{}_t\overline{k}(t)]^2 = \frac{\overline{l^2} - \bar{l}^2}{\bar{l}^3}\, t + \text{constant} $$

$$ = \frac{\overset{\vee}{l}}{\bar{l}^3}\, t + \text{constant} \quad \text{for large } t, \qquad (11.15.76) $$

which corresponds with Equation 7.2.77. The variance of the number of renewals grows linearly with t when t is large at a rate equal to the variance of the lifetime distribution divided by the cube of the mean lifetime. When we substitute the moments $\bar{l}$ and $\overset{\vee}{l}$ from Equation 11.15.9 for the double exponential lifetime process into Equation 11.15.76, we immediately obtain the asymptotic form for the variance of that process found in Equation 11.15.39.

11.16 CONCLUSION

The results developed in this chapter for the continuous-time semi-Markov process provide a theoretical completeness to our earlier work. However, as we realize from even the simple examples we have considered, the possibility of using exponential transform analysis for the solution of even very small Markovian models is slim. Therefore, we should think of the exponential transform formulation as an aid to developing insight rather than computational results.

The geometric transform is quite another story, however, because we can convert the geometric transform equations into recursive equations eminently suitable for computer analysis. Therefore the results of this chapter are far surpassed in practicality by those developed in Chapter 10. If we want to find the statistics of practical models, sooner or later we revert to formulating the problem as a discrete-time process, either implicitly or explicitly. Interestingly, if analog computers were more technologically advanced than digital computers, then we would far prefer the continuous-time formulation of this chapter.

PROBLEMS

The company has also found that the density functions for the time the trips take is given by the holding time density function matrix:

$$ P = \mathit{From} \begin{matrix} A \\ B \end{matrix} \overset{\displaystyle \mathit{To} \atop \displaystyle A \qquad B}{\begin{bmatrix} 0.6 & 0.4 \\ 0.1 & 0.9 \end{bmatrix}} $$

The company has also found that the density functions for the time the trips take is given by the holding time density function matrix:

$$H(t) = \text{From} \begin{matrix} & \text{To} \\ & \begin{matrix} A & B \end{matrix} \\ \begin{matrix} A \\ B \end{matrix} & \begin{bmatrix} te^{-t} & e^{-t} \\ 4te^{-2t} & 2e^{-2t} \end{bmatrix} \end{matrix}$$

(Assume there is no delay between trips.)

a) If a driver starts his day in A, what is the probability that he will be in A after n trips?

b) If a driver starts his day in A, what is the expected time until his first arrival in B?

c) If a driver has started in A and made two trips, what is the expected amount of time that he has spent traveling between A and B (i.e., in $A \to B$ and $B \to A$ trips)?

d) If a driver starts in A and if at the end of each trip there is a 10% chance that he will be called back into the garage for servicing, what is the expected amount of time he will spend on the road before being called in?

2. We have considered the marketing example with transition probability matrix:

$$\text{Last Purchase} \begin{matrix} & \text{Next Purchase} \\ & \begin{matrix} A & B \end{matrix} \\ \begin{matrix} A \\ B \end{matrix} & \begin{bmatrix} 0.8 & 0.2 \\ 0.3 & 0.7 \end{bmatrix} \end{matrix}$$

Suppose now that the time to consume each brand is exponentially distributed with a mean of 1 week for brand A and 0.5 week for brand B. Assume that purchases are instantaneous after the product has been consumed.

a) If a customer has just purchased brand A, what is the probability that he is consuming a brand B purchase t weeks later?

b) During those t weeks, what is the expected number of times that he will switch from brand A to brand B?

c) If we are now given the additional information that at time t the customer is consuming brand B, what is the expected number of times that he switched from A to B?

d) If a customer has just purchased brand A, what is the probability density function for the time until his next purchase of brand A? What is the mean of this distribution?

3. For the following two-state continuous-time semi-Markov process,

$$P = \begin{bmatrix} 0.6 & 0.4 \\ 0.2 & 0.8 \end{bmatrix} \qquad H(t) = \begin{bmatrix} 2e^{-2t} & e^{-t} \\ 2(e^{-t} - e^{-2t}) & te^{-t} \end{bmatrix},$$

find:

a) The interval transition probability $\phi_{12}(t)$.

b) The entrance rate into state 2 if the process starts in state 2, $e_{22}(t)$.

c) The probability density function for the first passage time θ_{12} from state 1 to state 2.

d) The matrix of mean first passage times $\overline{\Theta}$.

e) The expected number of times the process will enter state 2 in a time interval t if it enters state 1 at the beginning of the interval.

f) The expected amount of time the process will spend in state 2 in a time interval t if it enters state 1 at the beginning of the interval.

4. For the marketing example of Problem 2 with a transition probability matrix

$$P = \begin{bmatrix} 0.8 & 0.2 \\ 0.3 & 0.7 \end{bmatrix},$$

suppose that the length of time between purchases is uniformly distributed between 0 and 1; i.e., $h_{ij}(t) = u(t) - u(t - 1)$ for all i, j. Find $\Phi(t)$ for $0 \leq t < 2$. Evaluate $\Phi(1)$ and $\Phi(2)$.

5. Develop a real transition equivalent of the continuous-time car rental example. Place it in competing process form.

6. A three-state continuous-time semi-Markov process is described by the competing process model. For all i, j the probability density functions $g_{ij}(\cdot)$ are defined by $g_{ij}(\tau) = 1$, $0 \leq \tau \leq 1$. Find the following process matrices: $C(\tau)$, P, $H(\tau)$, $P(\tau)$, $W(\tau)$.

7. If the core matrix $C(\cdot)$ for a semi-Markov process is known, consider how we might calculate the matrix of density functions $G(\cdot)$ for a competing process that will have the same behavior as the original semi-Markov process.

a) In particular, derive the first order linear differential equation that $g_{ij}(\cdot)$ must satisfy. [The coefficients will be time-varying and will involve the elements of the known core matrix $C(\cdot)$.]

b) For the special case in which $h_{ij}(\tau) = \lambda_i e^{-\lambda_i \tau}$ for all j, use the equation in a) to solve for $g_{ij}(t)$.

8. Let $\bar{k}_i(t)$ be the expected number of special transitions incurred in time t after starting in state i. For an N-state semi-Markov process with transition matrix P, holding-time density matrix $H(t)$, and all transitions to states $1, 2, \ldots M$, $(M < N)$ considered as special,

a) Find a set of integral-difference equations for the $\bar{k}_i(\cdot)$ functions by considering all possible first transitions.

b) Take the exponential transform of these equations.

c) Draw the flow graph whose outputs are $\bar{k}_1{}^e(s)$ and $\bar{k}_2{}^e(s)$ for the following process:

$$P = \begin{bmatrix} 0.9 & 0.1 \\ 0.4 & 0.6 \end{bmatrix} \qquad H(t) = \begin{bmatrix} h_{11}(t) & h_{12}(t) \\ h_{21}(t) & h_{22}(t) \end{bmatrix}$$

where $M = 1$.

9. If a customer in Problem 2 started with brand A and has never purchased brand A twice in a row, what is the probability that he is consuming brand A at some time t later? Evaluate your answer for large t.

10. A certain company manufactures two products, 1 and 2. Because of the impact of customers telling one another about the products, the generation of new customers can best be described by the following process: If a new customer has just arrived whose first purchase is brand 1, then with probability p_{11} the next customer to be generated will also start off as a brand 1 customer; with probability $p_{12} = 1 - p_{11}$, he will start as a brand 2 customer. The probability density functions for the times between arrivals of these new customers is $h_{11}(\cdot)$ and $h_{12}(\cdot)$, respectively. Similarly, if a new customer has just arrived whose first purchase is brand 2, then with probability p_{21} and after a time described by the probability density function $h_{21}(\cdot)$, the next customer to be generated will start as a brand 1 customer; he will start as a brand 2 customer with probability p_{22} and after a time described by the probability density function $h_{22}(\cdot)$.

Once a customer has arrived he continues to buy the two products according to the following dynamics:

q_{ij} = {next purchase will be brand j | last purchase was brand i}

$g_{ij}(\cdot)$ = probability density function for time of next purchase if he has just purchased brand i and his next purchase is brand j

$v_{ik}(t)$ = the *number of customers* using brand k at time t if the first customer arrived at $t = 0$ and purchased brand i for his first purchase

Draw a flow graph in terms of the p's, h's, q's, and g's whose transmission from input node i to output node k is $\bar{v}_{ik}^{e}(s)$. [Note: You may find it useful to define the random variable $x_{jk}(\xi, t)$ to be equal to one if a customer who bought brand j for the first time at time ξ is currently using brand k at time t, and equal to zero otherwise.]

11. For Problem 2 it is known that after both products are put on the market there is an initial waiting period before either product is purchased. The length of this waiting period is exponentially distributed with a mean of 2.5 weeks. At the end of this period the probability of a brand A purchase is 0.5.

a) What is the probability that a customer is a brand B customer t weeks after both products are put on the market?

b) An obscure market analyst states that he can reduce the above semi-Markov process to another semi-Markov process with no virtual transitions and with identical interval transition probability matrices. Can he? If so, what will be the P and $H(t)$ matrices for the new process?

12. Mr. Jones has one light bulb in his attic that he replaces as soon as it burns out. He has found that the probability density function for the lifetime of attic bulbs is uniform between one and two months, i.e., $h(t) = 1$ for $1 \leq t \leq 2$ and $h(t) = 0$ otherwise. Let $e(t)\,\Delta$ be the probability that Mr. Jones makes a replacement between t and $t + \Delta$ if Mr. Jones puts in a new bulb at $t = 0$. Sketch $e(t)$ for $0 \leq t \leq 6$ months and find the steady-state value of $e(t)$.

13. Consider a piece of equipment whose time until failure has a hyper-exponential distribution, i.e., probability σ that the lifetime is selected from $2\sigma\mu e^{-2\sigma\mu t}$ and probability $1 - \sigma$ that the lifetime is selected from $2(1 - \sigma)\mu e^{-2(1-\sigma)\mu t}$. Each time a piece fails it is immediately replaced by a new piece. We start with a new piece at time zero.

Let $p(t)$ = density function of the equipment lifetime.

a) If $r(t)\,\Delta$ is the probability that a machine will break down between t and $t + \Delta$ for small Δ, find $r(t)$, the replacement rate for this process.

b) What is the steady-state value of $r(t)$?

c) Find $n(t)$, the expected number of replacements through time t.

d) Using your answer to part c), how would you react to the following situation? At time zero a manufacturer gives you the choice of a new piece or a piece that has been running for some unknown time. You want to minimize the expected number of replacements in the next t hours. Which piece should you select?

14. Some concern has been expressed about the replacement of pencil sharpeners in a certain university. Through long years of experience it has been found that if a new pencil sharpener is placed in a particular location, then the expected number of replacements during the next t years is

$$\bar{k}(t) = (1/2)t - 1/4 + (1/4)e^{-2t}.$$

a) What is the lifetime distribution for the pencil sharpeners?

b) If at some time you are given the choice between a new pencil sharpener and one that has been in use for some unknown time, which pencil sharpener should you use to minimize the expected number of replacements during the next t years?

15. A certain machine when first started has a breakdown time with density function

$$f(t) = \mu^2 te^{-\mu t}.$$

Once the machine breaks down it is repaired. The repair time has density function,

$$g(t) = \lambda e^{-\lambda t}.$$

a) Model this system as a two-state semi-Markov process. Draw the flow graph and find $\phi_{11}^e(s)$ and $\phi_{12}^e(s)$. Find the steady-state probability that the machine is in repair.

b) The density function $f(t)$ is also the density function for the sum of two independent random variables with individual density functions $\mu e^{-\mu t}$. Now model the above problem as a three-state process with only exponentially distributed holding times. Draw the flow graph for this process. How are the elements of $\Phi^e(s)$ for this process related to those for the original process? Show that the steady-state probability that the machine is in repair agrees with the result of part a). If the machine emerges from repair at time zero, what is the probability that it is running at time t?

16. Mr. Smith is visiting his car dealer where they are having a big sale on his favorite model of car (a marked-off model?). Through long experience Mr. Smith has found that whenever he buys a car there is a probability p that the car will be a "lemon" and have a lifetime density function $h_\ell(\cdot)$ and a mean lifetime of $\bar{\tau}_\ell$. The lifetime density function for normal cars is $h_n(\cdot)$ with a mean of $\bar{\tau}_n$. Every time Mr. Smith's car wears out, he buys a new one immediately.

a) What is the exponential transform of the expected number of lemons Mr. Smith will purchase by time t if he purchases a new car at time zero?

b) In the steady-state, what is the expected number of lemons purchased per unit time? What fraction of the time will Mr. Smith be driving a lemon?

c) Mr. Smith has been buying cars for some time and pays $\$c$ for a car. However, he has recently been given the opportunity to purchase his cars from another dealer. The new dealer will guarantee that none of his cars are lemons. How much should Mr. Smith be willing to pay for cars purchased from the new dealer?

12 CONTINUOUS-TIME MARKOV PROCESSES

We can construct a theory of continuous-time Markov processes as a special case of the theory of continuous-time semi-Markov processes. Because the continuous-time Markov process has a much simpler theoretical structure than the continuous-time semi-Markov process, we often find it useful to prepare analytical models of the continuous-time Markov type before proceeding to the more complicated numerical analyses required by continuous-time semi-Markov models. The discussion of the continuous-time Markov process will provide the last of the four models in the discrete- and continuous-time, Markov and semi-Markov framework.

12.1 DEFINING RELATIONSHIPS

The continuous-time Markov process must possess one basic property if it is to deserve description as a Markov process: The only factor that influences the probability assignments to the future trajectory of the process must be the state presently occupied by the process. In particular, the length of time that the state has been occupied must be irrelevant both in predicting its destination state and in assigning a probability distribution to the remainder of the holding time in its present state. We have already observed in our discussion of semi-Markov processes that the first requirement of irrelevance between holding time and destination probability implies that the process must be an independent semi-Markov process. That is, the holding time density functions for all transitions out of a state must be identical and therefore must equal the waiting time density function for that state. However, these waiting time density functions may be different for different states.

In accordance with the discussion of Section 11.6, we know that the conditional transition probability matrix $P(\tau)$ is equal to the unconditional transition probability matrix P for such an independent semi-Markov process, and thus that the core matrix equation,

$$C(\tau) = P \,\square\, H(\tau) = W(\tau)P(\tau), \qquad (12.1.1)$$

becomes simply

$$C(\tau) = P \,\square\, H(\tau) = W(\tau)P. \qquad (12.1.2)$$

A necessary condition for the continuous-time Markov process is therefore that the process be an independent continuous-time semi-Markov process.

Independence of Lapsed Time

However, a second necessary property of the continuous-time Markov process concerns the waiting times for all states: The density function of time remaining until the next transition must be the same regardless of how long the state has already been occupied. As in Section 11.9, we call the lapsed occupancy time the lapsed time. To understand the requirement of independence of lapsed time, let us suppose that the process is known to have occupied state i through time t and that we are interested in the probability that it will remain there for at least an additional time Δ, $\Delta \geq 0$. For the process to be a Markov process, this probability must be a function only of Δ for any value of t. Formally,

$$\mathscr{P}\{\tau_i > t + \Delta | \tau_i > t\} = g(\Delta), \tag{12.1.3}$$

where τ_i is the waiting time in state i and $g(\cdot)$ is a function only of Δ. By the definition of conditional probability and the fact that the event $\tau_i > t + \Delta$ implies $\tau_i > t$,

$$\mathscr{P}\{\tau_i > t + \Delta | \tau_i > t\} = \frac{\mathscr{P}\{\tau_i > t + \Delta, \tau_i > t\}}{\mathscr{P}\{\tau_i > t\}} = \frac{\mathscr{P}\{\tau_i > t + \Delta\}}{\mathscr{P}\{\tau_i > t\}} = g(\Delta) \tag{12.1.4}$$

or

$$\mathscr{P}\{\tau_i > t + \Delta\} = \mathscr{P}\{\tau_i > t\}g(\Delta). \tag{12.1.5}$$

Since this equation must hold for all values of t including $t = 0$ and since $\mathscr{P}\{\tau_i > 0\} = 1$, we immediately see that

$$g(\Delta) = \mathscr{P}\{\tau_i > \Delta\} \tag{12.1.6}$$

and therefore write Equation 12.1.5 as

$$\mathscr{P}\{\tau_i > t + \Delta\} = \mathscr{P}\{\tau_i > t\}\mathscr{P}\{\tau_i > \Delta\} \qquad t \geq 0, \Delta \geq 0. \tag{12.1.7}$$

Our notation for the complementary cumulative probability distribution for waiting times allows us to place this equation in the form

$${}^{>}w_i(t + \Delta) = {}^{>}w_i(t)\, {}^{>}w_i(\Delta) \qquad t \geq 0, \Delta \geq 0. \tag{12.1.8}$$

We have now developed in Equation 12.1.8 a formal statement of the requirement that must be placed on the waiting time distribution for state i if the time the state has already been occupied is to be irrelevant in assessing the remaining time it will be occupied. Note that when Δ or t equals zero, for consistency we must insist that

$${}^{>}w_i(0) = 1. \tag{12.1.9}$$

Of course, this requirement is already met by all waiting time distributions that we are considering: A zero waiting time must have zero probability.

Implications for the Discrete-Time Markov Process

We can confirm Equation 12.1.8 by showing that it leads to the waiting time structure of the discrete-time Markov process if we allow holding times to take on only positive integral values. When $\Delta = 1$, Equation 12.1.8 becomes

$$^{>}w_i(n+1) = {}^{>}w_i(n)\,{}^{>}w_i(1) \qquad n = 0, 1, 2, \ldots . \tag{12.1.10}$$

Now we substitute the successive values $n = 1, 2, 3, \ldots$ and write

$$\begin{aligned} ^{>}w_i(2) &= {}^{>}w_i(1)\,{}^{>}w_i(1) = [{}^{>}w_i(1)]^2 \\ ^{>}w_i(3) &= {}^{>}w_i(2)\,{}^{>}w_i(1) = [{}^{>}w_i(1)]^3 \end{aligned} \tag{12.1.11}$$

or, in general,

$$^{>}w_i(n) = [{}^{>}w(1)]^n \qquad n = 1, 2, 3, \ldots . \tag{12.1.12}$$

The waiting time probability mass function $w_i(m)$ is then

$$w_i(m) = \mathscr{P}\{\tau_i = m\} = {}^{>}w_i(m-1) - {}^{>}w_i(m) = [1 - {}^{>}w_i(1)][{}^{>}w_i(1)]^{m-1}$$
$$m = 1, 2, 3, \ldots \tag{12.1.13}$$

which is, of course, just the geometric probability distribution we discussed in Section 4.2 as the distribution governing the time to the first Head in coin tossing.

Therefore we have found that the discrete-time Markov process must have geometrically distributed waiting times. If we consider that the process makes a transition at every time instant, then $^{>}w_i(1) = 0$ for every state and all waiting time distributions become the degenerate case of the geometric distribution where the entire probability mass is concentrated at the point $m = 1$. However, we can also allow each state to have a different geometric waiting time distribution, as we saw in Section 4.3. Thus we can consider the discrete-time Markov process as an independent discrete-time semi-Markov process where the waiting time probability mass functions for each state are all geometric distributions, possibly different for different states.

Implications for the Continuous-Time Markov Process

We can use the same type of reasoning to determine the necessary form of the waiting time probability density functions for the continuous-time Markov process. We begin once more with Equation 12.1.8, but consider it to have continuous arguments,

$$^{>}w_i(t+\Delta) = {}^{>}w_i(t)\,{}^{>}w_i(\Delta) \qquad t \geq 0, \Delta \geq 0. \tag{12.1.14}$$

Then we differentiate with respect to Δ,

$$ {}^{>}w_i'(t+\Delta) = {}^{>}w_i(t)\,{}^{>}w_i'(\Delta) \tag{12.1.15}$$

and evaluate the result at $\Delta = 0$,

$$ {}^{>}w_i'(t) = {}^{>}w_i(t)\,{}^{>}w_i'(0). \tag{12.1.16}$$

We write this equation as

$$ \frac{{}^{>}w_i'(t)}{{}^{>}w_i(t)} = {}^{>}w_i'(0). \tag{12.1.17}$$

If we note that the derivative of the complementary cumulative waiting time probability distribution at the origin is just the negative of the waiting time density function at the origin, and if we assume that the density function has a finite value $w_i(0)$ at that point, then Equation 12.1.17 becomes

$$ \frac{{}^{>}w_i'(t)}{{}^{>}w_i(t)} = -w_i(0). \tag{12.1.18}$$

Now we integrate both sides of this equation from zero to t to produce

$$ \ln {}^{>}w_i(t) = -w_i(0)t \tag{12.1.19}$$

or

$$ {}^{>}w_i(t) = e^{-w_i(0)t}. \tag{12.1.20}$$

The corresponding waiting time density function then emerges as

$$ w_i(\tau) = -\frac{d}{d\tau}\,{}^{>}w_i(\tau) = w_i(0)e^{-w_i(0)\tau}, \tag{12.1.21}$$

which is, of course, the exponential density function we discussed in Section 11.1.

We have therefore found that the continuous-time Markov process is an independent continuous-time semi-Markov process where the waiting time in each state is exponentially distributed, possibly with a different exponential waiting time density function for each state. For convenience we shall let $w_i(0)$, the value for state i of the waiting time density function at the origin, be simply the quantity λ_i. Then the equations for the exponential waiting time density function and its complementary cumulative probability distribution have the simple appearance,

$$ w_i(\tau) = \lambda_i e^{-\lambda_i \tau}, \quad \tau \geq 0; \qquad {}^{>}w_i(t) = e^{-\lambda_i t}, \quad t \geq 0. \tag{12.1.22}$$

Matrix Forms

We can present the values of λ_i for the process by an N by N diagonal matrix Λ whose ith diagonal element is λ_i,

$$ \Lambda = \begin{bmatrix} \lambda_1 & 0 & 0 & 0 \\ 0 & \lambda_2 & & \\ 0 & & \ddots & \\ 0 & & & \lambda_N \end{bmatrix}. \tag{12.1.23}$$

Since the mean of a variable that is exponentially distributed with rate parameter λ is $1/\lambda$, the mean waiting time matrix M is just the inverse of Λ,

$$M = \begin{bmatrix} \bar{\tau}_1 & 0 & 0 & 0 \\ 0 & \bar{\tau}_2 & & \\ 0 & & \ddots & \\ 0 & & & \bar{\tau}_N \end{bmatrix} = \Lambda^{-1} = \begin{bmatrix} \frac{1}{\lambda_1} & 0 & 0 & 0 \\ 0 & \frac{1}{\lambda_2} & & \\ 0 & & \ddots & \\ 0 & & & \frac{1}{\lambda_N} \end{bmatrix}. \tag{12.1.24}$$

The Λ or M matrices and the transition probability matrix P thus provide a complete distribution of the continuous-time Markov process.

Irrelevance of Random Entry

At this point we can confirm that entering a continuous-time Markov process at a random time rather than when a transition is completed does not affect the statistics of the process in any way. Equation 11.14.9 shows how the core matrix element ${}_{\mathrm{r}}c_{ij}(\tau)$ for the next transition under random starting is related to the other process parameters,

$${}_{\mathrm{r}}c_{ij}(\tau) = \frac{p_{ij}\,{}^{>}h_{ij}(t)}{\bar{\tau}_i}. \tag{12.1.25}$$

For the continuous-time Markov process, ${}^{>}h_{ij}(t) = {}^{>}w_i(t) = e^{-\lambda_i t}$ and $1/\bar{\tau}_i = \lambda_i$. Therefore,

$${}_{\mathrm{r}}c_{ij}(\tau) = p_{ij}\lambda_i e^{-\lambda_i \tau} = w_i(\tau)p_{ij} = c_{ij}(\tau); \tag{12.1.26}$$

the core matrix for the first transition after random starting is the same as the core matrix governing all future transitions. Knowing that the initial state of the process was selected by observation at a random time has no bearing on the probability assignments to future trajectories.

The Continuous-Time Markov Process

The continuous-time Markov process is just like a discrete-time Markov process except that the time between transitions must be distributed exponentially rather than geometrically. We are not surprised by this result because the exponential distribution is just the continuous analog of the geometric distribution. We shall see that the relations we develop for the continuous-time Markov process bear a strong similarity to those we have already established for the discrete-time Markov process.

12.2 INTERVAL TRANSITION PROBABILITIES OF THE CONTINUOUS-TIME MARKOV PROCESS

The interval transition probability $\phi_{ij}(t)$ for the continuous-time Markov process is the probability that the process occupies state j at time t given that it occupied state i at time zero. Note that we need not require that the process enter state i at time zero because, in the light of the previous section, such knowledge would have no relevance to the prediction of the future trajectory.

We can find the interval transition probability $\phi_{ij}(t)$ and its matrix form $\Phi(t)$ directly from the results of Chapter 11 for the continuous-time semi-Markov process. The exponential transform $\Phi^e(s)$ of $\Phi(t)$ appears in Equation 11.5.6,

$$\Phi^e(s) = [I - P \,\Box\, H^e(s)]^{-1}\, {}^{>}W^e(s). \tag{12.2.1}$$

In view of Equation 12.1.2 for the independent semi-Markov process we immediately have

$$C^e(s) = P \,\Box\, H^e(s) = W^e(s)P \tag{12.2.2}$$

and therefore

$$\begin{aligned} \Phi^e(s) &= [I - W^e(s)P]^{-1}\, {}^{>}W^e(s) \\ &= [({}^{>}W^e(s))^{-1} - ({}^{>}W^e(s))^{-1} W^e(s)P]^{-1}. \end{aligned} \tag{12.2.3}$$

Because of the exponential nature of the waiting times expressed by Equation 12.1.22 and the transform of the exponential distribution from Equation 11.4.31, the exponential transforms of the matrices of waiting time density functions and complementary cumulative probability distributions are:

$$W^e(s) = \begin{bmatrix} \dfrac{\lambda_1}{s+\lambda_1} & 0 & \cdots & 0 \\ 0 & \dfrac{\lambda_2}{s+\lambda_2} & \cdots & 0 \\ \vdots & \vdots & \ddots & \\ 0 & 0 & \cdots & \dfrac{\lambda_N}{s+\lambda_N} \end{bmatrix}$$

$${}^{>}W^e(s) = \frac{1}{s}[I - W^e(s)] = \begin{bmatrix} \dfrac{1}{s+\lambda_1} & 0 & \cdots & 0 \\ 0 & \dfrac{1}{s+\lambda_2} & \cdots & 0 \\ \vdots & \vdots & \ddots & \\ 0 & 0 & & \dfrac{1}{s+\lambda_N} \end{bmatrix} \tag{12.2.4}$$

Therefore Equation 12.2.3 assumes the form,

$$\Phi^e(s) = \left[\begin{pmatrix} s+\lambda_1 & 0 & \cdots & 0 \\ 0 & s+\lambda_2 & \cdots & 0 \\ \vdots & \vdots & \ddots & \vdots \\ 0 & 0 & \cdots & s+\lambda_N \end{pmatrix} - \begin{pmatrix} \lambda_1 & 0 & \cdots & 0 \\ 0 & \lambda_2 & \cdots & 0 \\ \vdots & \vdots & \ddots & \vdots \\ 0 & 0 & \cdots & \lambda_N \end{pmatrix} P\right]^{-1} \tag{12.2.5}$$

or

$$\Phi^e(s) = [sI + \Lambda(I - P)]^{-1}. \tag{12.2.6}$$

The Transition Rate Matrix

Now we define the transition rate matrix A of the continuous-time Markov process by

$$A = -\Lambda(I - P) = \Lambda(P - I). \tag{12.2.7}$$

Thus A has the form:

$$A = \begin{bmatrix} a_{11} & a_{12} & \cdots & a_{1N} \\ a_{21} & a_{22} & \cdots & a_{2N} \\ \vdots & \vdots & \ddots & \vdots \\ a_{N1} & a_{N2} & \cdots & a_{NN} \end{bmatrix}$$

$$= \begin{bmatrix} -\lambda_1 \sum_{j \neq 1} p_{1j} & \lambda_1 p_{12} & \lambda_1 p_{13} & \cdots & \lambda_1 p_{1N} \\ \lambda_2 p_{21} & -\lambda_2 \sum_{j \neq 2} p_{2j} & \lambda_2 p_{23} & \cdots & \lambda_2 p_{2N} \\ \vdots & \vdots & \vdots & \ddots & \vdots \\ \lambda_N p_{N1} & \lambda_N p_{N2} & \lambda_N p_{N3} & \cdots & -\lambda_N \sum_{j \neq N} p_{Nj} \end{bmatrix} \tag{12.2.8}$$

The rows of the transition rate matrix A sum to zero rather than 1; as you remember, we call such a matrix a differential matrix. Note that the off-diagonal elements are positive, while the on-diagonal elements are the negative sum of the off-diagonal elements in the same row. The transition rate matrix plays the same central role for continuous-time Markov processes as the transition probability matrix P does for discrete-time Markov processes.

When we substitute the transition rate matrix A into Equation 12.2.6, we obtain a very simple matrix expression for the transform of the interval transition probability matrix,

$$\Phi^e(s) = [sI - A]^{-1}. \tag{12.2.9}$$

The exponentially transformed interval transition probability matrix is just the inverse of the matrix formed by subtracting the transition rate matrix from s times the identity matrix.

The Explicit Matrix Solution

We have therefore solved our problem of writing an explicit expression for the interval transition probability matrix $\Phi(t)$. In view of relation 26 of Table 11.4.1, we write $\Phi(t)$ as

$$\Phi(t) = e^{At} \qquad t \geq 0, \tag{12.2.10}$$

where the matrix function e^{At} is to be interpreted in the sense of Equation 11.4.19. Thus, for example, we see that $\Phi(0) = I$, as we would expect.

Equation 12.2.10 corresponds to the equation

$$\Phi(n) = P^n \qquad n = 0, 1, 2, \ldots \tag{12.2.11}$$

that produced the multistep transition probabilities in the discrete-time case. We shall soon see that the exponential transform equation 12.2.9 allows us to calculate explicit expressions for $\Phi(t)$ with the same ease that the geometric transform equation

$$\Phi^{\mathscr{g}}(z) = [I - zP]^{-1} \tag{12.2.12}$$

afforded us in the discrete-time case.

State Probabilities

We define $\phi_i(t)$ as the probability that the continuous-time Markov process occupies state i at time t and let $\boldsymbol{\phi}(t)$ be the row vector of state probabilities for all states. We then relate the state probability vector to the interval transition probability matrix by

$$\boldsymbol{\phi}(t) = \boldsymbol{\phi}(0)\Phi(t) = \boldsymbol{\phi}(0)e^{At}. \tag{12.2.13}$$

Thus if we know the initial state probability vector we can find the state probability vector for any future time.

Since the chain structure of the continuous-time Markov process is the same as that of the discrete-time Markov process with corresponding transition probability matrix, we know that there can exist all types of chain structure in the continuous-time Markov process that we have already observed in the discrete-time Markov process. The monodesmic, or one-chain, process is, as usual, of greatest practical interest. We know that for such a process the state probability vector $\boldsymbol{\phi}(t)$ will approach a limiting state probability vector $\boldsymbol{\phi}$ when t is large and that this limiting state probability vector will be the same for any initial probability vector $\boldsymbol{\phi}(0)$.

We can find a simple method for computing the limiting state probability vector $\boldsymbol{\phi}$ for a monodesmic continuous-time Markov process by differentiating Equation 12.2.13 with respect to t. In view of Equation 11.4.19 this differentiation produces the result

$$\frac{d}{dt}\boldsymbol{\phi}(t) = \boldsymbol{\phi}(0)\frac{d}{dt}e^{At} = \boldsymbol{\phi}(0)e^{At}\cdot A \tag{12.2.14}$$

or

$$\frac{d}{dt}\boldsymbol{\phi}(t) = \boldsymbol{\phi}(t)A. \tag{12.2.15}$$

The derivative of the state probability vector is just the state probability vector postmultiplied by the transition rate matrix A. Now as t becomes large, $\boldsymbol{\phi}(t)$ approaches $\boldsymbol{\phi}$ and the derivative of $\boldsymbol{\phi}(t)$ becomes zero. Therefore the limiting state probability vector must satisfy the equation

$$\boldsymbol{\phi}A = 0. \tag{12.2.16}$$

However, since the vector $\boldsymbol{\phi}$ in this equation can be multiplied by any constant without changing the equation, this relation alone does not suffice to produce the limiting state probabilities. What we need in addition is the requirement that the limiting state probabilities sum to one,

$$\sum_{j=1}^{N} \phi_i = 1, \tag{12.2.17}$$

the same requirement we had to impose in the discrete-time case. Simultaneous solution of Equations 12.2.16 and 12.2.17 provides a direct method of evaluating the limiting state probability vector for a monodesmic continuous-time Markov process.

12.3 A CONTINUOUS-TIME TAXICAB PROBLEM AND OTHER EXAMPLES

The nature of our results will become much clearer if we examine numerical examples.

A Continuous-Time Taxicab Problem

We shall first study a three-state continuous-time Markov process based on the taxicab problem of Chapter 1. In fact, the state interpretations will be exactly the same as before and we shall use the same transition probability matrix

$$P = \begin{bmatrix} 0.3 & 0.2 & 0.5 \\ 0.1 & 0.8 & 0.1 \\ 0.4 & 0.4 & 0.2 \end{bmatrix}. \tag{12.3.1}$$

The only difference we shall introduce is that instead of having each trip require exactly one time unit, we shall assume that the time for each trip is selected from an exponential density function with a mean of 1; that is, the waiting time density functions for the three states are

$$w_1(\tau) = w_2(\tau) = w_3(\tau) = e^{-\tau} \qquad \tau \geq 0, \tag{12.3.2}$$

and the matrix Λ becomes simply the 3 by 3 identity matrix I. With these definitions we can find the transition rate matrix A directly as

$$A = \Lambda(P - I) = \begin{bmatrix} -0.7 & 0.2 & 0.5 \\ 0.1 & -0.2 & 0.1 \\ 0.4 & 0.4 & -0.8 \end{bmatrix}. \tag{12.3.3}$$

The Real Transition Equivalent

There are other process definitions that lead to the same transition rate matrix. Thus, according to the discussion in Section 4.3, we can consider that the process makes only real transitions by defining transitions to be only those trips that result in a change of town. The transition probability matrix for real transitions only is given in Equation 4.3.22,

$$P^{\mathrm{r}} = \begin{bmatrix} 0 & 2/7 & 5/7 \\ 1/2 & 0 & 1/2 \\ 1/2 & 1/2 & 0 \end{bmatrix}. \tag{12.3.4}$$

If we want the mean waiting times for the process to be the same for both the discrete-time and continuous-time examples, then we must choose λ_1, λ_2, and λ_3 to be consistent with Equation 4.3.8,

$$\lambda_1^{\mathrm{r}} = \frac{1}{\bar{\tau}_1} = 0.7, \qquad \lambda_2^{\mathrm{r}} = \frac{1}{\bar{\tau}_2} = 0.2, \qquad \lambda_3^{\mathrm{r}} = \frac{1}{\bar{\tau}_3} = 0.8 \tag{12.3.5}$$

and use the matrix Λ defined by

$$\Lambda^{\mathrm{r}} = \begin{bmatrix} 0.7 & 0 & 0 \\ 0 & 0.2 & 0 \\ 0 & 0 & 0.8 \end{bmatrix}. \tag{12.3.6}$$

Since this real-transition-only process represents a change in viewpoint rather than in the basic structure of the process, Equations 12.3.4 and 12.3.6 should lead to the same transition rate matrix found in Equation 12.3.3 when substituted into the equation

$$A = \Lambda^{r}(P^{r} - I), \tag{12.3.7}$$

and they do.

Transform Analysis

Continuing now with our analysis, we first write the matrix $sI - A$,

$$sI - A = \begin{bmatrix} s + 0.7 & -0.2 & -0.5 \\ -0.1 & s + 0.2 & -0.1 \\ -0.4 & -0.4 & s + 0.8 \end{bmatrix} \tag{12.3.8}$$

and then find its determinant,

$$|sI - A| = s^3 + 1.7s^2 + 0.6s = s(s + 0.5)(s + 1.2). \tag{12.3.9}$$

Note that the determinant is a polynomial in s, that it contains a factor s, and that its other two factors are very simple for this example. The determinant $|sI - A|$ always contains a factor s for the same reason that $|I - zP|$ contains a factor $1 - z$: the existence of a limiting interval transition probability matrix.

Next we evaluate the inverse matrix $[sI - A]^{-1}$,

$$[sI - A]^{-1} = \frac{1}{s(s + 0.5)(s + 1.2)} \times \begin{bmatrix} s^2 + s + 0.12 & 0.2s + 0.36 & 0.5s + 0.12 \\ 0.1s + 0.12 & s^2 + 1.5s + 0.36 & 0.1s + 0.12 \\ 0.4s + 0.12 & 0.4s + 0.36 & s^2 + 0.9s + 0.12 \end{bmatrix} \tag{12.3.10}$$

and write it in the partial fraction expansion form,

$$[sI - A]^{-1} = \frac{1}{s}\begin{bmatrix} 0.2 & 0.6 & 0.2 \\ 0.2 & 0.6 & 0.2 \\ 0.2 & 0.6 & 0.2 \end{bmatrix} + \frac{1}{s + 0.5}\begin{bmatrix} 13/35 & -26/35 & 13/35 \\ -1/5 & 2/5 & -1/5 \\ 8/35 & -16/35 & 8/35 \end{bmatrix} + \frac{1}{s + 1.2}\begin{bmatrix} 3/7 & 1/7 & -4/7 \\ 0 & 0 & 0 \\ -3/7 & -1/7 & 4/7 \end{bmatrix}. \tag{12.3.11}$$

We obtain the interval transition probability matrix by inverse exponential transformation as

$$\Phi(t) = e^{At} = \begin{bmatrix} 0.2 & 0.6 & 0.2 \\ 0.2 & 0.6 & 0.2 \\ 0.2 & 0.6 & 0.2 \end{bmatrix} + e^{-0.5t}\begin{bmatrix} 13/35 & -26/35 & 13/35 \\ -1/5 & 2/5 & -1/5 \\ 8/35 & -16/35 & 8/35 \end{bmatrix} + e^{-1.2t}\begin{bmatrix} 3/7 & 1/7 & -4/7 \\ 0 & 0 & 0 \\ -3/7 & -1/7 & 4/7 \end{bmatrix} \qquad t \geq 0. \tag{12.3.12}$$

As an initial check we note that substituting $t = 0$ in this expression produces the identity matrix I as required. We observe that $\Phi(t)$ is the sum of a set of matrices each multiplied by a coefficient that may be a function of time: The N-state monodesmic continuous-time Markov process will have N component matrices forming $\Phi(t)$. The matrix having coefficient 1 is the limiting interval transition probability matrix Φ. Since our example is a monodesmic Markov process, all rows of Φ are identical and are equal to the limiting state probability vector $\boldsymbol{\phi}$ for the process. Although Φ is a stochastic matrix, the other terms of $\Phi(t)$ with decaying exponential coefficients are differential matrices. These components of $\Phi(t)$ vanish when t is large.

General Observations

The general form of $\Phi(t)$ for an N-state monodesmic continuous-time Markov process is therefore the sum of a stochastic matrix with identical rows and $N - 1$ differential matrices with exponentially decaying coefficients. The exponential decay rates are just the characteristic values of A since they are found by solving the equation $|sI - A| = 0$. Thus the transition rate matrix A must have at least one characteristic value equal to zero to produce the limiting interval probability matrix in the solution. The other characteristic values must have negative real parts so that they will cause exponential decay rather than exponential growth in the transient components.

However, the analysis works as well for the polydesmic case. The number of characteristic values equal to zero is the number of chains in the process. If a particular characteristic value a other than zero occurs k times, it will cause coefficients of the form te^{-at}, t^2e^{-at}, up through $t^{k-1}e^{-at}$, a result evident from the table of exponential transforms. Thus the exponential transform analysis of the continuous-time Markov process is as general as the geometric transform analysis of the discrete-time Markov process. We can use exponential transform methods to produce a closed-form expression for the matrix function e^{At} for any process regardless of its chain structure.

Limiting Behavior

If we compare Equation 12.3.12 with Equation 1.6.44, we observe that the matrix terms are identical and that only the coefficients are different. The geometric sequences we found in the discrete-time case have been replaced by decaying exponentials in this continuous-time version of the example. Note that the coefficient $e^{-1.2t}$ does not oscillate the way $(-1/5)^n$ does. All transient components of $\Phi(t)$ in this continuous-time Markov process approach their limiting values without oscillation.

If we were interested only in the limiting state probability vector of this process, we could use the simultaneous equations 12.2.16 and 12.2.17 to find this vector directly. Equations 12.2.16 are

$$\begin{aligned} -0.7\phi_1 + 0.1\phi_2 + 0.4\phi_3 &= 0 \\ 0.2\phi_1 - 0.2\phi_2 + 0.4\phi_3 &= 0 \\ 0.5\phi_1 + 0.1\phi_2 - 0.8\phi_3 &= 0. \end{aligned} \tag{12.3.13}$$

We note that the last equation is the negative sum of the first two, and write Equation 12.2.17

$$\phi_1 + \phi_2 + \phi_3 = 1. \tag{12.3.14}$$

We can solve this expanded set of equations uniquely to produce the limiting state probability vector

$$\boldsymbol{\phi} = [0.2 \quad 0.6 \quad 0.2]. \tag{12.3.15}$$

If we cannot obtain a unique solution to the expanded set of equations, we have encountered a polydesmic process. The number of undetermined constants in the solution is the number of chains.

Graphical Representation—Shrinkage

We can think of the problem of how to represent graphically the possible convergence of $\Phi(t)$ to Φ when t is large. The geometric interpretations of the possible regions for $\Phi(t)$ that we discussed in Chapter 1 (Volume I) still apply to the continuous-time Markov process (as of course they do to semi-Markov processes). The possible regions must now be measured not only after each transition, but rather as a function of time. Thus we could draw a figure like Figure 1.4.6 to represent $\Phi(t)$ as given by Equation 12.3.12. As the time argument t increases from zero the possible region starts to shrink from the entire triangle toward the limiting point [0.2, 0.6, 0.2]. However, as we see from Equation 12.3.12, the shrinkage is continuous, without any of the reversals in orientation of the possible region that we observed in the discrete-time case.

The nature of the shrinkage becomes even clearer when we examine the vector interpretation of Figure 1.6.4. The vectors for the continuous- and the discrete-time examples are the same. The only differences are that they shrink geometrically in the discrete-time case, whereas they shrink exponentially in the continuous-time case, and that they never reverse direction. Thus the vector **a** shrinks according to the exponential $e^{-0.5t}$, while the vector **b** shrinks according to the exponential $e^{-1.2t}$. Eventually both vectors vanish and the rows of $\Phi(t)$ each become just the limiting state probability vector.

However, we observe that the shrinkage of **a** by the factor $e^{-0.5t}$ and the shrinkage of **b** by the factor $e^{-1.2t}$ imply that the area of the possible region shrinks as the product $e^{-0.5t}e^{-1.2t} = e^{-1.7t}$. In general, we see that each dimension of the possible region will shrink as one of the exponential decay factors and therefore that the area of the possible region will shrink at an exponential rate equal to the sum of the exponential rates of the decay factors. We shall call the exponential rate at which the possible region shrinks the "shrinkage rate" (sr) of the process. Since we know that the rates of the exponential decay factors are just the characteristic values of the transition rate matrix A, it follows that the shrinkage rate of the process must be just the sum of the characteristic values of the transition rate matrix. Thus for the example the shrinkage rate is -1.7 because the characteristic values of the matrix A in Equation 12.3.3 are 0, -0.5, and -1.2.

Finally, we recall from matrix theory that the sum of the characteristic values of any matrix is just the sum of the diagonal elements of the matrix. Therefore the shrinkage rate for a continuous-time Markov process is just the sum of the diagonal elements of the transition rate matrix A. Since these diagonal elements are non-positive real numbers, the shrinkage rate must be a non-positive real number. By referring to Equation 12.3.3, we see immediately that the shrinkage rate for the example must be -1.7.

It is no coincidence that each characteristic value 0, -0.5, and -1.2 of this A matrix equals one less than the characteristic values 1, 1/2, and $-1/5$ we found for the P matrix that described the discrete-time version of the example. When all waiting times in the continuous-time Markov process have unit exponential density functions, then Λ is just the identity matrix I. In this case Equation 12.2.7 shows that the characteristic values of A must be just one less than the characteristic values of P. Since the three-state continuous-time taxicab example satisfies the requirement that $\Lambda = I$, we could have predicted the shrinkage rate -1.7 from our earlier results.

Other Examples

We shall find it illuminating to analyze the continuous-time counterparts of other examples we discussed in Chapter 1. In all cases we shall assume for convenience that $\Lambda = I$; that is, the waiting times are all exponential density functions with means of 1. Since A is now equal simply to $P - I$, Equations 12.2.16 and 12.2.17 for finding the limiting state probability vector directly become the same equations we solved in the corresponding discrete-time cases and we need not discuss them further.

A duodesmic process

We begin with the three-state multiple-chain example with transition probability matrix

$$P = \begin{bmatrix} 1 & 0 & 0 \\ 0 & 1 & 0 \\ 0.3 & 0.2 & 0.5 \end{bmatrix}. \tag{12.3.16}$$

The corresponding transition rate matrix A is then

$$A = \Lambda(P - I) = P - I = \begin{bmatrix} 0 & 0 & 0 \\ 0 & 0 & 0 \\ 0.3 & 0.2 & -0.5 \end{bmatrix}. \tag{12.3.17}$$

We note that trapping states correspond to rows entirely filled with zeroes in the transition rate matrix. Next we compute $sI - A$,

$$sI - A = \begin{bmatrix} s & 0 & 0 \\ 0 & s & 0 \\ -0.3 & -0.2 & s + 0.5 \end{bmatrix}, \tag{12.3.18}$$

its determinant,

$$|sI - A| = s^2(s + 0.5), \tag{12.3.19}$$

and its inverse,

$$\Phi^e(s)[sI - A]^{-1} = \frac{1}{s^2(s+0.5)}\begin{bmatrix} s(s+0.5) & 0 & 0 \\ 0 & s(s+0.5) & 0 \\ 0.3s & 0.2s & s^2 \end{bmatrix}$$

$$= \begin{bmatrix} \frac{1}{s} & 0 & 0 \\ 0 & \frac{1}{s} & 0 \\ \frac{0.3}{s(s+0.5)} & \frac{0.2}{s(s+0.5)} & \frac{1}{s+0.5} \end{bmatrix}$$

$$= \frac{1}{s}\begin{bmatrix} 1 & 0 & 0 \\ 0 & 1 & 0 \\ 0.6 & 0.4 & 0 \end{bmatrix} + \frac{1}{s+0.5}\begin{bmatrix} 0 & 0 & 0 \\ 0 & 0 & 0 \\ -0.6 & -0.4 & 1 \end{bmatrix}. \tag{12.3.20}$$

The interval transition probability matrix is therefore

$$\Phi(t) = \begin{bmatrix} 1 & 0 & 0 \\ 0 & 1 & 0 \\ 0.6 & 0.4 & 0 \end{bmatrix} + e^{-0.5t}\begin{bmatrix} 0 & 0 & 0 \\ 0 & 0 & 0 \\ -0.6 & -0.4 & 1 \end{bmatrix} \qquad t \geq 0. \tag{12.3.21}$$

The fact that we have two characteristic values $s = 0$ shows that we have two chains and therefore that the rows of Φ are not equal. Since the number of chains plus the number of exponentially decaying differential matrices must be N, the number of states, we have only one exponentially decaying term in this example; the rate of this decay is -0.5. Since the three characteristic values of A are therefore 0, 0, and -0.5, the shrinkage rate for the process is -0.5, a result confirmed by the sum of the diagonal elements of A. We can visualize the shrinkage of the possible region by referring to Figure 1.4.7. The altitude of the triangular possible region now falls exponentially at the rate -0.5. The final location of the possible region is again just the line joining vertices 1 and 2. The position that the process will occupy on that line again depends on the initial state probability vector of the process.

The identity process

Next we examine the three-state three-chain process, which has the identity matrix as its transition probability matrix,

$$P = I = \begin{bmatrix} 1 & 0 & 0 \\ 0 & 1 & 0 \\ 0 & 0 & 1 \end{bmatrix}. \tag{12.3.22}$$

When we compute the transition rate matrix A,

$$A = P - I = \begin{bmatrix} 0 & 0 & 0 \\ 0 & 0 & 0 \\ 0 & 0 & 0 \end{bmatrix}, \tag{12.3.23}$$

we find that it is a matrix composed entirely of zeroes because every state is a trapping state. Then we immediately have $sI - A = sI$,

$$sI - A = \begin{bmatrix} s & 0 & 0 \\ 0 & s & 0 \\ 0 & 0 & s \end{bmatrix}, \tag{12.3.24}$$

with determinant $|sI - A| = s^3$ and inverse $\Phi^e(s) = [sI - A]^{-1} = (1/s)I$. The interval transition probability matrix $\Phi(t)$ is therefore the identity matrix I: $\Phi(t) = I$, $t \geq 0$. Since all three characteristic values of A are equal to zero, we confirm that the process has three chains. Furthermore, since the shrinkage rate must be zero, the limiting possible region is the entire triangle.

The periodic process

We turn finally to the three-state periodic process. Though we may consider our previous extensions of discrete-time examples to continuous-time as routine, here is the point where we shall encounter an important new feature of the continuous-time Markov process.

Since the transition probability matrix P for the process is

$$P = \begin{bmatrix} 0 & 1 & 0 \\ 0 & 0 & 1 \\ 1 & 0 & 0 \end{bmatrix}, \tag{12.3.25}$$

we write the transition rate matrix as

$$A = P - I = \begin{bmatrix} -1 & 1 & 0 \\ 0 & -1 & 1 \\ 1 & 0 & -1 \end{bmatrix}. \tag{12.3.26}$$

Then we have

$$sI - A = \begin{bmatrix} s+1 & -1 & 0 \\ 0 & s+1 & -1 \\ -1 & 0 & s+1 \end{bmatrix} \tag{12.3.27}$$

with determinant

$$\begin{aligned}|sI - A| &= (s + 1)^3 - 1\\ &= s^3 + 3s^2 + 3s\\ &= s(s^2 + 3s + 3)\\ &= s[s + (1/2)(3 + j\sqrt{3})][s + (1/2)(3 - j\sqrt{3})]. \end{aligned} \tag{12.3.28}$$

The characteristic values of the transition rate matrix are therefore 0, $-(1/2) \times (3 + j\sqrt{3})$, and $-(1/2)(3 - j\sqrt{3})$. The complex nature of two of these characteristic values requires no change in our usual approach. We proceed by writing the transformed interval transition probability matrix:

$$\begin{aligned}\Phi^e(s) &= (sI - A)^{-1}\\ &= \frac{1}{s[s + (1/2)(3 + j\sqrt{3})][s + (1/2)(3 - j\sqrt{3})]}\\ &\quad \times \begin{bmatrix} (s+1)^2 & s+1 & 1 \\ 1 & (s+1)^2 & s+1 \\ s+1 & 1 & (s+1)^2 \end{bmatrix}\\ &= \frac{1}{s}\begin{bmatrix} 1/3 & 1/3 & 1/3 \\ 1/3 & 1/3 & 1/3 \\ 1/3 & 1/3 & 1/3 \end{bmatrix} + \frac{-(1/6)(1 + j\sqrt{3})}{s + (1/2)(3 + j\sqrt{3})}\\ &\quad \times \begin{bmatrix} -(1/2)(1 - j\sqrt{3}) & -(1/2)(1 + j\sqrt{3}) & 1 \\ 1 & -(1/2)(1 - j\sqrt{3}) & -(1/2)(1 + j\sqrt{3}) \\ -(1/2)(1 + j\sqrt{3}) & 1 & -(1/2)(1 - j\sqrt{3}) \end{bmatrix}\\ &\quad + \frac{-(1/6)(1 - j\sqrt{3})}{s + (1/2)(3 - j\sqrt{3})}\\ &\quad \times \begin{bmatrix} -(1/2)(1 + j\sqrt{3}) & -(1/2)(1 - j\sqrt{3}) & 1 \\ 1 & -(1/2)(1 + j\sqrt{3}) & -(1/2)(1 - j\sqrt{3}) \\ -(1/2)(1 - j\sqrt{3}) & 1 & -(1/2)(1 + j\sqrt{3}) \end{bmatrix}\\ &= \frac{1}{s}\begin{bmatrix} 1/3 & 1/3 & 1/3 \\ 1/3 & 1/3 & 1/3 \\ 1/3 & 1/3 & 1/3 \end{bmatrix} + \frac{2/3}{s + (1/2)(3 + j\sqrt{3})}\end{aligned}$$

$$\times \begin{bmatrix} 1/2 & -(1/4)(1-j\sqrt{3}) & -(1/4)(1+j\sqrt{3}) \\ -(1/4)(1+j\sqrt{3}) & 1/2 & -(1/4)(1-j\sqrt{3}) \\ -(1/4)(1-j\sqrt{3}) & -(1/4)(1+j\sqrt{3}) & 1/2 \end{bmatrix}$$

$$+ \frac{2/3}{s+(1/2)(3-j\sqrt{3})}$$

$$\times \begin{bmatrix} 1/2 & -(1/4)(1+j\sqrt{3}) & -(1/4)(1-j\sqrt{3}) \\ -(1/4)(1-j\sqrt{3}) & 1/2 & -(1/4)(1+j\sqrt{3}) \\ -(1/4)(1+j\sqrt{3}) & -(1/4)(1-j\sqrt{3}) & 1/2 \end{bmatrix} \quad (12.3.29)$$

We can now write the interval transition probability matrix as

$$\Phi(t) = \begin{bmatrix} 1/3 & 1/3 & 1/3 \\ 1/3 & 1/3 & 1/3 \\ 1/3 & 1/3 & 1/3 \end{bmatrix} + (2/3)e^{-(3/2)t}e^{-j(\sqrt{3}/2)t}$$

$$\times \begin{bmatrix} 1/2 & -(1/4)(1-j\sqrt{3}) & -(1/4)(1+j\sqrt{3}) \\ -(1/4)(1+j\sqrt{3}) & 1/2 & -(1/4)(1-j\sqrt{3}) \\ -(1/4)(1-j\sqrt{3}) & -(1/4)(1+j\sqrt{3}) & 1/2 \end{bmatrix}$$

$$+ (2/3)e^{-(3/2)t}e^{+j(\sqrt{3}/2)t}$$

$$\times \begin{bmatrix} 1/2 & -(1/4)(1+j\sqrt{3}) & -(1/4)(1-j\sqrt{3}) \\ -(1/4)(1-j\sqrt{3}) & 1/2 & -(1/4)(1+j\sqrt{3}) \\ -(1/4)(1+j\sqrt{3}) & -(1/4)(1-j\sqrt{3}) & 1/2 \end{bmatrix}. \quad (12.3.30)$$

By using the relation that $e^{j\theta} = \cos\theta + j\sin\theta$, we can change $\Phi(t)$ into the more convenient form,

$$\Phi(t) = \begin{bmatrix} 1/3 & 1/3 & 1/3 \\ 1/3 & 1/3 & 1/3 \\ 1/3 & 1/3 & 1/3 \end{bmatrix} + (2/3)e^{-(3/2)t}$$

$$\times \begin{bmatrix} \cos(\sqrt{3}/2)t & \begin{matrix} -(1/2)\cos(\sqrt{3}/2)t \\ +(\sqrt{3}/2)\sin(\sqrt{3}/2)t \end{matrix} & \begin{matrix} -(1/2)\cos(\sqrt{3}/2)t \\ -(\sqrt{3}/2)\sin(\sqrt{3}/2)t \end{matrix} \\ \begin{matrix} -(1/2)\cos(\sqrt{3}/2)t \\ -(\sqrt{3}/2)\sin(\sqrt{3}/2)t \end{matrix} & \cos(\sqrt{3}/2)t & \begin{matrix} -(1/2)\cos(\sqrt{3}/2)t \\ +(\sqrt{3}/2)\sin(\sqrt{3}/2)t \end{matrix} \\ \begin{matrix} -(1/2)\cos(\sqrt{3}/2)t \\ +(\sqrt{3}/2)\sin(\sqrt{3}/2)t \end{matrix} & \begin{matrix} -(1/2)\cos(\sqrt{3}/2)t \\ -(\sqrt{3}/2)\sin(\sqrt{3}/2)t \end{matrix} & \cos(\sqrt{3}/2)t \end{bmatrix}$$

$$t \geq 0. \quad (12.3.31)$$

This form shows clearly the differential nature of the second matrix. However, we shall find interpretation easier if we use trigonometric identities once more to describe $\Phi(t)$ as

$$\Phi(t) = \begin{bmatrix} 1/3 & 1/3 & 1/3 \\ 1/3 & 1/3 & 1/3 \\ 1/3 & 1/3 & 1/3 \end{bmatrix} + (2/3)e^{-(3/2)t}$$

$$\times \begin{bmatrix} \cos\frac{\sqrt{3}}{2}t & \cos\left(\frac{\sqrt{3}}{2}t - \frac{2\pi}{3}\right) & \cos\left(\frac{\sqrt{3}}{2}t + \frac{2\pi}{3}\right) \\ \cos\left(\frac{\sqrt{3}}{2}t + \frac{2\pi}{3}\right) & \cos\frac{\sqrt{3}}{2}t & \cos\left(\frac{\sqrt{3}}{2}t - \frac{2\pi}{3}\right) \\ \cos\left(\frac{\sqrt{3}}{2}t - \frac{2\pi}{3}\right) & \cos\left(\frac{\sqrt{3}}{2}t + \frac{2\pi}{3}\right) & \cos\frac{\sqrt{3}}{2}t \end{bmatrix}$$

$$t \geq 0. \quad (12.3.32)$$

The differential matrix has an interesting periodic behavior. Whenever t is a multiple of $2\pi/(\sqrt{3}/2) = 4\pi/\sqrt{3}$, the matrix assumes the same value,

$$\begin{bmatrix} 1 & -(1/2) & -(1/2) \\ -(1/2) & 1 & -(1/2) \\ -(1/2) & -(1/2) & 1 \end{bmatrix}, \quad (12.3.33)$$

that it has when $t = 0$. By referring to Figure 1.4.9, we can interpret the differential matrix as the cause of rotation of the possible region by 360° whenever t increases by $4\pi/\sqrt{3}$. However, the exponential decay factor $e^{-(3/2)t}$ is a phenomenon we do not encounter in the discrete-time example. Not only does the possible region rotate, it also shrinks exponentially in each dimension at the rate $-3/2$. The shrinkage rate for the possible region is therefore -3, the sum of the three characteristic values 0, $-(1/2)(3 + j\sqrt{3})$, and $-(1/2)(3 - j\sqrt{3})$, and is, of course, also the sum of the diagonal elements of A in Equation 12.3.26. The combination of rotation and shrinkage produces a spiral decay of the possible region toward the limiting state probability vector $\boldsymbol{\phi} = [1/3 \quad 1/3 \quad 1/3]$.

Thus continuous-time Markov processes that are periodic with respect to the sequence of their transitions do not produce interval transition probabilities that are indefinitely oscillating functions of time. Rather they produce periodic functions that decay exponentially to a unique limiting probability vector. This finding should not surprise us because the continuous-time periodic process corresponds quite closely to a discrete-time periodic Markov process that allows virtual transitions.

Such a process would have a transition probability matrix like

$$P = \begin{bmatrix} 1-a & a & 0 \\ 0 & 1-a & a \\ a & 0 & 1-a \end{bmatrix} \qquad 0 < a < 1. \tag{12.3.34}$$

We can interpret its behavior as that of a real transition discrete-time Markov process with transition probability matrix given in Equation 12.3.25 and waiting time probability mass functions that have the geometric distribution

$$w_i(m) = a(1-a)^{m-1} \qquad m = 1, 2, 3, \ldots; i = 1, 2, 3. \tag{12.3.35}$$

Although this process is periodic with respect to transitions, the possible region experiences the same kind of rotation and shrinkage that we observed in the continuous-time periodic process. We readily compute the shrinkage factor to be

$$\text{sf} = \|P\| = 1 - 3a + 3a^2. \tag{12.3.36}$$

Note that the shrinkage factor approaches 1 as a approaches 0 because the process tends toward the identity process. The shrinkage factor also approaches 1 as a approaches 1 because the process tends toward the no-virtual-transition periodic process that we studied extensively in Chapter 1. A quick calculation shows that maximum shrinkage occurs when $a = 1/2$; the shrinkage factor then becomes 1/4. In this case the possible region shrinks to 1/64 of its original size after only three time instants.

Thus the periodic continuous-time Markov process does not introduce any really new phenomenon, but rather the necessity to understand the real-virtual transition question in discrete-time Markov processes. The exponential waiting time distributions of continuous-time processes correspond completely to the geometric waiting time distributions we observed in real transition discrete-time Markov processes.

12.4 FLOW GRAPH ANALYSIS

We develop the matrix flow graph that produces $\Phi^e(s)$ by writing Equation 12.2.9 in the form

$$\Phi^e(s) = [sI - A]^{-1} = \left[I - \frac{1}{s}A\right]^{-1}\frac{1}{s} = \left[I - \frac{1}{s}A\right]^{-1}\frac{1}{s}I. \tag{12.4.1}$$

This relation shows that $\Phi^e(s)$ is the transmission of the matrix flow graph shown in Figure 12.4.1, a loop with transmission $(1/s)A$ followed by an identity system with a multiplicative factor $1/s$.

$$\Phi^e(s) = \quad \xrightarrow{\frac{1}{s}I} \quad \bullet = [I - \tfrac{1}{s}A]^{-1}\tfrac{1}{s}I = [sI - A]^{-1}$$

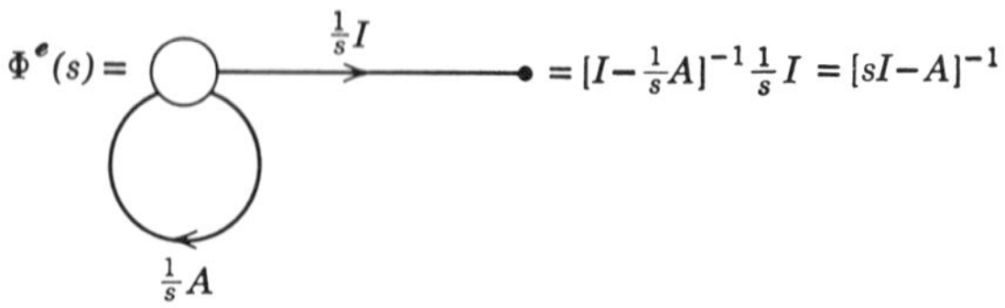

Figure 12.4.1 Matrix flow graph for the continuous-time Markov process.

Figure 12.4.2 illustrates the detailed flow graph that corresponds to this matrix flow graph. The branch transmission from node i to node j of this graph is just the transition rate a_{ij} divided by s. Associated with each node there is an output branch with transmission $1/s$. The transformed interval transition probability $\phi_{ij}^e(s)$ is therefore the transmission of the flow graph from node i to the output node associated with node j.

If we view the continuous-time Markov process as a special case of the continuous-time semi-Markov process, then we know that Figure 11.7.2 must be the general form of the detailed flow graph. By using Equations 12.2.2 and 12.2.4 we find that the detailed flow graph for the continuous-time Markov process must possess the form shown in Figure 12.4.3, a form that at first glance appears quite different from that of Figure 12.4.2.

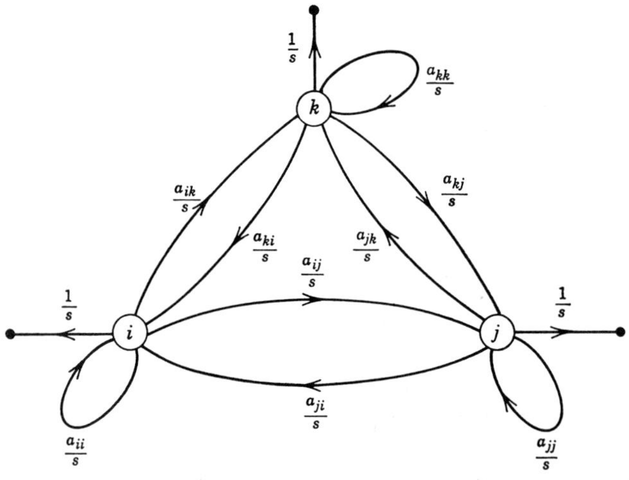

Figure 12.4.2 Flow graph for the continuous-time Markov process.

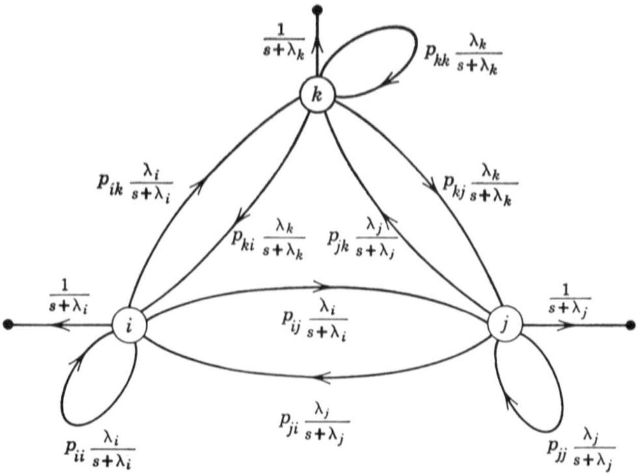

Figure 12.4.3 Flow graph for the continuous-time Markov process as a special form of that for the semi-Markov process.

To reconcile the two representations we proceed according to Figure 12.4.4. We note that each loop with transmission $p_{jj}[\lambda_j/(s + \lambda_j)]$ in Figure 12.4.3 can be replaced by a loop with transmission a_{jj}/s followed by a branch with transmission $(s + \lambda_j)/s$. If we perform this conversion on all nodes of Figure 12.4.3, we find that we have simply caused the transmissions of the loop around each node j to be a_{jj}/s,

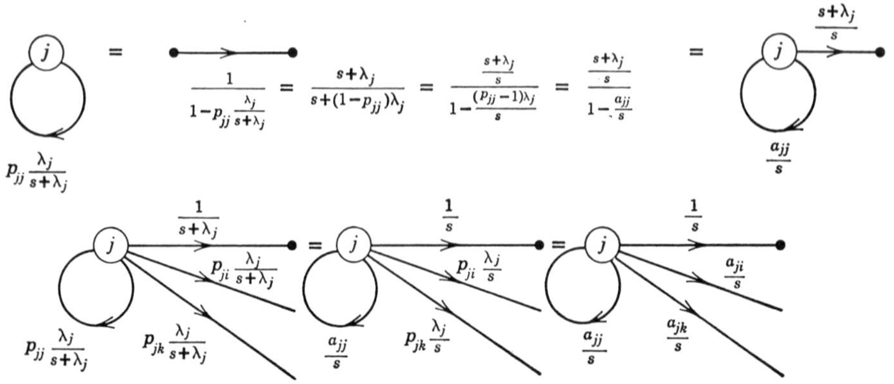

Figure 12.4.4 Flow graph operations necessary to show the equivalence of Figures 12.4.2 and 12.4.3.

the branch transmission from node j to node k to be a_{jk}/s, and the branch transmission of the output branch to be $1/s$. Thus we have transformed the flow graph of Figure 12.4.3 into that of Figure 12.4.2.

The Taxicab Problem

The transition rate matrix A given by Equation 12.3.3 for the continuous-time taxicab problem implies the flow graph representation of Figure 12.4.5. Each element a_{ij} of the transmission rate matrix has been divided by s and written as the transmission of the branch from node i to node j. An output branch with transmission $1/s$ appears at each node. The sum of the loop products for this graph is

$$\Delta = 1 + \frac{1.7}{s} + \frac{0.60}{s^2} \tag{12.4.2}$$

since the terms in $1/s^3$ turn out to have a zero coefficient. Note that this expression is not the determinant of the matrix $sI - A$, but rather the determinant of $I - (1/s)A$. Because each element of $sI - A$ must be divided by s to produce $I - (1/s)A$, the ratio of $|sI - A|$ to $|I - (1/s)A|$ is s^N for an N-state process. Comparing Equations 12.3.9 and 12.4.2 shows that this ratio is s^3 for the example.

We can calculate any interval transition probability or the entire matrix of interval probabilities for the continuous-time taxicab problem by computing the transmissions of the flow graph of Figure 12.4.5. Thus the transmission from

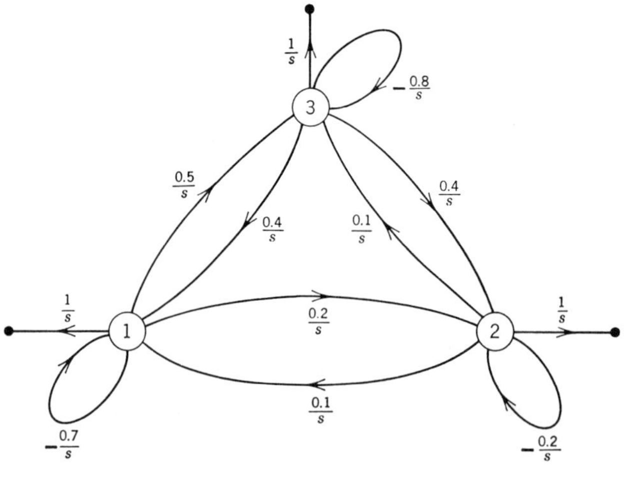

Figure 12.4.5 Flow graph for the continuous-time taxicab problem.

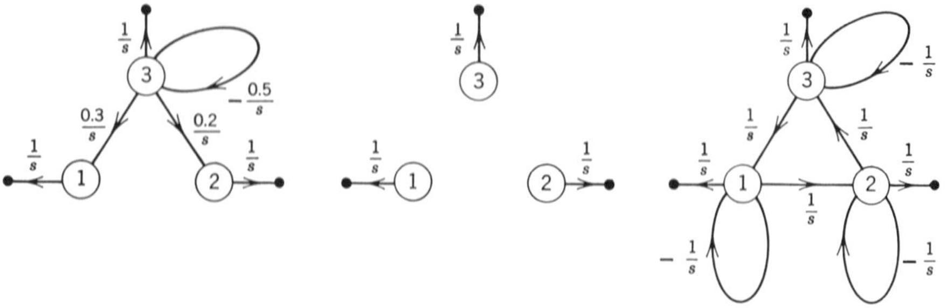

Figure 12.4.6 Flow graphs for three examples.

node 1 to the output node associated with node 2 is $\phi_{12}^e(s)$, the exponential transform of the probability that the process will occupy state 2 at time t if it occupied state 1 at time zero. We find

$$\phi_{12}^e(s) = \frac{1}{\Delta}\left[\frac{0.2}{s}\left(1 + \frac{0.8}{s}\right) + \left(\frac{0.5}{s}\right)\left(\frac{0.4}{s}\right)\right]\frac{1}{s} = \frac{0.2s + 0.36}{s(s^2 + 1.7s + 0.6)}$$

$$= \frac{0.2s + 0.36}{s(s + 0.5)(s + 1.2)} = \frac{0.6}{s} + \frac{-26/35}{s + 0.5} + \frac{1/7}{s + 1.2}, \qquad (12.4.3)$$

a result confirmed by the 12 element of the matrices in Equations 12.3.10 and 12.3.11. The inverse exponential transform produces the interval transition probability from state 1 to state 2,

$$\phi_{12}(t) = 0.6 - (26/35)e^{-0.5t} + (1/7)e^{-1.2t} \qquad t \geq 0, \qquad (12.4.4)$$

the 12 element of $\Phi(t)$ in Equation 12.3.12.

Other Examples

Figure 12.4.6 shows the flow graphs for the duodesmic, identity, and periodic examples we studied in the last section. These graphs were drawn directly from the transition rate matrices in Equations 12.3.17, 12.3.23, and 12.3.26. Their transmissions immediately confirm the $\Phi^e(s)$ matrices computed in Section 12.3.

12.5 INTERPRETATION AS COMPETING EXPONENTIAL PROCESSES

Let us now explore a competing process, real transition model for the mechanism determining destination state and waiting time in a continuous-time Markov process. The development parallels the general formulation of Section 11.6. We imagine that when the process enters state i it begins to observe $N-1$ random processes, one for each state $k \neq i$ to which the next transition might be made. The kth process produces an independent time as a candidate for the next real transition time by selecting a sample from an exponential distribution with rate parameter λ_{ik}. Thus the kth exponential process is governed by the density function

$$g_{ik}(t) = \lambda_{ik}e^{-\lambda_{ik}t} \qquad t \geq 0 \qquad k = 1, 2, \ldots, N, k \neq i \tag{12.5.1}$$

and by a complementary cumulative probability distribution

$$^{>}g_{ik}(t) = e^{-\lambda_{ik}t} \qquad t \geq 0 \quad k = 1, 2, \ldots, N, k \neq i. \tag{12.5.2}$$

Suppose that process j of these $N-1$ processes produces the smallest candidate value for waiting time and that this value is τ. Then we decree that the Markov process will make its next transition after waiting a time τ and that the transition will be made to state j. Thus we consider the selection of transition time and destination to be a race between exponential processes. The process that produces the lowest time determines both the destination state and the transition time. Of course once the transition is made, the selection process begins again using the exponential rates appropriate to the new state.

Relationship to Core Matrix Formulation

We can relate this model to the core matrix by noting that $c_{ij}(\tau)$, $i \neq j$—the core matrix element specifying the joint probability-probability density function for destination and transition time—is just the exponential density function $g_{ij}(\tau)$ multiplied by the probability that all other exponential processes produce values larger than τ,

$$\begin{aligned} c_{ij}(\tau) &= g_{ij}(\tau) \prod_{\substack{k=1 \\ k \neq i,j}}^{N} {}^{>}g_{ik}(\tau) = \lambda_{ij}e^{-\lambda_{ij}\tau} \prod_{\substack{k=1 \\ k \neq i,j}}^{N} e^{-\lambda_{ik}\tau} \\ &= \lambda_{ij} \prod_{\substack{k=1 \\ k \neq i}}^{N} e^{-\lambda_{ik}\tau} = \lambda_{ij} \exp\left(-\sum_{\substack{k=1 \\ k \neq i}}^{N} \lambda_{ik}\tau\right) \qquad i \neq j\cdot \end{aligned} \tag{12.5.3}$$

Of course, when $i = j$, the core matrix element is zero.

We compute the transition probability p_{ij} from the core matrix as

$$\begin{aligned} p_{ij} &= \int_0^\infty d\tau \; c_{ij}(\tau) = \lambda_{ij} \int_0^\infty d\tau \exp\left(-\sum_{\substack{k=1 \\ k \neq i}}^{N} \lambda_{ik}\tau\right) \\ &= \frac{\lambda_{ij}}{\sum\limits_{\substack{k=1 \\ k \neq i}}^{N} \lambda_{ik}} \qquad i \neq j \end{aligned} \tag{12.5.4}$$

and

$$p_{ij} = 0 \qquad i = j. \tag{12.5.5}$$

We see that the probability of a transition from state i to state j is proportional to the exponential rate λ_{ij} with the proportionality constant required to make the transition probabilities sum to one.

The holding time density function $h_{ij}(\tau)$ is just $c_{ij}(\tau)$ divided by p_{ij} or

$$h_{ij}(\tau) = \frac{c_{ij}(\tau)}{p_{ij}} = \sum_{\substack{k=1 \\ k \neq i}}^{N} \lambda_{ik} \exp\left(-\sum_{\substack{k=1 \\ k \neq i}}^{N} \lambda_{ik}\tau\right) = w_i(\tau), \tag{12.5.6}$$

which is, of course, just an exponential density function with rate parameter $\sum_{k=1,k\neq i}^{N} \lambda_{ik}$. Note that the holding time density function does not depend on the destination state j and is therefore the same as the waiting time density function. Thus we see that the process we have defined is an independent continuous-time semi-Markov process with exponentially distributed waiting times, or in other words, a continuous-time Markov process.

Relationship to Transition Rate Matrix

In view of Equations 12.5.4, 12.5.5, and 12.5.6, we can write the matrices P and Λ that describe the continuous-time Markov process as

$$P = \begin{bmatrix} 0 & \dfrac{\lambda_{12}}{\sum_{k=2}^{N} \lambda_{1k}} & \dfrac{\lambda_{13}}{\sum_{k=2}^{N} \lambda_{1k}} & \cdots & \dfrac{\lambda_{1N}}{\sum_{k=2}^{N} \lambda_{1k}} \\ \dfrac{\lambda_{21}}{\sum_{\substack{k=1 \\ k\neq 2}}^{N} \lambda_{2k}} & 0 & \dfrac{\lambda_{23}}{\sum_{\substack{k=1 \\ k\neq 2}}^{N} \lambda_{2k}} & \cdots & \dfrac{\lambda_{2N}}{\sum_{\substack{k=1 \\ k\neq 2}}^{N} \lambda_{2k}} \\ \vdots & & & & \vdots \\ \dfrac{\lambda_{N1}}{\sum_{k=1}^{N-1} \lambda_{Nk}} & \dfrac{\lambda_{N2}}{\sum_{k=1}^{N-1} \lambda_{Nk}} & \dfrac{\lambda_{N3}}{\sum_{k=1}^{N-1} \lambda_{Nk}} & \cdots & 0 \end{bmatrix},$$

$$\Lambda = \begin{bmatrix} \sum_{k=2}^{N} \lambda_{1k} & 0 & 0 & \cdots & 0 \\ 0 & \sum_{\substack{k=1 \\ k\neq 2}}^{N} \lambda_{2k} & 0 & \cdots & 0 \\ 0 & 0 & 0 & \cdots & 0 \\ 0 & 0 & 0 & \cdots & \sum_{k=1}^{N-1} \lambda_{Nk} \end{bmatrix}. \tag{12.5.7}$$

The transition rate matrix A is therefore

$$A = \Lambda(P - I) = \begin{bmatrix} -\sum_{k=2}^{N} \lambda_{1k} & \lambda_{12} & \lambda_{13} & \cdots & \lambda_{1N} \\ \lambda_{21} & -\sum_{\substack{k=1 \\ k \neq 2}}^{N} \lambda_{2k} & \lambda_{23} & \cdots & \lambda_{2N} \\ \vdots & & & & \vdots \\ \lambda_{N1} & \lambda_{N2} & \lambda_{N3} & \cdots & -\sum_{k=1}^{N-1} \lambda_{Nk} \end{bmatrix}. \tag{12.5.8}$$

The form of this matrix is expressed by the equations

$$a_{ij} = \lambda_{ij}, \quad i \neq j; \qquad a_{ii} = -\sum_{\substack{k=1 \\ k \neq i}}^{N} \lambda_{ik}. \tag{12.5.9}$$

Thus when i is not equal to j, the transition rate a_{ij} is just the exponential rate parameter λ_{ij}. Each diagonal transition rate a_{ii} is just the negative sum of the off-diagonal transition rates in the same row.

We have thus found a direct interpretation of the transition rate matrix for a continuous-time Markov process in terms of the rate parameters of exponential processes that compete to determine the transition time and destination when each state is occupied. We shall be able to exploit this interpretation in our future work.

The Transition Rate Diagram

The identification of the off-diagonal elements of A with the rates of exponential processes leads us to a compact representation of a continuous-time Markov

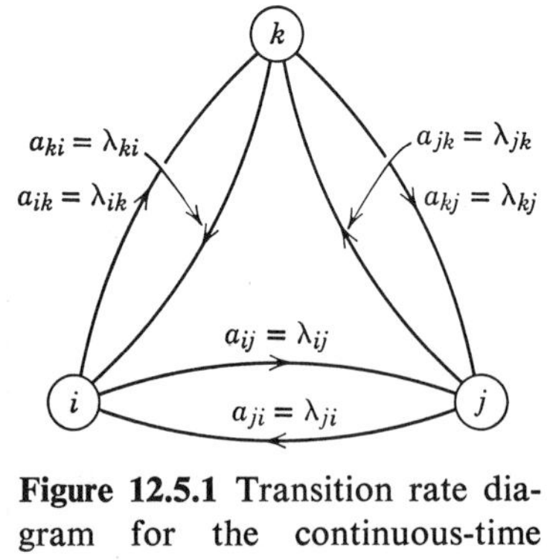

Figure 12.5.1 Transition rate diagram for the continuous-time Markov process.

process—the transition rate diagram. We identify a node in the diagram to correspond to each state in the process and then draw a branch from node i to node j, $i \neq j$, having a branch transmission equal to $a_{ij} = \lambda_{ij}$. Figure 12.5.1 illustrates such a diagram. The elimination from the transition rate diagram of the output branches, loops around each node, and factors of $1/s$ that appear in the flow graph allows us to grasp more readily the relations of the process.

12.6 CONTINUOUS-TIME BIRTH AND DEATH PROCESSES

An important type of continuous-time Markov processes is the birth and death process. As in the discrete-time case, this process is one whose state indices represent the number of units in the system and which can make transitions only to immediately neighboring states. We number the states in the process from 0 through N to allow for the possibility of having no units in the system. When the process is in state k because there are k units in the system, its next transition must be either to state $k - 1$ or to state $k + 1$ according to whether the next transition is the result of a death or a birth. Determination of whether a birth or death will next occur and when it will occur depends on the outcome of a race between two exponential processes in state k. The birth process for state k is an exponential process with rate parameter b_k, the birth rate for state k. The death process for this state is an exponential process with rate parameter d_k, the death rate for state k. Of course, if the process is in state 0 then only births can occur ($d_0 = 0$) with birth rate b_0; similarly, if it is in state N then only deaths can occur ($b_N = 0$) with death rate d_N.

The Transition Rate Matrix

In view of Equation 12.5.8 this description of the continuous-time birth and death process leads directly to a transition rate matrix A defined by:

$$A = \begin{bmatrix} -b_0 & b_0 & 0 & & & 0 \\ d_1 & -(b_1 + d_1) & b_1 & 0 & & 0 \\ 0 & d_2 & -(b_2 + d_2) & b_2 & 0 & 0 \\ 0 & 0 & d_k & -(b_k + d_k) & b_k & 0 \\ 0 & & 0 & d_{N-1} & -(b_{N-1} + d_{N-1}) & b_{N-1} \\ 0 & 0 & & 0 & d_N & -d_N \end{bmatrix} \tag{12.6.1}$$

Thus the transition rate matrix for the birth and death process has non-zero entries only on the main diagonal and just above and below it. This form for the transition rate matrix shows that the shrinkage rate for a continuous-time birth and death process is just the negative sum of all birth and death rates in the process,

$$\text{sr} = -\sum_{k=1}^{N}(b_{k-1} + d_k) = -\sum_{k=0}^{N}(b_k + d_k). \tag{12.6.2}$$

In general, the larger the birth and death rates, the faster will be the collapse of the possible region, and the sooner shall we be able to assign only steady-state probabilities to the states of the process.

By referring to Equation 12.5.7, we can represent A in terms of the matrices P and Λ:

$$P = \begin{bmatrix} 0 & 1 & 0 & & & & 0 \\ \frac{d_1}{b_1 + d_1} & 0 & \frac{b_1}{b_1 + d_1} & 0 & & & 0 \\ 0 & \frac{d_2}{b_2 + d_2} & 0 & \frac{b_2}{b_2 + d_2} & 0 & & 0 \\ 0 & & & \frac{d_k}{b_k + d_k} & 0 & \frac{b_k}{b_k + d_k} & 0 \\ 0 & & & 0 & \frac{d_{N-1}}{b_{N-1} + d_{N-1}} & 0 & \frac{b_{N-1}}{b_{N-1} + d_{N-1}} \\ 0 & & & & & 1 & 0 \end{bmatrix}$$

$$\Lambda = \begin{bmatrix} b_0 & 0 & & & & 0 \\ 0 & b_1 + d_1 & 0 & & & 0 \\ 0 & 0 & b_2 + d_2 & 0 & & 0 \\ 0 & & 0 & b_k + d_k & 0 & 0 \\ 0 & & & 0 & b_{N-1} + d_{N-1} & 0 \\ 0 & & & & 0 & d_N \end{bmatrix} \tag{12.6.3}$$

The shrinkage rate is therefore the sum of the elements in the Λ matrix for the birth and death process. Note that when the process is in state k, the probability that its next transition is to state $k + 1$ is $b_k/(b_k + d_k)$, and to state $k - 1$ is $d_k/(b_k + d_k)$; in other words, the transition probabilities are proportional to the birth and death rates. The waiting time in state k is an exponential probability density function

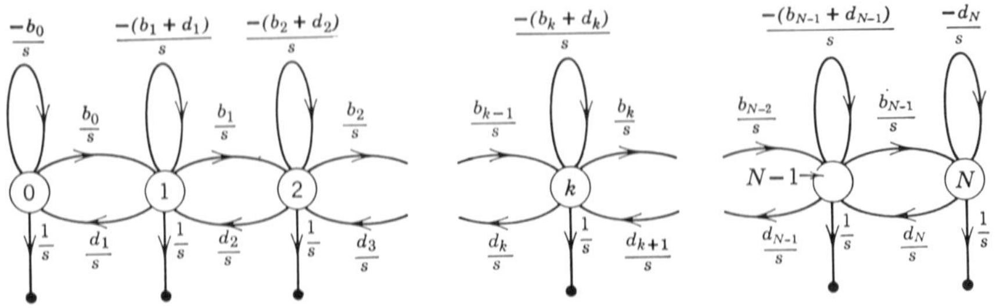

Figure 12.6.1 Flow graph for the continuous-time birth and death process.

with rate parameter $b_k + d_k$. Of course, in each end state, 0 or N, the process must make its next transition to state 1 or $N - 1$ with exponential rate b_0 or d_N, respectively.

Graphical Representations

Figure 12.6.1 shows the flow graph for the birth and death process implied by the transition rate matrix A of Equation 12.6.1. It is, of course, very similar in form to the transition diagram of the discrete-time birth and death process shown in Figure 7.5.1. By direct operations on this flow graph or by using the results of Equation 12.6.3 in the flow graph structure of Figure 12.4.3, we represent the flow graph for the continuous-time birth and death process in the semi-Markov form shown in Figure 12.6.2. Note that this form requires no loops around each node.

We obtain an even more compact representation of the continuous-time birth and death process by drawing its transition rate diagram as shown in Figure 12.6.3. The transition rate diagram contains all the information necessary to construct a flow graph representation of the process.

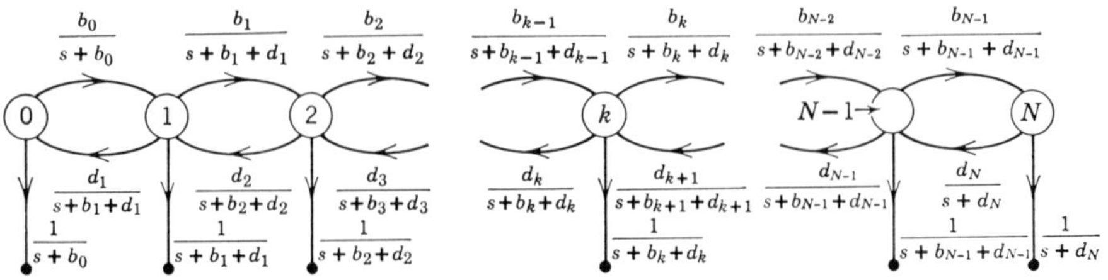

Figure 12.6.2 Semi-Markov type flow graph for the continuous-time birth and death process.

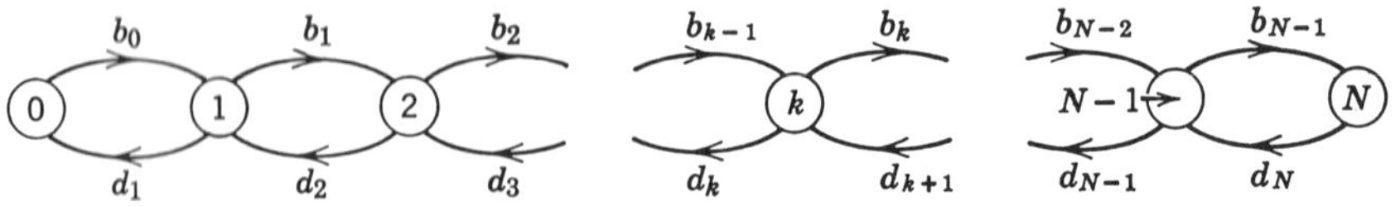

Figure 12.6.3 Transition rate diagram for the continuous-time birth and death process.

A Two-State Machine Repair Example

Consider a machine facility that comprises one machine and one repairman. Every time the machine breaks down the repairman goes to work to place it back in operation. Then the machine breaks down again, etc. We assume that the time required for the machine to fail after it is placed in operation is an exponentially distributed random variable with rate parameter λ. We assume that when the machine fails, the time required to make it operative is also an exponentially distributed random variable, but with rate parameter μ. Thus the mean operating period is $1/\lambda$ and the mean repair time is $1/\mu$. If we let the state of the system be the number of machines that are broken down, then we need only two states—state 0 and state 1. The transition rate matrix for this simplest of continuous-time birth and death processes is therefore

$$A = \begin{bmatrix} -\lambda & \lambda \\ \mu & -\mu \end{bmatrix}. \tag{12.6.4}$$

Equation 12.6.3 shows that this representation is equivalent to using the transition probability matrix P and the Λ matrix given by

$$P = \begin{bmatrix} 0 & 1 \\ 1 & 0 \end{bmatrix} \qquad \Lambda = \begin{bmatrix} \lambda & 0 \\ 0 & \mu \end{bmatrix}. \tag{12.6.5}$$

Thus as far as transitions are concerned, the process is a two-state, periodic continuous-time Markov process. Whenever the machine is working, we can be sure that the next transition the machine makes will be to the failure state. Whenever it has failed, we know that the next transition will be back to the operating state. The exponential waiting time distribution for state 0 has rate parameter λ, the failure rate; for state 1 it has parameter μ, the repair rate. We should note that the transition rate matrix in Equation 12.6.4 represents the most general two-state continuous-time Markov process.

Interval transition probabilities

We now proceed to find the interval transition probabilities for the example. First we form $sI - A$,

$$sI - A = \begin{bmatrix} s+\lambda & -\lambda \\ -\mu & s+\mu \end{bmatrix}; \tag{12.6.6}$$

evaluate its determinant $|sI - A|$,

$$|sI - A| = s(s + \lambda + \mu); \tag{12.6.7}$$

and then write its inverse $(sI - A)^{-1}$,

$$\Phi^e(s) = (sI - A)^{-1} = \frac{1}{s(s + \lambda + \mu)} \begin{bmatrix} s + \mu & \lambda \\ \mu & s + \lambda \end{bmatrix}$$

$$= \frac{1}{s} \begin{bmatrix} \frac{\mu}{\lambda + \mu} & \frac{\lambda}{\lambda + \mu} \\ \frac{\mu}{\lambda + \mu} & \frac{\lambda}{\lambda + \mu} \end{bmatrix} + \frac{1}{s + \lambda + \mu} \begin{bmatrix} \frac{\lambda}{\lambda + \mu} & \frac{-\lambda}{\lambda + \mu} \\ \frac{-\mu}{\lambda + \mu} & \frac{\mu}{\lambda + \mu} \end{bmatrix}. \tag{12.6.8}$$

We could also have formed $\Phi^e(s)$ by evaluating the transmissions of either of the two flow graph representations in Figure 12.6.4. Next we invert the exponential transform to produce

$$\Phi(t) = e^{At} = \begin{bmatrix} \frac{\mu}{\lambda + \mu} & \frac{\lambda}{\lambda + \mu} \\ \frac{\mu}{\lambda + \mu} & \frac{\lambda}{\lambda + \mu} \end{bmatrix} + e^{-(\lambda + \mu)t} \begin{bmatrix} \frac{\lambda}{\lambda + \mu} & \frac{-\lambda}{\lambda + \mu} \\ \frac{-\mu}{\lambda + \mu} & \frac{\mu}{\lambda + \mu} \end{bmatrix} \qquad t \geq 0. \tag{12.6.9}$$

We check that $\Phi(0) = I$, as required.

We can readily interpret Equation 12.6.9 in terms of the example. Thus

$$\phi_{00}(t) = \frac{\mu}{\lambda + \mu} + \frac{\lambda}{\lambda + \mu} e^{-(\lambda + \mu)t} \qquad t \geq 0 \tag{12.6.10}$$

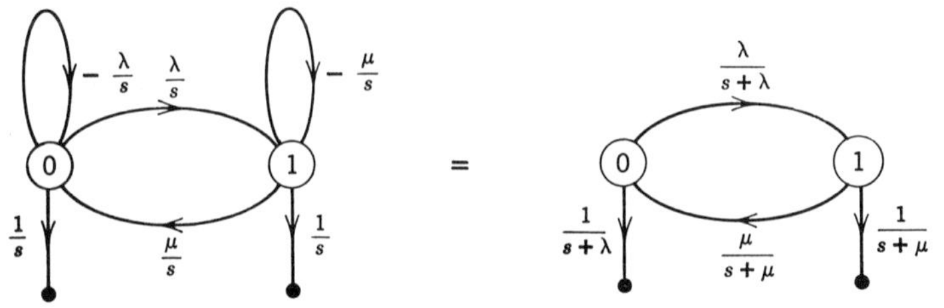

Figure 12.6.4 Flow graph for the one-machine–one-repairman example.

shows the probability that the machine is operating at time t if it is known to be operating at time zero. If t is very large, this probability becomes $\phi_0 = \mu/(\lambda + \mu)$, the steady-state probability of finding the machine in the operative state. Note that this probability approaches one as the repair rate μ increases and the failure rate λ decreases.

The transient part of $\Phi(t)$ decreases at the exponential rate $\lambda + \mu$, the sum of the failure and repair rates. The factor $\lambda + \mu$ is, of course, just the shrinkage rate for this process as computed from Equation 12.6.2.

A Three-State Machine Repair Example

We now turn to a larger machine facility with two machines and two repairmen. Only one repairman at a time can work on a broken machine. Thus if one machine fails, one repairman goes to work; only if both machines fail are both repairmen busy. Again we assume that each machine has a time of operation that is independently exponentially distributed with rate parameter λ, and that the repair time for one man to fix one machine is exponentially distributed with rate parameter μ. We let the state of the system be the number of machines that are broken—0, 1, or 2.

If both machines are working, then the next transition of the system must be to the state where one is broken. The chance of the simultaneous breakdown of two machines is negligible compared with the chance of a single breakdown. The probability that the first breakdown will occur beyond time t is the product of the probabilities that the first machine will break down beyond t and that the second will break down beyond t; this product is $e^{-\lambda t} \cdot e^{-\lambda t} = e^{-2\lambda t}$, and is the complementary cumulative distribution for the time to the first breakdown. Therefore, the time to the first breakdown must have an exponential distribution with rate parameter 2λ, the sum of the failure rates for the two machines. By the same argument, when both machines are broken down and undergoing repair, the time to the first repair must have an exponential density function with rate parameter 2μ, the sum of the repair rates for the two machines.

These results are just a special case of our finding in the last section that the time to the first event produced by competing exponential processes is exponentially distributed with a rate equal to the sum of the process rates. By the same arguments regarding competing exponential processes, when exactly one machine is undergoing repair, the chance that it will be fixed before the other fails is $\mu/(\lambda + \mu)$; while the chance that the other will fail before the first is fixed is $\lambda/(\lambda + \mu)$. The time until one or the other of these events occurs is exponentially distributed with parameter $\lambda + \mu$, the sum of the failure and repair rates.

These considerations lead us directly to a representation of the two-machine–

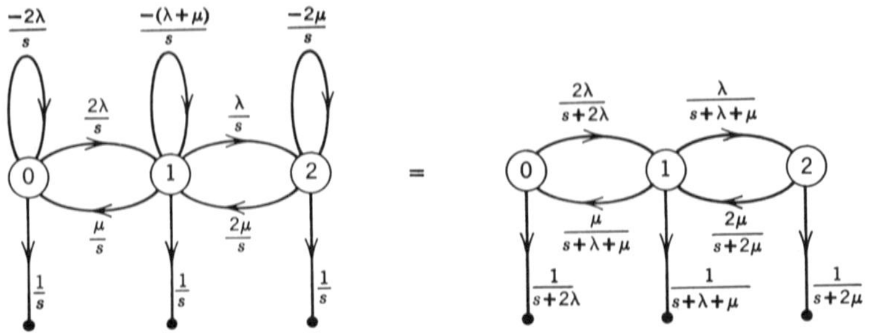

Figure 12.6.5 Flow graph for the two-machine–two-repairman example.

two-repairman problem as a continuous-time birth and death process with transition rate matrix A given by

$$A = \begin{bmatrix} -2\lambda & 2\lambda & 0 \\ \mu & -(\lambda + \mu) & \lambda \\ 0 & 2\mu & -2\mu \end{bmatrix}, \tag{12.6.11}$$

or to a formulation in terms of P and Λ as

$$P = \begin{bmatrix} 0 & 1 & 0 \\ \dfrac{\mu}{\lambda + \mu} & 0 & \dfrac{\lambda}{\lambda + \mu} \\ 0 & 1 & 0 \end{bmatrix} \qquad \Lambda = \begin{bmatrix} 2\lambda & 0 & 0 \\ 0 & \lambda + \mu & 0 \\ 0 & 0 & 2\mu \end{bmatrix}. \tag{12.6.12}$$

These forms in turn allow us to draw the flow graph for the process in the two versions shown in Figure 12.6.5.

Interval transition probabilities

We can compute the transformed interval transition probability matrix either from the transmissions of these flow graphs or by the usual matrix operations:

$$sI - A = \begin{bmatrix} s + 2\lambda & -2\lambda & 0 \\ -\mu & s + \lambda + \mu & -\lambda \\ 0 & -2\mu & s + 2\mu \end{bmatrix} \tag{12.6.13}$$

$$|sI - A| = s(s + \lambda + \mu)[s + 2(\lambda + \mu)] \tag{12.6.14}$$

$$\Phi^e(s) = [sI - A]^{-1} = \frac{1}{s(s + \lambda + \mu)[s + 2(\lambda + \mu)]}$$

$$\times \begin{bmatrix} s^2 + (\lambda + 3\mu)s + 2\mu^2 & 2\lambda(s + 2\mu) & 2\lambda^2 \\ \mu(s + 2\mu) & (s + 2\lambda)(s + 2\mu) & \lambda(s + 2\lambda) \\ 2\mu^2 & 2\mu(s + 2\lambda) & s^2 + (3\lambda + \mu)s + 2\lambda^2 \end{bmatrix}$$

$$= \frac{1}{s}\begin{bmatrix} \frac{\mu^2}{(\lambda+\mu)^2} & \frac{2\lambda\mu}{(\lambda+\mu)^2} & \frac{\lambda^2}{(\lambda+\mu)^2} \\ \frac{\mu^2}{(\lambda+\mu)^2} & \frac{2\lambda\mu}{(\lambda+\mu)^2} & \frac{\lambda^2}{(\lambda+\mu)^2} \\ \frac{\mu^2}{(\lambda+\mu)^2} & \frac{2\lambda\mu}{(\lambda+\mu)^2} & \frac{\lambda^2}{(\lambda+\mu)^2} \end{bmatrix}$$

$$+ \frac{1}{s + \lambda + \mu}\begin{bmatrix} \frac{2\lambda\mu}{(\lambda+\mu)^2} & \frac{2\lambda(\lambda-\mu)}{(\lambda+\mu)^2} & \frac{-2\lambda^2}{(\lambda+\mu)^2} \\ \frac{\mu(\lambda-\mu)}{(\lambda+\mu)^2} & \frac{(\lambda-\mu)^2}{(\lambda+\mu)^2} & \frac{\lambda(\mu-\lambda)}{(\lambda+\mu)^2} \\ \frac{-2\mu^2}{(\lambda+\mu)^2} & \frac{2\mu(\mu-\lambda)}{(\lambda+\mu)^2} & \frac{2\lambda\mu}{(\lambda+\mu)^2} \end{bmatrix}$$

$$+ \frac{1}{s + 2(\lambda + \mu)}\begin{bmatrix} \frac{\lambda^2}{(\lambda+\mu)^2} & \frac{-2\lambda^2}{(\lambda+\mu)^2} & \frac{\lambda^2}{(\lambda+\mu)^2} \\ \frac{-\lambda\mu}{(\lambda+\mu)^2} & \frac{2\lambda\mu}{(\lambda+\mu)^2} & \frac{-\lambda\mu}{(\lambda+\mu)^2} \\ \frac{\mu^2}{(\lambda+\mu)^2} & \frac{-2\mu^2}{(\lambda+\mu)^2} & \frac{\mu^2}{(\lambda+\mu)^2} \end{bmatrix} \quad (12.6.15)$$

Then we write the interval transition probability matrix as

$$\Phi(t) = \begin{bmatrix} \frac{\mu^2}{(\lambda+\mu)^2} & \frac{2\lambda\mu}{(\lambda+\mu)^2} & \frac{\lambda^2}{(\lambda+\mu)^2} \\ \frac{\mu^2}{(\lambda+\mu)^2} & \frac{2\lambda\mu}{(\lambda+\mu)^2} & \frac{\lambda^2}{(\lambda+\mu)^2} \\ \frac{\mu^2}{(\lambda+\mu)^2} & \frac{2\lambda\mu}{(\lambda+\mu)^2} & \frac{\lambda^2}{(\lambda+\mu)^2} \end{bmatrix}$$

$$+ e^{-(\lambda+\mu)t}\begin{bmatrix} \frac{2\lambda\mu}{(\lambda+\mu)^2} & \frac{2\lambda(\lambda-\mu)}{(\lambda+\mu)^2} & \frac{-2\lambda^2}{(\lambda+\mu)^2} \\ \frac{\mu(\lambda-\mu)}{(\lambda+\mu)^2} & \frac{(\lambda-\mu)^2}{(\lambda+\mu)^2} & \frac{\lambda(\mu-\lambda)}{(\lambda+\mu)^2} \\ \frac{-2\mu^2}{(\lambda+\mu)^2} & \frac{2\mu(\mu-\lambda)}{(\lambda+\mu)^2} & \frac{2\lambda\mu}{(\lambda+\mu)^2} \end{bmatrix}$$

$$+ e^{-2(\lambda+\mu)t}\begin{bmatrix} \frac{\lambda^2}{(\lambda+\mu)^2} & \frac{-2\lambda^2}{(\lambda+\mu)^2} & \frac{\lambda^2}{(\lambda+\mu)^2} \\ \frac{-\lambda\mu}{(\lambda+\mu)^2} & \frac{2\lambda\mu}{(\lambda+\mu)^2} & \frac{-\lambda\mu}{(\lambda+\mu)^2} \\ \frac{\mu^2}{(\lambda+\mu)^2} & \frac{-2\mu^2}{(\lambda+\mu)^2} & \frac{\mu^2}{(\lambda+\mu)^2} \end{bmatrix} \quad t \geq 0. \quad (12.6.16)$$

We observe once more the standard form of solution: a stochastic matrix plus $N - 1$ differential matrices weighted by exponential coefficients. Note that if λ and μ and states 0 and 2 are interchanged, the expression remains the same. This result is a direct consequence of the symmetry of the matrix A with respect to λ and μ. The shrinkage rate is, of course, just $3(\lambda + \mu)$, the sum of the elements of Λ, a result confirmed by the exponential factors $e^{-(\lambda+\mu)t}$ and $e^{-2(\lambda+\mu)t}$ in $\Phi(t)$.

The interval transition probability matrix provides the basic probabilistic solution of the two-machine–two-repairman example. Thus $\phi_{12}(t)$, the probability that both machines will be broken at time t if it is known that exactly one was broken at time zero, is the element at the right end of the middle row of $\Phi(t)$,

$$\phi_{12}(t) = \frac{\lambda^2}{(\lambda+\mu)^2} + \frac{\lambda(\mu-\lambda)}{(\lambda+\mu)^2} e^{-(\lambda+\mu)t} + \frac{-\lambda\mu}{(\lambda+\mu)^2} e^{-2(\lambda+\mu)t} \quad t \geq 0. \quad (12.6.17)$$

Note that this solution is not simply the probability that the other machine failed during $(0, t)$; it is the sum of the probabilities of all trajectories that could lead from a situation with one machine failed at time 0 to two machines failed at time t. Thus, for example, the original machine could have been repaired and then both could have failed.

When t is large the probability of finding both machines failed is $\lambda^2/[(\lambda + \mu)^2]$, the steady-state probability of state 2. The entire limiting state probability vector,

$$\boldsymbol{\phi} = \left[\frac{\mu^2}{(\lambda+\mu)^2} \quad \frac{2\lambda\mu}{(\lambda+\mu)^2} \quad \frac{\lambda^2}{(\lambda+\mu)^2}\right], \quad (12.6.18)$$

shows that state 0 becomes more likely as the repair rate μ increases, while state 2 becomes more likely as the failure rate λ increases.

Limiting Behavior

The limiting state probability vector $\boldsymbol{\phi}$ for the continuous-time birth and death process is governed by Equations 12.2.16 and 12.2.17 for the continuous-time Markov process,

$$\boldsymbol{\phi}A = 0, \qquad \sum_{i=1}^{N} \phi_i = 1. \quad (12.6.19)$$

However, in view of the special form of the transition rate matrix for the birth and death process shown in Equation 12.6.1, these relations immediately become the set of equations we developed earlier in Section 7.5 as Equations 7.5.8. The only change is that ϕ_i replaces π_i. We found the solution in Equation 7.5.13; we write it now as

$$\phi_k = \phi_0 \frac{b_0}{d_1} \cdot \frac{b_1}{d_2} \cdots \frac{b_{k-1}}{d_k} = \phi_0 \prod_{i=1}^{k} \frac{b_{i-1}}{d_i} \qquad k = 1, 2, \ldots, N. \qquad (12.6.20)$$

The limiting state probability of state k is the limiting state probability of state 0 multiplied by successive ratios of the birth rate to the death rate for the intervening states. As before, we find ϕ_0 from the normalizing requirement that the limiting state probabilities sum to one.

We know that in developing the solution we obtain the relation

$$b_k \phi_k = d_{k+1} \phi_{k+1} \qquad k=0, 1, \ldots, N-1, \qquad (12.6.21)$$

which implies that the average rate at which the system leaves state k due to births must be the average rate at which it enters state k as the result of deaths. This is a special case of a more general result for continuous-time Markov processes: There must be equal net transition rates in both directions across any boundary placed in the transition rate diagram.

Equation 12.6.20 has a simple visualization in terms of the transition rate diagram of Figure 12.6.3. The limiting state probability of any state k is the limiting state probability of state 0 multiplied by the ratio of birth to death rates on each pair of branches that successively connects states 0 and k.

The one-machine–one-repairman example

Returning to the one-machine–one-repairman example, we draw the transition rate diagram of Figure 12.6.6 directly from the transition rate matrix of Equation 12.6.4. We find

$$\phi_1 = \phi_0 \cdot \frac{b_0}{d_1} = \phi_0 \cdot \frac{\lambda}{\mu} \cdot \qquad (12.6.22)$$

The requirement that ϕ_0 and ϕ_1 sum to one immediately produces the solution

$$\boldsymbol{\phi} = \begin{bmatrix} \frac{\mu}{\lambda + \mu} & \frac{\lambda}{\lambda + \mu} \end{bmatrix}, \qquad (12.6.23)$$

which we have already found as the common row of the stochastic matrix Φ that is the first term of $\Phi(t)$ in Equation 12.6.9.

Of course, the transition probability matrix P in Equation 12.6.5 has a limiting state probability vector $\boldsymbol{\pi} = [1/2 \quad 1/2]$, showing that the process will on the average

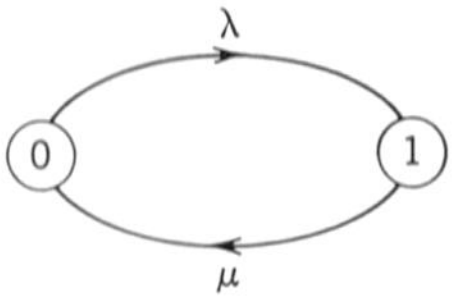

Figure 12.6.6 Transition rate diagram for the one-machine–one-repairman example.

make half its transitions to each state. However, the mean waiting time matrix for the process is just the reciprocal of the Λ matrix,

$$M = \Lambda^{-1}, \tag{12.6.24}$$

and for this example is

$$M = \begin{bmatrix} \dfrac{1}{\lambda} & 0 \\ 0 & \dfrac{1}{\mu} \end{bmatrix}. \tag{12.6.25}$$

We can therefore use the relationships developed for semi-Markov processes to relate $\boldsymbol{\phi}$ and $\boldsymbol{\pi}$,

$$\phi_i = \frac{\pi_i \bar{\tau}_i}{\sum_{i=0}^{N} \pi_i \bar{\tau}_i} \qquad i = 0, 1, \ldots, N. \tag{12.6.26}$$

We find

$$\phi_0 = \frac{\frac{1}{2}\left(\frac{1}{\lambda}\right)}{\frac{1}{2}\left(\frac{1}{\lambda}\right) + \frac{1}{2}\left(\frac{1}{\mu}\right)} = \frac{\mu}{\lambda + \mu}; \qquad \phi_1 = \frac{\frac{1}{2}\left(\frac{1}{\mu}\right)}{\frac{1}{2}\left(\frac{1}{\lambda}\right) + \frac{1}{2}\left(\frac{1}{\mu}\right)} = \frac{\lambda}{\lambda + \mu}. \tag{12.6.27}$$

The limiting probabilities measured in time are different from those measured in transitions because of the disparate mean waiting times of the two states.

The two-machine–two-repairman example

Turning now to the two-machine–two-repairman example, we use the transition rate matrix of Equation 12.6.11 to draw the transition rate diagram of Figure 12.6.7 and then write

$$\phi_1 = \phi_0 \cdot \frac{b_0}{d_1} = \phi_0 \frac{2\lambda}{\mu}; \qquad \phi_2 = \phi_0 \cdot \frac{b_0}{d_1} \cdot \frac{b_1}{d_2} = \phi_0 \cdot \frac{2\lambda}{\mu} \cdot \frac{\lambda}{2\mu} = \phi_0 \frac{\lambda^2}{\mu^2}. \tag{12.6.28}$$

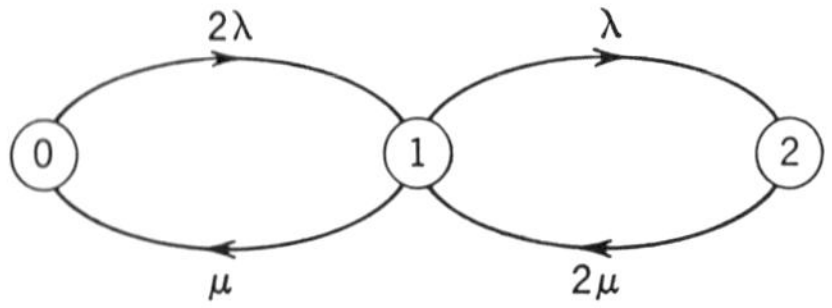

Figure 12.6.7 Transition rate diagram for the two-machine–two-repairman example.

The requirement that ϕ_0, ϕ_1, and ϕ_2 sum to one then produces the limiting state probability vector

$$\boldsymbol{\phi} = \left[\frac{\mu^2}{(\lambda + \mu)^2} \quad \frac{2\lambda\mu}{(\lambda + \mu)^2} \quad \frac{\lambda^2}{(\lambda + \mu)^2}\right]. \tag{12.6.29}$$

This is, of course, the limiting state probability vector of Equation 12.6.18.

We find the limiting state probability vector $\boldsymbol{\pi}$ in terms of transitions directly from the transition probability matrix P of Equation 12.6.12,

$$\boldsymbol{\pi} = \left[\frac{(1/2)\mu}{\lambda + \mu} \quad \frac{1}{2} \quad \frac{(1/2)\lambda}{\lambda + \mu}\right]. \tag{12.6.30}$$

We observe that, on the average, one-half of the transitions will be transitions to state 1. We write the mean waiting time matrix for this example from Equations 12.6.12 and 12.6.24 as

$$M = \Lambda^{-1} = \begin{bmatrix} \frac{1}{2\lambda} & 0 & 0 \\ 0 & \frac{1}{\lambda + \mu} & 0 \\ 0 & 0 & \frac{1}{2\mu} \end{bmatrix}. \tag{12.6.31}$$

To use this result in Equation 12.6.26 we first write

$$\sum_{i=0}^{2} \pi_i \bar{\tau}_i = \frac{(1/2)\mu}{\lambda + \mu}\cdot\frac{1}{2\lambda} + \frac{1}{2}\cdot\frac{1}{\lambda + \mu} + \frac{(1/2)\lambda}{\lambda + \mu}\cdot\frac{1}{2\mu} = \frac{\lambda + \mu}{4\lambda\mu}. \tag{12.6.32}$$

As we recall from our semi-Markov process work, this quantity is $\bar{\tau}$, the mean time between transitions in the process. Then we immediately obtain the elements of $\boldsymbol{\phi}$ as

$$\phi_0 = \frac{\pi_0 \bar{\tau}_0}{\bar{\tau}} = \frac{\mu^2}{(\lambda + \mu)^2}; \qquad \phi_1 = \frac{\pi_1 \bar{\tau}_1}{\bar{\tau}} = \frac{2\lambda\mu}{(\lambda + \mu)^2};$$
$$\phi_2 = \frac{\pi_2 \bar{\tau}_2}{\bar{\tau}} = \frac{\lambda^2}{(\lambda + \mu)^2}. \tag{12.6.33}$$

Servicing Problems

We can consider a number of interesting examples as special cases of birth and death processes. We shall place them all in the machine–repairman context for economy of presentation.

An infinite-machine–one-repairman example

Suppose that we have a very, very large number of machines and that the time between machine failures for the machine population is exponentially distributed with rate λ. We assume that we have only one repairman, that he can work on only one machine at a time, and that his time to repair a machine is exponentially distributed with rate μ. Further, the entire installation is shut down (no further failures occur) whenever N machines are out of order. We maintain our convention that the state indices of the system represent the number of machines that have failed; the state entries therefore range from 0 through N in this example. From the statement of the problem we can write the birth and death rates as

$$\begin{aligned} b_k &= \lambda, \quad k = 0, 1, \ldots, N-1; \qquad b_N = 0; \\ d_0 &= 0; \qquad d_k = \mu, \quad k = 1, 2, \ldots, N; \end{aligned} \tag{12.6.34}$$

and thus draw the transition rate diagram of Figure 12.6.8. It is clear from the structure of this diagram that

$$\phi_k = \phi_0 \left(\frac{\lambda}{\mu}\right)^k \qquad k = 0, 1, \ldots, N. \tag{12.6.35}$$

Then, since the limiting state probabilities must sum to one,

$$\sum_{k=0}^{N} \phi_k = 1 = \phi_0 \sum_{k=0}^{N} \left(\frac{\lambda}{\mu}\right)^k = \phi_0 \frac{1 - \left(\frac{\lambda}{\mu}\right)^{N+1}}{1 - \frac{\lambda}{\mu}}, \tag{12.6.36}$$

or

$$\phi_0 = \frac{1 - \frac{\lambda}{\mu}}{1 - \left(\frac{\lambda}{\mu}\right)^{N+1}}. \tag{12.6.37}$$

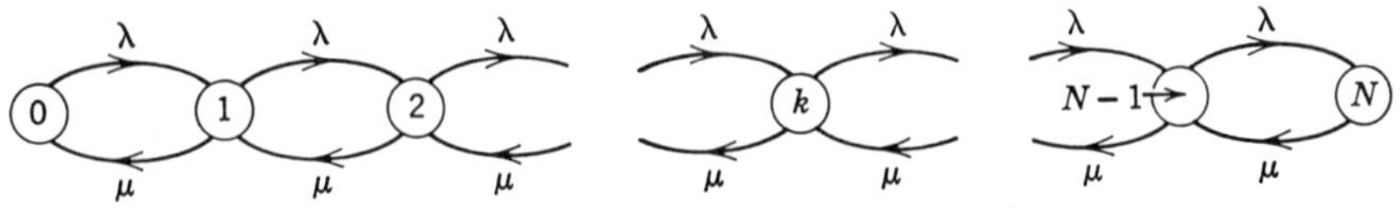

Figure 12.6.8 Transition rate diagram for the infinite-machine–one-repairman example with at most N machines in the service system.

Finally we have the complete solution

$$\phi_k = \frac{1 - \dfrac{\lambda}{\mu}}{1 - \left(\dfrac{\lambda}{\mu}\right)^{N+1}} \left(\frac{\lambda}{\mu}\right)^k \qquad k = 0, 1, \ldots, N, \tag{12.6.38}$$

a geometric relationship among the limiting state probabilities. By summing the birth and death rates for all states we learn that the shrinkage factor governing the approach to this limiting distribution is

$$\text{sr} = N(\lambda + \mu). \tag{12.6.39}$$

We note that if we take $N = 1$ in this solution, we reduce this example to the one-machine–one-repairman problem we have already studied. In this circumstance we see that Equation 12.6.38 produces the limiting state probabilities found in Equation 12.6.23.

If we allow N (the maximum number of machines out of order) to become very large, and if $\lambda < \mu$, then Equation 12.6.38 becomes

$$\phi_k = \left(1 - \frac{\lambda}{\mu}\right)\left(\frac{\lambda}{\mu}\right)^k \qquad k = 0, 1, 2, \ldots. \tag{12.6.40}$$

Of course, a steady-state solution will exist for this system only when the failure rate λ is less than the repair rate μ.

An infinite-machine–K-repairman example

In our next servicing model we again limit the maximum number of machines that can be out of order to be N, but assume that we have $K \leq N$ repairmen available. Each machine that fails can receive the services of only one repairman; the time to repair it is still exponentially distributed with rate parameter λ. From this statement we establish the birth and death rates for states 0 through N as

$$\begin{aligned} b_k &= \lambda, \quad k = 0, 1, \ldots, N-1; \qquad b_N = 0; \\ d_0 &= 0; \qquad d_k = k\mu, \quad k = 1, 2, \ldots, K; \\ d_k &= K\mu, \quad k = K+1, K+2, \ldots, N; \end{aligned} \tag{12.6.41}$$

and draw the transition rate diagram of Figure 12.6.9. By inspection of this diagram we write the limiting state probability relations as

$$\begin{aligned} \phi_k &= \phi_0\left(\frac{\lambda}{\mu}\right)^k \cdot \frac{1}{k!} & k &= 0, 1, \ldots, K \\ \phi_k &= \phi_0\left(\frac{\lambda}{\mu}\right)^K\left(\frac{1}{K!}\right)\left(\frac{\lambda}{K\mu}\right)^{k-K} & k &= K+1, K+2, \ldots, N. \end{aligned} \tag{12.6.42}$$

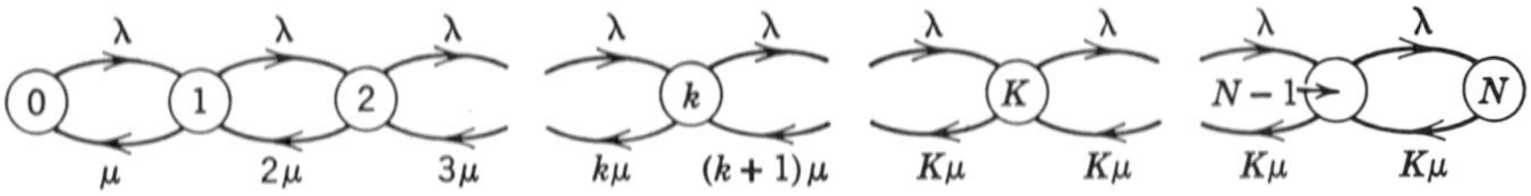

Figure 12.6.9 Transition rate diagram for the infinite-machine–K-repairman example with at most $N(\geq K)$ machines in the service system.

The quantity ϕ_0 is again determined by requiring that the limiting state probabilities must sum to one. We readily write the shrinkage rate governing the rate at which the steady state distribution is approached as

$$\begin{aligned} \text{sr} = \sum_{k=0}^{N} (b_k + d_k) &= N\lambda + (1/2)K(K+1)\mu + (N-K)K\mu \\ &= N(\lambda+\mu) + [-N + (1/2)K(K+1) + (N-K)K]\mu \\ &= N(\lambda+\mu) + [N - (1/2)K](K-1)\mu. \end{aligned} \tag{12.6.43}$$

Note that the increased service capability increases the magnitude of the shrinkage rate over that found for the earlier model in Equation 12.6.39.

We should realize that if we desire to let N become indefinitely large, we shall be able to write a steady-state solution only when $\lambda < K\mu$, that is, when the failure rate of the system is less than the total available repair rate.

The trunking problem

An important special case of this example arises when we remove the limits on both N, the number of machines in service, and on K, the number of repairmen available. We can regard this case as the situation where each machine that fails generates a repairman to service it. Equation 12.6.42 shows that the solution is

$$\phi_k = \phi_0 \left(\frac{\lambda}{\mu}\right)^k \cdot \frac{1}{k!} \qquad k = 0, 1, 2, \ldots. \tag{12.6.44}$$

By normalizing this result to make the limiting state probabilities sum to one, we find

$$\begin{aligned} \sum_{k=0}^{\infty} \phi_k = 1 &= \phi_0 \sum_{k=0}^{\infty} \left(\frac{\lambda}{\mu}\right)^k \cdot \frac{1}{k!} \\ &= \phi_0 \left[1 + \left(\frac{\lambda}{\mu}\right) + \frac{1}{2!}\left(\frac{\lambda}{\mu}\right)^2 + \frac{1}{3!}\left(\frac{\lambda}{\mu}\right)^3 + \cdots\right] \\ &= \phi_0 e^{\lambda/\mu} \end{aligned} \tag{12.6.45}$$

or

$$\phi_0 = e^{-(\lambda/\mu)}. \tag{12.6.46}$$

Then Equation 12.6.44 becomes

$$\phi_k = \frac{\left(\frac{\lambda}{\mu}\right)^k e^{-(\lambda/\mu)}}{k!} \qquad k = 0, 1, 2, \ldots. \tag{12.6.47}$$

The probability mass function for the number of machines out of order in the steady state is therefore just the Poisson probability mass function with mean λ/μ.

The service model just solved is often called the telephone trunking problem because of its continuing application to the problem of determining the number of telephone trunks required to provide a given level of service. In this application, machine failures are replaced by originating calls requiring the assignment of a trunk; repairs are replaced by termination of calls and the release of a trunk. Telephone experience indicates that both the time between arrivals and the duration of calls are well approximated by exponentially distributed random variables. Equation 12.6.47 states that when the number of trunks is very large, the probability that k trunks are in use in the steady state is given by a Poisson distribution with mean equal to the ratio of call incidence to call termination rates.

Finite machine population

For our last service model we consider a finite population of M machines and assign each machine an exponential failure rate λ rather than using λ as a composite rate for the entire machine population. We limit the number of repairmen to $K \leq M$ and make the same assumptions about each repairman's capabilities that we made before. Because the population of machines is finite, the system failure rate will decrease as machines fail. We require states 0 through M to describe the possible number of machines that could be out of order at any time. The specific birth and death rates for the process are then

$$\begin{aligned} &b_k = (M - k)\lambda, \quad k = 0, 1, \ldots, M; \\ &d_k = k\mu, \quad k = 0, 1, \ldots, K; \qquad d_k = K\mu, \quad k = K + 1, K + 2, \ldots, M. \end{aligned} \tag{12.6.48}$$

The transition rate diagram appears in Figure 12.6.10. We write the limiting state probabilities as

$$\begin{aligned} \phi_k &= \phi_0 \frac{M(M-1)\cdots(M-k+1)}{k!} \left(\frac{\lambda}{\mu}\right)^k & k &= 0, 1, \ldots, K \\ \phi_k &= \phi_0 \frac{M(M-1)\cdots(M-k+1)}{K!\, K^{k-K}} \left(\frac{\lambda}{\mu}\right)^k & k &= K + 1, K + 2, \ldots, M \end{aligned} \tag{12.6.49}$$

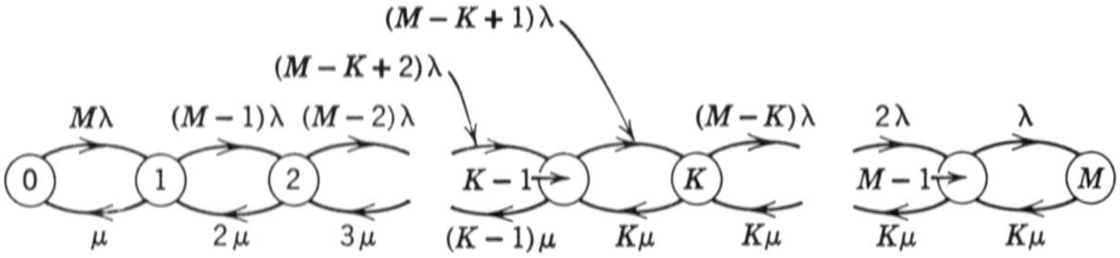

Figure 12.6.10 Transition rate diagram for the M-machine–$K(\leq M)$-repairman example.

or

$$\phi_k = \phi_0 \binom{M}{k}\left(\frac{\lambda}{\mu}\right)^k \qquad k = 0, 1, \ldots, K$$
$$\phi_k = \phi_0 \frac{k!}{K!\, K^{k-K}} \binom{M}{k}\left(\frac{\lambda}{\mu}\right)^k \qquad k = K+1, K+2, \ldots, M, \tag{12.6.50}$$

where the normalization for ϕ_0 can be performed as usual. We compute the shrinkage rate as

$$\text{sr} = \sum_{k=0}^{M} (b_k + d_k) = (1/2)M(M+1)\lambda + (1/2)K(K+1)\mu + (M - K)\mu. \tag{12.6.51}$$

The case when $K = M$ is of special interest for then we have enough repairmen to assign one to each machine. The shrinkage rate becomes $(1/2)M(M+1)(\lambda + \mu)$. The solution of Equation 12.6.50 is simply

$$\phi_k = \phi_0 \binom{M}{k}\left(\frac{\lambda}{\mu}\right)^k \qquad k = 0, 1, \ldots, M. \tag{12.6.52}$$

Through normalization we find

$$\sum_{k=0}^{M} \phi_k = \phi_0 \sum_{k=0}^{M} \binom{M}{k}\left(\frac{\lambda}{\mu}\right)^k = \phi_0\left(1 + \frac{\lambda}{\mu}\right)^M \tag{12.6.53}$$

or

$$\phi_0 = \frac{1}{\left(1 + \dfrac{\lambda}{\mu}\right)^M}. \tag{12.6.54}$$

We can therefore write the solution in the form

$$\phi_k = \binom{M}{k}\left(\frac{\lambda}{\lambda + \mu}\right)^k \left(\frac{\mu}{\lambda + \mu}\right)^{M-k} \qquad k = 0, 1, \ldots, M. \tag{12.6.55}$$

We see that the probability mass function for the number of machines undergoing repair in the steady state is a binomial probability mass function with M as the number of trials and $\lambda/(\lambda + \mu)$ as the probability of success on each trial. The mean $\bar{k}$ and variance $\check{k}$ of the number of machines under repair in the steady state are therefore

$$\bar{k} = M\frac{\lambda}{\lambda + \mu}, \qquad \check{k} = \frac{M\lambda\mu}{(\lambda + \mu)^2}. \tag{12.6.56}$$

We note that when $M = 1$ and $M = 2$, this model becomes, successively, the one-machine–one-repairman problem and the two-machine–two-repairman problem we have previously analyzed. Thus Equation 12.6.55 produces immediately the limiting state probability vectors found in Equations 12.6.23 and 12.6.29.

This service model has been applied to estimating the number of a group of M welders who will be connected to an electricity supply at any time when each welder has an exponential connection rate λ and disconnection rate μ. It has also been used to estimate the number of telephone subscribers to expect at any time in a population group of known size where each potential subscriber has known exponential rates λ and μ for requesting and discontinuing service.

We have only indicated a few of the more common continuous-time birth and death process service models. Finding the limiting state probabilities of these models is quite simple since the computation requires little more than inspection of the transition rate diagram. We are indeed fortunate when we can model the systems we must analyze in such simple terms.

12.7 TRANSIENT PROCESSES AND FIRST PASSAGE TIMES

The analysis of transient continuous-time Markov processes is a special case of the development of Section 11.10. If we wish to find the exponential transform of the probability density function for the time spent in the process before reaching a trapping state, we first construct the semi-Markov type flow graph for the process and then remove all branches that leave the trapping state node including the associated output branch. The transmission of the resulting modified flow graph from any node i to the trapping state node is then the exponential transform of the probability density function for the time to reach the trapping state from state i.

An important application of this transient process lies in determining the first passage time statistics of the process. If we wish to find the first passage time from state i to state j, $j \neq i$, we draw a semi-Markov type flow graph and then treat node j as a trapping state by removing all branches that leave node j including the associated output branch. The transmission of the resulting flow graph from node i to node j is then $f_{ij}^e(s)$, the exponential transform of the density function for the first passage time from node i to node j.

When $i = j$ we call the first passage time the recurrence time of state i. To find the exponential transform of the recurrence time density function for state i, we draw the semi-Markov type flow graph of the process and then transfer all branches that enter node i to another i node with no departing branches. The transmission of this graph from the original node i to the added node i is then the required $f_{ii}^e(s)$. The construction rests on separating the role of state i as the originator from its role as the terminator of recurrence times.

The One-Machine–One-Repairman Problem

We can apply these ideas to find selected first passage times in some of the machine repair examples we have considered. Thus in the one-machine–one-repairman problems whose semi-Markov flow graph appeared as the second representation of Figure 12.6.4, the recurrence time of state 0 has a density function whose exponential transformation $f_{00}^e(s)$ is the transmission of the modified flow graph of Figure 12.7.1,

$$f_{00}^e(s) = \frac{\lambda\mu}{(s+\lambda)(s+\mu)} = \frac{-\dfrac{\lambda\mu}{\lambda-\mu}}{s+\lambda} + \frac{\dfrac{\lambda\mu}{\lambda-\mu}}{s+\mu}. \qquad (12.7.1)$$

Note the check that $f_{00}^e(0) = 1$. The first passage time density function is therefore

$$f_{00}(t) = \frac{\lambda\mu}{\lambda-\mu}[e^{-\mu t} - e^{-\lambda t}] \qquad t \geq 0. \qquad (12.7.2)$$

This equation specifies the density function for the time required for an operating machine to experience a breakdown and be returned to the operating state. It is, of course, just the exponential time to failure distribution with rate parameter λ convolved with the exponential time to repair distribution with rate parameter μ.

The probability density function $f_{00}(\cdot)$ was in fact used in Section 11.15 as the lifetime distribution of the continuous-time renewal example; we called it the

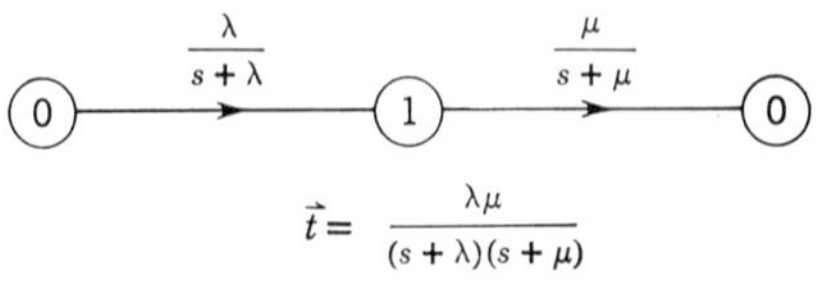

Figure 12.7.1 Modified flow graph for recurrence time of state 0 in the one-machine–one-repairman example.

double exponential lifetime distribution. The results of Section 11.15 are therefore directly relevant to the recurrence time problem we have just solved. Thus Equation 11.15.7 shows the complementary cumulative distribution of the recurrence time of state 0; Equation 11.15.9 provides the mean $\bar{\theta}_{00}$, second moment $\overline{\theta_{00}^2}$, and variance $\check{\theta}_{00}$ of the recurrence time; Equation 11.15.35 specifies the expected number of recurrences through time t; and Equation 11.15.39 illustrates the behavior of the variance of the number of recurrences in time t when t is large. We should note that by the symmetry of the process, states 0 and 1 both have the same recurrence time statistics.

The Two-Machine–Two-Repairman Problem

As a second example, consider the first passage time from state 0 to state 2 of the two-machine–two-repairman problem whose semi-Markov flow graph is the second flow graph representation of Figure 12.6.5. We construct the modified flow graph of Figure 12.7.2 to represent the transient process implied by this first passage. Thus, for convenience, all branches leaving node 2 have been eliminated as have all associated output branches. The transmission of this flow graph is then

$$f_{02}^e(s) = \vec{t}_{02} = \frac{\dfrac{2\lambda^2}{(s + 2\lambda)(s + \lambda + \mu)}}{1 - \dfrac{2\lambda\mu}{(s + 2\lambda)(s + \lambda + \mu)}} = \frac{2\lambda^2}{s^2 + (3\lambda + \mu)s + 2\lambda^2}. \qquad (12.7.3)$$

We again check that $f_{02}^e(0) = 1$. Since the roots of the denominator are

$$s = (1/2)[-(3\lambda + \mu) \pm \sqrt{\lambda^2 + 6\lambda\mu + \mu^2}],$$

we perform the partial fraction expansion as

$$\begin{aligned} f_{02}^e(s) &= \frac{2\lambda^2}{[s + (1/2)(3\lambda + \mu - \sqrt{\lambda^2 + 6\lambda\mu + \mu^2})] \times [s + (1/2)(3\lambda + \mu + \sqrt{\lambda^2 + 6\lambda\mu + \mu^2})]} \\ &= \frac{\dfrac{2\lambda^2}{\sqrt{\lambda^2 + 6\lambda\mu + \mu^2}}}{s + (1/2)(3\lambda + \mu - \sqrt{\lambda^2 + 6\lambda\mu + \mu^2})} \\ &\quad + \frac{\dfrac{-2\lambda^2}{\sqrt{\lambda^2 + 6\lambda\mu + \mu^2}}}{s + (1/2)(3\lambda + \mu + \sqrt{\lambda^2 + 6\lambda\mu + \mu^2})}. \end{aligned} \qquad (12.7.4)$$

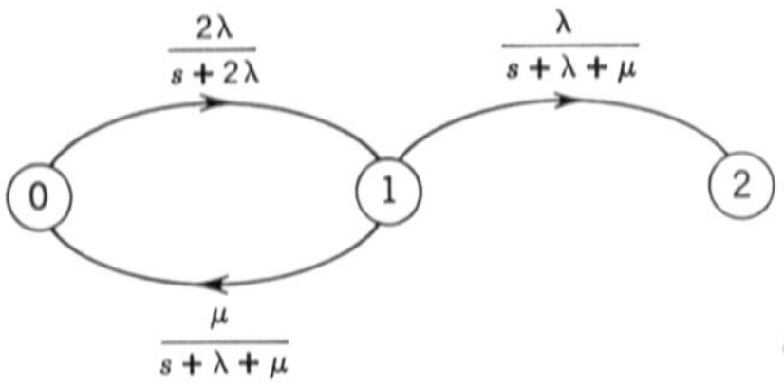

Figure 12.7.2 Modified flow graph for first passage time from state 0 to state 2 in the two-machine–two-repairman example.

Then we invert the exponential transform to produce the density function for first passage time from state 0 to state 2 as

$$\begin{aligned} f_{02}(t) &= \frac{2\lambda^2}{\sqrt{\lambda^2 + 6\lambda\mu + \mu^2}} [e^{-(1/2)(3\lambda+\mu)t} e^{\sqrt{\lambda^2+6\lambda\mu+\mu^2}t} - e^{-(1/2)(3\lambda+\mu)t} e^{-\sqrt{\lambda^2+6\lambda\mu+\mu^2}t}] \\ &= \frac{2\lambda^2}{\sqrt{\lambda^2 + 6\lambda\mu + \mu^2}} e^{-(1/2)(3\lambda+\mu)t} [e^{\sqrt{\lambda^2+6\lambda\mu+\mu^2}t} - e^{-\sqrt{\lambda^2+6\lambda\mu+\mu^2}t}] \\ &= \frac{4\lambda^2}{\sqrt{\lambda^2 + 6\lambda\mu + \mu^2}} e^{-(1/2)(3\lambda+\mu)t} \sinh \sqrt{\lambda^2 + 6\lambda\mu + \mu^2}t \qquad t \geq 0. \end{aligned} \quad (12.7.5)$$

This density function describes the time required for the system to pass for the first time from the situation where both machines are working to the situation where both machines have failed. Of course, many single machine failures can occur and be remedied before both machines are out of order at the same time.

Mean first passage time

Finding the moments of the first passage time from state 0 to state 2 is awkward using the density function $f_{02}(\cdot)$. But we can find moments readily by differentiating the exponential transform $f_{02}{}^e(s)$ in Equation 12.7.3. Thus $\bar{\theta}_{02}$, the mean first passage time from state 0 to state 2, is simply

$$\bar{\theta}_{02} = -\frac{d}{ds} f_{02}{}^e(s)\bigg|_{s=0} = \frac{2\lambda^2(2s + 3\lambda + \mu)}{[s^2 + (3\lambda + \mu)s + 2\lambda^2]^2}\bigg|_{s=0} = \frac{3\lambda + \mu}{2\lambda^2}. \quad (12.7.6)$$

We can check this result by noting that when $\mu = 0$, no repair is performed and the mean time required for both machines to break down is the mean time for the first failure, $1/2\lambda$, plus the mean additional time for the second failure, $1/\lambda$. This sum is $3/2\lambda$, the value of $\bar{\theta}_{00}$ when $\mu = 0$.

As you recall from our discussion of semi-Markov processes, we can find the mean time spent in each state of a transient process by drawing the transition

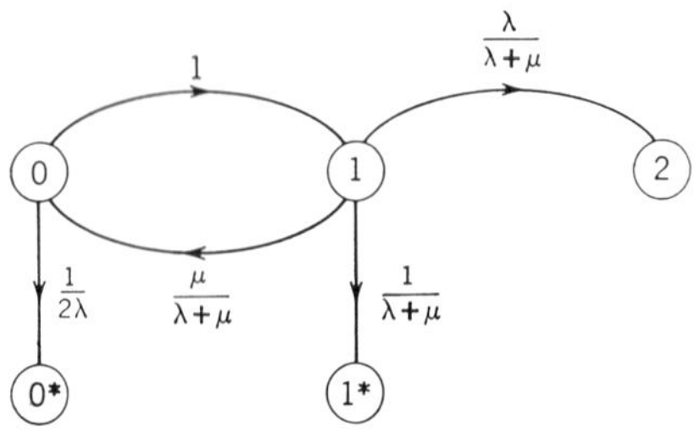

Figure 12.7.3 Augmented transition diagram for first passage from state 0 to state 2 in the two-machine–two-repairman example.

diagram of the process and then associating with each node internal to the transient process an output branch whose transmission is the mean waiting time in the corresponding state. The resulting graph is called the augmented transition diagram and is just the semi-Markov flow graph for the process evaluated at $s = 0$ with all branches leaving the trapping state removed. The transmission of the augmented transition diagram from node i to the output node associated with state j is then the mean time the process will spend in state j before trapping given that it was started in state i.

The augmented transition diagram for the transient process representing a first passage from state 0 to state 2 of the two-machine–two-repairman example appears in Figure 12.7.3. We compute the mean first passage time $\bar{\theta}_{02}$ as the sum of the mean times the process will spend in states 0 and 1 given that it started in state 0,

$$\bar{\theta}_{02} = \vec{t}_{00*} + \vec{t}_{01*} = \frac{1}{1 - \dfrac{\mu}{\lambda + \mu}} \cdot \frac{1}{2\lambda} + \frac{1}{1 - \dfrac{\mu}{\lambda + \mu}} \cdot \frac{1}{\lambda + \mu} = \frac{3\lambda + \mu}{2\lambda^2}, \quad (12.7.7)$$

which concurs with the result of Equation 12.7.6.

12.8 THE INFINITE-STATE CONTINUOUS-TIME MARKOV PROCESS

We can apply our methods of analysis to the solution of infinite-state continuous-time Markov processes if the structure of the process has an exploitable regularity. Just as in the discrete-time case, the most convenient type of infinite-state process to study is the infinite-state birth and death process. As an example, we shall consider the case where all states have an exponential birth rate λ and all states except state zero have an exponential death rate μ. We have already considered this

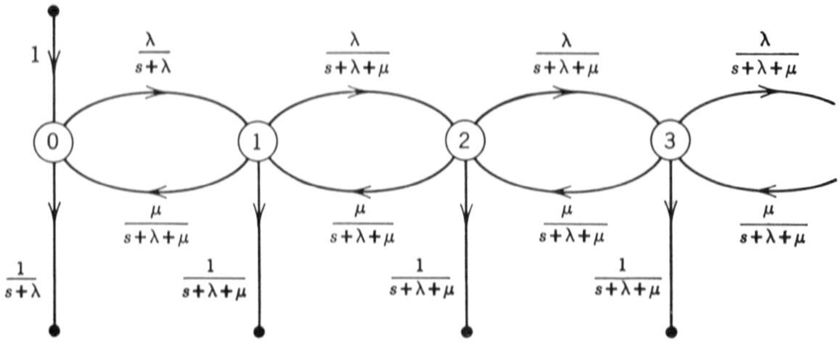

Figure 12.8.1 Flow graph for infinite-state example.

example in the form of a service model for an infinite population of machines with average breakdown rate λ and a single repairman with repair rate μ. The transition rate diagram is just like the one in Figure 12.6.8, except that the structure continues indefinitely to the right. We have already found the limiting state probability distribution as the geometric distribution of Equation 12.6.40 and have noted that the steady-state solution exists only when the failure rate λ is less than the repair rate μ, a condition we shall assume in what follows.

In this section we are not content with knowing just the limiting state probability vector for this infinite-state service model: We want to be more ambitious and develop the interval transition probabilities that provide the transient solution. We proceed by drawing the infinite-state semi-Markov flow graph representation of the process as shown in Figure 12.8.1. State 0 represents the situation where the system is empty, that is, where no machines are out of order.

From Empty to Empty

Perhaps the most interesting transition probability is $\phi_{00}(t)$, the probability that the system will be empty at time t if it is empty at time zero. We know that $\phi_{00}{}^{e}(s)$, the exponential transform of this transition probability, is the transmission of the flow graph from node 0 through the associated output branch. To find this transmission, we first make use of the observation that the portion of the flow graph to the right of node 1 is an infinite flow graph of the type we studied in Section 7.4, and whose transmission we evaluated in Figure 7.4.3. Thus we denote the transmission of the infinite-node graph to the right of node 1 as $\vec{t}_{\mathrm{I}}$ and represent the infinite flow graph by a loop with transmission $\vec{t}_{\mathrm{I}}$ about node 1. Figure 12.8.2 shows the evaluation of the transmission $\vec{t}_{\mathrm{I}}$ of the infinite flow graph and the representation of the original flow graph in terms of $\vec{t}_{\mathrm{I}}$. By finding the transmission

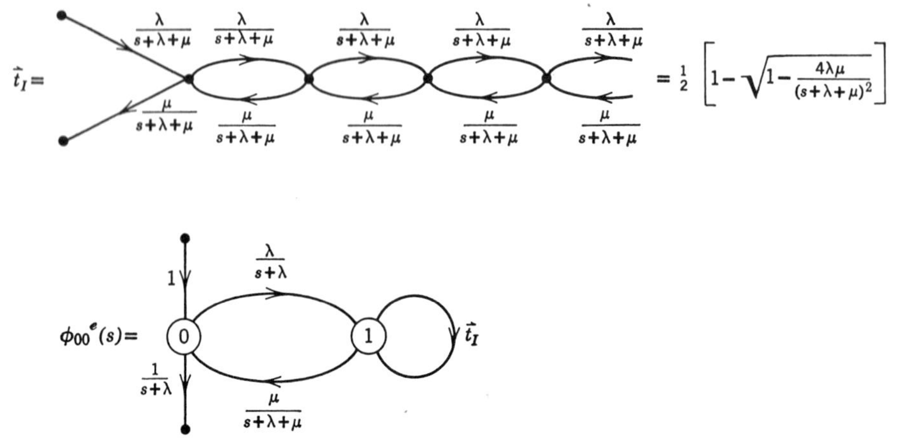

Figure 12.8.2 Collapse of the infinite flow graph.

of the representation from node 0 through its associated output branch, we write $\phi_{00}{}^e(s)$ as

$$\phi_{00}{}^e(s) = \frac{\dfrac{1}{s+\lambda}(1 - \vec{t}_I)}{1 - \dfrac{\lambda}{s+\lambda}\cdot\dfrac{\mu}{s+\lambda+\mu} - \vec{t}_I} \tag{12.8.1}$$

where

$$\vec{t}_I = \frac{1}{2}\left[1 - \sqrt{1 - \frac{4\lambda\mu}{(s+\lambda+\mu)^2}}\right] = \frac{1}{2}\left[\frac{s+\lambda+\mu - \sqrt{(s+\lambda+\mu)^2 - 4\lambda\mu}}{s+\lambda+\mu}\right]. \tag{12.8.2}$$

Algebraic simplification then produces

$$\phi_{00}{}^e(s) = \frac{2}{s+\lambda-\mu+\sqrt{(s+\lambda+\mu)^2 - 4\lambda\mu}}. \tag{12.8.3}$$

We observe that the exponential transform of $\phi_{00}(t)$ has a form quite different from any of the exponential transforms we have already encountered. The square root in the denominator places it outside the realm of our transform table. Such irrational transforms are the usual consequence of infinite-state systems.

Limiting behavior

When t is large, $\phi_{00}(t)$ should become the limiting probability that the system is empty, regardless of its starting state. If we apply the initial value theorem to

$\phi_{00}{}^e(s)$ and recall that $\mu > \lambda$, we obtain

$$\phi_{00}(\infty) = \lim_{s\to 0} s\phi_{00}{}^e(s) = \lim_{s\to 0} \frac{2s}{s + \lambda - \mu + \sqrt{(s + \lambda + \mu)^2 - 4\lambda\mu}}$$

$$= \frac{0}{\lambda - \mu + \sqrt{(\mu - \lambda)^2}} = \frac{0}{0}, \tag{12.8.4}$$

which is indeterminate. However, using L'Hôpital's rule we write

$$\phi_{00}(\infty) = \lim_{s\to 0} s\phi_{00}{}^e(s) = \lim_{s\to 0} \frac{2}{1 + (s + \lambda + \mu)[(s + \lambda + \mu)^2 - 4\lambda\mu]^{-1/2}}$$

$$= \frac{2}{1 + \dfrac{\lambda + \mu}{\mu - \lambda}}$$

$$= 1 - \frac{\lambda}{\mu} = \phi_0 \tag{12.8.5}$$

and we have obtained the limiting probability of being empty given by Equation 12.6.40.

Explicit solution

We can write the inverse transform of Equation 12.8.3 by methods that lie beyond the scope of this book in the form

$$\phi_{00}(t) = e^{-(\lambda+\mu)t}\left[I_0(2\sqrt{\lambda\mu}t) + \sqrt{\frac{\mu}{\lambda}}\, I_1(2\sqrt{\lambda\mu}t) + \left(1 - \frac{\lambda}{\mu}\right)\sum_{n=2}^{\infty}\left(\sqrt{\frac{\mu}{\lambda}}\right)^n I_n(2\sqrt{\lambda\mu}t)\right]$$

$$t \geq 0 \tag{12.8.6}$$

where $I_n(\cdot)$ denotes the nth order modified Bessel function. The main value in seeing this explicit result is that it should properly discourage anyone from considering the analytical transient solution to an infinite-state Markov process unless he is willing to make a large investment in time and effort.

From Empty to k

We might ask whether it is difficult to find the interval transition probability from state 0 to some other state in the system. Of course, $\phi_{0k}{}^e(s)$, the exponential transform of $\phi_{0k}(t)$, is just the transmission of the flow graph of Figure 12.8.1 from node 0 to the output node associated with node k. However, instead of finding this transmission directly, we shall first change the flow graph into an alternate form. We make the change by multiplying the transmissions of the branches leaving each node by the factor necessary to make the transmission from the node to its associated output branch equal to one. To maintain the appropriateness of the flow graph, we must then divide the transmissions of all branches entering each node by the same factor.

We illustrate this procedure in Figure 12.8.3. The branches leaving node 0 have their transmissions multiplied by $s + \lambda$, and the transmissions of the branches entering node 0 are divided by $s + \lambda$. All other nodes in the graph have the transmissions of the branches leaving the nodes multiplied by $s + \lambda + \mu$ and the transmissions of the branches entering the nodes divided by $s + \lambda + \mu$. The alternate form of the flow graph that we obtain in Figure 12.8.3 by following this procedure is very similar to the original graph; in fact, the only changes are that the factor $1/(s + \lambda)$ appears on the input rather than the output branch of node 0 and that the transmissions of the branches linking nodes 0 and 1 have been altered.

As the result of this change in form we can represent a typical section of the flow graph for the process as shown in Figure 12.8.4. Note that the representation holds even when $k = 1$. The relationships of this flow graph imply the equation

$$\phi_{0k}{}^{e}(s) = \frac{\lambda}{s + \lambda + \mu}\phi^{e}_{0,k-1}(s) + \vec{t}_{\mathrm{I}}\,\phi_{0k}{}^{e}(s) \qquad k = 1, 2, 3, \ldots \tag{12.8.7}$$

or

$$\phi_{0k}{}^{e}(s) = \frac{\lambda}{s + \lambda + \mu}\cdot\frac{1}{1 - \vec{t}_{\mathrm{I}}}\,\phi^{e}_{0,k-1}(s) \qquad k = 1, 2, 3, \ldots . \tag{12.8.8}$$

Thus we have been able to relate the transforms of the interval transition probabilities from state 0 to state k and from state 0 to state $k - 1$. This recursive equation leads directly to an explicit expression for $\phi_{0k}{}^{e}(s)$ as

$$\phi_{0k}{}^{e}(s) = \phi_{00}{}^{e}(s)\left[\frac{\lambda}{s + \lambda + \mu}\cdot\frac{1}{1 - \vec{t}_{\mathrm{I}}}\right]^{k} \qquad k = 0, 1, 2, \ldots . \tag{12.8.9}$$

By simple operations on Equation 12.8.2 we find

$$\frac{\lambda}{s + \lambda + \mu}\cdot\frac{1}{1 - \vec{t}_{\mathrm{I}}} = \frac{2\lambda}{s + \lambda + \mu + \sqrt{(s + \lambda + \mu)^2 - 4\lambda\mu}}, \tag{12.8.10}$$

and therefore we have our desired transform,

$$\phi_{0k}{}^{e}(s) = \frac{2}{s + \lambda - \mu + \sqrt{(s + \lambda + \mu)^2 - 4\lambda\mu}} \times \left(\frac{2\lambda}{s + \lambda + \mu + \sqrt{(s + \lambda + \mu)^2 - 4\lambda\mu}}\right)^{k} \qquad k = 0, 1, 2 \ldots . \tag{12.8.11}$$

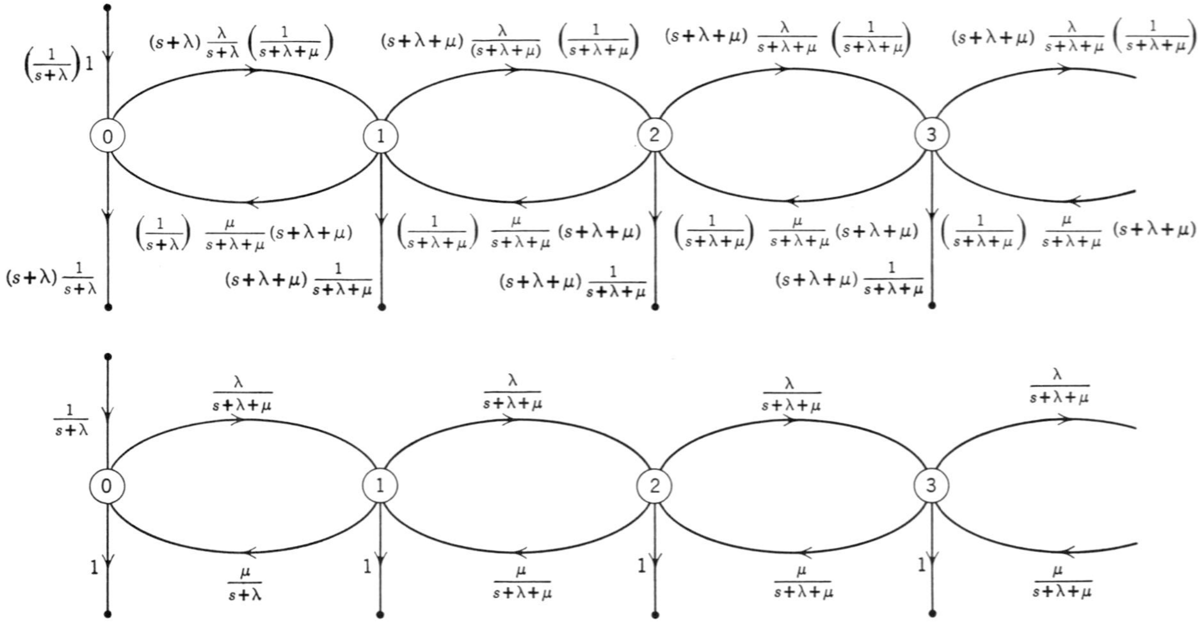

Figure 12.8.3 An alternate flow graph for the infinite-state example.

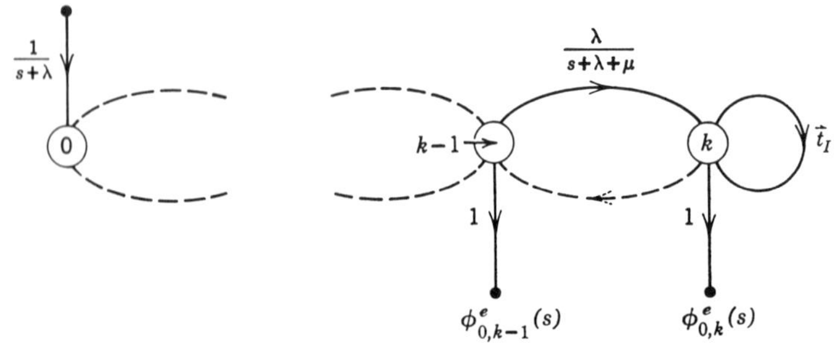

Figure 12.8.4 A representative section of the alternate flow graph.

Explicit solution

The inverse of this more complicated transform, the probability that a system empty at time 0 will contain k units at time t, is

$$\phi_{0k}(t) = e^{-(\lambda+\mu)t}\left[\left(\sqrt{\frac{\mu}{\lambda}}\right)^{-k} I_{-k}(2\sqrt{\lambda\mu t}) + \left(\sqrt{\frac{\mu}{\lambda}}\right)^{1-k} I_{1+k}(2\sqrt{\lambda\mu t}) + \left(1-\frac{\lambda}{\mu}\right)\left(\frac{\lambda}{\mu}\right)^{k} \sum_{n=k+2}^{\infty} \left(\sqrt{\frac{\mu}{\lambda}}\right)^{n} I_n(2\sqrt{\lambda\mu t})\right]$$

$$t \geq 0;\ k \geq 0, 1, 2, \ldots, \quad (12.8.12)$$

which must be of interest to somebody.

Limiting behavior

Once again we can determine whether the transform $\phi_{0k}{}^e(s)$ implies the correct limiting behavior as t grows large. Using the initial value theorem on Equation 12.8.9 we have

$$\phi_{0k}(\infty) = \lim_{s\to 0} s\phi_{0k}{}^e(s) = \lim_{s\to 0} s\phi_{00}{}^e(s)\left[\frac{\lambda}{s+\lambda+\mu}\cdot\frac{1}{1-\vec{t}_I}\right]^k. \quad (12.8.13)$$

In view of Equations 12.8.5 and 12.8.10, we can express the limit as

$$\begin{aligned}\phi_{0k}(\infty) &= \lim_{s\to 0} s\phi_{00}{}^e(s) \lim_{s\to 0}\left[\frac{\lambda}{s+\lambda+\mu}\cdot\frac{1}{1-\vec{t}_I}\right]^k \\ &= \left(1-\frac{\lambda}{\mu}\right)\left[\frac{2\lambda}{\lambda+\mu+\sqrt{(\mu-\lambda)^2}}\right]^k \\ &= \left(1-\frac{\lambda}{\mu}\right)\left(\frac{\lambda}{\mu}\right)^k = \phi_k \qquad \mu > \lambda, \qquad k = 0, 1, 2, \ldots, \quad (12.8.14)\end{aligned}$$

which is just the expression of Equation 12.6.40 for the limiting probability that there will be k units in the system regardless of starting condition.

First Passage Times

Computing first passage time and recurrence time statistics in an infinite-state continuous-time Markov process is also a large order, but it can be done in simple cases. For example, suppose that the process is now empty and that we are interested in the time at which it will *become* empty again following the next one or more breakdowns and subsequent repairs. The density function for this time is $f_{00}(\cdot)$, the recurrence time density function for state 0. Its exponential transform $f_{00}{}^e(s)$ is just the transmission of the flow graph obtained by removing node zero from the graph of Figure 12.8.1. The resulting flow graph appears in Figure 12.8.5, where it is reduced to a simple flow graph by using the transmission $\vec{t}_{\text{I}}$ of the infinite graph. We then find

$$f_{00}{}^e(s) = \frac{s + \lambda + \mu}{s + \lambda}\vec{t}_{\text{I}} = \frac{1}{2}\left[\frac{s + \lambda + \mu - \sqrt{(s + \lambda + \mu)^2 - 4\lambda\mu}}{s + \lambda}\right] \tag{12.8.15}$$

as the exponential transform of the recurrence time for state 0.

We know that the exponential transform $f_{00}{}^e(s)$ of the recurrence time of state 0 is related to the exponential transform $\phi_{00}{}^e(s)$ by Equation 11.11.8 with $y = 1$. We find

$$\phi_{00}{}^e(s) = \frac{{}^{>}w_0{}^e(s)}{1 - f_{00}{}^e(s)} = \frac{\dfrac{1}{s + \lambda}}{1 - \dfrac{1}{2}\left[\dfrac{(s + \lambda + \mu) - \sqrt{(s + \lambda + \mu)^2 - 4\lambda\mu}}{s + \lambda}\right]}$$

$$= \frac{2}{s + \lambda - \mu + \sqrt{(s + \lambda + \mu)^2 - 4\lambda\mu}}, \tag{12.8.16}$$

which is the result of Equation 12.8.3.

We expect that when the failure rate λ exceeds the repair rate μ, the number of machines broken down will tend to grow with time so that no limiting-state probability distribution will exist. We expect further in this case that the recurrence time density functions will not integrate to one but rather to p_R, the probability that the renewal process represented by returns to the state is in fact recurrent. Since the exponential transform $f_{00}{}^e(s)$ evaluated at $s = 0$ is just the area under the recurrence time density function for state zero, we have

$$f_{00}{}^e(0) = p_R = \begin{cases} \dfrac{1}{2\lambda}(\lambda + \mu - \sqrt{(\lambda - \mu)^2}) = \dfrac{\mu}{\lambda} & \lambda > \mu \\ \dfrac{1}{2\lambda}(\lambda + \mu - \sqrt{(\mu - \lambda)^2}) = 1 & \lambda \leq \mu. \end{cases} \tag{12.8.17}$$

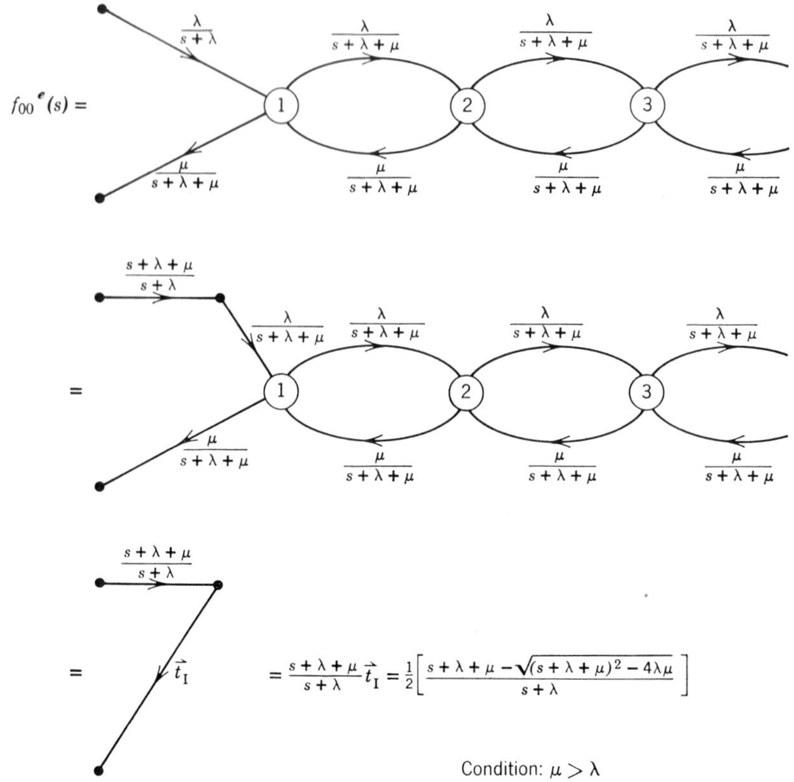

Figure 12.8.5 Flow graph for computing the transform of the recurrence time density function for state 0.

Therefore returns to state 0 are recurrent renewal processes only when the failure rate λ does not exceed the repair rate μ.

Mean recurrence time

When $\lambda \leq \mu$, we can compute a mean recurrence time $\bar{\theta}_{00}$ for state zero by differentiating $f_{00}{}^{e}(s)$,

$$\bar{\theta}_{00} = -\frac{d}{ds} f_{00}{}^{e}(s)\bigg|_{s=0} = \frac{\mu}{\lambda(\mu - \lambda)}\,. \tag{12.8.18}$$

Thus if the failure rate λ is one per unit time and the repair rate μ is 3 per unit time, the mean recurrence time of state 0 is 3/2 time units. Note that when $\lambda = \mu$ the mean recurrence time is infinite even though the probability of ultimate recurrence is one. We observed just this kind of behavior in the infinite-state discrete-time birth and death process coin-tossing models.

The mean recurrence time $\bar{\theta}_{00}$ for the empty state can be related to earlier results. Thus from Equation 11.11.12, we know that it is the reciprocal of the entrance rate of the empty state,

$$\bar{\theta}_{00} = \frac{1}{e_0}. \tag{12.8.19}$$

Since the entrance rate is given by Equation 11.9.13 as the ratio of limiting state probability to mean waiting time, we have

$$\bar{\theta}_{00} = \frac{1}{e_0} = \frac{\bar{\tau}_0}{\phi_0}. \tag{12.8.20}$$

Using $\bar{\tau}_0 = 1/\lambda$ and $\phi_0 = 1 - \lambda/\mu$ from Equation 12.8.5 we obtain

$$\bar{\theta}_{00} = \frac{\frac{1}{\lambda}}{1 - \frac{\lambda}{\mu}} = \frac{\mu}{\lambda(\mu - \lambda)}, \tag{12.8.21}$$

which is Equation 12.8.18.

12.9 COUNTING TRANSITIONS

All the relations for counting transitions that we developed for the semi-Markov process apply here as well; however, we can more often obtain analytical results for the continuous-time Markov process.

An Important Example

As a very simple but important example, consider a one-state continuous-time Markov process whose exponential waiting time distribution has rate λ. We want to find the probability $\phi_{11}(n|t)$ that the process will make n transitions into state 1 in time t. We see that we can consider this problem as the problem of counting renewals in a continuous-time renewal process whose lifetime distribution is exponential with rate λ. We proceed by drawing the semi-Markov type flow graph of Figure 12.9.1 to represent the process. Each transition of the process is counted by the discrete transform variable z. The transmission of the graph is $\phi_{11}{}^{ge}(z|s)$, the geometric-exponential transform of $\phi_{11}(n|t)$. We find it to be

$$\phi_{11}{}^{ge}(z|s) = \frac{1}{1 - \frac{z\lambda}{s + \lambda}} \cdot \frac{1}{s + \lambda} = \frac{1}{s + \lambda - \lambda z}. \tag{12.9.1}$$

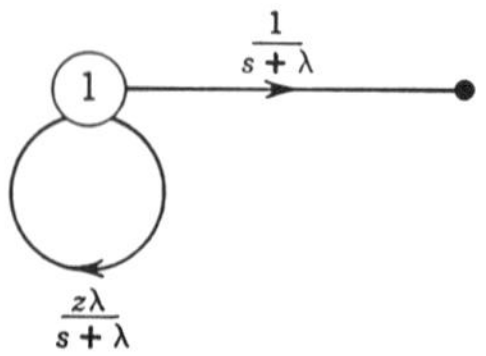

Figure 12.9.1 Flow graph for counting transitions in the one-state continuous-time Markov process.

We can invert this double transform in either of two ways. In the first approach, we write the transform in the form

$$\phi_{11}{}^{ge}(z|s) = \frac{1}{s+\lambda}\cdot\frac{1}{1-\left(\dfrac{\lambda}{s+\lambda}\right)z} \tag{12.9.2}$$

and then invert the geometric transform,

$$\phi_{11}{}^{\cdot e}(n|s) = \frac{1}{s+\lambda}\left(\frac{\lambda}{s+\lambda}\right)^n = \frac{\lambda^n}{(s+\lambda)^{n+1}} \qquad n = 0, 1, 2.\ldots \tag{12.9.3}$$

Finally, we invert the exponential transform using the table to obtain

$$\phi_{11}(n|t) = \frac{(\lambda t)^n e^{-\lambda t}}{n!} \qquad n = 0, 1, 2, \ldots; 0 \leq t. \tag{12.9.4}$$

In the second approach, we inverse transform the exponential transform first to produce

$$\begin{aligned}\phi_{11}{}^{g\cdot}(z|t) &= e^{-(\lambda-\lambda z)t}\\ &= e^{-\lambda t}e^{\lambda z t}\\ &= e^{-\lambda t}\left[1 + (\lambda z t) + \frac{(\lambda z t)^2}{2!} + \cdots\right] \qquad 0 \leq t.\end{aligned} \tag{12.9.5}$$

By observing the coefficient of the nth power of z in the expansion, we immediately obtain the result of Equation 12.9.4. Of course, $\phi_{11}(n|t)$ is just the Poisson distribution with mean λt: Thus we have shown that the probability distribution for the number of renewals in time t of a renewal process with an exponential lifetime distribution is the Poisson distribution. The counting distributions of more general continuous-time Markov processes seldom have such a familiar form.

12.10 PROCESSES WITH PARTIAL INFORMATION: INFERENCE

The analysis of semi-Markov processes with partial information is very analogous to the corresponding discrete-time Markov process analysis of Chapter 6. We shall illustrate the procedure by an example interpretable as a continuous-time Markov process.

A Transient Repair Process

Consider a system consisting of one machine that is subject to failure. When a machine fails and is replaced by a new machine, the lifetime distribution of the new machine is exponential with failure rate λ. However when a new machine fails, it is not certain that it will be replaced by a new machine; in fact, it will be repaired with probability a and replaced by a new machine with probability $1 - a$. A repaired machine has a lifetime distribution that is also exponential, but with failure rate μ, $\mu \geq \lambda$. Once a machine that has been repaired fails, it is never replaced by a new machine, but repaired once more. Thus if a is not zero, as we shall assume, the installation will ultimately contain a repaired machine with failure rate μ. We shall call this system a transient repair process.

We model the system by the two-state continuous-time semi-Markov process shown diagrammatically in Figure 12.10.1. State 1 is the state of the installation when it contains a new (unrepaired) machine; state 2 is the state when it contains a repaired machine. The transition probability from state 1 to state 2 is a, and therefore the transition probability from state 1 to state 1 is $1 - a$. The transition probability from state 2 to state 2 is 1. Clearly, state 1 is a transient state while state 2 is a trapping state.

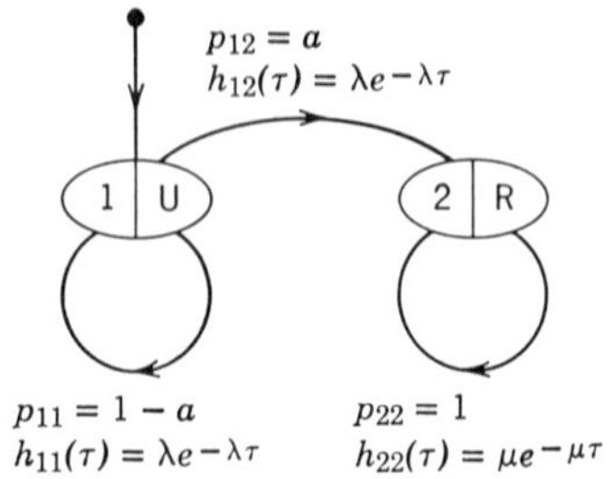

Figure 12.10.1 Diagram showing transition probabilities and holding time density functions for a transient repair process.

The holding time density functions for the transition from state 1 to state 1 and for the transition from state 1 to state 2 are the same and given by

$$h_{11}(\tau) = h_{12}(\tau) = \lambda e^{-\lambda\tau} \qquad \tau \geq 0. \tag{12.10.1}$$

The waiting time density function is therefore

$$w_1(\tau) = \lambda e^{-\lambda\tau}, \tag{12.10.2}$$

with complementary cumulative waiting time distribution

$$^{>}w_1(\tau) = e^{-\lambda t}. \tag{12.10.3}$$

For state 2 we also have identical holding and waiting time density functions

$$h_{22}(\tau) = w_2(\tau) = \mu e^{-\mu\tau} \tag{12.10.4}$$

and, consequently, the complementary cumulative waiting time distribution

$$^{>}w_2(t) = e^{-\mu t}. \tag{12.10.5}$$

As the diagram indicates, the installation initially contains a new machine and, therefore, the process begins in state 1.

Inference on Transitions

We may ask many questions of even this simple model. We begin with a problem of incorporating partial information. Suppose we know that the process is still in state 1 at some time. What is the probability that it has made various numbers of transitions? In this process a transition represents a failure of the machine; as usual, we let n be the number of transitions. In our customary notation we shall write t for the event that time t has passed since the process began and write S_1 for the event that the process occupies state 1. The quantity we seek is $\{n|S_1, t\}$, the probability that n transitions have been made given that the state at time t is 1 and, implicitly, that the system started in state 1 at time zero.

There are many ways we might reason to find $\{n|S_1, t\}$. One is as follows: Since we know that the process was in state 1 at time zero and in state 1 at time t, it must have occupied state 1 throughout the entire $(0, t)$ time interval. This conclusion follows directly from the observation that there are no ways for the process to reenter state 1 if it ever leaves state 1. Since the process was in state 1 throughout the $(0, t)$ interval, the time between transitions of the process had the exponential density function $\lambda e^{-\lambda\tau}$, i.e., the waiting time density function for state 1. In other words, the times between transitions of the process were exponential with rate λ. From probability theory or the results of Section 12.9, it follows that the probability of n transitions in time t is Poisson with mean λt. We can then use Equation 12.9.4

to write

$$\{n|S_1, t\} = \frac{(\lambda t)^n}{n!} e^{-\lambda t} \qquad n = 0, 1, 2, \ldots \tag{12.10.6}$$

However before accepting this answer, let us try to confirm it using an alternate approach.

An alternate approach

Another way to solve this problem would be to proceed more formally by using flow graph techniques. By the definition of conditional probability we can write $\{n|S_1, t\}$ as the ratio

$$\{n|S_1, t\} = \frac{\{n, S_1|t\}}{\{S_1|t\}}. \tag{12.10.7}$$

Here $\{n, S_1|t\}$ is the probability of the joint event that the process will have made n transitions and will be in state 1 given that it started in state 1 at time zero and that time t has elapsed. In our alternate notation, we see immediately that

$$\{n, S_1|t\} = \phi_{11}(n|t). \tag{12.10.8}$$

The expression $\{S_1|t\}$ in Equation 12.10.7 is just the sum of this joint probability over all values of n; it represents the probability that the process will occupy state 1 at time t, i.e., the interval transition probability $\phi_{11}(t)$. Hence,

$$\{S_1|t\} = \sum_{n=0}^{\infty} \phi_{11}(n|t) = \phi_{11}(t). \tag{12.10.9}$$

We thus see that the key to solving the problem in this form is to find $\phi_{11}(n|t)$. Fortunately, as we observed in Section 12.9, we can obtain the geometric-exponential transform $\phi_{11}{}^{g}(z|s)$ as the transmission from node 1 to the output node associated with node 1 of the tagged flow graph for the process. We draw this flow graph as Figure 12.10.2. The transmission between any two states is the product

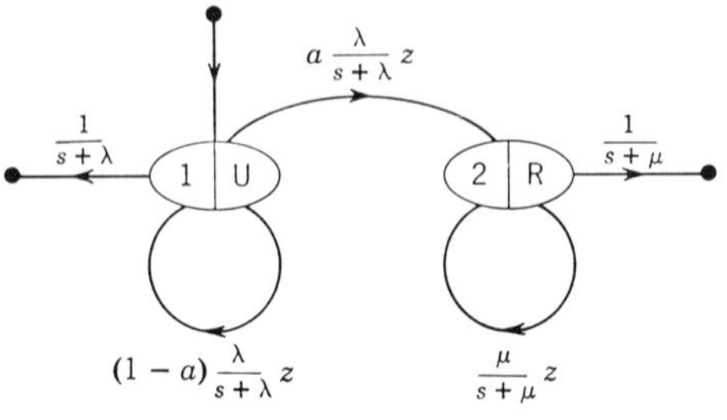

Figure 12.10.2 Tagged flow graph for a transient repair process.

of three quantities—the transition probability, the exponential transform of the holding time density function, and the tagging variable z. The transmission of the output branch associated with node 1 is the exponential transform of the complementary cumulative waiting time density function of Equation 12.10.3,

$$ {}^{>}w_1{}^e(s) = \frac{1}{s + \lambda}. \tag{12.10.10} $$

We obtain the transmission of the output branch associated with node 2 from Equation 12.10.5,

$$ {}^{>}w_2{}^e(s) = \frac{1}{s + \mu}. \tag{12.10.11} $$

When we compute $\phi_{11}{}^{ge}(z|s)$ as the transmission from node 1 to the output node associated with node 1, we may neglect the entire section of the graph to the right of the node 1 because node 1 receives no input from that section. Consequently, we may quickly write

$$ \phi_{11}{}^{ge}(z|s) = \frac{\dfrac{1}{s + \lambda}}{1 - (1 - a)\dfrac{\lambda}{s + \lambda} z} = \frac{1}{s + \lambda - (1 - a)\lambda z}. \tag{12.10.12} $$

Following the procedures of the last section, we first invert the geometric transform,

$$ \phi_{11}{}^{\cdot e}(n|s) = \frac{1}{s + \lambda}(1 - a)^n \left(\frac{\lambda}{s + \lambda}\right)^n = (1 - a)^n \frac{\lambda^n}{(s + \lambda)^{n+1}}, \tag{12.10.13} $$

and then the exponential transform to obtain

$$ \phi_{11}(n|t) = \{n, S_1|t\} = (1 - a)^n \frac{(\lambda t)^n}{n!} e^{-\lambda t}. \tag{12.10.14} $$

Now that we have found the joint probability of being in state 1 and of having made n transitions after time t, we can find the marginal probability $\phi_{11}(t)$ of being in state 1 by summing this expression over all values of n as indicated in Equation 12.10.9. However, an easy route to this expression is to realize that its transform $\phi_{11}{}^e(s)$ is just $\phi_{11}{}^{ge}(z|s)$ evaluated at $z = 1$,

$$ \phi_{11}{}^e(s) = \phi_{11}{}^{ge}(1|s) = \frac{1}{s + a\lambda}. \tag{12.10.15} $$

Therefore, we immediately have

$$ \phi_{11}(t) = \{S_1|t\} = e^{-a\lambda t}. \tag{12.10.16} $$

Now we are ready to return to Equation 12.10.7. We write

$$\{n|S_1, t\} = \frac{\{n, S_1|t\}}{\{S_1|t\}} = \frac{\phi_{11}(n|t)}{\phi_{11}(t)} = \frac{(1 - a)^n \frac{(\lambda t)^n}{n!} e^{-\lambda t}}{e^{-a\lambda t}}$$

$$= \frac{[(1 - a)\lambda t]^n}{n!} e^{-(1-a)\lambda t}. \qquad (12.10.17)$$

The probability that a process which started with a new machine will make n transitions (experience n failures) given that time t has elapsed and that it now occupies state 1 (the present machine has not been repaired) is described by a Poisson distribution with mean $(1 - a)\lambda t$. But wait a minute. By a chain of reasoning that culminated in Equation 12.10.6, we showed that this very same probability was given by a Poisson distribution with mean λt. What is the trouble?

Resolution

The trouble is that the chain of reasoning that led to Equation 12.10.6 is fallacious. We committed the same error here that we warned against in Section 6.2. You cannot make probability assignments on the basis that certain transitions *could not* occur just because you have information that they *did not* occur.

One way of showing the correctness of the probability distribution of Equation 12.10.17, rather than that of Equation 12.10.6, is to consider the case where a is close to 1. In this case, every failure-transition of the process that occurs in state 1 will have a high probability of carrying the process to state 2. Now suppose that a long time has elapsed and that the process is still in state 1. Because even a few transitions by the process would make it very likely that state 1 would have been left, the evidence that the system is still in state 1 causes us to assign high probabilities to those situations where very, very few transitions were made. Consequently, the probability distribution $\{n|S_1 t\}$ should have its mean very small when a is close to 1. Equation 12.10.17 satisfies this requirement, while Equation 12.10.6 does not.

Inference on State

A computationally more complicated, but possibly less confusing problem associated with this transient repair process is the following. Given the time the installation has been operating since a new machine was installed and the number of failures that have occurred, what is the probability that the installation contains an unrepaired machine? We thus seek the probability that the process occupies state 1 given that it has made n transitions and that it has been operating for a time t. Using the same notation as before, we write this probability as $\{S_1|n, t\}$. By the definition of conditional probability we can write $\{S_1|n, t\}$ as

$$\{S_1|n, t\} = \frac{\{n, S_1|t\}}{\{n|t\}} \tag{12.10.18}$$

where the numerator is the joint probability of n transitions and occupancy of state 1 by time t, the quantity $\phi_{11}(n, t)$ found in Equation 12.10.14.

The denominator is the probability that the process will make n transitions (experience n failures) in time t. This probability is the sum of the probabilities of two mutually exclusive events. The first event is that the process will make n transitions and occupy state 1 by time t; this event is, of course, the same event whose probability $\{n, S_1|t\}$ is the numerator in Equation 12.10.18. The second event is that the process will make n transitions and occupy state 2 by time t; we write the probability of this event by analogy as $\{n, S_2|t\}$. Therefore, we have

$$\{S_1|n, t\} = \frac{\{n, S_1|t\}}{\{n, S_1|t\} + \{n, S_2|t\}} \tag{12.10.19}$$

or in our usual notation,

$$\{S_1|n, t\} = \frac{\phi_{11}(n|t)}{\phi_{11}(n|t) + \phi_{12}(n|t)}. \tag{12.10.20}$$

Transform analysis

The only task remaining is to calculate $\phi_{12}(n|t)$. In principle this calculation is quite simple because the geometric-exponential transform of this quantity, $\phi_{12}{}^{ge}(z|s)$, is just the transmission of the flow graph of Figure 12.10.2 from node 1 to the output node associated with node 2. We obtain

$$\phi_{12}{}^{ge}(z|s) = \frac{\left(a\dfrac{\lambda}{s+\lambda}z\right)\left(\dfrac{1}{s+\mu}\right)}{\left(1-(1-a)\dfrac{\lambda}{s+\lambda}z\right)\left(1-\dfrac{\mu}{s+\mu}z\right)}$$

$$= \frac{a\lambda z}{[s+\lambda-(1-a)\lambda z][s+\mu-\mu z]}. \tag{12.10.21}$$

The inversion of this transform is more tedious than difficult. We begin by considering it as an exponential transform and by making a partial fraction expansion,

$$\phi_{12}{}^{ge}(z|s) = \frac{a\lambda z}{\mu-\lambda-\mu z+(1-a)\lambda z}\left[\frac{1}{s+\lambda-(1-a)\lambda z} - \frac{1}{s+\mu-\mu z}\right]. \tag{12.10.22}$$

We can now invert the exponential transform,

$$\phi_{12}{}^{g\text{-}}(z|t) = \frac{a\lambda z}{\mu - \lambda - \mu z + (1-a)\lambda z}\,[e^{-\lambda t}e^{(1-a)\lambda zt} - e^{-\mu t}e^{\mu zt}]. \quad (12.10.23)$$

Let us consider separately the case $\lambda = \mu$. We find

$$\phi_{12}{}^{g\text{-}}(z|t) = e^{-\lambda t}e^{\lambda zt} - e^{-\lambda t}e^{(1-a)\lambda zt}$$

$$= e^{-\lambda t}\sum_{n=0}^{\infty}\frac{(\lambda t)^n}{n!}z^n - e^{-\lambda t}\sum_{n=0}^{\infty}\frac{[(1-a)\lambda t]^n}{n!}z^n \qquad \lambda = \mu, \quad (12.10.24)$$

from which we may readily write the inverse geometric transform,

$$\phi_{12}(n|t) = \frac{(\lambda t)^n}{n!}e^{-\lambda t} - \frac{[(1-a)\lambda t]^n}{n!}e^{-\lambda t}$$

$$\lambda = \mu;\, n = 0, 1, 2, \ldots;\, 0 \le t. \quad (12.10.25)$$

When λ is not equal to μ, we can write Equation 12.10.23 as

$$\phi_{12}{}^{g\text{-}}(z|t) = \frac{\dfrac{a\lambda}{\mu-\lambda}z}{1 - \left(1 + \dfrac{a\lambda}{\mu-\lambda}\right)z}\,[e^{-\lambda t}e^{(1-a)\lambda zt} - e^{-\mu t}e^{\mu zt}]$$

$$= \left[\sum_{l=1}^{\infty}\frac{a\lambda}{\mu-\lambda}\left(1 + \frac{a\lambda}{\mu-\lambda}\right)^{l-1}z^l\right]$$

$$\times \left[e^{-\lambda t}\sum_{m=0}^{\infty}\frac{[(1-a)\lambda t]^m}{m!}z^m - e^{-\mu t}\sum_{m=0}^{\infty}\frac{(\mu t)^m}{m!}z^m\right]$$

$$\lambda \ne \mu. \quad (12.10.26)$$

Presenting the transform in this way shows that it is the product of two transforms whose inverses are evident. The first inverse has the form

$$u(l-1)\frac{a\lambda}{\mu-\lambda}\left(1 + \frac{a\lambda}{\mu-\lambda}\right)^{l-1} \qquad l = 0, 1, 2, \ldots. \quad (12.10.27)$$

The second has the form

$$\frac{[(1-a)\lambda t]^m}{m!}e^{-\lambda t} - \frac{(\mu t)^m}{m!}e^{-\mu t}. \quad (12.10.28)$$

Since $\phi_{12}{}^{g\text{-}}(z|t)$ is the product of the geometric transforms of these expressions,

$\phi_{12}(n|t)$ must be equal to their convolution,

$$\phi_{12}(n|t) = \sum_{m=0}^{n} u(n - m - 1)\frac{a\lambda}{\mu - \lambda}\left(1 + \frac{a\lambda}{\mu - \lambda}\right)^{n-m-1} \times \left[\frac{[(1 - a)\lambda t]^m}{m!}e^{-\lambda t} - \frac{(\mu t)^m}{m!}e^{-\mu t}\right]$$

$$\lambda \neq \mu; n = 0, 1, 2, \ldots; 0 \leq t. \quad (12.10.29)$$

Solution

We are now ready to answer the original problem. First, when $\lambda = \mu$, we substitute Equations 12.10.14 and 12.10.25 into Equation 12.10.20 to obtain

$$\{S_1|n, t\} = \frac{\phi_{11}(n|t)}{\phi_{11}(n|t) + \phi_{12}(n|t)}$$

$$= \frac{\dfrac{[(1 - a)\lambda t]^n}{n!}e^{-\lambda t}}{\dfrac{[(1 - a)\lambda t]^n}{n!}e^{-\lambda t} + \dfrac{(\lambda t)^n}{n!}e^{-\lambda t} - \dfrac{[(1 - a)\lambda t]^n}{n!}e^{-\lambda t}}$$

$$= (1 - a)^n \qquad \lambda \neq \mu; n = 0, 1, 2, \ldots; 0 \leq t. \quad (12.10.30)$$

We verify the appropriateness of this simple answer by noting that when $\lambda = \mu$ the two states have the same waiting time distributions, and hence, the duration of the interval t provides no additional information on state once the number of transitions in the interval is known. The probability that the process will occupy state 1 after making n transitions is just the probability that it will return to state 1 on each transition raised to the nth power.

When $\lambda \neq \mu$, we use the results of Equations 12.10.14 and 12.10.29 in Equation 12.10.20,

$$\{S_1|n, t\} = \frac{\phi_{11}(n|t)}{\phi_{11}(n|t) + \phi_{12}(n|t)}$$

$$= \frac{\dfrac{[(1 - a)\lambda t]^n}{n!}e^{-\lambda t}}{\dfrac{[(1 - a)\lambda t]^n}{n!}e^{-\lambda t} + \sum_{m=0}^{n} u(n - m - 1)\dfrac{a\lambda}{\mu - \lambda}\left(1 + \dfrac{a\lambda}{\mu - \lambda}\right)^{n-m-1} \times \left[\dfrac{[(1 - a)\lambda t]^m}{m!}e^{-\lambda t} - \dfrac{(\mu t)^m}{m!}e^{-\mu t}\right]}$$

$$\lambda \neq \mu; n = 0, 1, 2, \ldots; 0 \leq t. \quad (12.10.31)$$

This expression gives the probability that the installation is currently using an unrepaired machine given any total time of operation and any number of failures within that time.

To illustrate, suppose that the failure rate of a new machine is $\lambda = 1$, that the failure rate of a repaired machine is $\mu = 2$, and that the probability that a failed machine will be repaired is $a = \frac{1}{2}$. For $n = 3$, $t = 2$, we calculate

$$\{S_1|n = 3, t = 2\} = 0.1398. \tag{12.10.32}$$

Thus if we know that three failures have occurred and that two time units have elapsed, we would assign probability 0.1398 to the event that the current machine is unrepaired. If we knew only that three failures had occurred, then we would assign probability $(1 - a)^3 = 0.125$ to this event; whereas if we knew only that two units of time had passed, we would use Equation 12.10.16 to assign probability $e^{-a\lambda t} = e^{-1} = 0.368$ to the same event.

Computational results

Figure 12.10.3 shows a more complete calculation for the example $\lambda = 1$, $\mu = 2$, $a = 1/2$. Here we have plotted $\{S_1|n, t\}$ for integral values of n from 1 to 20 and of t from 1 to 10. For ease in reading, the plots for constant t are shown as continuous functions of n although they are, in fact, meaningful only for integral values of n. We observe that for any value of n the probability of being in state 1 increases with t. This is true because the longer the time interval to achieve a given number of transitions, the more likely that the time between transitions was generated by the exponential process with mean $1/\lambda = 1$ associated with state 1, rather than by the faster exponential process with mean $1/\mu = 1/2$ associated with state 2.

Time unknown. For comparison we show in the same figure a plot of the probability of being in state 1 after n transitions when t is not known, $\{S_1|n\} = (1 - a)^n = (0.5)^n$. This function appears as a straight line on the figure as a result of the logarithmic ordinate scale. Suppose, for example, that we know only that the process has made $n = 10$ transitions. The probability that it still occupies state 1 is $(0.5)^{10} = 9.766 \times 10^{-4}$. Now if we are told, in addition, that t, the time of process operation, is no greater than 7, we would, according to the figure, assign a lower probability to being in state 1 than we have just calculated. Similarly, if we are told that t is at least 8, we would assign a higher probability. It appears from the figure that a statement that t was approximately 7.2 would leave our probability assignment unchanged.

Transitions unknown. We also show in this figure the probability of being in state 1 after time t when the number of transitions n is not known, $\{S_1|t\} = e^{-a\lambda t} = e^{-0.5t}$ from Equation 12.10.16. For each value of t, the value of this function is shown by a small circle on the curve for $\{S_1|n, t\}$. We can use this plot to determine the effect of additional information on the number of transitions n when the operating time t is known.

For example, suppose we know only that $t = 7$. Then we would assign a probability $e^{-0.5(7)} = 0.030$ to occupancy of state 1, as shown by the small circle on the $t = 7$ curve. We observe that if we were told in addition that $n = 7$ transitions had been made, our probability assignment would be virtually unchanged. However, if we learned that fewer than 7 transitions had been made, we would assign a higher probability to the event that the process is occupying state 1; conversely, if we learned that more than 7 transitions had been made, we would assign a lower probability. In fact, if we conduct this same investigation for values of t from 1 through 10, we find that learning that n is approximately equal to t causes virtually no change in the probability assignment from that made on the basis of

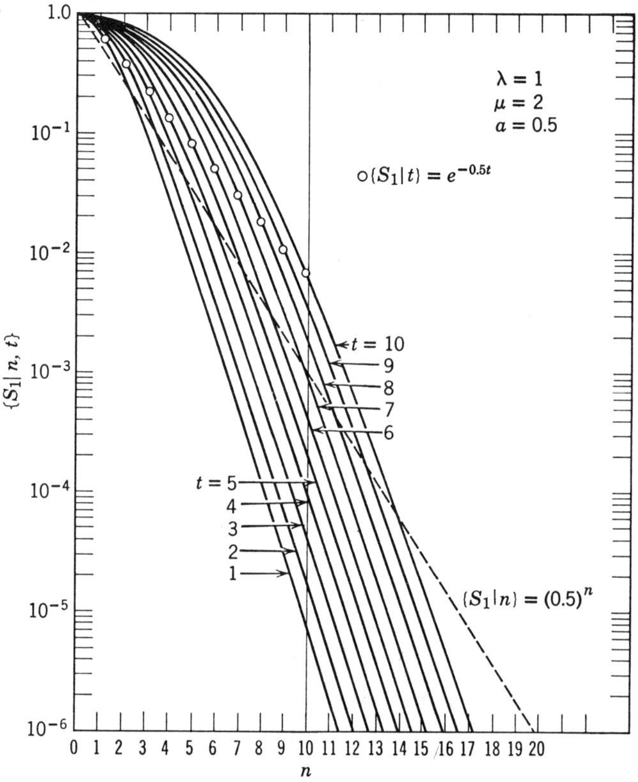

Figure 12.10.3 Probability of occupying state 1 after n transitions and time t for transient repair process. Dashed line shows $(s_1|n)$. ooo indicates $(s_1|t)$.

t alone, while values of n that differ from t cause the same type of modification in probability assignment that we have just observed.

The lack of symmetry in the effects of additional information on n or t is quite interesting. We have found that if we know that $n = 10$, then finding that t is about 7.2 will not change substantially the probability 9.766×10^{-4} that we assign to state 1's being occupied. However, if we know that $t = 7$, then learning that $n = 7$ will not materially change the probability assignment 3×10^{-2}, while learning that $n = 10$ will reduce the probability to 8.398×10^{-4}. Thus Figure 12.10.3 shows graphically for the transient repair process the importance of joint information on transitions and time in assigning state probabilities.

Inference on Operating Time

Up to this time we have been discussing the problem of making probability assignments on the state and number of transitions given the time that the process has been operating. We can also address ourselves to the inverse problem of finding the probability density function for the operating time t given some rule that states how operating time will be determined from other features of the process. This is analogous to the problem of inference under conditions of natural termination that we studied in Section 6.3.

Suppose, for example, we wish to find $\{t, S_j | Q_n, S_{0i}\}$, the joint density function on operating time t and probability that the state at the end of the operating time is j given that the process stops operating (quits) after n transitions and that it is started at time zero in state i. We might think that this quantity is difficult to calculate, but careful consideration of the conditions for stopping shows that we have already solved the problem.

We observe that the trajectories starting in state i that have operating time t and terminal state j because they have completed n transitions are just those trajectories in which the nth transition is made exactly at time t into state j. We defined the joint density function-probability of such a trajectory in Section 11.9 as the entrance rate $e_{ij}(n|t)$. Therefore we immediately have

$$\{t, S_j | Q_n S_{0i}\} = e_{ij}(n|t). \qquad (12.10.33)$$

Thus the probabilities of major events associated with natural termination in a given number of transitions follow directly from the relatively easily calculated entrance rates. We have a choice of developing these entrance rates from the integral equation 11.9.1 or of finding them by transform methods. As we showed in Section 11.9, the geometric-exponential transform $e_{ij}^{ge}(z|s)$ of $e_{ij}(n|t)$ is the transmission of the process flow graph from node i to node j rather than to the output node associated with node j.

The transient repair process

Let us demonstrate these concepts using the transient repair process. Suppose we are interested in $\{t|S_1, Q_n, S_{01}\}$, the density function on operating time given that the process stopped after n transitions and that it was in state 1 at that time, and also that the process started in state 1. We can write this quantity as

$$\{t|S_1, Q_n, S_{01}\} = \frac{\{t, S_1|Q_n, S_{01}\}}{\{S_1|Q_n, S_{01}\}}, \tag{12.10.34}$$

or as

$$\{t|S_1, Q_n, S_{01}\} = \frac{e_{11}(n|t)}{\int_0^\infty dt\, e_{11}(n|t)}. \tag{12.10.35}$$

Transform analysis. The transform of the numerator is $e_{11}{}^{ge}(z|s)$; the transform of the denominator is $e_{11}{}^{ge}(z|0)$. We find $e_{11}{}^{ge}(z|s)$ as the transmission of the flow graph in Figure 12.10.2 from the input to node 1,

$$e_{11}{}^{ge}(z|s) = \frac{1}{1 - (1 - a)\dfrac{\lambda}{s + \lambda} z}. \tag{12.10.36}$$

We first invert the geometric transform,

$$e_{11}{}^{\cdot e}(n|s) = (1 - a)^n\left(\frac{\lambda}{s + \lambda}\right)^n, \tag{12.10.37}$$

and then the exponential transform,

$$\{t, S_1|Q_n, S_{01}\} = e_{11}(n|t) = (1 - a)^n\lambda^n \frac{t^{n-1}}{(n - 1)!} e^{-\lambda t}. \tag{12.10.38}$$

The geometric transform of the denominator in Equations 12.10.34 or 12.10.35 is obtained directly from Equation 12.10.36

$$e_{11}{}^{ge}(z|0) = \frac{1}{1 - (1 - a)z}. \tag{12.10.39}$$

We therefore can immediately write the denominator as

$$\{S_1|Q_n, S_{01}\} = \int_0^\infty dt\, e_{11}(n|t) = (1 - a)^n. \tag{12.10.40}$$

Finally, we use Equations 12.10.38 and 12.10.40 to write

$$\{t|S_1, Q_n, S_{01}\} = \frac{\{t, S_1|Q_n, S_{01}\}}{\{S_1|Q_n S_{01}\}} = \lambda \frac{(\lambda t)^{n-1}}{(n - 1)!} e^{-\lambda t} \tag{12.10.41}$$

as the density function for the operating time of the process given that it was destined to stop after n transitions and that it stopped in state 1.

This is a well-known density function called the gamma distribution. It is the density function that represents the sum of n independent exponential variables, each with rate λ. Of course, since under the conditions specified the process had to make the n transitions into state 1, the operating time of the process is just the sum of the n independent exponential holding times, each with rate λ.

Alternate gamma derivation

We can verify these comments in another way by recalling the flow graph of Figure 12.9.1 for the simple exponential process. If we permit this process to operate until it makes n transitions, the density function $\{t|n\}$ for the time of operation t will be $e_{11}(n|t)$. The geometric-exponential transform of this quantity is $e_{11}^{ge}(z|s)$, which we obtain from Figure 12.9.1 as the transmission of the flow graph through node 1,

$$e_{11}^{ge}(z|s) = \frac{1}{1 - \dfrac{\lambda}{s + \lambda} z}. \tag{12.10.42}$$

Inversion produces

$$e_{11}^{\cdot e}(n|s) = \left(\frac{\lambda}{s + \lambda}\right)^n \tag{12.10.43}$$

and

$$\{t|n\} = e_{11}(n|t) = \lambda \frac{(\lambda t)^{n-1}}{(n - 1)!} e^{-\lambda t}, \tag{12.10.44}$$

which is, of course, the gamma distribution of Equation 12.10.41.

Thus for a simple exponential process, the probability of n transitions in time t will be Poisson as we found in Equation 12.9.4, while the density function of the time t to obtain n transitions will be the gamma density function. The similarity in forms of Equations 12.9.4 and 12.10.44 should not be allowed to obscure the fundamentally different problems that they answer.

We have demonstrated in this section that the reasoning we developed in Chapter 6 for problems of partial information and inference in Markov processes carries over directly to the semi-Markov case. This is fortunate, because some of the most challenging problems in the practical analysis of semi-Markov models arise in the inference area.

12.11 THE CONTINUOUS-TIME CHAPMAN-KOLMOGOROV EQUATIONS

Since the continuous-time process we have been discussing is a Markov process, its interval transition probabilities must satisfy the Chapman-Kolmogorov equations. However, the equations must now be formulated to be consistent with the continuous-time basis.

Formulation

The development of the equations closely parallels the discussion in Section 9.1. We begin by considering three successive time points τ, σ, and t ($\tau \leq \sigma \leq t$) at which the system occupies states i, k, and j, respectively. Figure 9.1.1 indicates the type of system trajectory considered. We define $\phi_{ij}(\tau, t)$ as the interval transition probability from time τ to time t, the probability that the system will occupy state j at time t if it occupied state i at the earlier time τ. If the process has the Markovian property that the future trajectory depends only on the state currently occupied, then the same argument that led to Equation 9.1.7 allows us to relate the interval transition probabilities by

$$\phi_{ij}(\tau, t) = \sum_{k=1}^{N} \phi_{ik}(\tau, \sigma)\phi_{kj}(\sigma, t) \qquad \begin{array}{l} i = 1, 2, \ldots, N \\ j = 1, 2, \ldots, N \\ \tau \leq \sigma \leq t. \end{array} \tag{12.11.1}$$

This equation is the Chapman-Kolmogorov equation for continuous-time processes, the defining equation for the continuous-time Markov process. In matrix form it becomes

$$\Phi(\tau, t) = \Phi(\tau, \sigma)\Phi(\sigma, t) \qquad \tau \leq \sigma \leq t. \tag{12.11.2}$$

Consistency requires that

$$\Phi(t, t) = I. \tag{12.11.3}$$

The Forward and Backward Equations

If the basic time period for the discrete-time Markov process is assumed to be very small, we can derive continuous-time analogs of the results of Section 9.1 very easily. For example, the forward Chapman-Kolmogorov equation for the discrete-time process, Equation 9.1.18, assumes the form

$$\frac{d}{dt}\Phi(\tau, t) = \Phi(\tau, t)A(t) \qquad \tau \leq t, \tag{12.11.4}$$

the forward Chapman-Kolmogorov equation for the continuous-time Markov process. The difference operator has become the derivative, and the differential matrix $D(n)$ has become the time-varying transition rate matrix $A(t)$, also differential. As the equation shows, we can think of $A(t)$ as a limit,

$$A(t) = \lim_{\tau \to t} \frac{d}{dt}\Phi(\tau, t). \tag{12.11.5}$$

The backward Chapman-Kolmogorov equation for the continuous-time Markov process follows directly from Equation 9.1.23, the discrete-time version,

$$\frac{d}{d\tau}\Phi(\tau, t) = -A(\tau)\Phi(\tau, t) \qquad \tau \leq t. \tag{12.11.6}$$

Solution

The common solution to Equations 12.11.4 and 12.11.6 follows directly from basic differential equation theory,

$$\Phi(\tau, t) = \exp\left(\int_{\tau}^{t} d\sigma\, A(\sigma)\right). \tag{12.11.7}$$

We interpret this equation for $\Phi(\tau, t)$ as a function of the matrix $\int_{\tau}^{t} A(\sigma)\, d\sigma$ in the sense of Section 11.4. Note that Equation 12.11.2 is also satisfied by this solution. Equation 12.11.7 is the continuous-time counterpart of Equation 9.1.25.

If the continuous-time Markov process is not time-varying, then it is governed by the same transition rate matrix A at all times. In this case $\Phi(\tau, t)$ becomes

$$\begin{aligned}\Phi(\tau, t) &= \exp\left(\int_{\tau}^{t} d\sigma\, A(\sigma)\right)\\ &= \exp\left(A\int_{\tau}^{t} d\sigma\right)\\ &= e^{A(t-\tau)} \qquad \tau \leq t.\end{aligned} \tag{12.11.8}$$

Finally, if we choose the starting time τ as zero, we have

$$\Phi(0, t) = \Phi(t) = e^{At} \qquad 0 \leq t, \tag{12.11.9}$$

and we have shown that the result of Equation 12.2.10 is the solution of the continuous-time Chapman-Kolmogorov equation for the time-invariant process.

12.12 CONCLUSION

The continuous-time Markov process can be developed as fully as the discrete-time Markov process. For example, we could consider population models, time-varying transition behavior, and the problem of the reverse process. However, as the methods are very similar to our previous developments, we shall not pursue them in detail. Summarizing our results on the Markov family of models up to this point, we observe that the semi-Markov models provide considerably more modeling generality than simple Markov models, but that they usually result in less tractable analytic expressions. However, the discrete-time rather than the continuous-time version of either type model produces readily computable expressions. Little or no penalty is paid for the additional flexibility of semi-Markov models *provided* that a discrete-time formulation is used.

PROBLEMS

1. The Renaissance Taxicab Company operates in towns A and B and has found that the trips its drivers make can be modeled by a semi-Markov process with the following transition probabilities:

$$\begin{array}{cc} & \textit{To} \\ & \begin{array}{cc} A & B \end{array} \\ \textit{From} \begin{array}{c} A \\ B \end{array} & \begin{bmatrix} 1/3 & 2/3 \\ 1/2 & 1/2 \end{bmatrix} \end{array}$$

The length of the trips are exponentially distributed; those originating in A have a mean of 1/3 hour and those originating in B have a mean of 1/2 hour. If Driver Iram Bick Pentameter's first trip of the day starts in town A, what is the probability that the dispatcher will find him in town B t hours later?

2. Consider the simple marketing example in which customers continuously choose between brand A and brand B. The probability that a customer will purchase brand A next if he has just chosen brand A is 0.8, and the probability that he will choose brand B again if he has just chosen brand B is 0.7. Now consider the time between purchases. If the customer has just chosen brand A, the time until his next purchase is exponentially distributed with a mean of one week; if he has just chosen brand B, it is exponentially distributed with a mean of 0.5 week. If a customer has just purchased brand A, what is the probability t weeks later that his last purchase was brand B?

3. A cosmic ray counter has been set up to detect incoming cosmic rays and classify them into groups A and B. A wandering analyst has suggested a continuous-time Markov process as a model for the incoming radiation. His model assumes that a group A ray will be followed by a group A ray with probability 0.9, and a group B ray will be followed by a group B ray with probability 0.7. He has found that the interarrival times of the rays are exponentially distributed with a mean of one hour if a group A ray has just occurred and 0.5 hour if a group B ray has just occurred. Our man defines the process to be in state A if a group A ray was last detected and in state B if a group B ray was last detected.

a) If a group A ray has just been detected, what is the probability density function for the *next* arrival of a group B ray?

b) If the process is in state A at time zero, what is the probability that it will be in state A at time t?

4. A businessman manages a parking lot with only three parking spaces. He runs the lot so that there is never a waiting line, i.e., as soon as all three spaces are filled, he closes the lot and only reopens it when someone leaves. Customers are known to arrive at a rate of λ customers per hour with an exponentially distributed interarrival time. The time each customer spends in the lot is exponentially distributed with a mean of $1/\mu$ hours.

a) What are the differential equations governing $\phi_0(t)$, $\phi_1(t)$, $\phi_2(t)$, and $\phi_3(t)$ where $\phi_k(t)$ is the probability that there are k people parked in the lot at time t?

b) What are the steady-state values of these probabilities?

5. Find $\lim_{t \to 0} \frac{d}{dt} \Phi(t)$ for a continuous-time semi-Markov process in terms of the process descriptors. Verify the expression by applying it to the continuous-time Markov process.

6. Under what conditions is it possible to construct a continuous-time Markov process with transition rate matrix A that will have the same state probabilities at integral times as a discrete-time Markov process with given transition probability matrix P? What is the relationship between A and P? Illustrate your answer for the two-state case where

$$P = \begin{bmatrix} 1 - a & a \\ b & 1 - b \end{bmatrix} = \text{the discrete-time transition probability matrix}$$

and

$$A = \begin{bmatrix} -\lambda & \lambda \\ \mu & -\mu \end{bmatrix} = \text{the transition rate matrix for the continuous-time model.}$$

7. Consider the problem of customers learning of a new business by word of mouth. If there is a probability $\lambda \Delta$ that in a small time Δ a customer will induce an aquaintance to become a customer, find $p(n, t)$, the probability that there are n customers at time t if the business starts with one customer at $t = 0$. Notice the applicability of this model to rumor generation, growth of microorganisms, and chain reactions.

8. The manager of the neighborhood supermarket has been clocking the arrival of customers at the checkout counter and has observed that interarrival times are exponential with a mean of 10 minutes. The time to check out a customer is also exponentially distributed with a mean of 10 minutes. Lately, the manager has noticed that the waiting lines have begun to be very long so he has instituted the following policy:

a) If there is 0 or 1 person *waiting*, use only a single checkout station.
b) Otherwise, use two checkout stations.

(Assume that customers wait in a single line and go to the first available checkout station.)
What fraction of time (in the steady state) will the second station be open?

9. A commercial airline service facility is experiencing an excessive number of planes waiting to be serviced. The facility can service only one plane at a time. Initial measurements indicate that planes arrive for service at random with exponentially distributed interarrival times of mean $1/\lambda$ and that they independently require an exponentially distributed servicing time of mean $1/\mu$. Two factions have proposed a solution. The first suggests that the size of the facility be doubled so that two planes may be serviced at the same time using present servicing techniques. The second suggests the purchase of improved servicing equipment that will double the average servicing rate at the present facility. You decide which action will minimize the number of planes that are *waiting*.

10. One attendant is assigned to care for two machines. The time between malfunctions of each machine is exponentially distributed with mean $1/\lambda$; the time required for the attendant to service a machine is exponentially distributed with mean $1/\mu$. The attendant can service only one machine at a time.

a) Find the exponential transform of the probability that at least one machine is out of order at time t if both were working at $t = 0$. Find this probability if $\mu = 2\lambda$. If $\lambda = 1$ breakdown/hour, find the probability that the foreman will find an out-of-order machine at a time 12 minutes after he last looked and found both working. Compare with the steady-state value. What does this probability become if the attendant has been taking a coffee break in the meantime?

b) It is found that a team of two attendants can service a machine three times as fast as a single man. Thus for one man $\mu = 2\lambda$, but for the team $\mu = 6\lambda$. Find the steady-state probabilities of the process for each scheme. If each hour of machine downtime costs \$25 and each man costs \$5/hour, should the single attendant or the team be used?

11. A certain Enatco gasoline service station (that's octane spelled backwards) has two gas pumps for servicing customers. The pumps are both located on a small island in the center of the station and, if necessary, may be used simultaneously with one auto on each side of the island. The construction of the station is such that customers wait in a single line, then enter service at the first free pump. If both are free, either pump is chosen. The proprietor has found that customers generally arrive at a rate of 6 per hour with an interarrival time that is exponentially distributed, and that the servicing time for each pump is exponentially distributed with a mean of 10 minutes.

a) What is the expected fraction of time when no customers will be in the gas station?

b) What is the expected length of the waiting line?

12. Dr. B. Ill (Dr. Bill to his friends) has a single waiting chair in his office. Because of these crowded conditions, he has given his nurse the following instructions: Whenever a patient arrives and *another patient* is waiting, she is to give *both* waiting patients an aspirin and *send them home.* The time between patient arrivals is exponentially distributed with mean $1/\lambda$, and Dr. Bill's service time is exponentially distributed with mean $1/\mu$. If the system has been in operation for a long time, what is the expected number of times that the nurse will "do the aspirin bit" in a unit time interval? Or alternatively, what is the probability that the nurse will give out aspirin in any small interval Δ?

13. Dr. Sawyer Bones has space for only one patient in his waiting room; anyone arriving when someone is waiting is given an aspirin by the nurse and sent home. Through long experience Dr. Bones has found that patient interarrival times are exponentially distributed with a mean of $1/\lambda$; his service time is also exponentially distributed but with a mean of $1/\mu$.

a) If Dr. Bones is helping a patient but the waiting room is empty, what is the probability that another patient will arrive before the doctor finishes with his present patient?

Now Dr. Bones has just finished with a patient and there is no patient waiting for his attention.

b) What is the exponential transform of the density function of the time for this event to occur again?

c) What is the expected length of time between the occurrences of these events when there are zero patients in the system?

d) If there are zero patients in the system, what is the probability that Dr. Bones will see only *one* patient before getting another rest.

14. A service facility is being constructed. A question has arisen as to how much space should be allowed for customers who are waiting. The service facility can handle only one customer at a time and will have a service time that is exponentially distributed with a mean of $1/\mu$. The times between customer arrivals are exponentially distributed with a mean of $1/\lambda$. The designer has been told that the cost of turning a customer away is c and the cost per unit time of maintaining m spaces for waiting customers is km. These are the only costs.

a) What is the total expected cost per unit time of a facility with m waiting spaces?

b) For $\lambda = 1$, $\mu = 2$, $k = 0.1$, and $c = 1$, what number of waiting spaces minimizes the total cost?

Note: In part a) let $\rho = \lambda/\mu$ for convenience. Also assume that customers *must* wait in one of the m waiting spaces; customers are turned away when all m spaces are full.

15. Sam and Jack are taxi drivers working in two different towns served by the same airport. On any one trip Sam has a 30% chance of going to the airport while Jack has only a 20% chance. The duration of Sam's trips is exponentially distributed with a mean of $1/\lambda_S$; the duration of Jack's is exponentially distributed with a mean of $1/\lambda_J$. Both men start the day in their respective towns at the same time (at $t = 0$). Sam has made a friendly wager with Jack that he will get to the airport for the first time before Jack does. What is the probability that Sam has won the bet by time t?

16. It is known that a certain three-state continuous-time Markov process has the following mean first passage times:

$$\overline{\Theta} = \begin{bmatrix} - & 1 & 3 \\ 2.5 & - & 2 \\ 4 & 2.2 & - \end{bmatrix}$$

a) What are the transition rates for this process?

b) Find the P and Λ matrices if the process has no virtual transitions.

17. Consider a monodesmic continuous-time Markov process defined by the usual matrices P and Λ. Suppose now that we interpret the process as always being between two states, e.g., the frog is always in the air. Thus a transition from i to j implies that the process will spend a certain amount of time between i and j. We define $w_{ijk}(t)$ as the amount of time that the process has spent going from j to k if it started in i at $t = 0$ and has been running for a time t.

a) Find $\bar{w}^e_{ijk}(s)$, the transform of the mean of $w_{ijk}(t)$, in terms of the elements of $\Phi^e(s)$, P, Λ, A, ϕ, or π.

b) Suppose now that we have measured the steady-state expected fraction of time spent between states for all pairs of states; that is, we know

$$f_{jk} = \lim_{t \to \infty} \left(\frac{1}{t}\right) \overline{w}_{ijk}(t) \qquad \text{for all } j \text{ and } k.$$

(Since the process is assumed to be monodesmic, f_{jk} will be independent of the starting state.) If you had no other knowledge of the parameters of the process, how would you calculate ϕ and P for the process from the f_{jk}'s?

c) From part b), what can you say about the mean waiting times for each state in the process?

18. Let $\tau_{ij}(t)$ be the amount of time that an N-state continuous-time Markov process spends in state j if it started in state i at $t = 0$ and has run for a time t.

a) Find the mean and mean square of $\tau_{ij}(t)$ in terms of integrals of the interval transition probabilities.

b) Find the exponential transform of the mean and mean square of $\tau_{ij}(t)$ in terms of the exponential transforms of the interval transition probabilities.

19. In the marketing model of Problem 2, a customer buys brand A at time 0 and at time t his last purchase was brand B. What is the probability that he never purchased brand A twice in a row?

20. a) Consider a taxicab driver for the Renaissance Taxicab Company in Problem 1. If his first trip of the day originates in town A, what is the probability that after t hours he will never have gone to the same town twice in a row, that is, have made no $A \to A$ or $B \to B$ trips?

b) A driver's first trip originated in town A and t hours later he has never gone to the same town twice in a row. What is the probability that he is in town B?

21. A machine has a time to breakdown density function that is exponential with mean $1/\lambda$; its repair time density function is also exponential with mean $1/\mu$.

a) If the machine is working at time 0 but is "down" at time t, what is the probability that it has broken down exactly once during this time interval?

b) The foreman of the shop arrives late in the day and does not know how long this process has been going on. However, he does know that the machine was in the "up" state when the process started; based on this information he assigns a density function $\alpha e^{-\alpha t}$ for the length of time t the process has been operating. If he now finds out that the machine is in the "down" state and has broken down only once since the process started, what density function does he assign for the length of time the process has been operating?

22. A computer has a time to failure that is exponentially distributed with mean $1/\lambda$ and a repair time that is exponentially distributed with mean $1/\mu$. At time T Joe calls up the confused computer operator and is told that the computer is operating with probability p. If the computer was operating at $t = 0$, what is the probability that it was operating at $t = \tau$ where $\tau \leq T$?

23. A supermarket has a single checkout counter. Through long experience, the manager has found that customers arrive at the checkout counter with an interarrival time that is exponentially distributed with a mean of $1/\lambda$. The service time is also exponentially distributed but with a mean of $1/\mu$. There is no restriction on the length of the waiting line and $\lambda < \mu$.

After the counter has been in operation for a long time, the manager observes that there is someone in service but that there is no one in line (i.e., there is one person in the system). He is given the additional information that no one has completed service in the last τ seconds. With this information, what is the probability that there was no one in the system τ seconds ago?

24. Consider a stationary N-state continuous-time Markov process that is in the *steady state*. Let ${}^{I}\phi_{ji}(\tau)$ be the probability that the system *was* in state i τ units of time ago if it is in state j now.

a) If ${}^{I}a_{ij}$ is the ijth element of the A matrix for this inverse process, find an expression for ${}^{I}a_{ij}$ in terms of the elements of the A matrix for the forward process and the steady-state probabilities.

b) If a reversible process is defined as one for which ${}^{I}A = A$, prove that all continuous-time birth and death processes are reversible. Explain the physical meaning of the conditions for reversibility.

13 REWARDS

Now that we have spent some time analyzing the probabilistic structure of Markov models, we shall extend their usefulness by adding a feature of great practical importance: the possibility of attaching rewards to the process. We can think generally of the reward as a random variable associated with the state occupancies and transitions, but it will simplify our terminology by considering it to be a reward of the economic type. The addition of a reward structure allows us to compute the operational characteristics of a wide variety of systems.

13.1 THE REWARD STRUCTURE FOR CONTINUOUS-TIME PROCESSES

Although we have several choices in how we associate rewards with the behavior of the process, we shall select a reward structure that affords considerable generality while retaining computational convenience. Consider the continuous-time semi-Markov process. According to our interpretation of the process, whenever the system enters a state i its first action is to select a successor state j according to the transition probabilities of the process p_{ij}. Then it determines how long it will spend in state i before making the transition to j by selecting a time interval from the holding time density function $h_{ij}(\cdot)$. We shall assume that while the process occupies state i having chosen a successor state j, it earns reward at a rate $y_{ij}(\sigma)$ at a time σ after entering state i. We call $y_{ij}(\sigma)$ the "yield rate" of state i at time σ when the successor state is state j. When the transition from state i to state j is actually made at some time τ, the process earns a bonus $b_{ij}(\tau)$, a fixed sum. Thus the yield rate is generally paid continuously for occupancy of state i whereas the bonus is a lump sum payment at the time of a transition, a payment that depends on the transition made and on the holding time in state i preceding the transition. The only requirement for the yield rates and bonuses in the process is that they be real numbers, positive or negative; thus rewards may, in fact, be costs.

The combination of yield rate and bonus structure provides a powerful modeling capability. For example, in an inventory system where the state represents the number of items in inventory and where transitions represent sales or additions to inventory, the yield rate will describe the costs of maintaining the inventory (such as carrying charges), while the bonus structure will describe the costs associated with placing an order and the revenue associated with a sale. If we were modeling a machine shop by letting the state be the number of machines in operating condition and a transition be a repair or a breakdown, then the yield rate would describe the hourly maintenance, operating, and repair costs of the shop while the bonus structure would provide flexibility in describing material losses due to machine breakdowns and the cost of repair parts.

Usually we shall not require all the generality that this model affords. Many systems are well modeled by yield rates that are constant during the occupancy of any state and by bonuses that do not depend on the holding time of the previously occupied state; thus,

$$y_{ij}(\sigma) = y_{ij} \qquad b_{ij}(\tau) = b_{ij}. \tag{13.1.1}$$

Further simplification results when the yield rate does not depend on the successor state,

$$y_{ij} = y_i. \tag{13.1.2}$$

Of course, many systems require a reward structure using either yield rates or bonuses, but not both.

Discounting

We often encounter situations where the payment of rewards stretches over a long time period, perhaps several years, so that we have to provide a capability for the discounting of future income or expenditures. The rationale is that a sum of money that will be received or paid in the future is worth less today because a smaller amount placed at interest beginning today could generate that larger sum in the future. We shall assume that a unit sum of money at time t in the future has a worth or present value of $e^{-\alpha t}$ today, $\alpha \geq 0$. That is, we shall perform continuous discounting at a rate α.

Suppose now that we have described a monetary prospect out into the future by a reward rate function $f(t)$ that prescribes the rate of income (if positive) or expenditure (if negative) at time t, $0 \leq t < \infty$. The present value of this reward rate function is then

$$\int_0^\infty dt\, e^{-\alpha t} f(t). \tag{13.1.3}$$

If the reward rate function grows in the positive or negative direction at a rate higher than the discount rate α, then, of course, its present value is unbounded.

However, we shall assume that it does not grow so quickly and therefore that the present value of reward rate functions with which we deal is always finite. In this case, by comparing Equation 13.1.3 with the definition of the exponential transform from Equation 11.4.1, we observe that the present value of a reward rate function discounted continuously at the rate α is just the exponential transform of the reward rate function evaluated at α,

$$\int_0^\infty dt\, e^{-\alpha t} f(t) = f^e(\alpha). \tag{13.1.4}$$

This observation provides an important connection between discounting and transform analysis.

On certain occasions we choose to interpret discounting as a method of incorporating uncertainty about the duration of the period during which rewards will be paid. Thus if we assign the exponential probability density function $\alpha e^{-\alpha\tau}$ to the random variable τ representing the duration of the income stream, then $e^{-\alpha t}$ is the probability that the stream will survive at least through time t and $f^e(\alpha)$ from Equation 13.1.4 becomes the expected earnings from the reward process. The expected duration of the reward process would be $1/\alpha$, the reciprocal of the quantity we previously interpreted as the discount rate.

Equivalent annuital reward rate

Since on occasion the present value can be so large as to be difficult to interpret, it is sometimes worthwhile to bring it into perspective using the concept of an equivalent annuital reward rate. We ask, what constant rate of reward ρ paid forever would have the present value $f^e(\alpha)$ of the reward process under consideration; we call ρ the equivalent annuital reward rate. Since the present value of the constant payment ρ at the discount rate α is

$$\int_0^\infty dt\, e^{-\alpha t} \cdot \rho = \rho/\alpha, \tag{13.1.5}$$

we set

$$\rho/\alpha = f^e(\alpha) \tag{13.1.6}$$

and find

$$\rho = \alpha f^e(\alpha). \tag{13.1.7}$$

The equivalent annuital reward rate is just the present value multiplied by the discount rate. When the reward process is interpreted to have uncertain duration as discussed above, it is also equal to the present value divided by the expected duration. Alternately in this case, it is the expected reward rate that will be paid at the moment the process stops.

13.2 THE CONTINUOUS-TIME SEMI-MARKOV REWARD PROCESS WITH DISCOUNTING

As you can imagine, the introduction of a reward structure into a semi-Markov process increases the complexity of analysis as well as the modeling convenience. The number of investigations that could be carried out is limitless, reminding one of the adage that a fool can ask more questions in a day than a wise man can answer in a lifetime. To provide some important answers while limiting the complexity of analysis, we shall focus our attention on determining the expected discounted reward that the process will generate in some time interval.

Formulation

Let us define $v_i(t, \alpha)$ as the expected present value of the reward the process will generate in a time interval of length t if it is placed in state i at the beginning of this interval. We shall assume that the previously described reward generation of the process stops when the time interval expires, but that the process generates an additional fixed reward payment $v_j(0)$ if it occupies state j at the end of the interval. This boundary reward structure allows us to model the scrap values or other terminal rewards of operating systems.

As a preliminary, we note that if a process enters state i at time 0 and leaves state i at time τ to enter state j, then the present value at time zero of the reward generated by the yield rate structure is

$$\int_0^\tau d\sigma\, e^{-\alpha\sigma} y_{ij}(\sigma). \tag{13.2.1}$$

If the process were interrupted at a time t before making its transition to state j, the present value at time zero of the reward generated by the yield rate structure would be the same as shown in Equation 13.2.1 except that the upper limit on the integral would be limited so as not to exceed the time of interruption.

Now we can write an integral equation for the expected present value of the rewards generated by the process as

$$v_i(t, \alpha) = \sum_{j=1}^{N} p_{ij} \int_t^\infty d\tau\, h_{ij}(\tau)\left[\int_0^t d\sigma\, e^{-\alpha\sigma} y_{ij}(\sigma) + e^{-\alpha t} v_i(0)\right]$$
$$+ \sum_{j=1}^{N} p_{ij} \int_0^t d\tau\, h_{ij}(\tau)\left[\int_0^\tau d\sigma\, e^{-\alpha\sigma} y_{ij}(\sigma) + e^{-\alpha\tau} b_{ij}(\tau) + e^{-\alpha\tau} v_j(t - \tau, \alpha)\right]$$
$$i = 1, 2, \ldots, N;\ t \geq 0. \tag{13.2.2}$$

We interpret the first summation in this equation as follows. The first transition out of state i can occur either before or after the time t. If it occurs after t then the process will spend the entire interval of length t in state i. In this case the process will generate rewards according to the yield rate structure for state i throughout the time t and will then generate the terminal reward $v_i(0)$. The rewards from the yield structure are discounted using Equation 13.2.1 with the upper limit of the integral equal to t; the terminal reward $v_i(0)$ has a present value $e^{-\alpha t}v_i(0)$. The first term in Equation 13.2.2 sums these discounted rewards multiplied by the probability of their occurrence over all possible successor states and over all holding times greater than t.

If on the other hand the first transition out of state i is made to state j at a time $\tau < t$, then the yield rate structure will provide discounted rewards according to Equation 13.2.1. In addition, the bonus $b_{ij}(\tau)$ will be paid at time τ and will have a present value at the beginning of the interval of $e^{-\alpha\tau}b_{ij}(\tau)$. Finally, the process will enter state j at a time when an amount $t - \tau$ of the original interval remains. The expected present value of future rewards at the time of entrance is therefore $v_j(t - \tau, \alpha)$. However, when we observe this quantity at the beginning of the interval of length τ, it must be multiplied by the discount factor $e^{-\alpha\tau}$ to account for the additional delay of τ in receiving these rewards. The second term in Equation 13.2.2 sums these reward terms multiplied by their probability of occurrence over all values of j and first transition times $\tau < t$.

Notation

We can simplify Equation 13.2.2 by introducing suitable notation. First we define $y_{ij}(\tau, \alpha)$ as the discounted yield contribution to reward during an occupancy, the present value of the reward generated by the yield rate structure during a holding time τ in state i with successor state j. Thus $y_{ij}(\tau, \alpha)$ is just the quantity in Equation 13.2.1,

$$y_{ij}(\tau, \alpha) = \int_0^\tau d\sigma\, e^{-\alpha\sigma} y_{ij}(\sigma). \tag{13.2.3}$$

With this notational change, Equation 13.2.2 becomes

$$\begin{aligned} v_i(t, \alpha) = &\sum_{j=1}^N p_{ij} \int_t^\infty d\tau\, h_{ij}(\tau)[y_{ij}(t, \alpha) + e^{-\alpha t}v_i(0)] \\ &+ \sum_{j=1}^N p_{ij} \int_0^t d\tau\, h_{ij}(\tau)[y_{ij}(\tau, \alpha) + e^{-\alpha\tau}b_{ij}(\tau) + e^{-\alpha\tau}v_j(t - \tau, \alpha)] \end{aligned} \tag{13.2.4}$$

or

$$\begin{aligned} v_i(t, \alpha) = &\sum_{j=1}^N p_{ij} y_{ij}(t, \alpha) \int_t^\infty d\tau\, h_{ij}(\tau) + e^{-\alpha t}v_i(0) \sum_{j=1}^N p_{ij} \int_t^\infty d\tau\, h_{ij}(\tau) \\ &+ \sum_{j=1}^N p_{ij} \int_0^t d\tau\, h_{ij}(\tau)[y_{ij}(\tau, \alpha) + e^{-\alpha\tau}b_{ij}(\tau)] \\ &+ \sum_{j=1}^N p_{ij} \int_0^t d\tau\, h_{ij}(\tau)e^{-\alpha\tau}v_j(t - \tau, \alpha). \end{aligned} \tag{13.2.5}$$

Now we make some further identifications. We see that the first term is the contribution to the expected present value of the yield rate structure when the first transition is made after t and give it the symbol ${}^{>}y_i(t, \alpha)$,

$$ {}^{>}y_i(t, \alpha) = \sum_{j=1}^{N} p_{ij} y_{ij}(t, \alpha) \int_t^{\infty} d\tau \; h_{ij}(\tau) = \sum_{j=1}^{N} p_{ij} y_{ij}(t, \alpha) \; {}^{>}h_{ij}(t). \qquad (13.2.6) $$

The third term is the contribution to the expected present value from both yield rate and bonus structures for first transitions that take place before time t; we denote it by $r_i(t, \alpha)$,

$$ r_i(t, \alpha) = \sum_{j=1}^{N} p_{ij} \int_0^t d\tau \; h_{ij}(\tau)[y_{ij}(\tau, \alpha) + e^{-\alpha\tau} b_{ij}(\tau)] $$

$$ = \sum_{j=1}^{N} p_{ij} \int_0^t d\tau \; h_{ij}(\tau) \left[\int_0^{\tau} d\sigma \; e^{-\alpha\sigma} y_{ij}(\sigma) + e^{-\alpha\tau} b_{ij}(\tau) \right]. \qquad (13.2.7) $$

Then Equation 13.2.5 becomes

$$ v_i(t, \alpha) = {}^{>}y_i(t, \alpha) + e^{-\alpha t} v_i(0) \; {}^{>}w_i(t) + r_i(t, \alpha) + \sum_{j=1}^{N} p_{ij} \int_0^t d\tau \, h_{ij}(\tau) e^{-\alpha\tau} v_j(t - \tau, \alpha). $$

$$ (13.2.8) $$

Here we have expressed the expected present value of being in state i with time t remaining in the process as the sum of four terms. The first is the discounted yield rate contribution from the case where the process makes no transition during time t; the second term is the discounted terminal reward contribution for this case. The third term is the discounted contribution of both yield and bonus rewards from the first transition for the case when it occurs before t; the last term is the discounted reward from future transitions when the first transition occurs before time t.

Transform analysis

We can readily place Equation 13.2.8 in the transform domain by taking its exponential transform,

$$ v_i^e(s, \alpha) = {}^{>}y_i^e(s, \alpha) + v_i(0) \; {}^{>}w_i^e(s + \alpha) + r_i^e(s, \alpha) + \sum_{j=1}^{N} p_{ij} h_{ij}^e(s + \alpha) v_j^e(s, \alpha), $$

$$ (13.2.9) $$

where we have used conventional notation and some of the relations from the transform table. Next we put this equation in matrix form by writing each of the single subscripted quantities as a column vector, with the exception of ${}^{>}w_i^e(s + \alpha)$

which becomes the diagonal matrix ${}^{>}W^e(s + \alpha)$,

$$\mathbf{v}^e(s, \alpha) = {}^{>}\mathbf{y}^e(s, \alpha) + {}^{>}W^e(s + \alpha)\mathbf{v}(0) + \mathbf{r}^e(s, \alpha) + [P \,\square\, H^e(s + \alpha)]\mathbf{v}^e(s, \alpha). \tag{13.2.10}$$

We solve this equation for $\mathbf{v}^e(s, \alpha)$ as

$$\mathbf{v}^e(s, \alpha) = [I - P \,\square\, H^e(s + \alpha)]^{-1}[{}^{>}\mathbf{y}^e(s, \alpha) + {}^{>}W^e(s + \alpha)\mathbf{v}(0) + \mathbf{r}^e(s, \alpha)]. \tag{13.2.11}$$

Thus we have developed an expression that produces the exponential transform of the expected present values of rewards generated by the process for each starting state in terms of the exponential transforms of the process parameters. However, the complexity of this relationship in all but the simplest cases limits its use to theoretical interpretation.

Limiting Behavior

One very important result we derive from Equation 13.2.11 is the form that the column vector $\mathbf{v}(t, \alpha)$ will assume when t is large and when $\alpha > 0$. From the final value theorem we have

$$\begin{aligned}\lim_{t\to\infty} \mathbf{v}(t, \alpha) = \lim_{s\to 0} s\mathbf{v}^e(s, \alpha) &= \lim_{s\to 0} [I - P \,\square\, H^e(s + \alpha)]^{-1} \\ &\times \lim_{s\to 0} [s\, {}^{>}\mathbf{y}^e(s, \alpha) + s\, {}^{>}W^e(s + \alpha)\mathbf{v}(0) + s\mathbf{r}^e(s, \alpha)].\end{aligned} \tag{13.2.12}$$

We now consider each of these limits in turn. Of course,

$$\lim_{s\to 0} [I - (P \,\square\, H^e(s + \alpha))]^{-1} = [I - P \,\square\, H^e(\alpha)]^{-1}, \tag{13.2.13}$$

and the inverse will exist because of our provision that α is strictly greater than zero. Next we write

$$\begin{aligned}\lim_{s\to 0} s\, {}^{>}y_i^e(s, \alpha) = \lim_{t\to\infty} {}^{>}y_i(t, \alpha) &= \lim_{t\to\infty} \sum_{j=1}^{N} p_{ij} y_{ij}(t, \alpha)\, {}^{>}h_{ij}(t) \\ &= \lim_{t\to\infty} \sum_{j=1}^{N} p_{ij} y_{ij}(t, \alpha) \lim_{t\to\infty} {}^{>}h_{ij}(t) \\ &= \sum_{j=1}^{N} p_{ij} y_{ij}^e(\alpha) \cdot 0 \\ &= 0,\end{aligned} \tag{13.2.14}$$

where we have used our assumption that the present value of the yield structure rewards for any occupancy is finite.

We proceed to evaluate the limit

$$\lim_{s\to 0} s\, {}^{>}w_i^e(s+\alpha)v_i(0) = \lim_{t\to\infty} e^{-\alpha t}\, {}^{>}w_i(t)v_i(0) = 0, \tag{13.2.15}$$

which is zero because both $e^{-\alpha t}$ and ${}^{>}w_i(t)$ tend to zero when t is large. Finally we investigate

$$\lim_{s\to 0} s r_i^e(s,\alpha) = \lim_{t\to\infty} r_i(t,\alpha) = \lim_{t\to\infty} \sum_{j=1}^{N} p_{ij} \int_0^t d\tau\, h_{ij}(\tau)[y_{ij}(\tau,\alpha) + e^{-\alpha\tau}b_{ij}(\tau)]$$
$$= r_i(\infty,\alpha) \tag{13.2.16}$$

which is just the expected present value of reward from the first transition out of state i regardless of when it occurs. We give it the shorter symbol $r_i(\alpha)$,

$$r_i(\alpha) = r_i(\infty,\alpha) = \sum_{j=1}^{N} p_{ij} \int_0^\infty d\tau\, h_{ij}(\tau)[y_{ij}(\tau,\alpha) + e^{-\alpha\tau}b_{ij}(\tau)]$$
$$= \sum_{j=1}^{N} p_{ij} \int_0^\infty d\tau\, h_{ij}(\tau)\left[\int_0^\tau d\sigma\, e^{-\alpha\sigma}y_{ij}(\sigma) + e^{-\alpha\tau}b_{ij}(\tau)\right], \tag{13.2.17}$$

and let $\mathbf{r}(\alpha)$ be the column vector giving this quantity for all states.

Expected present values

Then by returning to Equation 13.2.12, we find that the vector $\mathbf{v}(t,\alpha)$ of expected discounted future rewards from starting in each state approaches a limiting vector $\mathbf{v}(\alpha)$ given by

$$\mathbf{v}(\alpha) = [I - P \,\square\, H^e(\alpha)]^{-1}\mathbf{r}(\alpha). \tag{13.2.18}$$

We observe that if we write Equation 13.2.18 in the form

$$\mathbf{v}(\alpha) = \mathbf{r}(\alpha) + P \,\square\, H^e(\alpha)\mathbf{v}(\alpha), \tag{13.2.19}$$

it implies the set of simultaneous equations

$$v_i(\alpha) = r_i(\alpha) + \sum_{j=1}^{N} p_{ij}h_{ij}^e(\alpha)v_j(\alpha) \qquad i = 1, 2, \ldots, N \tag{13.2.20}$$

which may be readily solved for the quantities $v_i(\alpha)$ representing the expected present values of occupying each state.

Thus if we want to calculate the expected present values $v_i(\alpha)$ of entering state i in a process that will continue indefinitely, we compute the expected present value of rewards from the first transition using Equation 13.2.17 and evaluate the exponential transform of each holding time distribution at the point $s = \alpha$. We then substitute these results into Equation 13.2.20 and solve for $v_i(\alpha)$.

Constant yield rates and bonuses

To illustrate this procedure let us consider the case of constant yield rates and bonuses indicated by Equation 13.1.1. We find from Equation 13.2.3

$$y_{ij}(\tau, \alpha) = \int_0^\tau d\sigma\, e^{-\alpha\sigma} y_{ij}(\sigma) = \int_0^\tau d\sigma\, e^{-\alpha\sigma} y_{ij} = y_{ij} \int_0^\tau d\sigma\, e^{-\alpha\sigma}$$

$$= \begin{cases} y_{ij} \dfrac{1}{\alpha} [1 - e^{-\alpha\tau}] & \alpha > 0 \\ y_{ij}\tau & \alpha = 0\,. \end{cases} \tag{13.2.21}$$

Then from Equation 13.2.17

$$r_i(\alpha) = \sum_{j=1}^{N} p_{ij} \int_0^\infty d\tau\, h_{ij}(\tau)[y_{ij}(\tau, \alpha) + e^{-\alpha\tau} b_{ij}(\tau)] \qquad \alpha > 0$$

$$= \sum_{j=1}^{N} p_{ij} \int_0^\infty d\tau\, h_{ij}(\tau)\left[y_{ij} \frac{1}{\alpha}(1 - e^{-\alpha\tau}) + b_{ij} e^{-\alpha\tau}\right]$$

$$= \sum_{j=1}^{N} p_{ij} y_{ij} \frac{1}{\alpha} [1 - h_{ij}{}^{e}(\alpha)] + \sum_{j=1}^{N} p_{ij} b_{ij} h_{ij}{}^{e}(\alpha)\,. \tag{13.2.22}$$

Thus in this case of constant yield and bonus structures the exponential transforms of the holding time distributions evaluated at $s = \alpha$ are as important in finding the expected present value of the first transition $r_i(\alpha)$ as they are in writing the Equations 13.2.20.

Interpretation as discounted occupancies

The interpretations of the expected present values described by Equation 13.2.18 or 13.2.20 are interesting and important to us. We develop the interpretations by considering the underlying semi-Markov process without rewards. We assume that the process will continue to make transitions and to hold in states until a time τ that is selected from the exponential density function with parameter α,

$$f_\tau(\tau_0) = \alpha e^{-\alpha\tau_0} \qquad 0 \le \tau_0\,. \tag{13.2.23}$$

Thus the mean time of operation for the process will be $1/\alpha$. We shall call a process terminated in this way a discounted process. We now calculate ${}^{d}\bar{\nu}_{ij}(\alpha)$, the expected number of times that state j will be occupied before the termination of the process if the process starts in state i and the initial occupancy is counted for $i = j$. We can write the equation

$${}^{d}\bar{\nu}_{ij}(\alpha) = \delta_{ij} + \int_0^\infty d\tau_0\, \bar{\nu}_{ij}(\tau_0)\alpha e^{-\alpha\tau_0}, \tag{13.2.24}$$

which relates ${}^{d}\bar{\nu}_{ij}(\alpha)$ to the quantity $\bar{\nu}_{ij}(\tau_0)$ developed in Chapter 11. As you recall, $\bar{\nu}_{ij}(t)$ is the expected number of times state j is occupied through time t given that the process started in state i and that the original occupancy is *not* counted when $i = j$. The quantity δ_{ij} in Equation 13.2.24 arises from the difference in treatment of the initial occupancy in the definitions of ${}^{d}\bar{\nu}_{ij}(\alpha)$ and $\nu_{ij}(\tau_0)$. The integral represents the expected number of occupancies given that the process terminates at any time τ_0, multiplied by the height of the density function for τ at τ_0, and integrated over all values of τ_0. We see immediately from the definition of the exponential transform $\bar{\nu}_{ij}{}^{e}(s)$ of $\bar{\nu}_{ij}(t)$ that Equation 13.2.24 can be written as

$$ {}^{d}\bar{\nu}_{ij}(\alpha) = \delta_{ij} + \alpha\bar{\nu}_{ij}{}^{e}(\alpha) \tag{13.2.25} $$

or in matrix form as

$$ {}^{d}\overline{\mathrm{N}}(\alpha) = I + \alpha\overline{\mathrm{N}}^{e}(\alpha). \tag{13.2.26} $$

Thus the matrix of discounted state occupancies ${}^{d}\overline{\mathrm{N}}(\alpha)$ is directly related to the exponential transform of the matrix of mean state occupancies through any time. Equation 11.12.13 of Chapter 11 shows that

$$ \overline{\mathrm{N}}^{e}(s) = \frac{1}{s}\{[I - C^{e}(s)]^{-1} - I\}. \tag{13.2.27} $$

Therefore,

$$ {}^{d}\overline{\mathrm{N}}(\alpha) = [I - C^{e}(\alpha)]^{-1} = [I - P \,\square\, H^{e}(\alpha)]^{-1}. \tag{13.2.28} $$

The matrix of discounted state occupancies is therefore equal to the inverse of I minus the exponential transform of the core matrix evaluated at $s = \alpha$.

Of course, it is evident from the definition of ${}^{d}\bar{\nu}_{ij}(\alpha)$ that the elements of ${}^{d}\overline{\mathrm{N}}(\alpha)$ must be non-negative. However, we can establish the result formally by noting that since $P \,\square\, H^{e}(\alpha)$ has all its characteristic values strictly less than one in magnitude for $\alpha > 0$,

$$ {}^{d}\overline{\mathrm{N}}(\alpha) = [I - P \,\square\, H^{e}(\alpha)]^{-1} = \sum_{m=0}^{\infty} [P \,\square\, H^{e}(\alpha)]^{m}. \tag{13.2.29} $$

Because all elements of $P \,\square\, H^{e}(\alpha)$ are non-negative, so will be all elements of ${}^{d}\overline{\mathrm{N}}(\alpha)$. Furthermore, we see that the diagonal elements of ${}^{d}\overline{\mathrm{N}}(\alpha)$ are at least equal to 1. We are thus in a position to interpret Equation 13.2.18, which we can now write as

$$ \mathbf{v}(\alpha) = {}^{d}\overline{\mathrm{N}}(\alpha)\mathbf{r}(\alpha), \tag{13.2.30} $$

or, in component form, as

$$ v_i(\alpha) = \sum_{j=1}^{N} {}^{d}\bar{\nu}_{ij}(\alpha) r_j(\alpha) \qquad i = 1, 2, \ldots, N. \tag{13.2.31} $$

The expected present value of starting in state i is therefore equal to the discounted number of state occupancies of state j for this starting state, multiplied by the expected present value of a single occupancy of state j, and summed over all states j of the process.

13.3 THE CONTINUOUS-TIME SEMI-MARKOV REWARD PROCESS WITHOUT DISCOUNTING

In modeling many operational systems the importance of discounting is negligible. Instead of dealing with expected present values we can examine total expected reward. Thus we define $v_i(t)$ to be the expected total reward the process will earn in a time t following the entrance of the process into state i, $v_i(t) = v_i(t, 0)$. We obtain the integral equation for $v_i(t)$ by writing Equation 13.2.2 with $\alpha = 0$,

$$v_i(t) = \sum_{j=1}^{N} p_{ij} \int_t^{\infty} d\tau\, h_{ij}(\tau)\left[\int_0^t d\sigma\, y_{ij}(\sigma) + v_i(0)\right]$$
$$+ \sum_{j=1}^{N} p_{ij} \int_0^t d\tau\, h_{ij}(\tau)\left[\int_0^{\tau} d\sigma\, y_{ij}(\sigma) + b_{ij}(\tau) + v_j(t-\tau)\right] \qquad \begin{array}{l} i = 1, 2, \ldots, N \\ t \geq 0. \end{array} \tag{13.3.1}$$

Now $y_{ij}(\tau, 0)$ is simply the reward the process earns from the yield structure by spending a time τ in state i before making a transition to state j,

$$y_{ij}(\tau, 0) = \int_0^{\tau} d\sigma\, y_{ij}(\sigma). \tag{13.3.2}$$

Therefore Equation 13.2.5 becomes

$$v_i(t) = \sum_{j=1}^{N} p_{ij} y_{ij}(t, 0) \int_t^{\infty} d\tau\, h_{ij}(\tau) + v_i(0) \sum_{j=1}^{N} p_{ij} \int_t^{\infty} d\tau\, h_{ij}(\tau)$$
$$+ \sum_{j=1}^{N} p_{ij} \int_0^t d\tau\, h_{ij}(\tau)[y_{ij}(\tau, 0) + b_{ij}(\tau)]$$
$$+ \sum_{j=1}^{N} p_{ij} \int_0^t d\tau\, h_{ij}(\tau) v_j(t-\tau). \tag{13.3.3}$$

Then following our earlier procedure, we let ${}^{>}y_i(t, 0)$ be the expected contribution to the total reward that is created by the yield structure in the case where the first transition occurs beyond time t,

$${}^{>}y_i(t, 0) = \sum_{j=1}^{N} p_{ij} y_{ij}(t, 0) \int_t^{\infty} d\tau\, h_{ij}(\tau) = \sum_{j=1}^{N} p_{ij} y_{ij}(t, 0)\, {}^{>}h_{ij}(t). \tag{13.3.4}$$

Similarly, we use $r_i(t, 0)$ to represent the expected profit from yield and bonus associated with the occurrence of the first transition before time t,

$$r_i(t, 0) = \sum_{j=1}^{N} p_{ij} \int_0^t d\tau\, h_{ij}(\tau)[y_{ij}(\tau, 0) + b_{ij}(\tau)]. \tag{13.3.5}$$

Then from this development or by taking $\alpha = 0$ in Equation 13.2.8 we obtain an expression for $v_i(t)$,

$$v_i(t) = {}^{>}y_i(t, 0) + v_i(0)\,{}^{>}w_i(t) + r_i(t, 0) + \sum_{j=1}^{N} p_{ij} \int_0^t d\tau\, h_{ij}(\tau) v_j(t - \tau). \tag{13.3.6}$$

We find the transform and matrix equations for the case without discounting by setting $\alpha = 0$ in Equations 13.2.9, 13.2.10, and 13.2.11:

$$v_i^e(s) = {}^{>}y_i^e(s, 0) + v_i(0)\,{}^{>}w_i^e(s) + r_i^e(s, 0) + \sum_{j=1}^{N} p_{ij} h_{ij}^e(s) v_j^e(s) \tag{13.3.7}$$

$$\mathbf{v}^e(s) = {}^{>}\mathbf{y}^e(s, 0) + {}^{>}W^e(s)\mathbf{v}(0) + \mathbf{r}^e(s, 0) + [P \,\square\, H^e(s)]\mathbf{v}^e(s) \tag{13.3.8}$$

$$\mathbf{v}^e(s) = [I - P \,\square\, H^e(s)]^{-1}[{}^{>}\mathbf{y}^e(s, 0) + {}^{>}W^e(s)\mathbf{v}(0) + \mathbf{r}^e(s, 0)] \tag{13.3.9}$$

Once more, this expression for the transform of the expected reward in time t for each starting state has more theoretical than practical uses. We ask again about the form of $v_i(t)$ when t is large. Since there is no discounting, we expected $v_i(t)$ to grow without bound as t increases—the only question is the type of growth.

Limiting Behavior

We begin our analysis of limiting behavior by writing Equation 13.3.9 in the form

$$\begin{aligned} \mathbf{v}^e(s) &= [I - P \,\square\, H^e(s)]^{-1}[\mathbf{r}^e(s, 0) + {}^{>}\mathbf{y}^e(s, 0)] + [I - P \,\square\, H^e(s)]^{-1}\,{}^{>}W^e(s)\mathbf{v}(0) \\ &= E^e(s)[\mathbf{r}^e(s, 0) + {}^{>}\mathbf{y}^e(s, 0)] + \Phi^e(s)\mathbf{v}(0), \end{aligned} \tag{13.3.10}$$

where we have substituted the exponentially transformed entrance probability matrix $E^e(s)$ from Equation 11.9.8 and the exponentially transformed interval transition probability matrix from Equation 11.5.6. To explore the behavior of $\mathbf{v}(t)$ when t is large, we first investigate the asymptotic properties of the terms in Equation 13.3.10.

Thus $r_i^e(s, 0)$ is the exponential transform of $r_i(t, 0)$ from Equation 13.3.5. When t is large, $r_i(t, 0)$ is just the expected reward from the first transition out of state i, a quantity we have already defined as $r_i(0)$ in Equation 13.2.17. Therefore the time function $r_i(t, 0)$ has a step component of magnitude $r_i(0)$ plus some other transient components that vanish for large values of t. We shall call its transient component $u_i(t)$ and write $r_i(t, 0)$ as

$$r_i(t, 0) = r_i(0) + u_i(t) \tag{13.3.11}$$

or in the transform domain as

$$r_i^e(s, 0) = \frac{1}{s} r_i(0) + u_i^e(s). \tag{13.3.12}$$

Then in vector form we have

$$\mathbf{r}^e(s, 0) = \frac{1}{s} \mathbf{r}(0) + \mathbf{u}^e(s). \tag{13.3.13}$$

The exponential transform ${}^{>}y_i^e(s, 0)$ is the transform of the time function ${}^{>}y_i(t, 0)$ defined in Equation 13.3.4. Since ${}^{>}y_i(t, 0)$ is the contribution to the expected total reward from having the first transition made beyond t, this quantity approaches zero when t is very large. Therefore ${}^{>}y_i^e(s, 0)$ and its vector form ${}^{>}\mathbf{y}^e(s, 0)$ exhibit no step component.

The other terms $E^e(s)$ and $\Phi^e(s)$ in Equation 13.3.10 have asymptotic forms that we have studied in detail. The entrance rate matrix for the semi-Markov process has a step component of magnitude E defined in Equation 11.9.11. We can express the transform $E^e(s)$ as the sum of the transform of this step component and a matrix of transforms $T^e(s)$ representing the transient components that vanish for large t,

$$E^e(s) = \left[\frac{1}{s} E + T^e(s)\right]. \tag{13.3.14}$$

Of course, the matrix $\Phi^e(s)$ also contains a step component represented by $(1/s)\Phi$ plus a matrix of transformed transient components that we shall call $T_\phi^e(s)$,

$$\Phi^e(s) = \left[\frac{1}{s} \Phi + T_\phi^e(s)\right]. \tag{13.3.15}$$

We are ready to substitute all these transform expressions into Equation 13.3.10,

$$\begin{aligned}\mathbf{v}^e(s) &= \left[\frac{1}{s} E + T^e(s)\right]\left[\frac{1}{s} \mathbf{r}(0) + \mathbf{u}^e(s) + {}^{>}\mathbf{y}^e(s, 0)\right] + \left[\frac{1}{s} \Phi + T_\phi^e(s)\right]\mathbf{v}(0) \\ &= \frac{1}{s^2} E\mathbf{r}(0) + \frac{1}{s} E\mathbf{u}^e(s) + \frac{1}{s} E\, {}^{>}y^e(s, 0) + \frac{1}{s} T^e(s)\mathbf{r}(0) \\ &\quad + T^e(s)\mathbf{u}^e(s) + T^e(s)\, {}^{>}y^e(s, 0) + \frac{1}{s} \Phi\mathbf{v}(0) + T_\phi^e(s)\mathbf{v}(0). \end{aligned} \tag{13.3.16}$$

We now identify which of these transform terms correspond to time components that will persist for large t. The term $(1/s^2)E\mathbf{r}(0)$ is easy to interpret: it represents the ramp component $tE\mathbf{r}(0)$, the asymptotic linear growth of $v(t)$ with t. The term $(1/s)E\mathbf{u}^e(s)$ contains a step component whose magnitude we evaluate by multiplying the term by s and evaluating the result at $s = 0$; we find that it is $E\mathbf{u}^e(0)$. Similarly, the term $(1/s)E\, {}^{>}\mathbf{y}^e(s, 0)$ contains a step of magnitude $E\, {}^{>}\mathbf{y}^e(0, 0)$, and the term $(1/s)T^e(0)\mathbf{r}(0)$ contains a step of magnitude $T^e(0)\mathbf{r}(0)$. The terms $T^e(s)\mathbf{u}^e(s)$

and $T^e(s)\ {}^{>}y^e(s, 0)$ contain only transient components and therefore do not contribute to $\mathbf{v}(t)$ when t is large. Finally, the term $(1/s)\Phi\mathbf{v}(0)$ is a step of magnitude $\Phi\mathbf{v}(0)$, while the term $T_\phi{}^e(s)\mathbf{v}(0)$ contains only transient components.

The Limiting Form

Therefore when t is large we are able to express $v(t)$ in terms of ramp and step components as

$$\mathbf{v}(t) = tE\mathbf{r}(0) + E[\mathbf{u}^e(0) + {}^{>}\mathbf{y}^e(0, 0)] + T^e(0)\mathbf{r}(0) + \Phi\mathbf{v}(0) \qquad \text{for large } t. \quad (13.3.17)$$

We can gain further insight by examining each of these terms. The matrix E is the matrix of limiting entrance rates for the process. The vector $\mathbf{r}(0)$ is a vector giving for each state the expected reward that will be generated as a direct result of entering that state. Since the entrance rates give the rate of entering each state per unit time and the reward vector $\mathbf{r}(0)$ gives the expected reward from each entrance, it is satisfying and intuitive that the rate of growth of expected total reward in the steady state should be just the product of these quantities.

Note that we have not required that the imbedded process be monodesmic; therefore the rows of E can be different. This means that the rate of growth of total reward can be different for different starting states. Of course, for a monodesmic process the asymptotic rate of growth of expected total reward would be the same for each state in which the process might be started. We define g_i as the asymptotic rate of growth of total reward if the process is started in state i and call it the "gain" of the process under the condition that the process is started in state i. For a monodesmic process the same gain g will apply for any starting condition. In this case we speak of g as the gain of the process without ambiguity.

Let us next examine $\mathbf{u}^e(0)$. Since the exponential transform evaluated at $s = 0$ is the integral under the inverse of the transform, the quantity $u_i^e(0)$ is just $\int_0^\infty dt\ u_i(t)$ or, in view of Equation 13.3.11, the integral of the difference between $r_i(t, 0)$ and its step component $r_i(0)$. Using Equation 13.3.5, we have

$$\begin{aligned} u_i^e(0) &= \int_0^\infty dt\ u_i(t) = \int_0^\infty dt\ [r_i(t, 0) - r_i(0)] \\ &= \int_0^\infty dt \left[\sum_{j=1}^N p_{ij} \int_0^t d\tau\ h_{ij}(\tau)[y_{ij}(\tau, 0) + b_{ij}(\tau)] \right. \\ &\qquad \left. - \sum_{j=1}^N p_{ij} \int_0^\infty d\tau\ h_{ij}(\tau)[y_{ij}(\tau, 0) + b_{ij}(\tau)]\right] \\ &= -\int_0^\infty dt \sum_{j=1}^\infty p_{ij} \int_t^\infty d\tau\ h_{ij}(\tau)[y_{ij}(\tau, 0) + b_{ij}(\tau)] \end{aligned}$$

$$= -\int_0^\infty d\tau \sum_{j=1}^N p_{ij} \int_0^\tau dt\, h_{ij}(\tau)[y_{ij}(\tau, 0) + b_{ij}(\tau)]$$

$$= -\sum_{j=1}^N p_{ij} \int_0^\infty d\tau\, h_{ij}(\tau) \cdot \tau \cdot [y_{ij}(\tau, 0) + b_{ij}(\tau)]. \qquad (13.3.18)$$

Therefore we can interpret $u_i^e(0)$ as the negative of the expected value of the product of the holding time and total reward associated with the first transition out of state i.

Using the same reasoning, we evaluate the term ${}^{>}\mathbf{y}^e(0, 0)$. The quantity ${}^{>}y_i^e(0, 0)$ is just the integral of ${}^{>}y_i(t, 0)$ from Equation 13.3.4,

$${}^{>}y_i^e(0, 0) = \int_0^\infty dt\, {}^{>}y_i(t, 0) = \int_0^\infty dt \sum_{j=1}^N p_{ij} y_{ij}(t, 0) \int_t^\infty d\tau\, h_{ij}(\tau)$$

$$= \sum_{j=1}^N p_{ij} \int_0^\infty d\tau\, h_{ij}(\tau) \int_0^\tau dt\, y_{ij}(t, 0)$$

$$= \sum_{j=1}^N p_{ij} \int_0^\infty d\tau\, h_{ij}(\tau) \int_0^\tau dt \int_0^t d\sigma\, y_{ij}(\sigma). \qquad (13.3.19)$$

Thus ${}^{>}y_i^e(0, 0)$ is the expectation for the first transition out of state i of the yield rate integrated twice with respect to time during the holding time of the first transition. If we combine the results of Equations 13.3.18 and 13.3.19 we have

$$u_i^e(0) + {}^{>}y_i^e(0, 0) = \sum_{j=1}^N p_{ij} \int_0^\infty d\tau\, h_{ij}(\tau)\left[\int_0^\tau dt\, y_{ij}(t, 0) - \tau[y_{ij}(\tau, 0) + b_{ij}(\tau)]\right]. \qquad (13.3.20)$$

This quantity is zero if the bonuses are zero and if the yield rates are impulses that occur when state i is entered. Thus $u_i^e(0) + {}^{>}y_i^e(0, 0)$ is associated with the time of generation of rewards during each occupancy of state i. Finally $E[\mathbf{u}^e(0) + {}^{>}\mathbf{y}^e(0, 0)]$ represents the weighting of these quantities by the limiting entrance rates for each state.

Next we examine the component $T^e(0)\mathbf{r}(0)$. The matrix $T^e(0)$ has an interesting and important interpretation that we have encountered before. Equations 11.12.15 and 11.12.16 show that the transformed mean state occupancy matrix $\overline{\text{N}}^e(s)$ is related to the transformed entrance rate matrix by

$$\overline{\text{N}}^e(s) = \frac{1}{s} E^e(s) \qquad (13.3.21)$$

for the case where the initial occupancies of each state are counted. If we write $E^e(s)$ in the form of Equation 13.3.14, then we have

$$\overline{\mathrm{N}}^e(s) = \frac{1}{s}\left[\frac{1}{s}E + T^e(s)\right] = \frac{1}{s^2}E + \frac{1}{s}T^e(s). \qquad (13.3.22)$$

This transform equation shows that the mean state occupancy matrix has a ramp component of magnitude E and a step component of magnitude $T^e(0)$; all other components vanish for large t. Therefore we can write $\overline{\mathrm{N}}(t)$ asymptotically as

$$\overline{\mathrm{N}}(t) = Et + T^e(0) \qquad \text{for large } t, \qquad (13.3.23)$$

an equation that provides considerable insight into the process. The ramp component of magnitude E in the expected number of state occupancies is directly responsible for the gain term $E\mathbf{r}(0)$ in the expression for $v(t)$ of Equation 13.3.17. The fact that expected occupancies grow linearly with time requires that the rewards grow linearly with time.

The quantity $T^e(0)$ represents the contribution to the expected number of occupancies caused by starting in one state rather than another. Thus $t_{ij}{}^e(0)$ is the difference in the expected number of occupancies of state j in an infinite time caused by starting the process in state i rather than simply entering some state of the process at a random time. Consequently $T^e(0)\mathbf{r}(0)$ is the column vector which shows for each state the difference in reward caused by starting the process in that state rather than starting it with steady-state conditions.

The final term $\Phi\mathbf{v}(0)$ in Equation 13.3.17 is the expected contribution from the terminal reward structure. Each terminal reward $v_j(0)$ is multiplied by the probability ϕ_{ij} that the process will be in state j after a very long time if it is started in state i.

We have now evaluated each term in Equation 13.3.17. We have found that the linear growth of $v(t)$ for large t is caused by the linear growth of state occupancies and that the step components of $v(t)$ arise from (1) the interaction of the probabilistic and reward structure during a holding time, (2) the difference in the expected number of state occupancies caused by starting in one state rather than another, and (3) the probability of receiving each terminal reward after a long time. If the process is monodesmic, then the rows of the E matrix are identical and the rows of the Φ matrix are identical. In this case the step components in $v_i(t)$ arising from $E[\mathbf{u}^e(0) + {}^{>}y^e(0, 0)]$ and $\Phi\mathbf{v}(0)$ are the same for all values of i. Only the step component $T^e(0)\mathbf{r}(0)$ will be different for each state i. Thus differences in the step component of expected reward for a monodesmic process arise only from differences in the expected number of state occupancies. Of course, these differences in the step component of expected reward are the real reason for preferring to start the process in one state rather than in another.

Gain

Let us now summarize these considerations by placing Equation 13.3.17 in a more compact form. First we simplify our notation by letting r_i represent $r_i(0)$, the expected total reward from the first occupancy of state i, given by Equation 13.2.17 as

$$r_i = r_i(0) = \sum_{j=1}^{N} p_{ij} \int_0^\infty d\tau \; h_{ij}(\tau)[y_{ij}(\tau, 0) + b_{ij}(\tau)]$$

$$= \sum_{j=1}^{N} p_{ij} \int_0^\infty d\tau \; h_{ij}(\tau)\left[\int_0^\tau d\sigma \; y_{ij}(\sigma) + b_{ij}(\tau)\right]. \tag{13.3.24}$$

Then we can write Equation 13.3.17 in component form as

$$v_i(t) = g_i t + v_i \qquad \text{for large } t, \tag{13.3.25}$$

where

$$g_i = \sum_{j=1}^{N} e_{ij} r_j \tag{13.3.26}$$

and v_i is the total magnitude of the step component of $v_i(t)$. We can express g_i, the gain conditional on starting in state i, in an alternate form by using the fact that $\phi_{ij} = e_{ij}\bar{\tau}_j$,

$$g_i = \sum_{j=1}^{N} \phi_{ij} \frac{r_j}{\bar{\tau}_j}. \tag{13.3.27}$$

If we define $r_j/\bar{\tau}_j$ to be q_j, the earning rate of state j,

$$q_j = \frac{r_j}{\bar{\tau}_j}, \tag{13.3.28}$$

then the gain conditional on starting in state i is just

$$g_i = \sum_{j=1}^{N} \phi_{ij} q_j, \tag{13.3.29}$$

the earning rates weighted by the limiting interval transition probabilities of each state conditional on starting in state i.

Gain in a monodesmic process

These relations become simpler for a monodesmic process. Thus in this case

$$v_i(t) = gt + v_i. \tag{13.3.30}$$

We have already observed that the step component v_i depends on i only because of the difference in the step components of expected state occupancies. However, the gain g is now the same for all states,

$$g = \sum_{j=1}^{N} e_j r_j = \sum_{j=1}^{N} \phi_j \frac{r_j}{\bar{\tau}_j} = \sum_{j=1}^{N} \phi_j q_j. \tag{13.3.31}$$

The expected average reward earned per unit time in the steady state is therefore the earning rates of the process weighted by the limiting interval transition probabilities.

If we introduce the limiting state probabilities π_i of the imbedded process, we can alternately express the gain as

$$g = \sum_{j=1}^{N} \phi_j q_j = \frac{\sum_{j=1}^{N} \pi_j \bar{\tau}_j q_j}{\sum_{j=1}^{N} \pi_j \bar{\tau}_j} = \frac{\sum_{j=1}^{N} \pi_j r_j}{\sum_{j=1}^{N} \pi_j \bar{\tau}_j} = \frac{\bar{r}}{\bar{\tau}}. \tag{13.3.32}$$

This relation shows that the gain is equal to the expected reward per occupancy divided by the mean time between transitions in the steady state.

Gain as equivalent annuital reward rate

Another interpretation of the gain is sometimes useful: The gain of a state is the equivalent annuital reward rate associated with the state as the discount rate approaches zero. From Equation 13.1.7,

$$g_i = \lim_{\alpha \to 0} \alpha v_i(\alpha). \tag{13.3.33}$$

Note that this result follows directly from the final value theorem for exponential transforms. If the process is monodesmic then the limit is the same for all i,

$$g = \lim_{\alpha \to 0} \alpha v_i(\alpha) \qquad i = 1, 2, \ldots, N. \tag{13.3.34}$$

Direct Gain Evaluation

We could readily find the gain of a monodesmic process by finding the limiting interval transition probabilities and then using them to weight the earning rates. However, finding the step components of value v_i would involve quite a large amount of manipulation. If we are interested only in which state of the process we would prefer to use as a starting state, then we would be happy to know the quantities v_i to within a constant because only the differences in the v_i's for different states would be significant to us. Happily, we have a direct method for finding the v_i's to within a constant.

The relative value equations

We begin by considering the form of Equation 13.3.6 when t is large. As we have already discussed, the terms ${}^{>}y_i(t, 0)$ and $v_i(0)\,{}^{>}w_i(t)$ vanish for large t. The term $r_i(t, 0)$ becomes $r_i(0) = r_i$, the expected reward from an occupancy of state i. Thus for large t we have

$$v_i(t) = r_i + \sum_{j=1}^{N} p_{ij} \int_0^\infty d\tau\, h_{ij}(\tau) v_j(t - \tau) \qquad \text{for large } t. \qquad (13.3.35)$$

Now we substitute for $v_i(t)$ and $v_j(t - \tau)$ the limiting form of Equation 13.3.30,

$$gt + v_i = r_i + \sum_{j=1}^{N} p_{ij} \int_0^\infty d\tau\, h_{ij}(\tau)[g(t - \tau) + v_j]$$

$$= r_i + gt - g\bar{\tau}_i + \sum_{j=1}^{N} p_{ij} v_j \qquad \text{for large } t \qquad (13.3.36)$$

and obtain

$$v_i + g\bar{\tau}_i = r_i + \sum_{j=1}^{N} p_{ij} v_j \qquad i = 1, 2, \ldots, N. \qquad (13.3.37)$$

Equation 13.3.37 relates the gain and the step components of expected total reward v_i to the expected rewards per occupancy r_i, the mean waiting times $\bar{\tau}_i$, and the transition probabilities p_{ij}. Note, however, that this set of equations is unchanged if we add the same constant to all v_i's; therefore, we can use these equations to find the v_i's only within a constant. We accomplish this by setting one of them, say v_N, equal to 0, and then solving the N equations for the gain g and the remaining $N - 1$ v_i's. We shall call the v_i's generated in this way the "relative values" of each state because we do not know their absolute magnitude. If the process is monodesmic, using this technique for solving Equation 13.3.37 will always provide a unique solution for the gain and relative values. Since, as we have already remarked, the relative values are the only quantities necessary for selecting the best starting state for an infinite duration process, we have found a simple method for making this decision.

We obtain a confirmation of one of our earlier results by multiplying Equation 13.3.37 by the limiting state probability of state i, π_i, and then summing over all values of i,

$$\sum_{i=1}^{N} \pi_i v_i + g \sum_{i=1}^{N} \pi_i \bar{\tau}_i = \sum_{i=1}^{N} \pi_i r_i + \sum_{i=1}^{N} \pi_i \sum_{j=1}^{N} p_{ij} v_j$$

$$= \sum_{i=1}^{N} \pi_i r_i + \sum_{j=1}^{N} v_j \sum_{i=1}^{N} \pi_i p_{ij}. \qquad (13.3.38)$$

But $\sum_{j=1}^{N} \pi_i p_{ij} = \pi_j$ and therefore the first and last terms of this equation are identical. Thus we obtain

$$g = \frac{\sum_{i=1}^{N} \pi_i r_i}{\sum_{i=1}^{N} \pi_i \bar{\tau}_i} = \sum_{i=1}^{N} \frac{\phi_i}{\bar{\tau}_i} r_i = \sum_{i=1}^{N} \phi_i q_i, \tag{13.3.39}$$

the same results expressed in Equations 13.3.31 and 13.3.32.

As a final point we shall note that if the yield rates and bonus are the constants shown in Equation 13.1.1, then the expected total reward r_i from a single occupancy of state i is computed from Equation 13.3.24 to be

$$\begin{aligned} r_i = r_i(0) &= \sum_{j=1}^{N} p_{ij} \int_0^\infty d\tau\, h_{ij}(\tau)\left[\int_0^\tau d\sigma\, y_{ij}(\sigma) + b_{ij}(\tau)\right] \\ &= \sum_{j=1}^{N} p_{ij} \int_0^\infty d\tau\, h_{ij}(\tau)[y_{ij}\tau + b_{ij}] \\ &= \sum_{j=1}^{N} p_{ij}[y_{ij}\bar{\tau}_{ij} + b_{ij}], \end{aligned} \tag{13.3.40}$$

a simple and intuitive result.

Gains in Polydesmic Processes

When the process is not monodesmic, the problem of finding the gain g_i and relative value v_i for each state becomes slightly more complicated. We must note first that the relative value of any state is meaningful only in comparing its expected earnings with those of other states in the same chain. To develop a convenient procedure for computing the gains and relative values of a multiple-chain process, we substitute the asymptotic form, Equation 13.3.25, into the asymptotic Equation 13.3.35 to obtain

$$\begin{aligned} g_i t + v_i &= r_i + \sum_{j=1}^{N} p_{ij} \int_0^\infty d\tau\, h_{ij}(\tau)[g_j(t - \tau) + v_j] \\ &= r_i + t\sum_{j=1}^{N} p_{ij} g_j - \sum_{j=1}^{N} p_{ij}\bar{\tau}_{ij} g_j + \sum_{j=1}^{N} p_{ij} v_j \qquad i = 1, 2, \ldots, N; \text{ for large } t. \end{aligned} \tag{13.3.41}$$

Since these equations must hold for any large value of t, by equating the coefficients of t and the constant terms in these equations, we develop the relations

$$g_i = \sum_{j=1}^{N} p_{ij} g_j \qquad i = 1, 2, \ldots, N \tag{13.3.42}$$

and

$$v_i = r_i - \sum_{j=1}^{N} p_{ij}\bar{\tau}_{ij} g_j + \sum_{j=1}^{N} p_{ij} v_j \qquad i = 1, 2, \ldots, N. \tag{13.3.43}$$

We observe that Equation 13.3.43 is invariant to the addition of a constant to all v_i's; we can set the value of one state in each chain equal to zero and find the values of other states in that chain relative to that state. These values are the relative values. Therefore, to find the complete set of gains and relative values for the process, we set the value of one state in each chain equal to zero and then solve the combined Equations 13.3.42 and 13.3.43 to produce the relative values of the remaining states and the gains of all states. Once we have set one relative value in each chain equal to zero, the combined equations will always have a unique solution.

We note that if the process is in fact monodesmic, then all $g_i = g$ and Equations 13.3.42 and 13.3.43 reduce to Equation 13.3.37. A more interesting, if less practical, case that demonstrates the use of the combined equations arises when the transition probability matrix for the process is the N by N identity matrix. In this case Equation 13.3.42 states only that $g_i = g_i$—a hardly informative result. However, because we know that there are N chains since each state is a trapping state, we must set the relative values v_i for all states equal to zero. Equation 13.3.43 then becomes

$$r_i = \sum_{j=1}^{N} p_{ij}\bar{\tau}_{ij} g_j = \bar{\tau}_{ii} g_i \tag{13.3.44}$$

or

$$g_i = \frac{r_i}{\bar{\tau}_{ii}} = q_i \qquad i = 1, 2, \ldots, N. \tag{13.3.45}$$

The gain of each state is therefore equal to its earning rate, as we would expect.

In most problems we can avoid the difficulty of multiple chains by carefully formulating the process model. The existence of multiple chains often means that we have not devoted enough effort to separating the problem into independent parts.

An Inventory Example

The semi-Markov process with a reward structure is an excellent model for many stochastic processes. It offers a method by which general results can often be obtained with little difficulty. For example, consider the problem of establishing the order quantity Q for an inventory system with the following characteristics. A single item is subject to random demand with the time between successive demands selected independently from the same probability density function; mean time between demands is $1/\lambda$. No stockouts are permitted, leadtime is zero (orders arrive immediately), there is a fixed cost a of placing an order, and a carrying charge of r per unit time to be assessed against each item in inventory.

Probabilistic structure

We see that we can model this inventory system as a semi-Markov process whose state index i represents the number of items in inventory at any time. The state index can range from 1 to Q, the order quantity. The state index cannot be zero because when the last item in inventory is sold, the amount of stock in inventory jumps instantaneously to Q. The transition probability structure is therefore very simple: The imbedded Markov process is periodic with period Q.

The transition diagram appears as Figure 13.3.1. The state index falls by one unit with each transition (demand) unless there is only one unit in inventory in

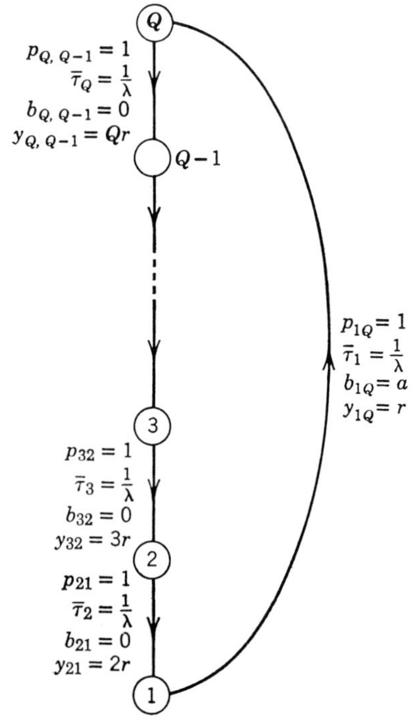

Figure 13.3.1 Transition diagram for an inventory problem.

which case it becomes Q. Therefore the limiting state probability for each state in the imbedded Markov process is just $1/Q$,

$$\pi_i = \frac{1}{Q} \qquad i = 1, 2, \ldots, Q. \tag{13.3.46}$$

The holding time in every state is the density function of time between demands. The mean holding time in any state is therefore

$$\bar{\tau}_i = \frac{1}{\lambda} \qquad i = 1, 2, \ldots, Q. \tag{13.3.47}$$

Since the expected holding time in all states is the same, we know that the limiting interval transition probabilities ϕ_i will be equal to the limiting state probabilities π_i,

$$\phi_i = \pi_i = \frac{1}{Q} \qquad i = 1, 2, \ldots, Q. \tag{13.3.48}$$

Reward structure

The reward structure for this example is also simple. Since this system can only lose money, we shall deal in costs rather than rewards. There is no bonus cost associated with any transition except the transition from state 1 to state Q. The cost associated with this transition is the ordering cost,

$$\begin{aligned} b_{1Q} &= a \\ b_{ij} &= 0 \qquad \text{otherwise}. \end{aligned} \tag{13.3.49}$$

The yield rate in any state is the inventory carrying charge rate of that state. For state i this will be ir,

$$y_{ij} = ir \qquad \begin{matrix} i = 1, 2, \ldots, Q \\ j = 1, 2, \ldots, Q. \end{matrix} \tag{13.3.50}$$

The reward structure also appears in Figure 13.3.1.

We can now calculate the earning rate in each state using Equations 13.3.28 and 13.3.40. We find

$$\begin{aligned} q_i = \frac{r_i}{\bar{\tau}_i} &= \frac{1}{\bar{\tau}_i}\left[\sum_{j=1}^{Q} p_{ij}(y_{ij}\bar{\tau}_{ij} + b_{ij})\right] \qquad i = 1, 2, \ldots, Q \\ &= \begin{cases} \dfrac{1}{\bar{\tau}_i}[y_{i,i-1}\bar{\tau}_i + b_{i,i-1}] & i = 2, 3, \ldots, Q \\ \dfrac{1}{\bar{\tau}_1}[y_{1Q}\bar{\tau}_1 + b_{1Q}] & i = 1 \end{cases} \\ &= \begin{cases} y_{i,i-1} & i = 2, 3, \ldots, Q \\ y_{1Q} + \dfrac{1}{\bar{\tau}_1} b_{1Q} & i = 1 \end{cases} \\ &= \begin{cases} ir & i = 2, 3, \ldots, Q \\ r + \lambda a & i = 1. \end{cases} \end{aligned} \tag{13.3.51}$$

Gain

Now that we have obtained both the limiting interval transition probabilities and the earning rates for the system, we can use Equation 13.3.31 to write the gain, which in this case is the average cost per unit time of operating the system in the steady state. We find

$$
\begin{aligned}
g &= \sum_{i=1}^{Q} \phi_i q_i = \frac{1}{Q} \sum_{i=1}^{Q} q_i \\
&= \frac{1}{Q} \left[\lambda a + r \sum_{i=1}^{Q} i \right] \\
&= \frac{1}{Q} \left[\lambda a + r \frac{Q(Q+1)}{2} \right] \\
&= \frac{\lambda a}{Q} + \frac{r(Q+1)}{2} .
\end{aligned}
\tag{13.3.52}
$$

All that remains is to find the value of Q that minimizes this average cost rate. If we assume that Q is large, we can ignore the discrete nature of Q, differentiate g with respect to Q, and set the derivative equal to zero. We find that the minimizing Q is given by

$$
Q = \sqrt{\frac{2a\lambda}{r}} \tag{13.3.53}
$$

which is, of course, the famous Wilson lot-size formula. The best integral value of Q can be found by direct evaluation, if necessary.

Note that the generality of the semi-Markov process has allowed us to establish this result for demand processes that range from Poisson to constant time between purchases. Such modifications as quantity-dependent ordering costs and inter-demand distributions that depend on the inventory level would complicate the model only slightly. Even the problem of multiple-demands occurring at the same time can be treated. The freedom to expand the problem under consideration in several interesting ways at small increase in difficulty is a particularly appealing feature of semi-Markov models.

Reprise

We have now analyzed the introduction of rewards to the continuous-time semi-Markov process. In the case where future rewards must be discounted, we have obtained transform equations for the expected present value of starting in each state and operating for a finite time interval. We also developed simultaneous equations that could be solved to give the expected present value of starting in each state when the process was going to operate indefinitely.

In the case where no discounting of future rewards was necessary, we produced transform equations for finding the expected total reward in a time period for a given starting state. We found that this expected total reward grows linearly with time when the time interval was large and developed an asymptotic expression for this growth. Finally, we developed ways of evaluating the asymptotic expressions for expected total reward to within a constant. These capabilities are important both for analyzing systems with rewards and, as we shall see later, for controlling such systems.

13.4 THE CAR RENTAL EXAMPLE AGAIN

As a vehicle for studying rewards in a continuous-time semi-Markov process let us turn once more to the continuous-time version of the car rental example whose transition diagram appears in Figure 11.2.1. Recall that the state of the system represents the town at which a car was last rented. We shall now add a reward structure to describe the income of the rental company. We assume that this structure has the form

$$y_{ij}(\tau) = 0 \qquad b_{ij}(\tau) = f_i\tau + f_{ij}. \tag{13.4.1}$$

The yield rate is zero because the company receives no income during the actual period of rental. However, if the car is rented in town i the company charges a rental fee f_i per unit time that the car is rented and a drop charge f_{ij} if the car is returned in town j; *the company receives its payment when the car is returned.* We assume that there is no drop charge if the car is returned to the same town at which it was rented. We shall think of the basic time unit as one week and use the following numerical values for the reward structure:

$$\begin{aligned} f_1 &= 120 \qquad f_{11} = 0 \qquad f_{12} = 45 \\ f_2 &= 60 \qquad f_{21} = 40 \qquad f_{22} = 0 \end{aligned} \tag{13.4.2}$$

Thus car rental in town 2 is more economical than rental in town 1 both because the charge per week is 1/2 as large and because the drop charge for leaving the car in town 1 is 5 less than it would be in the reverse situation. Our task is to examine the company's expected earnings using this charge structure. Of course, we assume that the transition probabilities and holding time densities used for the process exist in the presence of this reward structure.

Analysis with Discounting

Although discounting would be a very minor factor in the real life situation corresponding to this example, we shall carry out an analysis that includes discounting to see the form of the results. We shall calculate $v_1(\alpha)$ and $v_2(\alpha)$, the expected present values of all future rewards from the process conditional on just having rented a car in town 1 or in town 2; there will be no limits on the duration of the process. We use Equation 13.2.18 for our calculations and therefore begin by computing $\mathbf{r}(\alpha)$, the vector showing the expected present value of rewards attributable to a single occupancy of each state. From Equations 13.2.17 and 13.4.1 we have

$$\begin{aligned} r_i(\alpha) &= \sum_{j=1}^{N} p_{ij} \int_0^\infty d\tau\, h_{ij}(\tau)[y_{ij}(\tau, \alpha) + e^{-\alpha\tau} b_{ij}(\tau)] \\ &= \sum_{j=1}^{N} p_{ij} \int_0^\infty d\tau\, h_{ij}(\tau) e^{-\alpha\tau} b_{ij}(\tau) \\ &= \sum_{j=1}^{N} p_{ij} \int_0^\infty d\tau\, h_{ij}(\tau) e^{-\alpha\tau} [f_i \tau + f_{ij}] \\ &= f_i \sum_{j=1}^{N} p_{ij} \int_0^\infty d\tau\, h_{ij}(\tau) e^{-\alpha\tau} \tau + \sum_{j=1}^{N} p_{ij} f_{ij} \int_0^\infty d\tau\, h_{ij}(\tau) e^{-\alpha\tau} \\ &= f_i \sum_{j=1}^{N} p_{ij} \left(-\frac{d}{d\alpha} h_{ij}{}^e(\alpha) \right) + \sum_{j=1}^{N} p_{ij} f_{ij} h_{ij}{}^e(\alpha). \end{aligned} \tag{13.4.3}$$

Thus the discounted rewards from the first occupancy depend on the fee structure, the transition probabilities, the exponential transforms of the holding time density functions, and the derivatives of these transforms with respect to their arguments.

From the data for the continuous-time semi-Markov process in Equations 11.2.1 and 11.2.4 we have

$$P = \begin{bmatrix} 0.8 & 0.2 \\ 0.3 & 0.7 \end{bmatrix} \quad H^e(s) = \begin{bmatrix} \dfrac{4}{s+4} & \dfrac{2}{s+2} \\ \dfrac{3}{s+3} & \dfrac{1}{s+1} \end{bmatrix} \quad -\frac{d}{ds} H^e(s) = \begin{bmatrix} \dfrac{4}{(s+4)^2} & \dfrac{2}{(s+2)^2} \\ \dfrac{3}{(s+3)^2} & \dfrac{1}{(s+1)^2} \end{bmatrix}. \tag{13.4.4}$$

Then we compute

$$r_1(\alpha) = f_1\left[p_{11}\left(-\frac{d}{d\alpha} h_{11}{}^e(\alpha)\right) + p_{12}\left(-\frac{d}{d\alpha} h_{12}{}^e(\alpha)\right)\right] + p_{11} f_{11} h_{11}{}^e(\alpha) + p_{12} f_{12} h_{12}{}^e(\alpha)$$

$$r_2(\alpha) = f_2\left[p_{21}\left(-\frac{d}{d\alpha} h_{21}{}^e(\alpha)\right) + p_{22}\left(-\frac{d}{d\alpha} h_{22}{}^e(\alpha)\right)\right] + p_{21} f_{21} h_{21}{}^e(\alpha) + p_{22} f_{22} h_{22}{}^e(\alpha) \tag{13.4.5}$$

and, with the numerical values,

$$
\begin{aligned}
r_1(\alpha) &= 120\left[0.8\frac{4}{(\alpha+4)^2} + 0.2\frac{2}{(\alpha+2)^2}\right] + 0 + 0.2(45)\frac{2}{\alpha+2} \\
&= \frac{384}{(\alpha+4)^2} + \frac{48}{(\alpha+2)^2} + \frac{18}{\alpha+2} \\
r_2(\alpha) &= 60\left[0.3\frac{3}{(\alpha+3)^2} + 0.7\frac{1}{(\alpha+1)^2}\right] + 0.3(40)\frac{3}{\alpha+3} + 0 \\
&= \frac{54}{(\alpha+3)^2} + \frac{42}{(\alpha+1)^2} + \frac{36}{\alpha+3}.
\end{aligned}
\tag{13.4.6}
$$

We have thus expressed the expected present value of a single occupancy of each state under the discount rate α.

The expected present values

Now we employ Equation 13.2.18 to write $\mathbf{v}(\alpha)$ using the expression for $[I - P \,\square\, H^e(s)]^{-1}$ from Equation 11.5.13,

$$\mathbf{v}(\alpha) = [I - P \,\square\, H^e(\alpha)]^{-1}\mathbf{r}(\alpha) \tag{13.4.7}$$

or

$$
\begin{bmatrix} v_1(\alpha) \\ v_2(\alpha) \end{bmatrix} = \frac{(\alpha+1)(\alpha+2)(\alpha+3)(\alpha+4)}{\alpha(\alpha^3 + 6.1\alpha^2 + 11.38\alpha + 6)} \begin{bmatrix} \dfrac{\alpha+0.3}{\alpha+1} & \dfrac{0.4}{\alpha+2} \\ \dfrac{0.9}{\alpha+3} & \dfrac{\alpha+0.8}{\alpha+4} \end{bmatrix}
\times \begin{bmatrix} \dfrac{384}{(\alpha+4)^2} + \dfrac{48}{(\alpha+2)^2} + \dfrac{18}{\alpha+2} \\ \dfrac{54}{(\alpha+3)^2} + \dfrac{42}{(\alpha+1)^2} + \dfrac{36}{\alpha+3} \end{bmatrix}.
\tag{13.4.8}
$$

We have thus found an expression for the expected present value of renting a car in either town for any discount factor α.

Table 13.4.1 shows the vector $\mathbf{v}(\alpha)$ for several values of α. For example, if $\alpha = 0.1$ (implying a discount of 10% per unit time), we find

$$v_1(0.1) = 1030.68 \qquad v_2(0.1) = 965.72. \tag{13.4.9}$$

Thus we observe that the expected present value of renting a car in town 1 is 64.96 higher than it is for town 2. When α is reduced to 0.01, the difference $v_1(\alpha) - v_2(\alpha)$ increases to $10212.94 - 10141.69 = 71.25$; the difference appears to be approaching a limit.

The last two columns show the equivalent annuital reward rates associated with each state computed according to Equation 13.1.7. Notice that as α approaches zero, both $\alpha v_1(\alpha)$ and $\alpha v_2(\alpha)$ appear to be approaching a limit in the vicinity of 102. The tendency was predicted for a monodesmic process in Equation 13.3.34: the common limit is the gain.

Analysis without Discounting

Of course, in the car rental example, discounting would not be important. We shall therefore concentrate on finding the gain, the average reward per unit time that the system will generate if it is allowed to operate for a long time. The first quantities we want to calculate are $r_1 = r_1(0)$ and $r_2 = r_2(0)$, the expected reward generated by a single rental in each town. The most convenient way to perform this calculation is to specialize the results of Equation 13.4.6 to the case $\alpha = 0$,

$$r_1 = r_1(0) = 45 \qquad r_2 = r_2(0) = 60. \tag{13.4.10}$$

Thus each rental of a car in town 1 is expected to generate a reward of 45 while each rental of a car in town 2 is expected to produce a reward of 60. The reason that rentals in town 2 produce a larger income in spite of the lower rate structure resides primarily in the mean rental periods from Equation 11.2.7,

$$\bar{\tau}_1 = 0.3 \qquad \bar{\tau}_2 = 0.8. \tag{13.4.11}$$

Cars are rented for a longer average time in town 2.

Perhaps this result is more apparent if we compute $r_i = r_i(0)$ directly from Equation 13.3.24 rather than as a special case of Equation 13.4.6,

$$\begin{aligned} r_i = r_i(0) &= \sum_{j=1}^{N} p_{ij} \int_0^\infty d\tau\, h_{ij}(\tau)[y_{ij}(\tau, 0) + b_{ij}(\tau)] \\ &= \sum_{j=1}^{N} p_{ij} \int_0^\infty d\tau\, h_{ij}(\tau)[f_i\tau + f_{ij}] \\ &= f_i \sum_{j=1}^{N} p_{ij}\bar{\tau}_{ij} + \sum_{j=1}^{N} p_{ij}f_{ij} \\ &= f_i\bar{\tau}_i + \sum_{j=1}^{N} p_{ij}f_{ij}. \end{aligned} \tag{13.4.12}$$

Then we have

$$\begin{aligned} r_1 &= f_1\bar{\tau}_1 + p_{11}f_{11} + p_{12}f_{12} = 120(0.3) + 0.8(0) + 0.2(45) = 45 \\ r_2 &= f_2\bar{\tau}_2 + p_{21}f_{21} + p_{22}f_{22} = 60(0.8) + 0.3(40) + 0.7(0) = 60. \end{aligned} \tag{13.4.13}$$

Thus the expected rewards from a single rental in each town depend only on the fee structure, the transition probabilities, and the mean rental periods.

Table 13.4.1 Present Values and Equivalent Annuital Reward Rates of All Future Rewards in Car Rental Example for Various Discount Rates α

Discount Rate	Present Value of State 1	Present Value of State 2	Difference in Present Values	Equivalent Annuital Reward Rate of State 1	Equivalent Annuital Reward Rate of State 2
α	$v_1(\alpha)$	$v_2(\alpha)$	$v_1(\alpha) - v_2(\alpha)$	$\alpha v_1(\alpha)$	$\alpha v_2(\alpha)$
0.01	10212.94	10141.69	71.25	102.13	101.42
0.10	1030.68	965.72	64.96	103.07	96.57
1.00	100.00	69.81	30.19	100.00	69.81
10.00	5.09	4.05	1.04	50.09	40.50

The gain

We can now compute the gain g of this monodesmic process from the limiting entrance rates by using Equations 13.3.31 and the limiting entrance rates from Equation 11.9.14,

$$g = \sum_{j=1}^{N} e_j r_j = e_1 r_1 + e_2 r_2 = 1.2(45) + 0.8(60) = 102. \qquad (13.4.14)$$

We therefore expect the system to earn 102 per unit time in the steady state. This value of gain is consistent with the limiting behavior of $\alpha v_1(\alpha)$ and $\alpha v_2(\alpha)$ as α approaches zero that was observed in Table 13.4.1.

We can also compute the gain by first calculating the earning rates of the process from Equation 13.3.28,

$$q_1 = \frac{r_1}{\bar{\tau}_1} = \frac{45}{0.3} = 150 \qquad q_2 = \frac{r_2}{\bar{\tau}_2} = \frac{60}{0.8} = 75. \qquad (13.4.15)$$

We observe that the earning rate is twice as high for state 1 as it is for state 2, primarily because of the shorter average rental time in state 1. Next we use the limiting interval transition probabilities for the process from Equation 11.5.17 and the alternate expression for the gain in Equation 13.3.31 to write the gain as

$$g = \sum_{i=1}^{N} \phi_i q_i = \phi_1 q_1 + \phi_2 q_2 = 0.36(150) + 0.64(75) = 102. \qquad (13.4.16)$$

The relative values

We shall now write and solve the relative value equations 13.3.37 to illustrate the convenience and insight provided by this form of analysis. The general equations are

$$v_i + g\bar{\tau}_i = r_i + \sum_{j=1}^{N} p_{ij} v_j \qquad i = 1, 2, \ldots, N. \qquad (13.4.17)$$

For our example they become

$$\begin{aligned} v_1 + g\bar{\tau}_1 &= r_1 + p_{11}v_1 + p_{12}v_2 \\ v_2 + g\bar{\tau}_2 &= r_2 + p_{21}v_1 + p_{22}v_2. \end{aligned} \tag{13.4.18}$$

To find a solution we must set one of the v_i's equal to zero; we shall choose $v_2 = 0$ and write

$$\begin{aligned} v_1 + g\bar{\tau}_1 &= r_1 + p_{11}v_1 \\ g\bar{\tau}_2 &= r_2 + p_{21}v_1. \end{aligned} \tag{13.4.19}$$

We introduce numerical values,

$$\begin{aligned} v_1 + g(0.3) &= 45 + 0.8v_1 \\ g(0.8) &= 60 + 0.3v_1, \end{aligned} \tag{13.4.20}$$

and obtain the standard form

$$\begin{aligned} 0.2v_1 + 0.3g &= 45 \\ -0.3v_1 + 0.8g &= 60. \end{aligned} \tag{13.4.21}$$

The solution is

$$g = 102 \qquad v_1 = 72. \tag{13.4.22}$$

Interpretation of relative values. The gain, of course, is the same number we found earlier. But how do we interpret v_1? We note that $v_1 - v_2 = 72$. Therefore the expected total rewards in a very long time starting in each state have step components that differ by 72,

$$\lim_{t\to\infty} v_1(t) - v_2(t) = v_1 - v_2 = 72. \tag{13.4.23}$$

This implies that in a long time we expect the process to earn 72 more units of reward by starting in state 1 rather than state 2, or in other words, by renting a car in town 1 rather than in town 2. We can thus interpret the number 72 as the amount that the car company would be just willing to pay for instantaneous transportation of a car from town 2 to town 1. As we found in Table 13.4.1, this number is reduced to 71.25 if future earnings are discounted at the discount rate 0.01, and to 64.96 at the discount rate 0.1.

Thus solving the relative value equations for the process is a simple and convenient way to evaluate the gain. The interesting and important relative values of starting in each state are produced at very little additional computational expense.

13.5 THE REWARD STRUCTURE FOR DISCRETE-TIME PROCESSES

We need to consider a reward structure for discrete-time semi-Markov processes both because we encounter situations where there is a fundamental periodic time scale to the process and because, as usual, the difference equations generated for this type of structure are far more manageable computationally than the integral equations or transform expressions for the continuous-time case. Therefore we may often consider the discrete-time process as an approximation to a continuous-time process for the purpose of computation.

The discrete-time reward structure is very similar to the continuous-time. We define $y_{ij}(\ell)$ to be the reward or yield that the system earns at time ℓ after entering state i for occupying state i during the interval $(\ell, \ell + 1)$ when its successor state is j. We define $b_{ij}(m)$ to be the bonus reward generated by the system at the time of transition for making a transition from state i to state j after a holding time m in state i. Thus if the system should enter state i and then make a transition to state j after holding m time units in state i, the total reward it would earn as a result of this action would be

$$b_{ij}(m) + \sum_{\ell=0}^{m-1} y_{ij}(\ell).$$

Again, a special and interesting reward structure arises when the same yield is paid during each time period and the bonus is independent of the holding time,

$$y_{ij}(\ell) = y_{ij} \qquad b_{ij}(m) = b_{ij}. \tag{13.5.1}$$

Discounting

According to our discussion of discounting for the continuous-time case, if a unit sum is paid n time units in the future, its present value is $e^{-\alpha n}$. For convenience we define a discount factor β by

$$\beta = e^{-\alpha} \tag{13.5.2}$$

and say that its present value is β^n. Streams of payments made on a periodic time scale are therefore reduced to a single present value by multiplying them by the successive terms of the geometric sequence $1, \beta, \beta^2, \ldots$ and then summing them. Thus if we describe a stream by a function $f(\cdot)$ where $f(n)$ is the amount of reward at time n, the present value of this reward stream is

$$\sum_{n=0}^{\infty} f(n)\beta^n, \tag{13.5.3}$$

but this is, of course, just the geometric transform of the stream evaluated at $z = \beta$,

$$\sum_{n=0}^{\infty} f(n)\beta^n = f^g(\beta). \tag{13.5.4}$$

We can therefore find the present value of any reward stream by evaluating its geometric transform at the value of the discount factor.

To interpret discounting in the discrete-time case as uncertainty about the duration of the reward process, we simply consider β to be the probability that the process will be allowed to continue at each discrete time instant. The expected duration of the process will then be $1/(1 - \beta)$ periods and the expected earnings from the process will be the quantity $f^g(\beta)$ from Equation 13.5.4.

Equivalent annuital payment

To extend the equivalent annuital concept to the discrete-time case, we consider an annuity that would pay an amount ρ at times $n = 0, 1, 2, \ldots$ ad infinitum. The present value of this annuity at a discount factor β is

$$\rho[1 + \beta + \beta^2 + \cdots] = \rho \cdot \frac{1}{1 - \beta} \cdot \tag{13.5.5}$$

The payment ρ that would make the present value of this annuity equal to the present value $f^g(\beta)$ of some reward stream would then be derived from

$$\rho \cdot \frac{1}{1 - \beta} = f^g(\beta) \tag{13.5.6}$$

to be

$$\rho = (1 - \beta)f^g(\beta). \tag{13.5.7}$$

The equivalent annuital payment is the present value multiplied by one minus the discount factor, or equivalently, divided by the expected duration of the uncertain duration process.

13.6 THE DISCRETE-TIME SEMI-MARKOV REWARD PROCESS WITH DISCOUNTING

We shall not carry out the analysis of the discrete-time process in as much detail as the analysis of the continuous-time process because it is so similar. However, we shall exhibit the basic equations because of their computational importance. To begin, we define $v_i(n, \beta)$ as the expected present value of rewards generated by the process during a time interval of length n if it is started in state i. Once more, we use $v_i(0)$ to represent the terminal rewards that the process receives if it occupies state i at the end of the interval. Then the discrete version of Equation 13.2.2 is

$$\begin{aligned} v_i(n, \beta) &= \sum_{j=1}^{N} p_{ij} \sum_{m=n+1}^{\infty} h_{ij}(m) \left[\sum_{\ell=0}^{n-1} \beta^{\ell} y_{ij}(\ell) + \beta^n v_i(0) \right] \\ &\quad + \sum_{j=1}^{N} p_{ij} \sum_{m=1}^{n} h_{ij}(m) \left[\sum_{\ell=0}^{m-1} \beta^{\ell} y_{ij}(\ell) + \beta^m b_{ij}(m) + \beta^m v_j(n - m, \beta) \right] \\ &\qquad i = 1, 2, \ldots, N;\ n = 1, 2, 3, \ldots . \end{aligned} \tag{13.6.1}$$

This equation can be solved recursively to find $v_i(n, \beta)$ for any value of n. Although it is computable in its present form, it may be useful to present the discrete-time forms of some of the quantities we defined in the continuous-time case. Thus we define

$$y_{ij}(m, \beta) = \sum_{\ell=0}^{m-1} \beta^{\ell} y_{ij}(\ell) \qquad m = 1, 2, 3, \ldots, \tag{13.6.2}$$

$$\begin{aligned} {}^{>}y_i(n, \beta) &= \sum_{j=1}^{N} p_{ij} y_{ij}(n, \beta) \sum_{m=n+1}^{\infty} h_{ij}(m) \\ &= \sum_{j=1}^{N} p_{ij} y_{ij}(n, \beta)\, {}^{>}h_{ij}(n), \end{aligned} \tag{13.6.3}$$

and

$$\begin{aligned} r_i(n, \beta) &= \sum_{j=1}^{N} p_{ij} \sum_{m=1}^{n} h_{ij}(m)[y_{ij}(m, \beta) + \beta^m b_{ij}(m)] \\ &= \sum_{j=1}^{N} p_{ij} \sum_{m=1}^{n} h_{ij}(m) \left[\sum_{\ell=0}^{m-1} \beta^{\ell} y_{ij}(\ell) + \beta^m b_{ij}(m) \right]. \end{aligned} \tag{13.6.4}$$

Their interpretations are the same as they were in the continuous-time case. We can then write Equation 13.6.1 as

$$v_i(n, \beta) = {}^{>}y_i(n, \beta) + \beta^n v_i(0)\, {}^{>}w_i(n) + r_i(n, \beta) + \sum_{j=1}^{N} p_{ij} \sum_{m=1}^{n} h_{ij}(m) \beta^m v_j(n - m, \beta)$$

$$i = 1, 2, \ldots, N;\ n = 1, 2, 3, \ldots. \tag{13.6.5}$$

This form may permit more efficient recursive computation than does Equation 13.6.1 of the expected present value of rewards generated during a time interval for a given starting state. As a matter of interest, the transform solution of this equation corresponding to Equation 13.2.11 is

$$\mathbf{v}^g(z, \beta) = [I - P \,\square\, H^g(\beta z)]^{-1}[{}^{>}\mathbf{y}^g(z, \beta) + {}^{>}W^g(\beta z)\mathbf{v}(0) + \mathbf{r}^g(z, \beta)]. \tag{13.6.6}$$

When the time interval n is very large, the expected present value of starting in each state i converges to a constant $v_i(\beta)$ provided that the discount factor β is less than 1. By the same arguments used in the continuous-time case, the terms ${}^{>}y_i(n, \beta)$ and $\beta^n v_i(0)\, {}^{>}w_i(n)$ in Equation 13.6.5 vanish for large n. The term $r_i(n, \beta)$ becomes simply $r_i(\infty, \beta) = r_i(\beta)$, the expected present value of rewards generated by a single occupancy of state i,

$$\begin{aligned} r_i(\infty, \beta) = r_i(\beta) &= \sum_{j=1}^{N} p_{ij} \sum_{m=1}^{\infty} h_{ij}(m)[y_{ij}(m, \beta) + \beta^m b_{ij}(m)] \\ &= \sum_{j=1}^{N} p_{ij} \sum_{m=1}^{\infty} h_{ij}(m) \left[\sum_{\ell=0}^{m-1} \beta^{\ell} y_{ij}(\ell) + \beta^m b_{ij}(m) \right]. \end{aligned} \tag{13.6.7}$$

Expected present values

Thus for large n we can substitute $v_i(\beta)$ for $v_i(n, \beta)$ in Equation 13.6.5 and write it as

$$v_i(\beta) = r_i(\beta) + \sum_{j=1}^{N} p_{ij} \sum_{m=1}^{\infty} h_{ij}(m)\beta^m v_j(\beta) \tag{13.6.8}$$

or

$$v_i(\beta) = r_i(\beta) + \sum_{j=1}^{N} p_{ij} h_{ij}{}^g(\beta) v_j(\beta), \tag{13.6.9}$$

which is, of course, just the discrete-time version of Equation 13.2.20 developed for the continuous-time case by a more formal analysis. This equation may be readily solved for the expected present value of rewards generated as the result of starting in any state. The matrix solution is

$$\mathbf{v}(\beta) = [I - P \,\Box\, H^g(\beta)]^{-1}\mathbf{r}(\beta). \tag{13.6.10}$$

If we consider β as the probability that the process will be allowed to continue at each time instant, then Equation 13.6.10 has the same interpretation as Equation 13.2.18: The vector of expected present values of reward is equal to the matrix of discounted state occupancies post-multiplied by the vector of expected present values of reward for a single occupancy.

13.7 THE DISCRETE-TIME SEMI-MARKOV PROCESS WITHOUT DISCOUNTING

If we do not want to discount future rewards, we simply take $\beta = 1$ in our previous analysis and let $v_i(n) = v_i(n, 1)$ be the expected total reward that the process will generate in a time interval of length n if it is started in state i. The recursive equations follow directly from Equations 13.6.1 or 13.6.5 by setting $\beta = 1$:

$$v_i(n) = {}^{>}y_i(n, 1) + v_i(0)\, {}^{>}w_i(n) + r_i(n, 1) + \sum_{j=1}^{N} p_{ij} \sum_{m=1}^{n} h_{ij}(m) v_j(n - m)$$
$$n = 1, 2, 3, \ldots; i = 1, 2, \ldots, N. \tag{13.7.1}$$

The geometric transform of the solution to this equation in matrix form follows directly from Equations 13.3.9 or 13.6.6:

$$\begin{aligned}\mathbf{v}^g(z) &= [I - P \,\Box\, H^g(z)]^{-1}[{}^{>}\mathbf{y}^g(z, 1) + {}^{>}W^g(z)\mathbf{v}(0) + \mathbf{r}^g(z, 1)] \\ &= E^g(z)[\mathbf{r}^g(z, 1) + {}^{>}\mathbf{y}^g(z, 1)] + \Phi^g(z)\mathbf{v}(0).\end{aligned} \tag{13.7.2}$$

Limiting Behavior

If we solve for $v_i(n)$ recursively using Equation 13.7.1, we again find that $v_i(n)$ grows linearly with n when n is large. By arguments exactly analogous to those of the continuous-time case, we express $v_i(n)$ in the asymptotic form

$$v_i(n) = g_i n + v_i. \tag{13.7.3}$$

Gain

Here again we call g_i the gain of the process conditional on starting in state i. However, as we would anticipate, the gain is now the expected reward per time period in the steady state rather than the expected reward per unit time. The constants v_i represent the step components in expected total reward for the discrete-time case; they correspond completely to those we found for the continuous-time case. The gain g_i is again found to be

$$g_i = \sum_{j=1}^{N} e_{ij} r_j \tag{13.7.4}$$

where e_{ij} is the limiting entrance probability of state j conditional on starting in state i and r_j is the expected reward generated from an occupancy of state i defined by

$$\begin{aligned} r_i = r_i(1) = r_i(\infty, 1) &= \sum_{j=1}^{N} p_{ij} \sum_{m=1}^{\infty} h_{ij}(m)[y_{ij}(m, 1) + b_{ij}(m)] \\ &= \sum_{j=1}^{N} p_{ij} \sum_{m=1}^{\infty} h_{ij}(m)\left[\sum_{\ell=0}^{m-1} y_{ij}(\ell) + b_{ij}(m)\right]. \end{aligned} \tag{13.7.5}$$

We can again define the earning rate q_j to be the ratio of r_j to $\bar{\tau}_j$ and write the gain in the form

$$g_i = \sum_{j=1}^{N} \frac{\phi_{ij}}{\bar{\tau}_j} r_j = \sum_{j=1}^{N} \phi_{ij} q_j, \tag{13.7.6}$$

in analogy with Equation 13.3.29.

If the process is monodesmic, then it has the same gain g for all starting states. The asymptotic expression for the total expected reward is then

$$v_i(n) = gn + v_i \tag{13.7.7}$$

where g is again given by

$$g = \sum_{j=1}^{N} e_j r_j = \sum_{j=1}^{N} \phi_j \frac{r_j}{\bar{\tau}_j} = \sum_{j=1}^{N} \phi_j q_j. \tag{13.7.8}$$

The interpretation of gain follows from the continuous-time case. The gain of a state is the equivalent annuital payment associated with the state as the discount factor approaches one. From Equation 13.5.7,

$$g_i = \lim_{\beta \to 1} (1 - \beta) v_i(\beta), \tag{13.7.9}$$

a result implied by the final value theorem for the geometric transform. Finally, for a monodesmic process, the limit is independent of the state,

$$g = \lim_{\beta \to 1} (1 - \beta) v_i(\beta). \tag{13.7.10}$$

Relative value equations

The same argument we used previously shows that if we wish to find the relative values of the process, we must solve the same set of equations we developed in Equation 13.3.37,

$$v_i + g\bar{\tau}_i = r_i + \sum_{j=1}^{N} p_{ij} v_j \qquad i = 1, 2, \ldots, N. \tag{13.7.11}$$

Finally, the special reward structure of Equation 13.5.1 leads once more to Equation 13.3.40 for the expected reward per occupancy of state i,

$$r_i = \sum_{j=1}^{N} p_{ij} [y_{ij} \bar{\tau}_{ij} + b_{ij}]. \tag{13.7.12}$$

Thus we find that extension to the discrete-time case of all our continuous-time results is direct. The primary advantage of the discrete-time formulation is the computational convenience of the recursive Equations 13.6.5 and 13.7.1.

13.8 THE DISCRETE-TIME CAR RENTAL EXAMPLE

The discrete-time car rental example of Chapter 10 will serve to illustrate the reward computations for a discrete-time process. The car rental times are all multiples of some basic time period. We shall assume the reward structure has the form

$$y_{ij}(m) = 0 \qquad b_{ij}(m) = f_i m + f_{ij}. \tag{13.8.1}$$

Thus, when the car is returned, a fee of f_i per time period is paid if it was rented in town i; in addition a drop charge f_{ij} is collected if the car was rented in town i and returned to town j. We shall think of the basic time period as representing one day and assign the following values to the reward parameters:

$$\begin{array}{lll} f_1 = 10 & f_{11} = 0 & f_{12} = 45 \\ f_2 = 5 & f_{21} = 40 & f_{22} = 0 \end{array} \tag{13.8.2}$$

The values of f_1 and f_2 are 1/12 the values given in Equation 13.4.2 for the continuous-time example to compensate for the fact that the time scales of the continuous-time and discrete-time versions of the example differ by a factor of 12. However, the drop charges f_{ij} remain the same. The transition probabilities and holding time mass functions that describe this process with rewards are those given in Equations 10.1.14 and 10.1.17.

Analysis by Recursion

We can apply the recursive method for finding the expected reward to be generated by the process in n time periods either with or without discounting. The basic recursive equation is Equation 13.6.1; however, in view of Equation 13.8.1 and the assumption that $v_i(0) = 0$ it reduces to

$$v_i(n, \beta) = \sum_{j=1}^{N} p_{ij} \sum_{m=1}^{n} h_{ij}(m)\beta^m[f_i m + f_{ij} + v_j(n - m, \beta)]$$

$$i = 1, 2, \ldots, N; n = 1, 2, 3, \ldots . \quad (13.8.3)$$

Table 13.8.1 shows the result of solving this equation recursively for values of n through 15 and for values of β that range from 0 to 1 in increments of 0.1. The case $\beta = 1$ corresponds, of course, to no discounting of future rewards.

The method of constructing Table 13.8.1 deserves special mention. The expected present values of each state are shown both as row and column entries to manifest the dependence of these values on both stage and discount factor.

If we examine the column of expected present values for either state at any stage, we observe that the expected present values increase rapidly as the discount factor grows toward 1. This property follows directly from the interpretation that high discount factors imply a long effective duration of the process.

If we study the row of expected present values for either state at any discount factor, we find that the expected present values increase with stage as expected. Furthermore, they appear to converge toward a limiting value. This limiting value is attained by stage 4 when the discount factor β assumes the low value 0.1, and by stage 10 when $\beta = 0.4$. However, for higher values of β, the limiting value is approached, but not reached, within the confines of the table. The limiting value represents, of course, the expected present value of all future rewards for a process of unbounded duration.

When the discount factor β equals 1, there is, as we have said, no discounting of future rewards—the expected present value of the process grows continually with stage. When the number of stages is very large, the growth in expected present value will be just the gain, or average reward per stage, of the process. For the monodesmic process we are considering, the gain will be the same for both states.

Table 13.8.1 Expected Present Values of States in Car Rental Problem as a Function of Stages Remaining

$v_i(n, \beta)$
Expected Present Value

Discount Factor β	State i \ Stage n	1: State 1	1: State 2	2: State 1	2: State 2	3: State 1	3: State 2	4: State 1	4: State 2	5: State 1	5: State 2
0	1	0		0		0		0		0	
	2		0		0		0		0		0
0.1	1	0.450		0.517		0.525		0.526		0.526	
	2		0.367		0.406		0.410		0.410		0.410
0.2	1	0.900		1.167		1.232		1.247		1.250	
	2		0.733		0.889		0.923		0.931		0.932
0.3	1	1.350		1.952		2.170		2.243		2.267	
	2		1.100		1.451		1.565		1.602		1.615
0.4	1	1.800		2.869		3.388		3.619		3.717	
	2		1.467		2.090		2.361		2.479		2.530
0.5	1	2.250		3.921		4.934		5.498		5.797	
	2		1.833		2.808		3.337		3.625		3.781
0.6	1	2.700		5.106		6.857		8.026		8.771	
	2		2.200		3.604		4.518		5.115		5.502
0.7	1	3.150		6.425		9.205		11.370		12.981	
	2		2.567		4.477		5.929		7.035		7.872
0.8	1	3.600		7.877		12.027		15.721		18.862	
	2		2.933		5.428		7.596		9.483		11.114
0.9	1	4.050		9.464		15.373		21.289		26.950	
	2		3.300		6.458		9.544		12.566		15.506
1.0	1	4.500		11.183		19.289		28.307		37.893	
	2		3.667		7.565		11.799		16.405		21.384

The row corresponding to $\beta = 1$ in Table 13.8.1 does indicate that the expected present values of both states are continually increasing with stage. However, the amount of increase from one stage to the next is the most interesting characteristic of this case.

The successive differences in expected present value for each state when $\beta = 1$ are shown in Table 13.8.2. We observe that these differences are generally increasing with stage for both states. The differences increase monotonically for state 2, but with some oscillation for state 1. Later in this section, we shall find that the actual gain of the process is 8.5. The generally slow convergence and oscillation exhibited

6		7		8		9		10		11	
State		State		State		State		State		State	
1	2	1	2	1	2	1	2	1	2	1	2
0		0		0		0		0		0	
	0		0		0		0		0		0
0.526		0.526		0.526		0.526		0.526		0.526	
	0.410		0.410		0.410		0.410		0.410		0.410
1.250		1.250		1.250		1.250		1.250		1.250	
	0.932		0.933		0.933		0.933		0.933		0.933
2.274		2.276		2.277		2.277		2.277		2.277	
	1.618		1.620		1.620		1.620		1.620		1.620
3.758		3.774		3.781		3.784		3.785		3.785	
	2.552		2.561		2.565		2.567		2.568		2.568
5.952		6.031		6.071		6.091		6.101		6.106	
	3.864		3.908		3.932		3.944		3.950		3.953
9.234		9.517		9.688		9.791		9.852		9.889	
	5.751		5.910		6.010		6.073		6.112		6.136
14.149		14.982		15.569		15.981		16.268		16.468	
	8.500		8.966		9.310		9.561		9.744		9.876
21.464		23.584		25.294		26.663		26.755		28.623	
	12.513		13.701		14.701		15.537		16.232		16.806
32.224		37.059		41.445		45.398		48.943		52.114	
	18.342		21.051		23.618		26.032		28.288		30.386
47.818		57.927		68.116		78.318		88.486		98.591	
	26.720		32.384		28.346		44.577		51.048		57.733

in Table 13.8.2 demonstrate that recursive computation of expected present values with $\beta = 1$ can be a relatively inefficient method of finding the gain of even a simple process.

Analytic Asymptotic Solution with Discounting

When the number of time periods remaining is large, we determine the expected present value of future rewards as a consequence of entering each state from Equation 13.6.10. The expected present value of rewards associated with a single

Table 13.8.1—*continued*

$v_i(n, \beta)$
Expected Present Value

Discount Factor β	State i \ Stage n	12 State 1	12 State 2	13 State 1	13 State 2	14 State 1	14 State 2	15 State 1	15 State 2
0	1	0		0		0		0	
	2		0		0		0		0
0.1	1	0.526		0.526		0.526		0.526	
	2		0.410		0.410		0.410		0.410
0.2	1	1.250		1.250		1.250		1.250	
	2		0.933		0.933		0.933		0.933
0.3	1	2.277		2.277		2.277		2.277	
	2		1.620		1.620		1.620		1.620
0.4	1	3.785		3.785		3.785		3.785	
	2		2.568		2.568		2.568		2.568
0.5	1	6.108		6.110		6.110		6.110	
	2		3.955		3.956		3.956		3.957
0.6	1	9.911		9.924		9.932		9.936	
	2		6.151		6.160		6.166		6.169
0.7	1	16.606		16.703		16.769		16.816	
	2		9.971		10.040		10.088		10.123
0.8	1	29.312		29.858		30.290		30.633	
	2		17.279		17.666		17.983		18.240
0.9	1	54.946		57.471		59.721		61.726	
	2		32.327		34.118		35.764		37.273
1.0	1	108.616		118.550		128.388		138.127	
	2		64.608		71.652		78.847		86.176

Table 13.8.2 Successive Differences in State Values of Car Rental Problem without Discounting ($\beta = 1$)

$v_i(n) - v_i(n-1)$

State i \ Stage n	1	2	3	4	5	6	7
1	4.500	6.683	8.106	9.018	9.586	9.925	10.109
2	3.667	3.898	4.234	4.606	4.979	5.336	5.664

State i \ Stage n	8	9	10	11	12	13	14	15
1	10.189	10.202	10.168	10.105	10.025	9.934	9.838	9.739
2	5.962	6.231	6.471	6.685	6.875	7.044	7.195	7.329

occupancy of stage i, $r_i(\beta)$, we find from Equations 13.6.7 and 13.8.1,

$$\begin{aligned} r_i(\beta) = r_i(\infty, \beta) &= \sum_{j=1}^{N} p_{ij} \sum_{m=1}^{\infty} h_{ij}(m)[y_{ij}(m, \beta) + \beta^m b_{ij}(m)] \\ &= \sum_{j=1}^{N} p_{ij} \sum_{m=1}^{\infty} h_{ij}(m)\beta^m[f_i m + f_{ij}] \\ &= f_i \sum_{j=1}^{N} p_{ij} \sum_{m=1}^{\infty} h_{ij}(m)\beta^m m + \sum_{j=1}^{N} p_{ij} f_{ij} \sum_{m=1}^{\infty} h_{ij}(m)\beta^m \\ &= f_i \sum_{j=1}^{N} p_{ij}\left[\beta \frac{d}{d\beta} h_{ij}{}^{g}(\beta)\right] + \sum_{j=1}^{N} p_{ij} f_{ij} h_{ij}{}^{g}(\beta). \end{aligned} \tag{13.8.4}$$

This equation relates the expected discounted rewards from a single occupancy to the reward parameters, transition probabilities, and holding time transforms of the discrete-time process in much the same way that Equation 13.4.3 related these quantities for the continuous-time process. From Equations 10.1.14 and 10.1.17 we have

$$P = \begin{bmatrix} 0.8 & 0.2 \\ 0.3 & 0.7 \end{bmatrix} \qquad H^g(z) = \begin{bmatrix} \dfrac{(1/3)z}{1 - (2/3)z} & \dfrac{(1/6)z}{1 - (5/6)z} \\ \dfrac{(1/4)z}{1 - (3/4)z} & \dfrac{(1/12)z}{1 - (11/12)z} \end{bmatrix}$$

$$z \frac{d}{dz} H^g(z) = \begin{bmatrix} \dfrac{(1/3)z}{[1 - (2/3)z]^2} & \dfrac{(1/6)z}{[1 - (5/6)z]^2} \\ \dfrac{(1/4)z}{[1 - (3/4)z]^2} & \dfrac{(1/12)z}{[1 - (11/12)z]^2} \end{bmatrix} \tag{13.8.5}$$

and therefore,

$$\begin{aligned} r_1(\beta) &= f_1\left[p_{11}\beta \frac{d}{d\beta} h_{11}{}^{g}(\beta) + p_{12}\beta \frac{d}{d\beta} h_{12}{}^{g}(\beta)\right] + p_{11} f_{11} h_{11}{}^{g}(\beta) + p_{12} f_{12} h_{12}{}^{g}(\beta) \\ r_2(\beta) &= f_2\left[p_{21}\beta \frac{d}{d\beta} h_{21}{}^{g}(\beta) + p_{22}\beta \frac{d}{d\beta} h_{22}{}^{g}(\beta)\right] + p_{21} f_{21} h_{21}{}^{g}(\beta) + p_{22} f_{22} h_{22}{}^{g}(\beta). \end{aligned} \tag{13.8.6}$$

When we substitute the numerical values of Equation 13.8.2, we obtain

$$r_1(\beta) = 10\left[0.8\frac{(1/3)\beta}{[1-(2/3)\beta]^2} + 0.2\frac{(1/6)\beta}{[1-(5/6)\beta]^2}\right] + 0 + 0.2(45)\frac{(1/6)\beta}{1-(5/6)\beta}$$

$$= \frac{(8/3)\beta}{[1-(2/3)\beta]^2} + \frac{(1/3)\beta}{[1-(5/6)\beta]^2} + \frac{(3/2)\beta}{1-(5/6)\beta},$$

$$r_2(\beta) = 5\left[0.3\frac{(1/4)\beta}{[1-(3/4)\beta]^2} + 0.7\frac{(1/12)\beta}{[1-(11/12)\beta]^2}\right] + 0.3(40)\frac{(1/4)\beta}{1-(3/4)\beta} + 0$$

$$= \frac{(3/8)\beta}{[1-(3/4)\beta]^2} + \frac{(7/24)\beta}{[1-(11/12)\beta]^2} + \frac{3\beta}{1-(3/4)\beta}. \tag{13.8.7}$$

Expected present values

Since the vector of expected present values is given by Equation 13.6.10 as

$$\mathbf{v}(\beta) = [I - P \,\square\, H^g(\beta)]^{-1}\mathbf{r}(\beta), \tag{13.8.8}$$

we can use $[I - P \,\square\, H^g(z)]^{-1}$ from Equation 10.3.25 to write

$$\begin{bmatrix} v_1(\beta) \\ v_2(\beta) \end{bmatrix} = \frac{[1-(2/3)\beta][1-(11/12)\beta][1-(3/4)\beta][1-(5/6)\beta]}{(1-\beta)[1-(4/5)\beta][1-(203/120)\beta + (1021/1440)\beta^2]}$$

$$\times \begin{bmatrix} \dfrac{1-(39/40)\beta}{1-(11/12)\beta} & \dfrac{(1/30)\beta}{1-(5/6)\beta} \\ \dfrac{(3/40)\beta}{1-(3/4)\beta} & \dfrac{1-(14/15)\beta}{1-(2/3)\beta} \end{bmatrix}$$

$$\times \begin{bmatrix} \dfrac{(8/3)\beta}{[1-(2/3)\beta]^2} + \dfrac{(1/3)\beta}{[1-(5/6)\beta]^2} + \dfrac{(3/2)\beta}{1-(5/6)\beta} \\ \dfrac{(3/8)\beta}{[1-(3/4)\beta]^2} + \dfrac{(7/24)\beta}{[1-(11/12)\beta]^2} + \dfrac{3\beta}{1-(3/4)\beta} \end{bmatrix}. \tag{13.8.9}$$

Table 13.8.3 shows this vector for several different values of β. Note the correspondence between these asymptotic results and the recursive solutions of Table

Table 13.8.3 Expected Present Values of States for Infinite Duration Car Rental Problem

Discount Factor, β	0	0.1	0.2	0.3	0.4	0.5	0.6	0.7	0.8	0.9	1.0
State 1											
Expected Present Value $v_1(\beta)$	0	0.526	1.2501	2.277	3.785	6.111	9.943	16.920	31.946	78.598	∞
State 2											
Expected Present Value $v_2(\beta)$	0	0.410	0.933	1.620	2.568	3.957	6.174	10.208	19.331	51.997	∞

13.8.1 when the number of stages is 15. We find that the expected present values of the infinite duration process have been achieved after only 15 stages for discount factors through 0.4. The differences between the 15-stage and infinite duration results increase as the discount factor grows from 0.5 to 1. When $\beta = 0.9$, for example, the expected present value of state 1 at stage 15 is 61.726 or 16.872 less than the 78.598 expected present value of the infinite duration process. Of course, when $\beta = 1.0$, the expected present values of the infinite duration process become infinite.

Analytic Asymptotic Solution without Discounting

To find the gain and relative values of the process, we first compute r_1 and r_2, the expected rewards received from a single occupancy of each state without discounting. The simplest way to do this is to take β equal to 1 in the expressions of Equation 13.8.7,

$$r_1 = r_1(1) = 45 \qquad r_2 = r_2(1) = 60. \tag{13.8.10}$$

Note that these quantities are the same as those found for the continuous-time case in Equation 13.4.10 because we have made compensating changes in the reward structure and the time scale.

Examination of the argument that leads to Equation 13.4.12 shows that the same result holds for the discrete-time case,

$$r_i = r_i(1) = f_i\bar{\tau}_i + \sum_{j=1}^{N} p_{ij}f_{ij}. \tag{13.8.11}$$

Since we know for the discrete-time problem from Equation 10.1.22 that

$$\bar{\tau}_1 = 3.6 \qquad \bar{\tau}_2 = 9.6, \tag{13.8.12}$$

we can compute r_1 and r_2 directly as

$$\begin{aligned} r_1 &= f_1\bar{\tau}_1 + p_{11}f_{11} + p_{12}f_{12} = 10(3.6) + 0 + 0.2(45) = 45 \\ r_2 &= f_2\bar{\tau}_2 + p_{21}f_{21} + p_{22}f_{22} = 5(9.6) + 0.3(40) + 0 = 60. \end{aligned} \tag{13.8.13}$$

Gain

To compute the gain of this monodesmic process from the expected rewards per occupancy r_1 and r_2, we use Equation 13.7.8 and the limiting entrance probabilities for the discrete-time problem from Equation 10.7.24,

$$g = \sum_{j=1}^{N} e_j r_j = e_1 r_1 + e_2 r_2 = (3/30)(45) + (2/30)(60) = 8.5. \tag{13.8.14}$$

The gain is 1/12 as large as the value of 102 we found in Equation 13.4.14 for the continuous-time case because of the change in time scale by a factor of 12.

The earning rates of the process are also lower by a factor of 12 because

$$q_1 = \frac{r_1}{\bar{\tau}_1} = \frac{45}{3.6} = 12.5 \qquad q_2 = \frac{r_2}{\bar{\tau}_2} = \frac{60}{9.6} = 6.25. \tag{13.8.15}$$

By using Equation 13.7.8 we can alternately express the gain in terms of these earning rates and the limiting interval transition probabilities of the discrete-time process from Equation 10.3.51,

$$g = \sum_{j=1}^{N} \phi_j q_j = \phi_1 q_1 + \phi_2 q_2 = 0.36(12.5) + 0.64(6.25) = 8.5. \tag{13.8.16}$$

Relative values

We now note that if we write the relative value Equations 13.7.11 for this example they will look exactly like Equations 13.4.20 except that the coefficients of g are now 12 times larger than they were before. Consequently, the solution for the relative values is the same, but the new equations will produce a solution for g that is 1/12 as large as its previous value. Therefore we obtain

$$g = (1/12)(102) = 8.5 \qquad v_1 = 72 \qquad v_2 = 0. \tag{13.8.17}$$

13.9 THE EFFECT OF LAPSED TIME ON EXPECTED REWARDS

A particularly interesting aspect of the study of rewards in semi-Markov processes is the manner in which such rewards are affected by the lapsed time in a state. As you recall, we say that the process has experienced a lapsed time τ_ℓ in state i if we observe that the process still occupies state i at a time τ_ℓ after it entered state i. The question is this: If a lapsed time τ_ℓ has been spent in a state i, what is the expected reward that the process will earn in the following time period of length t, either with or without discounting?

To investigate this question we let $v_i^\ell(\tau_\ell, t, \alpha)$ be the expected discounted reward that will be generated by the process if it has spent a lapsed time τ_ℓ in state i, time t remains for the operation of the process, and the discount rate is α. We recall that the total waiting time in any state can be considered as the sum of the lapsed time τ_ℓ and the remaining time τ_r. Then by using our previously developed reward notation and the results of Equations 13.2.4 and 11.9.26 we can write the equation

$$\begin{aligned} v_i^\ell(\tau_\ell, t, \alpha) &= \sum_{j=1}^{N} p_{ij} \int_t^\infty d\tau_r \, \frac{h_{ij}(\tau_\ell + \tau_r)}{{}^>w_i(\tau_\ell)} \left[\int_0^t d\sigma \, e^{-\alpha\sigma} y_{ij}(\tau_\ell + \sigma) + e^{-\alpha t} v_i(0)\right] \\ &\quad + \sum_{j=1}^{N} p_{ij} \int_0^t d\tau_r \, \frac{h_{ij}(\tau_\ell + \tau_r)}{{}^>w_i(\tau_\ell)} \\ &\quad \times \left[\int_0^{\tau_r} d\sigma \, e^{-\alpha\sigma} y_{ij}(\tau_\ell + \sigma) + e^{-\alpha\tau_r} b_{ij}(\tau_\ell + \tau_r) + e^{-\alpha\tau_r} v_j(t - \tau_r, \alpha)\right]. \end{aligned} \tag{13.9.1}$$

Note that this equation relates the lapsed time expected rewards to the expected rewards we have already studied; thus we have in essence solved the problem as stated.

However, as we shall see, the specializations of Equation 13.9.1 are particularly interesting. First, we can consider the indefinite duration process and use the notation

$$v_i^{\ell}(\tau_\ell, \alpha) = v_i^{\ell}(\tau_\ell, \infty, \alpha), \tag{13.9.2}$$

where $v_i^{\ell}(\tau_\ell, \alpha)$ is the expected present value of the rewards generated by the indefinite duration process when the process has spent a lapsed time τ_ℓ in state i and the discount rate is α. We now write

$$v_i^{\ell}(\tau_\ell, \alpha) = \sum_{j=1}^{N} p_{ij} \int_0^\infty d\tau_r \frac{h_{ij}(\tau_\ell + \tau_r)}{{}^>w_i(\tau_\ell)} \times \left[\int_0^{\tau_r} d\sigma\, e^{-\alpha\sigma} y_{ij}(\tau_\ell + \sigma) + e^{-\alpha\tau_r} b_{ij}(\tau_\ell + \tau_r) + e^{-\alpha\tau_r} v_j(\alpha)\right] \tag{13.9.3}$$

since the first term of Equation 13.9.1 becomes of no importance. It is clearly advantageous to define

$$r_i^{\ell}(\tau_\ell, \alpha) = \sum_{j=1}^{N} p_{ij} \int_0^\infty d\tau_r \frac{h_{ij}(\tau_\ell + \tau_r)}{{}^>w_i(\tau_\ell)} \left[\int_0^{\tau_r} d\sigma\, e^{-\alpha\sigma} y_{ij}(\tau_\ell + \sigma) + e^{-\alpha\tau_r} b_{ij}(\tau_\ell + \tau_r)\right] \tag{13.9.4}$$

where $r_i^{\ell}(\tau_\ell, \alpha)$ is the expected present value of rewards generated by the process during the remaining time it spends in state i if it has spent a lapsed time τ_ℓ in state i and the discount rate is α. With this simplification in notation, Equation 13.9.3 becomes

$$\begin{aligned} v_i^{\ell}(\tau_\ell, \alpha) &= r_i^{\ell}(\tau_\ell, \alpha) + \sum_{j=1}^{N} p_{ij} \int_0^\infty d\tau_r \frac{h_{ij}(\tau_\ell + \tau_r)}{{}^>w_i(\tau_\ell)} e^{-\alpha\tau_r} v_j(\alpha) \\ &= r_i^{\ell}(\tau_\ell, \alpha) + \frac{1}{{}^>w_i(\tau_\ell)} \sum_{j=1}^{N} p_{ij} v_j(\alpha) \int_0^\infty d\tau_r\, h_{ij}(\tau_\ell + \tau_r) e^{-\alpha\tau_r}. \end{aligned} \tag{13.9.5}$$

Since this equation allows us to compute the lapsed time expected rewards from the expected rewards we have developed earlier, it constitutes a complete solution to the indefinite duration problem with discounting. If we wish to consider how the relative value of state i depends on τ_ℓ in the indefinite duration monodesmic case without discounting, we simply set $\alpha = 0$ in Equations 13.9.4 and 13.9.5. The only change worthy of note is that the relative values v_j rather than the expected present values of future rewards $v_j(\alpha)$ for each state will appear in Equation 13.9.5.

One-State System

The one-state lapsed time computation is especially interesting because we can use it as the basis for a theory of depreciation. Since there will be only one state, we do not need subscripts on any of our quantities. Further, we can write $h(\cdot)$ for both the holding time and waiting time density functions for the state because there will be no distinction between them. Thus Equations 13.9.4 and 13.9.5 assume the simpler forms,

$$r^{\ell}(\tau_\ell, \alpha) = \int_0^\infty d\tau_r \frac{h(\tau_\ell + \tau_r)}{{}^{>}h(\tau_\ell)} \left[\int_0^{\tau_r} d\sigma\, e^{-\alpha\sigma} y(\tau_\ell + \sigma) + e^{-\alpha\tau_r} b(\tau_\ell + \tau_r)\right] \qquad (13.9.6)$$

and

$$v^{\ell}(\tau_\ell, \alpha) = r^{\ell}(\tau_\ell, \alpha) + \frac{1}{{}^{>}h(\tau_\ell)} v(\alpha) \int_0^\infty d\tau_r\, h(\tau_\ell + \tau_r) e^{-\alpha\tau_r}. \qquad (13.9.7)$$

The expected discounted reward from a single occupancy of the state, $r(\alpha)$, is related to $r^{\ell}(\tau_\ell, \alpha)$ by

$$r(\alpha) = r^{\ell}(0, \alpha) = \int_0^\infty d\tau_r\, h(\tau_r) \left[\int_0^{\tau_r} d\sigma\, e^{-\alpha\sigma} y(\sigma) + e^{-\alpha\tau_r} b(\tau_r)\right], \qquad (13.9.8)$$

which, of course, agrees with Equation 13.2.17. The expected discounted reward for all future time from entering this state, $v(\alpha)$, is derived from Equation 13.9.7 as

$$v(\alpha) = v^{\ell}(0, \alpha) = r(\alpha) + v(\alpha) \int_0^\infty d\tau_r\, h(\tau_r) e^{-\alpha\tau_r} = r(\alpha) + v(\alpha) h^e(\alpha), \qquad (13.9.9)$$

or

$$v(\alpha) = \frac{r(\alpha)}{1 - h^e(\alpha)} \qquad (13.9.10)$$

in correspondence with Equation 13.2.18 for the one-state case. Now if we are given any yield-bonus structure for the state, we can use Equations 13.9.8, 13.9.10, 13.9.6, and finally Equation 13.9.7 to find its lapsed time expected reward $v^{\ell}(\tau_\ell, \alpha)$

Book Value

Suppose that we are going to purchase a facility for a business. The facility will have a purchase cost, operating and maintenance costs, and, when it is worn out, a scrap value. If we include all these costs in the yield and bonus structure for the one-state process we have been considering, then $v(\alpha)$ will be the present value of all future costs just after we have purchased a new facility under the assumption that when it is worn out we shall replace it by another facility with the same associated costs. The lapsed time quantity $v^{\ell}(\tau_\ell, \alpha)$ will be the present value of all future costs given that the facility has been operating for a time τ_ℓ. We call the value for the facility that we should carry on our books if it has been operating for a time τ_ℓ the book value for the facility at this age and give it the symbol $v^b(\tau_\ell, \alpha)$. If this book value is to reflect the savings in future costs because we already have a facility of age τ_ℓ and therefore do not have to buy a new one, then it must be given by

$$v^b(\tau_\ell, \alpha) = v(\alpha) - v^\ell(\tau_\ell, \alpha). \tag{13.9.11}$$

In this equation we interpret $v(\alpha)$ as measuring future expected costs just before the purchase of a new facility and $v^\ell(0, \alpha)$ as just after the purchase of a new facility.

An example

The idea is best illustrated by a simple example. Suppose that a new machine costs P, lasts exactly T years, and has a scrap value S ($P > S$). We assume that the operating costs do not change with age so that they may be omitted from the problem. To place these costs in our yield-bonus framework, we see that there is an impulse of magnitude P in yield at the origin and that the bonus is $-S$,

$$y(\sigma) = P\,\delta(\sigma) \qquad b(\tau) = -S. \tag{13.9.12}$$

We now begin our computations with Equation 13.9.8. Since the constant life T implies a holding time density function consisting of a unit impulse at T,

$$r(\alpha) = P - e^{-\alpha T}S. \tag{13.9.13}$$

The present value of costs associated with a state occupancy is just the price of the new machine less the present value of its scrap value. Since $h^e(\alpha) = e^{-\alpha T}$, Equation 13.9.10 shows that the present value of costs associated with all future replacement cycles just before a replacement is

$$v(\alpha) = \frac{P - e^{-\alpha T}S}{1 - e^{-\alpha T}}. \tag{13.9.14}$$

Next we use Equation 13.9.6 to compute the present value of the costs in the remainder of the cycle if time τ_ℓ in the cycle has lapsed,

$$r^\ell(\tau_\ell, \alpha) = -e^{-\alpha(T-\tau_\ell)}S, \tag{13.9.15}$$

which is just the scrap value discounted over the time remaining in the cycle. Finally from Equation 13.9.7 we compute the present value of all future costs if a time τ_ℓ has lapsed,

$$\begin{aligned} v^\ell(\tau_\ell, \alpha) = r^\ell(\tau_\ell, \alpha) + v(\alpha)\cdot e^{-\alpha(T-\tau_\ell)} &= -e^{-\alpha(T-\tau_\ell)}S + e^{-\alpha(T-\tau_\ell)}\frac{P - e^{-at}S}{1 - e^{-\alpha T}} \\ &= (P - S)\frac{e^{-\alpha(T-\tau_\ell)}}{1 - e^{-\alpha T}}. \end{aligned} \tag{13.9.16}$$

From Equation 13.9.11 we then have the book value as

$$v^b(\tau_\ell, \alpha) = v(\alpha) - v^\ell(\tau_\ell, \alpha) = P\frac{1 - e^{-\alpha(T-\tau_\ell)}}{1 - e^{-\alpha T}} + S\frac{e^{-\alpha(T-\tau_\ell)} - e^{-\alpha T}}{1 - e^{-\alpha T}}. \tag{13.9.17}$$

We note that the book value of a new machine is P, ($v^b(0, \alpha) = P$), and that the book value of a machine about to be replaced is S, ($v^b(T, \alpha) = S$), two satisfying results.

To explore the nature of this book value in more detail, let $f(\tau_\ell, \alpha)$ be defined by

$$f(\tau_\ell, \alpha) = \frac{e^{-\alpha(T-\tau_\ell)} - e^{-\alpha T}}{1 - e^{-\alpha T}} = \frac{e^{-\alpha T}}{1 - e^{-\alpha T}}(e^{\alpha \tau_\ell} - 1). \tag{13.9.18}$$

Then Equation 13.9.17 becomes

$$v^b(\tau_\ell, \alpha) = P[1 - f(\tau_\ell, \alpha)] + Sf(\tau_\ell, \alpha) \tag{13.9.19}$$

or

$$v^b(\tau_\ell, \alpha) = P - (P - S)f(\tau_\ell, \alpha). \tag{13.9.20}$$

By using Equations 13.9.20 and 13.9.18, we can easily produce the plot of book value shown in Figure 13.9.1. Note that the book value falls ever more rapidly as the age of the machine increases.

Depreciation

We call the depreciation of a facility of age τ_ℓ the amount by which its book value is lower than that of a new facility and give it the symbol $v^d(\tau_\ell, \alpha)$. Formally, the depreciation is given by

$$v^d(\tau_\ell, \alpha) = v^b(0, \alpha) - v^b(\tau_\ell, \alpha). \tag{13.9.21}$$

Since for our example $v^b(0, \alpha) = P$, we have

$$v^d(\tau_\ell, \alpha) = P - v^b(\tau_\ell, \alpha) = (P - S)f(\tau_\ell, \alpha) \tag{13.9.22}$$

or

$$v^d(\tau_\ell, \alpha) = (P - S)\frac{e^{-\alpha T}}{1 - e^{-\alpha T}}(e^{\alpha \tau_\ell} - 1). \tag{13.9.23}$$

We therefore see that the depreciation of the machine increases with its age as the difference between an exponential and a constant (see Figure 13.9.1).

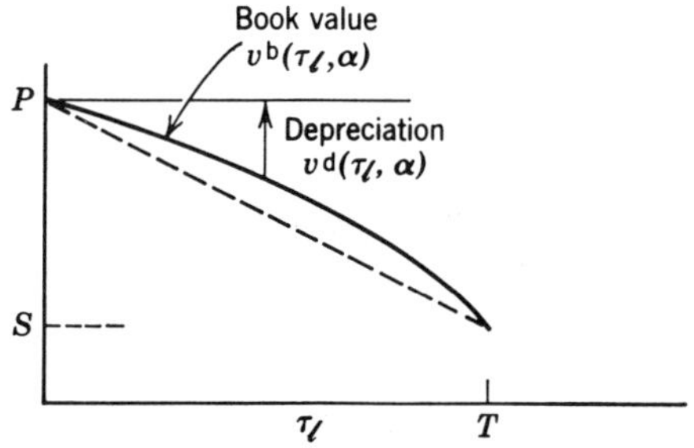

Figure 13.9.1 The book value and depreciation of a fixed life machine.

Depreciation rate

Sometimes it is helpful to be able to speak of the rate of depreciation, which is the derivative of depreciation with respect to the lapsed time. From Equation 13.9.22, we see that the depreciation rate for our example is given by

$$\frac{d}{d\tau_\ell} v^{\mathrm{d}}(\tau_\ell, \alpha) = (P - S) \frac{d}{d\tau_\ell} f(\tau_\ell, \alpha) \tag{13.9.24}$$

and therefore by

$$\frac{d}{d\tau_\ell} v^{\mathrm{d}}(\tau_\ell, \alpha) = (P - S) \frac{\alpha e^{-\alpha T}}{1 - e^{-\alpha T}} \cdot e^{\alpha \tau_\ell} . \tag{13.9.25}$$

The rate of depreciation increases exponentially with age.

Low discount rate

The results we have computed for this example assume an interesting form when the discount rate α is small enough so that for values of $\tau \leq T$, $e^{-\alpha\tau}$ can be approximated by $1 - \alpha\tau$. When this is the case, Equation 13.9.18 becomes

$$f(\tau_\ell, \alpha) = \frac{[1 - \alpha(T - \tau_\ell)] - [1 - \alpha T]}{1 - [1 - \alpha T]} = \frac{\tau_\ell}{T} . \tag{13.9.26}$$

From Equations 13.9.20 and 13.9.22 we obtain

$$v^{\mathrm{b}}(\tau_\ell, \alpha) = P - (P - S) \frac{\tau_\ell}{T} \tag{13.9.27}$$

and

$$v^{\mathrm{d}}(\tau_\ell, \alpha) = (P - S) \frac{\tau_\ell}{T} . \tag{13.9.28}$$

The book value of the machine falls linearly with time as shown by the dotted line in Figure 13.9.1; consequently, the depreciation increases linearly with time, and the rate of depreciation is a constant. We call this type of depreciation "straight line" depreciation—it is widely used. We note that it is based on the assumption that the compounding of interest is not an important factor over the life of the facility.

Depreciation with Random Lifetimes

We can treat depreciation in a more general context by allowing τ, the life of the facility, to be a random variable with density function $h(\tau)$ and exponential transform $h^e(s)$. If we use the same purchase price P and salvage value S, Equation 13.9.8 shows that $r(\alpha)$ is given by

$$r(\alpha) = P - h^e(\alpha) S . \tag{13.9.29}$$

Then from Equation 13.9.10, $v(\alpha)$ becomes

$$v(\alpha) = \frac{P - h^e(\alpha)S}{1 - h^e(\alpha)}. \tag{13.9.30}$$

We compute the lapsed time quantities from Equations 13.9.6 and 13.9.7 as

$$r^{\ell}(\tau_\ell, \alpha) = -S\int_0^\infty d\tau_r \frac{h(\tau_\ell + \tau_r)e^{-\alpha\tau_r}}{{}^{>}h(\tau_\ell)} \tag{13.9.31}$$

and

$$\begin{aligned} v^{\ell}(\tau_\ell, \alpha) &= r^{\ell}(\tau_\ell, \alpha) + \frac{1}{{}^{>}h(\tau_\ell)} v(\alpha)\int_0^\infty d\tau_r\, h(\tau_\ell + \tau_r)e^{-\alpha\tau_r} \\ &= [v(\alpha) - S]\frac{1}{{}^{>}h(\tau_\ell)}\int_0^\infty d\tau_r\, h(\tau_\ell + \tau_r)e^{-\alpha\tau_r}. \end{aligned} \tag{13.9.32}$$

By using Equation 13.9.30, we can write $v^{\ell}(\tau_\ell, \alpha)$ in the form

$$v^{\ell}(\tau_\ell, \alpha) = (P - S)\frac{1}{1 - h^e(\alpha)} \cdot \frac{1}{{}^{>}h(\tau_\ell)}\int_0^\infty d\tau_r\, h(\tau_\ell + \tau_r)e^{-\alpha\tau_r}. \tag{13.9.33}$$

We are now in a position to write the book value $v^{b}(\tau_\ell, \alpha)$ from Equation 13.9.11 using these results,

$$\begin{aligned} v^{b}(\tau_\ell, \alpha) = v(\alpha) - v^{\ell}(\tau_\ell, \alpha) &= P\frac{1}{1 - h^e(\alpha)}\left[1 - \frac{1}{{}^{>}h(\tau_\ell)}\int_0^\infty d\tau_r\, h(\tau_\ell + \tau_r)e^{-\alpha\tau_r}\right] \\ &\quad + S\frac{1}{1 - h^e(\alpha)}\left[\frac{1}{{}^{>}h(\tau_\ell)}\int_0^\infty d\tau_r\, h(\tau_\ell + \tau_r)e^{-\alpha\tau_r} - h^e(\alpha)\right]. \end{aligned} \tag{13.9.34}$$

We again find it useful to define a quantity $f(\tau_\ell, \alpha)$. In this case we define it by

$$f(\tau_\ell, \alpha) = \frac{1}{1 - h^e(\alpha)}\left[\frac{1}{{}^{>}h(\tau_\ell)}\int_0^\infty d\tau_r\, h(\tau_\ell + \tau_r)e^{-\alpha\tau_r} - h^e(\alpha)\right]. \tag{13.9.35}$$

We see that with this definition Equation 13.9.34 assumes the form shown in Equation 13.9.19 or 13.9.20. Consequently, the depreciation equations 13.9.21 and 13.9.22 and the depreciation rate equation 13.9.24 apply as well to random lifetimes. Of course, if we let $h(\tau) = \delta(\tau - T)$ so that $h^e(s) = e^{-sT}$ and $h^e(\alpha) = e^{-\alpha T}$, then all the expressions for the case of random lifetimes reduce to those developed earlier for the case of a definite lifetime T.

Low discount rate

The expressions for book value and depreciation for the case of random lifetime assume a special form when the discount rate is small. We first note that when α is small, we can approximate $h^e(\alpha)$ by

$$\begin{aligned} h^e(\alpha) &= 1 + \left.\frac{dh^e(\alpha)}{d\alpha}\right|_{\alpha=0} \cdot \alpha \\ &= 1 - \bar{\tau}\alpha, \end{aligned} \tag{13.9.36}$$

where $\bar{\tau}$ is the mean lifetime; moreover, we can approximate $e^{-\alpha\tau}$ by $1 - \alpha\tau$. With these approximations, Equation 13.9.35 becomes

$$\begin{aligned} f(\tau_\ell, \alpha) &= \frac{1}{1 - (1 - \bar{\tau}\alpha)} \left[\frac{1}{{}^{>}h(\tau_\ell)} \int_0^\infty d\tau_r\, h(\tau_\ell + \tau_r)[1 - \alpha\tau_r] - (1 - \bar{\tau}\alpha) \right] \\ &= \frac{1}{\bar{\tau}\alpha} \left[\bar{\tau}\alpha - \alpha \frac{1}{{}^{>}h(\tau_\ell)} \int_0^\infty d\tau_r\, h(\tau_\ell + \tau_r)\cdot\tau_r \right] \\ &= 1 - \frac{1}{\bar{\tau}} \left[\frac{1}{{}^{>}h(\tau_\ell)} \int_0^\infty d\tau_r\, h(\tau_\ell + \tau_r)\tau_r \right]. \end{aligned} \quad (13.9.37)$$

The quantity in brackets in this equation is the expected lifetime remaining given that the facility has already reached age τ_ℓ. We designate this expectation by $\bar{\tau}_r(\tau_\ell)$,

$$\bar{\tau}_r(\tau_\ell) = \frac{1}{{}^{>}h(\tau_\ell)} \int_0^\infty d\tau_r\, h(\tau_\ell + \tau_r)\cdot\tau_r\,. \quad (13.9.38)$$

Then Equation 13.9.37 becomes simply

$$f(\tau_\ell, \alpha) = 1 - \frac{\bar{\tau}_r(\tau_\ell)}{\bar{\tau}}. \quad (13.9.39)$$

From Equation 13.9.19 we see that the book value must depend on lapsed time in the form

$$v^{b}(\tau_\ell, \alpha) = P\frac{\bar{\tau}_r(\tau_\ell)}{\bar{\tau}} + S\left[1 - \frac{\bar{\tau}_r(\tau_\ell)}{\bar{\tau}}\right] \quad (13.9.40)$$

and from Equation 13.9.22 that the depreciation function is

$$v^{d}(\tau_\ell, \alpha) = (P - S)\left[1 - \frac{\bar{\tau}_r(\tau_\ell)}{\bar{\tau}}\right]. \quad (13.9.41)$$

Thus, when the discount rate is low, the book value and depreciation depend primarily on how the expected remaining life of the facility varies with the life already elapsed. Note that when the lifetime is fixed at T, then $\bar{\tau} = T$, $\bar{\tau}_r(\tau_\ell) = T - \tau_\ell$, and all these expressions reduce to those developed for the straight-line depreciation case.

Exponential lifetime

We obtain insight into the depreciation process by noting the forms of our expressions when the lifetime of the facility is exponentially distributed. Thus we shall consider the case

$$h(\tau) = \lambda e^{-\lambda\tau} \quad \tau \geq 0; \qquad {}^{>}h(t) = e^{-\lambda t}; \qquad h^{e}(s) = \frac{\lambda}{s + \lambda}. \quad (13.9.42)$$

From Equation 13.9.35 we have

$$f(\tau_\ell, \alpha) = \frac{1}{1 - \dfrac{\lambda}{\alpha + \lambda}} \left[\frac{1}{e^{-\lambda\tau_\ell}} \int_0^\infty d\tau_r\, \lambda e^{-\lambda(\tau_\ell + \tau_r)} e^{-\alpha\tau_r} - \frac{\lambda}{\alpha + \lambda} \right]$$

$$= \frac{\alpha + \lambda}{\alpha} \left[\lambda \int_0^\infty d\tau_r\, e^{-(\alpha+\lambda)\tau_r} - \frac{\lambda}{\alpha + \lambda} \right]$$

$$= \frac{\alpha + \lambda}{\alpha} \left[\frac{\lambda}{\alpha + \lambda} - \frac{\lambda}{\alpha + \lambda} \right]$$

$$= 0. \tag{13.9.43}$$

Therefore, from Equations 13.9.20 and 13.9.22, we have

$$v^{\mathrm{b}}(\tau_\ell, \alpha) = P; \qquad v^{\mathrm{d}}(\tau_\ell, \alpha) = 0. \tag{13.9.44}$$

If a facility has an exponential lifetime, it should be carried on the books at its purchase price and not depreciated. The reason is that when a facility has an exponential lifetime, the probability distribution for its remaining life is the same regardless of its age.

We can use this example to confirm Equation 13.9.39 developed for the case of small discount rates. For the exponential example, $\bar{\tau} = \bar{\tau}_r(\tau_\ell) = 1/\lambda$; therefore, Equation 13.9.39 shows that $f(\tau_\ell, \alpha) = 0$, in agreement with Equation 13.9.43.

Double exponential lifetime

As a further example, let us consider the case where the lifetime is the sum of two independent random variables, each with the exponential density function of the preceding example. We then have

$$h(\tau) = \lambda^2 \tau e^{-\lambda\tau}; \qquad {}^{>}h(t) = (\lambda t + 1)e^{-\lambda t}; \qquad h^e(s) = \left(\frac{\lambda}{s + \lambda}\right)^2. \tag{13.9.45}$$

By using Equation 13.9.35, we obtain

$$f(\tau_\ell, \alpha) = \frac{1}{1 - \left(\dfrac{\lambda}{\alpha + \lambda}\right)^2} \left[\frac{1}{(\lambda\tau_\ell + 1)e^{-\lambda\tau_\ell}} \int_0^\infty d\tau_r\, \lambda^2(\tau_\ell + \tau_r) e^{-\lambda(\tau_\ell + \tau_r)} e^{-\alpha\tau_r} - \left(\frac{\lambda}{\alpha + \lambda}\right)^2 \right]$$

$$= \frac{(\alpha + \lambda)^2}{\alpha^2 + 2\alpha\lambda} \left[\frac{1}{\lambda\tau_\ell + 1} \int_0^\infty d\tau_r\, \lambda^2(\tau_\ell + \tau_r) e^{-(\alpha+\lambda)\tau_r} - \left(\frac{\lambda}{\alpha + \lambda}\right)^2 \right]$$

$$= \frac{(\alpha + \lambda)^2}{\alpha^2 + 2\alpha\lambda} \left[\frac{1}{\lambda\tau_\ell + 1} \left(\frac{\lambda^2 \tau_\ell}{\alpha + \lambda} + \frac{\lambda^2}{(\alpha + \lambda)^2} \right) - \left(\frac{\lambda}{\alpha + \lambda}\right)^2 \right]$$

$$= \frac{(\alpha + \lambda)^2}{\alpha^2 + 2\alpha\lambda} \left[\frac{\alpha\lambda^2 \tau_\ell}{(\lambda\tau_\ell + 1)(\alpha + \lambda)^2} \right]$$

$$= \frac{\lambda\tau_\ell \cdot \dfrac{\lambda}{\alpha + 2\lambda}}{\lambda\tau_\ell + 1}. \tag{13.9.46}$$

From Equations 13.9.20 and 13.9.22 we immediately write the book value and depreciation as

$$v^b(\tau_\ell, \alpha) = P - (P - S)\frac{\lambda\tau_\ell \cdot \dfrac{\lambda}{\alpha + 2\lambda}}{\lambda\tau_\ell + 1}; \qquad v^d(\tau_\ell, \alpha) = (P - S)\frac{\lambda\tau_\ell \cdot \dfrac{\lambda}{\alpha + 2\lambda}}{\lambda\tau_\ell + 1}. \quad (13.9.47)$$

A plot of these quantities appears as Figure 13.9.2. We observe that the book value starts at P, the purchase price, when $\tau_\ell = 0$ and falls to $P - (P - S)\lambda/(\alpha + 2\lambda)$ when the lapsed time is very large. Therefore, the maximum depreciation of the facility is $(P - S)\lambda/(\alpha + 2\lambda)$ regardless of how old it is.

We find the rate of depreciation from Equation 13.9.47,

$$\frac{d}{d\tau_\ell} v^d(\tau_\ell, \alpha) = (P - S)\lambda \cdot \frac{\lambda}{\alpha + 2\lambda} \cdot \frac{1}{(\lambda\tau_\ell + 1)^2}. \quad (13.9.48)$$

The rate of depreciation decreases markedly with the age of the facility in contrast with the fixed lifetime case.

Low discount rate. If the discount rate is small, we can use Equations 13.9.40 13.9.41 to find the book value and depreciation. From Equation 13.9.45, we first compute that the mean lifetime is $\bar{\tau} = 2/\lambda$. Then we use Equation 13.9.38 to compute the expected remaining lifetime as a function of the lapsed time,

$$\begin{aligned}\bar{\tau}_r(\tau_\ell) &= \frac{1}{(\lambda\tau_\ell + 1)e^{-\lambda\tau_\ell}} \int_0^\infty d\tau_r\, \lambda^2(\tau_\ell + \tau_r)e^{-\lambda(\tau_\ell + \tau_r)}\tau_r \\ &= \frac{1}{\lambda\tau_\ell + 1} \int_0^\infty d\tau_r\, \lambda^2(\tau_\ell + \tau_r)e^{-\lambda\tau_r}\tau_r \\ &= \frac{1}{\lambda\tau_\ell + 1}\left[\tau_\ell + \frac{2}{\lambda}\right] \\ &= \frac{\lambda\tau_\ell + 2}{\lambda(\lambda\tau_\ell + 1)}. \end{aligned} \quad (13.9.49)$$

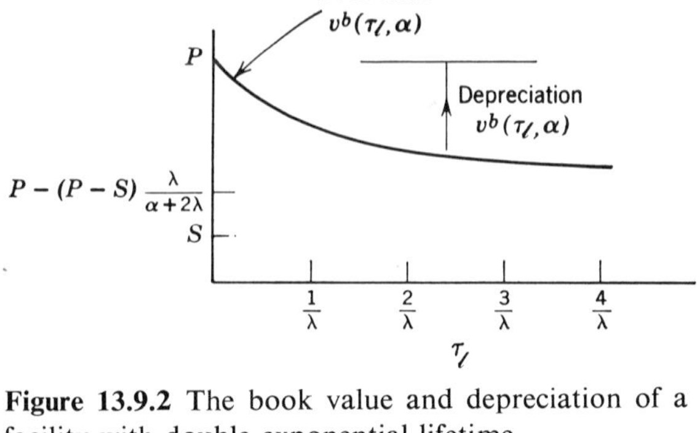

Figure 13.9.2 The book value and depreciation of a facility with double exponential lifetime.

We check this expression by noting that $\bar{\tau}_r(0) = \bar{\tau} = 2/\lambda$ as expected. Then from Equation 13.9.40 we have

$$v^{\mathrm{b}}(\tau_\ell, \alpha) = P\frac{\lambda\tau_\ell/2 + 1}{\lambda\tau_\ell + 1} + S\frac{\lambda\tau_\ell/2}{\lambda\tau_\ell + 1}$$

$$= P - (P - S)\frac{\lambda\tau_\ell/2}{\lambda\tau_\ell + 1} \tag{13.9.50}$$

and from Equation 13.9.41

$$v^{\mathrm{d}}(\tau_\ell, \alpha) = (P - S)\frac{\lambda\tau_\ell/2}{\lambda\tau_\ell + 1}\cdot \tag{13.9.51}$$

The forms of Equations 13.9.50 and 13.9.51 are the same as those shown in Figure 13.9.2. We note that Equations 13.9.50 and 13.9.51 are just the expressions we obtain if we take α small in Equation 13.9.47.

Depreciation or appreciation?

In our preceding examples we have seen that we can interpret depreciation as the decrease in the value of a facility caused by increasing age. In the case of the facility with exponentially distributed lifetime, no depreciation was called for. But can we experience the reverse situation, where we should increase the book value of a facility as it ages? To settle this question, let us consider an example. Suppose that a facility has two possible lifetimes, one time unit and two time units, with equal probability; that is,

$$h(\tau) = (1/2)\delta(\tau - 1) + (1/2)\delta(\tau - 2); \qquad h^e(s) = (1/2)e^{-s} + (1/2)e^{-2s}. \tag{13.9.52}$$

To compute the book value and depreciation we first invoke Equation 11.9.35 in two different regions of τ_ℓ. For $0 < \tau_\ell < 1$,

$$f(\tau_\ell, \alpha) = \frac{1}{1 - h^e(\alpha)}\left[\frac{1}{{}^{>}h(\tau_\ell)}\int_0^\infty d\tau_r\, h(\tau_\ell + \tau_r)e^{-\alpha\tau_r} - h^e(\alpha)\right]$$

$$= \frac{1}{1 - (1/2)e^{-\alpha} - (1/2)e^{-2\alpha}}$$

$$\times\ [(1/2)e^{-\alpha(1-\tau_\ell)} + (1/2)e^{-\alpha(2-\tau_\ell)} - (1/2)e^{-\alpha} - (1/2)e^{-2\alpha}]$$

$$= \frac{1}{2}\frac{(e^{\alpha\tau_\ell} - 1)(e^{-\alpha} + e^{-2\alpha})}{1 - (1/2)e^{-\alpha} - (1/2)e^{-2\alpha}} \tag{13.9.53}$$

and for $1 < \tau_\ell < 2$,

$$f(\tau_\ell, \alpha) = \frac{1}{1 - (1/2)e^{-\alpha} - (1/2)e^{-2\alpha}}[e^{-\alpha(2-\tau_\ell)} - (1/2)e^{-\alpha} - (1/2)e^{-2\alpha}]. \tag{13.9.54}$$

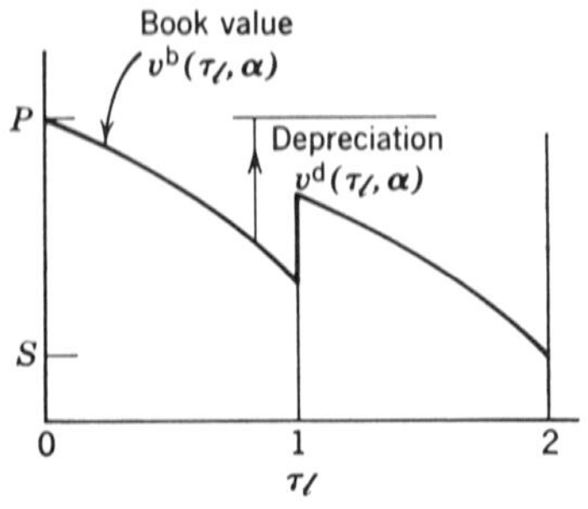

Figure 13.9.3 The book value and depreciation of a facility with two possible lifetimes.

Equations 13.9.20 and 13.9.22 then show the book value and depreciation; the results are plotted in Figure 13.9.3. We see that while the book value generally decreases with lapsed lifetime, it increases suddenly at the end of one time unit. Thus at the end of one time unit, we can justifiably say that the facility appreciates rather than depreciates. The reason for this behavior is clear from the lifetime distribution. If the lapsed time is just less than one time unit, the expected remaining life of the facility is 1/2; if it is just greater than one time unit, the expected remaining life is 1. The increase in expected life that results from surviving a possible failure at one time unit is directly responsible for the observed appreciation.

We should note that we could construct any number of examples that exhibit appreciation. We could create a smoother transition from depreciation to appreciation by using a continuous density function with its mass lumped at one and two time units rather than the impulse form we did use. We could even have the facility appreciate so much that its book value exceeded its purchase price. For example, if the facility were equally likely to fail immediately or to last for one year, then its book value would jump to $2P$ immediately after the threat of initial failure had passed. From that point it would fall gradually through the value P until it became S at one time unit.

The one-state depreciation model is only one of many uses for the lapsed time reward structure. For example, we can think of many-state models for depreciation of dependent equipment. We could explore fields beyond accounting for other applications. The important realization is that we can treat expected rewards in semi-Markov processes even if we begin to observe the process at an arbitrary time.

13.10 REWARDS IN TRANSIENT PROCESSES

Let us consider an N-state semi-Markov process divided into a set of transient states $\mathscr{T}$ and trapping states $\mathscr{R}$. Suppose that we start the process in a transient state and allow it to run until it enters a trapping state. Suppose further that we can assign a value to the process's entering each trapping state. Then how do we compute v_i, the expected reward that the process will earn if it starts in transient state i? We first recall that we have defined r_i as the expected reward from a single occupancy of state i. Then for each transient state we can write the equation

$$v_i = r_i + \sum_{j=1}^{N} p_{ij} v_j \qquad i \in \mathscr{T}. \tag{13.10.1}$$

The value v_j for each trapping state j is set equal to its assigned value. We now have

$$v_i = r_i + \sum_{k \in \mathscr{T}} p_{ik} v_k + \sum_{j \in \mathscr{R}} p_{ij} v_j \qquad i \in \mathscr{T}. \tag{13.10.2}$$

This equation has a particularly interesting form. By referring to the discussion of Section 4.1 where we first treated transient processes and specifically to Equation 4.1.34, we see that we can express its solution in the form

$$v_i = \sum_{k \in \mathscr{T}} \bar{\nu}_{ik} \left(r_k + \sum_{j \in \mathscr{R}} p_{kj} v_j \right) \qquad i \in \mathscr{T}, \tag{13.10.3}$$

where $\bar{\nu}_{ij}$ is the expected number of times transient state j will be occupied in the transient process if it is started in state i. We can express Equation 13.10.3 in terms of the transmissions of the modified transition diagram by using Equation 4.1.34,

$$\begin{aligned} v_i &= \sum_{k \in \mathscr{T}} \vec{t}_{ik} r_k + \sum_{j \in \mathscr{R}} \sum_{k \in \mathscr{T}} \vec{t}_{ik} p_{kj} v_j \\ &= \sum_{k \in \mathscr{T}} \vec{t}_{ik} r_k + \sum_{j \in \mathscr{R}} \vec{t}_{ij} v_j \qquad i \in \mathscr{T}. \end{aligned} \tag{13.10.4}$$

Since $\vec{t}_{ij}$ when i is transient and j is a trapping state is just ϕ_{ij}, the probability that a process starting in transient state i will ultimately be trapped by trapping state j, we obtain the easily interpretable form

$$v_i = \sum_{k \in \mathscr{T}} \bar{\nu}_{ik} r_k + \sum_{j \in \mathscr{R}} \phi_{ij} v_j \qquad i \in \mathscr{T}. \tag{13.10.5}$$

The expected reward from starting the process in transient state i is equal to: 1) the sum over all transient states of the expected number of times the process will visit each transient state times the expected reward from its visit plus 2) the sum over all trapping states of the probability that the process will be trapped by each trapping state times the value of the trapping state, all computations to be conditional on starting the process in state i. This result is intuitive and important in a variety of applications.

The Problem of Points

We can illustrate the usefulness of this discussion with an example from the dawn of probability theory. In 1654, Pascal wrote a letter to Fermat investigating a problem posed by an associate, the Chevalier de Méré, who was reputedly a gambler. The problem is called the Problem of Points, stated as follows. Two players who have equal probability of winning a point on each trial play a game in which the first to reach a given number of points will win. If they separate without playing out the game, how should the stakes be divided between them? Pascal wrote:

> The following is my method for determining the share of each player, when, for example, two players play a game of three points and each player has staked 32 pistoles.
>
> Suppose that the first player has gained two points and the second player one point; they have now to play for a point on this condition, that if the first player gains he takes all the money which is at stake, namely 64 pistoles, and if the second player gains each player has two points, so that they are on terms of equality, and if they leave off playing each ought to take 32 pistoles. Thus, if the first player gains, 64 pistoles belong to him, and if he loses, 32 pistoles belong to him. If, then, the players do not wish to play this game, but to separate without playing it, the first player would say to the second "I am certain of 32 pistoles even if I lose this game, and as for the other 32 pistoles perhaps I shall have them and perhaps you will have them; the chances are equal. Let us then divide these 32 pistoles equally and give me also the 32 pistoles of which I am certain." Thus the first player will have 48 pistoles and the second 16 pistoles.
>
> Next, suppose that the first player has gained two points and the second player none, and that they are about to play for a point; the condition then is that if the first player gains this point he secures the game and takes the 64 pistoles, and if the second player gains this point the players will then be in the situation already examined, in which the first player is entitled to 48 pistoles, and the second to 16 pistoles. Thus if they do not wish to play, the first player would say to the second "If I gain the point I gain 64 pistoles; if I lose it I am entitled to 48 pistoles. Give me then the 48 pistoles of which I am certain, and divide the other 16 equally, since our chances of gaining the point are equal." Thus the first player will have 56 pistoles and the second player 8 pistoles.
>
> Finally, suppose that the first player has gained one point and the second player none. If they proceed to play for a point the condition is that if the first player gains it the players will be in the situation first examined, in which the first player is entitled to 56 pistoles; if the first player loses the point each player has then a point, and each is entitled to 32 pistoles. Thus if they do not wish to play, the first player would say to the second "Give me the 32 pistoles of which I am certain and divide the remainder of the 56 pistoles equally, that is, divide 24 pistoles

equally." Thus the first player will have the sum of 32 and 12 pistoles, that is 44 pistoles, and consequently the second will have 20 pistoles.†

Pascal then proceeded to generalize certain aspects of the problem, but his example will suffice for us.

Transient process solution

We shall solve it by using the idea of rewards in a transient Markov process. The state description will be the pair of numbers representing the opponent's score and our score; thus, 12 is the state where the opponent has one point and we have two. The modified transition diagram for this process appears as Figure 13.10.1. The branches all bear the 1/2 probability that each player will gain a point. The state -3

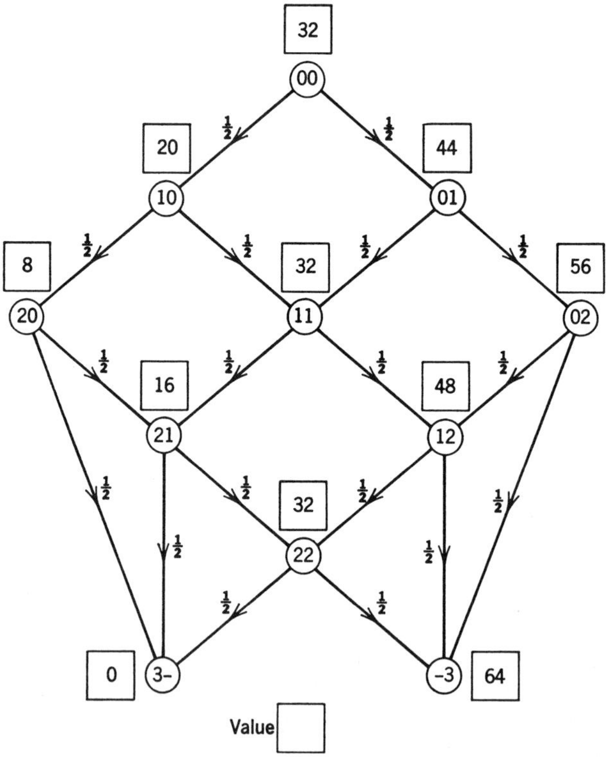

Figure 13.10.1 Modified transition diagram for the problem of points.

† Todhunter, I., *A History of the Mathematical Theory of Probability*, Chelsea, New York, 1949.

represents the situation where we have won; the state 3-, a win by our opponent, Only these two trapping states have any values, the state -3 representing a return of 64 to us and the state 3- representing no return. All the transient states have an expected reward per occupancy r_i that is equal to zero. The game starts in the transient state 00, but play may be interrupted in any transient state. We would like to find the expected reward that will be generated upon entering any transient state, for this will be the fair gain to us if the game is terminated at that point.

We could solve the problem immediately by writing Equation 13.10.1 for each of the nine transient states and finding the solution. However, let us instead employ the symmetry inherent in the problem. By symmetry we know that the payment to us if the game ends in states 00, 11, or 22 should be 32 because both we and our opponent have equal chances of winning from these states; we therefore enter 32 on the modified transition diagram as their values v_{00}, v_{11} and v_{22}.

Suppose now that we write Equation 13.10.1 for v_{12}, a task we can do by inspection of Figure 13.10.1,

$$\begin{aligned} v_{12} &= (1/2)v_{22} + (1/2)v_{-3} \\ &= (1/2)(32) + (1/2)(64) \\ &= 48. \end{aligned} \tag{13.10.6}$$

We should therefore receive a payment of 48 if the game is stopped when our opponent has one point and we have two. Having evaluated v_{12}, we can write a similar equation for v_{02},

$$\begin{aligned} v_{02} &= (1/2)v_{12} + (1/2)v_{-3} \\ &= (1/2)(48) + (1/2)(64) \\ &= 56. \end{aligned} \tag{13.10.7}$$

If our opponent has no points and we have two at the interruption of the game, we shall receive a payment of 56. We can finally find v_{01},

$$\begin{aligned} v_{01} &= (1/2)v_{11} + (1/2)v_{02} \\ &= (1/2)(32) + (1/2)(56) \\ &= 44. \end{aligned} \tag{13.10.8}$$

Thus, if our opponent has no points and we have one, the fair payment to us is 44. Note that the equations we have written follow closely the reasoning of Pascal. By continuing the procedure we have followed or by symmetry we can quickly find the values of all states in the diagram. It is not uncommon in practical problems to find a simple structure in the modified transition diagram that allows the values to be established by inspection rather than by formal solution of Equations 13.10.1.

Transition diagram solution

Another method of finding the values of each state is implicit in Equation 13.10.5. Since r_i is zero for all transient states, this equation becomes

$$\begin{aligned} v_i &= \sum_{j\in\mathscr{R}} \phi_{ij}v_j \qquad i \in \mathscr{T} \\ &= \phi_{i,\text{-}3}v_{\text{-}3} + \phi_{i,3\text{-}}v_{3\text{-}} \\ &= \phi_{i,\text{-}3}(64) + \phi_{i,3\text{-}}(0) \\ &= 64\phi_{i,\text{-}3}. \end{aligned} \tag{13.10.9}$$

The value of each transient state i is just 64 times the probability of reaching the state -3 from state i during transient operation. Since this probability is the transmission $\vec{t}_{i,\text{-}3}$ of the transition diagram from state i to state -3, we have a simple implementation of the result. Thus to find v_{12}, v_{02}, and v_{01}, we compute $\vec{t}_{12,\text{-}3}$, $\vec{t}_{02,\text{-}3}$, and $\vec{t}_{01,\text{-}3}$ from the modified transition diagram as:

$$\vec{t}_{12,\text{-}3} = \frac{1}{2} + \frac{1}{2}\cdot\frac{1}{2} = \frac{3}{4} = \phi_{12,\text{-}3}$$

$$\vec{t}_{02,\text{-}3} = \frac{1}{2} + \frac{1}{2}\cdot\frac{1}{2} + \frac{1}{2}\cdot\frac{1}{2}\cdot\frac{1}{2} = \frac{7}{8} = \phi_{02,\text{-}3}$$

$$\vec{t}_{01,\text{-}3} = \frac{1}{2}\cdot\frac{1}{2} + \frac{1}{2}\cdot\frac{1}{2}\cdot\frac{1}{2} + \frac{1}{2}\cdot\frac{1}{2}\cdot\frac{1}{2} + \frac{1}{2}\cdot\frac{1}{2}\cdot\frac{1}{2}\cdot\frac{1}{2} + \frac{1}{2}\cdot\frac{1}{2}\cdot\frac{1}{2}\cdot\frac{1}{2} + \frac{1}{2}\cdot\frac{1}{2}\cdot\frac{1}{2}\cdot\frac{1}{2} = \frac{11}{16} = \phi_{01,\text{-}3} \tag{13.10.10}$$

Then we use Equation 13.10.9 to obtain

$$\begin{aligned} v_{12} &= 64\phi_{12,\text{-}3} = 48 \\ v_{02} &= 64\phi_{02,\text{-}3} = 56 \\ v_{01} &= 64\phi_{01,\text{-}3} = 44, \end{aligned} \tag{13.10.11}$$

in agreement with our previous values.

We should note that the machinery we have developed in this problem is capable of solving a much more complicated version of the problem of points. For example, the probabilities of winning on each trial need not be symmetric, and intermediate payoffs can be introduced. However, this simple example of rewards in Markov processes illustrates that Pascal used a logic of solution that three centuries have not improved.

13.11 CONCLUDING REMARKS

The study of expectations of reward in a Markov process is a simple extension of our earlier results. As we would expect, computations are particularly easy if performed recursively. We note, however, that finding the asymptotic behavior of total expected reward for a given starting state requires only the solution of simultaneous equations whether or not future rewards are discounted. In the case of no discounting, the gain or average reward per unit time of a monodesmic Markov process provides an important descriptor of its reward-generating potential.

Reward as a Non-Economic Statistic

If we are alert in applications to interpret rewards broadly, we can often use the reward structure to find non-economic process statistics quickly. For example, if the boundary values $v_i(0)$ and bonuses $b_{ij}(\tau)$ are all zero and the yield rates are given by

$$y_{ij}(\sigma) = \begin{Bmatrix} 1 & i = r \\ 0 & i \neq r \end{Bmatrix} \quad 0 \leq \sigma \qquad \begin{matrix} i = 1, 2, \ldots, N \\ j = 1, 2, \ldots, N, \end{matrix} \tag{13.11.1}$$

then $v_i(t)$ from Equation 13.3.1 is the expected amount of time the process will spend in state r in the time interval $(0, t)$ given that it starts in state i.

If, with the same boundary values and bonuses, the yield rates are specified as the impulse functions

$$y_{ij}(\sigma) = \begin{Bmatrix} \delta(\sigma) & i = r \\ 0 & i \neq r \end{Bmatrix} \quad 0 \leq \sigma \qquad \begin{matrix} i = 1, 2, \ldots, N \\ j = 1, 2, \ldots, N, \end{matrix} \tag{13.11.2}$$

then $v_i(t)$ is the expected number of times the process will enter state r in the time interval $(0, t)$ given that it starts in state i.

If both boundary values and yield rates $y_{ij}(\sigma)$ are all set to zero, but the bonuses are established as

$$b_{ij}(\tau) = \begin{Bmatrix} 1 & i = r, j = s \\ 0 & \text{otherwise} \end{Bmatrix} \quad 0 \leq \tau \qquad \begin{matrix} i = 1, 2, \ldots, N \\ j = 1, 2, \ldots, N, \end{matrix} \tag{13.11.3}$$

then $v_i(t)$ is the expected number of transitions the process will make from state r to state s in the time interval $(0, t)$ given that it starts in state i.

PROBLEMS

1. The taxi company in Problem 1, Chapter 12 is trying to decide on a pricing system. The first system charges \$0.50 per trip for trips from A to A and B to B and \$1.00 otherwise. The second system charges \$1.75 per hour for a trip regardless of its origin or destination. If we only consider the steady-state operation of the company (i.e., ignore transients), which system should be used to maximize income? Explain why.

2. A gasoline service station has a single gas pump for servicing customers. Because of space limitations, there is only room for a single car to wait while another is being serviced. The proprietor has found that customers arrive a rate of 6 per hour with an interarrival time that is exponentially distributed, and that the servicing time is also exponentially distributed with a mean of 10 minutes. The owner of the station has determined that he makes \$10 per hour when a customer is in service. If he installs a second pump it will cost him \$3 per hour for an additional attendant. The second pump will work in parallel with the first pump, will earn the same amount of money, and will accept customers from the single waiting space. Should the owner install the second pump? Explain.

3. A taxi company operates between two towns and uses the following continuous-time Markov process to model the behavior of its drivers:

$$P = \begin{bmatrix} 0.9 & 0.1 \\ 0.4 & 0.6 \end{bmatrix} \qquad H(t) = \begin{bmatrix} 10e^{-10t} & 10e^{-10t} \\ 2.5e^{-2.5t} & 2.5e^{-2.5t} \end{bmatrix}$$

According to the company's rate schedule, each customer is charged a fixed amount of \$0.20 and \$0.40 for a trip originating in town 1 and town 2, respectively. In addition, the driver collects $\$y_{ij}$ per hour for a trip from town i to town j where

$$Y = \begin{bmatrix} 4 & 14 \\ 10 & 5 \end{bmatrix}.$$

Sam Hacker lives in town 1 and charges the company \$5 if he ends the day in town 2.

a) Sam starts the day in town 1 and works for t hours. At the end of that time he takes his passenger to his destination and then quits for the day. Find the exponential transform for the expected amount of money earned by Sam during the time t.

b) Find the asymptotic form for the expected amount earned by Sam if he starts in town 1 and operates for t hours. Do the same for the case where Sam starts in town 2. For what values of t are your asymptotic values a good approximation to the expected earnings?

c) Is it more profitable in the long run for Sam to start in town 1 or town 2?

4. For the preceding problem, suppose that the amount of time worked by Sam is uncertain. The probability density function for the length of Sam's working day is exponential with a mean of one hour (Sam is not very ambitious).

a) What is the expected amount earned by Sam if he starts in town 1? If he starts in town 2?

b) Is it more profitable for Sam to start in town 1 or town 2? By how much?

5. The Huge Kluge Manufacturing Company managers are trying to decide what their inventory policy should be. Through long experience they have found that the time between sales opportunities of Huge Kluge is exponentially distributed with a mean of 1 year. Because of the uncertainties in the labor market, etc., the time to build a Huge Kluge is also exponentially distributed with a mean of 1 year. The company never has more than one Huge Kluge under construction at any time. Because of the competitiveness of the market, the company has found that if a Huge Kluge is not available when a sales opportunity arises, the opportunity is lost, i.e., no back-ordering.

The company's inventory policy is completely characterized by N, the maximum inventory allowed; when this level is reached, no more Huge Kluge's are produced until one is sold. The company makes a profit of \$$b$ on each Huge Kluge that is sold, but each Huge Kluge in inventory accrues a storage cost at the rate of \$$c$ per year. For a fixed inventory policy N:

a) Let $v_n(t)$ be the total net profit over the next time interval t if there are currently n Huge Kluge's in inventory. Write an equation for $v_n(t)$. Do this for $n = 0$, $0 < n < N$, and $n = N$.

b) If the process has been in operation for a long time, find the steady-state fraction of time there will be an inventory of n Huge Kluge's.

c) Use your answer in b) (but not in a)) to find the long-run net profit per unit time. Do this by considering the net profit over a short time interval in the steady state.

d) If $b = 4c$ what should be the inventory policy, i.e., what value of N will maximize the long-run profit per year?

6. A certain computer has a habit of breaking down. If the machine is up, its time to the next breakdown is exponentially distributed with a mean of $1/\lambda$. The repair time for the computer is exponentially distributed with a mean of $1/\mu$. When the machine is working, it earns revenue at the rate of \$$r$ per hour. Every time the machine breaks down, there is a fixed cost of \$$c$ to repair it. Let:

$v_u(t)$ = total expected profit during the next t hours if the machine is working initially

$v_d(t)$ = total expected profit during the next t hours if the machine is not working initially

a) Write integral equations for $v_u(t)$ and $v_d(t)$ in terms of λ, μ, r, c, $v_u(\cdot)$, and $v_d(\cdot)$.

b) Find the exponential transform of $v_u(t)$.

c) For what values of r will the system make a profit in the steady state?

d) If $1/\lambda = 10$ hours and $1/\mu = 0.5$ hour, how long must we wait before the transients in the system have fallen to e^{-3} of their initial values?

7. A concessionaire operates a fleet of 10 outboard motor boats each summer. The boats cost him \$1000 apiece. On the average, half can be operated for three summers; the other half lasts only two. He can sell the boats he retires for \$200 each.

a) What is his average expenditure per year for new boats?

b) If he carries new boats on his books at \$1000, at what book-value should he carry a one-year-old boat? A two-year-old boat?

c) What fraction of the boats in service during any one summer are boats with a three-year lifetime?

d) How much should the concessionare be willing to pay for a new boat that is known to have a three-year lifetime?

8. Two evenly matched golfers play so that on half the holes they are even. On the remaining half, each of the two players is equally likely to pick up one stroke. They are playing for a \$10 bet on the game with a proviso that at the start of any hole either player can double the bet. The other must either accept the double or forfeit his \$10 immediately. The bet may be doubled only once during a game. With three holes left to play, the first player is one stroke up and doubles. Should the second player accept the double? Was the first player wise to double?

9. A manufacturing company has two products. However, the company only manufactures one product during any one month. Because of the effect of sales, availability of raw products, etc., the company's production policy from month to month can be modeled as a two-state discrete-time Markov process with $s(n) = i$ corresponding to the manufacture of the ith product during the nth month. The company has two alternative policies and must select one of these to use for the indefinite future:

Policy I

$$P = \begin{bmatrix} 0.8 & 0.2 \\ 0.3 & 0.7 \end{bmatrix} \qquad \mathbf{q} = \begin{bmatrix} 2 \\ 1 \end{bmatrix}$$

Policy II

$$P = \begin{bmatrix} 0.9 & 0.1 \\ 0.4 & 0.6 \end{bmatrix} \qquad \mathbf{q} = \begin{bmatrix} 1 \\ 2 \end{bmatrix}$$

In the above, q_i is the expected profit for each month that the company manufactures the ith product. Unfortunately, the company's monthly discount factor β is not known.

a) Find the present value of future profits for each policy and for each starting state. Express the answers as a function of β.

b) Find the policy as a function of β that will maximize the company's present value of future profits for each starting state.

10. A factory uses a special machine to manufacture its product. The probability density function for the lifetime of each machine is known to be $h(\cdot)$. When the machine fails, a new one is purchased for \$$c$. The yield of a machine is dependent on the age τ of the machine and is $ye^{-\lambda\tau}$ dollars per year; there is no salvage value for a machine. The discount rate for the factory is α.

a) If the company has just purchased a new machine, what is the exponential transform of the present value of expected earnings from the factory during the following time interval of length t?

b) What is the present value of expected future earnings if the factory is going to operate for a very long time?

c) Suppose survival of the factory is in doubt, so that the probability density function for the lifetime of the factory is exponentially distributed with a mean of $1/\mu$. Find the present value of the factory's expected future earnings for this case.

d) Repeat c) if the factory's lifetime density function is $\mu^2 te^{-\mu t}$.

11. Consider the special case of the preceding problem in which

$$h(t) = \begin{cases} 1 & \text{for } 0 \le t \le 1 \\ 0 & \text{otherwise} \end{cases}$$

and $\mu = 0$.

a) What should be the book value of a machine τ years old?

b) What should be the depreciation of a machine τ years old? The depreciation rate?

12. A small town has two supermarkets, A and B. The town housewives shop exactly once a week, and each shops in only one supermarket on her shopping day. Supermarket A plans an advertising campaign to be conducted over a test period of n consecutive weeks. They have developed a brochure (including bonus stamps, etc.) to be mailed out only to certain "special" customers. On the weekend prior to the first week of the test period a brochure will be sent to each customer who shopped in supermarket A during the previous week—these will be the "special" customers.

However, our executives are not sure how to approach their supermarketing problem. As the supermarketing consultant, you are given two strategies to study:

Strategy 1: Keep sending *all* "special" customers a brochure every weekend regardless of where each shops.
Strategy 2: If a customer does not shop in A during the first week of the test period, do not send her any further brochures.

You find that a customer's behavior can be modeled by a Markov process. However, the transition probabilities are affected by whether or not a brochure was received on the past weekend. If a customer has received a brochure on the past weekend, her transition probability matrix is:

$$\begin{array}{c} \\ \\ {}_1P = \end{array} \begin{array}{cc} & \\ & \\ \textit{last} & A \\ \textit{week} & B \end{array} \begin{array}{c} \textit{this week} \\ \begin{array}{cc} A & B \end{array} \\ \begin{bmatrix} 0.8 & 0.2 \\ 0.5 & 0.5 \end{bmatrix} \end{array}$$

If a customer has *not* received a brochure on the past weekend, her transition probability matrix is:

$$\begin{array}{c} \\ \\ {}_2P = \end{array} \begin{array}{cc} & \\ & \\ \textit{last} & A \\ \textit{week} & B \end{array} \begin{array}{c} \textit{this week} \\ \begin{array}{cc} A & B \end{array} \\ \begin{bmatrix} 0.6 & 0.4 \\ 0.4 & 0.6 \end{bmatrix} \end{array}$$

The executives also tell you that the average profit made by supermarket A when a customer shops is \$2.00. Each brochure costs \$0.40, including mailing charges.

a) Under each strategy, what is the expected number of times that a "special" customer will shop in supermarket A during the n week test period?

b) If the store's objective is to maximize expected net profit during the test period, which strategy should be used? Is one strategy better for all possible lengths of test period?

c) Briefly criticize the store's objective and suggest alternate objectives and strategies that might be preferable.

14 DYNAMIC PROGRAMMING

Dynamic programming is a mathematical technique for solving certain types of sequential decision problems. We characterize a sequential decision problem as a problem in which a sequence of decisions must be made, with each decision affecting future decisions. We need to consider such problems because rarely do we encounter an operational situation where the implications of a decision do not extend far into the future: The best way to invest funds this year depends upon how the proceeds from this year's investments can be employed next year; the best maintenance policy for our machinery this year depends upon what we intend to do with this machinery in the future. Examples are as numerous as the fields of man's endeavor.

14.1 THE STRUCTURE OF SEQUENTIAL DECISION PROCESSES

Dynamic programming is based on only a few concepts. Some of these it shares with other models; others are unique.

State Variable

The first concept that we must understand is that of a state variable. As you recall from our discussion in Chapter 1, the state variables of a process are variables whose values completely specify the instantaneous situation of the process. The values of these variables tell us all we need to know about the system for the purpose of making decisions about it.

The designation of system descriptors as state variables is quite arbitrary. For example, in the investment problem we might require as a state variable only the total amount of our present investment. Or we could define two state variables to describe the income and the capital growth of the investment. Or we might require a state variable for investment in each industry, or even in each company. Although the number of state variables can theoretically be made as large as we please, the difficulty of solving a problem increases dramatically with the number of state variables involved. Thus it is to our advantage to minimize the number of state variables we use until any further simplification would destroy the utility of our model. In general, it is better to start simply and then complicate rather than to proceed in the reverse order. We usually speak of the values of all state variables as specifying the "state" of the system.

Decision

Having defined the state variables of the problem, we introduce the concept of a decision as an opportunity to change these state variables, perhaps probabilistically. For example, in the investment problem the decision to sell a certain amount of one stock and buy another would lead to a change in state variables. However, because of the vagaries of the market, the net change in the state variables over some time period is subject to considerable uncertainty.

Reward

But why bother to make decisions that affect the state? Because we can realize a profit or equivalently avoid a loss by having the state variables change in different ways. We imagine that each change of state has associated with it a reward, which may be positive or negative. The rewards generated by each decision depend only on the starting and ending states for that decision and therefore may be added for a sequence of decisions. Our job is to make decisions that will yield the highest possible total reward.

Stage

Finally, we suppose that our ability to make decisions about the system occurs only at certain points of time called "stages". At each stage we make a decision, change the state, and consequently, earn a reward. At the next stage we must make another decision using the values of the state variables that resulted from the preceding decision, and so on. Using these terms, we can describe our goal more precisely as a desire to maximize the expected total reward we shall receive when the number of stages available and the initial values of the state variables are fixed. In terms of the investment problem this might mean maximizing expected profit over a ten-year interval using a starting capital of $1000.

We shall make all these ideas more precise in later sections, but first let us describe how dynamic programming solves a sequential decision problem and illustrate the procedure with some examples.

14.2 THE SOLUTION CONCEPTS OF DYNAMIC PROGRAMMING

Perhaps the most interesting idea used in dynamic programming is: When a function is maximized, the maximum value it can attain depends only on the constraints on the maximization and not on the procedure used to determine the maximum value. This idea is best illustrated by examples.

Suppose we have available a cannon with a fixed muzzle velocity and our job is to hurl the projectile as far as possible on level ground. The important point is that the maximum range we can achieve depends only on the muzzle velocity allowed. From basic physics we know if air resistance can be neglected, the maximum range can be achieved by firing at an inclination of 45°. The actual range achieved will, of course, depend on the inclination angle *used*, but it will be a maximum only at the inclination 45°. Therefore if we are sponsors of a cannon-firing contest, we know that the only factor limiting the *maximum* range is the muzzle velocity allowed. The actual range achieved by any contestant will depend on this muzzle velocity and also on his intelligence in selecting the inclination angle. Thus we see that the *maximum* value of the function (range) depends only on the constraints (muzzle velocity) and not on the technique used to achieve it (inclination angle).

Perhaps another example will help. We all remember the problem of the farmer who wanted to enclose the maximum rectangular area with a fixed amount of fencing. We know he will achieve the maximum area by using his fencing around a square plot. We might have solved the problem by trial and error, but more probably by calculus. Suppose we hold a rectangular fencing contest among farmers, supplying to each the same perimeter of fencing. We know that the maximum area anyone can enclose is determined only by the amount of fencing we provide and that it well be achieved only by a square design. Individual farmers may try a wide variety of rectangular solutions, but the one who comes closest to the square will do best. Here again we see that the *maximum* of the function (area enclosed) depends only on the constraints (fencing supplied) and not on the technique used to achieve it (shape of rectangle).

The Portable Genius

Since we have found that the best anyone can do in a decision problem depends only on the constraints, we find it worthwhile to postulate a portable genius—a person who invariably achieves the maximum in a decision problem. The portable genius is a valuable resource: He knows that cannons should be fired at a 45° inclination to achieve maximum range on level ground and that square plots have the maximum area of all rectangular plots with the same perimeter. We find it hard to hire people with this capability, but fortunately we shall find that we don't have to.

Once we have a portable genius we use him in solving a sequential decision problem by defining a function that is the total reward he could achieve if he were faced with a certain number of remaining stages and certain starting values of state variables. Since he can solve the problem, he can provide his total reward or value, as we shall call it, upon request.

We are now ready to solve the sequential decision problem. First we must make one decision at the beginning of a long sequence of decisions. The problem is difficult because you and I as mere mortals seem to have no way of evaluating the influence of our present decision on the future. After all, how can we tell what is going to happen as a result of making this decision if we still don't know what we are going to do in the future? This is where we use our portable genius to break our multiple stage decision problem into single stage decision problems.

We reason this way. In the present state a number of different decisions are available to us. Each decision would create some reward and place the system in some new state for the next stage. We ask our portable genius to tell us what we shall make in the future if we are now in this new state with one less stage remaining. He tells us, we add it to the reward from the present stage, and thus obtain the total profit from making this decision. Similarly, we compute the total profit from each of the other possible decisions and then compare them. The decision with the highest total profit is the one to choose.

When we have the portable genius there is no difficulty in solving sequential decision problems where the profits are additive because he can tell us the implications for the future of any present action. If he tells us the value of being in each state with n stages remaining, then we can figure out what to do when we have $n + 1$ stages remaining. Thus if he tells us how we shall fare when there is only one stage remaining, we can compute the best decisions when there are two stages remaining. Now that we have evaluated what to do with two stages remaining we can compute for three stages remaining, and so on. Therefore we need the portable genius only for the case when there is only one stage remaining.

But we do not need him even here, because when there is only one stage remaining, there are no future decisions and the present decision can be based only on the profit that it will directly generate. Consequently, we do not need the portable genius at all, although he was a useful crutch in developing our thinking about sequential decision problems.

Therefore, sequential decision problems are solved by induction using the concept of values supplied by the portable genius, a genius who turns out never to be needed. This solution process we call dynamic programming, although as you can see, a better name might be recursive programming because of the form in which the solution is generated. *In everyday terms, the fundamental concept is that the best way to where you are going has nothing to do with how you got to where you are now.*

However, let us postpone further general comments on dynamic programming until we have achieved more feeling for the process through examples.

14.3 A PRODUCTION SCHEDULING EXAMPLE

Suppose a company must produce a total quantity Q in K monthly periods. We shall let n be the index for months remaining at any time and use p_n for the quantity that will be produced in the nth month from the end of the K-month-long production period. Figure 14.3.1 illustrates a possible production plan. There are many production plans that meet the requirements:

$$\sum_{n=1}^{K} p_n = Q; \quad p_n \geq 0 \qquad n = 1, 2, \ldots, K \tag{14.3.1}$$

Therefore, to make the problem definite, we assign a non-negative weighting factor w_n to the square of production in the nth month from the end of the allowable time, and then require that the production plan minimize the sum of the weighted squares of production over the K-month period. The effect of the weighting factor would be to allow management to penalize production in some months more than others. We shall not discuss the merit of such a control procedure, but simply consider it as an instructive example. Thus our problem is to

$$\min_{p_1, p_2, \ldots, p_K} \sum_{n=1}^{K} w_n p_n^2 \tag{14.3.2}$$

subject to the constraints in Equation 14.3.1.

The Dynamic Programming Formulation

We could solve this problem in many ways ranging from trial and error to calculus of variations. We choose to use dynamic programming and therefore

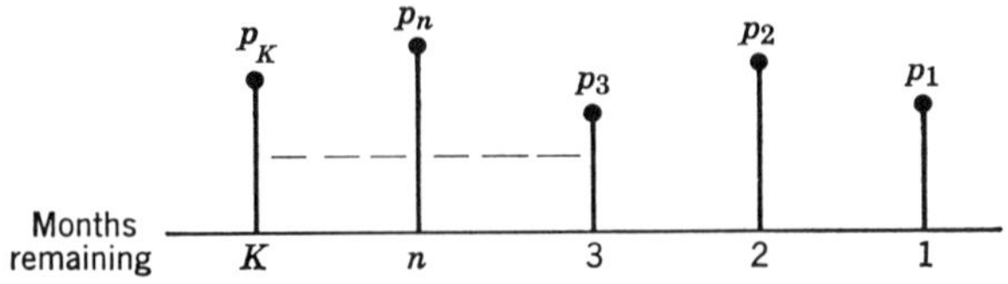

Figure 14.3.1 A possible production plan.

proceed to cast the problem in dynamic programming terms. Our first task is to identify the state variables of the process. We see that if we enter the process in the middle of a production plan when there remain n months in which to make a quantity s, we cannot affect the production levels that have already occurred—we can only influence the amounts to be made in each month in the future. What determines the weighted sum of squares of production we shall achieve in the future is the amount s that remains to be made and the number of months n that are left in which to make the amount s. We can consider both n and s as the state variables of the process or, alternatively and for convenience, we can call n the stage variable and s the state variable of the process. This terminology is reasonable because stages are the times at which decisions can be made, and every remaining month is an opportunity to set a production level for that month.

If we present anyone with this problem and tell him n, the number of production periods he is allowed, and s, the total amount he has to make, then in the light of our previous discussion we have already established the minimum weighted sum of squares that he will be able to obtain. Of course, he will not come up with a production plan to attain this minimum unless he is intelligent and diligent, but he can do no better than the minimum determined by n and s. We call this minimum $v(s|n)$, the value of being in state s with n stages remaining. It represents the minimum weighted sum of squares obtainable if the total amount to be made is s and if n periods remain. Our portable genius is able to attain this minimum and to tell us its value when requested.

We also need a terminology for the decision in order to specify the production plan that will be our answer. We let $p(s|n)$ be the optimum amount to be produced in the nth period from the end if a quantity s remains to be made in n monthly periods. If we knew this function, we would find it very easy to construct a production plan.

Let us now consider the situation where we have an amount s to be made in n months. If we make an amount p_n in the present month, then we shall have to make a total quantity $s - p_n$ in the remaining $n - 1$ months. The contribution to the weighted sum of squares of making p_n in the present month is $w_n p_n^2$. The minimum weighted sum of squares that can be achieved in the remaining $n - 1$ months starting with a quantity $s - p_n$ to be produced is reported by our portable genius to be $v(s - p_n|n - 1)$. Therefore, the total weighted sum of squares we shall achieve by making p_n now and doing the best anyone can do in the remaining months is $w_n p_n^2 + v(s - p_n|n - 1)$. Of course, we want to choose p_n so as to make this total weighted sum of squares as small as possible. If we do, then we can say that this quantity is $v(s|n)$, the best that can be done with a total quantity s to produce in n months. We therefore have the equation

$$v(s|n) = \min_{0 \le p_n \le s} \{w_n p_n^2 + v(s - p_n|n - 1)\} \qquad s \ge 0; n = 2, 3, 4, \ldots . \quad (14.3.3)$$

Note that we restrict the quantity p_n that can be made in the present month to be non-negative and to be less than or equal to s, the total quantity to be made throughout the n months. Of course, the value of p_n that minimizes the sum in Equation 14.3.3 is $p(s|n)$, the amount that should be made in the nth month from the end of an n-month period in which a total quantity s is to be produced so as to minimize the weighted sum of squares of production. Notice that the sum is composed of two parts, the immediate effect of the decision to make p_n, $w_n p_n^2$, and the long-run effect of the decision, $v(s - p_n|n - 1)$. This structure is typical of the dynamic programming approach: It provides the correct balance of short- and long-run consequences.

The Recursive Procedure

Well, we have solved the problem if we have a portable genius, but we don't have him. What do we do? We say that when only one month remains we don't need him and that Equation 14.3.3 then shows us how to dispense with him when more than one month remains.

One month remaining

Let us consider the situation when there is only one month in which to make a total quantity s. Then there is not much choice—the total quantity s must be produced in this month and the weighted sum of squares incurred will be $w_1 s^2$,

$$\begin{aligned} p(s|1) &= s \\ v(s|1) &= w_1 s^2. \end{aligned} \tag{14.3.4}$$

Thus the problem becomes trivial when only one month remains.

Two months remaining

But now that we know what to do with one month remaining, we can figure out what to do with two months remaining by writing Equation 14.3.3 with $n = 2$,

$$v(s|2) = \min_{0 \le p_2 \le s} \{w_2 p_2^2 + v(s - p_2|1)\}. \tag{14.3.5}$$

Since we already know the function $v(\cdot|1)$ from Equation 14.3.4, the minimization is clearly identified. We have many techniques that can be applied to perform this type of minimization. The easiest one to use in this case is differentiation of the expression and setting the result equal to zero. When we differentiate the quantity in braces with respect to p_2 and set the result equal to zero, we obtain

$$\frac{d\{\ \}}{dp_2} = 2w_2 p_2 - v'(s - p_2|1) = 0. \tag{14.3.6}$$

From Equation 14.3.4 we observe that the derivative of $v(s|1)$ with respect to its argument is

$$v'(s|1) = 2w_1 s \tag{14.3.7}$$

so that we can write Equation 14.3.6 as

$$2w_2 p_2 - 2w_1(s - p_2) = 0 \tag{14.3.8}$$

or

$$p_2 = p(s|2) = \frac{w_1}{w_1 + w_2} s. \tag{14.3.9}$$

Thus if we have two months in which to make a total quantity s, we should make a fraction $w_1/(w_1 + w_2)$ of the quantity in the present month to assure that the weighted sum of squares will be a minimum.

We find $v(s|2)$, the minimum weighted sum of squares that we can obtain in producing a total quantity s in a two-month period, by evaluating the quantity in braces in Equation 14.3.5 at the minimizing value of p_2 given by Equation 14.3.9. We obtain

$$\begin{aligned} v(s|2) &= \left\{w_2 p_2^2 + v(s - p_2|1)\right\}_{p_2 = [w_1/(w_1 + w_2)]s} \\ &= w_2\left(\frac{w_1}{w_1 + w_2}\right)^2 s^2 + v\left(\frac{w_2}{w_1 + w_2} s|1\right) \\ &= \frac{w_2 w_1^2}{(w_1 + w_2)^2} s^2 + \frac{w_1 w_2^2}{(w_1 + w_2)^2} s^2 \\ &= \frac{w_1 w_2}{w_1 + w_2} s^2. \end{aligned} \tag{14.3.10}$$

This is, of course, just the weighted sum of squares that will result from making $[w_1/(w_1 + w_2)]s$ in the present month and $[w_2/(w_1 + w_2)]s$ in the last month.

Equation 14.3.9 yields the policy to follow at the second stage, the amount that should be produced at present to insure that the decision will be the best possible as far as future decisions are concerned. Equation 14.3.10 provides the value, the weighted sum of squares, that will result by taking the optimum present decision and also following an optimum course in the future.

Three months remaining

Now that we have evaluated what to do when one or two months remain, we can continue to the case where three months remain. Then Equation 14.3.3 takes the form

$$v(s|3) = \min_{0 \le p_3 \le s} \{w_3 p_3^2 + v(s - p_3|2)\}. \tag{14.3.11}$$

We again perform the minimization by differentiation and write

$$\frac{d\{\ \}}{dp_3} = 2w_3p_3 - v'(s - p_3|2) = 0. \tag{14.3.12}$$

Equation 14.3.10 shows that the derivative of the function $v(s|2)$ with respect to its argument is

$$v'(s|2) = 2\frac{w_1w_2}{w_1 + w_2}s. \tag{14.3.13}$$

When we substitute this result into Equation 14.3.12 we find

$$2w_3p_3 - 2\frac{w_1w_2}{w_1 + w_2}(s - p_3) = 0,$$

$$p_3(w_1w_2 + w_1w_3 + w_2w_3) = w_1w_2s \tag{14.3.14}$$

or

$$p_3 = p(s|3) = \frac{w_1w_2}{w_1w_2 + w_1w_3 + w_2w_3}s. \tag{14.3.15}$$

The amount that should be made at present if three months remain in which to make a total quantity s is a fraction of s equal to the product of the weights in the last two months divided by the sum of the products of all possible pairs of weights for the three months.

If we substitute this value for p_3 into Equation 14.3.11, we obtain $v(s|3)$, the minimum weighted sum of squares obtainable throughout the three-month period,

$$\begin{aligned} v(s|3) &= \left\{w_3p_3^2 + v(s - p_3|2)\right\}_{p_3=[w_1w_2/(w_1w_2+w_1w_3+w_2w_3)]s} \\ &= \left\{w_3p_3^2 + \frac{w_1w_2}{w_1 + w_2}(s - p_3)^2\right\}_{p_3=[w_1w_2/(w_1w_2+w_1w_3+w_2w_3)]s} \\ &= \frac{w_1w_2w_3}{w_1w_2 + w_1w_3 + w_2w_3}s^2. \end{aligned} \tag{14.3.16}$$

Thus Equation 14.3.15 provides the policy (or what to do) and Equation 14.3.16 provides the value (or how much we shall benefit by doing it) for the case when three months remain.

General solution

We could continue to use the recursive equation 14.3.3 to solve the problem for higher and higher numbers of months or stages remaining. However, what we have already done is sufficient to see the form of the solution. For the *policy* we observe that

$$p(s\,|\,n) = \frac{\dfrac{1}{w_n}}{\displaystyle\sum_{i=1}^{n} \frac{1}{w_i}}\, s \qquad n = 1, 2, 3, \ldots \tag{14.3.17}$$

is consistent with the results of Equations 14.3.4, 14.3.9, and 14.3.15. It is clear that the reciprocals of the weights appear more naturally in the problem than do the weights themselves. Similarly, for the *value* we see that

$$v(s\,|\,n) = \frac{1}{\displaystyle\sum_{i=1}^{n} \frac{1}{w_i}}\, s^2 \tag{14.3.18}$$

is a general form for the results of Equations 14.3.4, 14.3.10, and 14.3.16. Furthermore, if we substitute the policy and value results from Equations 14.3.17 and 14.3.18 directly into Equation 14.3.3, we find that Equation 14.3.3 is satisfied. Therefore Equations 14.3.17 and 14.3.18 constitute a complete solution to the problem.

Interpretation

A word is in order about the form in which the solution has been generated. Although we seek a production plan for a specific total quantity Q to be made in a time period specified to be K months long, we have in fact solved a more general problem. The more general problem is that of finding how much to make in the present month for any amount to be produced s and for any number of months remaining n. We can solve not only the specific problem proposed, but also the whole class of problems. The generality that is provided and required by the dynamic programming procedure is called "imbedding" the problem in a larger class of problems. As you might expect, imbedding is a very good idea when you would like to have a general solution. However, it may also lead to higher computational requirements than if the specific problem posed were solved directly. The point is: In dynamic programming we always get more than we bargained for, even if we don't want it.

Note that when we finally get around to solving a specific problem, we must interpret our general solution as a rule for generating and evaluating optimum production plans rather than as a production plan itself. The policy tells us how much to make in the present month if we know the total amount to be made and the number of months remaining. Once we take this action, we then proceed to the next decision point with a lesser quantity to be made and one less month remaining. The policy for this stage again tells what to make in the present month, and we continue to generate the production plan in this way. However, at any stage and state, the value function tells us the minimum weighted sum of squares we shall be able to obtain in the future, even though at this point we have not yet found the explicit production plan that will be followed in the future. In other words, the value function tells our farmer contestant the maximum rectangular area he will be able to enclose even before it tells him the dimensions to use. Thus the policy and value functions provide powerful, if somewhat unusual, aid in solving decision problems.

Perhaps the structure of the solution appears most clearly in the case when all weights are equal; for simplicity, let us say equal to unity. Then the policy of Equation 14.3.17 becomes

$$p(s|n) = \frac{1}{n}s \qquad n = 1, 2, 3, \ldots. \tag{14.3.19}$$

This equation states that when n months remain in which to make a total quantity s, an amount $(1/n)s$ should be made in the present month. We know from the symmetry of the problem that when all weights are equal, equal amounts should be produced in each of the remaining months. Equation 14.3.19 presents this result implicitly rather than explicitly. For example, suppose that three months remain to make a total quantity Q. Then according to Equation 14.3.19, $(1/3)Q$ should be made in the present month. Next month a quantity $(2/3)Q$ will remain; Equation 14.3.19 shows that one half of it or $(1/3)Q$ should be produced next month. That will leave $(1/3)Q$ to be produced during the last month; Equation 14.3.19 states, of course, that all of it must be produced in that month. The net result is that we have produced $(1/3)Q$ in each of the three remaining months by applying the result of Equation 14.3.19 recursively.

Equation 14.3.18 shows that the value function for the case of equal unity weights is

$$v(s|n) = \frac{1}{n}s^2 \qquad n = 1, 2, 3, \ldots. \tag{14.3.20}$$

For the production schedule we have just developed, the weighted sum of squares is

$$\left(\frac{1}{3}Q\right)^2 + \left(\frac{1}{3}Q\right)^2 + \left(\frac{1}{3}Q\right)^2 = \frac{1}{3}Q^2, \tag{14.3.21}$$

which is the result of Equation 14.3.20 when a total quantity Q must be made in three months. The interpretation of a policy as a decision rule rather than as a specific plan and the interpretation of the value function as an overall measure of policy rather than of any part of it are fundamental to the dynamic programming approach.

Numerical Results

Suppose that we want to minimize the weighted sum of squares of production over a three-month period in which we must make 9 units. Thus $K = 3$, $Q = 9$. The weighting factors for the three months are $w_1 = 2$, $w_2 = 3$, $w_3 = 6$, as shown in Figure 14.3.2. We begin by deciding how much to make in the third month from the end. From Equation 14.3.17.

$$p(9|3) = \frac{\frac{1}{w_3}}{\frac{1}{w_1} + \frac{1}{w_2} + \frac{1}{w_3}}(9) = \frac{\frac{1}{6}}{\frac{1}{2} + \frac{1}{3} + \frac{1}{6}}(9) = 1.5 . \qquad (14.3.22)$$

We find that we should make 1.5 units in the present month when three months remain. Manufacturing 1.5 units might be a problem if our product were automobiles, but we shall assume that it is a bulk product for the moment and return to the quantization problem later.

From Equation 14.3.18 we compute the value of being in state 9 with three stages left,

$$v(9|3) = \frac{1}{\frac{1}{w_1} + \frac{1}{w_2} + \frac{1}{w_3}}(9)^2 = \frac{1}{\frac{1}{2} + \frac{1}{3} + \frac{1}{6}}(81) = 81 . \qquad (14.3.23)$$

Thus the minimum weighted sum of squares we shall be able to obtain is 81. We have not yet specified what our production plan will be (except for the first month and we have not used the result of that calculation) and still we can predict how well we shall do by following it.

Now we come to two months remaining with a total quantity $9 - 1.5 = 7.5$ yet to be produced. The amount of production for this middle month we compute from Equation 14.3.17 as

$$p(7.5|2) = \frac{\frac{1}{w_2}}{\frac{1}{w_1} + \frac{1}{w_2}}(7.5) = \frac{\frac{1}{3}}{\frac{1}{2} + \frac{1}{3}}(7.5) = 3. \qquad (14.3.24)$$

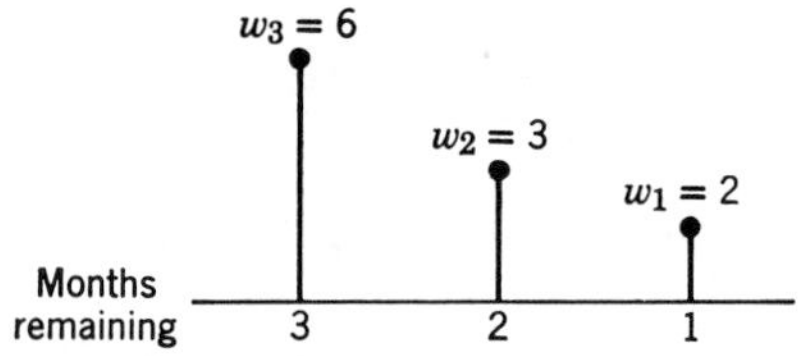

Figure 14.3.2 Weighting factors for the example.

Table 14.3.1 The Best Production Plan

Months remaining	n	3	2	1	
Weighting factor	w_n	6	3	2	
Production	p_n	1.5	3.0	4.5	
	p_n^2	2.25	9.0	20.25	
	$w_n p_n^2$	13.5	27.0	40.5	$\sum_{n=1}^{3} w_n p_n^2 = 81$

From Equation 14.3.18 we compute the minimum weighted sum of squares for the last two months,

$$v(7.5|2) = \frac{1}{\dfrac{1}{w_1} + \dfrac{1}{w_2}} (7.5)^2 = \frac{1}{\dfrac{1}{2} + \dfrac{1}{3}} (56.25) = 67.5 . \tag{14.3.25}$$

Notice that since our production of 1.5 units in the third month from the end contributed $w_3 p_3^2 = 6(1.5)^2 = 13.5$ to the weighted sum of squares, the predictions of Equations 14.3.23 and 14.3.25 are consistent.

In the last month we have still to produce $9 - 1.5 - 3 = 4.5$ units; of course, Equation 14.3.17 states that they all must be produced in this month,

$$p(4.5|1) = 4.5 . \tag{14.3.26}$$

Equation 14.3.18 then shows that the contribution to the sum of squares of this last month is

$$v(4.5|1) = \frac{1}{\dfrac{1}{w_1}} (4.5)^2 = 2(20.25) = 40.5 . \tag{14.3.27}$$

The complete production plan along with the weighted squares of production for the plan appears in Table 14.3.1. We observe that the predictions of Equations 14.3.23, 14.3.25, and 14.3.27 about the weighted sum of squares to be obtained in the future of the plan at different stages are substantiated by these results. The weighted sum of squares for the entire plan is 81 as predicted initially by $v(9|3)$. No other production plan can achieve so low a weighted sum of squares.

The Variational Approach

We observe that the best production plan has the property that the product of the production and weighting factor ($p_n w_n$) in any month is always 9. We can explain this behavior by solving this same problem using a variational approach. Thus to perform the minimization of Equation 14.3.2 subject to the constraints of Equation 14.3.1, we would first form the quantity

$$\sum_{n=1}^{K} w_n p_n^2 + \lambda\left(\sum_{n=1}^{K} p_n - Q\right) \qquad (14.3.28)$$

and then differentiate it both with respect to p_n and with respect to λ. We obtain for these differentiations

$$2w_n p_n + \lambda = 0 \qquad n = 1, 2, \ldots, K \qquad (14.3.29)$$

and

$$\sum_{n=1}^{K} p_n = Q. \qquad (14.3.30)$$

Then

$$p_n = -\frac{\lambda}{2w_n} \qquad n = 1, 2, \ldots, K, \qquad (14.3.31)$$

and we use Equation 14.3.30 to find λ,

$$\sum_{n=1}^{K} p_n = Q = -\frac{\lambda}{2}\sum_{n=1}^{K}\frac{1}{w_n} \qquad (14.3.32)$$

or

$$\lambda = \frac{-2Q}{\sum_{n=1}^{K}\frac{1}{w_n}}. \qquad (14.3.33)$$

Finally we substitute this result into Equation 14.3.31 to produce the solution

$$p_n = \frac{\frac{1}{w_n}}{\sum_{n=1}^{K}\frac{1}{w_n}} Q \qquad n = 1, 2, \ldots, K. \qquad (14.3.34)$$

Happily, the production quantities turn out to be positive so we do not have to worry about the constraint that they be positive.

Equation 14.3.31 shows immediately that the product of production quantity and weighting factor in any month will be a constant. Equation 14.3.33 shows further that this constant is just the total quantity to be produced divided by the sum of the reciprocals of the weighting factors for the months involved; we have therefore checked our numerical example.

However, the important thing to note in the variational solution is that Equation 14.3.34 describes the production quantity for each month rather than a rule for constructing the production quantity when the amount yet to be made is known. The solution is explicit rather than in the recursive form of Equation 14.3.17. Since both expressions look virtually identical, they differ only in interpretation, but the difference is critical.

If we evaluate the weighted sum of squares of production for the production plan, we find

$$\sum_{n=1}^{K} w_n p_n^2 = \sum_{n=1}^{K} w_n \frac{\left(\frac{1}{w_n}\right)^2}{\left(\sum_{n=1}^{K} \frac{1}{w_n}\right)^2} Q^2 = \frac{1}{\sum_{n=1}^{K} \frac{1}{w_n}} Q^2, \tag{14.3.35}$$

in agreement with Equation 14.3.18 when Q must be produced in K months.

It is clear that solving the production problem by variational methods is simpler than solving it by dynamic programming. We chose the less efficient route initially because it is a good way to illustrate the dynamic programming process. Yet if variational methods are better, why do we need dynamic programming? The answer is that dynamic programming provides a convenient approach to problems that are difficult to treat by variational methods. For example, the requirement that the production quantities must be positive is difficult to incorporate in the variational approach. We were fortunate that this constraint was not violated in the present problem. But what if it had been? The dynamic programming approach can easily handle this type of difficulty. At most it would mean that we could not use the differentiation method for finding the minimum of the quantities in braces in Equations 14.3.5 and 14 3.11; however, other methods are available. Similarly, we can use dynamic programming to treat the case where there are limits on the production in each month. But perhaps the most dramatic illustration of the advantage of dynamic programming arises when we require that the amount of production in each month be an integer.

The Effect of Integer Constraints

Let us consider the same example of producing 9 units in three months so as to minimize the weighted sum of squares of production using the weights of Figure 14.3.2. Only now we shall require that the number of units made during each month be integral. The only change that we have to make in our previous analysis is that the values of p_n considered in carrying out the minimization in Equation 14.3.3 must be limited to the integer values 0, 1, 2, . . ., s; that is,

$$v(s|n) = \underset{p_n=0,1,2,\ldots,s}{\text{Min}} \{w_n p_n^2 + v(s - p_n|n - 1)\}$$

$$s = 0, 1, 2, \ldots; n = 2, 3, 4, \ldots. \tag{14.3.36}$$

Since the quantity to be made must always be specified as an integer, Equation 14.3.4 still applies,

$$\begin{aligned} p(s|1) &= s \\ v(s|1) &= w_1 s^2 . \end{aligned} \tag{14.3.37}$$

Consequently, Equations 14.3.36 and 14.3.37 constitute a complete formal statement of the problem of finding the best integral production schedule.

We demonstrate the computational solution by writing $p(s|1)$ and $v(s|1)$ in Table 14.3.2 for values of s ranging from 0 through 10. We choose 10 simply to illustrate that we are not solving a particular problem, but rather a class of problems.

We continue now to the second stage and write Equation 14.3.36 as

$$\begin{aligned} v(s|2) &= \min_{p_2 = 0,1,2,\ldots,s} \{w_2 p_2^2 + v(s - p_2|1)\} \\ &= \min_{p_2 = 0,1,2,\ldots,s} \{3p_2^2 + v(s - p_2|1)\} \qquad s = 0, 1, 2, \ldots . \end{aligned} \tag{14.3.38}$$

For $s = 0$,

$$v(0|2) = \min_{p_2 = 0} \{3p_2^2 + v(-p_2|1)\} = v(0|1), \tag{14.3.39}$$

an obvious result.

For $s = 1$,

$$\begin{aligned} v(1|2) &= \min_{p_2 = 0,1} \{3p_2^2 + v(1 - p_2|1)\} \\ &= \text{Min} \begin{cases} p_2 = 1: & 3 + v(0|1) = 3 + 0 = 3 \\ p_2 = 0: & 0 + v(1|1) = 0 + 2 = 2 \end{cases} \\ &= 2 \text{ at } p_2 = 0. \end{aligned} \tag{14.3.40}$$

Table 14.3.2 Computation of Integral Production Problem at First Stage

s	$p(s\|1) = s$	$v(s\|1) = w_1 s^2 = 2s^2$
0	0	0
1	1	2
2	2	8
3	3	18
4	4	32
5	5	50
6	6	72
7	7	98
8	8	128
9	9	162
10	10	200

Therefore when one unit must be made in two months, it should not be made in the present month, but made in the last month. The weighted sum of squares so incurred will be 2.

For $s = 2$,

$$v(2|2) = \min_{p_2=0,1,2} \{3p_2^2 + v(2 - p_2|1)\}$$

$$= \operatorname{Min} \begin{cases} p_2 = 2: & 12 + v(0|1) = 12 + 0 = 12 \\ p_2 = 1: & 3 + v(1|1) = 3 + 2 = 5 \\ p_2 = 0: & 0 + v(2|1) = 0 + 8 = 8 \end{cases}$$

$$= 5 \text{ at } p_2 = 1. \tag{14.3.41}$$

Therefore when there are two units to be made in two months, one should be made in each month; a weighted sum of squares of 5 will be achieved.

We could continue in this way to compute all values of $v(s|2)$ from $v(s|1)$, but let us examine the general procedure we have been following. Suppose $s = 3$. Then we are constructing a column $3p_2^2$ for $p_2 = 3, 2, 1, 0$ and adding to each entry the value of $v(3 - p_2|1)$ from Table 14.3.2. Thus:

p_2	$3p_2^2$		$v(3 - p_2\|1)$	
3	27	+	0	= 27
2	12	+	2	= 14
1	3	+	8	= 11
0	0	+	18	= 18

(14.3.42)

The smallest value of the sum is 11, occurring when $p_2 = 1$. Therefore if 3 units must be made in two months, one should be made in the present month and two in the last month. The total weighted sum of squares will then be 11.

Thus a simple way to compute $v(s|2)$ would be to construct a vertical paper strip with columns containing entries p_2 and $3p_2^2$ with the highest possible value of p_2 at the top. This strip could be moved beside the column $v(s|1)$ from Table 14.3.1 and the value of $3p_2^2 + v(s - p_2|1)$ could be computed mentally through row s of Table 14.3.2. The smallest value of this quantity would be $v(s|2)$; the value of p_2 at which it occurred would be $p(s|2)$. Then the strip would be moved down one space and the computation would be repeated for the next higher value of s, and so on. By proceeding in this way with a paper strip, the calculation of $v(s|2)$ from $v(s|1)$ becomes straightforward. When we continue on to calculate $v(s|3)$ from $v(s|2)$, we use the same procedure, but use a paper strip containing the values of p_3 and $6p_3^2$ since $w_3 = 6$. The values on this strip are added mentally to the values of $v(s - p_2|2)$ already obtained to perform the optimization at the third stage. Since we can continue this process indefinitely, we can find $v(s|n)$ for any value of n we like.

Computational results

Table 14.3.3 shows the result of following this computational procedure for the first three stages. The table provides a solution for any number of months remaining through 3 and any quantity to be produced through 10. To see how to use this table, suppose we determine the production schedule corresponding to the requirement of producing 9 units in three months. From the table we observe $p(9|3) = 1, 2$. That is, when we have three months remaining and 9 units to make, we have a choice of making either 1 or 2 in the present month. The choice arises because we find in determining the minimum value of $v(9|3)$ in the computational procedure that two different values of p_3, 1 and 2, produce the same minimum value of 83. Suppose that we decide to make 1 unit in month 3. Then 8 units must be made in the last two months. Since $p(8|2) = 3$, we find that we must make 3 units in month 2. That leaves $9 - 1 - 3 = 5$ units to be made in month 1, and, of course, $p(5|1) = 5$.

If on the other hand we choose to make 2 units in month 3, then $9 - 2 = 7$ units remain to be made in the last two months. Since $p(7|2) = 3$, again we make 3 units in month 2. That leaves $9 - 2 - 3 = 4$ units to be made in month 1, and $p(4|1) = 4$. Therefore we have our choice of two production plans:

$$\begin{aligned} &\text{Plan 1:}\quad p(9|3) = 1 \quad p(8|2) = 3 \quad p(5|1) = 5 \\ &\text{Plan 2:}\quad p(9|3) = 2 \quad p(7|2) = 3 \quad p(4|1) = 4 \end{aligned} \tag{14.3.43}$$

We can make the 9 units in the order 1, 3, 5 or in the order 2, 3, 4. The monthly contributions to the weighted sum of squares for each plan are:

		$n = 3$	$n = 2$	$n = 1$	Total
	w_n	6	3	2	
Plan 1	$w_n p_n^2$	6	27	50	83
Plan 2	$w_n p_n^2$	24	27	32	83

(14.3.44)

We see that both plans produce a weighted sum of squares of 83. We observe that $v(8|2) = 77$ gives the correct prediction of the weighted sum of squares in the last two months for plan 1 and that $v(7|2) = 59$ gives the corresponding correct prediction for plan 2.

Hence the requirement that the amount of production in each month be integral has caused the minimum weighted sum of squares to increase by two units from the value of 81 we observed in Equation 14.3.23 for the case where this constraint was not imposed. This exemplifies the general result that adding a constraint in a problem can never help and may hinder the attainment of the maximum or minimum value obtainable without the constraint. The effect of adding constraints has philosophical as well as mathematical implications.

Table 14.3.3 Result of Three Stages for Integral Production Problem

s	$p(s\|1)$	$v(s\|1)$	$p(s\|2)$	$v(s\|2)$	$p(s\|3)$	$v(s\|3)$
0	0	0	0	0	0	0
1	1	2	0	2	0	2
2	2	8	1	5	0	5
3	3	18	1	11	0,1	11
4	4	32	2	20	1	17
5	5	50	2	30	1	26
6	6	72	2	44	1	36
7	7	98	3	59	1	50
8	8	128	3	77	1	65
9	9	162	4	98	1,2	83
10	10	200	4	120	2	101

Uniqueness of Value and Policy

Finally, we should note that the value function must be unique, but the policy function need not be. The value function is unique because it represents the results obtainable by our portable genius—the best anyone could do. Clearly the best cannot have two different values. However, the policy need not be unique. As in this problem, there may be two or more different sets of decisions that lead to the same optimum solution of the decision problem. Many roads of equal length may lead to Rome. We should regard this possibility with gratitude because it allows us in some situations a set of policies that are equally good from a formal point of view, but within which we may be able to exercise a preference on some secondary basis such as ease of explanation. Of course, we could also include more and more of these secondary considerations into the formal statement of the problem and ultimately make the optimum policy unique. Rarely, however, is such an approach necessary or desirable.

14.4 AN ACTION-TIMING PROBLEM

As a further example of dynamic programming we consider what we shall call an "action-timing" problem. In this problem a certain action may be taken only once, and the question is: When should it be taken? The problem we shall solve could serve as a useful model for a wide variety of situations. For example, suppose we are riding in an automobile and will soon enter a turnpike. We are low on gasoline and decide to fill up. However, we know the gasoline on the turnpike is expensive and the stations before the turnpike vary in their gasoline prices. The problem is: If we know the number of stations remaining and observe the price at the present station, should we or should we not fill up here? The same problem could arise in hiring if we were allowed to interview several applicants for a single vacancy but had to reach an irrevocable decision on whether to hire each one after he was interviewed before we could interview the next applicant. Or we might encounter the problem in a commodity market where we had to make a purchase before a certain deadline and we wanted to know whether today's price is sufficiently low to make the purchase. We can find an application even in amateur photography. Suppose that we have only a single frame of film left and no possibliity of obtaining any more. How do we determine whether a given scene is worthy of a shot when we have only expectations about the scenes we have remaining? Finally, the problem of getting married can be posed in these terms, but perhaps it is not wise to pursue that example further.

The Dynamic Programming Formulation

We shall develop a model general enough to allow considering all these possibilities. A known number of opportunities for action will be presented to us. At any of them we can take action and thereby terminate the problem. We can observe the merit of each opportunity before deciding whether or not to act. However, we do not know the merits of future opportunities. We assume that the merit of each opportunity is measured on a scale ranging from 0 to 1 with 0 being the lowest possible merit and 1 the highest. Thus the merit of 1 corresponds to the cheapest possible gasoline, the most capable employee, the best possible commodity bargain, the unforgettable picture, and the ideal spouse. We assume further that the merits presented on successive opportunities are selected independently from the same probability distribution. Our initial choice for this distribution is the uniform distribution of Figure 14.4.1. All values of merit between 0 and 1 are equally likely to be presented at each opportunity.

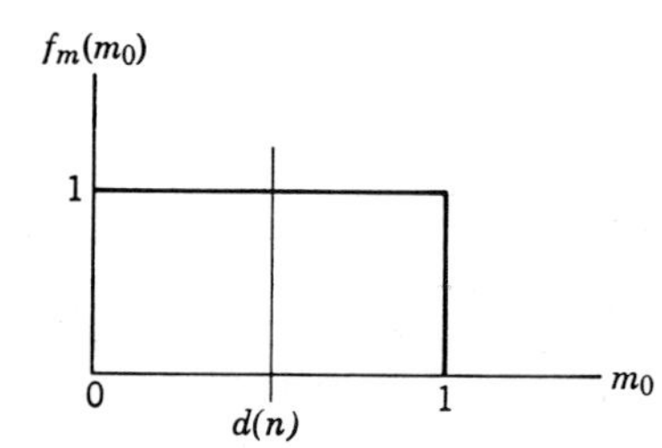

Figure 14.4.1 A uniform density function for the merit presented at each opportunity.

We shall let n represent the number of opportunities remaining at any time; in our previous terminology n is a stage variable. The essential problem is this: If we have arrived at a point where we have n opportunities remaining and have not yet acted, should we accept the present merit and act now? What we would really like to have is a decision criterion $d(n)$ for accepting the merit m offered with n opportunities remaining. That is, we would like to know a number $d(n)$ such that if m equals or exceeds $d(n)$ we shall act now, while if m is less than $d(n)$ we shall not act now. Therefore, for any n,

$$\begin{aligned} m \geq d(n) &\quad \text{implies ACT} \\ m < d(n) &\quad \text{implies DO NOT ACT.} \end{aligned} \tag{14.4.1}$$

To calculate $d(n)$, we begin by noting that we must be in one of two states at any time—the expectant state where we have not already taken the action, and the consummated state where we have already acted. We define $v(n)$ as the value or expected merit of being in the expectant state when n opportunities remain. There is no value of being in the consummated state beyond that received when the action is taken.

However, there is an expected merit to be derived from being in the expectant state when n opportunities remain. If we set the criterion level $d(n)$ at some value, then we will take action if m is at least as large as $d(n)$, and otherwise we will not act. Since the merit m that will be presented is a random variable, the probability that we will act when m is revealed is the probability that m will equal or exceed $d(n)$, i.e., $\mathscr{P}\{m \geq d(n)\}$. If we do act, then we will obtain the expected merit of an opportunity conditional on the merit's not being less than $d(n)$, $\langle m|m \geq d(n)\rangle$. We will also receive the value of being in the consummated state, but, as we have said, this position has no value in itself. The probability that we will not take action is 1 minus the probability that we will take action. In this case we find ourselves once more in the expectant state, but this time with one less opportunity remaining. The value of this situation is $v(n - 1)$; it must be supplied by the portable genius. Of course, our problem is to select the $d(n)$ that will yield the highest expected merit from the process. Therefore we have the recursive equation,

$$v(n) = \operatorname*{Max}_{0 \leq d(n) \leq 1} \{\mathscr{P}\{m \geq d(n)\}\langle m|m \geq d(n)\rangle + [1 - \mathscr{P}\{m \geq d(n)\}]v(n - 1)\}$$

$$n = 1, 2, 3, \ldots \tag{14.4.2}$$

The value $v(0)$ of being in the expectant state with no opportunities remaining must be specified as part of the problem statement. However, once $v(0)$ is known, Equation 14.4.2 can be used to find $v(n)$ for $n = 1, 2, 3, \ldots$ and thereby we can avoid using the portable genius.

Uniform Merit Distribution

We shall now specialize our results to the uniform density function for m shown in Figure 14.4.1. It is clear that the probability that m will exceed $d(n)$ is just the area under this density function between $d(n)$ and 1 or $1 - d(n)$. The expected value of m given that m is greater than or equal to $d(n)$ is just half-way between $d(n)$ and 1 or $(1/2)[1 + d(n)]$. Therefore Equation 14.4.2 becomes simply

$$\begin{aligned} v(n) &= \operatorname*{Max}_{d(n)} \{[1 - d(n)](1/2)[1 + d(n)] + d(n)v(n-1)\} \\ &= \operatorname*{Max}_{0 \le d(n) \le 1} \{(1/2)[1 - (d(n))^2] + d(n)v(n-1)\} \qquad n = 1, 2, 3, \ldots . \end{aligned} \tag{14.4.3}$$

Policy

The problem now is to find the value of $d(n)$ between 0 and 1 that maximizes the quantity in braces when $v(n-1)$ is known. Once more, differentiation is an efficient procedure. We differentiate the quantity in the braces with respect to $d(n)$ and set the result equal to zero,

$$\begin{aligned} -d(n) + v(n-1) &= 0 \\ d(n) &= v(n-1) \qquad n = 1, 2, 3, \ldots . \end{aligned} \tag{14.4.4}$$

From the second derivative we confirm that this solution represents a maximum rather than a minimum. We have therefore found that when n opportunities remain we should set the criterion level equal to the value of not having taken action when $n - 1$ opportunities remain: The form of the policy is very simple.

Value

We find how well we shall do under this policy by evaluating the quantity in braces in Equation 14.4.3 at the value of $d(n)$ given by Equation 14.4.4,

$$\begin{aligned} v(n) &= \Big\{(1/2)[1 - (d(n))^2] + d(n)v(n-1)\Big\}_{d(n)=v(n-1)} \\ &= (1/2)[1 - (v(n-1))^2] + (v(n-1))^2 \\ &= (1/2)[1 + (v(n-1))^2] \qquad n = 1, 2, 3, \ldots . \end{aligned} \tag{14.4.5}$$

The expected merit to be derived from not having acted when n opportunities remain is equal to 1/2 of 1 plus the square of the expected merit when $n - 1$ opportunities remain, but only, of course, if the optimum policy specified by Equation 14.4.4 is followed.

Specification of terminal value

Two special cases are of interest. The first is where $v(0) = 1$. This means that the highest merit is assured even if we never take advantage of any of the opportunities. In this case Equations 14.4.4 and 14.4.5 show that

$$v(n) = d(n) = 1 \qquad n = 0, 1, 2, \ldots . \tag{14.4.6}$$

Because $d(n) = 1$, no action will ever be taken at any opportunity. Because $v(n) = 1$, we are assured of achieving the highest possible merit by following this policy. It is reassuring that even in this very unusual case the formulation provides the appropriate result.

However, a more interesting case arises when $v(0) = 0$. This value for $v(0)$ means that we are assured of the lowest possible merit if we do not take advantage of any opportunity. The values of $d(n)$ and $v(n)$ generated for this case using Equations 14.4.4 and 14.4.5 appear in Table 14.4.1. As we would expect, the criterion level when only one opportunity remains is 0—we are forced to act. However, the criterion level increases gradually with n, showing that we are getting more and more selective as the number of opportunities available to us increases. Furthermore, the expected merit that would be gained by following the optimum policy increases with the number of opportunities n. The rate of increase is greater when n is small than it is when n is large. The quantities $d(n)$ and $v(n)$ approach 1 and each other asymptotically as n becomes larger and larger. Thus we can become arbitrarily choosy about accepting an opportunity and very optimistic about how well we shall do in expected merit provided that a large enough number of opportunities remain.

Note that the policy is very easy to implement. All we need is a card showing the decision criterion $d(n)$ for each n. The first time we encounter an opportunity

Table 14.4.1 Results for a Uniform Distribution of Opportunity Merit

Opportunities Remaining n	Decision Criterion $d(n) = v(n-1)$	Value $v(n) = 0.5 + 0.5(v(n-1))^2$
0	—	0
1	0	0.50000
2	0.50000	0.62500
3	0.62500	0.69531
4	0.69531	0.74173
5	0.74173	0.77508
6	0.77508	0.80037
7	0.80037	0.82030
8	0.82030	0.83644
9	0.83644	0.84982
10	0.84982	0.86110
11	0.86110	0.87074
12	0.87074	0.87910
13	0.87910	0.88641
14	0.88641	0.89286
15	0.89286	0.89860
16	0.89860	0.90374

whose merit equals or exceeds the corresponding $d(n)$, we act. Thus implementation would be practical for a truck driver buying gasoline.

A non-optimum policy

To convince ourselves that we have found the optimum policy for this problem, let us consider another policy: Act the first time the merit of an opportunity is better than average unless only one opportunity remains, in which case act regardless of the merit presented. This policy requires

$$d(1) = 0 \qquad d(n) = 0.5 \qquad n = 2, 3, 4, \ldots . \tag{14.4.7}$$

We observe that Equation 14.4.3 without the maximization allows us to evaluate any policy, even non-optimal ones, if we use the actual values of $d(n)$ rather than the optimizing values of Equation 14.4.4. We therefore have

$$v(n) = (1/2)[1 - (d(n))^2] + d(n)v(n - 1) \qquad n = 1, 2, 3, \ldots . \tag{14.4.8}$$

Using the policy of Equation 14.4.7, we find

$$\begin{aligned} v(1) &= 0.500, \\ v(n) &= (1/2)[1 - (0.5)^2] + 0.5v(n - 1) \\ &= 0.375 + 0.5v(n - 1) \qquad n = 2, 3, 4, \ldots . \end{aligned} \tag{14.4.9}$$

Table 14.4.2 Evaluation of a Non-Optimum Policy

Opportunities Remaining n	Decision Criterion $d(n)$	Value $v(n) = 0.375 + 0.5v(n - 1)$
0	—	0
1	0	0.50000
2	0.5	0.62500
3	0.5	0.68750
4	0.5	0.71875
5	0.5	0.73438
6	0.5	0.74219
7	0.5	0.74610
8	0.5	0.74805
9	0.5	0.74903
10	0.5	0.74952
11	0.5	0.74976
12	0.5	0.74988
13	0.5	0.74994
14	0.5	0.74997
15	0.5	0.74999
16	0.5	0.75000

Table 14.4.2 shows the values of $v(n)$ computed from this equation. We must remember that $v(n)$ is now the value of being in the expectant state with n opportunities remaining when we are using the policy of Equation 14.4.7.

By comparing Tables 14.4.1 and 14.4.2, we observe that when $n = 1$ or 2 the value or expected merit from the process under both policies and, in fact, the policies themselves are identical. However, when n exceeds 2, then the expected merits for the optimum policy shown in Table 14.4.1 always exceed the expected merits for the present policy shown in Table 14.4.2 for the same value of n. Moreover, the asymptotic expected merit when n is large under the present policy is 0.75 rather than 1. The present policy does not provide the appropriate balance of birds in the hand and birds in the bush. Note, for example, that when 16 opportunities remain the decision maker will obtain an increase of about 0.15 in expected merit by following the optimum policy rather than the policy of Equation 14.4.7.

Grafting optimum policies

Suppose that for some reason we are forced to use a non-optimum policy for some portion of our sequential decision process. How should we make decisions beyond this unfortunate region? Imagine that the non-optimum policy of Equation 14.4.7 must be followed only when 8 or fewer opportunities remain. What should we do when more than 8 opportunities remain? We already know the answer. Equation 14.4.4 states that regardless of where $v(n - 1)$ came from, the best thing to do is to make $d(n) = v(n - 1)$. Table 14.4.3 shows the result of this idea. The portion of the table for $n \leq 8$ is the same as the corresponding part of Table 14.4.2 for the non-optimum policy. However, when $n = 9$ we know that we should make $d(9) = v(8)$, no matter how $v(8)$ was produced. Since we are now operating under the optimum policy, $v(9)$ is computed from $v(8)$ using Equation 14.4.5. Thus the rows in Table 14.4.3 corresponding to $n = 9$ through 16 are obtained by applying Equations 14.4.4 and 14.4.5 from the point where the non-optimum policy stopped. We observe that both $d(n)$ and $v(n)$ will once more approach 1 asymptotically when n is large.

However, it is important to note that the values for $d(n)$ and $v(n)$ in the rows from $n = 9$ through 16 in Table 14.4.3 are *not* the same as the corresponding policy and value numbers in Table 14.4.1 where the optimum policy could be followed throughout. The difference is not too large when $n = 16$, but it exists and is important. We could easily verify by computation that using the values for $d(n)$, $n = 9, 10, \ldots, 16$ given by Table 14.4.1 would lead to lower values of $v(n)$ than do the values of $d(n)$, $n = 9, 10, \ldots, 16$ indicated in Table 14.4.3. It is just not true that if we are forced to use a non-optimum policy for the final stages of the decision process, then we should use for decisions beyond that point the same decisions we would have made if we had been able to follow an optimum policy

Table 14.4.3 Results for the Case of an Optimum Policy Grafted onto a Non-Optimum Policy

Opportunities Remaining n	Decision Criterion $d(n)$	Value $v(n)$	
0	—	0	
1	0	0.50000	Non-Optimum $v(n) = 0.375 + 0.5v(n-1)$
2	0.5	0.62500	
3	0.5	0.68750	
4	0.5	0.71875	
5	0.5	0.73438	
6	0.5	0.74219	
7	0.5	0.74610	
8	0.5	0.74805	
9	0.74805 $d(n) = v(n-1)$	0.77979	Optimum $v(n) = 0.5 + 0.5(v(n-1))^2$
10	0.77979	0.80404	
11	0.80404	0.82324	
12	0.82324	0.83886	
13	0.83886	0.85184	
14	0.85184	0.86282	
15	0.86282	0.87223	
16	0.87223	0.88039	

throughout. However, the decision rule for the optimum policy does apply in this event; it serves well in computing the appropriate decision criteria to use in the range for n where the policy is allowed to be anything we please. The nature of a dynamic programming solution is perhaps better evidenced by the question of grafting an optimum policy than by any other single topic we have discussed.

Triangular Merit Distribution

We might be interested in how much the nature of our results depends on the uniform distribution of merit of Figure 14.4.1. Let us therefore suppose that the merit distribution is the triangular distribution of Figure 14.4.2. The effect of this change is to make higher merits more prevalent than before. We still assume that the merits presented at successive opportunities are independently selected from this triangular distribution.

The two quantities that we need to provide in Equation 14.4.2 are the probability that m will equal or exceed $d(n)$ and the expected value of m given that it does. The probability that m will equal or exceed $d(n)$ is the area under the triangular probability distribution between $d(n)$ and 1, an area readily found to be $1 - (d(n))^2$. The density function for m conditional on m equalling or exceeding

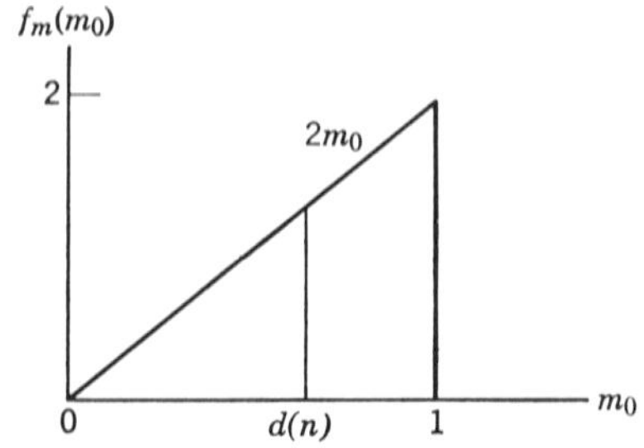

Figure 14.4.2 A triangular density function for the merit presented at each opportunity.

$d(n)$ is then $2m_0/[1 - (d(n))^2]$ for $d(n) \leq m_0 \leq 1$. Consequently, the expected value of m given that m equals or exceeds $d(n)$ is

$$\langle m|m \geq d(n)\rangle = \int_{d(n)}^{1} dm_0 \frac{m_0 \cdot 2m_0}{1 - (d(n))^2} = \frac{(2/3)[1 - (d(n))^3]}{1 - (d(n))^2}. \quad (14.4.10)$$

When we substitute these results into Equation 14.4.2 we obtain

$$v(n) = \underset{d(n)}{\text{Max}} \left\{[1 - (d(n))^2] \frac{(2/3)[1 - d(n))^3]}{[1 - (d(n))^2]} + (d(n))^2 v(n - 1)\right\}$$

$$= \underset{0 \leq d(n) \leq 1}{\text{Max}} \{(2/3)[1 - (d(n))^3] + (d(n))^2 v(n - 1)\}$$

$$n = 1, 2, 3, \ldots . \quad (14.4.11)$$

We observe that the denominator of the conditional expectation is just the probability that m equals or exceeds n. Therefore the contribution of the first term within the braces is just the integral of $m_0 f_m(m_0)$ from $d(n)$ to 1, a partial expectation.

Policy

We again find the maximizing value of $d(n)$ by differentiating the quantity in braces with respect to $d(n)$ and setting the result equal to zero,

$$-2(d(n))^2 + 2d(n)v(n - 1) = 0$$
$$d(n) = v(n - 1). \quad (14.4.12)$$

We have found once again that the decision criterion $d(n)$ when n opportunities remain should be the expected merit to be derived from the process when $n - 1$ opportunities remain. The policy rule is exactly the same as before.

Value

However, the computation of the value function $v(n)$ produces a different result. When we substitute the optimizing value of $d(n)$ from Equation 14.4.12 into the recursive equation 14.4.11, we find

$$\begin{aligned} v(n) &= \left\{(2/3)[1 - (d(n))^3] + (d(n))^2 v(n-1)\right\}_{d(n)=v(n-1)} \\ &= (2/3)[1 - (v(n-1))^3] + (v(n-1))^3 \\ &= (2/3) + (1/3)(v(n-1))^3 \qquad n = 1, 2, 3, \ldots . \end{aligned} \tag{14.4.13}$$

Thus the procedure for constructing $v(n)$ from $v(n-1)$ is changed from the one prescribed by Equation 14.4.5.

Table 14.4.4 shows the decision criteria and expected merits computed from Equations 14.4.12 and 14.4.13 for the case of the triangular merit distribution. By comparing these results with those of Table 14.4.1 we find that for a given number of opportunities remaining, the triangular distribution of merit requires a higher decision criterion and also predicts a higher expected merit from the process. This is not surprising because in the triangular distribution case, higher merits are more prevalent; therefore, the decision maker can be more selective with the expectation of obtaining a better result.

Table 14.4.4 Results for a Triangular Distribution of Opportunity Merit

Opportunities Remaining n	Decision Criterion $d(n) = v(n-1)$	Value $v(n) = (2/3) + (1/3)(v(n-1))^3$
0	—	0
1	0	0.6667
2	0.6667	0.7654
3	0.7654	0.8161
4	0.8161	0.8478
5	0.8478	0.8698
6	0.8698	0.8860
7	0.8860	0.8985
8	0.8985	0.9084
9	0.9084	0.9165
10	0.9165	0.9233
11	0.9233	0.9290
12	0.9290	0.9339
13	0.9339	0.9382
14	0.9382	0.9419
15	0.9419	0.9452
16	0.9452	0.9481

General Merit Distribution

Finding the same rule for establishing decision criteria for both the uniform and triangular distributions of merit presented leads us to inquire if this rule might not apply to any arbitrary merit distribution. We know that for any merit distribution $f_m(\cdot)$, the expected contribution to merit from acting now is just the partial expectation of the merit between $d(n)$ and 1. Furthermore, we shall obtain $v(n-1)$ with the probability we do not act, a probability that is the area of the merit density function between 0 and $d(n)$. Therefore, for a general merit density function, we can write Equation 14.4.2 as

$$v(n) = \underset{0 \leq d(n) \leq 1}{\text{Max}} \left\{ \int_{d(n)}^{1} dm_0\, m_0 f_m(m_0) + v(n-1) \int_{0}^{d(n)} dm_0\, f_m(m_0) \right\}. \quad (14.4.14)$$

Policy

We now find the optimizing value of $d(n)$ by differentiating the quantity in braces with respect to $d(n)$ and setting the result equal to zero. To perform this differentiation we must recall the rules for differentiating with respect to a variable appearing in the limits of an integral. We obtain

$$-d(n) f_m(d(n)) + v(n-1) f_m(d(n)) = 0. \quad (14.4.15)$$

Therefore our policy rule is

$$d(n) = v(n-1), \quad (14.4.16)$$

provided only that the density function is not zero at the point $d(n)$. Of course, when the density function is zero, then there is no possibility of a merit arising in that region and no difficulty can result. Therefore we have shown that regardless of the probability density function for the merit presented at each opportunity, the optimum rule for establishing decision criteria is to make each decision criterion equal to the expected merit to be obtained from the process when one less opportunity remains.

Of course, a moment's reflection shows that this result is just what we would expect. If n opportunities remain and we pass up our present opportunity, then what we can expect in the future is $v(n-1)$. We would be silly to accept any merit for the present opportunity that was lower than $v(n-1)$ and equally silly to refuse any that was higher. Therefore we should establish our decision criteria just as Equation 14.4.16 prescribes.

Value

We obtain an equation for the value $v(n)$ for a general merit distribution by evaluating Equation 14.4.14 at the value of $d(n)$ indicated by Equation 14.4.16,

$$v(n) = \int_{v(n-1)}^{1} dm_0\, m_0 f_m(m_0) + v(n-1) \int_{0}^{v(n-1)} dm_0\, f_m(m_0). \quad (14.4.17)$$

This equation will not be very easy to evaluate if $f_m(\cdot)$ assumes a complicated form.

Monotonicity of value

If we substitute the value of the lower limit $v(n-1)$ for the quantity m_0 in the integrand of the first integral in Equation 14.4.17, we develop an interesting inequality,

$$v(n) \geq \int_{v(n-1)}^{1} dm_0\, v(n-1) f_m(m_0) + v(n-1) \int_0^{v(n-1)} dm_0\, f_m(m_0),$$

$$v(n) \geq v(n-1)\left[\int_{v(n-1)}^{1} dm_0\, f_m(m_0) + \int_0^{v(n-1)} dm_0\, f_m(m_0)\right],$$

$$v(n) \geq v(n-1)\left[\int_0^1 dm_0\, f_m(m_0)\right],$$

$$v(n) \geq v(n-1). \tag{14.4.18}$$

Thus the value of having n opportunities remaining must be monotonically nondecreasing in n. This is a property we have observed in our examples and one that we would expect to hold for even a general density function of merit.

Apparent and Real Complications

The action-timing problem we have analyzed can be generalized in some ways at little cost and in others only with great difficulty. For example, suppose that the density function for merit presented was different for each opportunity. This would cause almost no increase in complexity over the problem we solved. The decision rule would still be given by Equation 14.4.16. All that would change is that the merit density function necessary in Equation 14.4.17 for computing the value function would require a subscript to indicate that it was the merit density function for the nth opportunity. Otherwise the analysis is unchanged. Since the assumption of the same merit density function for all opportunities is the criticism most easily leveled at the model we considered, we are fortunate that changing this requirement causes no difficulty whatsoever.

However, if we desired to generalize the problem by allowing the merits of successive opportunities to be not only uncertain, but dependent on one another (as might be the case, for example, if the gasoline service stations were having a price war), then we have made the problem considerably more difficult. The state of the system would have to specify not only whether or not the action had been taken, but also the merits observed at the opportunities not taken in the past. There would have to be a strong incentive for solving this model before the effort could be justified.

To summarize, we can usually allow a dynamic programming problem to be very general in the dependence of its variables upon the stage of the process without incurring any serious computational difficulty. As soon as the variables of the process become dependent from one stage to the next or when the concept of stage itself becomes confused, then we should expect stormy weather.

Uncertainty in the Number of Opportunities Remaining

We can see many advantages in having a version of this problem suitable when the number of opportunities remaining is uncertain. One case that is particularly easy to treat arises when there is a constant probability β that another opportunity for action beyond the present one will be available. Thus after each opportunity there is a probability $1 - \beta$ that no further opportunities for action will be presented. We assume that an opportunity exists at the moment. The probability that i opportunities after the present one will be available is given by the geometric distribution $(1 - \beta)\beta^i$, $i = 0, 1, 2, \ldots$. The expected number of opportunities including the present one is $1/(1 - \beta)$.

We shall use the case of uniform distribution of opportunity merit to illustrate. Let v be the expected merit of the opportunity selected if an optimum decision rule is followed in this process of uncertain duration. Note that the decision criterion d does not now depend on any stage index. Then the recursive equation for v is similar to Equation 14.4.3,

$$v = \max_{0 \le d \le 1} [(1/2)(1 - d)^2 + d\beta v]. \tag{14.4.19}$$

However, the same value v appears on both sides of the equation because if the process continues to another opportunity, the value will be equal once more to v. The probability of continuing is just d (the probability that the present opportunity has a merit less than d) times β (the probability that another opportunity is presented). We observe that Equation 14.4.19 is the same equation we would write if the process were to continue indefinitely, but merit received one time period in the future were to be multiplied by the discount factor β; consequently, all our present investigations are relevant to that case.

Solution

To solve Equation 14.4.19, we first find the value of d that will maximize the quantity in brackets for a fixed value of v. We do this by differentiating the bracketed quantity with respect to d and setting the result equal to zero; we obtain

$$d = \beta v. \tag{14.4.20}$$

The decision criterion should be equal to β times the value v, which, as before, is just the expected merit that will result if the present opportunity is not taken.

We now write an explicit expression for v by substituting d from Equation 14.4.20

as the maximizing value of d in Equation 14.4.19,

$$\begin{aligned} v &= (1/2)[1 - (\beta v)^2] + \beta v \cdot \beta v \\ &= (1/2)[1 + \beta^2 v^2]\,, \end{aligned} \tag{14.4.21}$$

and then by solving this quadratic equation to produce

$$v = \frac{1}{\beta^2}[1 \pm \sqrt{1 - \beta^2}]. \tag{14.4.22}$$

Since v can at most be 1, we choose the minus sign and obtain

$$v = \frac{1}{\beta^2}[1 - \sqrt{1 - \beta^2}]. \tag{14.4.23}$$

Then from Equation 14.4.20,

$$d = \beta v = \frac{1}{\beta}[1 - \sqrt{1 - \beta^2}]. \tag{14.4.24}$$

Checks

Equations 14.4.23 and 14.4.24 show the expected merit, or value, and decision criterion for this process of uncertain duration. We can check these results by taking $\beta = 1$ and $\beta = 0$. When $\beta = 1$, the process continues indefinitely; we should become very choosy, select a decision criterion near 1, and obtain an expected value near 1. Equations 14.4.23 and 14.4.24 confirm this intuition by showing $v = d = 1$. When $\beta = 0$, then the present opportunity is the last; we should accept it by setting the decision criterion to zero and thereby obtain an expected value equal to the mean of the uniform distribution, 1/2. By taking the limit of v from Equation 14.4.23 as β approaches zero we obtain the value 1/2; Equation 14.4.24 then confirms that $d = 0$.

A numerical example

As an example, let us consider the case where there is a 3/5 probability of presenting another opportunity. This value of β implies a mean number of total opportunities equal to $1/(1 - \beta) = 2.5$. From Equation 14.4.23 we write

$$v = \frac{1}{(3/5)^2}[1 - \sqrt{1 - (3/5)^2}] = (25/9)[1 - \sqrt{16/25}] = 5/9 = 0.55555. \tag{14.4.25}$$

The expected merit of the opportunity taken under the optimum policy would therefore be 5/9. The decision criterion is then given by

$$d = \beta v = (3/5)(5/9) = 1/3 = 0.33333. \tag{14.4.26}$$

The optimum policy is to select the first opportunity with a merit greater than 1/3.

The decision criterion d and expected value v from Equations 14.4.23 and 14.4.24 are shown for several values of continuation probability β in Table 14.4.5. By

Table 14.4.5 Results for a Uniform Distribution of Opportunity Merit for Various Continuation Probabilities β

Continuation Probability	Expected Duration	Value	Decision Criterion
β	$\frac{1}{1-\beta}$	$v = \frac{1}{\beta^2}[1 - \sqrt{1-\beta^2}]$	$d = \beta v = \frac{1}{\beta}[1 - \sqrt{1-\beta^2}]$
0	1	0.50000	0.0
0.1	1.111	0.50126	0.05013
0.2	1.250	0.50510	0.10102
0.3	1.428	0.51179	0.15354
0.4	1.667	0.52178	0.20871
0.5	2.000	0.53590	0.26795
0.6	2.500	0.55555	0.33333
0.7	3.333	0.58338	0.40837
0.8	5.000	0.62500	0.50000
0.9	10	0.69643	0.62679
0.95	20	0.76205	0.72395
1.0	∞	1.00000	1.00000

comparing this table with Table 14.4.1, we see that this process of uncertain duration has a much lower expected value than the fixed duration process of length equal to the expected duration of the uncertain duration process. Indeed, even when $\beta = 0.95$ and the expected duration of the process is 20, its expected value is only about the same as the fixed duration process of length 5.

This model of uncertain duration was once proposed for the problem of a bachelor seeking a bride. We observe that if he is to do well in the marriage sweepstakes, he will need a large β.

14.5 THE DYNAMIC PROGRAMMING FORMALISM

We began by describing the general theory of dynamic programming in rough terms and then proceeded to a pair of examples that indicated the types of problem to which the theory is applied. Now we are ready to present the subject of dynamic programming in more formal terms to establish the generality of the concept.

State

Suppose that we wish to describe a system by M state variables s_i. The composite state of the system at any time can then be represented by an M-component state vector $\mathbf{s}$ with components s_i,

$$\mathbf{s} = \{s_1, s_2, \ldots, s_M\}. \tag{14.5.1}$$

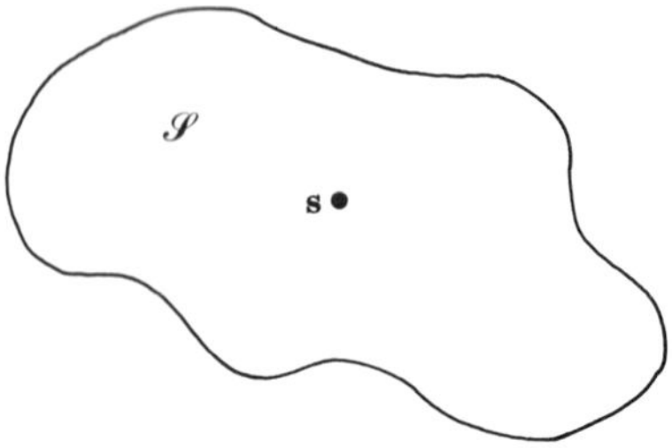

Figure 14.5.1 The state space.

Depending on the model we construct, the components of the state variable could represent pressure, temperature, voltage, energy, investments, or accounts receivable.

We can visualize every state vector **s** as a point in the M-dimensional state space $\mathcal{S}$ shown in Figure 14.5.1. The representation is unique: every state vector corresponds to a point in the state space and every point in the state space corresponds to a state vector. If the values of the state variables change, then the position of the corresponding state vector **s** in the state space changes.

Transformation

Suppose now that we have available a box of "transformations." Each transformation when applied to a state vector will change it into another state vector in the state space. A transformation in a physical problem might be an application of heat or the firing of a rocket. In a business problem it might represent a change in investment portfolio or the purchase of stock for inventory. Every transformation in the box is labeled with a number k for identification; thus T^k is the kth transformation. If T^k is applied to the system when it is described by the state vector **s**, the new state vector afterwards will be $T^k(\mathbf{s})$, another point in the state space $\mathcal{S}$. Figure 14.5.2 shows the box of transformations and a few transformations with

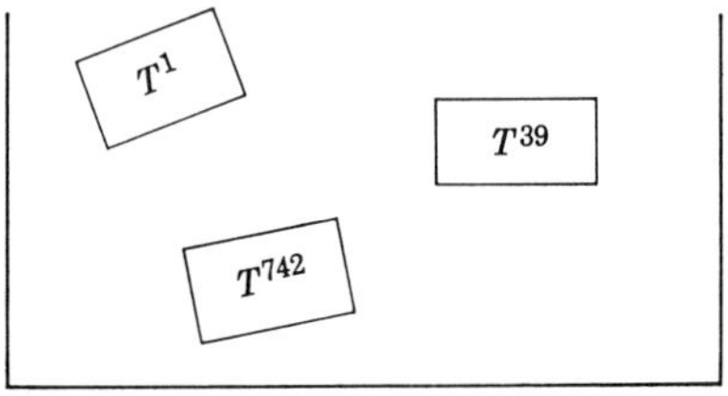

Figure 14.5.2 The box of transformations.

their labels. The number of transformations in the box may be finite or countably infinite.

Suppose now that we choose n transformations from the box of transformations. We can choose the same transformation again and again as we like—the transformations need not be different. Then we apply the n transformations in some order to the system. The transformations and their order could look like

$$T^{23}, T^{59}, T^{12}, T^{59}, T^{231}, \ldots, T^{77}. \tag{14.5.2}$$

We shall call the first transformation applied to the system T_1, the second T_2, etc. We must remember to distinguish between the identification number of a transformation and the number that indicates the order in which it is applied.

Trajectory

We shall specify that the system is originally described by the state vector $\mathbf{s}$. We denote its state vector by $\mathbf{s}_1$ after the first transformation T_1 is applied, by $\mathbf{s}_2$ after the second transformation T_2, etc. The sequence of state vectors for the system therefore satisfies the successive equations,

$$\begin{aligned} \mathbf{s}_1 &= T_1(\mathbf{s}) \\ \mathbf{s}_2 &= T_2(\mathbf{s}_1) \\ \mathbf{s}_3 &= T_3(\mathbf{s}_2) \\ &\vdots \\ \mathbf{s}_n &= T_n(\mathbf{s}_{n-1}). \end{aligned} \tag{14.5.3}$$

This sequence of state vectors establishes a trajectory in the state space, a trajectory shown in Figure 14.5.3. The particular trajectory that will be produced depends on the initial state vector $\mathbf{s}$, the n transformations selected from the box, and the order in which they are applied.

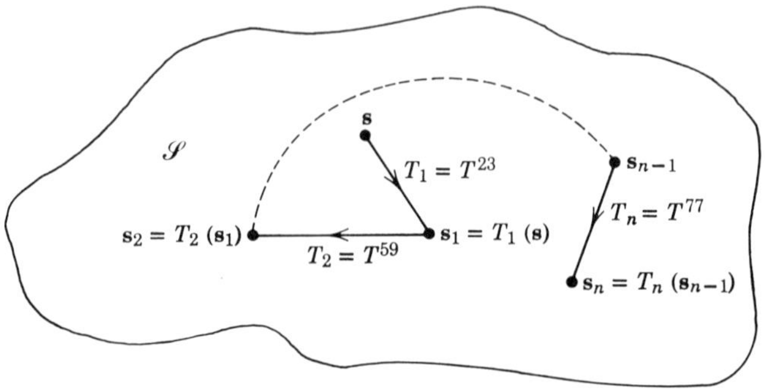

Figure 14.5.3 Trajectory in state space.

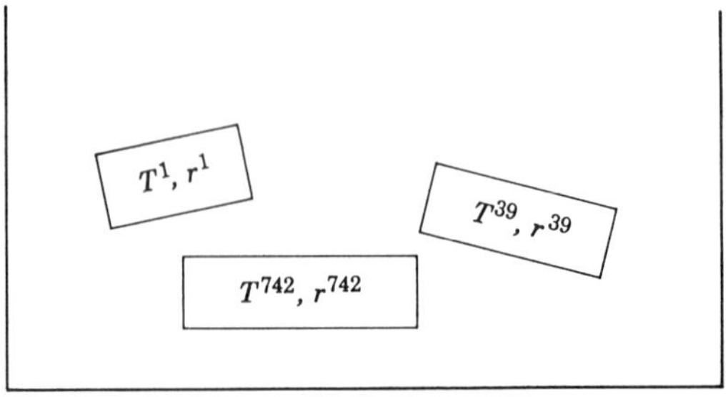

Figure 14.5.4 The box of transformations with associated rewards.

Reward

To make trajectories interesting, we assume that associated with the kth transformation in the box there is a reward function $r^k(\mathbf{s})$ that specifies the reward (money, fuel, power, etc.) that will be gained by applying the kth transformation to the system when it is described by the state vector $\mathbf{s}$. Rewards may, of course, be either positive or negative. Each trajectory of the system will therefore have an associated set of rewards. For the particular trajectory we illustrated in Figure 14.5.3 the sequence of rewards is

$$r^{23}(\mathbf{s}),\ r^{59}(\mathbf{s}_1),\ r^{12}(\mathbf{s}_2),\ \ldots,\ r^{77}(\mathbf{s}_{n-1}). \tag{14.5.4}$$

We denote this sequence by

$$r_1(\mathbf{s}),\ r_2(\mathbf{s}_1),\ r_3(\mathbf{s}_2),\ \ldots,\ r_n(\mathbf{s}_{n-1}) \tag{14.5.5}$$

in accordance with our notation for the sequence of transformations.

Figure 14.5.4 shows the box of transformations, each with an associated reward function. Figure 14.5.5 shows the system trajectory and the rewards generated by the application of each transformation. We now add one last feature to the model.

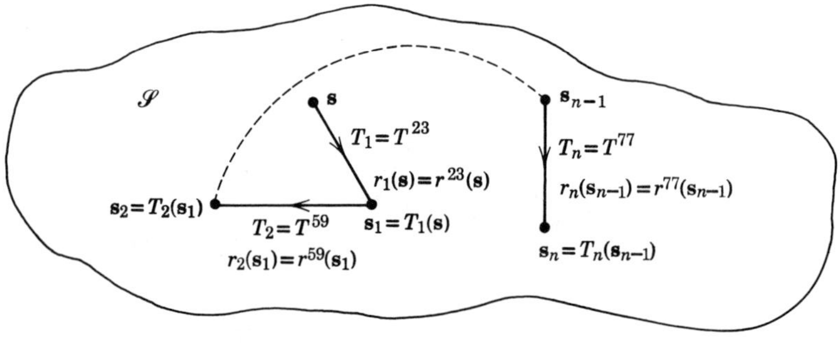

Figure 14.5.5 The system trajectory with rewards.

We associate with each state vector **s** in the state space a terminal reward function $r_0(\mathbf{s})$ that specifies the additional reward to be gained if the system has state vector **s** after all transformations have been applied. We require such a function because in many problems no reward is paid while transformations are being applied but only after they cease. These are called "terminal-value" problems; they are good approximations to a broad class of control problems including the guidance of planetary probes. A more mundane use for terminal rewards is to include the effect of scrap value in machinery replacement problems.

Policy

Let us use P to indicate the policy, the rule for determining the next transformation to be applied given the number of transformations remaining and the current state vector. The total reward $r(\mathbf{s}|n, P)$ from being allowed to choose n transformations depends on the policy P and the starting state vector **s**. Thus for a particular policy,

$$r(\mathbf{s}|n, P) = r_1(\mathbf{s}) + r_2(\mathbf{s}_1) + \cdots + r_n(\mathbf{s}_{n-1}) + r_0(\mathbf{s}_n). \tag{14.5.6}$$

We can now imagine a game where the starting state vector **s** and the number of transformations allowed n are specified, and we have to decide what transformations to use in what order so as to maximize the total reward from the trajectory that results. That is, we must find the best policy.

Value

As we have said before, some of us will be better at this game than others and will be able to achieve higher total rewards. However, the maximum total reward that anyone can achieve is a function only of the starting state vector **s** and the number of transformations allowed n—these are the ultimate constraints on performance. Our portable genius knows how to achieve the maximum; we define the value function $v(\mathbf{s}|n)$ as the total reward he will obtain, the best anyone can do. Formally,

$$v(\mathbf{s}|n) = \underset{P}{\text{Max}}\, r(\mathbf{s}|n, P) \tag{14.5.7}$$

where the maximization is carried out over all possible policies that can be constructed with n transformations.

Principle of Optimality

Now we begin the solution for the best policy. If the system has state vector **s**, if we have n transformations to use, and if we use transformation k now, we shall obtain the reward $r^k(\mathbf{s})$ and produce a new state vector $T^k(\mathbf{s})$ for the system. Our problem is to find what it is worth to have the system described by a state vector $T^k(\mathbf{s})$ when we have $n - 1$ transformations left to use. We consult the portable genius; the answer is $v(T^k(\mathbf{s})|n - 1)$. When we add this future reward to the present reward $r^k(\mathbf{s})$, we have obtained the total reward to be expected from applying transformation k now. We examine all transformations in this way to see which produces the highest total reward—the one that does is selected as the first transformation we apply. These results are summarized in the recursive equation

$$v(\mathbf{s}|n) = \underset{k}{\text{Max}}\,\{r^k(\mathbf{s}) + v(T^k(\mathbf{s})|n - 1)\} \qquad n = 1, 2, 3, \ldots$$
$$T_1 = T^k \qquad r_1(\mathbf{s}) = r^k(\mathbf{s}). \tag{14.5.8}$$

Figure 14.5.6 indicates the sequential nature of the result. If the value function is available when $n - 1$ transformations remain, we can find it when n transformations remain. Of course, we must realize that this evaluation must be performed for every possible state vector in the state space. This computation can be prohibitively difficult if the number of possible state vectors is very large. However, at least theoretically, Equation 14.5.8 shows us how to solve the problem if only someone will specify the function $v(\mathbf{s}|0)$. Yet this is just the reward to be gained by having the system described by the state vector $\mathbf{s}$ when no transformations remain; therefore it is equal to the terminal reward,

$$v(\mathbf{s}|0) = r_0(\mathbf{s}). \tag{14.5.9}$$

Thus we have been able to eliminate the necessity for the portable genius. The sequence of functions $v(\mathbf{s}|n)$ and the optimum policy are computable directly from the specifications of the problem.

This completes our formalization of the solution principle of dynamic programming. The principle that any portion of the optimal trajectory must be optimal with respect to the first transformation in that portion is called the "principle of optimality"; it results in recursive equations with the form of Equation 14.5.8. We see in the general formulation that the value function must *always* be unique, while the policy function need not be.

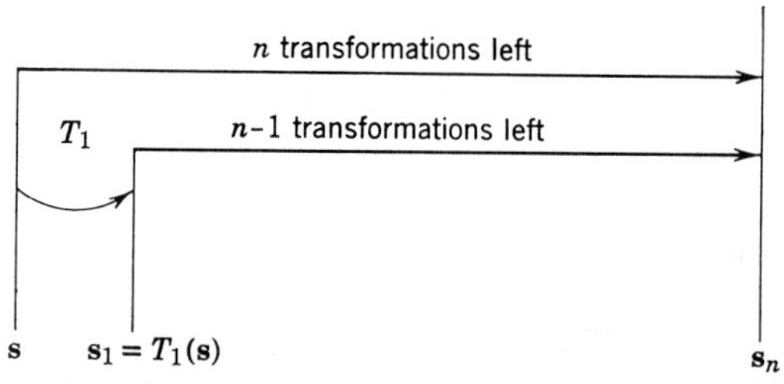

Figure 14.5.6 The sequencing relationship.

Probabilistic Systems

There is one last point we should mention on the general formalism. In some situations the results of applying transformations to the system may not be deterministic. Rather the new state vector, the reward generated, or both may have to be described by random variables. However, we can define an expected total reward $\bar{v}(\mathbf{s}|n)$ by analogy with Equation 14.5.7. We let $\mathbf{s}'$ be a possible new state vector generated by the probabilistic process and let $\mathscr{P}\{\mathbf{s}'|\mathbf{s}, T^k\}$ be the probability that the new state vector will be $\mathbf{s}'$ if the original state vector is $\mathbf{s}$ and transformation T^k is applied. Since the expected value of a sum is the sum of the expected values, we can write a recursive relation for $\bar{v}(\mathbf{s}|n)$ directly from Equation 14.5.8,

$$\bar{v}(\mathbf{s}|n) = \operatorname*{Max}_k \left\{\bar{r}^k(\mathbf{s}) + \sum_{\mathbf{s}'} \bar{v}(\mathbf{s}'|n-1)\mathscr{P}\{\mathbf{s}'|\mathbf{s}, T^k\}\right\} \qquad n = 1, 2, 3, \ldots$$

$$T_1 = T^k \qquad \bar{r}_1(\mathbf{s}) = \bar{r}^k(\mathbf{s}). \tag{14.5.10}$$

Here we have used $\bar{r}^k(\mathbf{s})$ to designate the expected reward received by applying transformation k to the system when it is described by state vector $\mathbf{s}$. To allow for the possibility that the terminal reward $r_0(\mathbf{s})$ may be a random variable, we replace Equation 14.5.9 by

$$\bar{v}(\mathbf{s}|0) = \bar{r}_0(\mathbf{s}). \tag{14.5.11}$$

Equations 14.5.10 and 14.5.11 now serve to find the policy that maximizes the expected value of total reward. However, since the solution rests on the linearity of the expectation operator, we should not find it surprising that using other criteria (as in finding the policy with the minimum reward variance) may be very difficult.

14.6 MULTIPLICATIVE REWARDS

We sometimes encounter problems in which the total reward generated by a trajectory is not simply the sum of the rewards due to each transformation. In these cases we can still apply dynamic programming if we can transform the reward structure into one that is additive.

For example, suppose that the reward generated by a trajectory equals the product of the rewards from applying each transformation. By measuring rewards in terms of their logarithms we would again obtain the additive property used in our development. We would then be maximizing the logarithm of the value function rather than the value function itself; but because of the monotonic property of the logarithmic function, the maximum of the log of the value function will be achieved by the same policy that maximizes the value function itself. Equations 14.5.8 and 14.5.9 in this case would become

$$\log v(\mathbf{s}|n) = \operatorname*{Max}_k \{\log r^k(\mathbf{s}) + \log v(T^k(\mathbf{s})|n-1)\} \qquad n = 1, 2, 3, \ldots$$
$$\log v(\mathbf{s}|0) = \log r_0(\mathbf{s}). \tag{14.6.1}$$

Of course, from this equation we see immediately that

$$\begin{aligned}\log v(\mathbf{s}|n) &= \operatorname*{Max}_k \{\log [r^k(\mathbf{s})v(T^k(\mathbf{s})|n-1)]\} \\ &= \log \operatorname*{Max}_k \{r^k(\mathbf{s})v(T^k(\mathbf{s})|n-1)\}\end{aligned} \tag{14.6.2}$$

or

$$\begin{aligned}v(\mathbf{s}|n) &= \operatorname*{Max}_k r^k(\mathbf{s})v(T^k(\mathbf{s})|n-1) \\ v(\mathbf{s}|0) &= r_0(s),\end{aligned} \tag{14.6.3}$$

where we now define $v(\mathbf{s}|n)$ to be the maximum product of rewards obtainable if the system starts with state vector **s** and is allowed n transformations. We have thus established that dynamic programming is readily applied to multiplicative rewards by changing the recursive equation from sum to product form.

A Reliability Example

We shall now demonstrate by example the procedure for solving multiplicative reward problems. A system is to be engineered so that its probability of failure will be as low as possible given a constraint on the system's total weight. The system is constructed by connecting together a number of components each of which can by itself sustain operation of the system; therefore, the system fails only if all its components fail. We have available five types of components whose weights and probabilities of failure appear in Table 14.6.1. We note that the

Table 14.6.1 Reliability Problem Components Available

Component Type i	Weight w_i	Failure Probability p_i
1	3	0.50
2	5	0.30
3	7	0.20
4	10	0.08
5	13	0.038

heaviest components are the most reliable. The total weight of the system is constrained to be not more than 19 pounds. We may use any combination of components within this constraint, for example, several components of the same type or a mixture of types. We assume that components fail independently and therefore that the failure probability for the system is just the product of the failure probabilities for its components. Our problem is to find how many of each type of component should be used to make this failure probability as low as possible within the weight allowance.

The dynamic programming formulation

The first step in the solution is to identify the state variable in the problem; of course, it is the weight available for construction of the system. We let w be the number of pounds of weight allowed for the system and then define $v(w)$ as the minimum system failure probability attainable within a weight allowance of w pounds. Every time we add a component to the system we reduce the weight available w by the weight of the component and, at the same time, multiply the lowest system failure probability that the system can achieve within its reduced weight allowance by the failure probability of the component. We want to add the component that makes the product of these two probabilities a minimum, for at that point we shall have achieved the minimum system failure probability within the weight allowance w. In recursive equation form,

$$v(w) = \begin{cases} \operatorname*{Min}_i p_i v(w - w_i) & \text{if some } w_i \le w \\ 1 & \text{if all } w_i > w \end{cases} \qquad w = 0, 1, 2, \ldots . \qquad (14.6.4)$$

Note that the minimization is carried out only over those components whose weights do not exceed the current weight allowance. If all components available weigh more than the weight allowance, then the system failure probability is, of course, 1. We consider only integral weights in pounds because the weight allowance and the weights of all components are measured in integral pounds.

Recursive solution

We are now ready to generate the solution by solving Equation 14.6.4 recursively for $w = 0, 1, 2, \ldots$. For $w = 0, 1$, or 2, $v(w) = 1$ because no components of weight less than three are available. For $w = 3$ or 4, only component 1 will fit and so it is used, producing $v(w) = 0.5$. When $w = 5$, we have a choice between components 1 and 2,

$$v(5) = \operatorname{Min} \begin{cases} p_1 v(5 - w_1) = 0.5v(2) = 0.5(1) = 0.5 \\ p_2 v(5 - w_2) = 0.3v(0) = 0.3(1) = 0.3; \end{cases} \qquad (14.6.5)$$

Table 14.6.2 Reliability Problem Solution

Weight Allowance w	Component Type To Be Introduced	Optimum System Failure Probability $v(w)$	Optimum System Component Mix
0	—	1.0	—
1	—	1.0	—
2	—	1.0	—
3	1	0.5	1
4	1	0.5	1
5	2	0.3	2
6	1	0.25	1,1
7	3	0.2	3
8	1 or 2	0.15	1,2
9	1	0.125	1,1,1
10	4	0.08	4
11	1 or 2	0.075	1,1,2
12	2 or 3	0.06	2,3
13	5	0.038	5
14	1 or 2	0.0375	1,1,1,2
15	2 or 4	0.024	2,4
16	1 or 5	0.019	1,5
17	3 or 4	0.016	3,4
18	2 or 5	0.0114	2,5
19	1 or 5	0.0095	1,1,5
20	4	0.0064	4,4

consequently, we use component 2. When $w = 6$, we again have a choice between components 1 and 2,

$$v(6) = \text{Min} \begin{cases} p_1 v(6 - w_1) = 0.5v(3) = 0.5(0.5) = 0.25 \\ p_2 v(6 - w_2) = 0.3v(1) = 0.3(1) = 0.3, \end{cases} \tag{14.6.6}$$

but this time we choose component 1.

We continue this procedure for higher and higher values of w to produce Table 14.6.2. Here we show in successive columns the weight allowance w; the component that would be used first with that weight allowance; the resulting minimum system failure probability $v(w)$; and finally, for convenience, the complete design of the system to produce the minimum system failure probability. The computations are performed for all weight allowances w from 0 to 20 pounds.

Interpretation of results

We observe that for some weight allowances like $w = 8$ there is a choice with respect to which component to install next in the optimum design caused by a tie in the minimization,

$$v(8) = \text{Min} \begin{cases} p_1 v(8 - w_1) = 0.5v(5) = 0.5(0.3) = 0.15 \\ p_2 v(8 - w_2) = 0.3v(3) = 0.3(0.5) = 0.15\ . \\ p_3 v(8 - w_3) = 0.2v(1) = 0.2(1) = 0.2 \end{cases} \qquad (14.6.7)$$

However, in this case there is no real choice in the design of the system: If we install component 1 at this point we shall have a remaining weight allowance of 5 pounds and, hence, will then install component 2; whereas if we install component 2 at this point, we shall have a remaining weight allowance of 3 pounds and therefore install component 1. Either way the optimum design of the system consists of one component of type 1 and one component of type 2, a fact recorded in the last column of the table.

To emphasize the distinction between the second and fourth columns, we note that when $w = 9$ the component to be selected according to the second column is component 1, thus reducing the weight allowance to $w = 6$. At $w = 6$ we find from the second column that component 1 should be used again, thereby reducing the weight allowance to $w = 3$. When $w = 3$ we see again from the second column that component 1 should be used. The design of the system is therefore three components of type 1 as shown in the fourth column for $w = 9$. The system failure probability $v(9) = 0.125$ is, of course, p_1^3.

The computation of Table 14.6.2 is a simple task for human or computer. A sliding paper strip of the type we discussed earlier facilitates manual computation.

We see that we have solved not only the problem originally posed, but also the optimum design of the system for any weight allowance up to 20 pounds. To answer the original question where the weight allowance was 19 pounds, we observe from the table that the optimum system consists of 2 components of type 1 and 1 component of type 5, thus requiring use of the entire 19 pounds allowed. The system failure probability for this system is $v(19) = 0.0095$. The table shows also that the design of the system is markedly affected by weight allowance. For example, if we were granted a 20-pound weight allowance, we would change the design of the system completely by specifying that it be constructed of two type 4 components. This system would have a failure probability of $v(20) = 0.0064$.

Dynamic programming is a very convenient tool for solving many problems of this type, which we might call "packing" problems. Additive or multiplicative reward structures are treated with the same ease. We can readily see how to extend the procedure to cases where there are additional constraints on volume or cost so that we require two or three state variables.

14.7 CONCLUSION

We have now seen both the general structure of dynamic programming and its application to representative examples. As the examples show, in the recursive procedure the number of points that must be evaluated increases rapidly both with the number of state variables and with the number of levels each state variable can assume. If there are a state variables, each assuming b levels, then we must consider b^a points in the state space. Clearly, this number becomes prohibitive very quickly for even the largest computers. Thus dynamic programming requires considerable insight on the part of the analyst if he is to avoid creating a computationally infeasible problem.

There is obviously an advantage in developing a dynamic programming formulation that is general enough to be suitable for broad classes of problems and yet computationally feasible. The most important formulation of this type is a decision model based on the Markov or semi-Markov process with rewards, a model developed and analyzed in the next chapter.

PROBLEMS

1. Use dynamic programming to solve the following problem:

$$\text{Max } x_1 x_2{}^2 x_3{}^3 \cdots x_n{}^n$$

$$x_1 + x_2 + x_3 + \cdots + x_n = y$$

$$x_i \geq 0 \qquad i = 1, 2, \ldots, n$$

a) Set up an appropriate recursive equation scheme in a function $v_N(\cdot)$.
b) Give explicit algebraic expressions for $v_1(\cdot)$, $v_2(\cdot)$, $v_3(\cdot)$.
c) Give a solution for $n = 3$, $y = 6$.

2. A weary desert traveler has x gallons of fuel left for his vehicle and enough rations remaining for n more days of travel. On any one day the traveler must decide how much fuel to use. He has found through experience that the distance he can travel during any one day on y gallons of fuel is $f(y)$ where $f'(w) > 0$ and $f''(w) < 0$ for all w. That is, there is a generally diminishing return on the use of additional fuel. Let $v_n(x)$ be the maximum distance the traveler can cover if he has x gallons of fuel remaining and n days of rations.

a) Write a recursive relation for $v_n(x)$.

b) Find the traveler's optimum policy and $v_n(x)$.

c) Suppose that $f(y)$ represents only the *expected* distance traveled on any one day if y gallons are used. Calculate $\bar{v}_n(x)$, the maximum *expected* distance covered if the traveler has x gallons of fuel remaining and n days of rations.

d) For part c), calculate the variance of the total distance traveled under the optimum policy. Let $\overset{\vee}{f}(y)$ represent the variance of the distance traveled on any one day if y gallons of fuel are used.

3. A factory has two production levels: It can produce either 2 items per week or 5 items per week. The cost of changing the production level is 5 units. The sales during the next three weeks are known to be 4, 1, and 5 items. The inventory cost for each item remaining in stock at the end of each week is one unit while the cost for each unfilled order at the end of each week is two units. Let x be the current number of items in stock where $x < 0$ corresponds to unfilled orders. For all integer $-5 \leq x \leq 5$, find the production policy that will minimize the total cost during the next three weeks. What is this minimum total cost for each x?

4. A company's sales during each month are known to be random with a mean and variance of $\bar{s}_i$ and $\check{s}_i$, respectively, for the ith month. The company must decide on its production policy for each month. If a production α_j is ordered during the jth month, the actual production that will occur is also random with a mean α_j and a variance σ_j^2. (Note that the variance of the production is independent of the ordered production.) The inventory cost during each month is equal to the square of the inventory at the end of the month—negative inventories correspond to unfilled orders. If the present inventory is x, find the optimum ordering policy and the corresponding expected total cost $v_n(x)$ during the next n months of operation.

5. A research coordinator must invest an amount x in various research project proposals. Only one proposal can be prepared during each month, and the coordinator must decide how much of his remaining budget to invest in the proposal for each month. Through long experience the coordinator knows that if he invests \$$y$ in a proposal, the probability of winning the project is $(1 - e^{-\lambda y})$. If he wins the project during month i, then his company accrues a reward r_i at the end of the month; if he loses, the company gains nothing. The potential reward from each project is known, but the rewards are not used to augment the research coordinator's budget. The company's monthly discount factor is β. Find:

a) $v_n(x)$ = the present worth of the total expected reward from an optimal investment of \$$x$ over the next n months. (Assume $v_0(x) = 0$.)

b) $\alpha_n(x)$ = the optimal amount to be invested in the proposal for the next month if the coordinator has n months remaining in which to invest a total of \$$x$.

Assume that the rewards r_i are sufficiently close and that β is near enough to unity that $0 < \alpha_n(x) < x$ for all $n > 1$.

6. A "challenge ladder" is often used in situations where a large number of people play the same game, but with varying degrees of skill. Consider the following continuous version of a challenge ladder: A person's position on the ladder can be any positive real number with zero corresponding to the lowest or least-skilled position. If a person's position is x, then he can challenge any position y that is higher than his own on the ladder. If he wins, then he takes the position y of the person challenged; if he loses, his position remains the same. Suppose further that:

i) If your position is x and you challenge y, the probability of winning a challenge is $\alpha e^{\mu x - \lambda y}$ where $\mu < \lambda$. (The μx term is intended to describe the improvement in your skill from stiffer competition, more self confidence, etc. resulting from a higher position on the ladder.)

ii) You only have time for n challenges per year.

iii) Your position on the ladder is only affected by the challenges *you* make.

Let $v_n(x)$ represent your expected position on the ladder at the end of the year if your present position is x and your remaining n challenges are delivered optimally. Let $y_n(x)$ be the optimal challenge if your present position is x and there are n challenges remaining.

a) Write a recursive equation for $v_n(x)$.

b) Find a general differential equation involving $v_{n-1}(\cdot)$ whose solution yields $y_n(x)$.

c) Find $y_1(x)$ and $v_1(x)$.

d) Find the transcendental equation whose solution yields $y_2(x)$.

7. A two-state Markov model has been proposed to describe the way a student learns a simple concept. There are two states of knowledge: In state 2 he knows it, and in state 1 he doesn't. The student is presented with a series of questions. If he is in state 1 he answers (i.e., guesses) correctly with probability g; in any case he goes to state 2 with probability p after we show him the correct answer. Of course, he always answers correctly if he is in state 2. Since an incorrect answer assures us that the student is in state 1, we keep track of the number of correct answers that the student has given since his last incorrect response.

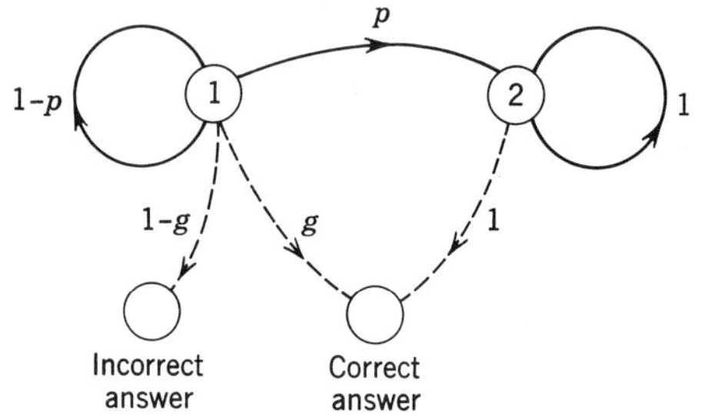

a) If a student has responded with j correct answers in a row since his last incorrect answer, what is the probability that he is still in state 1?

b) It costs us \$1 to present a question to the student and \$$c$ if we stop the process while he is in state 1. There is no cost if we stop in state 2. Let v_j = the total expected future cost to us of teaching a student if he has answered j successive questions correctly and we stop so as to minimize the total expected cost. Write an equation for v_j in terms of v_{j+1} and v_0.

c) Suppose that a certain student has answered j questions in a row correctly. Consider the two policies: (i) stop the instruction for all j, and (ii) stop the instruction for $j \geq 1$ but go on for $j = 0$. For what range of c is policy (i) preferred over (ii)?

8. A wealthy playboy wants to buy two horses of identical ancestry. In order that the two horses can work together as a team, he insists that the ages of the two horses should be no more than one year apart. He has bought an option on the next n foals of a particular brood mare but would like to know how to exercise his option in a way that will maximize the sum of the values for the two horses he will obtain. The probability density function for the value of each foal is $f(\cdot)$; the value of successive foals is independent; and the mare produces only one foal per year. Each time a foal is born, he must decide whether or not to exercise his option to buy the foal and the foal from the preceding year. Let:

$d_n(x)$ = the decision criterion for the next foal if there are n opportunities left and the last foal had a value x, i.e., he accepts the next foal if and only if its value exceeds $d_n(x)$

$v_n(x)$ = the expected summed value of the two horses if there are n opportunities left, the last foal had a value x, and an optimum policy is followed

a) Find $d_1(x)$, $v_1(x)$, $d_2(x)$, $v_2(x)$, and $d_3(x)$ in terms of μ, the mean of $f(\cdot)$.
b) Find $v_3(x)$ and $d_4(x)$ if $f(y)$ is uniform from zero to one.

9. Suppose in the previous problem that the playboy relaxes the restriction that the horses' ages differ by no more than one year. If there are n opportunities remaining, there are i horses still to be chosen, and an optimum selection policy is followed, let $v_i(n)$ and $d_i(n)$ be the expected value of the horses remaining to be chosen and the decision criterion, respectively. Each time a foal is born, the playboy must decide whether or not to buy it.

a) If the probability density function for the value of each foal is $f(\cdot)$, find the equation for $d_2(n)$ in terms of $v_1(n - 1)$ and $v_2(n - 1)$.

b) If $f(\cdot)$ is uniform from zero to one, find $d_1(n)$, $d_2(n)$, $v_1(n)$, and $v_2(n)$ for $n =$ 0, 1, 2, 3, 4, and 5.

c) Repeat part a) and *explain* how you would do part b) for the case in which the playboy wishes to buy m foals with no age constraints.

10. Mr. Otto B. Cautious has been given the opportunity to buy some property for one of his clients. He is told that he has a time period t to make a single purchase and his commission will be proportional to the value of the property purchased. The time between opportunities to make a purchase is an exponentially distributed random variable with mean $1/\lambda$ (i.e., the arrival of opportunities is a Poisson process). Furthermore, the probability density function $f(x)$ for the value x of the property that can be purchased is identical for each opportunity. Otto would like to find the policy he should follow so as to maximize the expected value of the purchased property. Let $v(t)$ be the expected value of the purchased property if Otto follows an optimum policy and has a time period t remaining to make the purchase. Let $d(t)$ be the decision criterion for an opportunity if there is a time t remaining; that is, Otto makes the purchase if the value is greater than $d(t)$ and refuses the purchase if the value is less than $d(t)$.

a) Write a recursive equation for $v(t)$ in terms of $d(\cdot)$ by considering the possible actions by Otto at the next opportunity.

b) Find the relationship between $d(\cdot)$ and $v(\cdot)$.

c) Find $v(t)$ and $d(t)$ if $f(x)$ is uniform between 0 and 1.

[*Hint*: The differential equation $du(t)/dt = ku^2(t)$ has the solution $u(t) = -1/k(t - a)$, where a is an arbitrary constant.]

15 SEMI-MARKOV DECISION PROCESSES

The most interesting problems in the treatment of dynamic probabilistic system models arise when we have the opportunity to control the system. In such problems we want to select from among the alternatives available for the operation of the system those alternatives that are in some sense most rewarding. In the first twelve chapters we discussed dynamic probabilistic system models. In Chapter 13 we introduced rewards, and in Chapter 14 the dynamic programming approach to optimization. Using all this earlier work, in this chapter we construct a model for decision-making in the semi-Markov process and develop procedures for determining the most rewarding policy in such processes.

15.1 THE DECISION STRUCTURE

Suppose we have described a system by the discrete- or continuous-time semi-Markov model with rewards developed in Chapter 13. We then augment the description by saying that whenever the system enters a state the probability and reward functions governing departure from it are not fixed, but rather may be selected from among a finite set of alternatives. Associated with the kth alternative in state i will be the transition probability to the next state, the holding time, the yield rate, the bonus, and the other probabilistic and reward measures derived from these quantities. Thus if we use superscript k to indicate the kth alternative in a given state, the process descriptors associated with the kth alternative in state i would appear as p_{ij}^k, $h_{ij}^k(\cdot)$, $y_{ij}^k(\cdot)$, $b_{ij}^k(\cdot)$, $r_i^k(t, \alpha)$, q_i^k, etc.

Note that we can only select an alternative when the system enters a state; when the selection is made, we have determined both the probabilistic and economic rules for the system until it makes its next transition. And of course, an alternative is a complete alternative—we cannot select the probabilistic functions from one alternative and the reward functions from another. The number of alternatives may differ from one state to another. Some states may have only one alternative and therefore allow us no choice whatsoever in the operation of the system whenever such a state is occupied.

As we have mentioned, the problem we want to solve is how to select the alternatives that will make operation of the system most rewarding. We shall say that the selection of an alternative for operation when the system enters a given state is called a decision, and that the set of decisions for all states constitutes a policy. Then the problem is to find the most rewarding or most profitable policy.

Criteria

To solve the problem we must specify more clearly what we mean by "most profitable." If the system is to operate for only a finite interval of time, then the maximum total reward it could earn would be finite and the expectation of this reward would be finite. In this case we might say that we wanted to maximize the expected total reward generated by the system over this time interval.

However, if the system is allowed to operate indefinitely, then the rewards generated by the system and the expected rewards generated by the system will generally grow without bound. In this case, maximizing the expected total reward becomes meaningless and we must turn to another criterion. As we showed in Chapter 13, if we operate a monodesmic system for an indefinite time, it will generate some average reward per unit time or gain. A reasonable criterion for monodesmic systems that will operate indefinitely is maximization of the gain. The essential difference introduced by the existence of either a finite or an infinite duration lies in the way we specify the policy. If the duration is finite, then the best alternative to select in each state will generally be a function of the time remaining for system operation; or briefly, the policy is a function of time. However, for a system that will operate indefinitely, the policy must be independent of time since the time variable will have no significance. The policy in this case is simply a specification of the number of the alternative to be selected whenever each state is entered. We shall call such a policy a stationary policy.

Criteria of choice

Thus for finite time intervals, our problem is to find the time-varying policy that will maximize the expected total reward generated by the system. For infinite time intervals, our problem is to find the stationary policy that will maximize the gain of the system. We shall usually assume in this case that our systems are monodesmic so that no ambiguity in gain can arise. Although our arguments can be extended to the multiple-chain case, the increased complexity is sufficient to justify organizing the problem so that this possibility is avoided.

Other criteria

The selection of these criteria for finding the optimum policy is, of course, quite arbitrary. One can think of many other criteria that would have important practical application. For example, we might desire to find the non-stationary policy that would maximize the probability of our earning a given amount in a given time interval. We do not discuss such problems only because for most of them we do not have computational techniques available that improve upon the obvious, but unwieldy, method of complete trajectory enumeration. Fortunately, we do have powerful computational methods for solving the problems we have posed.

Criteria under discounting

Our final remarks on criteria are concerned with discounting of future rewards. The major effect of discounting, as we found in Chapter 13, is to allow us to characterize by their present value the rewards generated by a process that operates indefinitely. Thus whether the process operates for a finite or infinite time interval, we can speak of the expected present value of future rewards, a finite quantity. Regardless of whether the process operates for a finite period or indefinitely, our criterion will therefore be maximization of the expected present value of future rewards. The only difference between the finite and infinite time duration is that the optimum policy will be time-varying in the first case and stationary in the second. We shall see that the introduction of discounting causes only minor modifications in our methods.

Solution Methods

Let us now discuss the matter of the solution procedures we shall develop. For the case of finite time intervals, whether or not discounting is present, we use dynamic programming to find the optimum time-varying policy. Because this method is convenient only for discrete time intervals, we restrict its use to the discrete-time semi-Markov decision process. If we want to solve a continuous-time semi-Markov decision process for a finite time interval, we must therefore transform it into a discrete-time version. We shall refer to the dynamic programming solution of the finite time interval problem as "value iteration."

We treat the case of infinite time intervals, whether or not discounting is present, by a method similar to, but not equivalent to, dynamic programming. We call this method "policy iteration." Policy iteration will find the stationary policy that maximizes the gain when no discounting is used and that maximizes the expected present value of future rewards in the case of discounting.†

In the next two sections we shall describe and illustrate both value iteration and policy iteration. But before we begin to consider solution methods, let us examine a semi-Markov decision problem to fix our ideas clearly.

† While our treatment of both value and policy iteration will be complete in itself, those who are interested in detailed large-size examples in such areas as baseball and automobile replacement are referred to the book, *Dynamic Programming and Markov Processes.*

The Car Rental Example—Again

We return once more to the discrete-time car rental example introduced in Chapter 10 and last discussed in Section 13.8. As you recall from Equation 13.8.2, there was a charge of 10 per day if the car was rented in town 1 and 5 per day if in town 2. There was a drop charge of 45 for returning the car to town 2 when it had been rented in town 1, and a drop charge of 40 for returning it to town 1 when it had been rented in town 2. The transition probabilities and holding time mass functions appear in Equations 10.1.14 and 10.1.17.

The decision problem

We now suppose that the company is considering a change in its operational policies and in its rate structure. The company has conducted a survey which indicates that it can require all cars rented in town 1 to be returned to town 2, maintain the same daily charge of 10 per day, and keep all of its cars busy, provided that it reduces the drop charge from 45 to 30. The same survey indicates that whether or not the company takes this action, it can require all cars rented in town 2 to be returned to town 1, maintain the same daily charge of 5 per day, and keep all its cars busy provided that it eliminates completely the 40 drop charge on such trips. The problem is whether the company should adopt either or both of these changes of practice.

The reward structure

To place this problem into our context, we identify the original operations of the company as constituting the first alternative in each of the two states, and the changes in operation as the second alternative in each state. We shall call the original alternative in each state the "free" alternative since the customer is free to choose his destination; the new alternative will be called the "limited" alternative. Thus according to Equation 13.8.2, the charges associated with state 1 for the free alternative are

$$f_1^{\,1} = 10 \qquad f_{11}^{\,1} = 0 \qquad f_{12}^{\,1} = 45, \tag{15.1.1}$$

whereas for the limited alternative they are

$$f_1^{\,2} = 10 \qquad f_{11}^{\,2} = 0 \qquad f_{12}^{\,2} = 30. \tag{15.1.2}$$

Similarly, charges for the free alternative in state 2 are

$$f_2^{\,1} = 5 \qquad f_{21}^{\,1} = 40 \qquad f_{22}^{\,1} = 0, \tag{15.1.3}$$

and for the limited alternative

$$f_2^{\,2} = 5 \qquad f_{21}^{\,2} = 0 \qquad f_{22}^{\,2} = 0. \tag{15.1.4}$$

The transition probabilities

Of course, the new alternatives affect the probabilistic structure of transitions as well as the rewards. Under the limited alternatives, a rented car is certain to make a transition to the town from which it was not rented. Thus the transition probabilities for the limited alternatives are

$$p_{11}{}^2 = 0 \qquad p_{12}{}^2 = 1$$
$$p_{21}{}^2 = 1 \qquad p_{22}{}^2 = 0. \tag{15.1.5}$$

The holding times

However, the survey reveals that the trip times would be described by the same distributions for both the free and limited alternatives, and therefore that the holding time mass functions would still be given by Equation 10.1.17,

$$h_{11}{}^1(m) = h_{11}{}^2(m) = (1/3)(2/3)^{m-1} \qquad h_{12}{}^1(m) = h_{12}{}^2(m) = (1/6)(5/6)^{m-1}$$
$$h_{21}{}^1(m) = h_{21}{}^2(m) = (1/4)(3/4)^{m-1} \qquad h_{22}{}^1(m) = h_{22}{}^2(m) = (1/12)(11/12)^{m-1}$$
$$m = 1, 2, 3, \ldots. \tag{15.1.6}$$

The mean holding times would consequently also be the same for the free and limited alternatives in each state and would be given by Equation 10.1.16,

$$\bar{\tau}_{11}{}^1 = \bar{\tau}_{11}{}^2 = 3 \qquad \bar{\tau}_{12}{}^1 = \bar{\tau}_{12}{}^2 = 6$$
$$\bar{\tau}_{21}{}^1 = \bar{\tau}_{21}{}^2 = 4 \qquad \bar{\tau}_{22}{}^1 = \bar{\tau}_{22}{}^2 = 12. \tag{15.1.7}$$

The waiting times

However, because the mean waiting times $\bar{\tau}_i$ involve both the transition probabilities and the mean holding times, they will be different for the free and limited alternatives. For the free alternatives, we find from Equation 10.1.22 that the mean waiting times are

$$\bar{\tau}_1{}^1 = 3.6 \qquad \bar{\tau}_2{}^1 = 9.6. \tag{15.1.8}$$

We compute them for the limited alternatives from Equations 15.1.5 and 15.1.7,

$$\bar{\tau}_1{}^2 = p_{11}{}^2\bar{\tau}_{11}{}^2 + p_{12}{}^2\bar{\tau}_{12}{}^2 = 0(3) + 1(6) = 6$$
$$\bar{\tau}_2{}^2 = p_{21}{}^2\bar{\tau}_{21}{}^2 + p_{22}{}^2\bar{\tau}_{22}{}^2 = 1(4) + 0(12) = 4. \tag{15.1.9}$$

The mean waiting times for the limited alternatives are, of course, equal to the mean holding times for the one transition possible.

Summary

The probabilistic and reward parameters for all alternatives appear in Table 15.1.1. We must now find whether one or both limited alternatives are more profitable for the company than the present free operations.

Table 15.1.1 The Car Rental Decision Problem

State	Alternatives	Transition Probabilities		Holding Time Mass Functions		Mean Holding Times		Mean Waiting Times	Day Charge	Drop Charge		Bonus $b_{ij}^k(m) = f_i^k m + f_{ij}^k$	
i	k	p_{i1}^k	p_{i2}^k	$h_{i1}^k(m)$	$h_{i2}^k(m)$	$\bar{\tau}_{i1}^k$	$\bar{\tau}_{i2}^k$	$\bar{\tau}_i^k$	f_i^k	f_{i1}^k	f_{i2}^k	$b_{i1}^k(m)$	$b_{i2}^k(m)$
1	1 (free)	0.8	0.2	$(1/3)(2/3)^{m-1}$	$(1/6)(5/6)^{m-1}$	3	6	3.6	10	0	45	$10m$	$10m + 45$
	2 (limited)	0	1	$(1/3)(2/3)^{m-1}$	$(1/6)(5/6)^{m-1}$	3	6	6	10	0	30	$10m$	$10m + 30$
2	1 (free)	0.3	0.7	$(1/4)(3/4)^{m-1}$	$(1/12)(11/12)^{m-1}$	4	12	9.6	5	40	0	$5m + 40$	$5m$
	2 (limited)	1	0	$(1/4)(3/4)^{m-1}$	$(1/12)(11/12)^{m-1}$	4	12	4	5	0	0	$5m$	$5m$

15.2 VALUE ITERATION

We shall now develop a procedure based on dynamic programming for finding the optimum time-varying policy for a discrete-time semi-Markov decision process over a finite time interval. The procedure will determine the policy that maximizes the expected total reward when no discounting is present and the expected present value of reward in the presence of discounting.

Let us suppose that the process will operate for a time interval of length n. We define a value function $v_i(n, \beta)$ to be the maximum expected present value of future rewards that can be generated by the process during the time interval of length n under the conditions that the process has just entered state i and that the discount factor per time period is β. In our dynamic programming terminology, $v_i(n, \beta)$ is the best anyone can achieve in terms of expected present value of reward if he is allowed a time interval of length n and required to start in state i. Of course, our expectations will be this high only if we make the best possible decision every time the system enters a state.

Suppose that the system has just entered state i with n time periods remaining and that we must select the alternative to govern the destination state, holding time, yield rate, and bonus associated with the departure from state i. If we knew the maximum expected present value to be attached to entering any state when less than n time periods remain, we could simply write the right-hand side of Equation 13.6.1 for each available alternative and then select the one that made this quantity the highest. Of course, this highest value for the right-hand side would be $v_i(n, \beta)$, the value function for n periods remaining when the process starts in state i. Thus we can find the value function for n periods remaining if we know it for less than n periods remaining. However, just as we found in our discussion of dynamic programming, we can solve the problem by induction by specifying $v_i(0)$, the value function when no time remains, and then recursively finding the function for higher and higher values of n. Thus we develop the formalism,

$$v_i(n, \beta) = \operatorname*{Max}_k \left\{ \sum_{j=1}^{N} p_{ij}{}^k \sum_{m=n+1}^{\infty} h_{ij}{}^k(m) \left[\sum_{\ell=0}^{n-1} \beta^\ell y_{ij}{}^k(\ell) + \beta^n v_i(0) \right] \right.$$
$$\left. + \sum_{j=1}^{N} p_{ij}{}^k \sum_{m=1}^{n} h_{ij}{}^k(m) \left[\sum_{\ell=0}^{m-1} \beta^\ell y_{ij}{}^k(\ell) + \beta^m b_{ij}{}^k(m) + \beta^m v_j(n-m, \beta) \right] \right\}$$
$$i = 1, 2, \ldots, N; n = 1, 2, 3, \ldots . \qquad (15.2.1)$$

The alternative k that produces $v_i(n, \beta)$ is, of course, the optimum decision to be made in state i when a time n remains. We designate this optimum decision by $d_i(n, \beta)$. The quantities $d_i(n, \beta)$ for $i = 1, 2, \ldots, N$ constitute a vector that specifies the decision to be made in each state if that state is entered when the time n remains. We call this vector the policy vector at time n and write it as $\mathbf{d}(n, \beta)$. The vectors $\mathbf{d}(m, \beta)$ for $m = 1, 2, 3, \ldots, n$ completely describe the optimum time-varying policy to be used throughout the time interval of length n. Thus by writing Equation 15.2.1 and performing the maximization for each i and n, we have a recursive method for constructing the optimum policy for a discrete-time semi-Markov decision process operating over a finite time interval with or without discounting. The case of no discounting requires only that we set $\beta = 1$ in our formulation.

Simplified Form

We can simplify Equation 15.2.1 by introducing the same notation we used in Chapter 13. Thus we write

$$y_{ij}^k(m, \beta) = \sum_{\ell=0}^{m-1} \beta^\ell y_{ij}^k(\ell) \tag{15.2.2}$$

for the present value under alternative k of all yields from the occupancy of state i through time m when the successor state is j;

$$\begin{aligned} {}^{>}y_i^k(n, \beta) &= \sum_{j=1}^{N} p_{ij}^k y_{ij}^k(n, \beta) \sum_{m=n+1}^{\infty} h_{ij}^k(m) \\ &= \sum_{j=1}^{N} p_{ij}^k y_{ij}^k(n, \beta)\, {}^{>}h_{ij}^k(n) \end{aligned} \tag{15.2.3}$$

for the contribution to the expected present value under alternative k of the yield from an occupancy of state i that arises from the situation where the system does not make any further transitions before the expiration of the time period of length n; and

$$r_i^k(n, \beta) = \sum_{j=1}^{N} p_{ij}^k \sum_{m=1}^{n} h_{ij}^k(m)[y_{ij}^k(m, \beta) + \beta^m b_{ij}^k(m)] \tag{15.2.4}$$

for the contribution to the expected present value under alternative k of both yield and bonus from an occupancy of state i that arises from the situation where the departure from state i occurs before the expiration of the time period of length n. We can now write Equation 15.2.1 in a form corresponding to Equation 13.6.5,

$$v_i(n, \beta) = \operatorname*{Max}_k \left\{ {}^{>}y_i^k(n, \beta) + \beta^n v_i(0)\, {}^{>}w_i^k(n) + r_i^k(n, \beta) + \sum_{j=1}^{N} p_{ij}^k \sum_{m=1}^{n} h_{ij}^k(m) \beta^m v_j(n-m, \beta) \right\} \qquad \begin{matrix} i = 1, 2, \ldots, N \\ n = 1, 2, 3, \ldots . \end{matrix} \tag{15.2.5}$$

To solve Equation 15.2.5 will require a computer for problems of practical interest; however, this type of formulation is particularly suitable for automatic computation. We shall now illustrate the technique by applying it to the car rental decision problem.

Value Iteration Solution of the Car Rental Problem

Suppose that the car rental company whose alternatives appear in Table 15.1.1 is interested in maximizing the expected present value of its earnings over some finite time period of length n measured in days. This could happen because the company desires to look most profitable in anticipation of its being sold or for tax reasons, but we shall not inquire further into its motivation. The company tells us that the inherent value of a car's being returned to either state at the end of the time period is zero; therefore, $v_1(0) = v_2(0) = 0$. Since both the daily rental charge and the drop charge are paid at the end of the rental, there is no yield, but only a bonus payment given by

$$b_{ij}{}^k(m) = f_i{}^k m + f_{ij}{}^k, \qquad (15.2.6)$$

as indicated in Equation 13.8.1 and tabulated for the car rental problem in Table 15.1.1. Note that cars returned beyond the end of the time period will not contribute to the profitability of the company during the period.

For the special conditions of the car rental problem, the value iteration equation 15.2.1 becomes

$$v_i(n, \beta) = \underset{k}{\text{Max}} \sum_{j=1}^{N} p_{ij}{}^k \sum_{m=1}^{n} h_{ij}{}^k(m)\beta^m[b_{ij}{}^k(m) + v_j(n - m, \beta)]$$
$$i = 1, 2, \ldots, N; n = 1, 2, 3, \ldots . \qquad (15.2.7)$$

Computational results

Table 15.2.1 shows the solution of this recursive equation and the optimum decisions $d_i(n, \beta)$ for values of β that range from 0 to 1 in increments of 0.1 and for values of n through 15.

The entries are in the format of Table 13.8.1 except that each entry now contains both the decision and the expected present value separated by a semicolon. We notice that the expected present values of a state increase with the discount factor β at any stage n.

If we examine how the optimum policy depends on stage for a fixed discount factor, we find that for β less than or equal to 0.6 the optimum policy immediately appears to converge to the policy of using the second alternative in state 1 and the first alternative in state 2. When $\beta = 0.7$, the same policy is optimal through 9

Table 15.2.1 Value Iteration Solution of Car Rental Decision Problem [Quantities shown are: decision, $d_i(n, \beta)$; expected present value, $v_i(n, \beta)$]

Discount Factor	State \ Stage n	1		2		3		4	
		State		State		State		State	
β	i	1	2	1	2	1	2	1	2
0	1	-;0		-;0		-;0		-;0	
	2		-;0		-;0		-;0		-;0
0.1	1	2;0.667		2;0.742		2;0.751		2;0.751	
	2		1;0.367		1;0.412		1;0.412		1;0.412
0.2	1	2;1.333		2;1.636		2;1.701		2;1.714	
	2		1;0.733		1;0.896		1;0.931		1;0.939
0.3	1	2;2.000		2;2.680		2;2.900		2;2.968	
	2		1;1.100		1:1.466		1;1.585		1;1.624
0.4	1	2;2.667		2;3.876		2;4.396		2;4.613	
	2		1;1.467		1;2.116		1;2.400		1;2.522
0.5	1	2;3.333		2;5.222		2;6.239		2;6.768	
	2		1;1.833		1;2.849		1;3.402		1;3.700
0.6	1	2;4.000		2;6.720		2;8.476		2;9.575	
	2		1;2.200		1;3.662		1;4.619		1;5.237
0.7	1	2;4.667		2;8.369		2;11.158		2;13.193	
	2		1;2.567		1;4.557		1;6.076		1;7.221
0.8	1	2;5.333		2;10.169		2;14.332		2;17.804	
	2		1;2.933		1;5.532		1;7.801		1;9.754
0.9	1	2;6.000		2;12.120		2;18.047		2;23.610	
	2		1;3.300		1;6.590		1;9.819		1;12.948
1.0	1	2;6.667		2;14.222		2;22.353		2;30.831	
	2		1;3.667		1;7.728		1;12.158		1;16.926

stages, but thereafter using the second alternative in each state becomes optimum. For $\beta = 0.8$, the transition between the two policies occurs on the sixth stage; the discount factor $\beta = 0.9$ produces this change on the fifth stage, but a further change occurs on the sixth stage to the policy of using the first alternative in state 1, the second in state 2. Finally, when $\beta = 1$ and thus there is no discounting, the optimum policy changes directly from the second-first policy to the first-second policy on the fifth stage.

In terms of the car rental example, the solution shows that when the number of days remaining is few or the discount factor is small, the town 1 customer should be limited to returning the car to town 2, while the town 2 customer should be free to choose his destination. However, for high discount factors even when only a few days remain, the reverse policy should be followed: the town 1 customer should be free to return the car to either town, while the town 2 customer should be limited to returning the car to town 1.

The question of whether for each discount factor the optimum policy has actually converged to a stationary policy when n is at least 15 cannot be answered within

5		6		7		8	
State		State		State		State	
1	2	1	2	1	2	1	2
-;0	-;0	-;0	-;0	-;0	-;0	-;0	-;0
2;0.751	1;0.412	2;0.751	1;0.412	2;0.751	1;0.412	2;0.751	1;0.412
2;1.717	1;0.940	2;1.718	1;0.941	2;1.718	1;0.941	2;1.718	1;0.941
2;2.989	1;1.636	2;2.996	1;1.640	2;2.998	1;1.641	2;2.998	1;1.642
2;4.702	1;2.574	2;4.737	1;2.596	2;4.752	1;2.605	2;4.757	1;2.609
2;7.039	1;3.859	2;7.176	1;3.943	2;7.244	1;3.986	2;7.278	1;4.009
2;10.249	1;5.631	2;10.656	1;5.881	2;10.901	1;6.037	2;11.046	1;6.135
2;14.649	1;8.074	2;15.677	1;8.703	2;16.396	1;9.163	2;16.896	1;9.498
2;20.643	1;11.416	2;22.933	2;13.133	2;24.806	2;14.897	2;26.367	2;16.357
2;28.726	2;16.444	1;33.457	2;20.697	1;38.172	2;24.739	1;42.506	2;28.600
1;39.673	2;23.923	1;49.569	2;31.971	1;59.755	2;40.703	1;70.144	2;49.965

the value iteration discussion. In fact, the query "Has it or hasn't it converged?" is one of the annoying dilemmas of value iteration computations. This difficulty was a major incentive for the development of the policy iteration technique we shall soon be discussing.

We observe in Table 15.2.1 for any discount factor that, although optimum policies may change as the number of stages increases, the expected present values of both states increase monotonically. For discount factors equal to 0.4 or less, the expected present values seem to have reached limiting values, but for higher values of β they are still increasing with the number of stages. Provided that β is less than 1, the expected present values will converge to those of the optimum policy for the unbounded duration process. When $\beta = 1$, the expected present values will increase with each stage by an amount that will asymptotically approach the gain of the process.

As an aid in observing this convergence, we have computed the successive differences in the expected present value of each state as given in the row for $\beta = 1.0$ of Table 15.2.1 and presented the results as Table 15.2.2. We see that the differences

Table 15.2.1—*continued*

Discount Factor β	State i \ Stage n	9 State 1	9 State 2	10 State 1	10 State 2	11 State 1	11 State 2
0	1	-;0		-;0		-;0	
	2		-;0		-;0		-;0
0.1	1	2;0.751		2;0.751		2;0.751	
	2		1;0.412		1;0.412		1;0.412
0.2	1	2;1.718		2;1.718		2;1.718	
	2		1;0.941		1;0.941		1;0.941
0.3	1	2;2.998		2;2.998		2;2.998	
	2		1;1.642		1;1.642		1;1.642
0.4	1	2;4.760		2;4.761		2;4.761	
	2		1;2.610		1;2.611		1;2.611
0.5	1	2;7.295		2;7.303		2;7.307	
	2		1;4.021		1;4.027		1;4.030
0.6	1	2;11.133		2;11.184		2;11.214	
	2		1;6.195		1;6.233		1;6.255
0.7	1	2;17.242		2;17.481		2;17.651	
	2		1;9.740		2;9.949		2;10.123
0.8	1	2;27.655		2;28.709		2;29.567	
	2		2;17.563		2;18.553		2;19.365
0.9	1	1;46.466		1;50.070		1;53.341	
	2		2;32.230		2;35.603		2;38.714
1.0	1	1;80.681		1;91.328		1;102.058	
	2		2;59.635		2;69.615		2;79.832

are monotonically increasing for both states and that the rate of increase indicates convergence toward a fixed value. In Section 15.3, we shall find that this fixed value, or gain of the process, is 11.14.

Value Iteration Applied to a Reservation Problem

A fundamental problem in the operation of airlines, hotels, and other enterprises where a highly perishable product is to be sold at a definite time is the question of reservations. Specifically, it is necessary to establish a policy on whether or not reservations will be accepted when all space for the activity has already been reserved. Of course, such a practice would be unethical if it were not for the fact that customers who hold reservations may sometimes cancel them. However, when reservation cancellations cause the departure of a plane with empty seats or the vacancy of hotel rooms, they occasion a real loss of revenue. Against this loss must be balanced the loss incurred if a customer with a reservation cannot be accommodated. We shall now explore a simple airline reservation model to illustrate how value iteration may be helpful in such problems.

12		13		14		15	
State		State		State		State	
1	2	1	2	1	2	1	2
-;0	-;0	-;0	-;0	-;0	-;0	-;0	-;0
2;0.751	1;0.412	2;0.751	1;0.412	2;0.751	1;0.412	2;0.751	1;0.412
2;1.718	1;0.941	2;1.718	1;0.941	2;1.718	1;0.941	2;1.718	1;0.941
2;2.998	1;1.642	2;2.998	1;1.642	2;2.998	1;1.642	2;2.998	1;1.642
2;4.761	1;2.611	2;4.761	1;2.612	2;4.761	1;2.612	2;4.761	1;2.612
2;7.309	1;4.031	2;7.310	1;4.032	2;7.310	1;4.032	2;7.311	1;4.033
2;11.232	1;6.269	2;11.243	1;6.278	2;11.249	1;6.283	2;11.253	1;6.286
2;17.773	2;10.245	2;17.860	2;10.330	2;17.922	2;10.391	2;17.966	2;10.434
2;30.262	2;20.027	2;30.825	2;20.565	2;31.278	2;21.002	2;31.643	2;21.356
1;56.304	2;41.564	1;58.985	2;44.165	1;61.409	2;46.530	1;63.598	2;48.677
1;112.855	2;90.230	1;123.704	2;100.767	1;134.598	2;111.413	1;145.529	2;122.142

System description

Suppose we are making reservations for a flight to be made at some date in the future. We begin by dividing the time to take-off into convenient time units, which we shall assume are days in our example. We then let n be the number of days until departure. We let r be the number of reservations that have been made as of any

Table 15.2.2 Successive Differences in State Values of Car Rental Decision Problem without Discounting ($\beta = 1.0$) [Quantities show result of $v_i(n, 1) - v_i(n - 1, 1)$.]

State i \ Stage n	1	2	3	4	5	6	7	8
1	6.667	7.555	8.131	8.478	8.842	9.896	10.186	10.389
2	3.667	4.061	4.430	4.768	6.997	8.048	8.732	9.262

State i \ Stage n	9	10	11	12	13	14	15
1	10.537	10.647	10.730	10.797	10.849	10.894	10.931
2	9.670	9.980	10.217	10.398	10.537	10.646	10.729

time. The pair (r, n) then specifies the state of the reservation system. The problem is to determine for a given (r, n) whether or not further reservations should be accepted. We assume that the policy we choose is fixed for the entire day and that cancellations of reservations occur at night. Thus each morning we shall decide on the basis of the number of days remaining n and the number of reservations made r whether or not to make additional reservations during the present day. If we do decide to accept reservations, then all customers who request a reservation will receive one; and if we decide not to accept reservations, then all customers will be turned away. We assume that after we have closed our office for the day some of the customers who have made reservations will cancel them. If this requirement of fixing a policy for a day at a time seems rather unrealistic, recall that the basic time period is arbitrary and that this period of fixed policy could be one hour or ten minutes.

Customer characteristics

The essence of determining the reservation policy is balancing the cost of over-reserving and the cost of empty seats. The balance depends, of course, on the uncertainties associated with the arrival of new customers and of cancellations.

We let $p_a(a_0)$ be the probability that a_0 customers will arrive during a day. For simplicity, we assume that the arrival distribution is a binomial with parameters p and N, where N is the maximum number of arrivals assumed possible in a day,

$$p_a(a_0) = \binom{N}{a_0} p^{a_0}(1 - p)^{N-a_0} \qquad a_0 = 0, 1, 2, \ldots, N. \tag{15.2.8}$$

In practice, a Poisson distribution might be more appropriate, but the binomial will serve our illustrative needs.

Again for simplicity, we assume that each customer who has a reservation at the end of each day has the same probability q of canceling it during the night. This leads us directly to a binomial distribution for $p_c(c_0|r)$, the probability that c_0 of the r reservations at the end of a day will cancel during the night,

$$p_c(c_0|r) = \binom{r}{c_0} q^{c_0}(1 - q)^{r-c_0} \qquad \begin{array}{r} c_0 = 0, 1, 2, \ldots, r \\ r = 0, 1, 2, \ldots . \end{array} \tag{15.2.9}$$

Value iteration solution

When we begin day n from the time of flight with r reservations, we must decide to follow alternative R, reject reservations during the day, or A, accept reservations during the day. The choice depends on which alternative has the higher expected profit. We define $v(r, n)$ to be the total profit to be expected from the flight in state (r, n) using an optimum reservation policy. (There is no need to consider discounting because of the relatively short time duration.) The relevant value iteration relation is therefore

$$v(r, n) = \underset{R,A}{\text{Max}} \begin{cases} R: & \sum_{c_0=0}^{r} p_c(c_0|r)v(r - c_0, n - 1) \\ A: & \sum_{a_0=0}^{N} p_a(a_0) \sum_{c_0=0}^{r+a_0} p_c(c_0|r + a_0)v(r + a_0 - c_0, n - 1) \end{cases}$$

$$n = 1, 2, 3, \ldots . \quad (15.2.10)$$

We observe that when the reject alternative is selected, the profit to be expected when $n - 1$ days remain will be $v(r - c_0, n - 1)$ if c_0 of the r reservations cancel during the night. Since the probability that c_0 of the r reservations will cancel is $p_c(c_0|r)$, the expected profit from the reject alternative is just $p_c(c_0|r)v(r - c_0, n - 1)$ summed over all numbers of cancellations from 0 through r that could occur.

If we decide to accept reservations, we have a similar expression with the exception that arrivals may occur. If a_0 customers arrive and if c_0 of the total of $r + a_0$ reserved customers at the end of the day cancel, then the expected profit when $n - 1$ days remain will be $v(r + a_0 - c_0, n - 1)$. The probability of a_0 arrivals and c_0 cancellations is $p_a(a_0)p_c(c_0|r + a_0)$. We find the expected profit of the accept alternative by multiplying the expected profit in the remaining $n - 1$ days by the probability of that expected profit and then summing over all possible numbers of arrivals a_0 from 0 through N and overall possible numbers of cancellations C_0 from 0 through $r + a_0$.

The only missing feature of Equation 15.2.10 is $v(r, 0)$, the value of having r reservations when the flight leaves. If K is the capacity of the flight, we expect $v(r, 0)$ to increase with r up to and including K, but to decrease with r when r exceeds K. A simple form is to let f be the fare per passenger carried and ℓ the loss incurred whenever a reserved passenger is not allowed to fly. Then,

$$v(r, 0) = \begin{cases} rf & r \le K \\ Kf - (r - K)\ell & r > K. \end{cases} \quad (15.2.11)$$

An example with high overbooking

We create a specific reservation problem by choosing the arrival distribution parameters p and N, the cancellation probability q, plane capacity K, fare f, and over-booking loss ℓ. Table 15.2.3 shows the expected profit computations for the problem,

$$p = 0.75 \quad N = 1 \quad q = 0.5 \quad K = 2 \quad f = 10 \quad \ell = 5, \quad (15.2.12)$$

where we have a very small plane, at most one arrival, and a relatively high cancellation probability. The result is considerable overbooking, that is, acceptance of

Table 15.2.3 Expected Profits for First Airplane Reservation Problem

$p = 0.75 \quad N = 1 \quad q = 0.5 \quad K = 2 \quad f = 10 \quad \ell = 5$

Number of reservations	Days before flight 0	1	2	3	4	5	6	7	8	9	10
0	0	3.75	5.63	6.46	6.86	7.04	7.14	7.18	7.21	7.22	7.22
1	10.00	8.75	7.86	7.51	7.36	7.29	7.26	7.24	7.24	7.23	7.23
2	20.00	12.34	9.70	8.45	7.84	7.53	7.38	7.30	7.27	7.25	7.24
3	15.00	14.06	11.13	9.30	8.29	7.77	7.50	7.36	7.30	7.26	7.24
4	10.00	14.38	12.19	10.04	8.72	7.99	7.62	7.42	7.33	7.28	7.25
5	5.00	14.22	12.91	10.70	9.12	8.22	7.73	7.48	7.36	7.29	7.26
6	0	13.13	13.36	11.26	9.50	8.43	7.85	7.54	7.39	7.31	7.27
7	−5.00	11.45	13.55	11.74	9.86	8.64	7.96	7.60	7.42	7.32	7.28
8	−10.00	9.41	13.59	12.15	10.20	8.85	8.07	7.66	7.45	7.34	7.28
9	−15.00	7.18	13.51	12.48	10.51	9.04	8.18	7.72	7.47	7.35	7.29
10	−20.00	4.82	13.25	12.75	10.80	9.24	8.29	7.77	7.50	7.37	7.30

Reject reservations ⟵ | ⟶ Accept reservations

reservations when the number of reservations is at least as great as the capacity of the plane. Thus one day before the flight, reservations are accepted even when three reservations already have been made. Two days before the flight, reservations are accepted even when seven have already been made. The line in Table 15.2.3 separates the "accept" and "reject" regions.

Note that the expected profits are quite sensitive to the number of reservations when the number of days remaining is small, but not when the number of days remaining is large. Thus when ten days remain, there is a difference of only 7.30 − 7.22 = 0.08 between having no reservations and ten reservations. We may gain insight into this result by noting that n days before the flight each reserved customer has a probability $1 - (1 - q)^n$ of cancelling before the time of departure. If there are r such customers, then the expected number of those who will cancel is $r[1 - (1 - q)^n]$. With $q = 0.5$, $r = 10$, and $n = 10$, the expected number of cancellations is 9.9. Clearly, having ten reservations ten days before the flight is not much more valuable than having none.

An example with low overbooking

Table 15.2.4 illustrates the problem

$$p = 0.2 \quad N = 5 \quad q = 0.1 \quad K = 5 \quad f = 10 \quad \ell = 10. \qquad (15.2.13)$$

We now have a much larger plane and an expected number of arrivals per day of (0.2)(5) = 1 rather than 0.75. However, the cancellation probability is much lower and the loss from each overbooking is twice as large as before. We see that the result of these changes is to make overbooking much less attractive. When only one or two days remain until the flight, we do not accept reservations if we already have at least five. If more than two but less than seven days remain until the flight, then we do not accept reservations if we already have at least six. We refuse further reservations on days seven through nine if we already have at least seven, and refuse on day ten if we already have at least eight.

Here again we observe that the expected profit is sensitive to the number of reservations only when the remaining time is small. When ten days remain, for example, there is less than a 4% difference between the lowest and highest expected profits recorded in the table. With $q = 0.1$, $r = 10$, and $n = 10$, the expression $r[1 - (1 - q)^n]$ for the expected number of cancellations before flight time in a group of r reserved customers n days before the flight yields 6.5. Since 7.5 ($= rp$) customers are expected to arrive in the ten-day period and the desired number of passengers is 5, having ten reservations ten days before the flight is of no great advantage.

Time-varying customer characteristics

Many criticisms could be made of this model for reservations. Perhaps the most cogent is that the probabilities of arrivals and cancellations will be a function of the

Table 15.2.4 Expected Profits for Second Airplane Reservation Problem

$p = 0.2 \quad N = 5 \quad q = 0.1 \quad K = 5 \quad f = 10 \quad \ell = 10$

Number of reservations	Days before flight 0	1	2	3	4	5	6	7	8	9	10	
0	0	9.00	17.04	23.84	29.15	33.06	35.80	37.69	38.98	39.86	40.46	
1	10.00	18.00	24.87	30.14	33.88	36.42	38.13	39.29	40.07	40.60	40.97	
2	20.00	26.92	32.06	35.41	37.54	38.90	39.81	40.42	40.84	41.13	41.34	
3	30.00	35.27	37.85	39.22	40.02	40.54	40.91	41.18	41.36	41.50	41.60	
4	40.00	41.16	41.44	41.45	41.44	41.51	41.58	41.64	41.69	41.73	41.77	
5	50.00	45.00	42.87	42.10	42.01	41.97	41.92	41.89	41.87	41.87	41.87	
6	40.00	43.37	43.59	43.03	42.48	42.17	42.00	41.97	41.96	41.94	41.93	Accept reservations
7	30.00	36.43	40.18	41.80	42.28	42.29	42.18	42.07	42.00	41.96	41.95	↑
8	20.00	27.89	34.09	38.16	40.42	41.50	41.92	42.03	42.03	42.00	41.97	↓
9	10.00	18.98	26.74	32.79	36.95	39.50	40.89	41.57	41.85	41.95	41.97	Reject reservations
10	0	10.00	18.89	26.41	32.25	36.36	38.99	40.52	41.33	41.71	41.88	

number of days before the flight. Fortunately, incorporating such time-varying probabilities introduces no computational difficulty. All we have to do is use the arrival and cancellation probability mass functions $p_a(\cdot)$ and $p_c(\cdot|r)$ that are pertinent to n days before the flight when we solve Equation 15.2.10. Thus every stage in the recursion will be performed with new arrival and cancellation probabilities. The ease with which we make this modification is a direct consequence of our observation in Chapter 14 that stage-dependent alternatives do not unduly complicate the formalism.

Loss assessment by greenback distribution

A question that is bound to arise in using this model is how to establish the loss ℓ that should be assigned to overbooking a customer. One allegedly practical way to do this is to confront a passenger with a reservation just after he has been told he cannot fly and observe his rage. Then slowly start counting out $10 bills to him, while keeping a close watch on his countenance. When his rage has turned to just the hint of a smile, stop counting and record your disbursement; the result is a measure of ℓ.

15.3 POLICY ITERATION

We could, of course, solve the problem of finding optimum policies for semi-Markov decision processes by value iteration. All we would have to do is solve the value iteration equations recursively for larger and larger values of the time period variable. There are some theoretical considerations as to whether the optimum policy without discounting would converge to the same set of decisions regardless of the length of the time interval for a large enough time interval. However, since cases where the optimum policy oscillates as the length of the time interval increases have to be artificially constructed, the possibility is of little practical consequence.

A practical problem might be caused in the case of no discounting by the growth beyond any bound of the expected rewards in the time interval. This problem usually may be readily solved by paying careful attention to the scaling of the $v_i(n, 1)$'s produced by Equation 15.2.1.

For example, at any stage n we could subtract from all the values $v_i(n, 1)$ the largest increase that occurred in them over the values at stage $n - 1$ for any state to create the normalized variables $v_i'(n, 1)$,

$$v_i'(n, 1) = v_i(n, 1) - \max_i [v_i(n, 1) - v_i(n - 1, 1)]. \qquad (15.3.1)$$

The normalization would not affect the optimization at the next stage because the maximization over alternatives is invariant to any constant added to all state values. This procedure would require keeping track of the amounts subtracted if the actual values $v_i(n, 1)$ were to be recovered at the conclusion of the value iteration. The successive differences in state values shown in Table 15.2.2 demonstrate the practicality of this approach in the car rental problem.

We would, in any case, prefer to solve the infinite duration problem directly. To do this, we need a way of searching among the possible stationary policies to find the one that maximizes the criterion of expected gain or expected present value. We can appreciate the magnitude of an exhaustive search by noting that if we were dealing with a process described by 50 states with 100 alternatives in each state, then we would have to search through $100^{50} = 10^{100}$ or a googol of different policies, calculating the gain or expected reward for each and then comparing.

We are fortunate to have available a much more efficient search procedure, which we call policy iteration. In this section we shall show the plausibility of policy iteration and then prove its properties for the case of no discounting. We shall base our developments on the continuous-time case since the discrete-time results follow directly as a special case.

The Policy Iteration Procedure without Discounting

Suppose that we use an arbitrary stationary policy to govern the process. We know that we can find the gain and relative values of this policy (if we assume that the resulting Markov process is monodesmic) by solving Equations 13.3.37,

$$v_i + g\bar{\tau}_i = r_i + \sum_{j=1}^{N} p_{ij}v_j \qquad i = 1, 2, \ldots, N, \tag{15.3.2}$$

with the relative value of some state, say state N, set equal to zero. In these equations, $\bar{\tau}_i$ is the mean waiting time for state i and r_i is the expected reward from a single occupancy of state i as defined in Equation 13.3.24,

$$r_i = r_i(0) = r_i(\infty, 0) = \sum_{j=1}^{N} p_{ij} \int_0^{\infty} d\tau\, h_{ij}(\tau)\left[\int_0^{\tau} d\sigma\, y_{ij}(\sigma) + b_{ij}(\tau)\right]. \tag{15.3.3}$$

We now solve Equation 15.3.2 for g,

$$g = \frac{r_i}{\bar{\tau}_i} + \frac{1}{\bar{\tau}_i}\left[\sum_{j=1}^{N} p_{ij}v_j - v_i\right] \qquad i = 1, 2, \ldots, N, \tag{15.3.4}$$

or in terms of the earning rate for each state, $q_i = r_i/\bar{\tau}_i$,

$$g = q_i + \frac{1}{\bar{\tau}_i}\left[\sum_{j=1}^{N} p_{ij}v_j - v_i\right] \qquad i = 1, 2, \ldots, N. \tag{15.3.5}$$

The heuristic development of the policy iteration procedure then follows. We note that we could substitute the quantities q_i^k, $\bar{\tau}_i^k$, and p_{ij}^k for another alternative k in state i into the right-hand side of this equation along with the relative values v_i from our arbitrary policy. If the result is a higher value for the right-hand side than the one for our arbitrary policy, we would have some tentative indication that the alternative k in state i would lead to a higher gain for the process than does the alternative used in state i under the arbitrary policy. When we have tested all alternatives in each state in the right-hand side of Equation 15.3.5 to find which produces the highest value, we shall have a new policy for the process. We then solve Equation 15.3.2 for the new policy and repeat the entire procedure. As we continue to change policies, we would expect the gain of the process to increase.

The Iteration Cycle

Let us now summarize the iterative procedure. We begin with an arbitrary policy for the system and then solve Equations 15.3.2 for the gain g and relative values v_i of the policy. Then we use these relative values to improve the policy by finding the alternative k in each state i that maximizes the test quantity Γ_i^k,

$$\Gamma_i^k = q_i^k + \frac{1}{\bar{\tau}_i^k}\left[\sum_{j=1}^{N} p_{ij}^k v_j - v_i\right]. \tag{15.3.6}$$

We note that the comparisons involving the test quantity are unchanged if any constant is added to all v_i's. This property justifies our use of the relative values rather than the true asymptotic intercepts of the value function.

We do not change the original decision in each state unless another alternative has a strictly greater value of the test quantity. When a new decision (possibly the same) has been reached in each state, we have found a new policy. We then evaluate the new policy, that is, find its gain and relative values using Equations 15.3.2, and repeat the attempted policy improvement. We continue to do this until the test quantity indicates that there is no reason to change the decision in any state. We shall later show formally that each new policy generated in the course of this iterative procedure cannot have a lower gain than its predecessor and that no other policy can have a gain higher than the final policy produced.

The iteration cycle appears in Figure 15.3.1. The upper box, policy evaluation, finds the gain and relative values for a particular policy. The lower box, policy improvement, finds a new policy that is an improvement over the original policy by using the values of the original policy. Then this new policy is evaluated, and so on.

Policy Evaluation

For the present policy solve

$$v_i + g\bar{\tau}_i = q_i\bar{\tau}_i + \sum_{j=1}^{N} p_{ij}v_j \qquad i = 1, 2, \ldots, N,$$

with $v_N = 0$, for the gain g, and the relative values $v_1, v_2, \ldots, v_{N-1}$.

Policy Improvement

For each state i find the alternative k that maximizes

$$\Gamma_i^k = q_i^k + \frac{1}{\bar{\tau}_i^k}\left[\sum_{j=1}^{N} p_{ij}^k v_j - v_i\right]$$

using the relative values v_i of the previous policy. Make this alternative the new decision in state i. Repeat for all states to find the new policy.

Figure 15.3.1. The iteration cycle.

Selection of initial policy

We are able to select the initial policy arbitrarily, but wisdom in this selection will gain more than caprice. We can choose the initial policy as one that seems intuitively consistent with a high gain, or we can make the choice more formally by, say, choosing as the initial decision in each state the alternative that maximizes the earning rate for that state. We observe that one way to do this is to enter the policy improvement procedure with all relative values equal to zero. We are, of course, protected from any long-run ill effects of our selection because of the ultimate optimum achieved by the policy iteration process. However, the number of iterative cycles necessary to reach the optimum will usually depend greatly on the extent to which we can initially guess the optimum policy.

Relevant process characteristics

We observe that the only characteristics of the semi-Markov decision process that enter into policy evaluation and policy improvement are for each state and alternative the transition probabilities p_{ij}^k, mean waiting times $\bar{\tau}_i^k$, and the expected rewards per occupancy r_i^k (or equivalently the earning rates $q_i^k = r_i^k/\bar{\tau}_i^k$). The actual probability distributions for holding times are important only insofar as they affect the mean waiting times and the expected rewards per occupancy. Furthermore, since all the arguments in this section apply with equal force to both continuous- and discrete-time processes, there is no need to make a distinction between the two time bases as far as infinite duration, no-discounting systems are concerned. The only place that the difference affects our calculations is in whether we use the continuous-time equation 13.3.24 or the discrete-time equation 3.7.5 in computing r_i, the expected reward per occupancy of state i.

Interpretation

Let us finish this discussion by commenting on the interpretation of Equation 15.3.5. This equation states that the gain of a process is the sum of the earning rate q_i for each state and a quantity

$$\frac{1}{\bar{\tau}_i}\left[\sum_{j=1}^{N} p_{ij}v_j - v_i\right] \tag{15.3.7}$$

which we may consider as the contribution to the gain derived from state i's relation to the other states. We characterize these two contributions as the immediate and subsequent contributions to the gain. The immediate contribution q_i^k of any alternative in any state is apparent; however, finding the subsequent contribution requires solution of the relative value equations for the policy.

Thus the policy iteration approach to finding the optimum policy involves estimating the subsequent contribution to the gain caused by using alternative i in state k. We do this by computing

$$\frac{1}{\bar{\tau}_i^k}\left[\sum_{j=1}^{N} p_{ij}^k v_j - v_i\right] \tag{15.3.8}$$

using the mean waiting time and transition probabilities for this alternative, but using the relative values of the previous policy. We add this estimate of the subsequent contribution to the immediate contribution q_i^k and consider the sum as the test quantity on the basis of which all alternatives in state i will be compared.

Of course, as the policy we are using becomes closer and closer to the optimal policy in the sense that its gain increases, we expect the estimates of subsequent contributions to approach the actual subsequent contributions for the optimal policy. When they do, the iterative procedure has converged, and we have found the optimum policy.

A practical consequence of these observations is that as a procedure for choosing our initial policy we may decide to provide direct estimates of the relative values of the process and, hence, of the subsequent contributions of each alternative. Passing through the policy improvement procedure will then produce an initial policy consistent with this set of relative values. To refine the procedure a little further, we may choose an initial policy on an intuitive basis and, at the same time, assign a set of relative values on an intuitive basis. When we compare the policy that results from using the policy improvement procedure on these relative values with the policy we devised intuitively, we may be able to choose an initial policy that is considerably closer to the optimum than either of these policies. However, we shall have more to say of this later.

Policy Iteration Solution of the Car Rental Problem

We shall now illustrate policy iteration by applying it to the discrete-time car rental example whose alternatives appear in Table 15.1.1. We solve the quite realistic problem where the car rental company is going to operate indefinitely, where discounting is not important, and where the company wishes to use the policy that maximizes its average reward per unit time or gain. We begin by computing the expected reward per occupancy r_i^k and earning rate q_i^k for each state i and alternative k. From Equation 13.8.11, we note that r_i^k is related to the day charge f_i^k, drop charge f_{ij}^k, mean waiting time $\bar{\tau}_i^k$, and transition probability p_{ij}^k by

$$r_i^k = f_i^k \bar{\tau}_i^k + \sum_{j=1}^{N} p_{ij}^k f_{ij}^k. \tag{15.3.9}$$

By using the information in Table 15.1.1, we find

$$\begin{aligned} r_1^1 &= 45 \qquad r_1^2 = 90 \\ r_2^1 &= 60 \qquad r_2^2 = 20. \end{aligned} \tag{15.3.10}$$

Of course, we have already seen r_1^1 and r_2^1 in Equation 13.8.13. The earning rates $q_i^k = r_i^k/\bar{\tau}_i^k$ are then

$$\begin{aligned} q_1^1 &= 12.5 \qquad q_1^2 = 15 \\ q_2^1 &= 6.25 \qquad q_1^2 = 5. \end{aligned} \tag{15.3.11}$$

The results from 15.3.10 and 15.3.11 together with the transition probabilities and mean waiting times for each alternative completely characterize the problem we face. Thus all relevant quantities are collected for convenience in Table 15.3.1.

Initial policy

We observe from this table that the second alternative in state 1, the limited alternative, has a higher value of both expected reward per occupancy and earning rate than does the first alternative, the free alternative. In state 2, however, the first alternative, the free alternative, has a higher value of both expected reward

Table 15.3.1 Pertinent Data for the Infinite Duration Car Rental Problem without Discounting

State	Alternative	Transition Probabilities		Mean Waiting Time	Expected Reward per Occupancy	Earning Rate
i	k	$p_{i1}{}^k$	$p_{i2}{}^k$	$\bar{\tau}_i{}^k$	$r_i{}^k$	$q_i{}^k = r_i{}^k/\bar{\tau}_i{}^k$
1	1 (free)	0.8	0.2	3.6	45	12.5
	2 (limited)	0	1	6	90	15
2	1 (free)	0.3	0.7	9.6	60	6.25
	2 (limited)	1	0	4	20	5

per occupancy and earning rate than does the second alternative, the limited alternative. Therefore, if we take earning rate as an approximation to the gain and if we use maximization of earning rate as the criterion for selection of the initial policy, then we should choose as our initial policy the second alternative in state 1 and the first alternative in state 2. It is convenient to describe a stationary policy by a vector **d** whose ith component is the number of the alternative to be used in state i. Thus our initial policy is $\mathbf{d} = [2 \quad 1]$: use the limited alternative in state 1 and the free alternative in state 2.

Evaluation. Now we must evaluate the initial policy by writing the policy evaluation equations 15.3.2. We find the process parameters associated with $\mathbf{d} = [2 \quad 1]$ from Table 15.3.1,

$$\begin{aligned} p_{11} &= p_{11}{}^2 = 0, \quad p_{12} = p_{12}{}^2 = 1, \quad \bar{\tau}_1 = \bar{\tau}_1{}^2 = 6, \quad r_1 = r_1{}^2 = 90 \\ p_{21} &= p_{21}{}^1 = 0.3, \quad p_{22} = p_{22}{}^1 = 0.7, \quad \bar{\tau}_2 = \bar{\tau}_2{}^1 = 9.6, \quad r_2 = r_2{}^1 = 60. \end{aligned} \tag{15.3.12}$$

We write Equations 15.3.2 for this policy as

$$\begin{aligned} v_1 + g\bar{\tau}_1 &= r_1 + p_{11}v_1 + p_{12}v_2 \\ v_2 + g\bar{\tau}_2 &= r_2 + p_{21}v_1 + p_{22}v_2. \end{aligned} \tag{15.3.13}$$

Setting $v_2 = 0$ arbitrarily and substituting the parameters from Equation 15.3.12, we obtain

$$\begin{aligned} v_1 + 6g &= 90 \\ 9.6g &= 60 + 0.3v_1. \end{aligned} \tag{15.3.14}$$

The solution of these equations is

$$g = 145/19 = 7\,12/19 = 7.63, \quad v_1 = 840/19 = 44\,4/19 = 44.21, \quad v_2 = 0. \tag{15.3.15}$$

We thus find that the gain of the process under the policy $\mathbf{d} = [2 \quad 1]$ will be 7.63 per time unit and that the relative value of starting in state 1 rather than state 2 is

44.21. Of course, we happen to know from Equation 13.8.14 that the gain of the original policy $\mathbf{d} = [1 \quad 1]$ is 8.5. Therefore, the initial policy we chose for the policy iteration procedure does not turn out to be as good as the free policy originally used by the car rental company. However, let us ignore this and use the policy improvement procedure to find a better policy than our initial guess $\mathbf{d} = [2 \quad 1]$.

First policy improvement

We illustrate the policy improvement in Table 15.3.2. Here we have calculated for each state and alternative the test quantity Γ_i^k of Equation 15.3.6 using the relative values v_1 and v_2 from Equation 15.3.15 and the alternative parameters from Table 15.3.1. We observe immediately that $\Gamma_1^2 = \Gamma_2^1 = 7.63 = g$, the gain of policy $\mathbf{d} = [2 \quad 1]$. This result is general: the test quantities associated with the policy from which the relative values were calculated will always be equal to the gain of that policy. The reason is clear when we reflect that the gain and relative values of any policy must satisfy Equation 15.3.5.

However, the reason we performed the policy improvement was to find a better policy. Since the first alternative in state 1 and the second alternative in state 2 produce a higher value of the test quantity than the other alternative in each state,

Table 15.3.2 First Policy Improvement for the Infinite Duration Car Rental Problem without Discounting

Present Policy: $\mathbf{d} = [2 \quad 1]$

Evaluation: $g = 7.63 \quad v_1 = 44.21 \quad v_2 = 0$

State	Alternative	Test Quantity
i	k	$\Gamma_i^k = q_i^k + \dfrac{1}{\bar{\tau}_i^k}\left[\sum_{j=1}^{N} p_{ij}^k v_j - v_i\right]$
		$= q_i^k + \dfrac{1}{\bar{\tau}_i^k}[p_{i1}^k v_1 + p_{i2}^k v_2 - v_i]$
1	1	$12.5 + \dfrac{1}{3.6}[0.8(44.21) - 44.21] = 10.04$
	2	$15 + \dfrac{1}{6}[-44.21] = 7.63$
2	1	$6.25 + \dfrac{1}{9.6}[0.3(44.21)] = 7.63$
	2	$5 + \dfrac{1}{4}[44.21] = 16.05$

Next Policy: $\mathbf{d} = [1 \quad 2]$

the next policy we should try is $\mathbf{d} = [1 \quad 2]$. The policy $\mathbf{d} = [1 \quad 2]$ is that of using free operation in town 1 and limited operation in town 2. Note that this policy is a complete change from our initial policy $\mathbf{d} = [2 \quad 1]$. We must now perform a policy evaluation on the policy $\mathbf{d} = [1 \quad 2]$ and continue our procedure because we have as yet no assurance that we have obtained the optimum policy.

Evaluation. For the policy $\mathbf{d} = [1 \quad 2]$, Table 15.3.1 shows

$$\begin{aligned} p_{11} &= p_{11}{}^1 = 0.8, \quad p_{12} = p_{12}{}^1 = 0.2, \quad \bar{\tau}_1 = \bar{\tau}_1{}^1 = 3.6, \quad r_1 = r_1{}^1 = 45 \\ p_{21} &= p_{21}{}^2 = 1, \quad p_{22} = p_{22}{}^2 = 0, \quad \bar{\tau}_2 = \bar{\tau}_2{}^2 = 4, \quad r_2 = r_2{}^2 = 20. \end{aligned} \tag{15.3.16}$$

With $v_2 = 0$, the policy evaluation equations 15.3.13 are then

$$\begin{aligned} v_1 + 3.6g &= 45 + 0.8v_1 \\ 4g &= 20 + v_1, \end{aligned} \tag{15.3.17}$$

with solution,

$$g = 245/22 = 11\ 3/22 = 11.14, \quad v_1 = 270/11 = 24\ 6/11 = 24.55, \quad v_2 = 0. \tag{15.3.18}$$

We find that the new policy $\mathbf{d} = [1 \quad 2]$ has a gain of 11.14, almost half again as much as the gain 7.63 for the previous policy $\mathbf{d} = [2 \quad 1]$. The policy improvement procedure has, in fact, improved the policy. Moreover, the policy $\mathbf{d} = [1 \quad 2]$ has a higher gain than the gain 8.5 for the policy $\mathbf{d} = [1 \quad 1]$, and thus is the best policy we have found up to this point. We note in passing that the relative value of state 1 over state 2 is now 24.55 rather than 44.21. However, we still may not have found the best policy so we must continue on to policy improvement.

Second policy improvement

Table 15.3.3 shows the test quantities $\Gamma_i{}^k$ for each state and each alternative using the relative values v_1 and v_2 found in Equation 15.3.18 for the policy $\mathbf{d} = [1 \quad 2]$. We observe once again that the test quantities associated with this policy are equal to the gain for the policy. Since the values of these test quantities are greater than those for any other alternative in either state, the policy improvement procedure produces once more the policy $\mathbf{d} = [1 \quad 2]$. Since the same policy has appeared twice in succession, it is the optimum policy. The highest gain possible for the car rental company is therefore 11.14. This gain is obtained by following the policy $\mathbf{d} = [1 \quad 2]$, using the original free alternative in town 1, but restricting customers to use of the limited alternative in town 2. The same policy appeared to be optimal in the value iteration solution of Table 15.2.1 with $\beta = 1$. The policy will produce a gain that is $11.14 - 8.50 = 2.64$ units greater than the company's former policy $\mathbf{d} = [1 \quad 1]$, which allowed free operation in both towns.

Table 15.3.3 Second Policy Improvement for the Infinite Duration Car Rental Problem without Discounting

Present Policy: $\mathbf{d} = [1 \quad 2]$
Evaluation: $g = 11.14 \quad v_1 = 24.55 \quad v_2 = 0$

State	Alternative	Test Quantity
i	k	$\Gamma_i^k = q_i^k + \dfrac{1}{\bar{\tau}_i^k}\left[\sum_{j=1}^{N} p_{ij}^k v_j - v_i\right]$
		$= q_i^k + \dfrac{1}{\bar{\tau}_i^k}[p_{i1}^k v_1 + p_{i2}^k v_2 - v_i]$
1	1	$12.5 + \dfrac{1}{3.6}[0.8(24.55) - 24.55] = 11.14$
	2	$15 + \dfrac{1}{6}[-24.55] = 10.91$
2	1	$6.25 + \dfrac{1}{9.6}[0.3(24.55)] = 7.02$
	2	$5 + \dfrac{1}{4}[24.55] = 11.14$

Optimum Policy: $\mathbf{d} = [1 \quad 2]$

We also note the credibility of 11.14 as the limiting value of the successive present value differences for each state developed in Table 15.2.2 using value iteration.

Exhaustive policy evaluation

Thus the policy iteration process has required two iteration cycles to find the best of the four possible policies. The advantage of the method over an exhaustive search naturally increases as problems become larger. We shall find it interesting however, to examine the exhaustive solution to the car rental problem. Since we have now evaluated all policies except $\mathbf{d} = [2 \quad 2]$ (the policy $\mathbf{d} = [1 \quad 1]$ was evaluated in Equation 13.8.17), evaluation of this policy is our only remaining task. We accomplish it by solving Equations 15.3.2 for this policy and find

$$g = 11 \qquad v_1 = 24 \qquad v_2 = 0. \tag{15.3.19}$$

The gains and relative values for the four policies appear in Table 15.3.4. We see that the optimum policy is confirmed to be $\mathbf{d} = [1 \quad 2]$ with a gain of 11.14. However, the policy $\mathbf{d} = [1 \quad 1]$ that we have just evaluated has a gain of 11, almost as large. This might lead us to ask whether anything that we have seen in our policy iteration calculations would have indicated the existence of another

Table 15.3.4 Result of Exhaustive Evaluation of All Policies for the Infinite Duration Car Rental Problem without Discounting

Policy $\mathbf{d} = [d_1 \quad d_2]$	Gain g	Relative Values v_1	v_2
[1 1]	8.5	72	0
[1 2]	11.14	24.55	0
[2 1]	7.63	44.21	0
[2 2]	11	24	0

policy with a close-to-optimum, if not optimum, gain. In fact, the policy improvement process is a storehouse of information, as we shall now see.

Bounds on Gain

We recall from Equation 13.3.31 that the gain of any policy is the sum of the earning rates for the policy weighted by the limiting interval transition probabilities,

$$g = \sum_{i=1}^{N} \phi_i \frac{r_i}{\bar{\tau}_i} = \sum_{i=1}^{N} \phi_i q_i . \tag{15.3.20}$$

For example, for the optimum policy $\mathbf{d} = [1 \quad 2]$ whose parameters appear in Equation 15.3.16, we readily find that the limiting interval transition probabilities are

$$\phi_1 = \frac{\pi_1 \bar{\tau}_1}{\sum_{i=1}^{2} \pi_i \bar{\tau}_i} = \frac{(5/6)(3.6)}{(5/6)(3.6) + (1/6)(4)} = \frac{9}{11}$$

$$\phi_2 = \frac{\pi_2 \bar{\tau}_2}{\sum_{i=1}^{2} \pi_i \bar{\tau}_i} = \frac{(1/6)(4)}{(5/6)(3.6) + (1/6)(4)} = \frac{2}{11} . \tag{15.3.21}$$

Then,

$$g = \sum_{i=1}^{N} \phi_i q_i = (9/11)(12.5) + (2/11)(5) = \frac{122.5}{11} = 11.14, \tag{15.3.22}$$

and we have found the same gain for this policy reported in Equation 15.3.18.

However, even without evaluating the limiting interval transition probabilities for any policy, we can learn much from Equation 15.3.20. Since the limiting interval transition probabilities for a policy are non-negative and sum to one, it follows that the gain of the policy must fall between the minimum and maximum earning rates for the policy. Thus by inspection of Table 15.3.1, we see that the gain for policy $\mathbf{d} = [1 \quad 1]$ must lie between 6.25 and 12.5; for policy $\mathbf{d} = [1 \quad 2]$ between 5 and 12.5; for policy $\mathbf{d} = [2 \quad 1]$ between 6.25 and 15; and for policy $\mathbf{d} = [2 \quad 2]$ between 5 and 15. Moreover, we can obtain bounds on the gain of the worst policy, the one with lowest gain, and on the gain of the optimum policy.

Bounds on gain of the worst policy

The worst policy cannot have a gain lower than the lowest earning rate for any alternative in any state. We call this the minimin earning rate, the minimum over all states of the minimum earning rate in each state. For our problem the minimin earning rate is 5, the earning rate of the second alternative in state 2.

The worst policy may have a gain no greater than the largest of the lowest earning rates in each state. We see this most easily by noting that if the worst policy were alleged to have a higher gain than this, we could construct a still worse policy composed of the alternatives in each state that have the lowest earning rates. We call the largest of the lowest earning rates the maximin earning rate, the maximum over all states of the minimum earning rate in each state. For our problem the maximin earning rate is 12.5, the earning rate of the first alternative in state 1. Thus the gain of the worst policy must fall between the minimin and the maximin earning rates, or between 5 and 12.5 for our example.

Bounds on gain of the optimum policy

To establish bounds on the gain of the optimum policy, we note first that the gain of the optimum policy cannot exceed the largest earning rate of any alternative in any state. We call this the maximax earning rate, the maximum over all states of the maximum earning rate in each state. The maximax earning rate for our problem is 15, the earning rate associated with the second alternative in state 1.

However, the gain of the optimum policy cannot be less than the smallest of the largest earning rates in each state. We call this the minimax earning rate, the minimum over all states of the maximum earning rate in each state. For the car rental problem, the minimax earning rate is 6.25, the earning rate of the first alternative in state 2. Thus the gain of the optimum policy must lie between the minimax and maximax earning rates, or between 6.25 and 15 for our problem.

The Relationship of Gain to Test Quantities

Finding that the gain of the worst policy must lie between 5 and 12.5 and that the gain of the optimum policy must lie between 6.25 and 15 may not seem to be very enlightening. However, when we combine the information we have derived from Equation 15.3.20 with another important result, we shall have learned a great deal. To state this result, consider the test quantities Γ_i^{BA} calculated for any policy

B in a policy improvement based on the relative values of *any* policy A. Then the gain g^{B} of policy B is equal to the quantities Γ_i^{BA} weighted by the limiting interval transition probabilities ϕ_i^{B} for policy B and summed,

$$g^{\mathrm{B}} = \sum_{i=1}^{N} \phi_i^{\mathrm{B}} \Gamma_i^{\mathrm{BA}}. \tag{15.3.23}$$

In simple terms, the gain of any policy is equal to its test quantities in *any* policy improvement, multiplied by its limiting interval transition probabilities, and summed,

$$g = \sum_{i=1}^{N} \phi_i \Gamma_i. \tag{15.3.24}$$

We shall soon prove this result, but we shall first confirm it and discuss its implications.

Confirmation in the car rental problem

We can confirm the result by applying it to the policy $\mathbf{d} = [1 \quad 2]$. We see from the first policy improvement of Table 15.3.2 that $\Gamma_1 = \Gamma_1^{\,1} = 10.04$, $\Gamma_2 = \Gamma_2^{\,2} = 16.05$. Then using the limiting interval transition probabilities of Equation 15.3.21, we have

$$g = \sum_{i=1}^{N} \phi_i \Gamma_i = (9/11)(10.04) + (2/11)(16.05) = \frac{122.5}{11} = 11.14, \tag{15.3.25}$$

the correct gain for the policy. For the second policy improvement of Table 15.3.3, $\Gamma_1 = \Gamma_1^{\,1} = \Gamma_2 = \Gamma_2^{\,2} = 11.14$, and therefore

$$g = \sum_{i=1}^{N} \phi_i \Gamma_i = 11.14. \tag{15.3.26}$$

This result is not surprising. We already know that when we base a policy improvement on the relative values of a policy, the test quantities for that policy will be equal to its gain.

Gain bounds from policy improvement

The main value of Equation 15.3.24 is the insight it provides into the meaning of the policy improvement calculations. We note, in particular, that if we replace the earning rate q_i with the test quantity Γ_i in our discussion of bounds on the gain, then we have a procedure for finding new bounds on the gain of any policy, or of the best or worst policies, every time we perform a policy improvement.

Gain bounds in the car rental problem

We illustrate this process in Table 15.3.5. Here we have indicated the bounds we can place on various gains for the car rental problem as the result of performing policy improvements. The first line of the table merely records the bounds we established earlier using the earning rates. The second line shows the bounds established by applying the same type of reasoning to the test quantities of the first policy improvement of Table 15.3.2 rather than to the earning rates. For example, since $\Gamma_1{}^2 = 7.63$ and $\Gamma_2{}^2 = 16.05$, we know that the gain of the policy $\mathbf{d} = [2 \quad 2]$ must lie between 7.63 and 16.05. Since the minimin and maximin test quantities are both 7.63, the gain of the worst policy must be 7.63. Since the minimax test quantity is 10.04 and the maximax test quantity is 16.05, the gain of the optimum policy must be between 10.04 and 16.05.

However, the ranges for gain in the second line of Table 15.3.5 reflect only the bounds implied by the first policy improvement. Since we already have information on bounds from the earning rates as shown in line one, we can combine the two sources of information to produce a new set of bounds as shown in the third line of Table 15.3.5. Here we compute the intersection of the ranges for gains from lines one and two. Thus since we know from the earning rates that the optimum policy has a gain between 6.25 and 15 and from the first policy improvement that it has a gain between 10.04 and 16.05, it follows that the gain of the optimum policy must lie between 10.04 and 15, the intersection of these ranges.

The fourth line of Table 15.3.5 shows the ranges for gain implied by the test quantities of the second policy improvement from Table 15.3.3. The last line gives the ranges on gain that result from using all three sources of information—the earning rates and the results of the first and second policy improvements. We see that in this example we have determined the gain of the worst policy as well as the gain of the optimum policy. However, more interesting are the results for particular policies. Without an exact calculation of the gains of either policy $\mathbf{d} = [1 \quad 1]$ or policy $\mathbf{d} = [2 \quad 2]$, we know that policy $\mathbf{d} = [2 \quad 2]$ has a higher gain than policy $\mathbf{d} = [1 \quad 1]$.

Bounds on the gain of the second-best policy

We can exploit these results to gain insight into a question that often arises. Once we have found the optimum policy, what can we say about the gain of the second-best policy, whatever it is? A moment's reflection shows that if we delete from the final policy improvement the alternatives corresponding to the optimum policy and then find the maximax test quantity among those alternatives that remain, it follows that this abridged maximax test quantity will be a lower bound on the gain of the second-best policy. All we have to do to prove this is to consider a policy that is identical with the optimum policy except that the alternative that

Table 15.3.5 Bounds on Gains in the Car Rental Problem Derived from Earning Rates and Policy Improvement Test Quantities

	Range of Gain					
	For Particular Policies **d**				For Worst Policy	For Best Policy
Information Source	[1 1]	[1 2]	[2 1]	[2 2]	minimin–maximin	minimax–maximax
(A) Earning Rates	6.25—12.5	5—12.5	6.25—15	5—15	5—12.5	6.25—15
(B) Test Quantities for First Policy Improvement	7.63—10.04	10.04—16.05	7.63	7.63—16.05	7.63	10.04—16.05
(A) + (B)	7.63—10.04	10.04—12.5	7.63	7.63—15	7.63	10.04—15
(C) Test Quantities for Second Policy Improvement	7.02—11.14	11.14	7.02—10.91	10.91—11.14	7.02—10.91	11.14
(A) + (B) + (C)	7.63—10.04	11.14	7.63	10.91—11.14	7.63	11.14

generates the abridged maximax test quantity is substituted for the alternative of the optimum policy in the state where it occurs. The policy so found will be different from the optimum policy, but will have a gain that is bounded by the abridged maximax test quantity and the gain of the optimum policy. Therefore, the second-best policy cannot have a gain lower than the abridged maximax test quantity, and, of course, it cannot have a gain higher than that of the optimum policy.

Bounds on the gain of the second-best policy in the car rental problem

We observe from the last policy improvement of the car rental problem in Table 15.3.3 that the abridged maximax test quantity is 10.91 and corresponds to the second alternative in state 1. Therefore the second-best policy and, in fact, the policy $\mathbf{d} = [2 \quad 2]$ must have a gain between 10.91 and 11.14. The exhaustive evaluation of Table 15.3.4 shows that this policy has a gain of 11. Since in many problems it is not convenient to include in our model such virtues of a policy as simplicity of implementation, we may be very appreciative of having a method like this for examining other close-to-optimum policies.

The range of gains we establish for the optimum policy as we progress through the problem using the procedure of Table 15.3.5 often has an important practical consequence. In very large problems where successive iterations are expensive, we may want to get some idea about how close the gain of a policy we have just evaluated is to the gain of the optimum policy. We would use this information to stop further iterations when we felt that the gain was close enough. In many problems examination of the bounds we have provided on the gain of the optimum policy yields sufficient information to settle this point.

Proof That the Gain Is the Weighted Sum of Test Quantities

Now let us prove the result stated in Equation 15.3.23: the gain for any policy B is equal to the sum of the policy improvement test quantities for policy B weighted by the limiting interval transition probabilities for policy B, regardless of the policy A from which the relative values used in the policy improvement were derived. We shall give all quantities a superscript A or B according to whether they pertain to policy A or policy B.

We begin by writing Equation 15.3.5 for policy B,

$$g^{\mathrm{B}} = q_i^{\mathrm{B}} + \frac{1}{\bar{\tau}_i^{\mathrm{B}}}\left[\sum_{j=1}^{N} p_{ij}^{\mathrm{B}} v_j^{\mathrm{B}} - v_i^{\mathrm{B}}\right] \qquad i = 1, 2, \ldots, N. \qquad (15.3.27)$$

We know, and have indicated most recently in Equation 15.3.20, that the gain of any policy is equal to the sum over all states of the product of limiting interval transition probability and earning rate in each state,

$$g^{\mathrm{B}} = \sum_{i=1}^{N} \phi_i^{\mathrm{B}} q_i^{\mathrm{B}}. \tag{15.3.28}$$

This expression reveals that the gain for the process depends ultimately only on the transition probabilities, mean waiting times, and earning rates. We therefore have an expression for gain that does not depend explicitly on the relative value variables in Equation 15.3.27.

Now we write the test quantity Γ_i^{BA} that will be calculated for state i under the alternative used in policy B for that state when the relative values v_i^{A} arose from some policy A,

$$\Gamma_i^{\mathrm{BA}} = q_i^{\mathrm{B}} + \frac{1}{\bar{\tau}_i^{\mathrm{B}}}\left[\sum_{i=1}^{N} p_{ij}^{\mathrm{B}} v_j^{\mathrm{A}} - v_i^{\mathrm{A}}\right]. \tag{15.3.29}$$

We subtract this equation from Equation 15.3.27 to obtain

$$g^{\mathrm{B}} = \Gamma_i^{\mathrm{BA}} + \frac{1}{\bar{\tau}_i^{\mathrm{B}}}\left[\sum_{i=1}^{N} p_{ij}^{\mathrm{B}}(v_j^{\mathrm{B}} - v_j^{\mathrm{A}}) - (v_i^{\mathrm{B}} - v_i^{\mathrm{A}})\right] \tag{15.3.30}$$

and then write $v_j^{\Delta} = v_j^{\mathrm{B}} - v_j^{\mathrm{A}}$ to produce

$$g^{\mathrm{B}} = \Gamma_i^{\mathrm{BA}} + \frac{1}{\bar{\tau}_i^{\mathrm{B}}}\left[\sum_{i=1}^{N} p_{ij}^{\mathrm{B}} v_j^{\Delta} - v_i^{\Delta}\right] \qquad i = 1, 2, \ldots, N. \tag{15.3.31}$$

These equations are the policy evaluation equations 15.3.27 for a policy that differs from policy B only in that the test quantities Γ_i^{BA} are substituted for the earning rates q_i. Therefore, in view of Equation 15.3.28, the solution for g^{B} must be

$$g^{\mathrm{B}} = \sum_{i=1}^{N} \phi_i^{\mathrm{B}} \Gamma_i^{\mathrm{BA}}, \tag{15.3.32}$$

and we have established Equation 15.3.23.

Proof of the Policy Iteration Method

Equation 15.3.32 shows the basic properties of policy improvement. We recall that $\Gamma_i^{\mathrm{AA}} = g^{\mathrm{A}}$. If policy B is produced as a successor policy to A by the policy improvement procedure, we must have for any state i, $\Gamma_i^{\mathrm{BA}} \geq \Gamma_i^{\mathrm{AA}} = g^{\mathrm{A}}$, and for at least one state i, $\Gamma_i^{BA} > \Gamma_i^{AA}$ unless policy A and B are identical. Therefore, if at least one of the states i for which $\Gamma_i^{BA} > \Gamma_i^{AA}$ is recurrent under policy B,

$$g^B = \sum_{i=1}^{N} \phi_i^B \Gamma_i^{BA} > \sum_{i=1}^{N} \phi_i^B g^A \tag{15.3.33}$$

or

$$g^B > g^A \qquad A \neq B. \tag{15.3.34}$$

Consequently, the gain of the process must increase under policy improvement if a change of policy occurs in any state that is recurrent under the new policy. In no case, however, can the gain decrease.

We show the ultimate convergence of the procedure by contradiction. Suppose that $g^B > g^A$, but that the policy improvement procedure has converged on policy A; therefore, $\Gamma_i^{BA} \leq \Gamma_i^{AA} = g^A$. By virtue of Equation 15.3.32,

$$g^B = \sum_{i=1}^{N} \phi_i^B \Gamma_i^{BA} \leq \sum_{i=1}^{N} \phi_i^B g^A \tag{15.3.35}$$

or

$$g^B \leq g^A. \tag{15.3.36}$$

Since by assumption $g^B > g^A$, we have reached a contradiction. The policy iteration procedure cannot converge on a non-optimum policy.

Gain change in policy improvement

We sometimes want to relate changes in gain directly to changes in test quantity and relative values. A convenient way to do this is to note that $g^A = \Gamma_i^{AA}$ and to subtract this relation from Equation 15.3.31,

$$g^B - g^A = \Gamma_i^{BA} - \Gamma_i^{AA} + \frac{1}{\bar{\tau}_i^B}\left[\sum_{j=1}^{N} p_{ij}^B v_j^\Delta - v_i^\Delta\right]. \tag{15.3.37}$$

Now we let $g^\Delta = g^B - g^A$, $\gamma_i^{BA} = \Gamma_i^{BA} - \Gamma_i^{AA}$ and write this equation as

$$g^\Delta = \gamma_i^{BA} + \frac{1}{\bar{\tau}_i^B}\left[\sum_{j=1}^{N} p_{ij}^B v_j^\Delta - v_i^\Delta\right] \tag{15.3.38}$$

or

$$v_i^\Delta + g^\Delta \bar{\tau}_i^B = \gamma_i^{BA} \bar{\tau}_i^B + \sum_{j=1}^{N} p_{ij}^B v_j^\Delta. \tag{15.3.39}$$

This equation relates the changes in relative values, gains, and test quantities in going from policy A to policy B to the transition probabilities and mean waiting times of policy B. Since Equation 15.3.38 is basically in the same form as Equation 15.3.5, we have immediately

$$g^{\Delta} = \sum_{i=1}^{N} \phi_i^{B} \gamma_i^{BA}. \tag{15.3.40}$$

The increase in gain is the increase in test quantity in each state multiplied by the limiting interval transition probability for the state and summed over all states. Of course, this is just another form of the result given by Equation 15.3.32.

The Nature of Relative Values

We have already described in Section 13.4 how the relative values of a process may be interpreted: $v_i - v_j$ is the difference in the total expected rewards over an infinite time interval caused by starting the process in state i rather than in state j. This interpretation can be very helpful in understanding the implications of any given policy.

For example, in Table 15.3.4 we showed the relative values for all possible policies for the car rental problem. Since v_2 was set equal to zero, the values of v_1 in this table represent the increase in total expected profit from starting the process in town 1 rather than in town 2. We can thus interpret v_1 as the break-even amount the company should be willing to pay for an instantaneous transfer of a car from town 2 to town 1. The table shows that the value of this transfer ranges from 24 to 72 for the four policies. The optimum policy has a transfer value from town 2 to town 1 of 24.55, neither the lowest nor the highest. Of course, there is generally no reason to expect that the policy selected to maximize gain would maximize the difference in relative values of any pair of states.

Relative value approximation

As we observed before, we can choose our initial policy for policy iteration by selecting a set of relative values and then performing a policy improvement. Sometimes a rough approximation to the relative values is helpful in doing this. We develop the approximation by solving Equation 15.3.2 for a particular v_i,

$$v_i + g\bar{\tau}_i = r_i + \sum_{j=1}^{N} p_{ij} v_j,$$

$$v_i + g\bar{\tau}_i = r_i + p_{ii} v_i + \sum_{\substack{j=1 \\ j \neq i}}^{N} p_{ij} v_j, \tag{15.3.41}$$

$$v_i = \frac{1}{1 - p_{ii}} [r_i - g\bar{\tau}_i] + \frac{1}{1 - p_{ii}} \sum_{\substack{j=1 \\ j \neq i}}^{N} p_{ij} v_j.$$

Now if we assume that all v_j's, $j \neq i$, are equal to zero, we have an equation for ${}^0v_i$, a rough approximation to v_i,

$$ {}^0v_i = \frac{r_i - g\bar{\tau}_i}{1 - p_{ii}}. \tag{15.3.42}$$

To use this approximation, we must make an estimation of what g will be for the optimum policy, perhaps by surveying the earning rates q_i^k in the problem, and then write the approximation ${}^0v_i^k$ for each alternative k in state i. Next we examine this set and select a relative value ${}^0v_i$ to represent state i, perhaps by averaging ${}^0v_i^k$ over all alternatives. When we have done this for all states, we have developed a set of relative values on which a policy improvement can be based to start the iteration procedure. The value of this approximation method could become important when iterations are expensive.

Relative value approximation in the car rental example

Table 15.3.6 illustrates this procedure for the car rental example. Since the gain of the present policy $\mathbf{d} = [1 \quad 1]$ is 8.5, and since the optimum policy cannot have a lower gain than this, we shall assume that the gain of the optimum policy will be 10. Then we use Equation 15.3.42 to calculate the approximate value for every alternative in every state. In state 1, we find approximate values of 30 and 45, suggesting that state 1 has a value of, say, 38 relative to other states and, in this case, relative to state 2. We observe also that the approximate values for state 2 are -20 and -120, indicating that state 2 has a value of, say, -70 relative to other

Table 15.3.6 Computation of Approximate Relative Values and Initial Policy for the Car Rental Problem

		Relative Value Approximation Assume: $g = 10$	Policy Improvement $v_1 = 50 \quad v_2 = 0$
i	k	${}^0v_i^k = \dfrac{r_i^k - g\bar{\tau}_i^k}{1 - p_{ii}^k}$	$\Gamma_i^k = q_i^k + \dfrac{1}{\bar{\tau}_i^k}\left[\sum_{i=1}^{N} p_{ij}^k v_j - v_i\right]$
1	1	$\dfrac{45 - 10(3.6)}{1 - 0.8} = 45$	9.72
	2	$\dfrac{90 - 10(6)}{1 - 0} = 30$	6.67
2	1	$\dfrac{60 - 10(9.6)}{1 - 0.7} = -120$	7.81
	2	$\dfrac{20 - 10(4)}{1 - 0} = -20$	17.50

Initial Policy $\mathbf{d} = [1 \quad 2]$

states and, in this case, relative to state 1. After viewing these results, we might decide on a number like 50 for the value of state 1 relative to state 2 and set $v_1 = 50$, $v_2 = 0$ as the basis for selecting an initial policy.

The final column of Table 15.3.6 shows the test quantities Γ_i^k that result from these relative values. We mention for completeness that even the test quantities in this table must satisfy Equation 15.3.24. We see that the initial policy selected is $\mathbf{d} = [1 \quad 2]$, which, after one policy evaluation and one more policy improvement attempt, we would find to be the optimum policy. Thus when we apply the approximate value procedure suggested by Equation 15.3.42 to the car rental example, we obtain the optimum policy as our initial policy. Although we shall not always be so fortunate, we can only benefit by at least considering as an initial policy the one that arises from the approximate relative values.

We have now finished our description of policy iteration for the infinite duration, no-discounting decision problem. Thus we need not search exhaustively through the impressively large number of policies in most problems; we can instead use a policy iteration procedure of repeatedly solving sets of simultaneous equations and making comparisons until we find the optimum policy. Although it is difficult to predict the number of iterations required in advance, the number has typically been so small as to make the procedure eminently practical.

Polydesmic Processes

When the process is not monodesmic, then our goal must be to maximize the gain g_i of every state i rather than the single gain of the process. The procedure for accomplishing this is a variation of the procedure we have just discussed. Once more we have iteration cycles of policy evaluation and policy improvement.

Policy evaluation

In policy evaluation, we solve Equations 13.3.42 and 13.3.43,

$$g_i = \sum_{j=1}^{N} p_{ij} g_j \qquad i = 1, 2, \ldots, N$$
$$v_i = r_i - \sum_{j=1}^{N} p_{ij} \bar{\tau}_{ij} g_j + \sum_{j=1}^{N} p_{ij} v_j \qquad i = 1, 2, \ldots, N, \tag{15.3.43}$$

to obtain the gains and relative values of all states. You recall that we must set the relative value of one state in each chain equal to zero to permit a unique solution.

Policy improvement

Policy improvement becomes a two-step procedure suggested by the right-hand side of Equation 13.3.41. After noting the importance of the coefficient of t, we first determine whether there is an alternative k in each state i that produces a higher value of the test quantity

$$\sum_{j=1}^{N} p_{ij}{}^{k} g_j \tag{15.3.44}$$

than does the present alternative in state i. If there is, then we change the decision in state i to the alternative with the highest value of this test quantity. Note that in this test we are using the gains for all states that result from the previous policy evaluation.

Suppose now that there is at least one other alternative in addition to the present decision that produces the same value of the test quantity (15.3.44). In that case we break the tie by referring to the constant terms on the right-hand side of Equation 13.3.41. Thus we select a new decision from among the tied alternatives by determining the alternative k that maximizes the test quantity,

$$r_i{}^{k} - \sum_{j=1}^{N} p_{ij}{}^{k} \bar{\tau}_{ij}{}^{k} g_j + \sum_{j=1}^{N} p_{ij}{}^{k} v_j \tag{15.3.45}$$

using both the gains and relative values of the present policy. If we again produce a tie with our present decision, then we leave our present decision unchanged.

The iteration cycle

Thus we now have a two-step policy improvement procedure. We attempt to improve our decision in each state first by using test quantity 15.3.44 and then by using test quantity 15.3.45 to resolve any ties generated by using the first test quantity. The ultimate result is a new policy for the problem, which is then evaluated from Equations 15.3.43, and the iteration cycle continues. The complete cycle is indicated in Figure 15.3.2. We note that this cycle reduces to that of Figure 15.3.1 when the process is in fact monodesmic. The iteration stops when the same policy is found on two successive iterations. The proof that this procedure has the desired properties follows closely the proof for the monodesmic case.† We select an initial policy arbitrarily; however, as before, the policy consisting of the alternatives that have the highest earning rate in each state has many merits when little other information on the structure of the optimum policy is available.

As we mentioned in Chapter 13, polydesmic models introduce computational difficulties that can seldom be justified by any increased insight into the problem.

† The analogous proof of the properties of policy iteration for the polydesmic case of the discrete-time Markov process appears in Chapter 6 of *Dynamic Programming and Markov Processes*.

Policy Evaluation

For the present policy solve

$$g_i = \sum_{j=1}^{N} p_{ij} g_j \qquad i = 1, 2, \ldots, N$$

$$v_i = r_i - \sum_{j=1}^{N} p_{ij} \bar{\tau}_{ij} g_j + \sum_{j=1}^{N} p_{ij} v_j \qquad i = 1, 2, \ldots, N$$

for all gains g_i and relative values v_i by setting the value of one v_i in each recurrent chain to zero.

Policy Improvement

For each state i find the alternative k that maximizes

$$\sum_{j=1}^{N} p_{ij}^{k} g_j$$

using the gains g_i of the previous policy. If only one alternative achieves the maximum, then make this alternative the new decision in state i. If a tie exists among alternatives that achieve the maximum, then resolve the tie in favor of the alternative that maximizes

$$r_i^k - \sum_{j=1}^{N} p_{ij}^{k} \bar{\tau}_{ij}^{k} g_j + \sum_{j=1}^{N} p_{ij}^{k} v_j$$

using both the gains and relative values of the previous policy. If a tie still exists and if the previous decision in state i is a member of the tie, then leave the decision unchanged; otherwise, any of the tied alternatives may be made the new decision. Repeat for all states to find the new policy.

Figure 15.3.2. The iteration cycle for polydesmic processes.

Since we can usually avoid polydesmic models by care in formulation, we would be wise to do so.

15.4 POLICY ITERATION WITH DISCOUNTING

As we found in Chapter 13, when we discount future rewards at some rate α, the total reward generated by the continuous-time process in an infinite operating period has an expected present value $v_i(\alpha)$ when the process starts in state i. The simultaneous equations 13.2.20 allow us to compute these present values for any given process,

$$v_i(\alpha) = r_i(\alpha) + \sum_{j=1}^{N} p_{ij} h_{ij}^e(\alpha) v_j(\alpha) \qquad i = 1, 2, \ldots, N. \tag{15.4.1}$$

To write these equations, we need the expected present value of a single occupancy of state i, $r_i(\alpha)$ as defined by Equation 13.2.17,

$$r_i(\alpha) = r_i(\infty, \alpha) = \sum_{j=1}^{N} p_{ij} \int_0^\infty d\tau\, h_{ij}(\tau) \left[\int_0^\tau d\sigma\, e^{-\alpha\sigma} y_{ij}(\sigma) + e^{-\alpha\tau} b_{ij}(\tau) \right]. \tag{15.4.2}$$

We also use the transition probabilities p_{ij} and the exponential transforms of the holding time density functions evaluated at $s = \alpha$.

The decision problem we face is how to select a stationary policy from among those available in such a way as to maximize the expected present value of starting in any state. It might appear that we would be faced with a dilemma in situations where we could increase the expected present value of one state only at the expense of the expected present value of another. However, as we shall see, we can find a policy whose expected present values are at least as high as the expected present values of any other policy in all states. This policy we shall call the optimum stationary policy, or simply the optimum policy.

To find the optimum policy by exhaustive evaluation would be as difficult as it is in the no-discounting case. Fortunately, however, we can develop a policy iteration procedure for the case with discounting that has all the advantages of the one we developed for the case where no discounting was present. Furthermore, the same procedure will apply to both monodesmic and polydesmic processes.

We again begin by showing plausibility. Suppose we had found the expected present values of some arbitrary policy using Equations 15.4.1. We call this process evaluating the policy. If we take these expected present values as approximations to the present values of the optimum policy, we would expect to find a better policy by writing the right-hand side of Equation 15.4.1 for each alternative in each state and then finding the alternative in each state that made this test quantity a maximum. By making our new policy consist of the alternative in each state with the highest value of this test quantity, we would have a new policy that we could evaluate. We would repeat the procedure until no further change in policy occurred. In fact, as we shall later show, this procedure will lead to the optimum policy.

The Iteration Cycle

Figure 15.4.1 summarizes the iteration cycle. We evaluate an arbitrary policy using Equations 15.4.1 and then compute the test quantity $V_i^k(\alpha)$,

$$V_i^k(\alpha) = r_i^k(\alpha) + \sum_{j=1}^{N} p_{ij}^k h_{ij}^{ek}(\alpha) v_j(\alpha), \tag{15.4.3}$$

for each state i and alternative k using the expected present values we have just found. We can interpret $V_i^k(\alpha)$ as an approximation to the expected present value $v_i(\alpha)$ of the optimum policy in rough analogy to our interpretation of Γ_i^k as an approximation to the gain of the optimum policy. We then form a new policy from the alternative in each state with the highest value of the test quantity, evaluate this policy, and repeat until the policies found on two successive iterations are identical. One of our ground rules is that we never change the decision in any state unless the test quantity is strictly greater for another alternative in that state. The final policy on which we converge in the procedure will be the optimum policy.

We can again select the initial policy for the iteration cycle intuitively or on a more formal basis. An appealing formal procedure is to choose for an initial policy the alternative in each state that maximizes the expected present value of a single

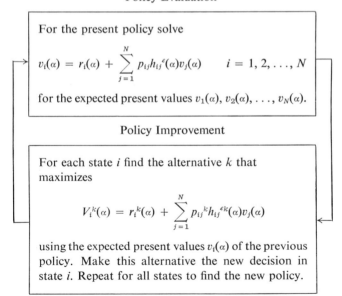

Policy Evaluation

For the present policy solve

$$v_i(\alpha) = r_i(\alpha) + \sum_{j=1}^{N} p_{ij} h_{ij}^{e}(\alpha) v_j(\alpha) \qquad i = 1, 2, \ldots, N$$

for the expected present values $v_1(\alpha), v_2(\alpha), \ldots, v_N(\alpha)$.

Policy Improvement

For each state i find the alternative k that maximizes

$$V_i^k(\alpha) = r_i^k(\alpha) + \sum_{j=1}^{N} p_{ij}^k h_{ij}^{ek}(\alpha) v_j(\alpha)$$

using the expected present values $v_i(\alpha)$ of the previous policy. Make this alternative the new decision in state i. Repeat for all states to find the new policy.

Figure 15.4.1. The continuous-time iteration cycle with discounting.

occupancy, $r_i^k(\alpha)$. This selection will be made automatically if we enter the policy evaluation with all expected present values $v_i(\alpha)$ equal to zero.

Policy Iteration for Discrete-Time Processes with Discounting

The policy iteration procedure for a discrete-time rather than continuous-time infinite duration process with discounting is derived by complete analogy to what we have done for the continuous-time case. The changes are that the policy iteration equations are now Equations 13.6.9,

$$v_i(\beta) = r_i(\beta) + \sum_{j=1}^{N} p_{ij} h_{ij}^{g}(\beta) v_j(\beta), \tag{15.4.4}$$

and that the test quantity is

$$V_i^k(\beta) = r_i^k(\beta) + \sum_{j=1}^{N} p_{ij}^k h_{ij}^{gk}(\beta) v_j(\beta). \tag{15.4.5}$$

Policy Evaluation

For the present policy solve

$$v_i(\beta) = r_i(\beta) + \sum_{j=1}^{N} p_{ij} h_{ij}^{g}(\beta) v_j(\beta) \qquad i = 1, 2, \ldots, N$$

for the expected present values $v_1(\beta), v_2(\beta), \ldots, v_N(\beta)$.

Policy Improvement

For each state i find the alternative k that maximizes

$$V_i^k(\beta) = r_i^k(\beta) + \sum_{j=1}^{N} p_{ij}^k h_{ij}^{gk}(\beta) v_j(\beta)$$

using the expected present values $v_i(\beta)$ of the previous policy. Make this alternative the new decision in state i. Repeat for all states to find the new policy.

Figure 15.4.2. The discrete-time iteration cycle with discounting.

The expected present value per occupancy of state i under alternative k with a discount factor β, $r_i^k(\beta)$, is computed from Equation 13.6.7,

$$r_i^k(\beta) = r_i^k(\infty, \beta) = \sum_{j=1}^{N} p_{ij}^k \sum_{m=1}^{\infty} h_{ij}^k(m)\left[\sum_{\ell=0}^{m-1} \beta^\ell y_{ij}^k(\ell) + \beta^m b_{ij}^k(m)\right]. \quad (15.4.6)$$

Of course, $h_{ij}^g(\beta)$ is just the geometric transform of the holding time mass function for the i to j transition evaluated at $z = \beta$. The iteration cycle for the discrete-time problem appears in Figure 15.4.2. All such considerations as choice of the initial policy, meaning of optimum policy, etc., are the same for both time bases.

Policy Iteration Solution of the Car Rental Problem with Discounting

We shall now apply policy iteration to find the optimum policy for the car rental problem whose alternatives appear in Table 15.1.1 in the case where earnings in future periods are to be discounted using a discounting factor $\beta = 0.9$. We can, of course, interpret this discount factor as the probability that the process will continue for one more time period. With this interpretation, the expected duration of the process would be $1/(1 - \beta) = 10$ time periods.

Evaluation of alternative characteristics

To carry out the solution, we must evaluate the quantities $r_i^k(\beta)$ and $h_{ij}^{gk}(\beta)$ that are necessary to perform policy evaluations and improvements using Equations 15.4.4 and 15.4.5. Since the yield is zero for the car rental problem, Equation 15.4.6 becomes simply

$$r_i^k(\beta) = \sum_{j=1}^{N} p_{ij}^k \sum_{m=1}^{\infty} h_{ij}^k(m)\beta^m b_{ij}^k(m), \quad (15.4.7)$$

and by incorporating the result of Equation 15.2.6,

$$r_i^k(\beta) = \sum_{j=1}^{N} p_{ij}^k \sum_{m=1}^{\infty} h_{ij}^k(m)\beta^m[f_i^k m + f_{ij}^k]. \quad (15.4.8)$$

Now we use the properties of the geometric transform to write

$$r_i^k(\beta) = \sum_{j=1}^{N} p_{ij}^k\left[f_i^k\beta \frac{d}{d\beta} h_{ij}^{gk}(\beta) + f_{ij}^k h_{ij}^{gk}(\beta)\right]$$

$$= f_i^k \sum_{j=1}^{N} p_{ij}^k \left[\beta \frac{d}{d\beta} h_{ij}^{gk}(\beta)\right] + \sum_{j=1}^{N} p_{ij}^k f_{ij}^k h_{ij}^{gk}(\beta), \quad (15.4.9)$$

a result that we first encountered as Equation 13.8.4. Since the holding time mass function for the kth alternative in state i for the example has the simple geometric form

$$h_{ij}^{k}(m) = (1 - \lambda_{ij}^{k})(\lambda_{ij}^{k})^{m-1} \qquad m = 1, 2, 3, \ldots,$$

we have immediately

$$h_{ij}^{gk}(z) = \frac{(1 - \lambda_{ij}^{k})z}{1 - \lambda_{ij}^{k}z}, \qquad z\frac{d}{dz}h_{ij}^{gk}(z) = \frac{(1 - \lambda_{ij}^{k})z}{(1 - \lambda_{ij}^{k}z)^2}. \tag{15.4.10}$$

Therefore, Equation 15.4.9 becomes

$$r_i^{k}(\beta) = f_i^{k}\sum_{j=1}^{N} p_{ij}^{k}\frac{(1 - \lambda_{ij}^{k})\beta}{(1 - \lambda_{ij}^{k}\beta)^2} + \sum_{j=1}^{N} p_{ij}^{k}f_{ij}^{k}\frac{(1 - \lambda_{ij}^{k})\beta}{1 - \lambda_{ij}^{k}\beta}. \tag{15.4.11}$$

For example, for the first alternative in state 1 we have from this equation and Table 15.1.1,

$$\begin{aligned} r_1^{1}(\beta) &= 10\left[0.8\frac{[1 - (2/3)]\beta}{[1 - (2/3)\beta]^2} + 0.2\frac{[1 - (5/6)]\beta}{[1 - (5/6)\beta]^2}\right] \\ &\quad + 0.8(0)\frac{[1 - (2/3)]\beta}{1 - (2/3)\beta} + 0.2(45)\frac{[1 - (5/6)]\beta}{1 - (5/6)\beta} \\ &= \frac{(8/3)\beta}{[1 - (2/3)\beta]^2} + \frac{(1/3)\beta}{[1 - (5/6)\beta]^2} + \frac{(3/2)\beta}{1 - (5/6)\beta}, \end{aligned} \tag{15.4.12}$$

a result that appears as $r_1(\beta)$ in Equation 13.8.7. However, for our present purpose we evaluate this expression at $\beta = 0.9$ to obtain $r_1^{1}(0.9) = 25.2$.

Initial policy

The discounted rewards per occupancy $r_i^{k}(0.9)$ appear in Table 15.4.1 along with the other quantities $p_{ij}^{k}h_{ij}^{gk}(0.9)$ necessary to perform policy evaluation and improvement for the car rental problem. We observe that the policy $\mathbf{d} = [2 \quad 1]$ has the highest discounted reward per occupancy in each state, namely, 42.0 for state 1 and 20.1 for state 2. We shall therefore begin our policy iteration with policy $\mathbf{d} = [2 \quad 1]$ as the initial policy.

Evaluation. Our first step is to evaluate the expected present values of policy $\mathbf{d} = [2 \quad 1]$ using Equations 15.4.4. We use Table 15.4.1 to produce these equations in the form

$$\begin{aligned} v_1(0.9) &= 42.0 + 0v_1(0.9) + 0.600v_2(0.9) \\ v_2(0.9) &= 20.1 + 0.208v_1(0.9) + 0.300v_2(0.9). \end{aligned} \tag{15.4.13}$$

Table 15.4.1 Pertinent Data for the Infinite Duration Car Rental Problem with Discounting ($\beta = 0.9$)

State	Alternative	Expected Discounted Reward per Occupancy	Transition Probabilities		Holding Time Geometric Transforms Evaluated at β			
i	k	$r_i^k(0.9)$	p_{i1}^k	p_{i2}^k	$h_{i1}^{gk}(0.9)$	$h_{i2}^{gk}(0.9)$	$p_{i1}^k h_{i1}^{gk}(0.9)$	$p_{i2}^k h_{i2}^{gk}(0.9)$
1	1	25.2	0.8	0.2	0.750	0.600	0.600	0.120
	2	42.0	0	1	0.750	0.600	0	0.600
2	1	20.1	0.3	0.7	0.692	0.429	0.208	0.300
	2	10.7	1	0	0.692	0.429	0.692	0

Their solution is

$$v_1(0.9) = 72.0 \qquad v_2(0.9) = 50.0. \tag{15.4.14}$$

Thus the expected present value of starting in state 1 with policy $\mathbf{d} = [2 \quad 1]$ is 72.0, and of starting in state 2 is 50.0.

First policy improvement

Next we attempt to find a better policy by performing the policy improvement shown in Table 15.4.2. The test quantities indicate that a better policy would be the one formed from the first alternative in state 1 and the second alternative in state 2, $\mathbf{d} = [1 \quad 2]$.

Table 15.4.2 First Policy Improvement for the Infinite Duration Car Rental Problem with Discounting ($\beta = 0.9$)

Present Policy: $\mathbf{d} = [2 \quad 1]$
Evaluation: $v_1(0.9) = 72.0 \qquad v_2(0.9) = 50.0$

State	Alternative	Test Quantity
i	k	$V_i^k(\beta) = r_i^k(\beta) + \sum_{j=1}^{N} p_{ij}^k h_{ij}^{\mathscr{g}k}(\beta) v_j(\beta)$
1	1	$25.2 + 0.600(72.0) + 0.120(50.0) = 74.4$
	2	$42.0 + 0\ (72.0) + 0.600(50.0) = 72.0$
2	1	$20.1 + 0.208(72.0) + 0.300(50.0) = 50.0$
	2	$10.7 + 0.692(72.0) + 0\ (50.0) = 60.5$

Next Policy: $\mathbf{d} = [1 \quad 2]$

We see by comparing Equations 15.4.4 and 15.4.5 that the policy improvement test quantities for the alternatives corresponding to the policy on which the policy improvement is based are equal to the expected present values of that policy. Thus from Table 15.4.2 and Equation 15.4.14, we verify that $V_1^2(0.9) = v_1(0.9) = 72.0$, $V_2^1(0.9) = v_2(0.9) = 50.0$.

Evaluation. Now we must evaluate the policy $\mathbf{d} = [1 \quad 2]$. We write Equations 15.4.4 using Table 15.4.1,

$$\begin{aligned} v_1(0.9) &= 25.2 + 0.600v_1(0.9) + 0.120v_2(0.9) \\ v_2(0.9) &= 10.7 + 0.692v_1(0.9) + 0v_2(0.9), \end{aligned} \tag{15.4.15}$$

and, by solving them, obtain

$$v_1(0.9) = 83.6 \qquad v_2(0.9) = 68.5. \tag{15.4.16}$$

We see that we have, in fact, produced a policy with higher expected present values than our previous policy by comparing Equations 15.4.16 and 15.4.14.

Second policy improvement

However, **d** = [1 2] may not be the optimum policy, so we must perform the policy improvement shown in Table 15.4.3. We find that the policy **d** = [1 2] cannot be improved, and it is therefore the optimum policy. The test quantities for this policy in Table 15.4.3 are, of course, the present values recorded in Equation 15.4.16.

We have thus found that the optimum policy for the car rental problem when the discount factor is 0.9 is the same as the optimum policy found earlier when we considered the same problem without discounting and sought to maximize gain. The company should use the free alternative in town 1 and the limited alternative in town 2. The optimum policies with and without discounting are the same in this problem because the discounting factor 0.9 moves the time horizon for the process out far enough to permit operation under the optimum no-discounting policy.

The test quantities in Table 15.4.3 indicate that alternative 2 in state 1 is almost as good an alternative as alternative 1. Therefore, the policy **d** = [2 2] should have a set of expected present values that are close to, if less than, the expected present values of the optimum policy **d** = [1 2]. If we write the policy evaluation equations for **d** = [2 2] and solve them, we find

$$v_1(0.9) = 82.8 \qquad v_2(0.9) = 67.9. \tag{15.4.17}$$

Table 15.4.3 Second Policy Improvement for the Infinite Duration Car Rental Problem with Discounting ($\beta = 0.9$)

Present Policy: **d** = [1 2]
Evaluation: $v_1(0.9) = 83.6 \quad v_2(0.9) = 68.5$

State	Alternative	Test Quantity
i	k	$V_i^k(\beta) = r_i^k(\beta) + \sum_{j=1}^{N} p_{ij}^k h_{ij}^{\mathscr{g}k}(\beta) v_j(\beta)$
1	1	$25.2 + 0.600(83.6) + 0.120(68.5) = 83.6$
	2	$42.0 + 0\ (83.6) + 0.600(68.5) = 83.1$
2	1	$20.1 + 0.208(83.6) + 0.300(68.5) = 58.1$
	2	$10.7 + 0.692(83.6) + 0\ (68.5) = 68.5$

Optimum Policy: **d** = [1 2]

By comparing these expected present values with those of Equation 15.4.16, we indeed confirm our expectations. Thus the test quantities $V_i^k(\beta)$ provide the same kind of insight into close-to-optimum policies that the test quantities Γ_i^k provided in the case without discounting.

Solution for various discount factors

We can repeat the policy iteration solution of this example for values of β other than 0.9. Table 15.4.4 shows the optimum policy and expected present values of each state for values of β that range up to 0.9 in increments of 0.1.† We observe that the policy $\mathbf{d} = [2 \quad 1]$ is optimal for β through 0.6; $\mathbf{d} = [2 \quad 2]$ is optimal for $\beta = 0.7$ and $\beta = 0.8$; finally, $\mathbf{d} = [1 \quad 2]$ is the best policy for $\beta = 0.9$. We already know from our results of the last section that $\mathbf{d} = [1 \quad 2]$ is also optimal for $\beta = 1.0$.

Table 15.4.4 Policy Iteration Solution of the Infinite Duration Car Rental Decision Problem with Discounting

Discount		Decision		Expected Present Value	
Factor β	State i	State 1	State 2	State 1	State 2
0	1	—		—	
	2		—		—
0.1	1	2		0.751	
	2		1		0.412
0.2	1	2		1.718	
	2		1		0.941
0.3	1	2		2.998	
	2		1		1.642
0.4	1	2		4.761	
	2		1		2.612
0.5	1	2		7.311	
	2		1		4.033
0.6	1	2		11.26	
	2		1		6.291
0.7	1	2		18.07	
	2		2		10.54
0.8	1	2		33.12	
	2		2		22.81
0.9	1	1		83.55	
	2		2		68.49

† For a discussion of how the optimum policy depends on the discount factor, see *Dynamic Programming and Markov Processes*, Chapter 7, and Richard D. Smallwood, "Optimum Policy Regions for Markov Processes with Discounting," *Operations Research*, Vol. 14, No. 4, July–August, 1966.

The present values of each state under the optimum policy increase with the discount factor as we would expect.

If we compare this table with Table 15.2.1 developed for the same problem using value iteration, we see that the optimum policy for every discount factor at 15 stages was, in fact, the optimum policy recorded in Table 15.4.4. In other words, in every case, value iteration had produced a convergence of policy within 15 stages. Of course, we could not be sure of this convergence until we had performed the policy iteration.

Comparing the expected present values at stage 15 with those of Table 15.4.4 shows that they, too, had converged under value iteration for values of β through 0.5. A small discrepancy between the two procedures appears when $\beta = 0.6$ and then increases with β until it is about 20 for $\beta = 0.9$. These results allow us to see the special value of the policy iteration procedure when future rewards are subjected to any realistic degree of discounting.

The Properties of Policy Improvement

We shall now prove that the policy iteration procedure we have used for processes with discounting will lead to the optimum policy. We shall base the proof on the continuous-time formulation; the discrete-time proof follows by direct analogy.

Suppose that policy A has been evaluated and has produced a successor policy B in the policy improvement procedure. The present values for the policies A and B must each satisfy Equations 15.4.1,

$$v_i^{\mathrm{B}}(\alpha) = r_i^{\mathrm{B}}(\alpha) + \sum_{j=1}^{N} p_{ij}^{\mathrm{B}} h_{ij}^{e\mathrm{B}}(\alpha) v_j^{\mathrm{B}}(\alpha) \qquad i = 1, 2, \ldots, N \tag{15.4.18}$$

$$v_i^{\mathrm{A}}(\alpha) = r_i^{\mathrm{A}}(\alpha) + \sum_{j=1}^{N} p_{ij}^{\mathrm{A}} h_{ij}^{e\mathrm{A}}(\alpha) v_j^{\mathrm{A}}(\alpha) \qquad i = 1, 2, \ldots, N. \tag{15.4.19}$$

Now we subtract Equation 15.4.19 from Equation 15.4.18 to obtain

$$v_i^{\mathrm{B}}(\alpha) - v_i^{\mathrm{A}}(\alpha) = r_i^{\mathrm{B}}(\alpha) - r_i^{\mathrm{A}}(\alpha) + \sum_{j=1}^{N} p_{ij}^{\mathrm{B}} h_{ij}^{e\mathrm{B}}(\alpha) v_j^{\mathrm{B}}(\alpha) - \sum_{j=1}^{N} p_{ij}^{\mathrm{A}} h_{ij}^{e\mathrm{A}}(\alpha) v_j^{\mathrm{A}}(\alpha). \tag{15.4.20}$$

Since policy B was produced from policy A as the result of policy improvement, we must have

$$V_i^{\mathrm{B}} \geq V_i^{\mathrm{A}} \qquad i = 1, 2, \ldots, N \tag{15.4.21}$$

or

$$r_i^{\text{B}}(\alpha) + \sum_{j=1}^{N} p_{ij}^{\text{B}} h_{ij}^{e\text{B}}(\alpha) v_j^{\text{A}}(\alpha) \geq r_i^{\text{A}}(\alpha) + \sum_{j=1}^{N} p_{ij}^{\text{A}} h_{ij}^{e\text{A}}(\alpha) v_j^{\text{A}}(\alpha) \qquad i = 1, 2, \ldots, N. \tag{15.4.22}$$

Let $\delta_i^{\text{BA}} = V_i^{\text{B}} - V_i^{\text{A}}$; then,

$$\delta_i^{\text{BA}} = r_i^{\text{B}}(\alpha) - r_i^{\text{A}}(\alpha) + \sum_{j=1}^{N} p_{ij}^{\text{B}} h_{ij}^{e\text{B}}(\alpha) v_j^{\text{A}}(\alpha) - \sum_{j=1}^{N} p_{ij}^{\text{A}} h_{ij}^{e\text{A}}(\alpha) v_j^{\text{A}}(\alpha) \geq 0 \qquad i = 1, 2, \ldots, N. \tag{15.4.23}$$

Finally, we subtract Equation 15.4.23 from Equation 15.4.20 and write $v_i^{\Delta} = v_i^{\text{B}}(\alpha) - v_i^{\text{A}}(\alpha)$ to produce

$$v_i^{\Delta} = \delta_i^{\text{BA}} + \sum_{j=1}^{N} p_{ij}^{\text{B}} h_{ij}^{e\text{B}}(\alpha) v_j^{\Delta} \qquad i = 1, 2, \ldots, N. \tag{15.4.24}$$

These equations have the same form as the policy evaluation equations 15.4.1 except that the increases δ_i^{BA} in the test quantity that caused the change from policy A to policy B have now replaced the expected discounted rewards per occupancy for policy B, $r_i^{\text{B}}(\alpha)$. We know from Equation 13.2.31 that the expected present values for policy B are related to the discounted state occupancies ${}^{d}\bar{v}_{ij}(\alpha)$ and the expected discounted reward per occupancy by

$$v_i^{\text{B}}(\alpha) = \sum_{j=1}^{N} {}^{d}\bar{v}_{ij}^{\text{B}}(\alpha) r_j^{\text{B}}(\alpha) \qquad i = 1, 2, \ldots, N. \tag{15.4.25}$$

Therefore, the solution for v_i^{Δ} of Equations 15.4.24 must be

$$v_i^{\Delta} = \sum_{j=1}^{N} {}^{d}\bar{v}_{ij}^{\text{B}}(\alpha) \delta_j^{\text{BA}} \qquad i = 1, 2, \ldots, N. \tag{15.4.26}$$

Since the discounted state occupancies ${}^{d}\bar{v}_{ij}^{\text{B}}(\alpha)$ are non-negative and at least 1 when $i = j$ and since the test quantity increases δ_i^{BA} are non-negative, v_i^{Δ} must be non-negative for every state. Furthermore, whenever we can increase the test quantity in any state j that can be reached from state i under policy B, the quantity v_i^{Δ} will be greater than zero and the expected present value of starting in state i will be greater under policy B than it was under policy A. Thus we see that it is generally advantageous to change alternatives in favor of higher test quantities in as many states as possible in each policy iteration.

The proof that the iteration process cannot stop until it has reached the highest possible expected present values for each state follows by analogy with the no-discounting case. If the iteration cycle has converged on policy A, then all $\delta_j^{BA} \leq 0$, whereupon Equation 15.4.26 shows that all $v_i^{\Delta} \leq 0$. Consequently, when the policy iteration cycle has converged on a policy, no other policy can have a higher expected present value in any state.

15.5 POLICY ITERATION IN TRANSIENT PROCESSES

In a large number of processes of practical importance we are more interested in the reward the process earns while passing through transient states than we are in the gain of the process. For example, we can often model terminal control systems with different possible trajectories by the kind of model we have been discussing—with all states but the terminal state transient. In this type of situation the total reward earned by the process before it enters the recurrent state is the quantity of greatest interest. We can learn about the behavior of such a transient process by writing the policy evaluation equation 15.3.2 in the form,

$$v_i = (q_i - g)\bar{\tau}_i + \sum_{j=1}^{N} p_{ij}v_j \qquad i = 1, 2, \ldots, N, \tag{15.5.1}$$

where $q_i = r_i/\bar{\tau}_i$. We interpret this equation by saying that the value of being in state i is equal to the difference between the earning rate and the gain multiplied by the mean waiting time in the state plus the sum of the relative values of all states weighted by the probability of reaching each of them on the next transition.

We can clarify the issues involved by assuming that all states but state N are transient and that state N is a trapping state. Since $p_{NN} = 1$, Equation 15.5.1 for $i = N$ produces immediately

$$g = q_N. \tag{15.5.2}$$

If the system were started in state N, then the total reward in time t would be simply $q_N t$. Therefore from Equation 13.3.30, v_N must be zero, and the other values are uniquely determined by Equation 15.5.1,

$$v_i = (q_i - g)\bar{\tau}_i + \sum_{j=1}^{N-1} p_{ij}v_j \qquad i = 1, 2, \ldots, N - 1. \tag{15.5.3}$$

The first term on the right side of this equation represents the contribution to the expected value of state i due to the present occupancy of this state; the second term represents the expectation of profit on later transitions.

Let $\mathbf{e}$ be an $N - 1$ element column vector with components $\{(q_i - g)\bar{\tau}_i\}$ and let P^* be the $N - 1$ by $N - 1$ matrix with elements $\{p_{ij}: i = 1, 2, \ldots, N - 1;$

$j = 1, 2, \ldots, N - 1\}$. Then Equation 15.5.3 becomes

$$\mathbf{v} = \mathbf{e} + P^*\mathbf{v} \tag{15.5.4}$$

or

$$\mathbf{v} = [I - P^*]^{-1}\mathbf{e}. \tag{15.5.5}$$

We recognize $[I - P^*]^{-1}$ as $\overline{\mathrm{N}}$, the matrix whose ijth element $\bar{\nu}_{ij}$ is the mean number of times the system will occupy state j in an infinite number of transitions. Then

$$\mathbf{v} = \overline{\mathrm{N}}\mathbf{e} \tag{15.5.6}$$

or

$$v_i = \sum_{j=1}^{N-1} \bar{\nu}_{ij}(q_j - g)\bar{\tau}_j \tag{15.5.7}$$

$$\begin{aligned} &= \sum_{j=1}^{N-1} \bar{\nu}_{ij} q_j \bar{\tau}_j - g \sum_{j=1}^{N-1} \bar{\nu}_{ij}\bar{\tau}_j \\ &= \sum_{j=1}^{N-1} \bar{\nu}_{ij} r_j - g \sum_{j=1}^{N-1} \bar{\nu}_{ij}\bar{\tau}_j. \end{aligned} \tag{15.5.8}$$

This equation says that the value of state i is equal to the sum over all transient states j of the expected earnings from a single occupancy of state j, $r_j = q_j\bar{\tau}_j$, multiplied by the expected number of times state j will be occupied if the system is started in state i less the gain of the system multiplied by the expected total time the system will spend in the transient process. The problem of maximizing the expected total reward from starting in a certain transient state in this process is therefore one of selecting the most favorable set of mean numbers of occupancies and expected rewards per occupancy, rather than one of selecting the most favorable set of limiting interval transition probabilities and earning rates. We might therefore expect that a slightly different iteration procedure would be advisable.

The Value-Oriented Policy Improvement Criterion

To establish such a procedure, we examine Equation 15.5.1. It suggests that v_i could be maximized by a policy improvement procedure, that maximized the test quantity,

$$V_i^k = (q_i^k - g)\bar{\tau}_i^k + \sum_{j=1}^{N} p_{ij}^k v_j \qquad i = 1, 2, \ldots, N, \tag{15.5.9}$$

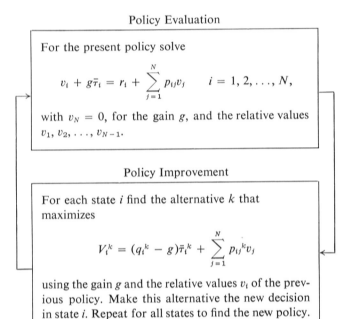

Policy Evaluation

For the present policy solve

$$v_i + g\bar{\tau}_i = r_i + \sum_{j=1}^{N} p_{ij}v_j \qquad i = 1, 2, \ldots, N,$$

with $v_N = 0$, for the gain g, and the relative values $v_1, v_2, \ldots, v_{N-1}$.

Policy Improvement

For each state i find the alternative k that maximizes

$$V_i^k = (q_i^k - g)\bar{\tau}_i^k + \sum_{j=1}^{N} p_{ij}^k v_j$$

using the gain g and the relative values v_i of the previous policy. Make this alternative the new decision in state i. Repeat for all states to find the new policy.

Figure 15.5.1. Policy iteration cycle using value-oriented criterion.

with respect to all alternatives k in state i. We shall call this test quantity the "value-oriented" criterion. Note that this criterion involves not only the relative values of state i under the previous policy, but also the gain of that policy.

Figure 15.5.1 shows the policy iteration cycle using the value-oriented criterion. We observe that when $g = 0$, it reduces to the policy iteration cycle of Figure 15.4.1 for the discounted process with $\alpha = 0$. Therefore, in a problem with zero gain, using the value-oriented criterion is equivalent to maximizing the expected present value of each state with no discounting of future rewards.

Value-maximization properties

Let us use the same type of proof we used before to find the properties of the new criterion. If policy B has been produced from policy A by using the value-oriented criterion in a policy improvement, then we can write the policy evaluation equations for each policy individually and subtract them. We obtain

$$v_i^{\mathrm{B}} - v_i^{\mathrm{A}} + g^{\mathrm{B}}\bar{\tau}_i^{\mathrm{B}} - g^{\mathrm{A}}\bar{\tau}_i^{\mathrm{A}} = q_i^{\mathrm{B}}\bar{\tau}_i^{\mathrm{B}} - q_i^{\mathrm{A}}\bar{\tau}_i^{\mathrm{A}} + \sum_{j=1}^{N} p_{ij}^{\mathrm{B}}v_j^{\mathrm{B}} - \sum_{j=1}^{N} p_{ij}^{\mathrm{A}}v_j^{\mathrm{A}}$$

$$i = 1, 2, \ldots, N. \qquad (15.5.10)$$

From the properties of the new type of policy improvement procedure,

$$(q_i^{\mathrm{B}} - g^{\mathrm{A}})\bar{\tau}_i^{\mathrm{B}} + \sum_{j=1}^{N} p_{ij}^{\mathrm{B}} v_j^{\mathrm{A}} \geq (q_i^{\mathrm{A}} - g^{\mathrm{A}})\bar{\tau}_i^{\mathrm{A}} + \sum_{j=1}^{N} p_{ij}^{\mathrm{A}} v_j^{\mathrm{A}} \qquad i = 1, 2, \ldots, N. \tag{15.5.11}$$

Let ζ_i^{BA} equal the difference between the left and right sides of this equation, the increase in the test quantity,

$$\zeta_i^{\mathrm{BA}} = (q_i^{\mathrm{B}} - g^{\mathrm{A}})\bar{\tau}_i^{\mathrm{B}} + \sum_{j=1}^{N} p_{ij}^{\mathrm{B}} v_j^{\mathrm{A}} - (q_i^{\mathrm{A}} - g^{\mathrm{A}})\bar{\tau}_i^{\mathrm{A}} - \sum_{j=1}^{N} p_{ij}^{\mathrm{A}} v_j^{\mathrm{A}} \qquad i = 1, 2, \ldots, N. \tag{15.5.12}$$

If we subtract Equation 15.5.12 from Equation 15.5.10, we find

$$v_i^{\mathrm{B}} - v_i^{\mathrm{A}} + (g^{\mathrm{B}} - g^{\mathrm{A}})\bar{\tau}_i^{\mathrm{B}} = \zeta_i^{\mathrm{BA}} + \sum_{j=1}^{N} p_{ij}^{\mathrm{B}}(v_j^{\mathrm{B}} - v_j^{\mathrm{A}}) \qquad i = 1, 2, \ldots, N \tag{15.5.13}$$

or, with $v_i^{\Delta} = v_i^{\mathrm{B}} - v_i^{\mathrm{A}}$ and $g^{\Delta} = g^{\mathrm{B}} - g^{\mathrm{A}}$, then

$$v_i^{\Delta} + g^{\Delta}\bar{\tau}_i^{\mathrm{B}} = \zeta_i^{\mathrm{BA}} + \sum_{j=1}^{N} p_{ij}^{\mathrm{B}} v_j^{\Delta} \qquad i = 1, 2, \ldots, N. \tag{15.5.14}$$

If we are dealing with a system in which only state N is recurrent and if the gain of that state is fixed, then $g^{\Delta} = 0$ and Equation 15.5.14 has the same form as Equation 15.5.3 with $g = 0$. Therefore by Equation 15.5.8,

$$v_i^{\Delta} = \sum_{j=1}^{N-1} \bar{\nu}_{ij}^{\mathrm{B}} \zeta_j^{\mathrm{BA}} \qquad i = 1, 2, \ldots, N - 1. \tag{15.5.15}$$

The change in values for each state is given by the sum of the mean number of transitions made to each state under the new policy multiplied by the increases in the test quantity. Since both of the factors are non-negative, all the v_i^{Δ} are non-negative. This iteration procedure will therefore converge on the policy with the largest values for the same reasons that were discussed in the case with discounting.

Effect on gain

We have found, therefore, a policy improvement criterion that will maximize the values of the transient states. We might ask about the effect that using this criterion in all problems would have upon the gain of a process that did not have this transient structure. Equations 15.5.14 still apply. We see that these equations are like Equations 15.3.2 except that they are written in terms of the differences in relative values and gains and that r_i has been replaced by ζ_i. Thus we can use Equations 13.3.31 or 15.3.20 to write

$$g^{\Delta} = \sum_{i=1}^{N} \phi_i^{\mathrm{B}} \frac{\zeta_i^{\mathrm{BA}}}{\bar{\tau}_i^{\mathrm{B}}}. \tag{15.5.16}$$

This equation shows that the increase in gain is not equal to the increases in the test quantities multiplied by the interval transition probabilities of policy B, but rather a division by $\bar{\tau}_i^{\mathrm{B}}$ is involved. Nevertheless, all the arguments about the necessity for the iteration procedure to increase the gain and ultimately to converge on the policy of highest gain apply equally well to this criterion. The value-oriented criterion may or may not increase the gain as quickly as the original criterion, but we do know that it will do so eventually and that it will maximize the values of a transient process.

Effect of Gain-Oriented Criterion on Values

There is a disturbing thought—how do we know that the original test quantity, which we shall call the "gain-oriented" criterion, does not maximize the values of a transient process just like the value-oriented criterion? Let us check. Equations 15.3.39, 15.5.14, and 15.5.15 show that in the situation with only state N recurrent and $g^{\Delta} = 0$, the v_i^{Δ} developed using the gain-oriented criterion must satisfy

$$v_i^{\Delta} = \sum_{j=1}^{N-1} \bar{\nu}_{ij}^{\mathrm{B}} \gamma_j^{\mathrm{BA}} \bar{\tau}_j^{\mathrm{B}}. \tag{15.5.17}$$

We see that increases in state value under the gain-oriented criterion involve not only the mean number of transitions to each state and the increases in test quantity but also the mean waiting times in each state. Yet all the arguments that show how Equation 15.5.15 implies a valid iteration procedure still apply. In other words, the gain-oriented criterion will also maximize the values of transient states.

Of course, Equations 15.3.40 and 15.5.16, and Equations 15.5.15 and 15.5.17 must be consistent. This would require that the test quantity increases for the two procedures be related by the equation

$$\zeta_i^{\mathrm{BA}} = \gamma_i^{\mathrm{BA}} \bar{\tau}_i^{\mathrm{B}}, \tag{15.5.18}$$

a result that is readily established.

The Efficiency of Gain- and Value-Oriented Criteria

We have now seen that both the gain-oriented and value-oriented test quantities will accomplish both tasks we require. The matter of their relative efficiency is

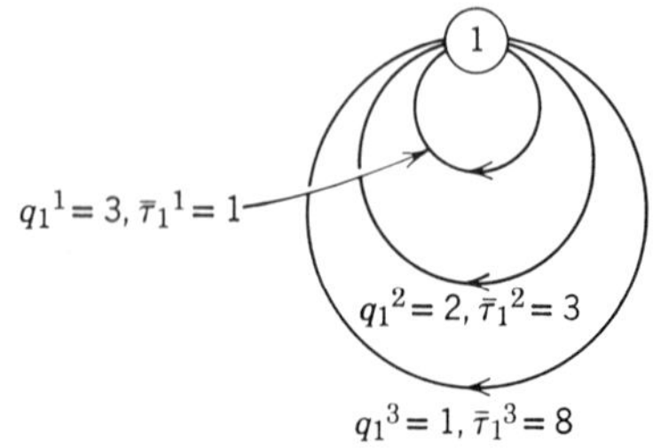

Figure 15.5.2 A one-state gain maximization example.

still open to question. However, it is easy to show that their efficiencies do differ by considering two examples.

A one-state gain maximization example

The first example is the one-state system with three alternatives in the state shown in Figure 15.5.2. The system can make only virtual transitions; the alternatives specify the earning rates and mean waiting times. The data are

$$\begin{array}{lll} q_1{}^1 = 3 & q_1{}^2 = 2 & q_1{}^3 = 1 \\ \bar{\tau}_1{}^1 = 1 & \bar{\tau}_1{}^2 = 3 & \bar{\tau}_1{}^3 = 8. \end{array} \qquad (15.5.19)$$

This trivial system has a trivial solution. Only the gain is involved—from Equation 15.5.2 we know that it is just equal to the earning rate of the state. Since alternative 1 produces the highest earning rate, 3, it is clear that this is the alternative on which we want any iteration scheme to converge. Suppose we start with a policy that specifies alternative 3, $\mathbf{d} = [3]$. How will solving the problem using the gain- and value-oriented criteria affect the number of iterations required for convergence?

Solution using gain-oriented criterion. We shall begin with the gain-oriented criterion. We already know that for the initial policy, $g = 1$, $v_1 = 0$. Therefore, the policy improvement procedure based on criterion 15.3.6 becomes simply $\text{Max}_k\, q_1{}^k$. We see that this leads immediately to the policy $\mathbf{d} = [1]$, and that the procedure has converged to give a gain $g = 3$ in one iteration.

Solution using value-oriented criterion. Now we shall solve the same problem using the value-oriented criterion 15.5.9. We see that the requirement becomes $\text{Max}_k\, (q_1{}^k - g)\bar{\tau}_1{}^k$. The test quantities for the three alternatives using the gain $g = 1$ of the original policy are then 2, 3, and 0. Therefore, the second alternative is best and we have a policy $\mathbf{d} = [2]$ with gain 2. Now we repeat the policy improvement

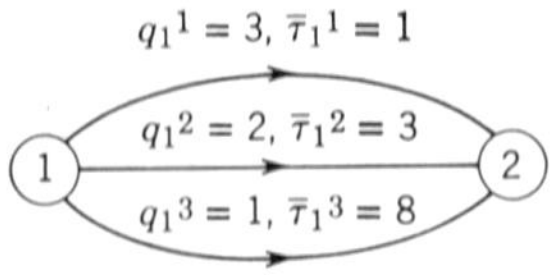

Figure 15.5.3 A two-state value maximization example.

again and obtain test quantities 1, 0, and −8. The first alternative is best and we have found the policy **d** = [1] with gain 3. Further attempts at improvement lead to the same policy.

We have just seen how in a particular example involving only gains, the gain-oriented test quantity was able to find the optimum policy in two fewer iterations. But is it always better for any problem? No, as we shall now see in a second example with two states.

A two-state value maximization example

Let state 2 be a trapping state with gain zero and let state 1 be a transient state that must enter state 2 on its first transition. State 1 has three alternative ways of going to state 2 described by the three alternatives in Equation 15.5.19 as shown in Figure 15.5.3. Since the process can earn money only while it occupies state 1 and since the expected amount it will earn doing this is $r_1 = q_1\bar{\tau}_1$, we see that it will earn the most, 8, by following alternative 3. In this problem we find quickly that $g = 0$, $v_2 = 0$, $v_1 = q_1\bar{\tau}_1$, so that solving the policy evaluation equation is no problem. Let us choose as our initial policy the first alternative in state 1 and indicate this choice simply by **d** = [1].

Solution using value-oriented criterion. Now we have to choose a test quantity. Let us begin this time with the value-oriented criterion 15.5.9. We find the alternative that maximizes $q_1^k\bar{\tau}_1^k$. We immediately decide, therefore, that the third alternative is the best, and we have converged on the optimum policy **d** = [3] with a value of 8 in only one iteration.

Solution using gain-oriented criterion. The gain-oriented criterion 15.3.6 reduces in this problem to the form

$$\operatorname*{Max}_k q_1^k - \frac{v_1}{\bar{\tau}_1^k}. \tag{15.5.20}$$

For the original policy, $v_1 = 3$, and so we have for the three test quantities, 0, 1, and 5/8. Therefore, alternative 2 is the best and we change to policy **d** = [2] for which $v_1 = 6$. Then we compute the test quantities again and find −3, 0, and 1/4.

Now alternative 3 is the best and we have found the optimum policy $\mathbf{d} = [3]$ with value $v_1 = 8$. Of course, further attempts at improvement lead to the same policy.

We have seen by example that the value-oriented criterion can save iterations in primarily value-maximization problems while the gain-oriented criterion can save iterations in primarily gain-maximization problems. However, either choice will always lead to an optimum policy.

The Value-Oriented Criterion in the Car Rental Problem

The car rental decision problem of Table 15.3.1 provides an opportunity for demonstrating that using the value-oriented criterion of Equation 15.5.9 will ultimately lead to the optimum policy.

Initial policy

If we choose our initial policy by assuming that the gain and relative values are zero and then attempt a policy improvement based on this criterion, we obtain initially a policy consisting of the alternative in each state that maximizes $q_i^k \bar{\tau}_i^k = r_i^k$, the expected reward per occupancy. For the car rental problem the initial policy will be $\mathbf{d} = [2 \quad 1]$, the same initial policy that maximized earning rate in each state.

First policy improvement

Since we have already evaluated this policy in Equation 15.3.15, we can immediately perform the policy improvement of Table 15.5.1 using the value-oriented criterion.

Table 15.5.1 First Policy Improvement for the Infinite Duration Car Rental Problem without Discounting Using the Value-Oriented Test Quantity

Present Policy: $\mathbf{d} = [2 \quad 1]$
Evaluation: $g = 7.63 \quad v_1 = 44.21 \quad v_2 = 0$

State	Alternative	Value-Oriented Test Quantity
i	k	$(q_i^k - g)\bar{\tau}_i^k + \sum_{j=1}^{N} p_{ij}^k v_j$
1	1	$(12.50 - 7.63)3.6 + 0.8(44.21) + 0.2(0) = 52.90$
	2	$(15.00 - 7.63)6 + 0(44.21) + 1(0) = 44.21$
2	1	$(6.25 - 7.63)9.6 + 0.3(44.21) + 0.7(0) = 0$
	2	$(5.00 - 7.63)4 + 1(44.21) + 0(0) = 33.69$

Next Policy: $\mathbf{d} = [1 \quad 2]$

Table 15.5.2 Second Policy Improvement for the Infinite Duration Car Rental Problem without Discounting Using the Value-Oriented Test Quantity

Present Policy: $\mathbf{d} = [1 \quad 2]$
Evaluation: $g = 11.14 \quad v_1 = 24.55 \quad v_2 = 0$

State	Alternative	Value-Oriented Test Quantity
i	k	$(q_i^k - g)\bar{\tau}_i^k + \sum_{j=1}^{N} p_{ij}^k v_j$
1	1	$(12.50 - 11.14)3.6 + 0.8(24.55) + 0.2(0) = 24.55$
	2	$(15.00 - 11.14)6 + 0(24.55) + 1(0) = 23.16$
2	1	$(6.25 - 11.14)9.6 + 0.3(24.55) + 0.7(0) = -39.58$
	2	$(5.00 - 11.14)4 + 1(24.55) + 0(0) = 0$

Optimum Policy: $\mathbf{d} = [1 \quad 2]$

We observe that the highest value of the test quantity occurs in state 1 for the first alternative and in state 2 for the second alternative. Thus a better policy is $\mathbf{d} = [1 \quad 2]$, the same policy found as a result of the gain-oriented policy improvement of Table 15.3.2.

Note that as a consequence of Equation 15.5.3, the value-oriented test quantities for the alternatives that make up the policy on which the policy improvement are based must be equal to the relative values of that policy. We can, of course, think of the value-oriented test quantities as successive approximations to the relative values of the optimum policy, just as the gain-oriented test quantities are successive approximations to the gain of the optimum policy.

Second policy improvement

Since we are not yet sure that $\mathbf{d} = [1 \quad 2]$ is the optimum policy, we use the evaluation of gain and relative values found in Equation 15.3.18 for this policy to perform the policy improvement of Table 15.5.2. Since the alternatives of the policy $\mathbf{d} = [1 \quad 2]$ have higher values of the test quantity than any other alternatives in each state, this policy is the optimum policy and the policy iteration has converged. The value-oriented test quantities for the optimum policy are, again, the relative values of that policy. We have thus found that solving the car rental problem by policy iteration using the value-oriented criterion is neither easier nor more difficult than its solution using the gain-oriented criterion.

15.6 EXAMPLES OF INFINITE DURATION PROCESSES

Since the measure of any proposed model is its ability to treat realistically the phenomena encountered in practice, we shall partially illustrate the variety of operational situations to which the semi-Markov decision process may be applied. We shall also attempt in this section to illustrate the connection between the semi-Markov formulation and the Markov formulation discussed in *Dynamic Programming and Markov Processes.*

The Foreman's Non-Exponential Dilemma

In Chapter 8 of *Dynamic Programming and Markov Processes* we discussed a problem called "The Foreman's Dilemma," wherein a foreman must choose maintenance and repair policies for a machinery installation. During this discussion the assumption is made that failure and repair are exponential processes, thus producing a final system that can be modeled by a continuous-time Markov process. However, the exponential assumption is not necessary to the solution of the problem once we expand our consideration to include semi-Markov models. We shall, therefore, restate the problem in semi-Markov terms and carry through its solution using policy iteration.

Alternative characteristics

Suppose that a single machine facility can be in either of two states. It is in state 1 when the machine is operating and in state 2 when the machine is out of order. When the machine is in state 1, it can be maintained with either normal or expensive maintenance; these two options are the alternatives in state 1. Under either maintenance alternative the machine will sooner or later break down so that $p_{11}{}^k = 0$, $p_{12}{}^k = 1$ for either option.

However, the density function for the time until the next breakdown will be different in each case. We believe that the effect of the more expensive maintenance is to increase the expected time until the next breakdown. Thus if we follow normal maintenance, alternative 1, we assume that the expected time until breakdown will be $\bar{\tau}_{12}{}^1 = 1/5$; whereas if we perform the expensive maintenance, alternative 2, we assume that the expected time until breakdown will be increased to $\bar{\tau}_{12}{}^2 = 1/2$. The actual density functions for time to breakdown for these two alternatives are completely arbitrary except for the means we have assumed.

The reward structure in state 1 is very simple. The yield rate of profit for normal maintenance will be higher than under expensive maintenance because of the lower maintenance cost; we assume $y_{12}{}^1 = 6$, $y_{12}{}^2 = 4$. Since we identify no bonus with the transition from state 1 to state 2, these yield rates are also the earning rates $q_1{}^1 = 6$, $q_1{}^2 = 4$. The expected rewards per occupancy are simply $r_1{}^1 = y_{12}{}^1\bar{\tau}_{12}{}^1 = 1.2$, $r_1{}^2 = y_{12}{}^2\bar{\tau}_{12}{}^2 = 2$.

When the system is in state 2 and the machine is out of order, there are again two alternatives, inside-plant and outside-plant repair crews. Under either alterna-

Table 15.6.1 Data for the Foreman's Non-Exponential Dilemma

State	Alternative	Transition Probabilities		Mean Waiting Time	Expected Reward per Occupancy	Earning Rate
i	k	p_{i1}^k	p_{i2}^k	$\bar{\tau}_i^k$	r_i^k	$q_i^k = \dfrac{r_i^k}{\bar{\tau}_i^k}$
1	1 (Normal maintenance)	0	1	1/5	1.2	6
	2 (Expensive maintenance)	0	1	1/2	2	4
2	1 (Inside-plant repair crew)	1	0	1/4	−3/4	−3
	2 (Outside-plant repair crew)	1	0	1/7	−5/7	−5

tive, the machine will sooner or later be fixed: $p_{21}^k = 1$, $p_{22}^k = 0$. The time for the repair, however, will have a different density function for each alternative. We call use of the inside-plant repair crew the first alternative in state 2 and use of the outside-plant repair crew the second alternative. We let the holding time density functions $h_{21}^1(\cdot)$ and $h_{21}^2(\cdot)$ be arbitrary, but specify that their means are $\bar{\tau}_{21}^1 = 1/4$ and $\bar{\tau}_{21}^2 = 1/7$. Thus the outside crew is expected to produce a faster repair.

However, the faster repair comes at a price: the inside-plant repair crew costs 1 per unit time, while the outside-plant repair crew costs 1.5 per unit time. In addition, after repair by either crew there is a fixed charge of 0.5 for restarting the machine. Thus we obtain the reward structure: $y_{21}^1 = -1$, $y_{21}^2 = -1.5$, $b_{21}^1 = b_{21}^2 = -0.5$. From Equation 13.3.40 we have the expected rewards per occupancy $r_2^1 = y_{21}^1\bar{\tau}_{21}^1 + b_{21}^1 = -3/4$, $r_2^2 = y_{21}^2\bar{\tau}_{21}^2 + b_{21}^2 = -5/7 = -.714$, and the earning rates $q_2^1 = r_2^1/\bar{\tau}_{21}^1 = -3$, $q_2^2 = r_2^2/\bar{\tau}_{21}^2 = -5$. The data for the example are summarized in Table 15.6.1.

Initial policy

Our goal is to find the maintenance-repair policy that will produce the most profitable operation of the facility. We take this to mean finding the policy that will maximize the gain of the non-discounted process. We shall use the policy iteration method and choose as our initial policy the one that maximizes the earning rate in each state. This policy consists of the first alternative in each state, the policy $\mathbf{d} = [1 \quad 1]$. We note that this policy requires the use of normal maintenance and the inside-plant repair crew.

Evaluation. We now write the policy evaluation equations 15.3.2 for the initial policy,

$$\begin{aligned} v_1 + (1/5)g &= 1.2 + v_2 \\ v_2 + (1/4)g &= -0.75 + v_1. \end{aligned} \tag{15.6.1}$$

When we set $v_2 = 0$ arbitrarily and add the equations, we immediately find the solution $g = 1$, $v_1 = 1$. The gain of the system under the initial policy is 1 per unit time.

First policy improvement

Now we try to improve the policy by maximizing in each state the test quantity Γ_i^k of Equation 15.3.6 using the relative values $v_1 = 1$, $v_2 = 0$ from the initial policy. Table 15.6.2 shows the results. We observe that the second alternative in each state now has the higher value of the test quantity. Therefore, we change to the better policy $\mathbf{d} = [2 \quad 2]$, which requires using expensive maintenance and the outside-plant repair crew.

Evaluation. We now solve the policy evaluation equations once more both to assure ourselves that the gain has increased and to provide the relative values v_i necessary for possible further improvement of the policy. The policy evaluation equations for $\mathbf{d} = [2 \quad 2]$ are

$$\begin{aligned} v_1 + (1/2)g &= 2 + v_2 \\ v_2 + (1/7)g &= -5/7 + v_1. \end{aligned} \tag{15.6.2}$$

With $v_2 = 0$, we obtain the solution $g = 2$, $v_1 = 1$. Thus the gain has doubled to 2 per unit time.

Table 15.6.2 First Policy Improvement for the Foreman's Non-Exponential Dilemma

Present Policy: $\mathbf{d} = [1 \quad 1]$
Evaluation: $g = 1 \quad v_1 = 1 \quad v_2 = 0$

State	Alternative	Test Quantity
i	k	$\Gamma_i^k = q_i^k + \dfrac{1}{\bar{\tau}_i^k}\left[\sum_{j=1}^{N} p_{ij}^k v_j - v_i\right]$
1	1	$6 + 5(-1) = 1$
	2	$4 + 2(-1) = 2$
2	1	$-3 + 4(1) = 1$
	2	$-5 + 7(1) = 2$

Next Policy: $\mathbf{d} = [2 \quad 2]$

Second policy improvement

However, if we now attempt policy improvement, we see that we shall coincidentally repeat the calculations in Table 15.6.2 because v_1 and v_2 have the same values as for the policy $\mathbf{d} = [1 \quad 1]$. Therefore, the policy found by the second alternative in each state has the highest gain of any possible policy; the policy iteration has converged. Thus the foreman will find it most profitable to operate his machine installation by using expensive maintenance and the outside-plant repair crew. We also note that since $v_1 - v_2 = 1$, the foreman should be willing to pay up to 1 unit to start operations with a just-repaired rather than a just-failed machine. We can therefore interpret $v_1 - v_2 = 1$ as the value of instantaneous repair.

The value of instantaneous repair

Perhaps the meaning of the observation that instantaneous repair is worth 1 unit will be more clear if we derive the value of this quantity by another method. Suppose that we had a third alternative in state 2 that corresponded to a method of repair requiring Δ time units and costing r monetary units. Then for this alternative,

$$\bar{\tau}_2^{\,3} = \Delta, \qquad r_2^{\,3} = -r, \qquad q_2^{\,3} = \frac{r_2^{\,3}}{\bar{\tau}_2^{\,3}} = \frac{-r}{\Delta}.$$

If we include this alternative in the policy improvement of Table 15.6.2, we would have obtained a value of the test quantity,

$$\Gamma_2^{\,3} = -\frac{r}{\Delta} + \frac{1}{\Delta}(1) = \frac{1}{\Delta}(1 - r). \tag{15.6.3}$$

If we assume Δ to be very small, then $\Gamma_2^{\,3}$ will be large and positive if r is less than 1 and large and negative if r is greater than 1. Thus if this virtually instantaneous repair costs more than one unit, the policy $\mathbf{d} = [2 \quad 2]$ will be preferable, while if it costs less than one unit, the policy $\mathbf{d} = [2 \quad 3]$ that incorporates the instantaneous repair will be preferable. Consequently, we see that the value of instantaneous repair is one unit, and substantiate our finding that $v_1 - v_2 = 1$.

The Speedy Taxicab Driver

In Chapter 5 of *Dynamic Programming and Markov Processes* we discuss the decision problem of a taxicab driver who makes trips among three towns that we identify with states 1, 2, and 3. In the first town he has three alternatives:

1. He can cruise in the hope of picking up a passenger by being hailed.
2. He can drive to the nearest cab stand and wait in line.
3. He can pull over and wait for a radio call.

Table 15.6.3 Data for the Speedy Taxicab Driver

State	Alternative	Transition Probabilities			Mean Waiting Time	Expected Reward per Occupancy	Earning Rate
i	k	p_{i1}^k	p_{i2}^k	p_{i3}^k	$\bar{\tau}_i^k$	r_i^k	$q_i^k = \dfrac{r_i^k}{\bar{\tau}_i^k}$
1	1 Cruise	1/2	1/4	1/4	τ	8	$8/\tau$
	2 Stand	1/16	3/4	3/16	1	2.75	2.75
	3 Radio	1/4	1/8	5/8	1	4.25	4.25
2	1 Cruise	1/2	0	1/2	1	16	16
	2 Stand	1/16	7/8	1/16	1	15	15
3	1 Cruise	1/4	1/4	1/2	1	7	7
	2 Stand	1/8	3/4	1/8	1	4	4
	3 Radio	3/4	1/16	3/16	1	4.5	4.5

He has the same alternatives in the third town, but in the second town the last alternative of waiting for a radio call is not available. The original problem was based on a Markov decision process: Transition probabilities were assigned and a reward per occupancy was computed for each state and alternative, but all trips were assumed to be of the same one-time-unit length.

Let us now abandon this last assumption in part. We shall assume that all trips require exactly one time unit with the exception that trips that originate in town 1 under alternative 1 require a fixed time τ. Table 15.6.3 summarizes the data for the amended problem. When τ is equal to one, we showed in *Dynamic Programming and Markov Processes* that if we performed policy iteration with the initial policy $\mathbf{d} = [1 \quad 1 \quad 1]$ we would find the optimum policy $\mathbf{d} = [2 \quad 2 \quad 2]$ in three iterations. This policy had gain $g = 13.34$ and relative values $v_1 = -1.18$, $v_2 = 12.66$, $v_3 = 0$. We shall now explore how the optimum policy and its evaluation change as we gradually decrease τ.

Policy iteration solution

Table 15.6.4 and Figure 15.6.1 show how the optimum policy and its gain and relative values depend on τ. In each case these results were obtained by carrying out the policy iteration procedure for the indicated value of τ until convergence on an optimum policy had been achieved. We note that as we decrease τ, the gain begins to increase because, although we are obtaining the same reward per occupancy of state 1, the time spent per occupancy is decreasing. However, the increase in gain as τ is decreased does not begin until τ falls below 0.9, since only at this point is the first alternative in state 1 introduced into the optimum policy. We also

Table 15.6.4 Dependence on τ of the Optimum Policy and Its Evaluation ($v_3 = 0$)

	Optimum Policy	Gain	Relative Value of State 1	Relative Value of State 2
τ	d	g	v_1	v_2
1.00	[2 2 2]	13.34	−1.18	12.66
0.90	[2 2 2]	13.34	−1.18	12.66
0.80	[1 2 2]	13.48	0.70	12.52
0.70	[1 2 2]	13.65	3.07	12.35
0.60	[1 2 2]	13.82	5.50	12.18
0.50	[1 2 2]	14.00	8.00	12.00
0.40	[1 2 2]	14.18	10.56	11.82
0.30	[1 2 3]	14.49	12.46	10.31
0.20	[1 1 3]	15.25	13.70	7.60
0.10	[1 1 3]	17.02	16.11	7.03
0.05	[1 1 3]	18.07	17.54	6.70
0.01	[1 1 3]	19.01	18.82	6.40
0.005	[1 1 3]	19.14	18.99	6.36

observe that as τ is decreased, v_1, the relative value of state 1, increases and v_2, the relative value of state 2, decreases.

As τ becomes small, the optimum policy becomes $\mathbf{d} = [1 \quad 1 \quad 3]$. This result is intuitive because as τ approaches zero, the earning rate for state 1 becomes very large. The object of the system must then be to return to state 1 as quickly as possible. Consequently, the best alternative in each of states 2 and 3 would be the one that had the highest probability of returning the system to state 1. Reference to Table 15.6.3 shows that we would choose the first alternative in state 2 and the third alternative in state 3, and thereby construct the policy $\mathbf{d} = [1 \quad 1 \quad 3]$.

To gain further understanding of these results, we should recall from Chapter 13 that the gain of a system is equal to its expected reward per occupancy divided by its expected waiting time per occupancy,

$$g = \frac{\sum_i \pi_i r_i}{\sum_i \pi_i \bar{\tau}_i} = \frac{\bar{r}}{\bar{\tau}}. \tag{15.6.4}$$

One important consequence of this equation is that even if a state has a non-zero reward per occupancy and a zero waiting time, the gain of the system can still be finite. This occurs in our present case when $\tau = 0$. To evaluate the gain, we note that the optimum policy when $\tau = 0$ is $\mathbf{d} = [1 \quad 1 \quad 3]$ and find the limiting state probability vector $\boldsymbol{\pi}$ for the policy $\mathbf{d} = [1 \quad 1 \quad 3]$ by our usual methods,

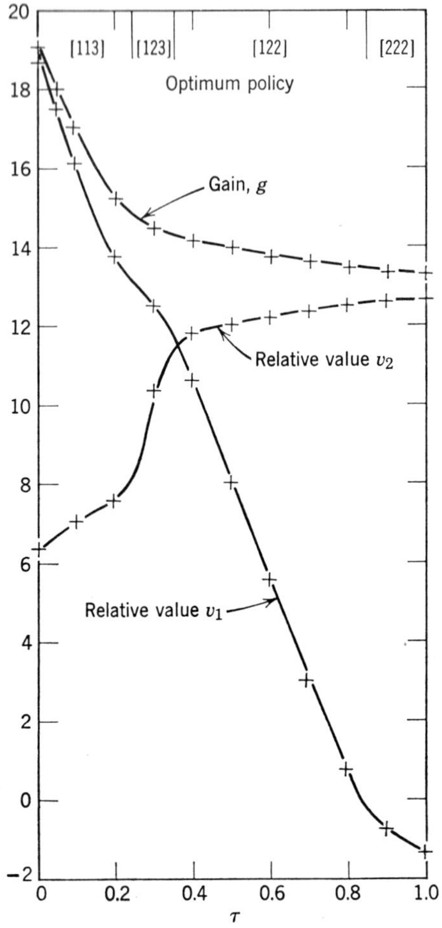

Figure 15.6.1 Dependence on τ of the optimal policy and its evaluation.

$\boldsymbol{\pi} = [25/44 \quad 7/44 \quad 12/44]$. Then we use this result and the data of Table 15.6.3 to obtain the gain when $\tau = 0$ from Equation 15.6.4,

$$g = \frac{\sum_i \pi_i r_i}{\sum_i \pi_i \bar{\tau}_i} = \frac{\bar{r}}{\bar{\tau}} = \frac{(1/44)[25 \cdot 8 + 7 \cdot 16 + 12 \cdot 4.5]}{(1/44)[25 \cdot 0 + 7 \cdot 1 + 12 \cdot 1]} = \frac{366/44}{19/44} = 19.26. \quad (15.6.5)$$

This calculation agrees with the behavior of g for small τ in Figure 15.6.1.

We see from Equation 15.6.4 that the gain depends inversely on the value of $\bar{\tau}$ for a given policy. In fact, the reciprocal of the gain is linear in τ if the first alternative in state 1 is included in the policy,

$$\frac{1}{g} = \frac{\sum_i \pi_i \bar{\tau}_i}{\sum_i \pi_i r_i} = \frac{1}{\bar{r}}[\pi_1 \tau + \pi_2 + \pi_3]. \tag{15.6.6}$$

This equation suggests plotting the reciprocal gain as a function of τ as we do in Figure 15.6.2. We observe that the curve is, in fact, piecewise linear. Of course, when the optimum policy is $\mathbf{d} = [2 \quad 2 \quad 2]$, the first alternative in state 1 is not included in the policy and there is no dependence of gain on τ. When the optimal policy is $\mathbf{d} = [1 \quad 1 \quad 3]$, we measure from the curve that its slope is

$$\frac{d\left(\frac{1}{g}\right)}{d\tau} = \frac{1/15.25 - 1/17.02}{0.2 - 0.1} = \frac{0.06557 - 0.05875}{0.1} = 0.0682. \tag{15.6.7}$$

From Equation 15.6.6 we find

$$\frac{d\left(\frac{1}{g}\right)}{d\tau} = \frac{\pi_1}{\bar{r}} = \frac{25/44}{366/44} = \frac{25}{366} = 0.0683, \tag{15.6.8}$$

thus confirming our measurement.

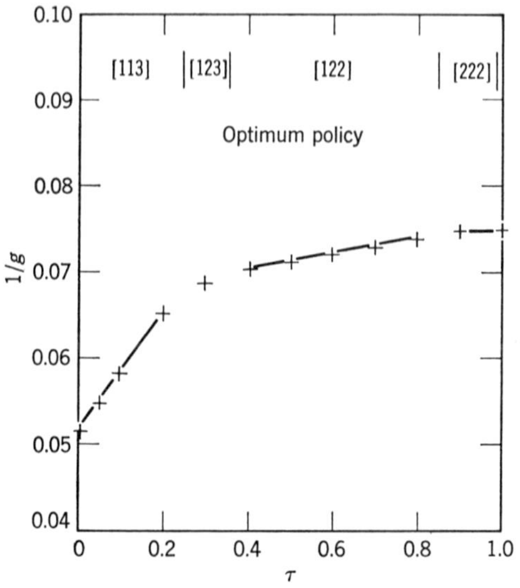

Figure 15.6.2 Dependence of reciprocal gain on τ.

This example indicates the type of parametric study that can be performed on one feature of a problem. Such studies play an important role in gaining the necessary insight into system relationships if we are to suggest new alternatives as well as optimum policies.

Machine Replacement

Let us now consider a machine replacement example that will demonstrate some of the choices we have in modeling a physical system. We shall treat the system initially as an infinite duration process and, as a final step, examine the effect of a finite horizon. We shall model the system first as a one-state semi-Markov process and then as a multiple-state Markov process.

The machine replacement example will emphasize the decisions to be made in maintaining and replacing a machine rather than the depreciation aspects of replacement considered in Chapter 13. We pose the case of a company that must always have available a certain machine to conduct its business. The machine wears out beyond repair at a random time; when it wears out, it must immediately be replaced. However, the yearly cost of operating and maintaining the machine increases with its age. Therefore, it may be wise for the company to replace the machine even before it wears out. This possibility is enhanced by the fact that the trade-in value of a machine of a given age is always higher if the machine is working rather than worn out.

The problem we analyze is this: Should the company allow the machine to wear out and then replace it or should it replace the machine at some age even when it is still working? If so, at what age?

Notation

To place the problem in quantitative form, we define the following quantities:

p = the price of a new machine.

τ = the life of a machine, a random variable. We measure the life of the machine in years (or periods) and consider only the integer values $0, 1, 2, \ldots$ for τ. The statement that $\tau = n$ implies that the actual life of the machine was at least $n - 1$ years but not so great as n years.

$f(n)$ = the probability that $\tau = n$, the probability mass function for machine life. We assume that $f(0) = 0$—there are no initial failures.

$y(n)$ = the cost to operate and maintain the machine from age $n - 1$ to age n.

${}^{\Sigma}y(n) = \sum_{m=1}^{n} y(m)$ = the total cost of operating and maintaining a machine from the time it is new until it reaches age n.

$s_0(n)$ = the trade-in, or scrap, value of a machine of age n that is worn out.

$s_1(n)$ = the trade-in, or scrap, value of a machine of age n that is still operable.

Semi-Markov process formulation

Now we are ready to begin analysis. We shall first model the system as a one-state semi-Markov process. We assume that the system enters the state immediately upon purchase of a new machine and holds there until either the machine wears out or is traded. In either case, the process will make a virtual transition, returning to the same state. The question then is one of defining the holding time and reward characteristics of this state and relating them to the system operating policy. We can specify the policy by an integer k that represents the age at which the machine will be traded if it has not previously worn out. We therefore reduce the problem to one of determining the value of k that will optimize our performance measure.

Let us choose as an initial performance measure the gain (average cost per unit time) that the system will incur if it is allowed to operate indefinitely. For this one-state system, we have immediately from Equation 15.3.20 that the gain is given by

$$g(k) = \frac{r(k)}{\bar{\tau}(k)}, \tag{15.6.9}$$

where $r(k)$ and $\bar{\tau}(k)$ are, respectively, the expected cost per occupancy and mean holding time of the state, given that it is our policy to trade the machine at age k if it has not failed previously. Naturally, we seek the value of k that will minimize the gain $g(k)$.

Mean holding time. We now examine the numerator and denominator of Equation 15.6.9 in detail. To express the denominator, we must first understand the effect of the trade-in policy upon the operation of the system. Figure 15.6.3 illustrates the relationship of the probability mass function for machine life to the holding time mass function of the model. A typical probability mass function for machine life appears as Figure 15.6.3(a). Since the machine is traded at age k if it has not previously worn out, the lifetime distribution is truncated because the longest possible holding time in the state is k. The probability that the holding time will equal k is just $f(k)$, the probability that the machine will wear out in the period from $k - 1$ to k, plus the probability $\sum_{n=k+1}^{\infty} f(n)$ that the machine will still be operating when it reaches age k. If we denote this summation that represents the probability that lifetime will exceed k by ${}^{>}f(k)$,

$${}^{>}f(k) = \sum_{n=k+1}^{\infty} f(n), \tag{15.6.10}$$

then we write the holding time probability mass function for the process under the policy of trading at k as

$$h(n) = \begin{cases} f(n) & n = 1, 2, \ldots, k - 1 \\ f(k) + {}^{>}f(k) & n = k \\ 0 & n = k + 1, k + 2, \ldots . \end{cases} \tag{15.6.11}$$

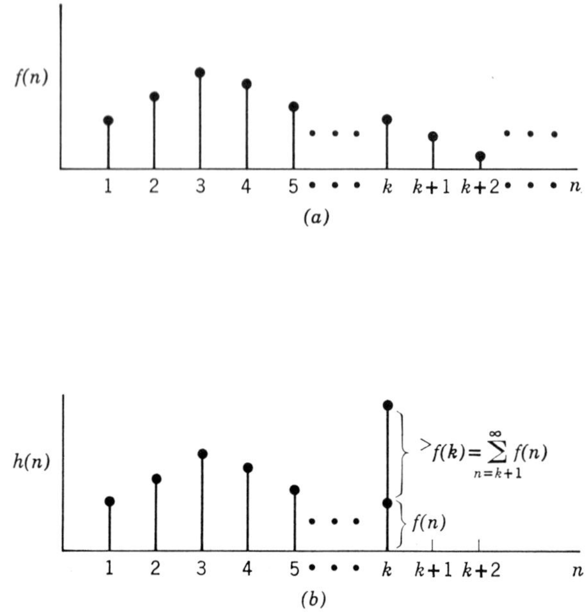

Figure 15.6.3 Construction of holding time probability mass function when policy is to trade an operable machine after k years.
(*a*) The lifetime probability mass function.
(*b*) The holding time probability mass function.

This holding time probability mass function is plotted as Figure 15.6.3(b). The mean of this function, which is the term $\bar{\tau}(k)$ that we need in the denominator of Equation 15.6.9, is then

$$\bar{\tau}(k) = \sum_{n=1}^{k} nf(n) + k\,{}^{>}f(k). \tag{15.6.12}$$

Expected cost per occupancy. Now we turn to the numerator of Equation 15.6.9, $r(k)$, the expected cost per occupancy of the state given that the policy is to trade after k years if the machine is still operable. If the machine fails at some time $n \leq k$, the total operating costs associated with its period of operation will be ${}^{\Sigma}y(n)$; its trade-in value will be $s_0(n)$; and, of course, the price of the new machine is p. The probability of a failure at age n is $f(n)$. Therefore, the contribution to the expected cost per occupancy caused by failures on or before year k is

$$\sum_{n=1}^{k} f(n)[{}^{\Sigma}y(n) + p - s_0(n)].$$

If the machine is still working at k, an event with probability ${}^{>}f(k)$, it will be traded for a new machine. The total operating cost in this case will be ${}^{\Sigma}y(k)$, the trade-in value will be the quantity $s_1(k)$ appropriate to a working machine, and the price of the new machine will still be p. The contribution to the expected cost per occupancy from machines that are traded is thus ${}^{>}f(k)[{}^{\Sigma}y(k) + p - s_1(k)]$.

The expected cost per occupancy is therefore

$$r(k) = \sum_{n=1}^{k} f(n)[{}^{\Sigma}y(n) + p - s_0(n)] + {}^{>}f(k)[{}^{\Sigma}y(k) + p - s_1(k)], \quad (15.6.13)$$

or, equivalently,

$$r(k) = \sum_{n=1}^{k} f(n)[{}^{\Sigma}y(n) - s_0(n)] + {}^{>}f(k)[{}^{\Sigma}y(k) - s_1(k)] + p. \quad (15.6.14)$$

By using the results of Equations 15.6.12 and 15.6.14 in Equation 15.6.9, we can write the gain of the process for the policy described by k as a function of the process characteristics,

$$g(k) = \frac{r(k)}{\bar{\tau}(k)} = \frac{\sum_{n=1}^{k} f(n)[{}^{\Sigma}y(n) - s_0(n)] + {}^{>}f(k)[{}^{\Sigma}y(k) - s_1(k)] + p}{\sum_{n=1}^{k} nf(n) + k\,{}^{>}f(k)}. \quad (15.6.15)$$

Once the data for the process are prescribed, finding the value of k that will minimize the average cost per unit time, $g(k)$, requires only successive substitution of k values into Equation 15.6.15.

Data. Now we shall make the example concrete by specifying numerical values. We shall take the price of a new machine p to be 10,000. We shall use as our lifetime probability mass function $f(\cdot)$ a discrete approximation to the beta distribution. We take the range from 0 to 30 years and use a beta whose mean and variance are both approximately 10. The actual probability mass function we shall use is the one marked N, for normal, in Figure 15.6.4. It is clear from this formulation that we assume that no machine can last longer than 30 years. The complementary cumulative ${}^{>}f(\cdot)$ corresponding to the lifetime probability mass function appears as the curve marked N in Figure 15.6.5.

We assume that the yearly operating expense has the linear form

$$y(n) = y_0 + y_1 n \qquad n = 1, 2, 3, \ldots. \quad (15.6.16)$$

We shall take $y_0 = 300$, $y_1 = 20$ so that yearly operating expense will increase by 20 each year. This function is plotted as the operating cost curve marked N in Figure 15.6.6(a).

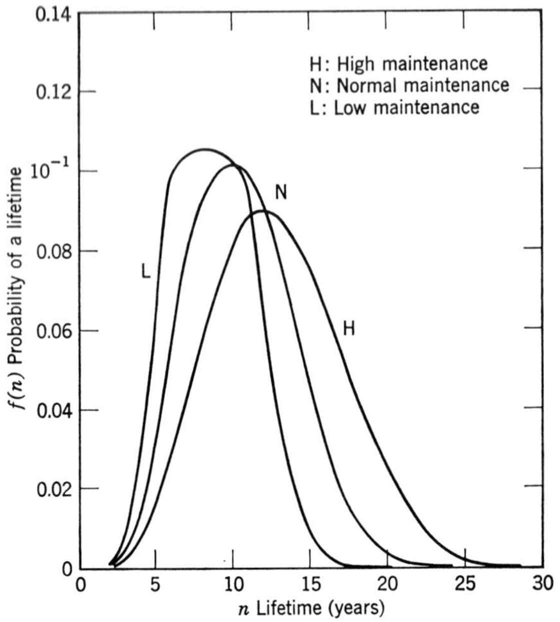

Figure 15.6.4 Lifetime probability mass functions (drawn as continuous curves).

For the trade-in or scrap value of a machine, we use an exponentially decreasing function. For the case where the machine is not working at trade-in, the form is

$$s_0(n) = a_0 + b_0 e^{-c_0 n}, \tag{15.6.17}$$

with $a_0 = 50$, $b_0 = 2000$, $c_0 = 1/7$. The plot of this function appears in Figure 15.6.6(b). Note that it implies a very marked decrease in the value of a relatively young machine if it is not operable. Furthermore, the scrap value decreases very quickly with time until it reaches what we may consider to be the value of the material it contains.

If the machine is working at the time of trade-in, we again use an exponentially decreasing function

$$s_1(n) = a_1 + b_1 e^{-c_1 n}, \tag{15.6.18}$$

but this time with parameters $a_1 = 1500$, $b_1 = 8000$, $c_1 = 1/10$. The plot of $s_1(n)$ in Figure 15.6.6(b) shows that working machines are quite valuable at any age, but their value, of course, decreases with age. The decrease is most rapid for young machines.

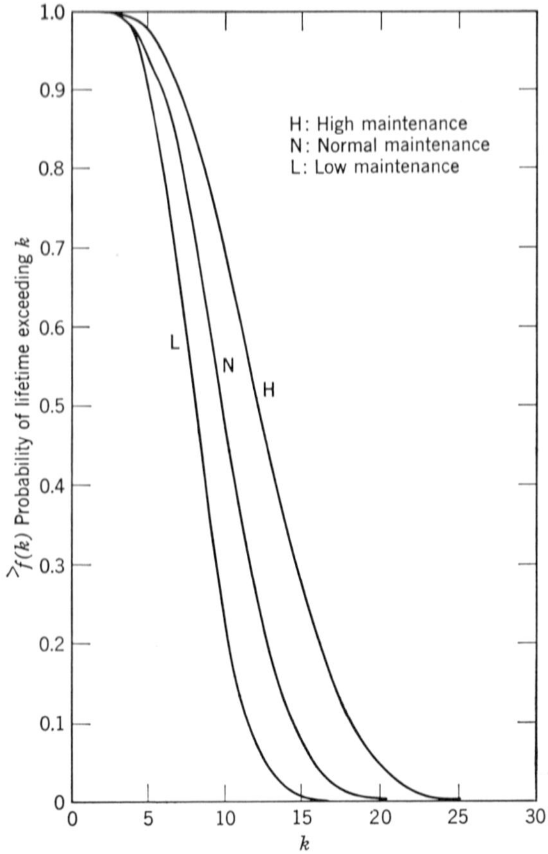

Figure 15.6.5 Lifetime complementary cumulative distributions (drawn as continuous curves).

Optimum replacement policy. Now that we have specified the data for the problem, we can compute the gain $g(k)$ for any value of k by using Equation 15.6.15. The results are plotted as the curve marked N in Figure 15.6.7. We find that the yearly gain $g(k)$ decreases from 1581 when $k = 1$ to a value of 1146 when $k = 5$ and then increases again to a value of 1326 when $k = 30$. The best value of k is therefore 5: machines should be traded when they are 5 years old if they have not failed earlier. The corresponding average yearly cost of operation for the machine installation will be 1146. We thus see how even a one-state semi-Markov model with a reward structure can be used to solve a fairly interesting problem without using a formal optimization procedure like value or policy iteration.

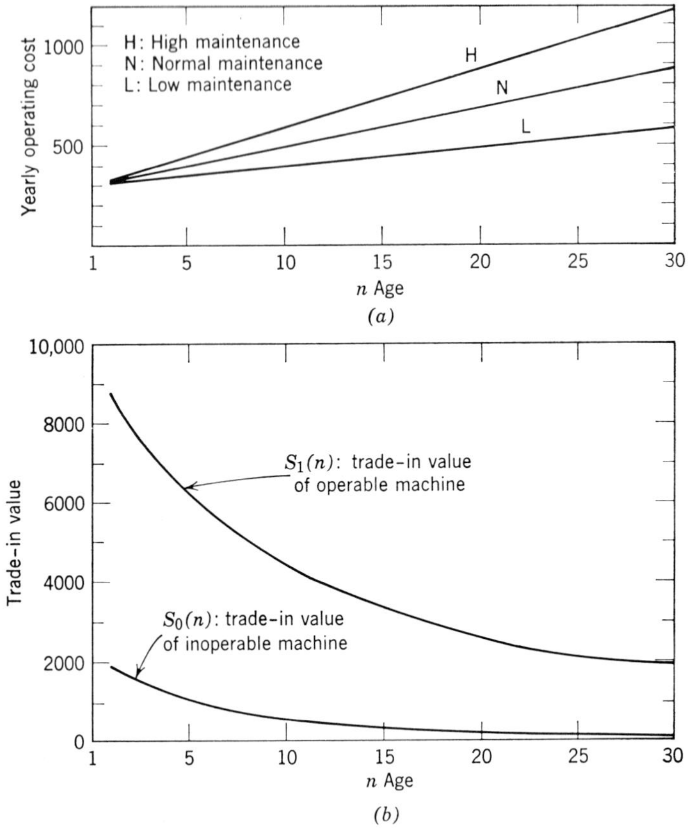

Figure 15.6.6 Operating cost and trade-in data. (*a*) Operating cost. (*b*) Trade-in value.

Maintenance alternatives. To make the problem more interesting, let us add some maintenance alternatives. We first remark that the probability that a machine will survive to reach at least age $n + 1$ given that it has reached age n is

$$\frac{\sum_{m=n+2}^{\infty} f(m)}{\sum_{m=n+1}^{\infty} f(n)} = \frac{{}^{>}f(n+1)}{{}^{>}f(n)}. \tag{15.6.19}$$

We shall call this quantity the conditional probability of survival at age n. By using the information in Figure 15.6.5 we can plot this probability for our problem as the curve marked N in Figure 15.6.8. Note that the conditional probability of

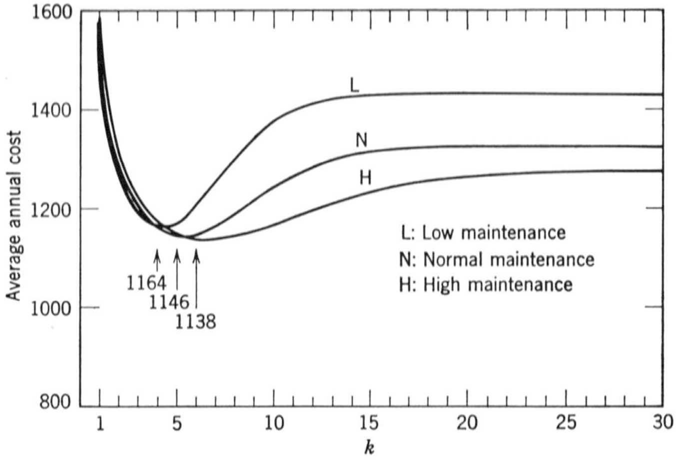

Figure 15.6.7 Average cost per year as a function of trade-in age k.

survival is a continually decreasing function of age. If the lifetime distribution were geometric, the conditional probability of survival would be constant with age.

Suppose now that in addition to the normal policy we have two other procedures for maintaining the machine throughout its life. The low maintenance policy has the same linearly increasing cost equation of Equation 15.6.16, but while $y_0 = 300$, y_1 is now 10, so that yearly costs now increase by only 10 per year rather than 20. The corresponding operating cost function appears as the curve marked L in Figure 15.6.6(a).

However, this cheaper maintenance has its effect on the life of the machine. We assume that this effect is described by saying that the conditional survival probabilities of the machine under low maintenance are the squares of the corresponding conditional survival probabilities under the normal maintenance policy. As shown in Figure 15.6.9, the square of any probability in the range $0 < p < 1$ must be less than the probability; therefore, at virtually any age, the machine that experiences low maintenance will have a lower probability of surviving at least another year. The conditional survival probabilities for the low maintenance policy appear as the curve marked L in Figure 15.6.8. This curve implies the complementary cumulative lifetime curve marked L in Figure 15.6.5 and the lifetime probability mass function marked L in Figure 15.6.4. We observe immediately that low maintenance will produce a shorter expected life.

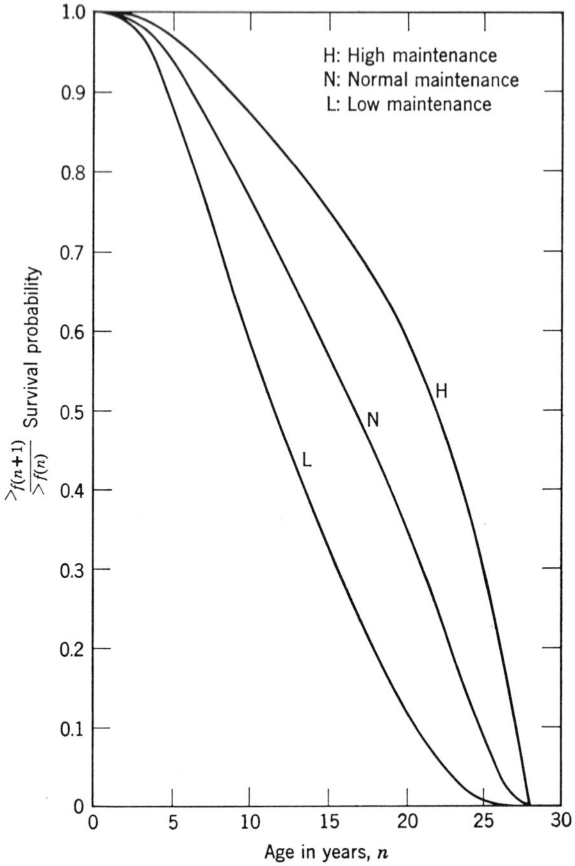

Figure 15.6.8 Conditional probability of survival as a function of age, ${}^{>}f(n + 1)/{}^{>}f(n)$.

We also have a high maintenance policy that is more expensive than the normal policy. The operating costs for this policy once more have the linear form of Equation 15.6.16, y_0 is still 300, but $y_1 = 30$. Thus yearly operating costs increase by 30 a year with the high maintenance policy rather than by 20 a year as they do for the normal maintenance policy. The resulting operating expense as a function of age is plotted as the operating expense curve marked H in Figure 15.6.6(a).

We would expect more expensive maintenance to be more effective, and it is. The conditional survival probabilities for the machine under high maintenance

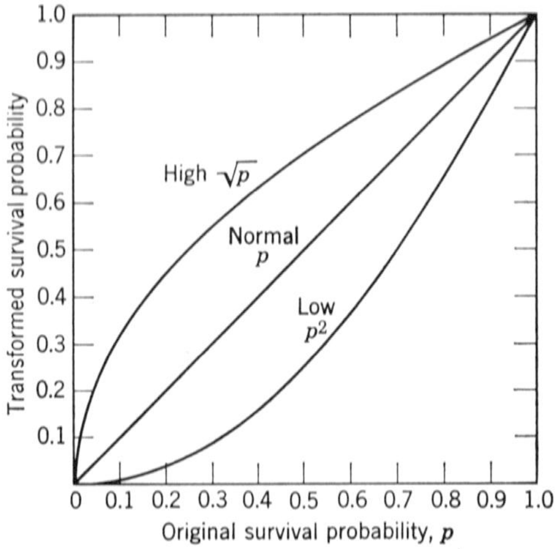

Figure 15.6.9 Illustration of effect of square and square root transformation of survival probabilities.

are the square roots of those for normal maintenance. Figure 15.6.9 shows that the square root of a probability in the range $0 < p < 1$ is greater than the probability. As confirmed by the plot marked H in Figure 15.6.8, the conditional survival probability of a machine receiving high maintenance will therefore be greater than that of a machine receiving normal maintenance at virtually any age. The complementary cumulative lifetime distribution for the high maintenance policy is the curve marked H in Figure 15.6.5; the corresponding lifetime probability mass function is the curve marked H in Figure 15.6.4. It is clear that the high maintenance policy implies a longer expected lifetime for the machine than does the normal maintenance policy.

Optimum maintenance policy. Now we can investigate the question of which maintenance policy will produce the lowest gain or average yearly cost of operation. We again use Equation 15.6.15 for $g(k)$, but we substitute the operating costs and lifetime distributions appropriate to the low and high maintenance policies as we evaluate the gain. The results appear in Figure 15.6.7. The curve marked L shows that the gain associated with the low maintenance policy falls from 1562 when $k = 1$ to 1164 when $k = 4$ and then rises to 1429 when $k = 30$. Therefore if the low maintenance policy were to be used, the machine should be traded at age 4. The resulting average cost per year, 1164, is higher than that for the normal policy where trades occur at age 5.

The high maintenance policy is more attractive as shown by the curve marked H. The gain decreases from 1591 when $k = 1$ to 1138 when $k = 6$ and then increases to 1272 when $k = 30$. If the system is operated according to the high maintenance policy, the machine should be traded at age 6; the corresponding average annual cost would be 1138. We observe that on the whole the high maintenance policy is the most desirable of the three because it achieves the lowest average annual cost. However, we should note that if we were forced to trade when a machine became 4 years old, the high maintenance policy would be the most expensive of the three by a small margin. In fact, trading at years 4 or 5 will produce a relatively low gain regardless of maintenance policy.

Discounting. A valid criticism of our model at this stage would be that it treats money spent in the future as equal in importance to money spent today. To overcome this objection we must introduce discounting. We shall let β be the discount factor appropriate to each year (or period). In the presence of discounting, the appropriate measure of performance is $v(k, \beta)$, the expected present value of all rewards (costs in this case) that will be produced by the infinite duration process. For the one-state example we are considering, Equation 13.6.10 shows that this expected present value will be given by

$$v(k, \beta) = \frac{r(k, \beta)}{1 - h^g(\beta)} \tag{15.6.20}$$

where, for the trading policy defined by k, $r(k, \beta)$ is the expected present value of all costs associated with a single entry of the state and $h^g(\beta)$ is the geometric transform of the holding time probability mass function evaluated at β.

To write $r(k, \beta)$, we first note that if we knew we had to operate the machine through age n, the present value ${}^{\Sigma}y(n, \beta)$ of the operating costs over this period would be

$${}^{\Sigma}y(n, \beta) = \sum_{m=1}^{n} \beta^m y(m). \tag{15.6.21}$$

If we knew that we had to trade the machine at a time n years in the future, we would multiply the difference between price and trade-in value of an n-year-old machine by β^n to obtain the present value of the exchange. With these remarks and the observation that we always enter the state having purchased a new machine, we can write $r(k, \beta)$ by direct analogy with Equation 15.6.13 as

$$r(k, \beta) = \sum_{n=1}^{k} f(n)[{}^{\Sigma}y(n, \beta) + \beta^n(p - s_0(n))] + {}^{>}f(k)[{}^{\Sigma}y(k, \beta) + \beta^k(p - s_1(k))]. \tag{15.6.22}$$

We find $h^g(\beta)$ for the denominator of Equation 15.6.20 by using either Equation 15.6.11 or Figure 15.6.3,

$$h^g(\beta) = \sum_{n=1}^{\infty} h(n)\beta^n = \sum_{n=1}^{k} f(n)\beta^n + {}^{>}f(k)\beta^k. \tag{15.6.23}$$

Optimum policy with discounting. We are now ready to determine the effect of discounting upon our replacement policy. We do this by finding for each maintenance policy and for each discount factor β the value of k that will make the present value of future costs $v(k, \beta)$ from Equation 15.6.20 as small as possible. The results are shown in Figure 15.6.10. The curve marked H shows how the optimum trade-in year k depends on the discount factor under the high maintenance policy; the other curves represent the other maintenance policies. We observe that for any value of β the optimum trade-in year will be greater for the high maintenance policy than for the normal maintenance policy, and greater for the normal than for the low. Furthermore, for any maintenance policy, as we decrease the discount factor from 1 and, hence, weight the future less and less heavily, the optimum trade-in year at first increases and then decreases.

Table 15.6.5 illustrates how the optimum policies indicated in Figure 15.6.10 compare in expected present value. The table shows that for small values of β the

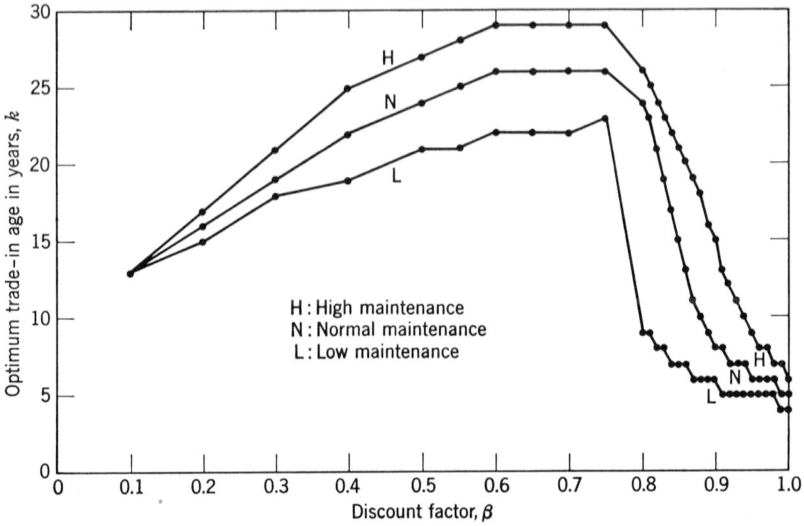

Figure 15.6.10 Optimum trading time for three maintenance practices as a function of discount factor.

Table 15.6.5 Expected Present Value of Future Costs for Three Optimized Maintenance Policies as a Function of Discount Factor

	Expected Present Value of Future Costs			Policy Ordering		
Discount Factor β	Low Maintenance (L)	Normal Maintenance (N)	High Maintenance (H)	Best Policy	Inter-mediate Policy	Worst Policy
0.1	34.8	35.9	37.1	L	N	H
0.2	79.8	82.1	84.8	L	N	H
0.3	142	145	149	L	N	H
0.4	237	236	240	N	L	H
0.50	399	384	383	H	N	L
0.55	528	497	489	H	N	L
0.60	714	657	636	H	N	L
0.65	989	892	847	H	N	L
0.70	1,409	1,251	1,166	H	N	L
0.75	2,077	1,825	1,676	H	N	L
0.80	3,195	2,805	2,555	H	N	L
0.85	5,137	4,632	4,221	H	N	L
0.90	9,041	8,501	7,932	H	N	L
0.95	20,690	20,050	19,450	H	N	L
0.99	114,000	111,900	110,600	H	N	L
0.999	1,161,000	1,143,000	1,135,000	H	N	L

low maintenance policy has the lowest present values of expected cost, while for high values of β the high maintenance policy has this property. The present values of expected cost for the normal maintenance policy are always between those of the other two policies except when β is in the neighborhood of 0.4, at which point the normal policy achieves the lowest present value of the three.

We observe in Table 15.6.5 that the present values of expected cost grow very rapidly with β. Let us take the high maintenance policy as an example. When β is 0.1, the present value of expected cost is 37, while for $\beta = 0.95$ it is 19450. Figure 15.6.11 exhibits this rapid growth of present value for the high maintenance policy graphically in a semi-logarithmic plot; we find that the growth is faster than exponential. The optimized low and normal maintenance policies manifest virtually the same behavior.

To see that this rapid growth of the expected present value as the discount factor approaches one is consistent with our understanding of the problem, refer to Table 15.6.6. The first two columns show the discount factor and the expected present value of future costs at that discount factor for the optimum high maintenance policy from Table 15.6.5. Since we have assumed that the process starts just after the purchase of a new machine, we must add the cost of this machine,

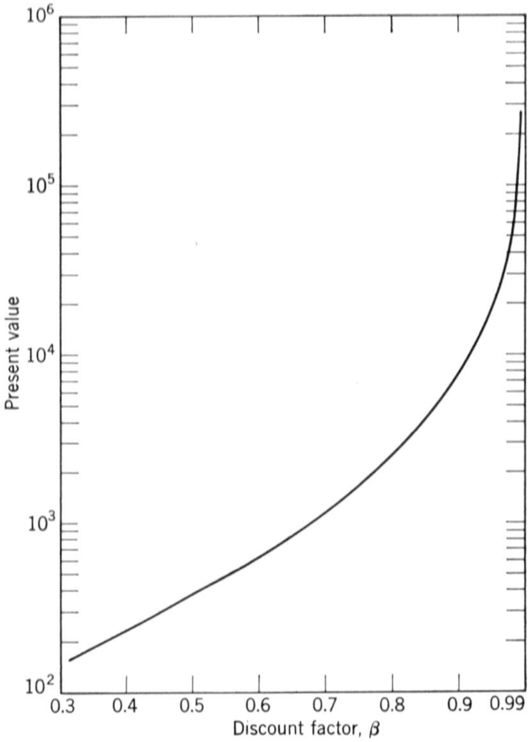

Figure 15.6.11 Present value of optimized high maintenance policy as a function of discount factor.

10,000, to the expected present value of future costs to obtain the expected discounted overall cost $v(\beta)$ of purchasing and maintaining the facility; the third column shows the result.

We call v the equivalent annuital cost of the system. It is computed according to Equation 13.5.7 in the fourth column of Table 15.6.6. As the discount factor increases, the equivalent annuital cost decreases. In fact, as β approaches one, the equivalent annuital cost becomes more and more nearly equal to the gain of this policy, 1138; as Equation 13.7.10 shows, in the limit it would equal the gain.

Finally, we may be curious about the yearly average costs or gains that we shall be incurring by following the optimum policies under discounting. Figure 15.6.12 shows for several values of β the gains of the three optimum maintenance policies described by Figure 15.6.10. It is obvious that the gains of the optimum policies for $\beta < 1$ must be less than those for $\beta = 1$ that we derived earlier, or else we

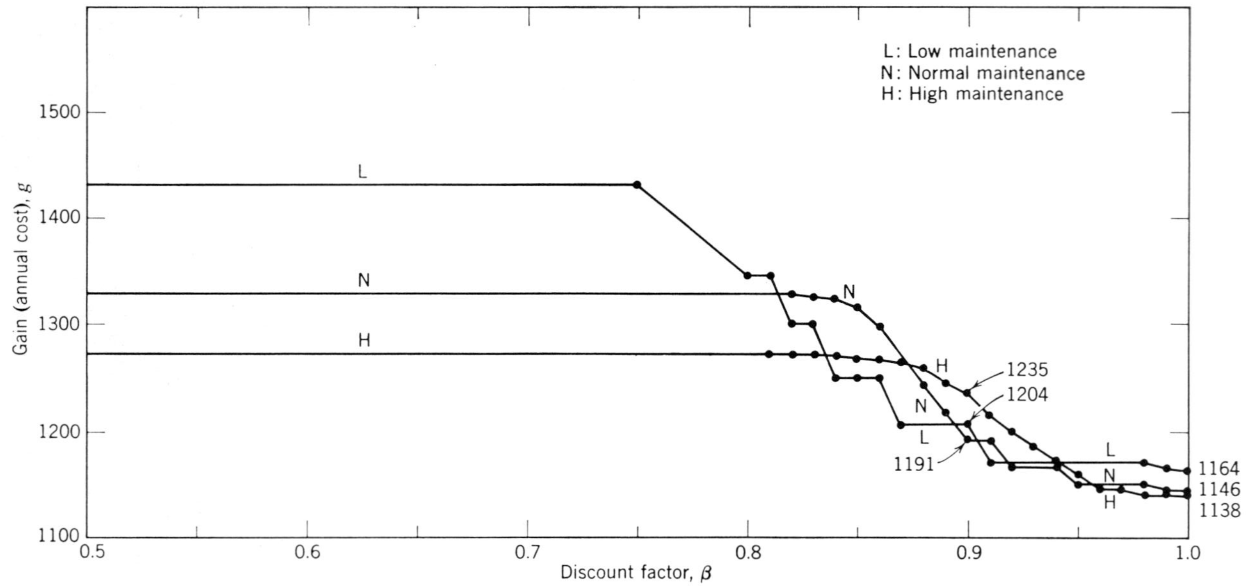

Figure 15.6.12 Gains of three optimized maintenance policies as a function of discount factor.

Table 15.6.6 Equivalent Annuital Cost as a Function of Discount Factor when Optimum High Maintenance Policy is Used.

Discount Factor β	Expected Present Value of Future Costs (Table 15.6.5)	Expected Discounted Over-all Cost: Machine Price (10,000) Plus Present Value of Future Costs $v(\beta)$	Equivalent Annuital Cost $(1 - \beta)v(\beta)$
0.1	37.1	10,037	9,033
0.2	84.8	10,085	8,068
0.3	149	10,149	7,104
0.4	240	10,240	6,144
0.50	383	10,383	5,192
0.55	489	10,489	4,720
0.60	636	10,636	4,254
0.65	847	10,847	3,796
0.70	1,166	11,166	3,350
0.75	1,676	11,676	2,919
0.80	2,555	12,555	2,511
0.85	4,221	14,221	2,133
0.90	7,932	17,932	1,793
0.95	19,450	29,450	1,473
0.99	110,600	120,600	1,206
0.999	1,135,000	1,145,000	1,145

would have a contradiction. What is interesting, however, is the price that must be paid in increased yearly average costs when we take a short-run rather than a long-run point of view. For example, both when $\beta = 1$ (no discounting) and when $\beta = 0.9$, the optimum maintenance procedure is to use the high maintenance policy. We know it is best without discounting because of our previous work; we know it is best when $\beta = 0.9$ from Table 15.6.5. Figure 15.6.10 shows that the best time to trade for the high policy is six years when $\beta = 1$ and fifteen years when $\beta = 0.9$. From Figure 15.6.12 we then learn that the average annual operating cost for the optimized high maintenance policy is 1138 when $\beta = 1$ and 1235 when $\beta = 0.9$, an increase in average annual cost of 97 as a result of discounting the future. Furthermore, although the high maintenance policy is the most profitable to use when $\beta = 0.9$, Figure 15.6.12 shows that it has the highest annual cost of the three maintenance policies under the same condition.

Markov process formulation

The one-state semi-Markov model that we have used has allowed us to obtain important insight into this maintenance-replacement process. However, there is another question we would like to investigate: How should maintenance policy depend on the age of the machine? In the model we have just used, we assumed that the machine was maintained in the same way throughout its lifetime, but that policy may not be optimum. Let us therefore address ourselves to this question by constructing a new model of the system, a simple Markov model.

Consider the replacement system as a Markov process with states that correspond to the possible ages of the machine. More precisely, we shall say that the system is in state i if the age of the machine is between $i - 1$ and i and if the machine was working when its age was $i - 1$. We therefore need as many states as the maximum life of the machine measured in years (or periods). Of course, we now have the possibility of using different maintenance policies for machines of each age.

Transition diagram. Figure 15.6.13 shows a typical section of the transition diagram for the Markov model. Each branch is described by two expressions separated by a semicolon. The first expression is the probability of the transition; the second is the discounted cost associated with it. We draw the diagram for the discounted case, although we are interested also in the problem without discounting, because we may obtain the transition diagram for the case without discounting simply by setting $\beta = 1$. In computing these discounted costs, we assume that operating costs associated with the period from $i - 1$ to i are paid just before i. Furthermore, we assume that if a failure occurs within the $i - 1$ to i time period, it occurs just before i. These considerations are sufficient to specify the transition probabilities and costs under a given policy of maintenance.

For example, suppose that the system is in state i and we are going to retain and maintain the machine rather than trade it. The probability that the machine will

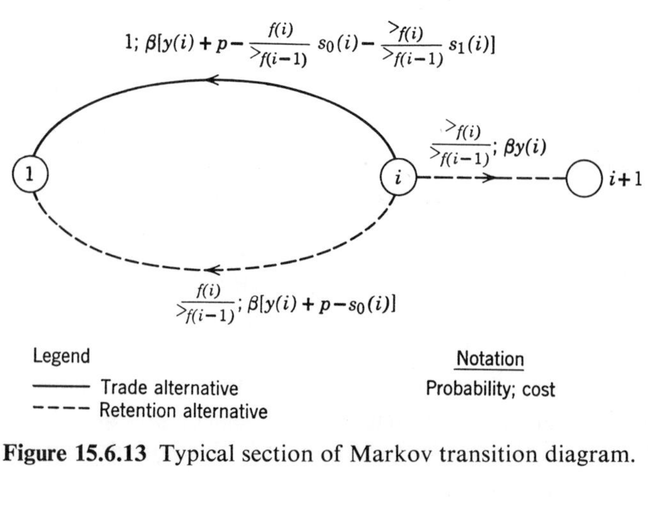

Figure 15.6.13 Typical section of Markov transition diagram.

achieve age i and, hence, enter state $i + 1$ is the conditional survival probability ${}^{>}f(i)/[{}^{>}f(i-1)]$. This is entered as the transition probability on the dashed branch linking state i to state $i + 1$. The cost of this transition is just the operating cost for this period, $y(i)$, multiplied by β to discount it to the beginning of the year. The probability that the machine in state i will fail before reaching age i is one minus the conditional survival probability, or $1 - [{}^{>}f(i)/{}^{>}f(i-1)] = f(i)/[{}^{>}f(i-1)]$. This quantity appears as the transition probability on the dashed branch from state i to state 1 because such a failure would require replacement by a new machine. Since we assume that failures occur just before i, the cost associated with this transition is the operating cost $y(i)$ plus the difference between the price p of the new machine and the trade-in value $s_0(i)$ of the worn-out i-year-old machine, with all these terms discounted by β.

Thus, the dashed lines in Figure 15.6.13 represent the transitions of the process if we never make a replacement unless we are forced to do so. But there is another alternative in each state—to trade in the machine. We assume that if we are in state i and decide to trade the machine, the trade takes place just before the machine reaches age i. The transition corresponding to the trading alternative in state i is the solid branch that links state i to state 1. The transition probability of this branch is, of course, 1. The cost associated with the branch is the operating cost $y(i)$ of the old machine plus the price p of the new machine less the trade-in value of the i-year-old machine. Since in what follows we shall assume that a machine that is to be traded is maintained by the high maintenance policy, the operating cost $y(i)$ will be the cost specified by that policy. Furthermore, the trade-in value is a random variable because the machine may not be working at the time of the trade. As we found in our discussion of the maintenance case, the probability that it is not working is $f(i)/[{}^{>}f(i-1)]$ while the probability that it is working is ${}^{>}f(i)/[{}^{>}f(i-1)]$; the probability calculations are again based on the use of the high maintenance policy. Since the corresponding trade-in values are $s_0(i)$ and $s_1(i)$, the expected net payment at the end of the year is $p - [f(i)/{}^{>}f(i-1)]s_0(i) - [{}^{>}f(i)/{}^{>}f(i-1)]s_1(i) + y(i)$. We multiply this by β to discount the cost to the beginning of the year and, hence, obtain the cost expression that appears on the solid branch of Figure 15.6.13.

The general form of the entire transition diagram for the model appears as Figure 15.6.14. Since there are, in fact, three maintenance policies for each state—low, normal, and high—we should think of three sets of dashed lines emanating from each state; however, only one is shown to simplify the diagram. Nevertheless, in a typical state of the process we have to choose among four alternatives: to trade the machine or to keep it using maintenance at one of the three levels.

Correspondence to semi-Markov formulation. A first question we might ask is how closely this model corresponds to the one-state semi-Markov model. To gain

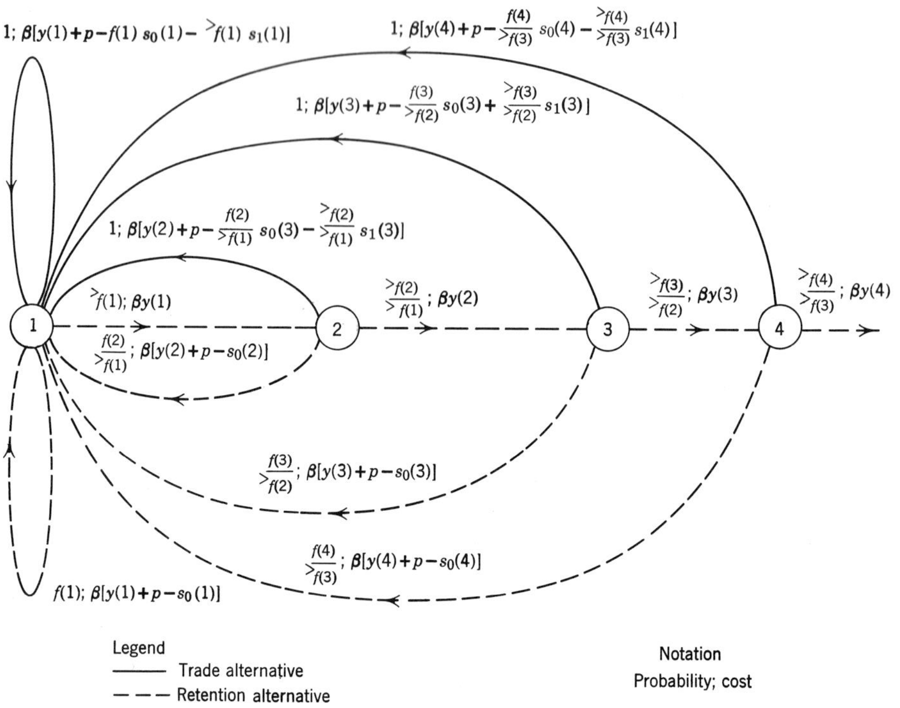

Figure 15.6.14 General form of Markov transition diagram.

insight into this question, we can set the decisions in the Markov model to be the same as those for the semi-Markov model reported in Figure 15.6.10. Suppose, for example, that we select the high maintenance policy. Then in each state of the Markov model we use the high maintenance alternative, but for the state corresponding to the optimum trading age for a given discount factor as given by Figure 15.6.10, we let the decision be to trade the machine. We thus have a Markov equivalent of the semi-Markov high maintenance policy for any β. Now we can compute the present value of state 1 for each β using the general procedures for finding the present values of each state in a discrete-time Markov process with rewards as described in Chapter 13. The results appear in Figure 15.6.15. The present value for each value of β is virtually identical to that shown in Figure 15.6.11 for the original semi-Markov high maintenance policy. The Markov model appears to capture effectively the behavior of the semi-Markov model.

Optimum maintenance policy given machine age. Now we shall exploit the Markov model in its own right. We begin by using policy iteration to see which alternative

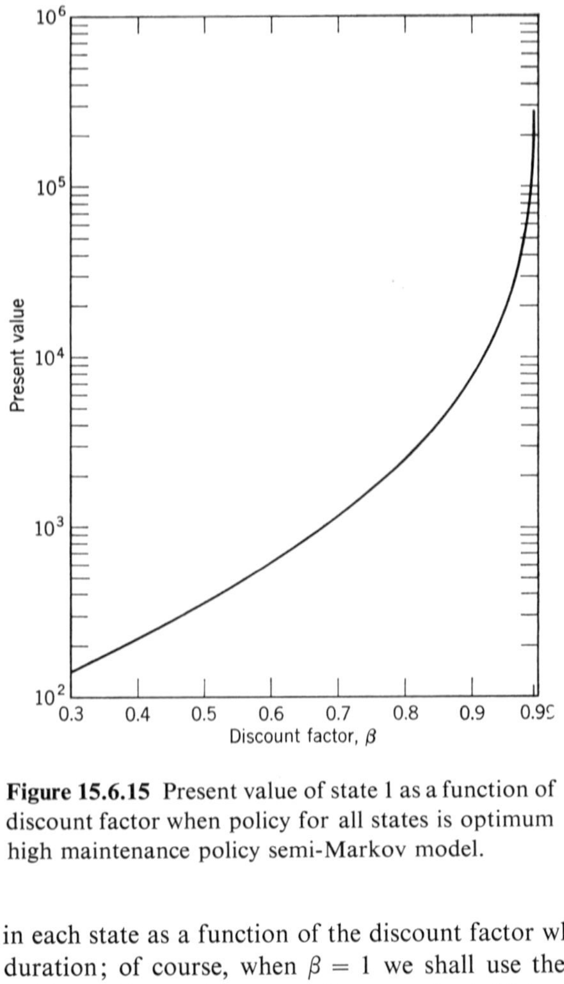

Figure 15.6.15 Present value of state 1 as a function of discount factor when policy for all states is optimum high maintenance policy semi-Markov model.

should be used in each state as a function of the discount factor when the process has an infinite duration; of course, when $\beta = 1$ we shall use the procedure for policy iteration without discounting. For all cases, the initial policy is chosen as the one that minimizes the immediate cost associated with each state.

Figure 15.6.16 shows the results. Along the top there is a plot of the number of iterations until convergence of the policy iteration cycle for each value of the discount factor used. The number of iterations ranges from 2 to 5; of course, at least one iteration is required in any event merely to confirm that the initial policy is optimum. Clearly, policy iteration is computationally efficient for this example.

The major part of Figure 15.6.16 specifies the best alternative to use in each state for discount factors between 0.5 and 1. For example, when $\beta = 1$, we find that we should use low maintenance until a machine is 3 years old, then switch to high

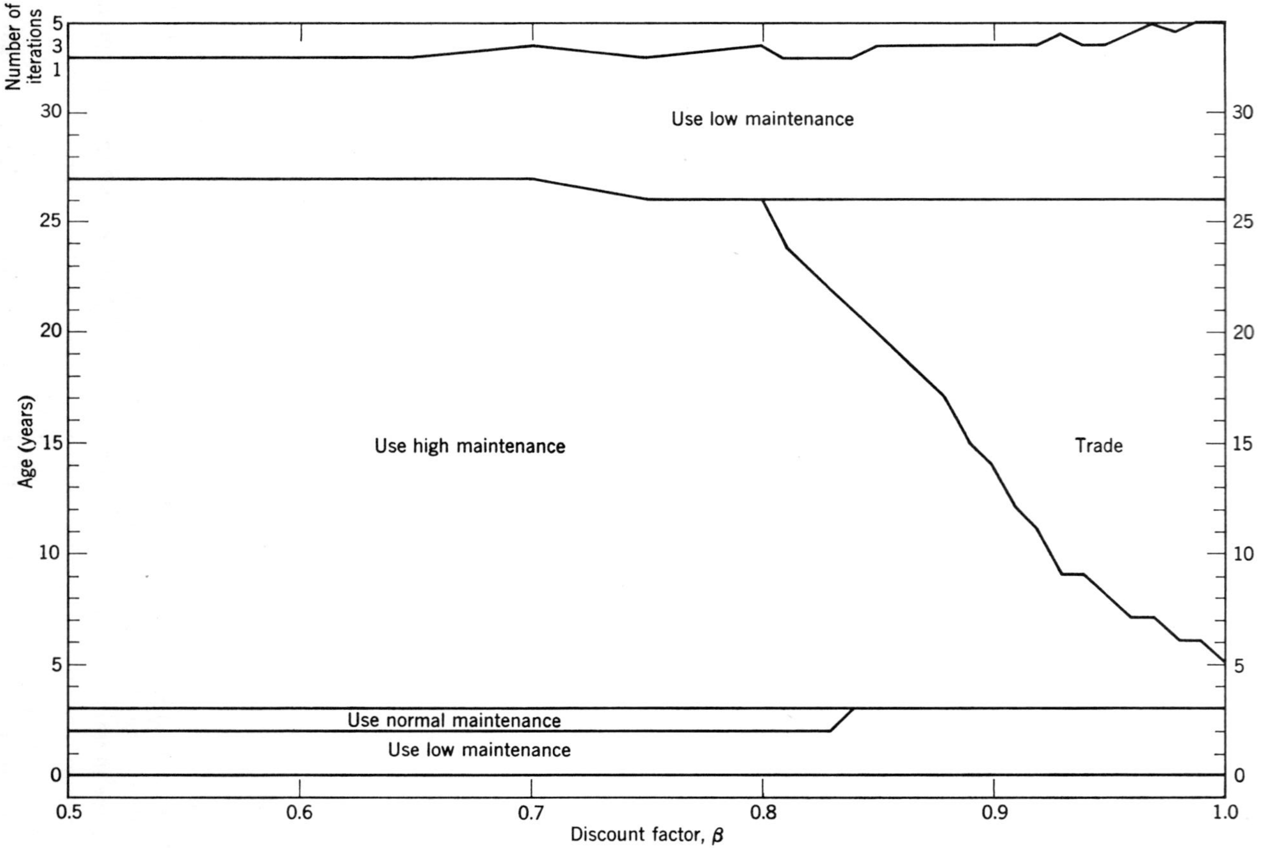

Figure 15.6.16 Optimum trade-maintenance decision as a function of discount factor and age of machine.

maintenance until it is 5, and then trade it. We may regard the specification of low maintenance for very old machines as an anomaly resulting from the finite machine lifetime.

Note that as the discount factor decreases, the major effect is to delay the time of trading until at $\beta = 0.8$ we have a "no-trade" policy for all ages. We also observe that when β falls below 0.84, normal maintenance becomes the best alternative for 2-year-old machines only. We have thus been able to accomplish just what we set out to do, namely, to show how the trade-maintenance policy should depend on the age of the machine.

Horizon effects. However, there is another aspect of the problem that is of some interest, even though it is not initially a proper part of this section. That is the question of how the trade-maintenance policy should change if there is a definite time or horizon at which the machine will no longer be necessary to the company's operations. We shall call the remaining time the horizon distance of the process and assume that the machine is worthless when the horizon arrives.

We can determine how the trade-maintenance policy should depend upon horizon distance as well as age by using the value iteration procedure of Equation 15.2.5 on the Markov model. When $\beta = 1$, we obtain the results shown in Figure 15.6.17. We see that when the horizon is distant, the policy approaches that for the infinite duration case of Figure 15.6.16. However, as the horizon approaches to within 8 years, the age at which the machine is traded increases from 4 years until no trading is done regardless of age when the horizon is only one year away. Thus as the horizon approaches, it is more profitable for the company to maintain the machine with high maintenance and to accept the risk of a breakdown than it is for it to undertake a trade. Such behavior in the face of a horizon is hardly surprising.

Figure 15.6.18 shows the corresponding policy regions for the case $\beta = 0.95$. The policy for a distant horizon agrees with that of Figure 15.6.16. The main lesson to be learned from this figure is that the approach of the horizon has only a small effect on the policy in this example when the future costs of the process are discounted.

Retrospection

We have now completed the discussion of the machine replacement problem. We have explored both problem complications and modeling alternatives. Perhaps the most important lesson to be drawn from this example is that we have considerable flexibility in fitting a Markov or semi-Markov model to a physical system. We can exploit this flexibility both to simplify computational procedures and to increase the spectrum of problems that may be meaningfully treated.

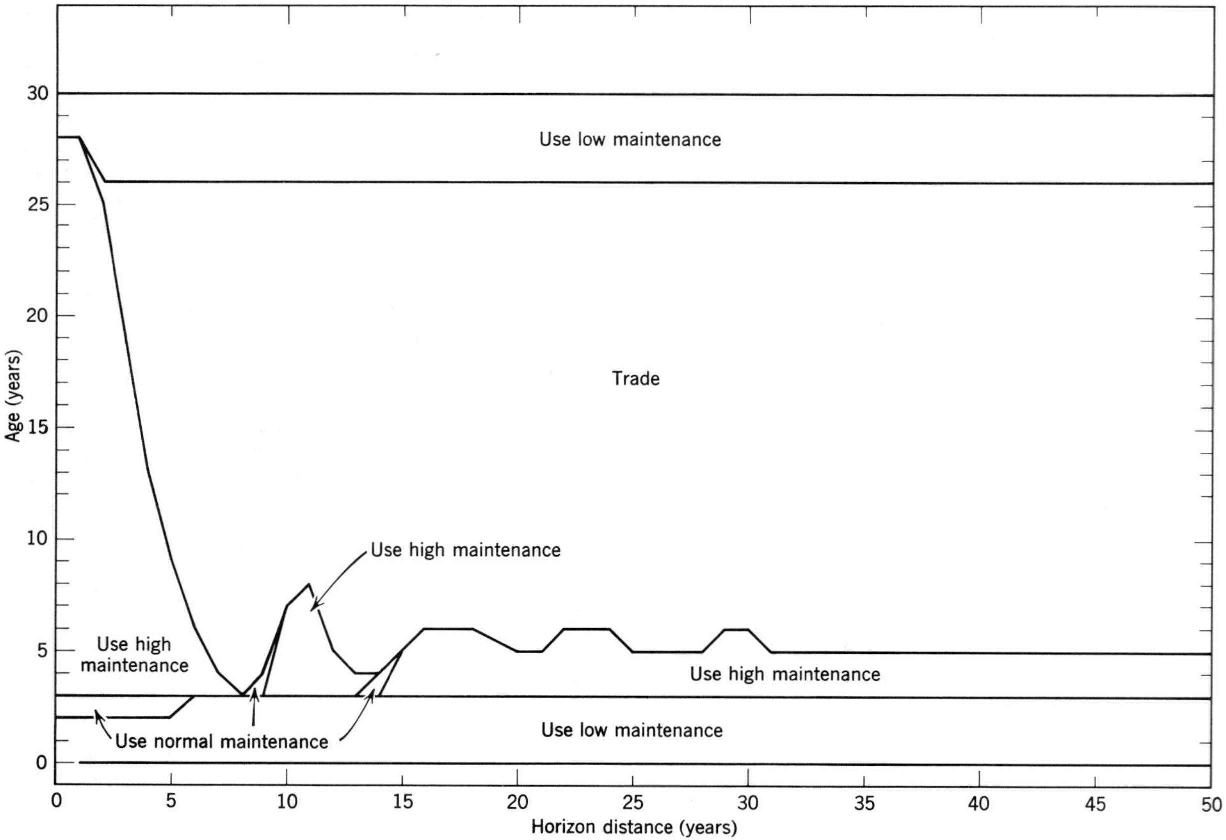

Figure 15.6.17 Optimum trade-maintenance decision as a function of process horizon and machine age with no discounting ($\beta = 1$).

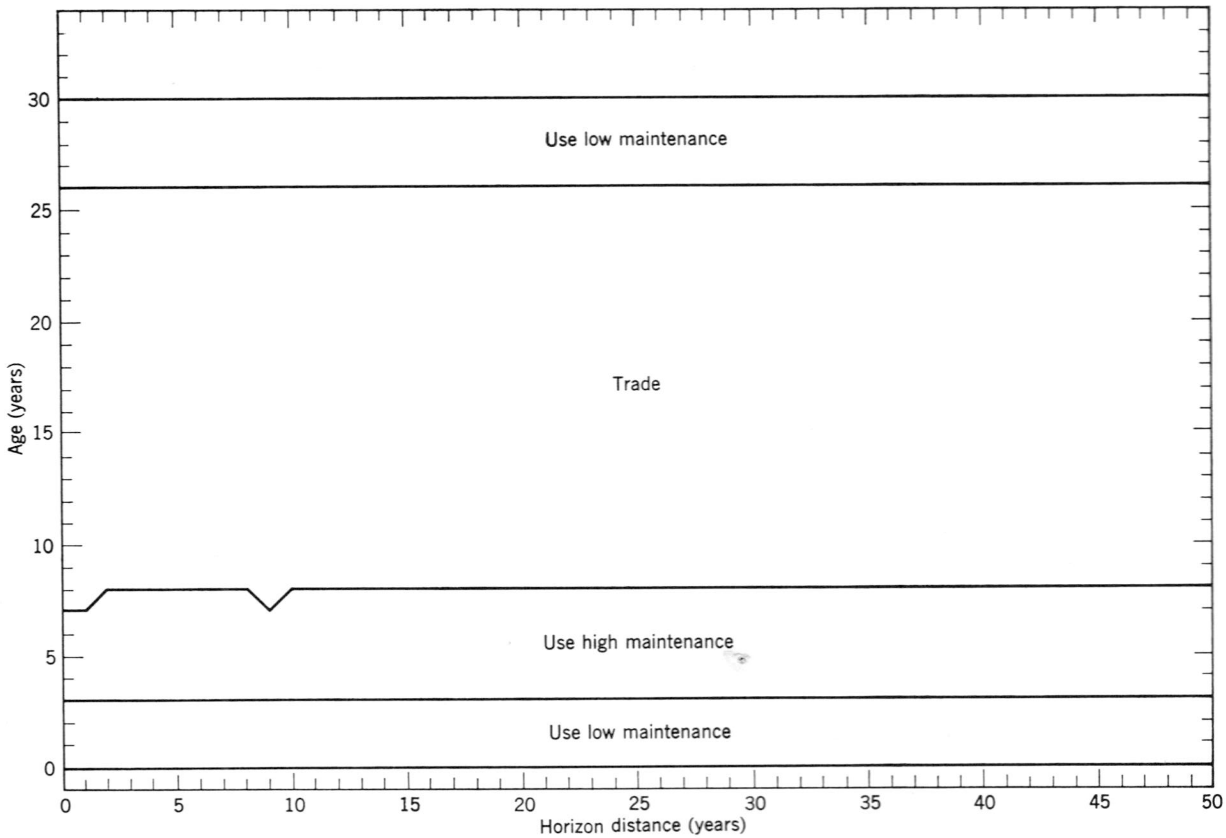

Figure 15.6.18 Optimum trade-maintenance decision as a function of process horizon and machine age for $\beta = 0.95$.

15.7 EXAMPLES OF TRANSIENT PROCESSES

As we learned in Section 15.5, the transient Markov or semi-Markov process with rewards readily lends itself to the policy iteration method. Since many physical processes may be adequately modeled by transient Markovian reward processes, we find this type of process very important in applications. The baseball example of *Dynamic Programming and Markov Processes* is an illustration of a transient Markov process with rewards, and we shall construct many others in the same vein. However, let us first concentrate on the deterministic transient Markov processes with rewards, for although it is a rather special and simple case, it provides insight into several important problems.

The Deterministic Transient Process with Rewards

Consider a transient Markov process with rewards where every transition probability is either 1 or 0. There is but one trapping state for the process, state N; rewards cease when this state is entered. When the system is in state i, it will make its next transition to a state j that depends on the alternative k used in this state. As a result of this transition, the system earns a reward r_{ij}^k. A selection of an alternative in each state constitutes a policy. We define v_i as the expected reward that the system will earn before entering the trapping state if it has just entered state i. In view of Equation 15.5.1, we know that for a given policy the quantities v_i must be related by the equations

$$v_i = \sum_{j=1}^{N} p_{ij}(r_{ij} + v_j) \qquad i = 1, 2, \ldots, N, \tag{15.7.1}$$

where r_{ij} is the reward for a transition to state j under the specified alternative in state i, and p_{ij} is equal to one only for the state j to which the alternative requires that the system must go. When we insist that $v_N = 0$, Equations 15.7.1 allow us to calculate the expected reward due to starting in each state for the policy specified.

Of course, what we are really interested in doing is finding the policy that will maximize the reward to be obtained by entering each state. We accomplish this by policy iteration. Since Equations 15.7.1 provide a policy evaluation procedure, we need only add a test criterion based on expression 15.5.9 to complete the iteration cycle. The test criterion is

$$\sum_{j=1}^{N} p_{ij}^k(r_{ij}^k + v_j), \tag{15.7.2}$$

where we realize again that the summation will always have exactly one term. By successive policy evaluation and policy improvement we are led ultimately to the

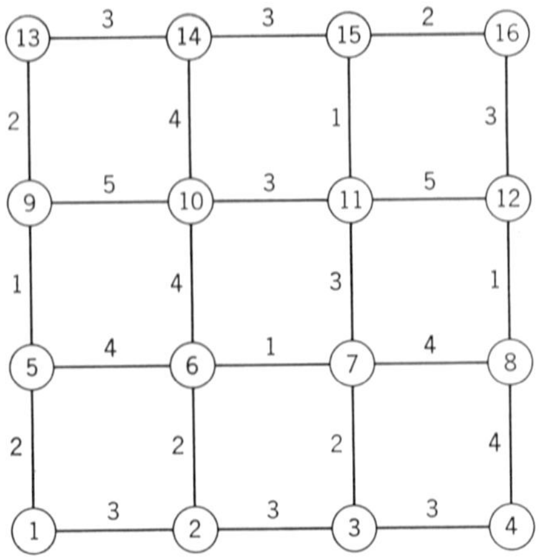

Figure 15.7.1 A network problem.

policy with the highest values of v_i. The fact that we are dealing only with deterministic processes allows us to carry out the policy iteration procedure in most cases by simple graphical methods. Since the problem is essentially one in state connectivity, we can think of the problem as one of finding the best way of connecting a network so as to produce a longest or shortest path through it. The analogy and computational procedure are best illustrated by an example.

A Network Example

Figure 15.7.1 shows a 16-state network with connecting branches. We can think of the 16 states as towns and the connecting branches as roads between the towns whose lengths are as indicated. The problem we pose is this: What is the shortest route between town 1 and town 16? We allow passage of each connecting road in either direction.

Initial policy

To solve this problem we begin by selecting an initial policy. A policy in this problem consists of specifying for each town the road to be used when leaving that town. For our initial policy we select arbitrarily the route specification indicated in Figure 15.7.2. Note that there is a unique way to reach town 16 from every town in the network. Now we perform a policy evaluation to see how far it will be from each town to town 16 under this policy. Although we are in fact solving Equations 15.7.1 for the values v_i, the computation is trivially done by inspection of the

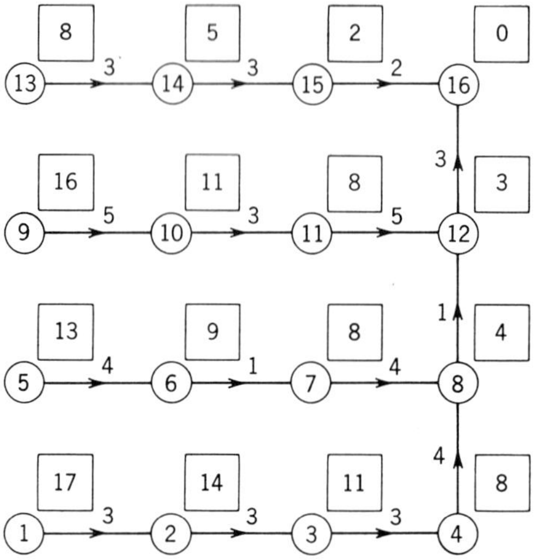

Figure 15.7.2 Initial policy evaluation.

figure. The values v_i for each state appear in the square boxes; thus we observe that the distance from town 5 to town 16 under this policy is $v_5 = 13$. However, we have no reason to believe that the distance 17 produced by this policy is the shortest distance from town 1 to town 16, so we perform a policy improvement using expression 15.7.2 as the quantity to be minimized.

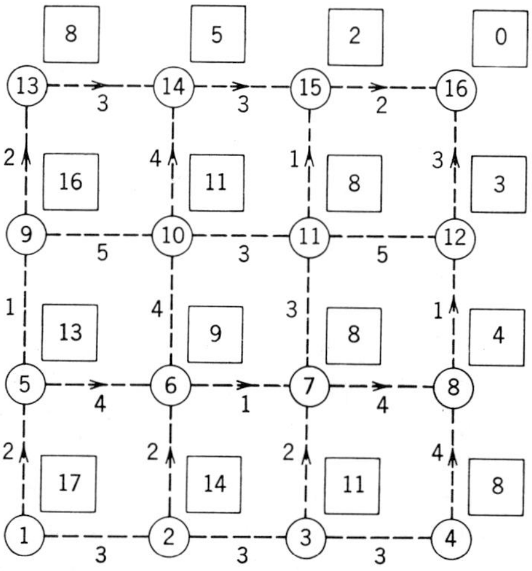

Figure 15.7.3 First policy improvement.

First policy improvement

The policy improvement is illustrated graphically in Figure 15.7.3. We first record by each state the values for the previous policy found in Figure 15.7.2. Then for each state we compute for each neighboring state the sum of the value of the neighboring state and the distance to it. The neighboring state with the lowest sum then is the preferred direction of leaving a state. Consider state 10, for example. State 10 has four neighbors, states 14, 11, 6, and 9. State 14 has a value of 5 and is at a distance 4 for a sum of 9; state 11 has a value of 8 and a distance 3 for a sum of 11; state 6 has a value of 9 and a distance of 4 for a sum of 13; and state 9 has a value of 16 and a distance of 5 for a sum of 21. The smallest sum is 9 and, hence, the best way to depart from state 10 is in the direction of state 14. We repeat this procedure for each state in the network; the states can be examined in any order. We note that if any of the branches were unidirectional, then the minimization would be carried out only on those neighboring states to which departures could be made.

The new policy that results from this procedure is indicated by the arrowheads in Figure 15.7.3. However, Figure 15.7.4 reveals the policy more clearly. We observe that the direction of leaving several towns has been changed. Policy evaluation in the same manner as before shows that the distance from town 1 to town 16 is now 15, a reduction of 2 over the previous policy. We find, further, that when we compare Figure 15.7.2 with 15.7.4 the values of all states have either decreased or remained unchanged.

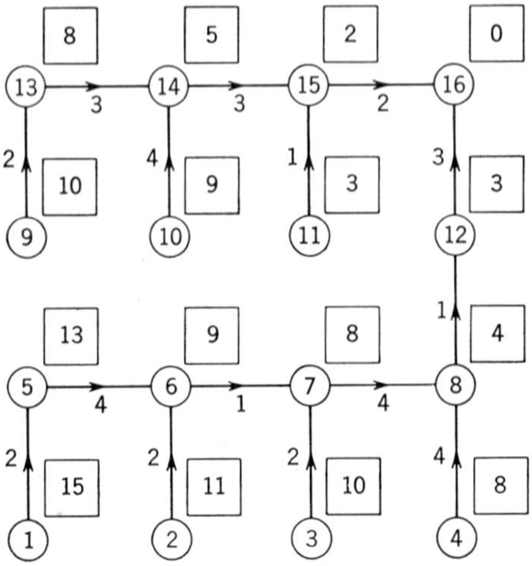

Figure 15.7.4 Second policy evaluation.

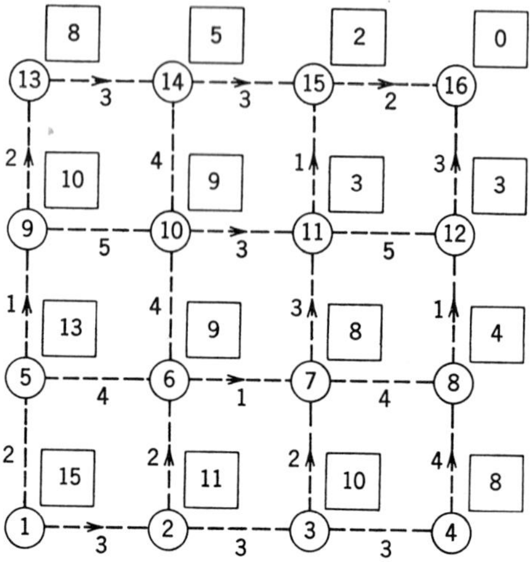

Figure 15.7.5 Second policy improvement.

Second policy improvement

However, we are still not sure that we have found the best policy and hence the shortest route. We therefore perform another policy improvement in Figure 15.7.5 using the values from Figure 15.7.4. The policy produced appears in Figure 15.7.6. The direction of leaving several states has again been changed. Policy

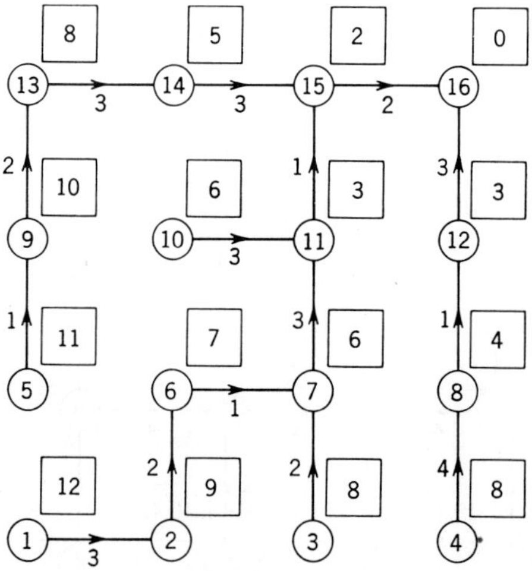

Figure 15.7.6 Third policy evaluation.

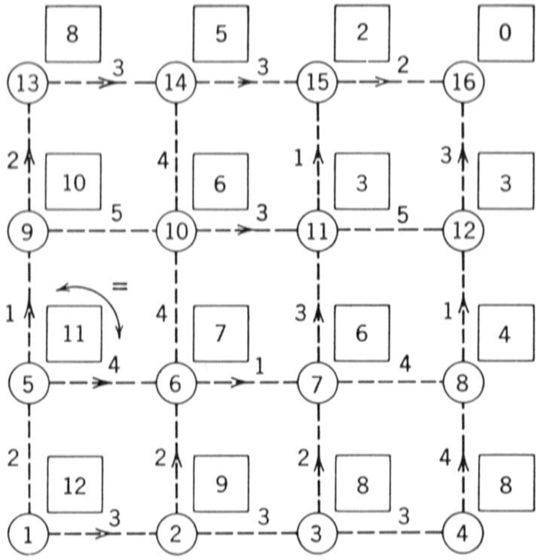

Figure 15.7.7 Third policy improvement.

evaluation shows that the distance from town 1 to town 16 is now 12, a reduction of 3. We next attempt another policy improvement in Figure 15.7.7, but we find that the policy of Figure 15.7.6 again appears; the process has converged. (We note in Figure 15.7.7, however, that leaving town 5 in the direction of town 6 or 9 produces the same minimum distance of 11.)

Thus Figure 15.7.6 shows that the shortest route from town 1 to town 16 is of length 12 and passes through towns 2, 6, 7, 11, and 15 in that order. Of course, the figure also shows the shortest route from any other town to town 16. Except for the confusion that would result in explaining the procedure, most of the computations we have performed could be accomplished on the same diagram.

The longest path

We see immediately that the same procedure can be used to find the longest path through a network by maximizing rather than minimizing in the policy improvement. However, we can only apply this procedure where the connectivity of the network or directional requirements on the branches eliminate the possibility of circular paths. Otherwise the policy iteration procedure would complete such a path in its attempt to maximize the gain of the system, and we would not have the transient process we desire. To pique interest in this version, we note that the longest route from town 1 to town 16 is of length 21 if all branches must be traversed in the direction from a low-numbered to a high-numbered town.

Application to trajectory optimization

The range of problems in which the deterministic transient process can be applied is wide, indeed. For example, we could consider Figure 15.7.1 to describe a rocket trajectory problem. We imagine a rocket to be launched from a point on the ground toward a point in the sky. We think of the states in Figure 15.7.1 as various altitude-distance stations, with state 1 representing the launch point and state 16 the desired terminal point. The numbers associated with the branches could then be the fuel cost incurred by having the rocket follow that branch. Of course, we would want to think of the branches as unidirectional and allow only movements up and to the right. Thus the trajectory 1, 5, 9, 13, 14, 15, 16 represents a vertical climb followed by a horizontal flight. On the other hand, the trajectory 1, 2, 3, 4, 8, 12, 16 indicates a horizontal flight followed by a vertical climb. The problem is to find which of the many possible trajectories will produce the lowest fuel consumption. We could also think of the numbers on the branches as times and then minimize the time to climb. In either case we have solved the problem.

Project Scheduling

A particularly interesting application of the deterministic transient Markov process lies in the area of project scheduling. It can be used to schedule N jobs so that they will be completed in the shortest possible time.

Project characteristics

As an example, let us consider the eight-job project ($N = 8$) for which the time t_i to complete each job i is shown in Table 15.7.1. The scheduling problem would be trivial but for the fact that some jobs must precede others: If we are building a house, we must plaster the walls before we paint them. We give the precedence information by a set of quantities x_{ij} defined by

$$x_{ij} = \begin{cases} 1 & \text{if job } i \text{ must immediately precede job } j \\ 0 & \text{otherwise.} \end{cases} \tag{15.7.3}$$

Note that if job i must immediately precede job j and if job j must immediately precede job k, then job i must precede job k, but not immediately. For our example we assume the precedence information in Table 15.7.2. Thus job 1 must be completed before either job 3 or job 4 can be started. From column 5 we see that only job 2

Table 15.7.1 Job Completion Times

Job, i	1	2	3	4	5	6	7	8
Completion time, t_i	3	1	4	6	2	3	5	4

Table 15.7.2 Job Precedences

$x_{ij} = 1$ if job i must immediately precede job j

x_{ij} i \ j	1	2	3	4	5	6	7	8
1			1	1				
2					1			
3								1
4						1	1	
5						1	1	
6								1
7								
8								

must immediately precede job 5. Because rows 7 and 8 contain no 1's, jobs 7 and 8 are the last jobs done in the project—no jobs follow them. Because columns 1 and 2 contain no 1's, jobs 1 and 2 are the first jobs done in the project—no jobs precede them.

The project network

We now proceed to find the minimum total time schedule. Our first step is to construct the project network shown in Figure 15.7.8. State i in this network represents the event that job i has begun. The precedence information of Table 15.7.2 is the basis for drawing the branches in this diagram: if $x_{ij} = 1$ then we draw a directed branch from state i to state j to indicate the precedence. The branches are labeled with the completion times for each job from Table 15.7.1. Thus the project network combines both completion time and precedence information into one easily visualized graphical structure. The project network is the key to solving project scheduling problems by using the deterministic transient Markov model.

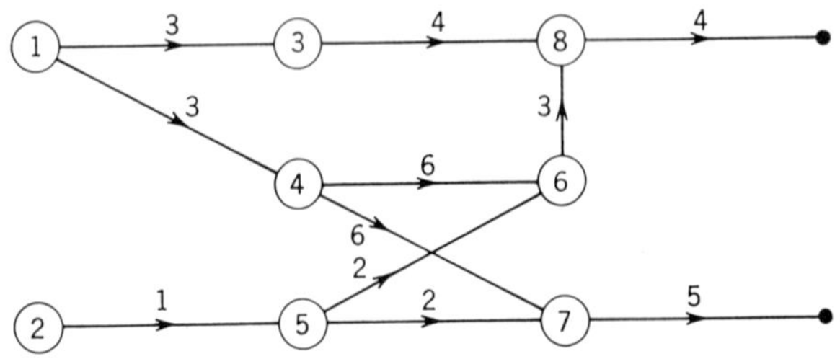

Figure 15.7.8 Project network.

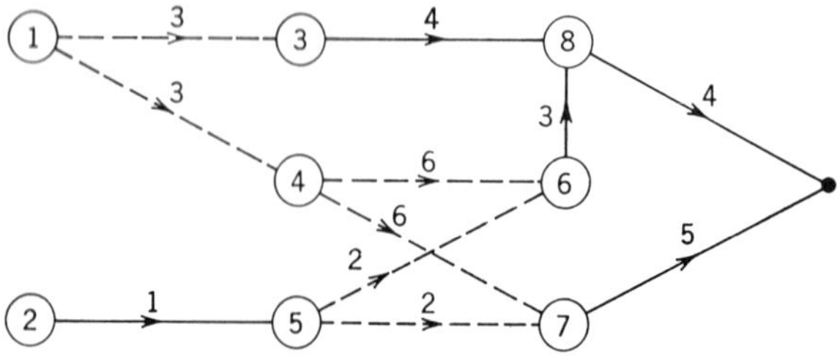

Figure 15.7.9 Project network based on latest starting times.

Latest starting times

We define ℓ_i to be the latest possible time we can start job i as measured from the end of the project. Since the latest possible time to start any job measured in this sense is the time to complete it plus the latest possible time to start any jobs that must follow this job, we have

$$\ell_i = t_i + \operatorname*{Max}_j x_{ij}\ell_j \qquad i = 1, 2, \ldots, N. \tag{15.7.4}$$

Although these equations cannot be solved by ordinary algebraic means, we note that if we draw the project network in the form shown in Figure 15.7.9, then the problem of finding the longest path through this directed network is exactly the same problem as determining the order in which the jobs should be done. We observe that only in states 1, 4, and 5 is there any choice concerning the path to be taken through the network. We use policy iteration to find out which choices should be made to maximize the distance through the network.

We begin by making arbitrary choices to produce the policy indicated in Figure 15.7.10. The evaluation of this policy shows that $\ell_1 = \ell_4 = 11$ is the longest

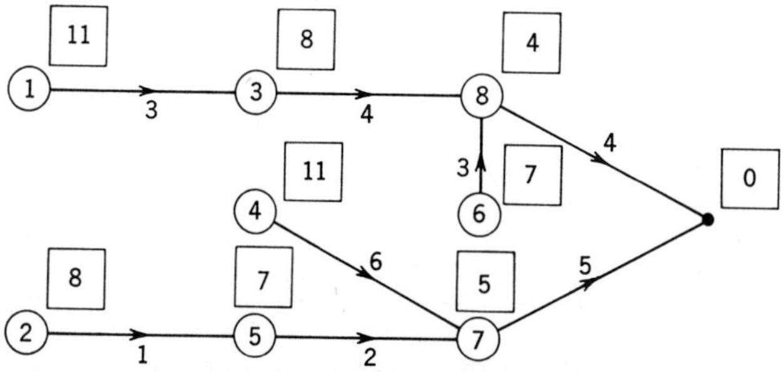

Figure 15.7.10 First policy for latest starting time network.

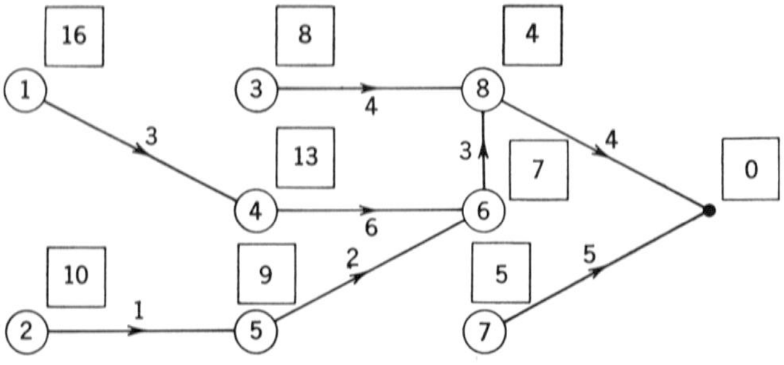

Figure 15.7.11 Second policy for latest starting time network.

distance through the network achieved with this policy. Our next step is a policy improvement based on these values of ℓ_i. Thus in state 1 both state 3 and state 4 lie at a distance of three, but since $\ell_3 = 8$, $\ell_4 = 11$, we can find a policy of longer paths by connecting state 1 to state 4. In the same way we find that states 4 and 5 should be connected to state 6. The resulting policy appears in Figure 15.7.11. Its evaluation shows that all values of ℓ_i either increase or stay the same. Policy improvement produces the same policy again; the policy iteration procedure has converged. The policy of Figure 15.7.11 is the policy that maximizes distance through the network and, hence, solves Equations 15.7.4.

Interpretation. There are a number of observations we can make about Figure 15.7.11. First, the time to complete the project T is equal to the maximum of the ℓ_i,

$$T = \operatorname*{Max}_{i} \ell_i, \tag{15.7.5}$$

which in this case is 16. Second, the longest path through the network, which consists of jobs 1, 4, 6, and 8, is the so-called "critical path" of the project. Shortening the time to complete a job in the critical path is a necessary condition for shortening the time to complete the project. Third, we can construct the Gantt chart, or time map of the jobs, shown in Figure 15.7.12 directly from the network of Figure 15.7.11. We observe from the Gantt chart that each noncritical job is begun as late as the precedences will allow. We note from the chart that this particular schedule requires that three jobs be simultaneously in progress between times 8 and 7 and between times 5 and 4 as measured from the end of the project.

Earliest starting time

We can solve the same problem in an alternative way by defining e_i to be the earliest time from the beginning of the project that job i can be started. Since no job can be started until all the jobs that must precede it have been completed, we have

$$e_i = \operatorname*{Max}_{j} x_{ji}(e_j + t_j) \qquad i = 1, 2, \ldots, N. \tag{15.7.6}$$

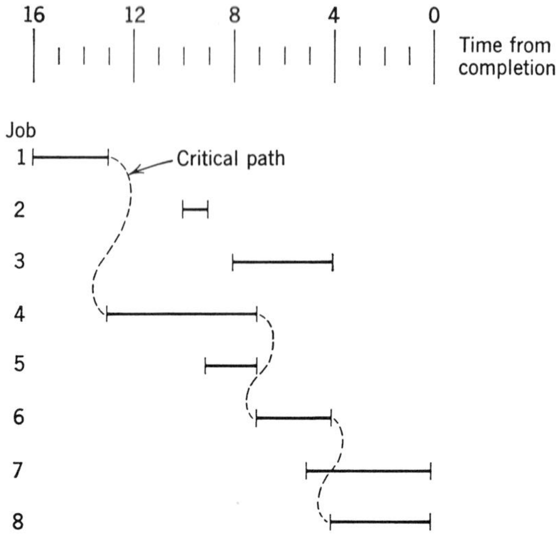

Figure 15.7.12 Gantt chart for latest starting time network.

Once again we can use the deterministic transient Markov policy iteration procedure to solve these equations by drawing the project network in the form shown in Figure 15.7.13. We coalesce nodes 1 and 2 because these jobs can be started immediately upon the inception of the project. Then the problem becomes one of finding the longest paths through the network from this state. Choices occur only in the direction *from* which states 6, 7, and 8 will be entered; we use policy iteration to make these choices.

We begin by using the deliberately inferior policy of Figure 15.7.14 as our initial policy. The evaluation of this policy shows a longest distance $e_8 + t_8 = 11$ through

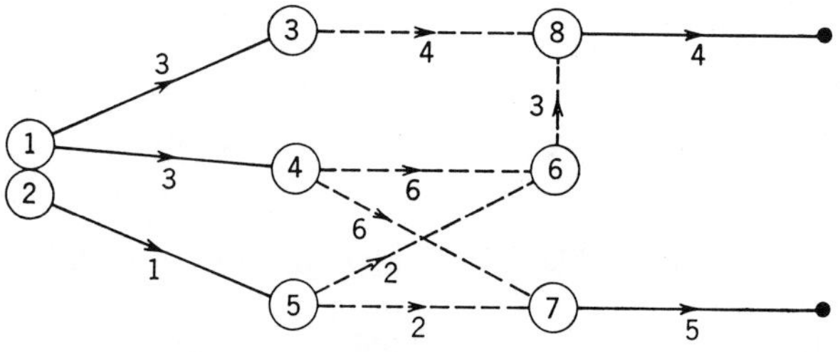

Figure 15.7.13 Project network based on earliest starting times.

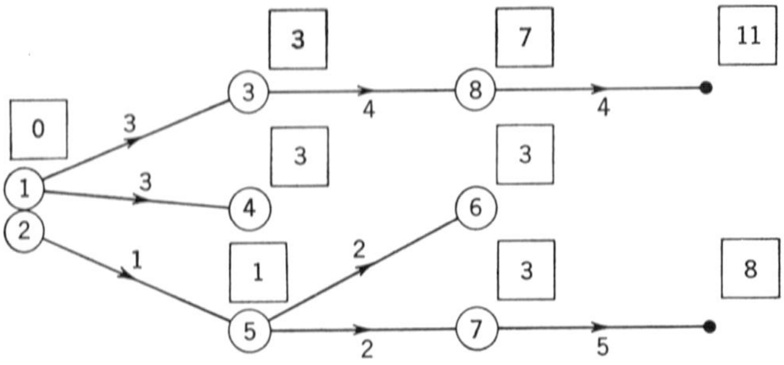

Figure 15.7.14 First policy for earliest starting time network.

the network. We use these values of e_i as the basis for a policy improvement. Thus, since states 3 and 6 must precede state 8, we compare $e_3 + t_3 = 3 + 4 = 7$ with $e_6 + t_6 = 3 + 3 = 6$, and choose to connect state 8 to state 3. A similar computation shows that states 6 and 7 should be connected to state 4.

The new policy and its evaluation appear in Figure 15.7.15. The longest distance through the network is now $e_7 + t_7 = 14$, but we still may not be finished. A policy improvement makes the change that state 8 should be connected to state 6 to produce the policy of Figure 15.7.16. The evaluation of this policy shows that the longest distance through the network is now $e_8 + t_8 = 16$. An attempt at further policy improvement produces the same policy; we have converged and, in the process, solved Equation 15.7.6.

Interpretation. The project network of Figure 15.7.16 is a complete solution to the problem. The time to complete the project is given by

$$T = \operatorname*{Max}_i \, (e_i + t_i) \tag{15.7.7}$$

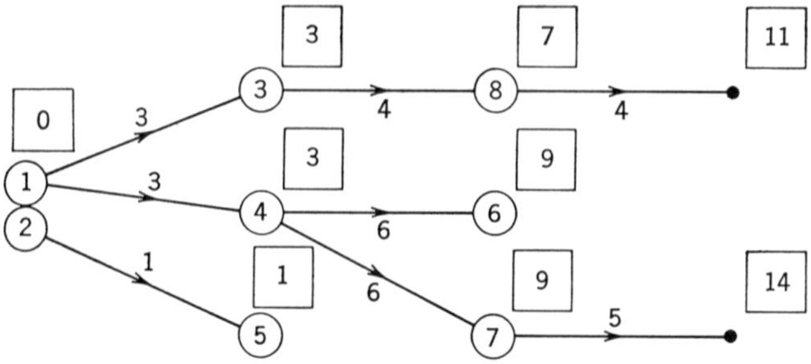

Figure 15.7.15 Second policy for earliest starting time network.

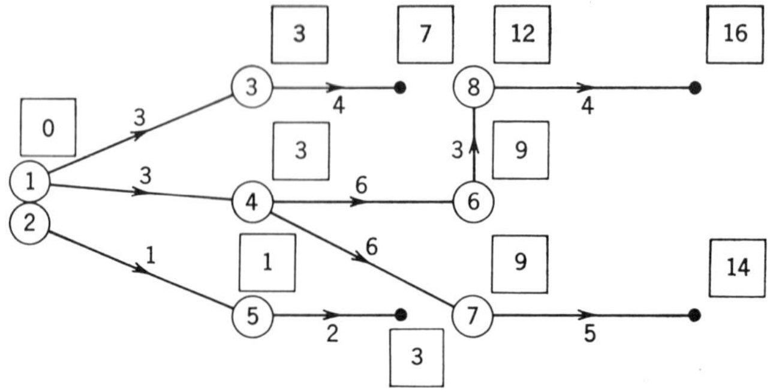

Figure 15.7.16 Third policy for earliest starting time network.

and is again, as we have noted, 16. It is, of course, also true that

$$T = \operatorname*{Max}_i \, (\ell_i + e_i). \tag{15.7.8}$$

The critical path remains the same as before: jobs 1, 4, 6, and 8.

The Gantt chart corresponding to this network appears as Figure 15.7.17. The critical path jobs are naturally in the same place as in the Gantt chart of Figure 15.7.12, but the noncritical jobs have been scheduled as early as possible consistent with the precedences. We note that this schedule never requires that more than

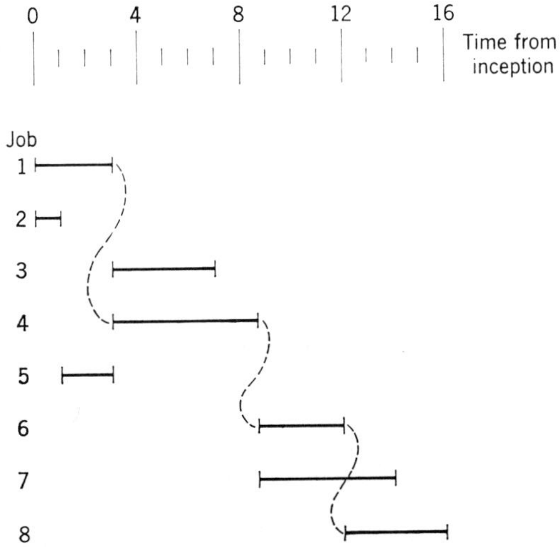

Figure 15.7.17 Gantt chart for earliest starting time network.

two jobs be worked on simultaneously. This observation may be a cogent reason for choosing this schedule over that of Figure 15.7.12.

Float

It is interesting to measure our freedom in scheduling job i by defining the slack or float associated with job i, f_i, by

$$f_i = T - e_i - \ell_i. \tag{15.7.9}$$

The float for each job for our example appears in Table 15.7.3. The jobs for which $f_i = 0$ are the critical jobs. As we have seen, solving the project scheduling problem in both ways is often helpful in demonstrating the flexibility of schedules.

The Probabilistic Transient Process with Rewards

Let us now turn to the case where the transitions are described by transition probabilities. We assume that the N-state semi-Markov process is monodesmic with a single recurrent state; we label this recurrent trapping state with index N. We assume further that all rewards cease when state N is entered. We may now consider the possibility that the process will operate indefinitely without any concern that the expected total reward will grow without limit.

Therefore, if we let $v_i(\beta)$ be the expected discounted reward that the process will earn when allowed to operate indefinitely with an optimum policy under a discount factor β, we can obtain an equation for this quantity from first principles by realizing that $v_i(n, \beta)$ in Equation 15.2.5 becomes $v_i(\beta)$ as n approaches infinity. After recalling that certain of the quantities in Equation 15.2.5 vanish for large n, we can write the equation as

$$v_i(\beta) = \underset{k}{\text{Max}} \left[r_i^k(\beta) + \sum_{j=1}^{N} p_{ij}^k h_{ij}^{gk}(\beta) v_j(\beta) \right] \qquad i = 1, 2, \ldots, N, \tag{15.7.10}$$

where $r_i^k(\beta) = r_i^k(\infty, \beta)$ is the expected present value of all rewards associated with a single entry into state i under alternative k with a discount factor β. This formulation implies the policy iteration cycle shown in Figure 15.4.2.

If we wish to consider the problem without discounting, we set $\beta = 1$, let $v_i = v_i(1)$, $r_i^k = r_i^k(1)$, and write

$$v_i = \underset{k}{\text{Max}} \left[r_i^k + \sum_{j=1}^{N} p_{ij}^k v_j \right] \qquad i = 1, 2, \ldots, N. \tag{15.7.11}$$

Table 15.7.3 Float for Each Job

Job, i	1	2	3	4	5	6	7	8
Float, f_i	0	6	5	0	6	0	2	0

Since the gain is zero, this equation merely confirms that the policy iteration cycle of Figure 15.5.1 based on the value-oriented criterion will lead to the policy with highest expected total reward starting from each transient state.

In either case, we find the policy that maximizes the total expected reward by policy iteration. All we do is select an initial policy and evaluate it by solving the equations without the maximization operation and with $v_N = 0$. Then we use the right-hand side of the equation as the test quantity for policy improvement and so continue the general procedure. In fact, we have just developed more general counterparts of the Equations 15.7.1 and 15.7.2 that we wrote for the deterministic transient Markov process. In summary, policy iteration provides a very useful approach to the problem of maximizing expected rewards in any transient process.

The triangular process

However, policy iteration is not the only approach; others may be quite useful in special situations. Suppose, for example, that the structure of connections among the transient states is such that we can assign them the indices $i = 1, \ldots, N - 1$ in such a way that each state may make transitions only to itself or to a higher numbered state. We shall call this a triangular process because its transition probability matrix has entries only on or above the main diagonal. In this case Equations 15.7.10 and 15.7.11 become

$$v_i(\beta) = \operatorname*{Max}_k \left[r_i^k(\beta) + \sum_{j=i}^{N} p_{ij}^k h_{ij}^{gk}(\beta) v_j(\beta) \right] \qquad i = 1, 2, \ldots, N \qquad (15.7.12)$$

and

$$v_i = \operatorname*{Max}_k \left[r_i^k + \sum_{j=i}^{N} p_{ij}^k v_j \right] \qquad i = 1, 2, \ldots, N \qquad (15.7.13)$$

where in each case the summation begins at i and extends to N. Since we know that $v_N = 0$, we can solve these equations recursively for $i = N - 1, N - 2, \ldots, 1$ and hence obtain the complete solution of the triangular process without iteration. Since triangular process models are not uncommon in practice, this special form of the solution procedure is worthy of study.

Planning space exploration

An interesting context in which to examine triangular models is that of space exploration. Suppose that the agency responsible for exploring Mars is concerned about which configurations of spacecraft to use to achieve its objectives. One limitation is that the launching of a spacecraft toward Mars is possible only every two years. The time required to design, build, and test a spacecraft makes advanced planning extremely important.

Space program model. We model the problem as follows. We recognize five levels of achievement L_0, L_1, L_2, L_3, L_4. The level L_0 corresponds to the current information available about Mars; the level L_4, to the state of information that would result from having conducted a life-detection experiment. The intermediate levels L_1, L_2, L_3 we can think of, respectively, as the states of information that result from orbiting, hard landing, and soft landing the spacecraft and conducting relevant experiments with the exception of life-detection. We measure the state of the system just prior to a launch and place the states in one-to-one correspondence with the levels of achievement. Thus state 1 means that the system had achieved L_0 before the launch; state 2 means that it had achieved L_1; etc. We have, therefore, a 5-state system.

We assume that at each launch-opportunity exactly one spacecraft configuration will be launched. In general, we could plan to have any one of four configurations available at a launch-opportunity. We call the configurations C_1, C_2, C_3, and C_4; they increase in sophistication in that order. Configuration C_i has the potential to achieve level L_i but no higher. It could, however, result in the achievement of a lower level than L_i. A level of achievement, once attained, cannot be undone by future mission failures; hence, we are interested only in advancing the level of achievement, not in repeating it. As a result, we never launch a configuration that could do no better than maintain the current level.

Data. Table 15.7.4 shows the data for this five-state Markov decision process. State 1 has four alternatives because any of the configurations may be launched. State 2 has only three because there would be no point in launching configuration C_1 when L_1 has already been achieved. By continuation of this reasoning, we see that each increase in the state index causes one alternative to be eliminated. In state 4, we are forced to use configuration C_4. State 5 is the trapping state that terminates the process; it, of course, requires no decision.

In general, we observe from the transition probabilities that at any level the simpler configurations are more likely to achieve some increase in level, regardless of magnitude. However, the more sophisticated configurations are the only ones that have the possibility of attaining large increases in achievement from a single launch. The question of which configuration to use depends ultimately on cost. The last column in the table shows the cost in millions of dollars associated with the launching of each configuration. The problem is to find the policy that will minimize the expected cost to reach level L_4 (state 5). Of course, to make the problem more realistic, we could make the state depend on the number of times each configuration has been launched and then base both costs and transition probabilities on this

Table 15.7.4 Data for Space Exploration Planning Problem

Present \ Successor		Level / State, j		L_0 / 1	L_1 / 2	L_2 / 3	L_3 / 4	L_4 / 5	
Level	State i	Alternative k	Configuration	Transition Probability p_{ij}^k					Cost r_i^k
L_0	1	1	C_1	0.10	0.90				575
		2	C_2	0.25	0.15	0.60			650
		3	C_3	0.30	0.10	0.20	0.40		800
		4	C_4	0.35	0.15	0.15	0.15	0.20	1000
L_1	2	1	C_2		0.30	0.70			650
		2	C_3		0.27	0.24	0.49		800
		3	C_4		0.37	0.19	0.19	0.25	1000
L_2	3	1	C_3			0.47	0.53		800
		2	C_4			0.47	0.23	0.30	1000
L_3	4	1	C_4				0.61	0.39	1000
L_4	5	1		0	0	0	0	1	0

history. We could also include the effect of discounting. However, the present version will illustrate the approach.

Solution. We begin by noting that we do, indeed, have a triangular process. Consequently, Equation 15.7.13 applies directly. Since $v_5 = 0$, we start our recursive process by computing v_4,

$$\begin{aligned} v_4 &= r_4^1 + p_{44}^1 v_4 + p_{45}^1 v_5 \\ &= 1000 + 0.61 v_4 \end{aligned} \tag{15.7.14}$$

or

$$v_4 = 2564. \tag{15.7.15}$$

Thus we find that when we have achieved level L_3 (state 4), the expected cost of the remainder of the program is 2564.

Now we can find the best alternative for state 3,

$$v_3 = \operatorname*{Max}_k \begin{cases} k = 1: & r_3^1 + p_{33}^1 v_3 + p_{34}^1 v_4 + p_{35}^1 v_5 = 800 + 0.47 v_3 + 0.53(2564) \\ k = 2: & r_3^2 + p_{33}^2 v_3 + p_{34}^2 v_4 + p_{35}^2 v_5 = 1000 + 0.47 v_3 + 0.23(2564). \end{cases} \tag{15.7.16}$$

By choosing $k = 1$ and $k = 2$, respectively, we find that v_3 is given by

$$\begin{aligned} v_3 &= 4073 \quad \text{for } k = 1 \\ v_3 &= 3000 \quad \text{for } k = 2. \end{aligned} \tag{15.7.17}$$

Therefore, the lower expected cost alternative in state 3 is $k = 2$, or that of using configuration C_4. The value we record for state 3 is then 3000.

To compute v_2, we write

$$v_2 = \operatorname*{Max}_k \begin{cases} k = 1: & r_2{}^1 + p_{22}{}^1 v_2 + p_{23}{}^1 v_3 + p_{24}{}^1 v_4 + p_{25}{}^1 v_5 \\ & \quad = 650 + 0.30v_2 + 0.70(3000) \\ k = 2: & r_2{}^2 + p_{22}{}^2 v_2 + p_{23}{}^2 v_3 + p_{24}{}^2 v_4 + p_{25}{}^2 v_5 \\ & \quad = 800 + 0.27v_2 + 0.24(3000) + 0.49(2564) \\ k = 3: & r_2{}^3 + p_{22}{}^3 v_2 + p_{23}{}^3 v_3 + p_{24}{}^3 v_4 + p_{25}{}^3 v_5 \\ & \quad = 1000 + 0.37v_2 + 0.19(3000) + 0.19(2564). \end{cases} \tag{15.7.18}$$

If we solve the equations with $k = 1, 2, 3$, we obtain

$$\begin{aligned} v_2 &= 3929 \quad \text{for } k = 1 \\ v_2 &= 3803 \quad \text{for } k = 2 \\ v_2 &= 3265 \quad \text{for } k = 3. \end{aligned} \tag{15.7.19}$$

Consequently, the best alternative in state 2 is alternative 3, the use of configuration C_4. The expected cost of the balance of the program given that level 1 has been reached is 3265.

Finally, we establish v_1 from

$$v_1 = \operatorname*{Max}_k \begin{cases} k = 1: & r_1{}^1 + p_{11}{}^1 v_1 + p_{12}{}^1 v_2 + p_{13}{}^1 v_3 + p_{14}{}^1 v_4 + p_{15}{}^1 v_5 \\ & \quad = 575 + 0.10v_1 + 0.90(3265) \\ k = 2: & r_1{}^2 + p_{11}{}^2 v_1 + p_{12}{}^2 v_2 + p_{13}{}^2 v_3 + p_{14}{}^2 v_4 + p_{15}{}^2 v_5 \\ & \quad = 650 + 0.25v_1 + 0.15(3265) + 0.60(3000) \\ k = 3: & r_1{}^3 + p_{11}{}^3 v_1 + p_{12}{}^3 v_2 + p_{13}{}^3 v_3 + p_{14}{}^3 v_4 + p_{15}{}^3 v_5 \\ & \quad = 800 + 0.30v_1 + 0.10(3265) + 0.20(3000) + 0.40(2564) \\ k = 4: & r_1{}^4 + p_{11}{}^4 v_1 + p_{12}{}^4 v_2 + p_{13}{}^4 v_3 + p_{14}{}^4 v_4 + p_{15}{}^4 v_5 \\ & \quad = 1000 + 0.35v_1 + 0.15(3265) + 0.15(3000) + 0.15(2564) \end{cases} \tag{15.7.20}$$

by setting k variously to 1, 2, 3, 4 to produce

$$\begin{aligned} v_1 &= 3904 \quad \text{for } k = 1 \\ v_1 &= 3920 \quad \text{for } k = 2 \\ v_1 &= 3933 \quad \text{for } k = 3 \\ v_1 &= 3577 \quad \text{for } k = 4. \end{aligned} \tag{15.7.21}$$

We thus learn that alternative 4, using configuration C_4, is the most economical and that the expected cost of the entire program is $v_1 = 3577$.

Interpretation. By reviewing our results we observe that configuration C_4 has been chosen at every level. Although this configuration is the most expensive, its performance justifies its use. Because we always use configuration C_4 at a cost of 1000, it follows that the expected number of launches required to achieve level L_4 is $3577/1000 = 3.577$.

The fact that one configuration is used throughout the program is a direct result of the cost structure. For example, if configuration C_1 cost 225 rather than 575, then v_1 would equal 3554 rather than 3904 for alternative 1. Since 3554 is less than the expected cost of 3577 for alternative 4, using configuration C_1 would be the preferred alternative when the system is at level L_0. Of course, configuration C_4 would be used at all higher levels if the rest of the cost structure were left unchanged.

This problem is a typical example of the use of triangular models. The form of the computations shows that very large triangular models may be solved very efficiently. However, policy iteration is just as valuable, if not as convenient, in solving nontriangular transient processes, as the following example shows.

How to Succeed in Business without Really Trying

Almost every young man faces the problem of negotiating his way through an organizational hierarchy. He must decide how to find his path to the top through the various levels, departments, and bosses that confront him. Perhaps as the final example of this section we can provide him with a rationale for success.

The model

We shall model the organization as an N-state discrete-time nontriangular semi-Markov process where each state represents a particular organizational position (usually specified in the real world by a job description). These states, or positions, form a hierarchy of prestige and financial gain. A person who enters a certain position will be promoted to a higher position, demoted to a lower position, or allowed to remain in that position indefinitely. We identify the time spent in a state or position as the holding time for that position; it will generally be a random variable whose probability mass function depends on the next position attained.

We might define as normal progression from a state the transition probabilities and holding time mass functions that will apply if the individual performs his job well, but neither invests heavily in future training or education, nor requests any transfers to other positions. Of course, it might be a very wise policy to follow one of these other courses. Therefore, in some states we shall allow for the possibility of what we shall call "education"; namely, an investment of money by the individual in further training to prepare himself for a higher position. This education will typically increase the transition probabilities and decrease the mean holding times to higher positions; however, it will cost money and hence decrease the yield of the present position.

Another alternative that might be useful is to allow the employee to request a transfer to another position. But we assume that transfers are restricted: A transfer must be requested at the time of assuming a new position, it must take place after a specified number of years in the new position, and it must be to a position that carries a salary no higher than the new position. We could think of several other alternatives, but these will be sufficient to illustrate the conceptual framework.

The organization

We shall choose for our example a 15-state industrial organization. As shown in Figure 15.7.18, six of these states represent positions for operating personnel, six represent positions of middle management, and three, positions of top management. The first twelve positions are again divided between the sales and engineering functions within the organization. In the circle corresponding to each state we have written the associated annual salary in dollars. If we consider the vertical dimension in this figure to represent the formal importance of the position, then we observe that at the levels of operating personnel, individuals in the engineering organization are paid more, stratum for stratum, than individuals in the sales organization. However, at the level of middle management, the trend is reversed: Sales executives of each stratum are paid more than their engineering counterparts. However, in top management, functional labels are unimportant. Individuals from both engineering and sales levels are indistinguishable in top management positions, including the presidency (position 15).

Data and assumptions

Now we must specify the data associated with the semi-Markov model. While the salary levels are supplied by the organization, the individual must assign his own transition probabilities and holding time mass functions. Thus a man who considers himself to be substantially more talented than average would want to incorporate his great expectations in his assignments.

The education and transfer alternatives require special treatment. The cost of the education alternative will be reflected in a lower yield rate for a state during the period in which education is being pursued, always one year. The transfer alternative will have the same salary and yield rate as the normal alternative, but the transition probability associated with it will be unity and the holding time will be a constant. For simplicity, we do not allow the possibility of requesting a transfer and at the same time pursuing education.

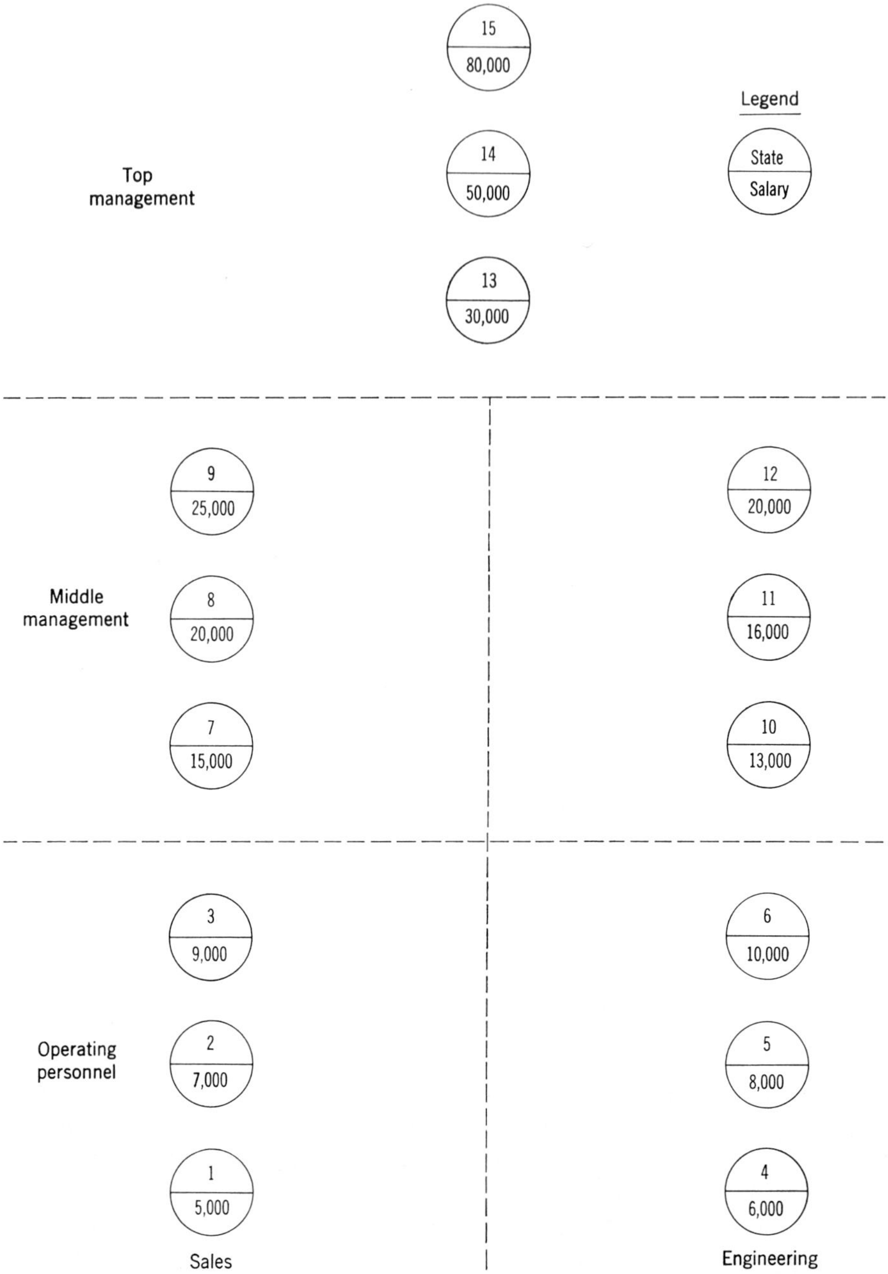

Figure 15.7.18 The organization.

Figure 15.7.19 exhibits the transition diagram for this semi-Markov organization model. Here we have assigned for each alternative that exists in a state and for each transition the transition probability, holding time mean, and holding time variance. To improve the clarity of Figure 15.7.19, these holding time means and variances are rounded approximations to the actual means and variances of the holding time mass functions. The actual holding time mass functions used in the problem appear with actual and approximate means and variances in Table 15.7.4.

On the transitions that represent the education alternative we have also written the cost applicable to the one year of training. The yield rate for the state during this year is thus the difference between the salary of the position and the education cost; for future years the yield rate is just the salary.

The normal alternative is present in all states; we represent its transitions by a solid line. One feature of special interest for transitions under both normal and education alternatives is that in some states, like state 1, there is a probability that the individual will make a virtual transition and return to the same state with a holding time of 50 years. We use this mechanism to represent a person's being trapped in his present position for an indefinite time.

Note that under the normal alternative, demotions can occur in states 2, 3, 6, 13, and 14; but the middle management levels of the organization are free from the threat of downward movement. In states 13, 14, and 15, the normal alternative is the only alternative. We assume education has no effect at this level; transfers are excluded by our ground rules.

All but states 9, 12, 13, 14, and 15 have an education alternative; its transitions are represented by dashed lines. This alternative decreases the yield during the first year, but enhances the transition probability–holding time characteristics of the state. Sometimes, as in state 8, it increases the transition probability to a higher state over the value it had with the normal alternative while leaving the holding time mass function unchanged. In other situations, like state 3, it leaves the transition probability unchanged, but decreases the expected time for the transition to a higher state. As we see in state 2, it may also have the combined effect. However, the net influence of education on the probabilistic structure is always favorable with respect to reaching higher levels in the organization more certainly or quickly.

We assume that every individual who enters the organization has fundamental engineering training to assure that transfers between the sales and engineering organizations are meaningful. Transfer probabilities are represented in Figure 15.7.19 by lines with alternating long and short dashes labeled with the transition probability (1) and the fixed time that the transfer requires. Since transfers may be made only to states whose salary does not exceed that of the present state, transfer possibilities are quite limited. We limit them further by considering transfers only to the same or next lower salary level positions in the other functional side of the

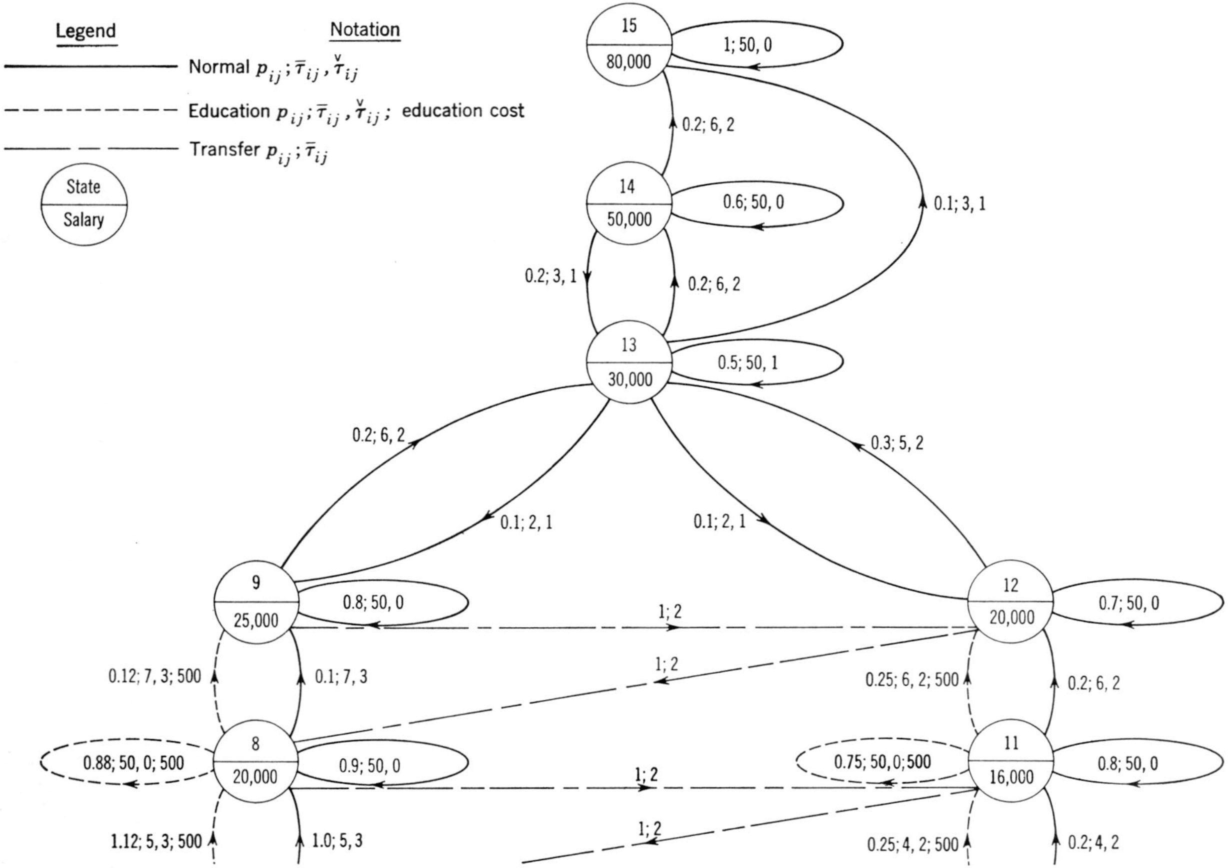

Legend
Notation
Normal $p_{ij}; \bar{\tau}_{ij}, \check{\tau}_{ij}$
Education $p_{ij}; \bar{\tau}_{ij}, \check{\tau}_{ij}$; education cost
Transfer $p_{ij}; \bar{\tau}_{ij}$
State
Salary
15
80,000
1; 50, 0
0.2; 6, 2
0.1; 3, 1
14
50,000
0.6; 50, 0
0.2; 3, 1
0.2; 6, 2
13
30,000
0.5; 50, 1
0.2; 6, 2
0.1; 2, 1
0.1; 2, 1
0.3; 5, 2
9
25,000
0.8; 50, 0
12
20,000
0.7; 50, 0
1; 2
1; 2
0.12; 7, 3; 500
0.1; 7, 3
0.25; 6, 2; 500
0.2; 6, 2
8
20,000
0.88; 50, 0; 500
0.9; 50, 0
11
16,000
0.75; 50, 0; 500
0.8; 50, 0
1; 2
1; 2
1.12; 5, 3; 500
1.0; 5, 3
0.25; 4, 2; 500
0.2; 4, 2

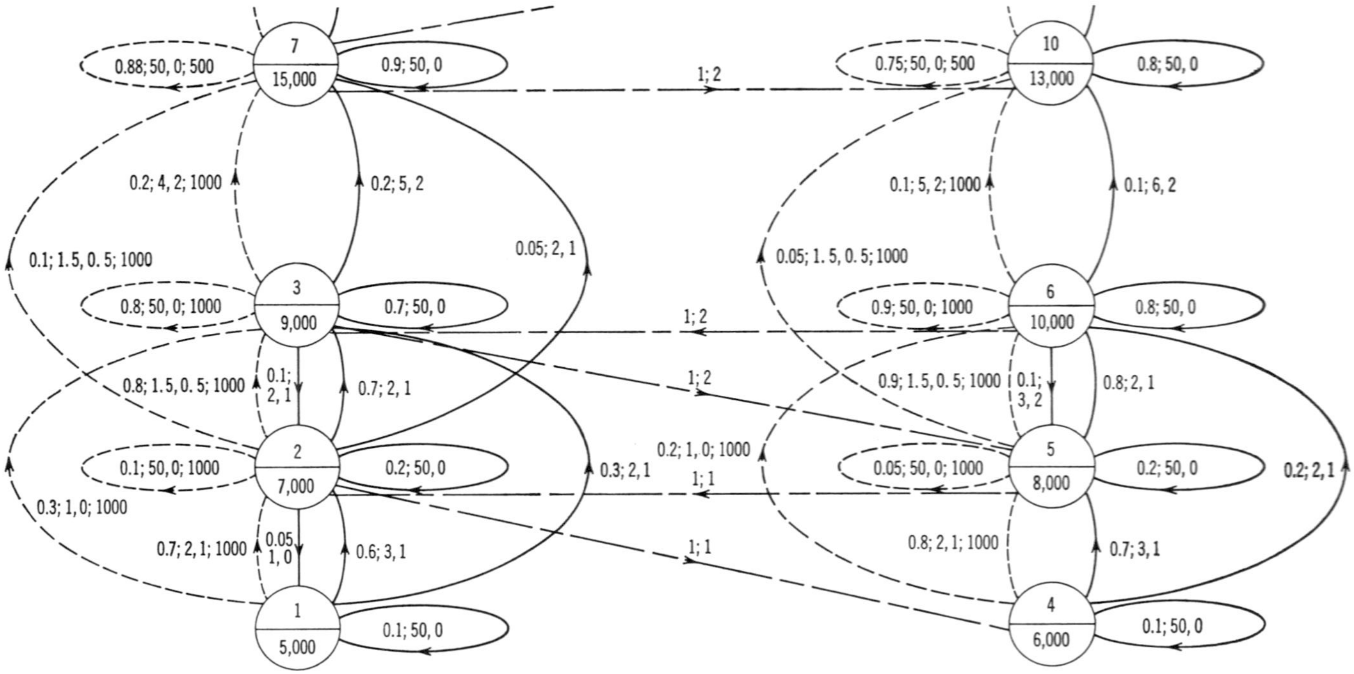

Figure 15.7.19 Transition diagram for organizational model.

Table 15.7.4 Holding Time Probability Mass Functions

Approximate		Actual		$h(n)$											
Mean	Variance	Mean	Variance	$n = 1$	2	3	4	5	6	7	8	9	10	11	12
1.5	0.5	1.62	0.516	0.500	0.400	0.080	0.020								
2	1	2.30	0.810	0.200	0.400	0.300	0.100								
3	1	2.70	0.810	0.100	0.300	0.400	0.200								
3	2	3.06	1.774	0.120	0.240	0.290	0.210	0.100	0.030	0.008	0.002				
4	2	3.99	1.857	0.031	0.110	0.221	0.278	0.223	0.112	0.022	0.003				
5	2	4.80	1.880	0.008	0.041	0.124	0.233	0.280	0.210	0.090	0.014				
5	3	4.80	2.764	0.017	0.064	0.142	0.214	0.229	0.178	0.102	0.042	0.010	0.002		
6	2	6.01	2.001	0.001	0.007	0.034	0.102	0.205	0.273	0.234	0.117	0.027			
7	3	6.85	2.963	0.001	0.005	0.020	0.060	0.128	0.199	0.228	0.190	0.112	0.045	0.010	0.002

organization; top management positions have no transfer possibilities. Observe that in the figure we have allowed transfers after only one year in the lowest states, whereas transfers at higher levels require a two-year commitment to the present position. This feature is designed to reflect a greater tolerance of horizontal mobility among the younger members of the organization.

How to become rich

Now that we have specified the organizational model in detail, we are ready to learn about the road to success that will produce the highest expected present value of wealth. We begin by using policy iteration to solve the problem with discounting. We shall use the discount factor $\beta = 0.95$, which corresponds approximately to 5% annual interest. In this case, as in all future policy iteration results on this problem, we develop the initial policy by choosing the alternative in each state that maximizes the expected present value of rewards generated by a single occupancy of that state. Finding the optimum policy required three iterations; the results appear in Figure 15.7.20.

Here we have shown adjacent to each state the optimum decision and the expected present value. In addition, we have drawn the complete transition diagram implied by the optimum policy. Note that the transition diagram is that of a transient process that will ultimately be trapped by state 15: According to the model, sooner or later a person starting anywhere will become president (if he lives long enough).

We observe that in the triplets of states (1, 2, 3), (4, 5, 6), (7, 8, 9), and (10, 11, 12) it is optimal to pursue the education alternative in the first two states of the triplet and the normal alternative in the last. In other words, within each hierarchy, education pays at the lower levels but not at the highest level. Of course, education is not an alternative in states 9 and 12.

The expected present values of the states are of particular interest. Each represents the expected discounted value of all future earnings starting from that position; we can think of this quantity simply as the value of the position. For example, the value of the presidency is the present value of state 15, the trapping state of the process. The value of this state should be the present value of the endless stream of 80,000 annual salaries discounted by the discount factor 0.95, or

$$80{,}000[1 + 0.95 + (0.95)^2 + (0.95)^3 + \cdots] = 80{,}000\,\frac{1}{1 - 0.95} = 1{,}600{,}000$$

as shown in Figure 15.7.20.

We can measure the value of a promotion from one position to another by computing the difference in the values of the positions. For example, if a person were following this optimum policy, a promotion from state 1 to state 2 would be

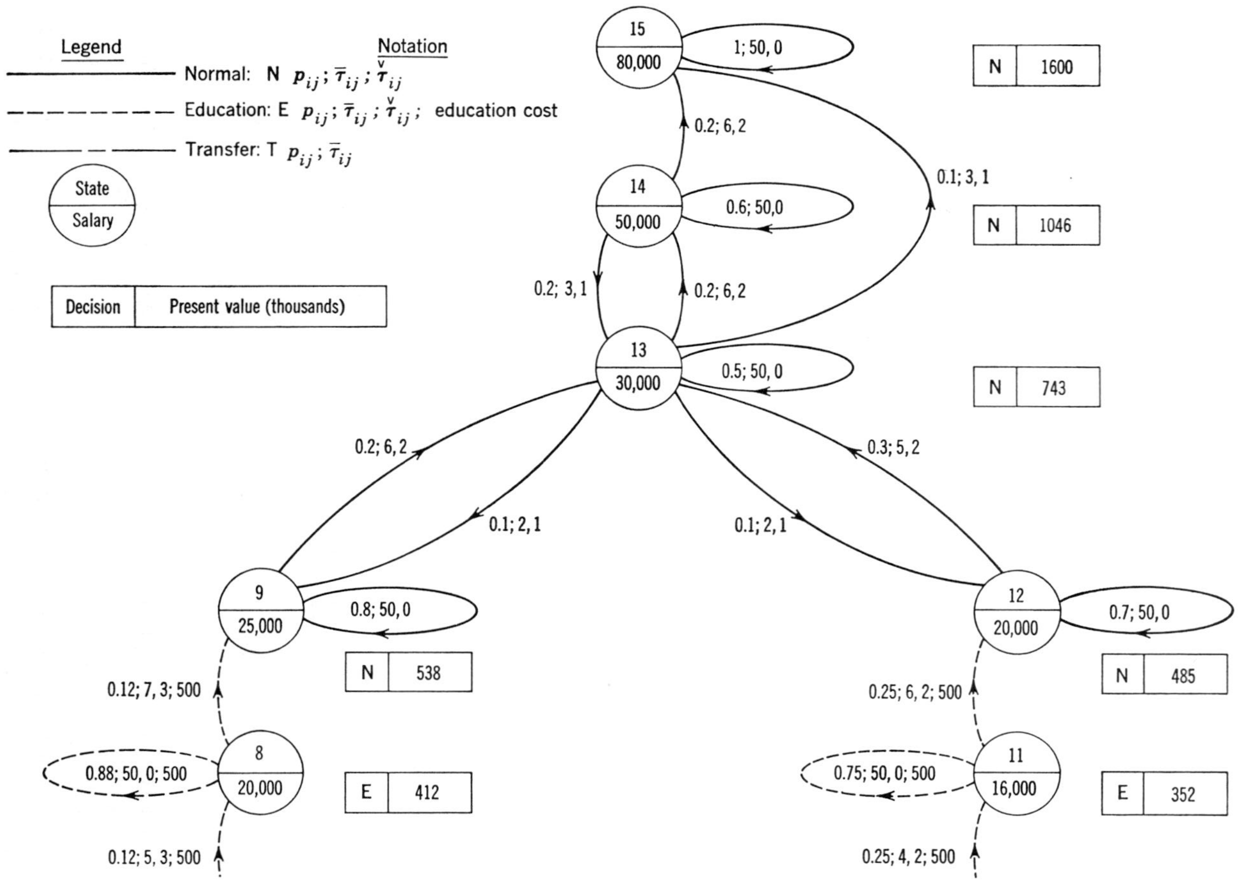
Legend
Notation
Normal: N p_{ij}; $\bar{\tau}_{ij}$; $\check{\tau}_{ij}$
Education: E p_{ij}; $\bar{\tau}_{ij}$; $\check{\tau}_{ij}$; education cost
Transfer: T p_{ij}; $\bar{\tau}_{ij}$
State
Salary
Decision
Present value (thousands)
15
80,000
1; 50, 0
N
1600
0.2; 6, 2
0.1; 3, 1
14
50,000
0.6; 50,0
N
1046
0.2; 3, 1
0.2; 6, 2
13
30,000
0.5; 50, 0
N
743
0.2; 6, 2
0.1; 2, 1
0.3; 5, 2
0.1; 2, 1
9
25,000
0.8; 50, 0
N
538
0.12; 7, 3; 500
8
20,000
0.88; 50, 0; 500
E
412
0.12; 5, 3; 500
12
20,000
0.7; 50, 0
N
485
0.25; 6, 2; 500
11
16,000
0.75; 50, 0; 500
E
352
0.25; 4, 2; 500

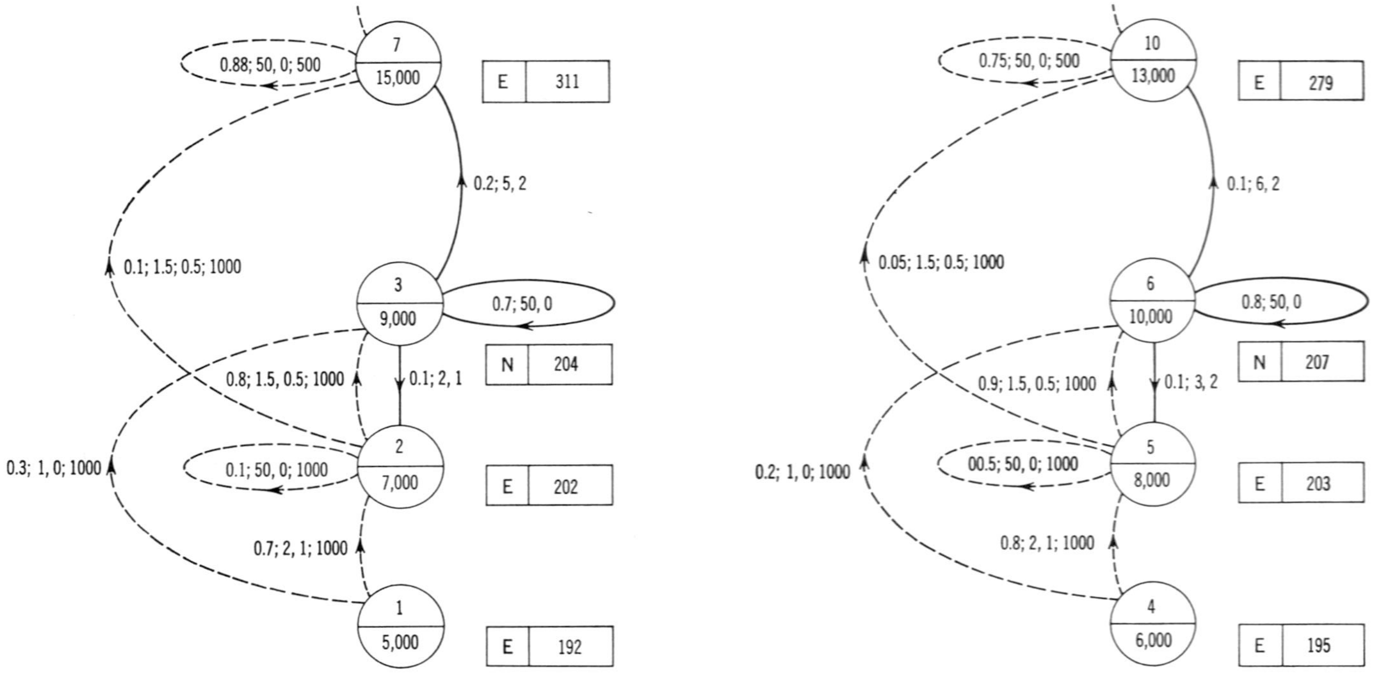

Figure 15.7.20 Transition diagram of optimal policy for discount factor $\beta = 0.95$.

worth 202 − 192 = 10 thousand dollars, while a promotion from state 2 to state 3 would be worth 204 − 202 = 2 thousand dollars. As we might expect, the most valuable promotions in the model are those that move one directly to the presidency.

We might comment on why no transfer alternatives appear in the optimum policy for the discount factor 0.95. If we examine each of the transfer possibilities in Figure 15.7.19, we find that in every case the transfer would be from a position of higher to lower value according to Figure 15.7.20. Consequently, there is no incentive for transfers with this discount factor.

States 8 and 12 provide an interesting comparison. Both have the same salary, yet the value of position 12 is 485 − 412 = 73 thousand dollars higher than that of position 8. The difference is due, of course, to the different prospects of each state. However, with this one exception, there is a direct positive correlation between position values and salary levels.

The effect of changing discount factors

We shall now examine the same problem for discount factors other than 0.95. Table 15.7.5 shows the results for discount factors in the range from 0.8 to 1.0. The specific discount factors recorded were selected by increasing β gradually from 0.8 and noting the results every time a new policy was produced. Thus the policies in Table 15.7.5 differ by exactly one decision for successive values of β. We have also shown in this table the policy iteration solution for the case without discounting. The optimum policy for this case is the same as that for $\beta = 0.999$.

The final column of the table shows the number of iterations required for the policy iteration procedure to find the optimum policy. In every case, the number of iterations was between 2 and 4.

As the discount factor increases, we observe an increase in the present value of each state. As the discount factor approaches one, the present values become measured in millions of dollars. However, the interest rates corresponding to these discount factors are too small to be realistic for mortal individuals.

Of particular interest is the case $\beta = 1$, where no discounting of the future occurs. Although, as we have said, the policy for this case is the same as that for $\beta = 0.999$, the relative values have an important interpretation. Since this example represents a transient process with a single trapping state, state 15, it is not surprising that the gain of the process is just the annual salary corresponding to this state. For convenience we set the value of state 15 equal to zero, and measure the values of all other states relative to state 15. Since state 15 is the most valuable state in the process, these other values are all negative.

By examining the last row of Table 15.7.5, for example, we find that the least valuable state when there is no discounting is state 6, whose relative value is −50,970,000. Thus the difference in values of states 6 and 15 is 50,970,000.

Note that when $\beta = 0.999$, state 6 is still the least valuable state, but the difference between its value and that of state 15 is now 80,000,000–47,200,000 = 32,800,000, or about 18,000,000 less than it is when there is no discounting. When $\beta = 0.99$, state 6 is no longer the state of lowest value, but the difference between its value and that of state 15 is 8,000,000 − 1,278,000 = 6,722,000, considerably less difference than when $\beta = 0.999$.

In fact, we observe from the table that as β increases, the difference between the values of any state and state 15 increases. The increase is quite dramatic when β nears one. However, the difference is definitely bounded when β equals one; the bounds appear as the relative values of the last row of the table. Thus even when there is no discounting, the positions have different values because of the finite difference in expected total rewards that will accrue by starting in one position rather than the other.

If we examine the types of change in policy that occur as we increase β, we find that for β between 0.8 and 0.965 they take the form of changes from the normal to the education alternative in various states. Above $\beta = 0.965$, policies generally change by switching from a normal or education alternative to a transfer alternative. The only exception occurs for β equal to 0.999 when a change from normal to education again occurs. These changes are all in the direction we would expect as concern for the future increases.

Within each three-state triplet the values of positions generally increase with state number for a given discount factor. However, we see that for high discount factors, there is a small reversal in the values of positions 2 and 3, and of positions 5 and 6. Furthermore, the values of states 1, 2, and 3 become higher than the values of their counterpart states 4, 5, and 6 even though they have lower salaries. The same phenomenon occurs for high discount factors in the triplets of states 7, 8, and 9 and 10, 11, and 12. When discount factors are high, sales-operating positions are preferred over engineering-operating positions even though they have lower salaries; at the middle management level the engineering positions are preferred in spite of their lower salaries.

These properties are a result of the complicated transfer patterns introduced by the policies for higher discount factors. Note, however, that transfers always take the employee to a state of higher value, as we would require.

How to become president

As we mentioned earlier, in this model a person starting anywhere will become president if he waits long enough. The emphasis of the model was to find the policy for the individual that would maximize the present value of his future expected earnings given some interest rate that he uses to discount future income. However, let us suppose that we are dealing with a person who measures his success only in terms of whether he achieves the presidency rather than in economic terms: He

Table 15.7.5 Decisions and Values of All Optimum Policies for Organizational Problem Generated by Discount Factors from 0.8 to 1.0

		Operating Personnel Sales			Operating Personnel Engineering		
Discount Factor, β	State Salary	1 5	2 7	3 9	4 6	5 8	6 10
0.800	Decision	E	E	E	E	E	N
	Present Value	37	44	47	40	46	50
0.830	Decision	E	E	N	E	E	N
	Present Value	46	53	56	49	55	59
0.870	Decision	E	E	N	E	E	N
	Present Value	64	71	74	67	74	78
0.887	Decision	E	E	N	E	E	N
	Present Value	75	83	86	79	86	90
0.965	Decision	E	E	N	E	E	N
	Present Value	287	298	298	287	296	298
0.968	Decision	E	E	N	E	T*	N
	Present Value	317	329	328	317	326	327
0.980	Decision	E	E	N	E	T	T*
	Present Value	540	554	549	539	551	547
0.988	Decision	E	E	T*	E	T	T
	Present Value	997	1,014	1,004	995	1,010	1,000
0.989	Decision	E	E	T	E	T	T
	Present Value	1,119	1,137	1,126	1,116	1,133	1,121
0.990	Decision	E	E	T	E	T	T
	Present Value	1,277	1,297	1,284	1,274	1,292	1,278
0.999	Decision	E	E	T	E	T	T
	Present Value	47,270	47,390	47,280	47,240	47,350	47,200
1.000	Decision	E	E	T	E	T	T
	Relative Value	−50,820	−50,620	−50,830	−50,900	−50,690	−50,970
	Gain = 80,000						

* Change of Decision

Decisions: N: Normal; E: Education; T: Transfer

would like to make the probability of being president within his lifetime as high as possible. We can help this gentleman by making some slight modifications in our model.

We begin by recalling that we can interpret the discount factor β as the probability that the process will survive for one more time period; the expected duration of the process is then $1/(1-\beta)$ time periods. In our problem we let β be the

Middle Management Sales			Middle Management Engineering			Top Management			No. of Iterations
7	8	9	10	11	12	13	14	15	
15	20	25	13	16	20	30	50	80	
N	N	N	N	N	N	N	N	N	2
76	101	127	66	81	107	165	249	400	
N	N	N	N	E*	N	N	N	N	2
90	119	151	78	96	128	198	294	471	
N	N	N	E*	E	N	N	N	N	2
118	156	199	104	128	171	265	388	615	
E*	N	N	E	E	N	N	N	N	2
136	179	230	120	148	200	308	449	708	
E	E*	N	E	E	N	N	N	N	4
448	595	785	407	518	722	1,094	1,515	2,286	
E	E	N	E	E	N	N	N	N	4
491	652	865	448	572	798	1,207	1,664	2,500	
E	E	N	E	E	N	N	N	N	3
800	1,068	1,446	753	976	1,378	2,035	2,727	4,000	
E	E	N	E	E	N	N	N	N	4
1,383	1,864	2,599	1,381	1,821	2,574	3,644	4,708	6,667	
T*	E	N	E	E	N	N	N	N	3
1,537	2,057	2,882	1,541	2,037	2,872	4,030	5,172	7,273	
T	T*	N	E	E	N	N	N	N	3
1,737	2,300	3,231	1,742	2,306	3,241	4,502	5,735	8,000	
T	T	E*	E	E	N	N	N	N	4
50,890	56,630	62,860	50,970	56,700	62,940	68,060	72,280	80,000	
T	T	E	E	E	N	N	N	N	4
−44,180	−33,850	−23,850	−44,050	−33,730	−23,740	−16,460	−10,610	0	

Entries are in thousands of dollars.

(assumed constant) probability that the individual will live for another year. For a middle-aged man we might take $\beta = 0.95$ and obtain a life expectancy of 20 years; for a young man β might be 0.98 with life expectancy 50 years.

Now we alter the structure of the problem slightly by introducing a new trapping state 16 and changing state 15 to a transient state whose only possible exiting transition is to state 16 with probability 1. Finally, we set the rewards for all states but state 15 equal to zero, and let the system earn a unit yield during its first time period in state 15 but no further reward. Now if we apply policy iteration with discounting to this system, it will operate so as to maximize the expected reward in the process. However, in this case the actual reward is one if the individual survives to the time he reaches the presidency and otherwise is zero. The expected reward is therefore the probability that the individual will reach the presidency while he is still alive. Consequently, the policy iteration procedure will maximize the probability that the individual will reach the presidency during his lifetime.

When the indicated modifications were made and the calculations carried out for $\beta = 0.95$ and 0.98, the results were as shown in Figure 15.7.21. For both discount factors, five iterations were required for the policy iteration procedure to converge on the optimum policy. We see that for both younger and middle-aged men, the policy turns out to be the same. In fact, it is the same policy reported in Table 15.7.5 for the maximization of expected present value of income using a discount factor of 0.999 or no discounting. This is not surprising because in the absence of discounting, the best strategy for the income maximizer would be to reach the presidency as soon as possible regardless of educational costs or immediate salary losses.

The probability that our client will achieve the presidency within his lifetime is shown in Figure 15.7.21 for each position and for both $\beta = 0.95$ and $\beta = 0.98$. Considering first the discount factor of 0.95, we observe that this probability ranges from a minimum of 2.313×10^{-4} for state 6 to 0.1770 for state 14. The probability generally increases with position in the organizational hierarchy. Note, however, that the probability of achieving the presidency is less for positions 3 and 6 than it is for the corresponding positions 1 and 4 that are designed to be the lowest positions in the organization. We can understand this by noting that men starting in positions 1 and 4 have the possibility of leapfrogging positions 3 and 6 as well as of passing through them. The transfer alternatives used by the optimum policy at the operating level make the most of this possibility.

The main effect of changing the discount factor from 0.95 to 0.98 is to increase the probability of reaching the presidency: young men have a better chance than middle-aged men. The probability is increased by roughly a factor of 10 at the operating level, a factor of 3 at the middle management level, and a factor of 1 1/2 at the top management level. The difference in factor is due to the fact that young men can make more of their natural advantage when they are at the operating level than they can in top management.

Wealth or prestige?

We shall now inquire into the effect on expected lifetime earnings of following a policy that maximizes the probability of being president. We do this by using the policy of Figure 15.7.21 in the original model of the problem in Figure 15.7.19 and then calculating the expected present value of each state for discount factors 0.95 and 0.98; the results appear in Figure 15.7.21. We find that the expected lifetime earnings increase with salary except for some small reversals at the operating level position.

However, it is more interesting to compare these expected lifetime earnings with those of someone who had started out to maximize his expected lifetime earnings in the first place. If we interpret the discount factors 0.95 and 0.98 as the probabilities of surviving from year to year, then we have already solved the problem of maximizing expected lifetime earnings for $\beta = 0.95$ in Figure 15.7.20 and for $\beta = 0.98$ in Table 15.7.5. We have copied in Figure 15.7.21 the values or expected lifetime earnings presented in those previous locations. Of course, the policies required to achieve them are not the same as the policy reported in Figure 15.7.21.

We observe that following the policy that maximizes the probability of achieving the presidency causes a significant decrease in expected lifetime earnings from those attained if expected lifetime earnings are maximized. For example, when $\beta = 0.95$, the expected lifetime earnings of state 1 falls from 192,000 to 174,000, a difference of 18,000. Similar decreases occur in the other positions at the operating level.

In positions 7, 8, and 9 of sales middle management, the loss is even larger. For example, the difference in the value of position 9 is 538,000 − 485,000 = 53,000 when $\beta = 0.95$ and 1,446,000 − 1,370,000 = 76,000 for $\beta = 0.98$. However, there is practically no difference in expected lifetime earnings for the policies of presidential pursuit and income maximization in the engineering middle management positions 10, 11, and 12 and in the top management positions 13, 14, and 15.

In fact, at the middle management level an income maximizer would prefer the sales positions 7, 8, and 9 to the corresponding engineering positions 10, 11, and 12. When $\beta = 0.95$, the difference between states 9 and 12 amounts to 538,000 − 485,000 = 53,000; for $\beta = 0.98$, it is 1,446,000 − 1,378,000 = 68,000. Similar differences appear at the other middle management positions.

By contrast, a person in pursuit of the presidency would prefer the engineering positions 10, 11, and 12 to the corresponding sales positions 7, 8, and 9. For example, when $\beta = 0.95$, position 12 has a presidential succession probability of 0.03061 compared to 0.02763 for position 9. Similar differences appear for the other middle management positions and for the discount factor 0.98. Yet at the operating level, the man in pursuit of the presidency would prefer the sales positions 1, 2, and 3 to the corresponding engineering positions 4, 5, and 6 in contrast to the preferences of an income maximizer. It is clear that a man on the move must specify his goals before we can give him any advice.

We may also regard the problem from the organization's point of view. The organization could use these models to consider the impact on promotions of changing organizational policy on transfer and education. It could even consider adjusting salary levels to make supposedly equivalent positions into positions of equal present value.

Legend
N: Normal
E: Education
T: Transfer

Key

State	Salary

Discount factor β	Goal: maximize probability of presidency		Goal: maximize expected lifetime income
0.95	Probability of presidency	Present value	Present value
0.98	Probability of presidency	Present value	Present value

Present value entries in thousands

Top management

State 15 (salary 80,000) — N

1.000	1600	1600
1.000	4000	4000

State 14 (salary 50,000) — N

1.770×10^{-1}	1045	1046
2.730×10^{-1}	2725	2727

State 13 (salary 30,000) — N

1.232×10^{-1}	738	743
1.909×10^{-1}	2025	2035

Middle management

Sales

State 9 (salary 25,000) — E

2.763×10^{-2}	485	538
6.704×10^{-2}	1370	1446

State 8 (salary 20,000) — T

5.401×10^{-3}	356	412
2.043×10^{-2}	976	1068

State 7 (salary 15,000) — T

1.171×10^{-3}	281	311
6.485×10^{-3}	752	800

Enginering

State 12 (salary 20,000) — N

3.061×10^{-2}	484	485
6.980×10^{-2}	1375	1378

State 11 (salary 16,000) — E

5.985×10^{-3}	352	352
2.127×10^{-2}	975	976

State 10 (salary 13,000) — E

1.297×10^{-3}	279	279
6.753×10^{-3}	752	753

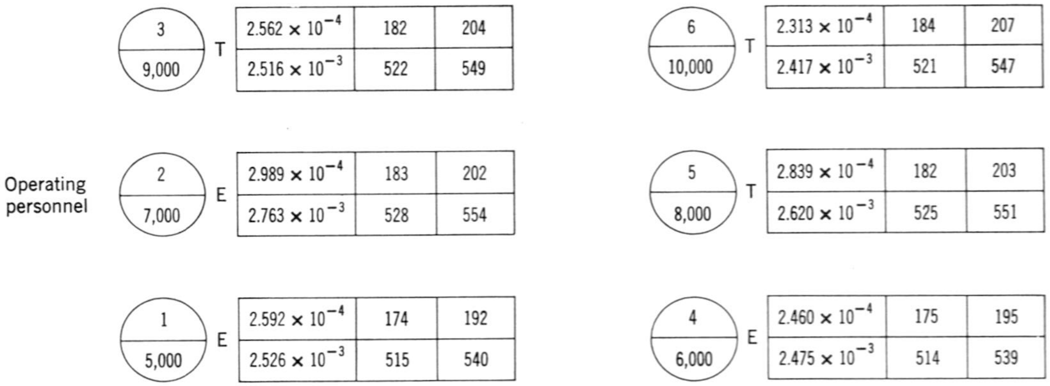

Figure 15.7.21 Optimal policy for maximizing probability of achieving presidency.

However, we would be wise not to take the intriguing results of this example too seriously. We should consider it as more indicative of the possibilities of the model than representative of practical application.

15.8 CONCLUSION

We have now described and illustrated methods for optimizing finite and infinite duration, discounted and undiscounted semi-Markov processes with rewards. Combinations of methods may have unique advantages. For example, there is the possibility of alternating value and policy iteration to achieve optimum policies more quickly than by using either one alone. The properties of the computational devices available will often dictate what is truly efficient.

An appropriate conclusion to this chapter is an indication of how the decision models we have developed have been applied to a variety of problems. Table 15.8.1 provides this indication. Each of its entries could be expanded into a chapter

Table 15.8.1 Applications of Markov Decision Models

Area	State	Transition	Reward	Optimization Problem
Inventory control	Number of items in stock	Sale or arrival of order	Profit from sale, carrying cost, ordering cost	Ordering policy
Production	Amount of each product in stock	Sale or production	Profit from sale, carrying cost, production cost	Production policy
Marketing	Last brand or amount purchased by customer	Purchase	Profit from sale less advertising cost	Advertising policy
Queuing	Number of each item in system	Arrival of new item or service of old one	Waiting cost plus service cost	Service policy (number of service units, priority)
Replacement	Age of item	Replacement of new item or passage of time	Operating cost, replacement cost	Replacement policy
Maintenance	Number of items working	Breakdown or repair	Operating profit, repair cost	Maintenance policy

Reliability	Number of units working	Total or partial failure, substitution of back-up unit	Expected system effectiveness	Design of system
Investment	Amount of portfolio in each investment opportunity	Purchase or sale of securities, receipt of dividends	Profit from exchange plus dividends	Investment policy
Routing	Location in network	Movement to another node	Cost of move	Minimum cost route
Human learning	Level of learning	Change in level of learning through presentation of material	Cost of presentation, value of learned concepts	Teaching procedures
Medical care demands	Phase of an illness or episode	Improvement or deterioration of patient's condition	Cost of care, morbidity, mortality	Level of care

or a book in its own right. However, the theoretical structure of the work would be based on the same models we have been discussing. Perhaps you will extend the table yourself.

PROBLEMS

1. A salesman works in two towns, A and B, and is trying to decide what his policy should be for visiting the two towns. On the morning of each day he can either remain in the town he is currently visiting, or he can travel to the other town and spend the day working there. Due to the distances involved it is impossible for him to work in both towns on the same day. For each day that he works in town A there is probability a of making a sale; the corresponding probability for town B is b. The reward for a sale is r and the cost of changing towns is c. The salesman is considering two alternatives for each town: i) Stay in the town until he makes a sale and then go to the other town; ii) Work in the town for one day and then go on to the other town whether or not a sale is made.

a) For each of the four possible policies find the salesman's long-run expected profit per day.

b) Find the range of the parameters a, b, r, and c for which each of the policies is optimum. Assume that $a > b$ and that all of the parameters are > 0.

2. A furrier buys coats at a cost of two for \$1500 and sells them for \$1000 apiece. In any given month the chance of a sale is 0.2; he never sells more than one coat a month. At the end of each month he examines his stock. Any coats in stock are reconditioned at a cost of \$40 each. If he is out of coats, he orders two.

a) What is the average monthly profit of the business?

b) If the furrier has one coat in stock, how much would he pay to buy a new coat in a special deal?

By discounting his price to \$900, the furrier can change his sales during a month so that he has probability 0.1 of selling two coats (provided there are two available), 0.2 of selling one coat, and 0.7 of selling none.

c) Under what inventory conditions, if any, should the furrier discount if he wishes to maximize his average monthly profit? Answer questions a) and b) for this policy.

3. Sam wants to take a three-day fishing trip a month from now in the wilds of Canada. There is considerable expense involved in flying his gear in and out of the wilderness and in his absence from work. Sam has decided to make the trip only if his expected net revenue is positive. His expenses per day would be \$50; but he assigns dollar values on the pleasures derived from fishing. However, the value is a function of the weather. On a sunny day (S), the value is \$100; on a cloudy day (C), \$50; and on a rainy day (R), \$10. Sam is convinced that the day-to-day weather can be represented as a Markov process with transition probability matrix:

$$P = \begin{matrix} & \begin{matrix} S & C & R \end{matrix} \\ \begin{matrix} S \\ C \\ R \end{matrix} & \begin{bmatrix} 3/4 & 1/8 & 1/8 \\ 1/4 & 3/8 & 3/8 \\ 0 & 3/8 & 5/8 \end{bmatrix} \end{matrix} .$$

[e.g., $p_{23} = \mathscr{P}\{\text{tomorrow is rainy} | \text{today is cloudy}\}$]

Sam will arrive at the end of a day and will have the option of returning home at the end of each day, including the day of arrival.

a) What should be Sam's policy toward coming home or staying?

b) What is the expected value of the trip to Sam?

c) For what expenses per day will he be indifferent toward the trip?

d) For the policy in a), what will be the expected length of Sam's trip?

4. Max E. Mhum is trying to find the infinite duration, non-discounted optimum policy for a monodesmic semi-Markov process. Max has already computed g^A and the v_i^A's for one policy A. He is now considering the case in which a new policy B is used for the first transition and then policy A is used from there on.

a) Let $v_i^B(t)$ be the total expected reward over the time interval t if the process has just entered state i and we use the policy sequence $(B, A, A, A, A, \ldots)$ mentioned above. Find the asymptotic values of $v_i^B(t)$ in terms of the gain g^A, the relative values v_i^A, and the parameters of policy B.

b) What test quantity should Max use if he decides to find the policy B that will maximize the relative values of the policy sequence $(B, A, A, A, \ldots)$? Compare your answer to the test quantities in Equations 15.3.6 and 15.5.9.

5. In a game of chance a player is allowed to buy up to two chips at \$1 each. The dealer then tosses two fair coins. For each head appearing on the coins, the dealer buys back a chip for \$2 as far as the player's chips last. If the player has chips left over, he must split them with the dealer; they toss for odd coins. Any chips remaining in the player's possession may be used on the next play. Find the strategy for the player that will maximize his average return.

6. Big Julie from Chicago is playing a game with a coin. Every time he flips a head he wins \$1 and every time he flips *two* tails *in a row* he loses \$3 (the sequence TTTT would result in the loss of \$9). The game is usually played with a fair coin, i.e., the probability of heads is 1/2. However, Big Julie has a two-headed coin that he has the option of using on each flip. Unfortunately, every time he uses this two-headed coin there is 40% chance that he will be caught *prior to flipping the coin*. When this occurs Big Julie is ejected from the game but suffers no additional cost.

We define: $v_1(n)$ = the maximum expected return from n flips if a head occurred on the last flip.

$v_2(n)$ = the maximum expected return from n flips if a tail occurred on the last flip.

a) Write expressions for $v_1(n)$ and $v_2(n)$ in terms of $v_1(n-1)$ and $v_2(n-1)$. Use the form:

$$v_1(n) = \text{Max} \begin{cases} \underline{\hspace{2cm}} \\ \underline{\hspace{2cm}} \end{cases} \text{etc.}$$

b) Find Big Julie's optimum policy and expected return if there were only two more flips in the game before everyone goes home. Do this for both states, i.e., find $v_1(2)$ and $v_2(2)$.

c) Suppose that Big Julie uses the policy in b) for *all* flips of the coin. If he starts the game and plays until he gets caught, what will be his total expected return?

d) What should be Big Julie's policy if there are no limits on the number of plays remaining in the game (unless he gets caught)? What will be Big Julie's total expected return for this policy? What will be the expected length of the game?

7. A boxer is one of 4 pugilists striving for the championship title. His manager, being an influential individual, can arrange a fight with any one of the 3 opponents. The expected earnings and the outcome of a match depend on the current rating of the boxer and his opponent. We define the possible states as:

State 1—Champion
State 2—No. 1 challenger
State 3—No. 2 challenger
State 4—No. 3 challenger
State 5—Washed up (he ends up in this state if he is beaten badly in a bout)

If a boxer wins a bout against a higher ranked opponent, he changes place with him; if he loses, they retain their pre-fight rankings. The probabilities for outcomes of fights are as follows:

$i \backslash j$	1	2	3	4
1	—	2/3	3/4	7/8
2	1/3	—	2/3	3/4
3	1/4	1/3	—	2/3
4	1/8	1/4	1/3	—

where the table entries are $p_{ij} = \mathscr{P}\{i \text{ beats } j\}$

Furthermore, any time a fighter loses, there is a 1/10 probability that he goes to state 5.

The expected earnings of each contestant for a specific match are fixed independent of the outcome as follows:

$i \backslash j$	1	2	3	4
1	—	10	8	6
2	7	—	6	5
3	4	5	—	3
4	2	3	3	—

where the table entries are e_{ij} = expected earnings for a fighter of rank i in a single bout against a fighter of rank j

Determine the strategy for the manager to follow:

a) if he merely wants to maximize the expected earnings on the very next two bouts. What are these expected earnings (starting in each of the four possible states) in the next two bouts under this strategy?

b) if he wants to maximize the expected overall earnings of his fighter before he eventually ends up in state 5. Using this strategy, if the fighter starts in state 4, what is the probability that he will ever become champion?

c) if he wants to maximize the probability that his fighter will become champion before his career is ended. What is the probability for states 2, 3, and 4 that a fighter will become champion under this policy?

8. Starting with policy (a, a, a), find the optimum policy and gain for the Markov model with transition probability matrix

$$P = \begin{matrix} 1\begin{cases} a \\ b \end{cases} \\ 2\begin{cases} a \\ b \end{cases} \\ 3\begin{cases} a \\ b \end{cases} \end{matrix} \overset{\begin{matrix} 1 & \;\;2 & \;\;3 \end{matrix}}{\begin{bmatrix} 0.8 & 0.1 & 0.1 \\ 0.6 & 0.2 & 0.2 \\ 0.3 & 0.4 & 0.3 \\ 0.2 & 0.5 & 0.3 \\ 0.2 & 0.6 & 0.2 \\ 0.3 & 0.5 & 0.2 \end{bmatrix}}$$

and bonus matrix

$$
B = \begin{matrix} 1\begin{cases} a \\ b \end{cases} \\ 2\begin{cases} a \\ b \end{cases} \\ 3\begin{cases} a \\ b \end{cases} \end{matrix}
\overset{\begin{matrix} 1 & 2 & 3 \end{matrix}}{\begin{bmatrix} 4 & 5 & 3 \\ 6 & 2 & 7 \\ 3 & 8 & 4 \\ 4 & 9 & 1 \\ 6 & 3 & 3 \\ 7 & 1 & 2 \end{bmatrix}}.
$$

9. By shrewd investments you have purchased the controlling interest in the Coronado Ranching Company. You wish to pick the best policy for operating the business. The Coronado Ranching Company buys fur-bearing animals, raises them, and markets them (or their fur) using the money to purchase young animals. For simplicity's sake, we may model the business by a two-state Markov process.

In the first state, you have new animals to raise; in the second, you are ready to market the animals. In state 1 you have two possible choices: You may buy very cheap food for your charges, or you may purchase very high quality food. In the latter case the cost is higher but the chances of being ready for market in the next month are greater. Whatever the decision, if the animals are not ready they must be fed for the following month.

Likewise, state 2 has two alternatives: The first is to sell the animals skinned; the second is to market them alive. Marketing them alive increases their chances of being sold but yields a smaller reward. In either case, if they are not sold, they must be stored; this costs more for live animals. With the states and decisions numbered as above, the transition probabilities and their associated bonuses are:

i	k	j	p_{ij}^k	b_{ij}^k	
1	1	1	1/2	−5	Cheap food
1	1	2	1/2	−3	
1	2	1	1/3	−10	High-quality food
1	2	2	2/3	−4	
2	1	1	2/5	20	Market them skinned
2	1	2	3/5	0	
2	2	1	3/4	14	Market them alive
2	2	2	1/4	−2	

Beginning with the policy that yields the greatest immediate expected rewards, use policy iteration to find the optimum policy as the number of months remaining grows large.

10. The manager of a supermarket wants to know what his policy for checkout counters should be. Customers arrive at the checkout counters with an interarrival time that is exponentially distributed with a mean of 1 minute. The service time is also exponential with a mean of 1 minute. The operating cost per minute for each checkout counter that is open is 1 unit, while the manager figures that the cost to him for each customer minute spent waiting for service is 2 units. (Note that there is no "waiting-cost" for a customer being serviced.) In addition, there is a "start-up cost" of 2 units every time a checkout counter is opened. Assume that counters may be opened and closed instantaneously and that there is a single waiting line for all counters.

a) If there are only 2 checkout counters available in the store, what should be the manager's policy for opening and closing counters, i.e., what should be $k(n)$, the number of counters open if there are n people in the system? What is the expected total cost per minute for this policy?

b) Discuss the applicability of policy iteration to the solution of this problem. If it is not applicable, explain why not.

c) If the manager builds a third checkout counter, find at least one policy that yields a lower expected total cost per unit time than the one in part a).

11. Consider the previous problem for the case in which:

i) the manager never allows more than four customers at the checkout area at one time. (Customers arriving when there are already four customers in the checkout area are handled by a separate process.)
ii) there are five checkout counters available for operation.
iii) there is no "start-up cost" for opening a checkout counter.

Find the optimum operating policy $k(n)$ for this case. What is the expected total cost per minute for this policy?

12. A factory relies on the operation of a certain machine that must be replaced from time to time. The price of a new machine is $p = 100$. The expense of operating a machine of age k periods until it is age $k + 1$ periods is $e(k)$. The trade-in value of a k-period-old machine is $t(k)$. These quantities are specified as:

k	$e(k)$	$t(k)$
0	10	—
1	12	70
2	16	50
3	22	40
4	30	35
≥ 5	40	32

Assume that no discounting is necessary. What is the best replacement policy? For this policy, what is the average total cost per period of operating the machine? What is the book value of a machine of age k under a policy of replacement every ℓ periods?

NOTATION

NOTATION (General)

x = a variable (perhaps a random variable)

$\mathbf{x}$ = a vector (represented by an underline at the blackboard)

x_i = the ith element of $\mathbf{x}$

X = a matrix

x_{ij} = the ijth element of X

$x(\cdot)$ = a function of a discrete or continuous argument

$x^g(z)$ = the geometric transform of a discrete function $x(\cdot)$, $= \sum_{n=0}^{\infty} z^n x(n)$

$x^{g'}(z) = \frac{d}{dz} x^g(z)$, derivative of $x^g(z)$

$x^{g''}(z) = \frac{d^2}{dz^2} x^g(z)$, second derivative of $x^g(z)$

$x^e(s)$ = the exponential transform of a continuous function $x(\cdot)$,
$= \int_0^\infty dt\, e^{-st} x(t)$

$x^{e'}(s) = \frac{d}{ds} x^e(s)$, derivative of $x^e(s)$

$x^{e''}(s) = \frac{d^2}{ds^2} x^e(s)$, second derivative of $x^e(s)$

$x^{gg}(y, z)$ = the double geometric transform of $x(k, n)$ where both arguments are discrete,
$= \sum_{k=0}^{\infty} y^k \sum_{n=0}^{\infty} z^n x(k, n)$

$x^{\cdot g}(k, z)$ = the geometric transform of $x(k, \cdot)$

$x^{g\cdot}(y, n)$ = the geometric transform of $x(\cdot, n)$

$x^{ge}(z, s)$ = the geometric-exponential transform of $x(n, t)$, where the first argument is discrete, the second continuous
$= \sum_{n=0}^{\infty} z^n \int_0^\infty dt\, e^{-st} x(n, t)$

$x^{\cdot e}(n, s)$ = the exponential transform of $x(n, \cdot)$

$x^{g}(z, t)$ = the geometric transform of $x(\cdot, t)$

$\bar{x} = \langle x \rangle$ = the expectation, or mean, of x

$\overline{x^m} = \langle x^m \rangle$ = the mth moment of x

$\overset{v}{x} = {}^{v}\langle x \rangle$ = the variance of x

If $x(n)$ = the probability that some random variable equals n,

then ${}^{\leq}x(n)$ = the probability that the random variable is less than or equal to n,

and ${}^{>}x(n)$ = the probability that the random variable is greater than n

I = the identity matrix with elements $\delta_{ij} = \begin{cases} 1 & \text{if } i = j \\ 0 & \text{if } i \neq j \end{cases}$

$\mathbf{s}$ = a column vector with all components equal to 1

U = the unity matrix, a square matrix with all elements = 1

NOTATION (Specific)

CHAPTER 10

Matrix	Symbol	
	N	= the number of states in the process
P	p_{ij}	= the probability that a semi-Markov process that entered state i on its last transition will enter state j on its next transition
	τ_{ij}	= the holding time for the transition $i \to j$, the time the process will spend in state i before making a transition to state j
$H(\cdot)$	$h_{ij}(\cdot)$	= the probability mass function for τ_{ij}, the holding time
	τ_i	= the waiting time for state i, the time that the process will spend in state i before making a transition
W	$w_i(\cdot)$	= the probability mass function for τ_i, the waiting time (W is a diagonal matrix)
$\Phi(n)$	$\phi_{ij}(n)$	= the interval transition probability, the probability that a discrete-time process will occupy state j at time n if it entered state i at time zero
$C(m)$	$c_{ij}(m)$	= the joint probability that a process that entered state i at time zero will make its next transition to state j and at time m
M		= a diagonal matrix of mean waiting times
Φ	ϕ_{ij}	= the limiting interval transition probability from i to j = $\lim_{n\to\infty} \phi_{ij}(n)$
π	π_i	= the limiting state probability for the imbedded Markov process described by the transition probability matrix P
	$\bar{\tau}$	= the mean time between transitions, $= \sum_{i=1}^{N} \pi_i \bar{\tau}_i$

Matrix	Symbol	
$\boldsymbol{\phi}$	ϕ_j	= the limiting interval transition probability for state j of a monodesmic semi-Markov process
$P(m)$	$p_{ij}(m)$	= the conditional transition probability from i to j at time m, the probability that a process that entered state i at time zero, and made its next transition at time m, will make that transition to state j
$\Phi(k\|n)$	$\phi_{ij}(k\|n)$	= the joint probability that the process is in state j and that it has made k transitions given the time is n and that at time zero it entered state i on its zeroth transition
$K^m(n)$	$k_{ij}{}^m(n)$	$= \sum_{n=0}^{\infty} k^m \phi_{ij}(k\|n)$
	$\overline{k_{ij}{}^m}(n)$	$= \dfrac{k_{ij}{}^m(n)}{\phi_{ij}(n)}$ = the mth moment of the number of transitions the process makes through time n given that it started in state i and ended in state j
$E(k\|n)$	$e_{ij}(k\|n)$	= the entrance probability, the probability that a process which enters state i at time zero and transition zero will enter state j at time n on its kth transition
$E(n)$	$e_{ij}(n)$	= the probability that a process that entered state i at time zero will enter state j at time n, $= \sum_{k=0}^{\infty} e_{ij}(k\|n)$
E	e_{ij}	= the limiting entrance probability, $= \lim_{n\to\infty} e_{ij}(n)$
$\mathbf{e}$	e_j	= the limiting entrance probability of state j for a monodesmic process
	$\gamma_{ijq}(k\|n)$	= the destination probability, the probability that a process started in state i at time zero and transition zero is in state j at time n, has made k transitions by that time, and will make its next transition to state q
	γ_{jq}	= the limiting destination probability for a monodesmic process $= \lim_{n\to\infty} \sum_{k=0}^{\infty} \gamma_{ijq}(k\|n)$
	$\gamma_{\Sigma q}$	= the limiting probability that a monodesmic semi-Markov process will make its next transition to state q, $= \sum_{j=1}^{N} \gamma_{jq}$
	$p_{ir}(k, n)$	= the joint probability that k transitions and time n are required for a process that enters state i to reach state r for the first time
N	ν_{ij}	= total time spent in state j of a transient semi-Markov process if it started in state i at time zero

Matrix	Symbol	
	$d_i(k, n)$	= the duration probability, the joint probability that k transitions and time n will be required for a system that entered state i at time and transition zero to enter some other state
$F(k, n)$	$f_{ij}(k, n)$	= the probability that a system that entered state i at time and transition zero will require k transitions and time n to make its first passage to state j
$F(n)$	$f_{ij}(n)$	= the probability that first passage from state i to state j will require time n
Θ	θ_{ij}	= the first passage time from state i to state j measured in time
$\mathrm{N}(n)$	$\nu_{ij}(n)$	= the number of times the process enters state j through time n given that it entered state i at time zero
$\Omega(k\|n)$	$\omega_{ij}(k\|n)$	= the probability that $\nu_{ij}(n) = k$
${}_fP$	${}_fp_{ij}$	= transition probability for first transition out of state i; similarly for other process descriptors
${}_f\Phi(k\|n)$	${}_f\phi_{ij}(k\|n)$	= same as $\phi_{ij}(k\|n)$ except that ${}_fp_{ij}$ and ${}_fh_{ij}(\cdot)$ govern the first transition out of state i; similarly for other process characteristics
	R	= the event that the holding time interval under examination was selected by a random entry procedure
${}_rP$	${}_rp_{ij}$, etc.	= the pre-subscript r implies random selection of time zero

Chapter 11

The notation of Chapter 11 is generally the same as that for Chapter 10. However, since the time variable is now continuous, the waiting time and holding time probability distributions are density functions rather than mass functions. Other process characteristics that depended on the discrete-time variable n will now depend on the continuous-time variable t.

$p(\cdot)$	= density function for the lifetime of a continuous-time renewal process
l	= the lifetime of a continuous-time renewal process
$e(t)$	= the renewal rate at time t
$k(t)$	= the number of renewals through time t

Chapter 12

Matrix	Symbol	
Λ	λ_i	= parameter of exponential waiting time density function for state i (Λ is a diagonal matrix)
A	a_{ij}	= the transition rate for the transition $i \to j$
	${}^{\mathrm{r}}$	= the superscript r refers to real-transition equivalent

Matrix	Symbol	
	sr =	the shrinkage rate of the possible region
	b_k =	the birth rate for state k
	d_k =	the death rate for state k
$\Phi(\tau, t)$	$\phi_{ij}(\tau, t)$ =	the interval transition probability from time τ to time t, the probability that the process will occupy state j at time t if it occupied state i at the earlier time τ
$A(t)$	$a_{ij}(t)$ =	the transition rate from i to j at time t

CHAPTER 13

Matrix	Symbol	
	$y_{ij}(\sigma)$ =	the yield rate of state i at time σ when the successor state is state j
	$b_{ij}(\tau)$ =	the bonus paid when the process makes a transition from state i to state j after occupying state i for a time τ
	y_{ij} =	yield rate of state i at any time during its occupancy when the successor state is state j
	b_{ij} =	bonus paid upon transition from state i to state j
	y_i =	the yield rate of state i at any time during its occupancy
	α =	the discount rate
	ρ =	the equivalent annuital payment
$\mathbf{v}(t, \alpha)$	$v_i(t, \alpha)$ =	the expected present value of the reward the process will generate through time t if it is placed in state i when $t = 0$
$\mathbf{v}(0)$	$v_j(0)$ =	the terminal reward associated with occupying state j
	$y_{ij}(\tau, \alpha)$ =	the present value of the reward generated by the yield rate structure during a holding time τ in state i with successor state j
${}^{>}\mathbf{y}(t, \alpha)$	${}^{>}y_i(t, \alpha)$ =	the contribution to the expected present value of the yield rate structure when the first transition is made after t
$\mathbf{r}(t, \alpha)$	$r_i(t, \alpha)$ =	the expected present value from both yield rate and bonus structures for first transitions that occur before time t
$\mathbf{r}(\alpha)$	$r_i(\alpha)$ =	$r_i(\infty, \alpha)$ = expected present value of reward from a single occupancy of state i
$\mathbf{v}(\alpha)$	$v_i(\alpha)$ =	the expected present value the process will generate if it is started in state i
${}^{d}\overline{\mathrm{N}}(\alpha)$	${}^{d}\bar{\nu}_{ij}(\alpha)$ =	the expected number of times state j will be occupied before the termination of the process if the process starts in state i
$\mathbf{v}(t)$	$v_i(t)$ =	$v_i(t, 0)$ = the expected total reward the process will earn through time t if it is placed in state i at time $t = 0$
	r_i =	$r_i(0)$ = the expected total reward from a single occupancy of state i
	g_i =	the gain conditional on starting in state i

Matrix	Symbol	
	v_i =	the step component of $v_i(t)$; also the relative value of state i
	q_i =	the earning rate of state i
	g =	the gain of a monodesmic process
	β =	discount factor
	n =	discrete time index (replaces t to convert from continuous-time formulation)
	τ_ℓ =	lapsed time, the time the process has already occupied a state without making a transition

CHAPTER 14

s	s_i =	the ith state variable
	$\mathscr{S}$ =	the state space
	T^k =	the kth transformation
	$r^k(\mathbf{s})$ =	the reward function for T^k
	$v(\mathbf{s}\|n)$ =	the value function for the state vector **s** when n transformations remain
	$r_0(\mathbf{s})$ =	the terminal reward function

CHAPTER 15

	k =	superscript to indicate the kth alternative in any state
	Γ_i^k =	the gain test quantity for alternative k in state i
	$V_i^k(\alpha)$ or $V_i^k(\beta)$ =	the discounted value test quantity for alternative k in state i
	$h_{ij}^{ek}(\alpha)$ =	the exponential transform of the holding time probability density function for the transition from state i to state j under alternative k in state i evaluated at the discount rate α
	$h_{ij}^{gk}(\beta)$ =	the geometric transform of the holding time probability mass function for the transition from state i to state j under alternative k in state i evaluated at the discount factor β
	V_i^k =	the value-oriented test quantity for alternative k in state i

APPENDIX

A PROPERTIES OF CONGRUENT MATRIX MULTIPLICATION

We find it convenient to define a matrix operation called congruent matrix multiplication. If two matrices A and B have the same dimensions, we say they are commensurate. The congruent product C of two commensurate matrices A and B is a matrix of the same dimensions as A and B and whose elements are related to those of A and B by

$$c_{ij} = a_{ij} b_{ij} \qquad \text{all } i, j. \tag{A.1}$$

Thus congruent matrix multiplication is multiplication of corresponding elements. We denote such multiplication by a "box" operator $\Box$ and write Equation A.1 in the matrix form

$$C = A \Box B. \tag{A.2}$$

Congruent multiplication is useful not only for manipulation of matrices but also for designation of portions of matrices. Recalling that the identity matrix I has elements δ_{ij} and the unity matrix U has elements 1, we see that if A is a square matrix then $A \Box I$ is a matrix composed only of the diagonal elements of A, with others set to zero, while $A \Box (U - I)$ is the same as A but with zero diagonal elements.

It is easy to show that congruent matrix multiplication has useful algebraic properties. For example, if A, B, and C are commensurate matrices it is easy to prove from the defining relation (A.1) that congruent matrix multiplication is:

$$\text{commutative,} \quad A \Box B = B \Box A, \tag{A.3}$$

$$\text{distributive,} \quad A \Box (B + C) = A \Box B + A \Box C, \tag{A.4}$$

$$\text{and associative,} \quad (A \Box B) \Box C = A \Box (B \Box C). \tag{A.5}$$

We can even define the congruent inverse A^* of matrix A from

$$A \Box A^* = A^* \Box A = U. \tag{A.6}$$

The elements of A^* are the reciprocals of corresponding elements of A.

Generally, however, congruent matrix multiplication and ordinary matrix multiplication are not commutative, and mixtures of the two operations are best investigated from the defining relations. For example, consider the expression $D = [A(B \square I)] \square I$ where A and B are commensurate square matrices. The definitions of ordinary and congruent matrix multiplication yield the component form

$$d_{ij} = \left[\sum_k a_{ik}(b_{kj}\delta_{kj})\right] \cdot \delta_{ij} = \sum_k (a_{ik}\delta_{ik})(b_{kj}\delta_{kj}) \tag{A.7}$$

and thus show that

$$\begin{aligned}[A(B \square I)] \square I &= (A \square I)(B \square I) = (B \square I)(A \square I) \\ &= [B(A \square I)] \square I.\end{aligned} \tag{A.8}$$

We can use this result to solve a matrix equation that is of interest to us in Chapter 10. Consider the equation

$$A - B(A \square I) = C \tag{A.9}$$

where A, B, and C are commensurate square matrices and we desire to find A given B and C. We first find the congruent product of this equation with I,

$$A \square I - [B(A \square I)] \square I = C \square I. \tag{A.10}$$

In view of Equation A.8, we have

$$A \square I - (B \square I)(A \square I) = C \square I \tag{A.11}$$

or

$$A \square I = [I - (B \square I)]^{-1}(C \square I) = (C \square I)[I - (B \square I)]^{-1}. \tag{A.12}$$

When we substitute this result into Equation A.9 we obtain the solution

$$A = C + B[I - (B \square I)]^{-1}(C \square I) = C + B(C \square I)[I - (B \square I)]^{-1}. \tag{A.13}$$

REFERENCES

R. Bellman, *Dynamic Programming*, Princeton University Press, Princeton, New Jersey, 1957, Chapter XI.

R. Bellman and S. Dreyfus, *Applied Dynamic Programming*, Princeton University Press, Princeton, New Jersey, 1962.

A. T. Bharucha-Reid, *Elements of the Theory of Markov Processes and Their Applications*, McGraw-Hill Book Company, Inc., New York.

E. B. Dynkin, *Theory of Markov Processes*, Prentice-Hall, Inc., Englewood Cliffs, New Jersey, 1961.

W. Feller, *An Introduction to Probability Theory and Its Applications*, Vol. I, 2nd Ed., John Wiley & Sons, Inc., 1962.

Ronald A. Howard, *Dynamic Programming and Markov Processes*, The M.I.T. Press, Cambridge, 1960.

W. H. Huggins, "Signal-Flow Graphs and Random Signals," *Proceedings of I.R.E.*, 45, 74 (1957).

J. G. Kemeny and J. L. Snell, *Finite Markov Chains*, D. Van Nostrand Company, Princeton, 1960.

S. J. Mason and H. J. Zimmermann, *Electronic Circuits, Signals, and Systems*, John Wiley & Sons, Inc., New York, 1960.

Operations Research Center, M.I.T., *Notes on Operations Research 1959*, Technology Press, Cambridge, 1969, Chapters 3, 5, and 7.

E. Parzen, *Stochastic Processes*, Holden-Day, Inc., San Francisco, 1962.

R. W. Sittler, "Systems Analysis of Discrete Markov Processes," I.R.E. *Transactions on Circuit Theory*, CT-3, No. 1, 257 (1956).

INDEX

Pages in Volume I are shown in italics.